THE LETTER OF JAMES

VOLUME 37 A

THE ANCHOR BIBLE is a fresh approach to the world's greatest classic. Its object is to make the Bible accessible to the modern reader; its method is to arrive at the meaning of biblical literature through exact translation and extended exposition, and to reconstruct the ancient setting of the biblical story, as well as the circumstances of its transcription and the characteristics of its transcribers.

THE ANCHOR BIBLE is a project of international and interfaith scope: Protestant, Catholic, and Jewish scholars from many countries contribute individual volumes. The project is not sponsored by any ecclesiastical organization and is not intended to reflect any particular theological doctrine. Prepared under our joint supervision, THE ANCHOR BIBLE is an effort to make available all the significant historical and linguistic knowledge which bears on the interpretation of the biblical record.

THE ANCHOR BIBLE is aimed at the general reader with no special formal training in biblical studies; yet it is written with the most exacting standards of scholarship, reflecting the highest technical accomplishment.

This project marks the beginning of a new era of co-operation among scholars in biblical research, thus forming a common body of knowledge to be shared by all.

William Foxwell Albright
David Noel Freedman
GENERAL EDITORS

THE ANCHOR BIBLE

THE LETTER OF JAMES

✦

A New Translation
with Introduction and Commentary

LUKE TIMOTHY JOHNSON

THE ANCHOR BIBLE
Doubleday
New York   London   Toronto   Sydney   Auckland

THE ANCHOR BIBLE
PUBLISHED BY DOUBLEDAY
a division of Bantam Doubleday Dell Publishing Group, Inc.
1540 Broadway, New York, New York 10036

THE ANCHOR BIBLE, DOUBLEDAY, and the portrayal
of an anchor with the letters A and B are trademarks of
Doubleday, a division of Bantam Doubleday Dell
Publishing Group, Inc.

Library of Congress Cataloging-in-Publication Data

Bible. N.T. James. English. Johnson. 1995.
    The Letter of James : a new translation with introduction and
commentary / by Luke Timothy Johnson. — 1st ed.
      p.   cm. — (The Anchor Bible : v. 37A)
    Includes bibliographical references and index.
    1. Bible. N.T. James—Commentaries.   I. Johnson, Luke Timothy.
II. Title.   III. Series: Bible. English. Anchor Bible. 1964:
37A.
BS192.2.A1   1964G3   vol. 37A
[BS2783]
227'.91077—dc20   94-40581
                                                        CIP

ISBN 0-385-41360-2

TO JOY

CONTENTS

Preface   xi
Abbreviations   xv

INTRODUCTION   1

I. THE CHARACTER OF THE WRITING: THE VOICE   3

A. The Text   4
   Bibliography   6
B. Language and Style   7
   Bibliography   11
C. Structure   11
   Bibliography   15
D. Genre   16
   Bibliography   25
E. Literary Relationships   26

   1. Greco-Roman Moralists   27
   2. The Old Testament   29
      a. *The Law*   30
      b. *Prophecy*   32
      c. *Wisdom*   33
   3. Jewish Literature   34
      a. *The* Pirke Aboth   34
      b. *Qumran:* 1QS, CD   36
      c. *The* Sentences of the Syriac Menander   37
      d. *The* Letter of Aristeas   38
      e. 4 Maccabees   39
      f. *The* Sentences of Pseudo-Phocylides   40
      g. *Philo*   41
      h. *The* Testaments of the Twelve Patriarchs   43
   Bibliography   46

    4. New Testament Writings 48
      a. Johannine Writings 53
      b. First Letter of Peter 54
      c. Synoptic Tradition 55
    Bibliography 57
      d. James and Paul 58
    Bibliography 64
    5. Noncanonical Christian Literature 66
      a. The Didache 69
      b. The Letter of Barnabas 69
      c. The Sentences of Sextus 70
      d. The Teachings of Silvanus 71
      e. 1 Clement 72
      f. The Shepherd of Hermas 75
    Bibliography 80
  F. Moral and Religious Perspectives 80

II. CIRCUMSTANCES OF COMPOSITION: WHOSE VOICE? 89

  A. James the Brother of the Lord 92

    1. New Testament Evidence 92
      a. Evidence in Paul 94
      b. Evidence in the Gospels 96
      c. Evidence in Acts 96
    2. Extracanonical Evidence 98
      a. Evidence in Josephus 98
      b. Evidence in Christian Writings 99
        1. Traditions of James' Death 99
        2. James' Authority and Character 100
          a. Clement/Hegesippus/Eusebius 100
          b. Gnostic Writings 101
          c. The Gospel of the Hebrews 102
          d. Protevangelium of James 103
          e. Pseudo-Clementine Literature 103
    Bibliography 106
  B. Theories of Authorship 108
  C. Loosening the Pauline Connection 111
    Bibliography 114
  D. The Question of Language 116
  E. Reasons for Early Dating 118
    Bibliography 121

III. HISTORY OF INTERPRETATION:
    HOW WAS THE VOICE HEARD? 124

  A. The Reception of James in the Church 126

Contents

B. The Use of James in the Eastern Church   130
C. James in the Latin Church   135
D. The Sixteenth Century   140
E. The Seventeenth and Eighteenth Centuries   143
F. Nineteenth-Century Battle Lines   146
G. Twentieth-Century Developments   152

    1. The Place of James in Christian History   153
    2. James and Paul   156
    3. Literary Aspects of James   156
    4. James' Theological and Moral Voice   159
    Bibliography   160

IV. EXPLANATION AND INTERPRETATION:
ON HEARING JAMES' VOICE   162

TRANSLATION AND COMMENTARY ON
THE LETTER OF JAMES   165

  I. GREETING 1:1   167

  II. EPITOME OF EXHORTATION 1:2–27   173

  III. THE DEEDS OF FAITH 2:1–26   217

  IV. THE POWER AND PERIL OF SPEECH 3:1–12   253

  V. CALL TO CONVERSION 3:13–4:10   267

  VI. EXAMPLES OF ARROGANCE 4:11–5:6   291

  VII. PATIENCE IN TIME OF TESTING 5:7–11   311

  VIII. SPEECH IN THE ASSEMBLY OF FAITH 5:12–20   325

Index of Scripture References   348
Index of Ancient Sources   382
Index of Pre-Modern Christian Writers   404
Index of Modern Authors   406

PREFACE

I was a young Benedictine monk in southern Louisiana in 1964 when I had my first conscious encounters with the Letter of James. The first came at the evening office of Compline. In those days, the entire Divine Office was in Latin. The only English Bible read was at this evening service from Ronald Knox's translation of the Vulgate. The reader was Father Charles Villere, a grizzled monk and missionary. His passionately harsh reading of James 2:1–8 against the backdrop of his own opposition to racial discrimination left an indelible impression that James' voice was not unlike the Paul I knew in 1 Corinthians and that this prophetic voice had immediate pertinence to the social crises of our own day.

The second encounter came through the reading of Bo Reicke's commentary on James in this ANCHOR BIBLE series. In Reicke's discussion of James 2:1–8, I saw for the first time how the knowledge of the social realities of the Greco-Roman world could deepen an understanding of the text.

These encounters affected my own approach to James when I began my formal work on the letter in a course at Yale Divinity School in 1981. It was, therefore, with great joy that I accepted David Noel Freedman's invitation to write the present commentary as the successor to Reicke's volume.

Bo Reicke's was the first of the Anchor New Testament commentaries. The series at that stage aimed at providing a fresh translation with some annotations and brief comments. Over the years, for better or worse, the character of the series changed, with volumes taking on a more scholarly character, and considerably more academic baggage.

One reason for a second run at James, then, was to standardize the series. Another reason may be more significant. It has become increasingly clear that compositions like James, 1 Peter, 2 Peter, and Jude are both too important and too disparate simply to be treated together. This is even more the case if, as the present commentary argues, James is not among the latest writings of the NT but among its earliest.

In the Introduction to the commentary, I try to provide a full discussion of all the issues pertinent to the understanding of James in its historical context. Apart from my favoring the traditional early dating of the letter, perhaps the most distinctive contribution of the Introduction is the amount of attention given to the entire history of interpretation. This discussion may be of interest primarily to specialists. But I thought it important to provide a fuller account of James' reception and interpretation than is anywhere available in English, above all to counter the creeping amnesia that afflicts American biblical scholarship. Even a cursory review of this narrative indicates that there is, indeed, very little new under the sun.

The commentary proper does not engage in extended discussions of scholarship. I give most attention to understanding James' language and logic. I do maintain a running conversation with some sixteen commentaries that I chose as "constant witnesses" to be consulted on critical points after I had done my own spadework; modern commentaries are cited by author and page, ancient ones simply by name. Since the time of Bede, commentaries have borrowed information and insight from their predecessors. Over the centuries, an enormous body of comparative material has also been compiled. Since some of this material has also simply been "borrowed," it is frequently erroneous. In addition to adding something to the collection of appropriate comparative material, I have done my best to ensure the accuracy of citation from the ancient sources.

My references themselves may appear idiosyncratic, since some titles are in Latin and some in English, some are abbreviated and some given in full. There is, in fact, no adequate system of abbreviation across the entire range of ancient literature. My main criterion has been usefulness: can the reader find the source from my reference? Finally, I have tried to enrich the commentary by providing a fuller sense of the ways in which James was read and used by patristic writers.

In the comments, I have tried to move from explanation to interpretation. In the case of exhortatory literature, this involves more than wrestling with the ideas presented. It means testing the claims of the text against the experience of life.

Many people have helped in the production of this book. The students in my classes on James at Yale Divinity School, Indiana University, Columbia Theological Seminary, and Emory University, all contributed insights that I probably have incorporated without proper acknowledgment. Among students who have made special contributions, I owe particular thanks to Mark Pitts, who researched the Greek patristic materials; to Laura Eggers, who uncovered the Gregorian catena tradition; and to James Norton for providing references to disputes on James 5:16. Ann Schechter and the late Todd Sullivan provided welcome debate.

Faculty and staff associates at Indiana and Emory were unfailingly supportive.

At Indiana, my colleagues Mary Jo Weaver, Steve Stein, Sam Preus, Richard Miller, Jim Hart, and Jim Ackerman provided welcome conversation, while Jenny Harrell and Jill Rogers provided warm and reliable assistance. At Emory, Carl Holladay has been a constant friend and valued consultant, John Hayes has provided key research help, while Hendrick Boers and Marilyn Schertz have given timely computer rescue. JoAnn Stone has alternately prodded and protected me, both to my benefit.

The research libraries at Indiana University and Boston College enabled me to find difficult to locate materials. But the Pitts Theological Library at Emory, especially through the efforts of Pat Graham and Ida Boers, was the perfect place for me to bring this project to completion.

For the past year and a half, Mary Foskett has been my research assistant on this project. Her intelligence, energy, and astonishing good cheer were extravagantly expended in every sort of assistance. Professor David Noel Freedman's impressive editorial alertness saved the manuscript from even more embarrassments than it retains.

This book is dedicated to Joy. For twenty years I have been with her. She has enabled me to learn something about wisdom from above and the word of truth and friendship with God. But most of all, she has been one of the perfect gifts that come from the father of lights. On this her birthday, a small gift back.

June 20, 1994

ABBREVIATIONS

Adamson	J. B. Adamson, *The Epistle of James*
AnBib	Analecta Biblica
ANRW	W. Haase and H. Temporini, *Aufstieg und Niedergang der Römischen Welt*
ATR	*Anglican Theological Review*
AUSS	*Andrews University Seminary Studies*
BA	*Biblical Archaeologist*
BAGD	Bauer-Arndt-Gingrich-Danker, *Greek-English Lexicon of the New Testament*
BETL	Biblioteca Ephemeridum theologicarum Lovaniensium
BfTh	Beihefte fuer Theologie
BFTh	Beiträge zur Förderung der christlichen Theologie
Bib	*Biblica*
BibLeb	*Bibel und Leben*
BJRL	*Bulletin of the John Rylands Library*
BN	*Biblische Notizen*
BR	*Biblical Research*
BSF	Biblische Studien, Freiburg
BT	*The Bible Translator*
BWANT	Beiträge zur Wissenschaft vom Alten und Neuen Testaments
BZ	*Biblische Zeitschrift*
BZNW	Beihefte zur Zeitschrift für die neutestamentliche Wissenschaft und die Kunde der älteren Kirche
CBQ	*Catholic Biblical Quarterly*
Cantinat	J. Cantinat, *Les Épîtres de Saint Jacques et de Saint Jude*

Chaine	J. Chaine, *L'Épître de Saint Jacques*
ConB	Coniectanea biblica
ConNT	Coniectanea Neotestamentica
CQR	*Church Quarterly Review*
CRINT	Compendium Rerum Iudicarum ad Novum Testamentum
CSCO	Corpus Scriptorum Christianorum Orientalium
CSEL	Corpus Scriptorum Ecclesiasticorum Latinorum
Davids	P. H. Davids, *The Epistle of James*
Dibelius	M. Dibelius, *James: A Commentary on the Epistle of James*
EBib	Études Bibliques
ETL	*Ephemerides Theologicae Lovanienses*
EvQ	*Evangelical Quarterly*
EvT	*Evangelische Theologie*
ExpT	*Expository Times*
FzB	Forschung zur Bibel
FRLANT	Forschungen zur Religion und Literatur des Alten und Neuen Testaments
GBS	Guides to Biblical Scholarship
GOTR	*Greek Orthodox Theological Review*
HE	Eusebius of Caesarea, *Historia Ecclesiastica*
HKNT	Handkommentar zum Neuen Testament
HNT	Handbuch zum Neuen Testament
HR	*History of Religions*
Hort	F. J. A. Hort, *The Epistle of St. James*
HTKNT	Herders theologischer Kommentar zum Neuen Testament
HTR	*Harvard Theological Review*
IBS	*Irish Biblical Studies*
ICC	International Critical Commentary
Int	*Interpretation*
JBL	*Journal of Biblical Literature*
JETS	*Journal of the Evangelical Theological Society*
JJS	*Journal of Jewish Studies*
JNES	*Journal of Near Eastern Studies*
JR	*Journal of Religion*
JRS	*Journal of Religious Studies*
JSNT	*Journal for the Study of the New Testament*
JSNTS	Journal for the Study of the New Testament Supplement
JSOT	*Journal for the Study of the Old Testament*
JSS	*Journal of Semitic Studies*

JTS	*Journal of Theological Studies*
KD	*Kerygma and Dogma*
Laws	S. Laws, A *Commentary on the Epistle of James*
LB	*Linguistica Biblica*
LSMJ	Liddell-Scott-McKenzie-Jones, *Greek-English Lexicon*
LXX	Septuagint
Mayor	J. B. Mayor, *The Epistle of St. James*
Martin	R. P. Martin, *James*
Marty	J. Marty, *l'Épître de Jacques; Étude Critique*
Metzger	B. Metzger, A *Textual Commentary on the Greek New Testament*
Mitton	C. L. Mitton, *The Epistle of James*
Moule	C. F. D. Moule, *Idiom Book of New Testament Greek* 2nd ed.
MT	Masoretic Text
Mussner	F. Mussner, *Der Jakobusbrief*
NAB	New American Bible
Neot	*Neotestamentica*
Nestle-Aland	E. Nestle and E. Aland, *Novum Testamentum Graece* 26th ed.
NHLE	J. M. Robinson, ed., *The Nag-Hammadi Library in English*
NKZ	*Neue kirchliche Zeitschrift*
NorTT	*Norsk teologisk Tidsskrift*
NovT	*Novum Testamentum*
NovTSup	Novum Testamentum, Supplements
NRSV	New Revised Standard Version
NTS	*New Testament Studies*
OTP	J. H. Charlesworth, ed., *The Old Testament Pseudepigrapha*
PA	*Pirke Aboth*
PG	J. Migne, ed., *Patrologia Graeca*
PL	J. Migne, cd., *Patrologia Latina*
PVTG	Pseudepigrapha Veteris Testamenti Graece
QD	Quaestiones Disputatae
RB	*Revue Biblique*
Reicke	B. Reicke, *The Epistles of James, Peter, and Jude*
RelS	*Religious Studies*
ResQ	*Restoration Quarterly*
RevistB	*Revista Biblica*
RevScRel	*Revue des sciences religieuses*
RGG	*Religion in Geschichte und Gegenwart*
RHE	*Revue d'histoire ecclésiastique*

RHPR	*Revue d'histoire et de philosophie religieuses*
RHR	*Revue de l'histoire des religions*
Ropes	J. H. Ropes, *A Critical and Exegetical Commentary on the Epistle of St. James*
RSPT	*Revue des sciences philosophiques et théologiques*
RSR	*Recherches de science religieuse*
RSV	Revised Standard Version
SB	Sources Bibliques
SBLDS	Society of Biblical Literature Dissertation Series
SBLMS	Society of Biblical Literature Monograph Series
SBLSP	*Society of Biblical Literature Seminar Papers*
SBLTT	Society of Biblical Literature Texts and Translations Series
Scr	*Scripture*
SE	*Studia Evangelica*
SecCent	*Second Century*
SJT	*Scottish Journal of Theology*
SNTSMS	Studiorum Novi Testamenti Societas, Monograph Series
SR	*Studies in Religion*
ST	*Studia Theologica*
SVTP	Studia in Veteris Testamenti Pseudepigrapha
TBl	*Theologische Blaetter*
TDNT	G. Kittel and G. Friedrich, eds., *Theological Dictionary of the New Testament*
THKNT	Theologischer Handkommentar zum Neuen Testament
TLZ	*Theologische Literaturzeitung*
TP	*Theologie und Philosophie*
TPQ	*Theologisch-praktische Quartalschrift*
TQ	*Theologische Quartalschrift*
TS	*Theological Studies*
TSK	*Theologische Studien und Kritiken*
TU	Text und Untersuchungen zur Geschichte der altchristlichen Literatur
TynB	*Tyndale Bulletin*
TZ	*Theologische Zeitschrift*
Vouga	F. Vouga, *l'Epitre de Saint Jacques*
Windisch	H. Windisch, *Die Katholischen Briefe*
WMANT	Wissenschaftliche Monographien zum Alten und Neuen Testament
WTJ	*Westminster Theological Journal*
WUNT	Wissenschaftliche Untersuchungen zum Neuen Testament

ZAW	*Zeitschrift für die alttestamentliche Wissenschaft*
Zerwick/Grosvener	M. Zerwick and Mary Grosvener, A *Grammatical Analysis of the Greek New Testament* Vol 2 (Rome: Biblical Institute, 1979)
ZHT	*Zeitschrift für historische Theologie*
ZKG	*Zeitschrift für Kirchengeschichte*
ZKT	*Zeitschrift für katholische Theologie*
ZKWKL	*Zeitschrift für kirchliche Wissenschaft und kirchliche Leben*
ZNW	*Zeitschrift für die neutestamentliche Wissenschaft*
ZRGG	*Zeitschrift für Religion und Geistengeschichte*
ZTK	*Zeitschrift für Theologie und Kirche*
ZWT	*Zeitschrift für wissenschaftliche Theologie*

INTRODUCTION

✦

I. THE CHARACTER
OF THE WRITING:
THE VOICE

✦

Even at first reading, the Letter of James is a remarkably accessible moral and religious exhortation. Its call to realize professed ideals in appropriate action has spoken with prophetic urgency to generations of readers who have found James' directives difficult to perform rather than to understand.

For readers seeking a fuller intellectual appreciation of this first-century Christian writing, however, James offers a number of difficulties, as well as an invitation to a richer reading. The present commentary takes as its goal both the clarification of difficulties and the pursuit of competent, if not comprehensive, understanding.

This extended Introduction seeks to provide the reader with a sense of the composition as a whole, so that the later detailed analysis of separate sections, however dense or tangled, can be seen to fit within a coherent frame of meaning. The Introduction proceeds as inductively as possible, so that at every stage the reader can grasp how larger interpretive issues emerge from questions posed by the text itself and be able to assess the evidence used to construct comprehensive interpretations.

The obvious starting point is the shape of the composition itself: what is the character of the writing, its *voice*? A fairly detailed review of the composition's language, style, structure, genre, literary and thematic relationships, will provide the reader with some sense of this voice. Only then is it appropriate to ask about the author and raise the question of *whose voice* is heard in the composition. Pursuing the question of authorship leads into the disputed territory concerning the social and historical setting within early Christianity suggested by the composition.

Any contemporary reading of the NT, however, is affected by centuries of interpretation. The third question asked by the Introduction, therefore, is *how was the voice heard*? The survey of interpretation is necessarily brief, but

3

includes both formal commentaries and some indications of how James was used (and thereby implicitly interpreted) by readers through the centuries.

The Introduction concludes by addressing the interaction between contemporary reader and ancient text: *how should the voice be heard*? This is a consideration that is raised, first, by James' character as moral and religious exhortation: practical wisdom is tested not against theory but against experience. It is a consideration raised as well by the fact that James is read within the context of a canon of Scripture.

A. THE TEXT

The translation and interpretation in the present commentary are based on the 26th edition of E. Nestle-K. Aland's *Novum Testamentum Graece* (Stuttgart: Deutsche Bibelstiftung, 1979). This critical edition is eclectic in character.[1] Rather than adopting a single manuscript tradition as the norm against which other evidence is tested, the eclectic method constitutes the text by a process of selection among witnesses, based on the relative strength of external attestation, as well as the basic rules of text criticism, which prefer shorter and harder readings.

For the text of James, the most important Greek witnesses are the great Uncials of the fourth and fifth centuries (‭א‬, B, A, C), which are supplemented by fragmentary papyri: $\mathfrak{P}^{20}$ from the third century includes 2:19–3:9; $\mathfrak{P}^{23}$ from the third century includes 1:10–12, 15–18; and $\mathfrak{P}^{74}$ from the seventh century includes some 70 verses through the entire letter. Other significant Greek witnesses are from the fifth century (048, 0166, 0173), the sixth century (0246), and the eighth and ninth centuries (K, P, Ψ, 33). Witnesses to the text of James also include early translations from the Greek into other languages, commonly called versions. These include several Egyptian dialects (Sahidic, Akhminic, Middle Egyptian, Coptic), Ethiopic, several Syriac versions (Peshitto, Philoxenian, Harclean, Palestinian), Armenian, and Georgian, as well as the Old Latin and the Vulgate. A third sort of witness is the citation of the text by patristic writers.[2]

Use of the eclectic method means, in effect, that the establishment of the text

---

[1] See Nestle-Aland, 43*; for the term "eclectic," see B. M. Metzger, *The Text of the New Testament* 2nd ed. (New York: Oxford University Press, 1968) 175–79, and G. D. Kilpatrick, "An Eclectic Study of the Text of Acts," *Biblical and Patristic Studies in Memory of Robert Pierce Casey*, ed. J. N. Birdsall and R. W. Thompson (Freiburg, 1963) 64–77; see also E. J. Epp, "The Eclectic Method in New Testament Textual Criticism: Solution or Symptom?" in *Studies in the Theory and Method of New Testament Textual Criticism*, ed. E. J. Epp et al. (Grand Rapids: Eerdmans, 1993) 141–73.

[2] For technical discussions of the various textual witnesses, see Ropes, 103–29; Mayor, cclxxx–cclxxxix; Dibelius, 57–61; Chaine, cviii–cxii; Mussner, 53–56.

already involves a certain amount of interpretation, as, for example, in the determination of what amounts to a "harder reading." The relative instability of any NT critical text must also be borne in mind when assessing the style and structure of a composition. Such evaluations sometimes turn on minutiae found in some witnesses but not all.[3] In fact, however, the text of James is relatively stable. To this point, for example, there has not appeared compelling evidence for a "Western" text of James that dramatically differs from the "Alexandrian" text and creates the sort of interpretive difficulties presented by the text traditions of the Acts of the Apostles.[4] Certainly the fact that Codex Bezae Cantabrigiensis (D) lacks James eliminates the most important evidence for the "Western" text, although it is possible that some medieval manuscripts together with some of the versions might still be shown to have consistent variations that might be called "Western."[5]

The relative homogeneity of James' text could be due to the fact that the late official recognition of James precluded the wider textual variations such as we find in the Gospels.[6] It may be due equally to the brevity of expression and tight framework of this composition (108 verses, fewer than 2000 words), which left little room for imaginative expansion. In any case, only some 44 verses contain variations of real significance. Even fewer verses contain textual difficulties demanding exegetical decisions (see, e.g., 1:3, 12, 17, 19, 27; 2:3, 20; 3:3, 6, 8, 9; 4:2; 5:7, 11).[7] Some of these passages, however, are so difficult that (beginning with Erasmus on 4:2) commentators have sometimes sought relief in emendations.[8] The temptation is understandable,[9] but is resisted in the present commentary.

The first interest of text criticism is establishing a text that approximates, as far as our evidence and skill allow, the "original text." But there is also much to be learned from the study of textual variants. They show how the text was understood in different regions and at different periods and, therefore, are evidence for "reception criticism" or the history of interpretation. This way of reading James is still in its infancy. No one has yet done for James what E. J.

---

[3]See, e.g., C. B. Amphoux, "Langue de l'épître de Jacques: études structurales," *RHPR* 53 (1973) 31–34.

[4]See, e.g., A. F. J. Klijn, A *Survey of the Researches into the Western Text of the Gospels and Acts* (NovTSup 21; Leiden: Brill, 1969).

[5]See C. B. Amphoux, "La parenté textuelle du Syr h et du groupe 2138 dans l'épître de Jacques," *Bib* 62 (1981) 259–71; ibid., "Quelques témoins grecs des formes textuelles les plus anciennes de l'épître de Jacques: le groupe 2138 (ou 614)," *NTS* 28 (1982) 91–115; C. B. Amphoux, Dom B. Outtier, "Les leçons des versions géorgiennes de l'épître de Jacques," *Bib* 65 (1984) 365–76.

[6]Dibelius, 61.

[7]See the slightly different list in Metzger, 679–86.

[8]See, e.g., E. Klostermann, "Zum Texte des Jakobusbriefes," *Verbum Dei Manet in Aeternum*, ed. W. Foerster (Witten: Luther-Verlag, 1953) 71–72.

[9]Dibelius, 61.

Epp has done for the Western text of Acts.[10] For a writing like James, which has a disputed early history, the study of the versions could have particular pertinence. If the Old Latin version underlying the Bobbio (fifth century) and Corbey (ninth/tenth century) manuscripts could be dated as early as the third century, for example, it would provide evidence of James' dissemination among Latin readers that preceded any certain use of James by Latin writers.[11]

BIBLIOGRAPHY

Amphoux, C. B., "Une relecture du chapitre I de l'épître de Jacques," *Bib* 59 (1978) 554–61.

Amphoux, C. B., "La parenté textuelle du Syr h et du groupe 2138 dans l'épître de Jacques," *Bib* 62 (1981) 259–71.

Amphoux, C. B., "Quelques temoins grecs des formes textuelles les plus anciennes de l'épître de Jacques: le groupe 2138 (ou 614)," *NTS* 28 (1982) 91–115.

Amphoux, C. B., and Outtier, B., "Les leçons des versions géorgiennes de l'épître de Jacques," *Bib* 65 (1984) 365–76.

Duplacy, J., "Les divisions du texte de l'épître de Jacques dans B (03) du Nouveau Testament," *Studies in New Testament Language and Text*, ed. J. K. Elliott (Leiden: Brill, 1976) 122–36.

Klostermann, E., "Zum Texte des Jakobusbriefes," *Verbum Dei Manet in Aeternum*, ed. W. Foerster (Witten: Luther-Verlag, 1953) 71–72.

Leloir, L., "Traduction latins des versions syriaques et arméniennes de l'épître de Jacques," *Le Muséon* 83 (1970) 189–208.

Metzger, B. M., *A Textual Commentary on the New Testament* (New York: United Bible Societies, 1975) 679–86.

Ropes, J. H., "The Text of the Epistle of James," *JBL* 28 (1909) 103–29.

Sanday, W., "Some Further Remarks on the Corbey St. James (ff)," *Studia Biblica: Essays in Biblical Archaeology and Criticism*, ed. S. R. Driver et al. (Oxford: Clarendon Press, 1885) 233–63.

Wordsworth, J., "The Corbey St. James (ff), and its Relation to Other Latin Versions, and to the original Language of the Epistle," *Studia Biblica:*

---

[10]E. J. Epp, *The Theological Tendency of Codex Bezae Cantabrigiensis in Acts* (SNTSMS 3; Cambridge: University Press, 1966). An interest in studying the Corbey Old Latin version for the evidence it might give for local Latin dialects is expressed by W. Sanday, "Further Remarks on the Corbey St. James (ff.)," *Studia Biblica: Essays in Biblical Archaeology and Criticism*, ed. S. R. Driver et al. (Oxford: Clarendon Press, 1885) 260–61.

[11]See J. Wordsworth, "The Corbey St. James (ff), and its Relation to Other Latin Versions, and to the original Language of the Epistle," *Studia Biblica: Essays in Biblical Archaeology and Criticism*, ed. S. R. Driver et al. (Oxford: Clarendon Press, 1885) 134–36.

Essays in Biblical Archeology and Criticism, ed. S. R. Driver et al. (Oxford: Clarendon Press, 1885) 113–50.

B. LANGUAGE AND STYLE

The language of James will be considered in detail throughout the commentary, as the peculiar density of its syntax and imagery and the multiple associations triggered by its diction are assessed. In general, it can be stated that James' Greek is a form of clear and correct *koine* with some ambitions toward rhetorical flourish.[12] Less idiosyncratic than the Greek of Paul and far more polished than that of John, James' language is comparable in quality, if less complex in texture, to that of Hebrews.[13]

His Greek can be located first in relationship to the Septuagint (LXX), the third century BCE translation of the Old Testament (OT). James explicitly cites the LXX in 2:8–11, 23, and 4:6. Other passages (e.g., 1:11; 2:25; 5:4, 5, 17, 20) contain verbal allusions to the LXX. Indeed, James' diction as a whole is that of the LXX. Only some thirteen of his words find no antecedent there.[14] Clearly dependent on the LXX are terms like *prosōpolēmpsia* (2:1) and *prosōpolēmptein* (2:9) ["impartiality"/"show impartiality"], which cannot be understood except as constructions deriving from *prosōpon labein*, the LXX translation of *naśa panîm* (see Lev 19:15). In the same way, James' various combinations with *poiein* ("doing") in 2:8, 12, 13, 19; 3:12, 18; 5:15 recall similar constructions in the LXX. In fact, phrases such as "doer of the word" (*poiētēs logou*) in 1:22 or "doer of the law" (*poiētēs nomou*) in 4:11 would be read by a Greek reader unfamiliar with the LXX as "poet" and "lawmaker."[15]

The Septuagintal connection also helps account for a number of grammatical "semitisms" that might otherwise be taken as evidence for a Hebrew or Aramaic original underlying James' Greek text. Among these is the heavy use of paratactic (1:11, 24; 4:7–11; 5:2–3, 4, 14–15, 17–18) and asyndetic sentence structure (1:16–18; 2:23; 3:8–9, 15; 4:7–10; 5:1–6, 8–10), as well as such "Hebraic" features as the articular infinitive (1:18, 19; 3:3; 4:2, 15; 5:17), the genitive of quality (1:17, 23, 25; 2:1, 4; 3:6, 13; 5:15), and cognate dative (5:17). The LXX might also have influenced James' slipping into the "prophetic past tense" in passages such as 1:11 (using the gnomic aorist) and 5:2–3 (using the perfect).[16]

---

[12]See A. Wifstrand, "Stylistic Problems in the Epistles of James and Peter," *ST* 1 (1948) 175.

[13]See Mayor, ccxliv–ccxlv.

[14]See S. C. Agourides, "The Origin of the Epistle of St. James," *GOTR* 9 (1963) 69.

[15]For a detailed discussion of James' diction, see Mayor, cclv–cclix.

[16]On semitisms in general, see C. F. D. Moule, *An Idiom Book of New Testament Greek* 2nd ed. (Cambridge: University Press, 1959) 171–91, and with particular reference to James, N. Turner, *Style* in J. H. Moulton, *A Grammar of New Testament Greek* IV (Edinburgh: T & T Clark, 1976) 116–20.

James' Greek is also affected by the exhortatory character of his composition. The sentences are generally short, with only a few relatively lengthy periods (2:2–4; 3:15–16; 4:13–15). The combination of brevity and asyndetic construction sometimes provides a staccato rhythm (see esp. 4:7–10). It is no surprise that the dominant mood of James' verbs is the imperative. In 108 verses, there are some 59 imperatives (46 in the second person, 13 in the third person). But by no means does James consist entirely of random or logically unconnected commandments. Imperatives are generally accompanied by explanations or warrants. For that purpose James uses participles (1:3, 14, 22; 2:9, 25; 3:1), *gar* clauses (1:6, 7, 11, 13, 20, 24; 2:11, 13, 26; 3:2, 16; 4:14), and *hoti* clauses (1:12, 23; 2:10; 3:1; 4:3; 5:8, 11). The commandments are also sometimes connected to purpose clauses (1:3; 5:8) and sometimes occur in the context of an implied argument signified by the use of *oun* (4:4, 7; 5:7, 16), *dio* (1:21; 4:6), or *houtōs* (1:11; 2:12, 17; 2:26; 3:5).

James also shows some striving for rhetorical effect, as in the rhythm of the (cited?) hexameter in 1:17; the pleonastic balance of *damazetai kai dedamastai* in 3:7, preceded by *phlogizousa/phlogizomenē* in 3:6; the rhyming endings (homoioteleuton) in 1:6, 14; 2:12; 3:17; 4:8. James is particularly fond of alliteration. He alliterates the initial letter *p* in 1:2, 3, 11, 17, 22; 3:2, the initial *d* in 1:1, 6, 21; 2:16; 3:8, and the combination of *p* and *d* in 1:21. He also alliterates *k* in 2:3 and 4:8, *l* in 1:4, *m* in 3:5. He uses parechesis (*apelēluthen/epelatheto*) in 1:24, and paronomasia in 1:1–2 (*chairein/charan*); 2:4 (*diekrithēte/kritai dialogismōn*); 2:20 (*erga/argē*); 3:17 (*adiakritos/anupokritos*), and 4:14 (*phainomenē/aphanizomenē*). A particularly subtle play on the form and meaning of words appears in 2:13, with its complex punning on *krisis/eleos/aneleos*).[17] Such complex and pervasive wordplay in the Greek makes it virtually certain that James was not simply the translation from a Hebrew or Aramaic original, but was originally written in Greek.

It has been pointed out that separate statements in James are frequently joined by catchwords, as in 1:4–5 (*leipomenoi/leipetai*), 1:12–13 (*peirasmon/peirazomenos*), 1:26–27 (*thrēskos/thrēskeia*), 2:12–13 (*krinesthai/krisis*), 3:17–18 (*karpōn/karpos*), 5:9–12 (*kritēs/krisis*), 5:19–20 (*epistrepsē/epistrepsas*).[18] It has also been amply demonstrated that such word-linkages are frequently found as a mnemonic device for organizing otherwise disparate materials in oral tradition.[19] But word-linkages in James need not necessarily serve the same purpose. Nor does the presence of such linkages demand that the sentences thus joined should be read in isolation from each other, as though they were joined only by sound and not by logic, revealing no "continuity in thought."[20]

---

[17]For a more complete list of rhetorical tropes, see E. Baasland, "Literarische Form, Thematik und geschichtliche Einordnung des Jakobusbriefes," ANRW II, 25.2 (1988) 3659–62.

[18]See Mayor, ccl; Dibelius, 7; Turner, *Style*, 116.

[19]See especially the full display in Dibelius, 7–11.

[20]The argument that word-linkages indicate a loose collection of disconnected aphorisms is central to Dibelius' overall approach to James (see 5–6).

The rhetorical effect of such linkages cannot be denied.[21] But it should be remembered that in the Greco-Roman world, rhetoric was not merely a matter of adornment. It was, above all, a matter of argumentation.[22] Each such word-linkage in James must, therefore, be examined without prejudgment concerning its literary or logical function. In some cases (see 1:12–13), continuity in thought may indeed be difficult to discern. In others, the linking of words may in fact form a rhetorical trope: the chain in 1:2–4, for example, is an obvious example of the figure called *sorites* or *gradatio*.[23]

Every careful reader of James in Greek is impressed by the freshness or "energy" of his language.[24] The impression derives particularly from James' vigorous use of those rhetorical devices found in many Greco-Roman moral discourses but associated especially with the *diatribe*.[25] The diatribe as a literary form will be considered more fully in the next section. For now, only the use of language associated with it needs noting. For example, James frequently addresses the readers directly, either as *adelphoi mou* (1:2; 2:1, 14; 3:1, 10, 12; 5:12, 19) or even more intimately as *adelphoi mou agapetoi* (1:16, 19; 2:5). The frequent use of second-person verbs intensifies the sense of direct address and dialogue (1:2, 16, 19, 21, 22; 2:1, 5, 12, 18; 3:1, 4, 5, 14; 4:7, 8, 9, 10, 11, 13; 5:1, 4, 7, 8, 9, 10, 11, 12, 16). James also makes use of an imaginary interlocutor (2:18–22), who can be addressed with unflattering epithets (2:20; 4:4) or in generalizing terms (4:13–16; 5:1–6). Four times James also allows other characters to speak: those who practice discrimination in the assembly (2:3); those who refuse help to the needy (2:16); those who have faith without deeds (2:18); and those who boast of future plans (4:13). Such "speech in character" (*prosōpopoiia*) also increases the dialogical character of the composition.[26]

Typical also of the diatribe is the posing of short questions that are immediately answered (3:13; 4:14; 5:13–14) and the asking of rhetorical questions, often in rapid sequence (2:4, 5, 6, 7, 14, 16, 20; 3:11, 12; 4:1, 4, 5; 5:6). Such rhetorical questions invite the readers' assent to what the author implies should be a shared conviction. Falling short of that shared perception, however, generates the energy of impatience, reflected in the use of short expletives and warnings: "Do not be mistaken" (1:16); "You know this" (1:19); "Do you wish to

---

[21]Dibelius, 38.

[22]See B. L. Mack, *Rhetoric and the New Testament* (GBS; Minneapolis: Fortress Press, 1990) 19–21; G. Kennedy, *The Art of Persuasion in Greece* (Princeton: Princeton University Press, 1963) 3–25.

[23]See the range of evidence provided by H. A. Fischel, "The Uses of Sorites (*Climax, Gradatio*) in the Tannaitic Period," *Hebrew Union College Annual* 44 (1973) 119–51.

[24]Mayor, cclix.

[25]This aspect of James' style has been particularly emphasized by Ropes, 10–18.

[26]Compare S. K. Stowers, "Romans 7:7–25 as a Speech in Character (*prosopopoiia*)," *Paul in his Hellenistic Setting*, ed. T. Engberg-Peterson (Minneapolis: Fortress Press, 1995) 180–202.

know?" (2:20); "What does it profit?" (2:14, 16); "Do you see?" (2:22); "You see" (2:24); "Behold" (*idou*, 3:4; 5:4, 9, 11); "This ought not to be so" (3:10); "Come now" (*age nyn*, 4:13; 5:1). The combination of reminder/complaint is perfectly realized in the rhetorical question, "Do you not know?" (4:4).[27]

The vividness of James' language is also strengthened by another characteristic of the diatribe: the frequent use of comparisons. James makes comparisons to natural phenomena such as a wave tossed by the wind (1:6), foliage that withers in the sun (1:10–11), a dead body (2:26), fire in the forest (3:5–6), fresh and bitter water (3:11), grapes and figs (3:12), vanishing mist (4:14), moths eating clothes (5:2), rust as active as fire (5:3), rain renewing the earth (5:18). He also makes comparisons to cultural realities, such as a person checking appearance in a mirror (1:23), the reining of a horse (3:3), the steering of a ship (3:4), the taming of wild animals (3:7), farmers waiting for rain (5:7). It is also characteristic of the diatribe to make use of exemplary figures of the past, as James does (2:21–25; 5:10–11, 17–18), and cite from authoritative writings, as James also does (2:8, 11, 23; 4:6).

Two final and interrelated aspects of James style have less to do with specific tropes than with overall impressions. First, James' language is characterized by brevity. Not only are his sentences short and often asyndetic; more impressively, with the short space of 108 verses, James manages to touch on an impressive variety of subjects with remarkable concision and insight. When one compares James' treatment of various *topoi* to those in other Hellenistic moral treatises, his appear as precise miniatures. It should be remembered that in ancient rhetorical theory, the quality of brevity (*brachylogia/brevitas*) was especially connected to youth, strength, discipline, and wisdom. James' style is therefore appropriate to moral exhortation.[28]

Second, brevity forces language into a compressed and sometimes paradoxical form. James is filled with paradoxes, statements striking both in form and content, whose power is enhanced by abbreviated formulation: the invitation to consider testing as "all joy" (1:2); the rich man "boasting in his humbling" (1:10); the God who is "untempted by evil and himself tempts no one" (1:13); the desire that becomes pregnant and gives birth to sin; the sin that reaches its term in giving birth to death (1:15); the Father-God who "gives birth" to humans (1:18); the demons who "believe and shudder" (1:19); the tongue that is a "world of wickedness" and "enflamed from Gehenna" (3:6); the "pleasures battling in your members" (4:1). The habituation of repeated and careless reading keeps us from appreciating the peculiar power of such language. It is a major concern of a commentary to restore something of its freshness.

---

[27]See the evidence displayed by S. Stowers, *The Diatribe and Paul's Letter to the Romans* (SBLDS 57; Chico: Scholars Press, 1981) 85–93; 125–33.

[28]See L. T. Johnson, "Taciturnity and True Religion: James 1:26–27," *Greeks, Romans, and Christians: Essays in Honor of Abraham J. Malherbe*, ed. D. L. Balch, E. Ferguson, W. A. Meeks (Minneapolis: Fortress Press, 1990) 329–32.

BIBLIOGRAPHY

Amphoux, C. B., "Vers une description linguistique de l'épître de Jacques," *NTS* 25 (1978–79) 58–92.

Baasland, E., "Literarische Form, Thematik und geschichtliche Einordnung des Jakobusbriefes," *ANRW* II, 25.2 (1988) 3659–62.

Turner, N., *Style* in J. H. Moulton, *Grammar of New Testament Greek* IV (Edinburgh: T & T Clark, 1976) 114–20.

Wifstrand, A., "Stylistic Problems in the Epistles of James and Peter," *ST* 1 (1948) 170–82.

C. STRUCTURE

The question of a literary composition's structure has to do first with its internal coherence: do the various parts of the composition reveal some ordering principle? The question of structure also has to do with the connection between form and meaning: does the presence or absence of a certain structure determine the reading of the composition?

One of the persistent problems in interpreting James has been the difficulty in determining its structure. At one extreme, M. Dibelius argues against any overarching structure: the pieces have been drawn together haphazardly by various forces of attraction, rather than by any formal principle or logical consistency. Dibelius adheres to this position so strongly that he excludes in principle any contextual reading.[29]

Few have been either so radical or so consistent, and theories concerning the structure of James flourish. The simplest are those that proceed thematically: James is divided into sections according to the topics that ostensibly are being discussed. Judgments concerning what those topics actually are provide considerable variation, and the divisions do not necessarily shed any great light on meaning, but they do function to provide some sense of coherence to the whole.[30] More complex are those thematic analyses that seek the interrelationship and possible convergence of themes,[31] especially when these are also joined to an analysis of genre.[32]

---

[29]Dibelius, 11; he was preceded in such views by A. Jülicher, *An Introduction to the New Testament*, trans. J. P. Ward (1st German ed. 1894; New York: Putnam, 1904) 216–18.

[30]See, e.g., Ropes, 4–5; Vouga, 20; Martin, ciii–civ; F. Stagg, "An Analysis of the Book of James," *Review and Expositor* 66 (1969) 365–68.

[31]See E. Pfeiffer, "Der Zusammenhang des Jakobusbriefes," *TSK* 1 (1850) 163–80; E. Fry, "The Testing of Faith. A Study of the Structure of the Book of James," *BT* 29 (1978) 427–35.

[32]See Davids, 22–29, using the premise of a double epistolary opening argued by F. Francis, "The Form and Function of the Opening and Closing Paragraphs of James and 1 John," *ZNW* 70 (1970) 110–26.

Some critics have responded to the difficulty of determining the structure from a thematic analysis by appealing to something external to the text. One version of this approach regards James as an allegorical writing. The key to its meaning is located in some other textual tradition,[33] or in coded ecclesiastical arrangements.[34] Another version seeks some framing key to James' structure: perhaps the composition should be divided on the basis of the length of lections for oral delivery,[35] or the length of lines (strophes),[36] or in the paragraph divisions provided by the ancient manuscripts.[37]

Other critics have sought the key to James' structure in a reading of the text that does not focus simply on the display of themes. This can take the form of a simple descriptive linguistics,[38] or a much more complex approach that combines straightforward grammatical/syntactical analysis with a more comprehensive understanding of how texts are structured.[39] It is noteworthy—and the point will be examined again later in this Introduction—that recent analyses have tended to recover a much older tradition by finding in James a specifically *rhetorical* structure.[40] Also supporting the coherence of James is an approach to its structure that adopts a semiotic reading.[41]

Before stating the approach to James' structure taken in this commentary, it is appropriate to sketch the problems in the text that have generated such diversity of views among scholars. We can begin with what is least problematic. Some sections of James are easily recognized as units that are internally unified and

---

[33]The most famous example is A. Meyer's attempt to explain James on the basis of the twelve patriarchs in *Das Rätsel des Jakobusbriefes* (BZNW 10; Giessen: Töpelmann, 1930), which was adopted by G. Hartmann, "Der Aufbau des Jakobusbriefes," ZKT 66 (1942) 63–70. Less notorious is the effort by A. Blenker to connect James to the Book of Job in "Jakobs brevs sammenhaeng," *Dansk teologisk Tidsskrift* 4 (1967) 193–202.

[34]See A. Cabaniss' effort to structure James on the basis of the various church officials, who are the targets of different instructions, in "A Note on Jacob's Homily," EvQ 47 (1975) 219–22.

[35]See P. B. R. Forbes, "The Structure of the Epistle of James," EvQ 44 (1972) 147–53.

[36]H. J. Cladder, "Die Anfang des Jakobusbriefes," ZKT 28 (1904) 37–57.

[37]See J. Duplacy, "Les divisions du texte de l'épître de Jacques dans B (03) du Nouveau Testament," *Studies in New Testament Language and Text*, ed. J. K. Elliott (Leiden: Brill, 1976) 122–36; C. B. Amphoux, "Systèmes anciens de division de l'épître de Jacques et composition littéraire," Bib 62 (1981) 390–400.

[38]C. B. Amphoux, "Langue de l'épître de Jacques: études structurales," RHPR 53 (1973) 7–45.

[39]See, e.g., W. H. Wuellner, "Der Jakobusbrief im Licht der Rhetorik und Textpragmatik," LB 43 (1978) 5–66; H. Frankemölle, "Das semantische Netz des Jakobusbriefes. Zur Einheit eines umstrittenen Briefes," BZ 34 (1990) 161–97; E. Baasland, "Literarische Form, Thematic und geschichtliche Einordnung des Jakobusbriefes," ANRW II.II, 25.5 (1988) 3655–59.

[40]See Baasland, 3659; Frankemölle, 175–93; Wuellner, 36–37. See H. Frankemölle's recent *Der Brief des Jakobus* (Ökumenischer Taschenbuch-Kommentar Zum Neven Testament 17/1–2; Gütersloh: Gütersloher Verlaghaus, 1994) 1:152–80.

[41]See T. B. Cargal, *Restoring the Diaspora: Discursive Structure and Purpose in the Epistle of James* (SBLDS 144; Atlanta: Scholars Press, 1993), who states, ". . . the Epistle of James is in fact a discourse that has been organized primarily on the basis of its 'discourse semantics' (thematization and figurativization) rather than its 'discursive syntax' " (45).

capable of being topically defined. Thus, 2:1–11 deals with the incompatibility of faith and discrimination; 2:14–26 deals with the inadequacy of faith without deeds; 3:1–12 condemns the misuse of speech; 3:13–4:10 opposes friendship with the world and friendship with God; 4:13–5:6 deals with offenses involving property; 5:7–11 reinforces appropriate eschatological attitudes; and 5:13–18 advocates the proper use of speech within the community. All readers recognize and can identify such "essays."

A much harder problem is presented by those verses that appear as unattached to these relatively self-contained essays. Are these verses merely intrusive? Or do they, upon closer examination, reveal themselves as transition statements? The clearest instance is 2:12–13. It can be read as an isolated maxim, or as a bridge that connects 2:1–11 and 2:14–26 into a single coherent essay, "Concerning faith and its deeds." Similarly, James 3:13–17, which is often read as an isolated unit concerning wisdom, can legitimately be considered as a transition connecting 3:1–12 and 4:1–10.

Other examples, however, are more resistant. It is extremely difficult to connect 4:11–12 directly either to the passage immediately preceding or following it. In similar fashion, 5:12 and 5:19–20 can appear to be statements disconnected from their environment.

The most daunting challenge to the position that James has an overall structure is posed by the opening verses (1:1–27). The "diatribal" elements found so frequently in the essays are here almost absent. These opening statements are far more aphoristic in character. They appear to be more joined by word-linkage than by logic. In one case, for example, the same word appears to bear different meanings in successive sentences (1:12–13). It is above all the disjointed appearance of 1:1–27, together with the isolated verses such as 4:11–12, 5:12, and 5:19–20, that most confound efforts to locate in James a single coherent literary structure.

Despite these difficulties, some decision concerning structure is demanded of every serious reader and directly affects any interpretation. On the one hand, a rejection of *any* coherence necessitates in principal the isolated, a-contextual treatment of every statement.[42] On the other hand, finding coherence in James not at the syntactical but only at the deep structural level can, despite its appeal, mask the very real difficulties posed at the level of surface discourse.[43] The present commentary's position concerning structure and its implications for interpretation, therefore, is a carefully qualified one:

1. No attempt is made here to locate or describe a complex structure based on the intricate connections of semantic signals. Such arrangements can

---

[42]It is precisely Dibelius' steadfast commitment to this principle that makes his commentary a splendid conversation partner and challenge to easy theories of textual coherence (see esp. pp. 6 and 214).

[43]This charge cannot be made against Cargal, *Restoring the Diaspora*, who works closely with the details of language and is open to a variety of approaches to the text (218–19).

legitimately be "found" in many texts, including that of James. But they are based in a spatial, visual apprehension of the text as it now appears on the printed page. A reading of James in closer conformity to its original rhetorical setting recognizes that, like all ancient compositions, it was composed first of all for oral presentation.[44] The text, as first experienced, unfolded its meaning through time rather than displaying it in space.

2. By no means does this suggest that a variety of structuring techniques were not employed which can now be located in the text. Authors obviously say more than they intend, and language falls into patterns of meaning unanticipated by speakers or writers. To take only the most obvious example, chiasm happens as much by accident as by design. Rather, I am suggesting that the proper premise for reading James is to assume that there *is* a surface and syntactically discernible connection between statements. Only if rigorous analysis fails to yield any such connection should that premise be abandoned, and then only for that segment of text.

3. Even if materials in James were originally gathered on the basis of mechanical mnemonic principles—a premise *not* adopted by this commentary—they would, once drawn into conjunction, take on a new level of meaning simply in virtue of their juxtaposition. Even the most haphazard ordering of proverbs generates a meaning larger than the message of each individual saying, even if only by the *selection* of material. In the case of James, the isolated verses between essays should seriously be considered as particularly important authorial commentary.

4. The present commentary argues that an important organizing (and selecting) principle in James is a central set of convictions concerning the absolute incompatibility of two construals of reality and two modes of behavior following from such diverse understandings. This "deep structure" of polar opposition between "friendship with the world" and "friendship with God" undergirds the inclusion and shaping of James' material.[45]

5. Finally, the reading in this commentary is based not only on the general conviction that there is thematic and literary coherence in James, but that the aphorisms of 1:1–27 can be aligned with the essays in 2:1–5:18 in fairly simple fashion. It has often been observed that the same topics treated by maxim in the first chapter reappear in the form of essays later. Thus, the

---

[44]On this point, Forbes, "Structure," 148, is correct.

[45]Cargal, *Restoring the Diaspora*, moves in the same direction and identifies most of the important oppositions (see, e.g., 229–32). Strangely, the tension that in this commentary is taken as fundamental, that between "friendship with the world" and "friendship with God," is not isolated as central by Cargal.

prayer of faith in 1:5–7 is advocated more elaborately in 5:13–18; the reversal of the fortunes of rich and poor in 1:9–10 is developed by 2:1–7 and 4:13–5:6; the theme of enduring testing in 1:2–4 and 12 is found further in 5:7–11; the contrast between wicked desire and God's gift in 1:12–18 is argued more extensively in 3:13–4:10; the use of the tongue in 1:19–20 is picked up by the essay in 3:1–12; the necessity of acting out religious convictions in 1:22–27 is elaborated by the essay in 2:14–26. As for the final statement in 5:19–20, it serves as an excellent conclusion, recommending that the reader do for others what the author has tried to do for the readers.

The commentary itself will obviously examine these connections and their implications more fully. For now it should be noted that chapter one functions as something of a "table of contents" for the treatise, or as an "overture" of its themes. In terms of ancient literary categories, chapter one serves as an *epitome* of the work as a whole.[46] The simple principles stated here enable us to assert the essential coherence of the work as a whole without being forced into a structural procrustean bed that predetermines every reading.

BIBLIOGRAPHY

Amphoux, C. B., "Langue de l'épître de Jacques: études structurales," *RHPR* 53 (1973) 7–45.

Amphoux, C. B., "Systèmes anciens de divisions de l'épître de Jacques et compositions littéraire," *Bib* 62 (1981) 390–400.

Baasland, E., "Literarische Form, Thematik und geschichtliche Einordnung des Jakobusbriefes," ANRW II.II, 25.5 (1988) 3646–84.

Blenker, A., "Jakobs brevs sammhaeng," *Dansk teologisk Tidsskrift* 4 (1967) 193–202.

Cabaniss, A., "A Note on Jacob's Homily," *EvQ* 47 (1975) 219–22.

Cargal, T. B., *Restoring the Diaspora: Discursive Structure and Purpose in the Epistle of James* (SBLDS 144; Atlanta: Scholars Press, 1993).

Cladder, H. J., "Die Anfang des Jakobusbriefes," ZKT 28 (1904) 37–57.

Duplacy, J., "Les divisions du texte de l'épître de Jacques dans B(03) du Nouveau Testament," *Studies in New Testament Language and Text*, ed. J. K. Elliott (Leiden: Brill, 1976) 122–36.

Forbes, P. B. R., "The Structure of the Epistle of James," *EvQ* 44 (1972) 147–53.

---

[46]For the term, see A. J. Malherbe, *Moral Exhortation: A Greco-Roman Sourcebook* (Library of Early Christianity; Philadelphia: Westminster Press, 1986) 85; for an example of an epitome serving as the preface to a wisdom writing, compare *The Sentences of Syriac Menander* (see below).

Francis, F. O., "The Form and Function of the Opening and Closing Paragraphs of James and 1 John," *ZNW* 70 (1970) 110–26.
Frankemölle, H., "Das semantische Netz des Jakobusbriefes. Zur Einheit eines umstrittenen Briefes," *BZ* 34 (1990) 161–97.
Fry, E., "The Testing of Faith. A Study of the Structure of the Book of James," *BT* 29 (1978) 427–35.
Hartmann, G., "Der Aufbau des Jakobusbriefes," *ZKT* 66 (1942) 63–70.
Meyer, A., *Das Rätsel des Jakobusbriefes* (BZNW 10; Giessen: 1930).
Pfeiffer, E., "Der Zusammenhang des Jakobusbriefes," *TSK* 1 (1850) 163–80.
Stagg, F., "An Analysis of the Book of James," *Review and Expositor* 66 (1969) 365–68.
Wuellner, W. H., "Der Jakobusbrief im Licht der Rhetorik und Textpragmatik," *LB* 43 (1978) 5–66.

D. GENRE

Discussions of literary genre frequently prove frustrating, not least because of disputes over what constitutes a genre (*Gattung*)[47] and how important the determination of genre is for locating meaning.[48] At the most elementary level, genre can be understood as a combination of certain culturally defined and recognizable conventions. These can include the use of certain sorts of materials (*topoi*), of certain rhetorical devices, and of certain formal characteristics. Certainty of judgment concerning genre is proportionate to the presence or absence of all three sorts of conventions. Since few literary compositions are totally defined by previous patterns, probability concerning generic decisions is more often realizable than certainty. This is true as much for ancient as for contemporary literature, for not only did ancient theorists disagree on classifications,[49] practice often failed to correspond to their ideal typologies.

The discussion of genre is important for NT writings for three interrelated reasons. The first is similar to the reason why understanding a composition's structure helps determine meaning: to some extent, function follows form. Second, the Greco-Roman world in particular was one in which literary

---

[47]See, e.g., the discussions in N. Frye, *Anatomy of Criticism* (New York: Athenaeum, 1969), 95–99 and 243–337; E. D. Hirsch, *Validity in Interpretation* (New Haven: Yale University Press, 1967) 68–126; R. Scholes, *Structuralism in Literature* (New Haven: Yale University Press, 1974) 117–41; A. Fowler, *Kinds of Literature: An Introduction to the Theory of Genres and Modes* (Cambridge: Harvard University Press, 1982), esp. 37–53; T. Kent, *Interpretation and Genre* (Lewisburg: Bucknell University Press, 1986) 59–80.

[48]See Fowler, *Kinds of Literature*, 256–76.

[49]See, e.g., the different sorts of classifications of letters and what they should include given by the handbooks of Pseudo-Demetrius and Pseudo-Libanius, in A. J. Malherbe, "Ancient Epistolary Theorists," *Ohio Journal of Religious Studies* 5 (1977) 3–77.

conventions were widely employed and recognized. The very course of educa-tion involved the imitation of works composed according to such conventions[50] and the mastering of the standard rhetorical conventions.[51] For writings reaching us from the Hellenistic world, therefore, determination of genre offers significant assistance in locating both authorial intention and audience expectation.[52] Third, the definition of genre also enables us to make some tentative conclusions concerning the social world (even if fictive) inhabited by writer and readers, since the use of certain literary genres in Hellenistic culture suggested social arrangements and relationships.[53]

Even works that closely conform to generic standards are capable of surpassing or subverting them. The more vibrant the piece of literature, the more likely it is to challenge casual definitions of form. James stands as a particularly forceful example. It is easy to see how it partially conforms to several kinds of ancient literary genres. But in each case, closer examination shows how much of James escapes confinement to any single category. Every reader recognizes that James is some variety of moral/religious exhortation. But does James fit into a conventional form of exhortation? We will pass the candidates in review.

An obvious candidate is that ancient form of exhortation called the *diatribe*.[54] We have already touched on the many stylistic elements that James shares with noteworthy examples of the diatribe (see above, pp. 9–10). But defining the diatribe as a genre is itself problematic. In its fullest realizations, the diatribe appears not simply as a loose collection of rhetorical devices, but as a form of argumentation in which a clear thesis is argued[55] within the (fictive or real) social setting of a school.[56] Nevertheless, diatribal elements can also be found within diverse literary vehicles. Noteworthy examples are the festival discourse called *4 Maccabees*[57] and Paul's *Letter to the Romans.*

Not everything within James, furthermore, fits even this loose definition of

---

[50]See H. Marrou, *A History of Education in Antiquity,* trans. G. Lamb (New York: Mentor, 1964) 238–42.

[51]See S. F. Bonner, *Education in Ancient Rome* (Berkeley: University of California Press, 1977) 250–76.

[52]For the role of genre in creating reader expectations, see Kent, *Interpretation and Genre,* 59–80.

[53]See K. Berger, "Hellenistische Gattungen im Neuen Testament," ANRW II. 25.2 (1984) 1041–44. Different perspectives on the question of social location and literary form are found in L. G. Perdue, "Paraenesis and the Letter of James," ZNW 72 (1981) 241–56; S. K. Stowers, "Social Typifications and the Classification of Ancient Letters," in *Social World of Formative Christianity and Judaism: Essays in Tribute to Howard Clark Kee,* ed. J. Neusner, P. Borgen, et al. (Minneapolis: Fortress Press, 1988) 78–89; V. K. Robbins, "The Social Location of the Implied Author of Luke-Acts," *The Social World of Luke-Acts,* ed. J. H. Neyrey (Peabody, Massachusetts: Hendrickson, 1991) 305–32.

[54]Ropes, 10–16.

[55]See K. Berger, "Hellenistische Gattungen" 1124–32.

[56]See Stowers, *The Diatribe and Paul's Letter to the Romans* 76–78.

[57]See S. K. Stowers, "4 Maccabees," *Harper's Bible Commentary,* ed. J. L. Mays (San Francisco: Harper and Row, 1985) 922–23.

diatribe. The distinctively "diatribal" features are found primarily within the "essays" of 2:1–5:11, rather than evenly throughout the composition. Nor does James state a clear thesis that is then argued by means of antithesis and demonstration, in the manner of Romans, the NT's most impressive example of the diatribe. Finally, although James can legitimately be seen as addressing a "party" or "sect" (*hairesis*)—insofar as his readers belong to the "faith of Jesus Christ"—and exhorting it to appropriate behavior, only by a considerable stretch can the readership be thought of as a "school" comparable to that of Epictetus (see *Discourses* III, 5; III, 23; IV, 1; IV, 5).

A second way of categorizing James is as *paraenesis*. Already in 1835, F. Kern described James as "paraenetische-sittlich,"[58] and M. Dibelius considered this generic classification to be pivotal for his entire interpretation.[59] There is certainly justification for calling James paraenetic, but there is also the need for some qualification, mainly because our understanding of paraenesis has advanced considerably beyond that of Dibelius. For Dibelius, paraenesis was not only the communication of traditional moral teaching, but it was so in a necessarily formless fashion. Paraenetic literature grew by a process of agglutination rather than by authorial intention. Dibelius in principle therefore rejected any contextual analysis; every statement had to be treated atomistically.[60] The designation of James as paraenesis also meant that no conclusions could be drawn from this composition about the social setting or historical occasion of the writing.[61]

Since the time of Dibelius, further research into Hellenistic moral literature has shown his conclusions to be in need of refinement.[62] At the purely literary level, for example, although paraenesis involves the transmission of traditional teaching (at least for the group concerned), it does not follow that paraenesis must be lacking in form or development in thought.[63] Paraenetic literature, in fact, tends to combine several consistent elements: traditional teaching is often attached to an emphasis on *memory*; memory, in turn, has to do not simply with learning lore, but with a process of *imitation* of character; imitation, in turn, is directed at some *model* or paradigm who exemplifies the sort of character to be emulated; the model, finally, is spelled out by means of *maxims*, short directives concerning specific attitudes and behavior, often arranged in an antithetical

---

[58]F. H. Kern, *Der Character und Ursprung des Briefes Jacobi* (Tübingen: Fues, 1835) 5.

[59]Dibelius, 1 and 6.

[60]Dibelius, 5–6.

[61]Dibelius, 21, 46; all of these conclusions are found also in H. Songer, "The Literary Character of the Book of James," *Review and Expositor* 66 (1969) 379–89.

[62]The discussion of paraenesis in K. Berger, "Hellenistische Gattungen," 1075–77, however, does not represent much of an advance, since it still tends to identify paraenesis with gnomic literature (1076).

[63]See, e.g., J. G. Gammie, "Paraenetic Literature: Toward the Morphology of a Secondary Genre," *Semeia* 50 (1990) 41–77.

pattern, "do this, avoid that."[64] Pseudo-Isocrates' *Ad Demonicum* is a perfect sample of how a writing that designates *itself* as "paraenesis" combines these elements in a highly formal arrangement.[65] Some moral exhortations that obviously have the "feel" of paraenesis, however, not only lack these specific elements but also have only a loose arrangement of materials. The perfect example of this type is *The Sentences of Pseudo-Phocylides*.[66]

It has also been shown that paraenesis can be fitted within more encompassing literary genres. The Rhetorical Handbook of Pseudo-Libanius, for example, which delineates various "letter types" as a guide for epistolographers, contains one designated as *epistolē parainetikē* ("paraenetic letter") and provides a sample containing just these same aspects of imitation, model, and antithetic maxims.[67] Finally, Dibelius' premise that no connection can be made between paraenesis and social setting has been challenged. Analysis of the full range of writings that might qualify as paraenetic leads to the conclusion that although the dominant (ostensible) setting for such literature is transgenerational, in which paraenesis communicates a culture's norms across the crisis presented by the change of generations,[68] some paraenetic literature can be called "counter-cultural," since it serves to reinforce the specific norms of a sectarian group in contrast to dominant cultural norms.[69] The social function of paraenesis in the first case is to legitimate and reinforce the values of the dominant culture; in the second case it is to challenge and subvert them from the standpoint of a culturally marginal group. Within Jewish wisdom literature, *Sirach* serves as a splendid example of paraenesis in the service of reinforcing traditional norms in the face of generational challenge, and the *Wisdom of Solomon* as an equally fine example of paraenesis reinforcing a minority group's (Jewish) identity over against that of the dominant (Hellenistic) culture. Getting at the social setting and function is difficult and uncertain at best. But some approximations can be made by careful comparison of form and content across the entire spectrum of wisdom traditions reaching from the ancient Near East to the Desert Fathers.[70]

In some respects, James obviously fits within the broad category of paraenesis.

---

[64]See, above all, A. J. Malherbe, "Hellenistic Moralists and the New Testament," ARNW II.II, 26.1 (1992) 278–93.

[65]See Malherbe, "Hellenistic Moralists," 282.

[66]Note that Berger, "Hellenistische Gattungen," 1073, locates it among gnomic literature.

[67]See Malherbe, "Ancient Epistolary Theorists," 71; and ibid., "Hellenistic Moralists," 284.

[68]See L. G. Perdue, "Paraenesis and the Letter of James," ZNW 72 (1981) 241–46; and ibid., "Liminality as a Social Setting for Wisdom Instruction," ZAW 93 (1981) 114–26; and ibid., "The Death of the Sage and Moral Exhortation: From Ancient Near Eastern Instructions to Greco-Roman Paraenesis," *Semeia* 50 (1990) 81–109.

[69]L. G. Perdue, "The Social Character of Paraenesis and Paraenetic Literature," *Semeia* 50 (1990) 14–27.

[70]See L. T. Johnson, "The Social World of James: Literary Analysis and Historical Reconstruction," *The Social World of the First Christians: Essays in Honor of Wayne A. Meeks*, eds. L. Michael White and O. Larry Yarbrough (Minneapolis: Fortress, 1995) 180–97.

There is the assumption that the readers should already know the exhortations here being delivered (1:3, 19; 2:5–7; 4:4; 5:20); the use throughout, but most notably in chapter one, of exhortations/maxims concerned with attitude and behavior; the combined themes of memory and mirror in 1:22–25; and the presentation of models for imitation (2:21–25; 5:10–11; 5:17–18).[71]

At the same time, it is equally clear that James does not display the sort of formal arrangement of these elements that is found, for example, in *Ad Demonicum*. As noted earlier, furthermore, some of these same elements are found also in the diatribe. Both paraenetic and diatribal classifications, then, point us to important features of James' text and reinforce our perception of it as exhortatory literature. But neither so comprehensively encompasses James as to allow judgments as to what James *must* or *must not* be on the basis of those classifications.

Far less attention has been paid to James as a form of *logos protreptikos*, or protreptic discourse, but an argument can be made also for this genre.[72] The protreptic discourse originated as an exhortation to follow a particular profession, arguing for the superiority of one profession or another.[73] Thus, Pseudo-Isocrates distinguishes between *paraenesis*, which has to do with character, and *protrepsis*, which, he says, has to do with proficiency in speech (*Ad Demonicum* 4).

But when the "profession" in question was that of the philosopher (*sophos*) rather than that of the rhetorician (*sophistēs*), then protreptic would have everything to do with moral character, for such was the very essence of philosophy in the Hellenistic age.[74] Thus, Epictetus speaks of *protrepsis* entirely in terms of its moral focus (*Discourse* III, 23, 57).

There are extant a number of such protreptic discourses that encourage the reader to a life dedicated to philosophy, understood precisely as a wholehearted commitment to the life of virtue.[75] These discourses often contain the same elements of memory, model, imitation, and maxims that are found also in paraenesis. But here they encourage commitment to a certain specified lifestyle or profession and are communicated with a certain urgency and conviction. Rather than simply maxims that spell out what one should "desire and avoid," for example, such discourses often present antithetical portraits of the "true" and "false" philosopher, with stereotypical polemic against opponents here finding a

---

[71]See L. T. Johnson, "The Mirror of Remembrance (James 1:22–25)," *CBQ* 50 (1988) 632–45.

[72]See E. Baasland, "Literarische Form," 3652.

[73]See K. Berger, "Hellenistische Gattungen," 1139–43, and esp. A. J. Malherbe, *Moral Exhortation, A Greco-Roman Sourcebook* (Library of Early Christianity; Philadelphia: Westminster Press, 1986) 122–24.

[74]See L. T. Johnson, *The Writings of the New Testament: An Interpretation* (Philadelphia: Fortress Press, 1986) 32–40.

[75]See, e.g., Epictetus, *Discourse* III, 22; Dio Chrysostom, *Oration* 77/78; Lucian of Samosata, *Nigrinus* and *Demonax*; Musonius Rufus, *Fragment* 16; Maximus of Tyre, *Discourse* 36.

secondary literary function as describing the negative example readers were to avoid.[76]

Insofar as James advocates a form of behavior that is consistent, not with the norms of society as a whole, but of that community defined in terms of being "heirs of the kingdom" or "faith" (2:5) or in terms of "friendship with God" (2:23, 4:4) or in terms of "the noble name invoked upon you" (2:7), its moral teaching is defined in terms of a certain specific "profession" of life. And insofar as its admonitions and warnings are fitted to this specific (even counter-cultural) profession, and are delivered with a passion appropriate to a call to conversion, then James can as legitimately be called a form of protreptic discourse.[77]

Thinking of James as a coherent discourse suggests that it can be taken seriously not simply as a compendium of *sententiae* but as a deliberately composed piece of rhetoric. Readers of James in the sixteenth and seventeenth centuries recognized the presence of rhetorical arguments within James (see, e.g., John Calvin, below, p. 143), and assumed the logical coherence of the composition as a whole. New Testament scholars have only recently recovered the awareness of rhetoric's pervasive influence in ancient literature and on the NT in particular,[78] although there has already been a very considerable body of scholarship devoted to it.[79] The pioneering efforts at locating James within the categories of ancient rhetoric have already been noted in our discussion of the composition's structure.[80] These efforts have been followed by the reading of specific sections of James in terms of rhetorical argument.[81] Although such efforts have primarily been concerned with demonstrating the validity of a

---

[76]See L. T. Johnson, "II Timothy and the Polemic against False Teachers: A Reexamination," *JRS* 6/7 (1978–79) 1–26; ibid., "The Anti-Jewish Slander of the New Testament and the Conventions of Ancient Polemic," *JBL* 103 (1989) 419–41.

[77]So also E. Baasland, "Literarische Form," 3654, who concludes that James is a wisdom protreptic discourse written in the form of a letter.

[78]See, e.g., B. L. Mack, *Rhetoric and the New Testament* (GBS; Minneapolis: Fortress Press, 1990); G. A. Kennedy, *New Testament Interpretation through Rhetorical Criticism* (Chapel Hill: University of North Carolina Press, 1984); M. Warner, ed., *The Bible as Rhetoric: Studies in Biblical Persuasion and Credibility* (London: Routledge, 1990).

[79]For a sampling of the literature devoted to the rhetorical analysis of Paul's letters, for example, see only T. H. Olbricht, "An Aristotelian Rhetorical Analysis of 1 Thessalonians," in *Greeks, Romans, and Christians*, ed. D. L. Balch et al. (Minneapolis: Fortress Press, 1990) 216–36, and M. M. Mitchell, *Paul and the Rhetoric of Reconciliation* (Louisville: Westminster/John Knox Press, 1991); and for the Gospels, see, e.g., B. L. Mack and V. K. Robbins, *Patterns of Persuasion in the Gospels* (Sonoma, California: Polebridge Press, 1989).

[80]See W. Wuellner, "Der Jakobusbrief im Licht der Rhetorik und Textpragmatik," H. Frankemölle, "Das semantische Netz des Jakobusbriefes," and E. Baasland, "Literarische Form."

[81]See, e.g., D. F. Watson, "James 2 in Light of Greco-Roman Schemes of Argumentation," *NTS* 39 (1993) 94–121; and ibid., "The Rhetoric of James 3:1–12 and a Classic Pattern of Argumentation," *NovT* 35 (1993) 48–64; W. H. Wachob, "*The Rich in Faith and the Poor in Spirit*": *The Socio-Rhetorical Function of a Saying of Jesus in the Epistle of James* (Ph.D. diss., Emory University, 1993).

certain way of reading, they have also successfully confirmed that James does have both literary cohesion and logic.

A final genre for consideration is that of the *letter*. James presents itself for such consideration by beginning with a classic epistolary greeting: "James, slave of God and of the Lord Jesus Messiah, to the twelve tribes that are in the diaspora, greeting" (*chairein*, 1:1). But is James a "real letter?" The question bears first on debates concerning epistolography in the Hellenistic period and secondly on the possible historical circumstances of composition.

The formal study of NT letters was deeply influenced by A. Deissmann. On the basis of his research into previously unexamined papyrological material, Deissmann claimed that a fundamental distinction could be made between letters and epistles.[82] The distinction was both literary and sociological.[83] In the papyri, Deissmann found what he considered as "real letters," spontaneous and informal missives occasioned by specific situations in life and responding to those situations: illness, death, business arrangements, family problems.[84] Such letters, he thought, were characteristic of the lower orders in the empire. In contrast, Deissmann termed as "epistles" those productions from the educated and cultured classes that were in the form of a letter but were in fact literary or moral exercises, such as the *epistulae morales* of Seneca.[85]

In light of this distinction, Deissmann could categorize Paul's letters as "real" correspondence, since they are so filled with incidental detail and so obviously occasioned by present circumstances rather than the hope for a reading by posterity.[86] The production of such "real letters," in turn, supported the view that Christianity was in the beginning a "lower-class" movement, whose amazing growth could be attributed to spiritual rather than cultural factors.[87] New Testament "letters" that did not reveal such obvious rootedness in circumstance could, conversely, be regarded as closer to the artificial literary productions of the Greco-Roman elite.[88] Deissmann's distinctions could be used by him and by others as a way of locating NT compositions chronologically and theologically.[89] When Deissmann characterizes James as "from the beginning literary," there-

---

[82]A. Deissmann, *Light from the Ancient East*, trans. L. R. M. Strachan (4th ed., 1922; Grand Rapids: Baker Book House, 1978) 1–61; 146–251.

[83]See A. J. Malherbe, *Social Aspects of Early Christianity* 2nd ed. (Philadelphia: Fortress Press, 1983) 31–36.

[84]See the examples provided by Deissmann, 149–233, and in J. L. White, *Light from Ancient Letters* (Philadelphia: Fortress Press, 1986).

[85]Deissmann, 148; 229–30.

[86]Deissmann, 233–42.

[87]Deissmann, 465–67.

[88]Deissmann, 242–45.

[89]Deissmann, 247–51; the same tendency is found in works as diverse in their approach as A. E. Barnett, *Paul Becomes a Literary Influence* (Chicago: University of Chicago Press, 1941) and M. Y. MacDonald, *The Pauline Churches: A Socio-Historical Study of Institutionalization in the Pauline and Deutero-Pauline Writings* (SNTMS 60; Cambridge: Cambridge University Press, 1988) 85–234.

fore, more is implied than at first appears: James is not part of the first, "creative" stage of the Christian movement, but "the beginnings of a Christian literature."[90]

Subsequent research has altered Deissmann's simple and powerful distinctions. More comprehensive social analysis of early Christianity suggests, in the first place, that it was not uniformly a movement made up of the oppressed and downtrodden, but at least in some urban areas, was comprised of the moderately prosperous population as well.[91] Second, analysis of rhetorical handbooks not only shows the variety of "letter types" there were in Greco-Roman culture,[92] but also that some at least of these "letter types" correspond to the "real letters" of Paul.[93] Such analysis also suggests a complex world of social status and relationship for diverse types of letters.[94] The simple distinctions of Deissmann must yield to subtler and more complex discriminations.

It is clear, for example, that if the letter is a genre, it is also capable of a variety of manifestations.[95] The NT contains examples of letters of commendation (Romans 16; Philemon; 3 John), of the friendly letter (Philippians), letters of rebuke (Galatians, Revelation), of the paraenetic letter (2 Timothy; 2 Peter), of the mandate letter (1 Timothy, Titus), of the diatribal letter (Romans), and of circular letters (Ephesians, 1 Peter, 1 John).[96] A decision on the epistolary character of James must be made with reference to this wide range of specific letter forms and functions.

Apart from the greeting in 1:1, what recommends consideration of James as a letter? Although it contains elements of paraenesis, it does not fit the sort of formal pattern suggested by the sample *epistolē parainetikē* in Pseudo-Libanius.[97] Still less do the aspects of James that can be described as diatribal suggest the sort of formal diatribal argument such as we find in Romans. Indeed, James lacks most of the formal elements familiar to us from many of Paul's letters. There is no thanksgiving period, no personal greetings, no formal farewell.

---

[90]Deissmann, 242–43; see also M. Dibelius, *A Fresh Approach to the New Testament and Early Christian Literature* (New York: Charles Scribner's Sons, 1936) 230.

[91]See, e.g., A. E. Judge, *The Social Pattern of Christian Groups in the First Century* (London: Tyndale, 1960); G. Theissen, *The Social Setting of Pauline Christianity*, ed. and trans. J. H. Schütz (Philadelphia: Fortress Press, 1982); W. A. Meeks, *The First Urban Christians: The Social World of the Apostle Paul* (New Haven: Yale University Press, 1983); A. J. Malherbe, *Social Aspects of Early Christianity* 2nd ed. (Philadelphia: Fortress Press, 1983).

[92]Malherbe, "Epistolary Theorists," 62–77.

[93]See the discussions and examples given by S. K. Stowers, *Letter Writing in Greco-Roman Antiquity* (Library of Early Christianity; Philadelphia: Westminster Press, 1986).

[94]See S. K. Stowers, "Social Typification and the Classification of Ancient Letters," *The Social World of Formative Christianity and Judaism*, ed. J. Neusner et al. (Philadelphia: Fortress Press, 1988) 78–89.

[95]See K. Berger, "Hellenistische Gattungen," 1327–40.

[96]See L. T. Johnson, *Writings of the New Testament*, 261, 306, 316–18, 341, 351, 367, 391, 396, 430, 445–49, 503–4.

[97]See Malherbe, "Epistolary Theorists," 71.

James addresses none of his readers by name. He makes mention of no specific incidents in the life of the author or readers. The situations mentioned tend to be general and typical in character rather than specific and local.[98] After the greeting (1:1), the author does not intrude himself except for the very oblique (implied) inclusion of himself among "teachers" in 3:1. If the conceit of ancient letter-writing was that the letter made the author present,[99] in the case of James that presence is mediated entirely by instructions.

On the other hand, some aspects of James do support classifying it as a letter.[100] The exhortatory rhetoric, with its use of direct address and vivid dialogical style is appropriate to letter-writing. The fact that the greeting portrays the readers as inhabiting an indefinite geographical area (the *diaspora*), furthermore, is compatible with considering James a circular letter intended for a broader readership than that of a local community. It would make sense, therefore, that the situations reflected in the letter be general and typical rather than specific and local. James can certainly be called a "letter" at least in the broad sense that *Aristeas to Philocrates* can be so designated, or Lucian of Samosata's *Nigrinus*.

The second question concerning James as a "real letter" has less to do with its formal elements so much as the veracity of its self-presentation and will be considered later under the topic of "whose voice?" If we decide that the author could have been the historical James, who was the brother of Jesus, writing from Jerusalem to diaspora believers in the first generation of the Christian movement, then we could consider James a "real letter" in a different sense than if we decide that it was a pseudonymous composition composed for a general readership of a later generation and given an epistolary greeting only in order to conform it to an already developing Christian literary tradition. Making such a decision does not involve the determination of genre so much as it does the assessment of the composition's contents.

In either case, however, it should be noted that even if James was written pseudonymously and to a fictional readership, whenever it was subsequently read out loud, it was experienced as a letter from "James the slave of God and of the Lord Jesus Christ." Whatever it was first intended to be, in other words, it has in fact become a letter.

In summary, the analysis of James' language, structure, and literary form support the conclusion that this is a literarily coherent composition written in a correct koine Greek with significant rhetorical dimensions (both stylistic and argumentative), and that it can be appropriately considered a protreptic discourse in the form of a letter.[101]

---

[98]Dibelius, 46–47.

[99]See Malherbe, "Epistolary Theorists," 15.

[100]This case has been most forcefully argued by F. O. Francis, "The Form and Function of the Opening and Closing Paragraphs of James and 1 John," ZNW 70 (1970) 110–26.

[101]Compare Baasland, "Literarische Form," 3654.

BIBLIOGRAPHY

Baasland, E., "Literarische Form, Thematik und geschichtliche Einordnung des Jakobusbriefes," *ANRW* II. II, 25. 5 (1988) 3646–84.

Berger, K., "Hellenistische Gattungen im Neuen Testament," *ANRW* II. 25.2 (1984) 1031–432.

Deissmann, A., *Light from the Ancient East,* trans. L. R. M. Strachan (4th ed., 1922; Grand Rapids, Baker Books, 1978).

Dibelius, M., *A Fresh Approach to the New Testament and Early Christian Literature* (New York: Charles Scribner's Sons, 1936).

Francis, F. O., "The Form and Function of the Opening and Closing Paragraphs of James and 1 John," *ZNW* 70 (1970) 110–26.

Gammie, J. G., "Paraenetic Literature: Toward the Morphology of a Secondary Genre," *Semeia* 50 (1990) 41–77.

Johnson, L. T., "The Social World of James: Literary Analysis and Historical Reconstruction," *The Social World of the First Christians: Essays in Honor of Wayne A. Meeks,* eds. L. Michael White and O. Larry Yarbrough (Minneapolis: Fortress, 1995) 180–97.

———, "The Mirror of Remembrance (James 1:22–25)," *CBQ* 50 (1988) 632–45.

Malherbe, A. J., "Ancient Epistolary Theorists," *Ohio Journal of Religious Studies* 5 (1977) 3–77.

———, "Hellenistic Moralists and the New Testament," *ANRW* II. II, 26. 1 (1992) 267–333.

———, *Moral Exhortation: A Greco-Roman Sourcebook* (Library of Early Christianity; Philadelphia: Westminster Press, 1986).

———, *Social Aspects of Early Christianity* 2nd ed. (Philadelphia: Fortress Press, 1983).

Perdue, L. G., "The Death of the Sage and Moral Exhortation: From Ancient Near Eastern Instructions to Greco-Roman Paraenesis," *Semeia* 50 (1990) 81–109.

———, "Liminality as a Social Setting for Wisdom Instruction," *ZAW* 93 (1981) 114–26.

———, "Paraenesis and the Letter of James," *ZNW* 72 (1981) 241–56.

———, "The Social Character of Paraenesis and Paraenetic Literature," *Semeia* 50 (1990) 14–27.

Songer, H., "The Literary Character of the Book of James," *Review and Expositor* 66 (1969) 379–89.

Stowers, S. K., *The Diatribe and Paul's Letter to the Romans* (SBLDS 57; Chico: Scholars Press, 1981).

———, *Letter Writing in Greco-Roman Antiquity* (Library of Early Christianity; Philadelphia: Westminster Press, 1986).

————, "Social Typifications and the Classification of Ancient Letters," *Social World of Formative Christianity and Judaism: Essays in Tribute to Howard Clark Kee*, ed. J. Neusner, et al. (Minneapolis: Fortress Press, 1988) 78–89.

Wachob, W. H., *"The Rich in Faith and the Poor in Spirit:" The Socio-Rhetorical Function of a Saying of Jesus in the Epistle of James* (Emory University Dissertation, 1993).

Watson, D. F., "James 2 in Light of Greco-Roman Schemes of Argumentation," *NTS* 39 (1993) 94–121.

————, "The Rhetoric of James 3:1–12 and a Classic Pattern of Argumentation," *NovT* 35 (1993) 48–64.

White, J. L., *Light from Ancient Letters* (Philadelphia: Fortress Press, 1986).

E. LITERARY RELATIONSHIPS

James stands within a great stream of exhortatory literature, both Greco-Roman and Jewish, from the ancient Mediterranean world, a literature that, in one way or another, has to do with the right ordering of practical life. James both draws from that stream and contributes to it. Part of distinguishing James' voice, therefore, involves locating it within these diverse literary traditions.

The task is made more complex by the tendencies of wisdom literature. Since wisdom deals with real human life, and since certain standard human situations tend to recur from culture to culture, even literature from widely disparate settings can contain remarkably similar perceptions. Both Heraclitus and Confucius compare life's transitoriness to a passing stream.[102] In the ancient Mediterranean world, moreover, wisdom was also international in another sense: it was both produced by and disseminated among those educated classes who clustered in the bureaucracies of empires, for whom the regular transmission and translation of legal lore provided the vehicle also for the sharing of practical wisdom. Wisdom literature, therefore, tends to be agglutinative in character, gathering materials here and there without obsessive concern for sources, and handing them on in turn to other collections.[103]

In order to distinguish the specific voice of James, the issue of literary

---

[102]See Heraclitus, "On the Universe," *frag.* 41; Confucius, *Analects* 9:17; likewise, Confucius declares that students should be "slow in speech and prompt in action" (*Analects* 4:24; compare James 1:19).

[103]The pioneering essays of Henry A. Fischel traced the transmutation of traditions within the Greco-Roman and Jewish wisdom schools; see esp. "Story and History: Observations on Greco-Roman Rhetoric and Pharisaism," *American Oriental Society West Branch Semi-Centennial Volume* (Asian Studies Research Institute, *Oriental Studies* 3, Indiana University), ed. D. Sinor (Bloomington, Indiana: 1969) 59–88; and "Studies in Cynicism and the Ancient Near East: The History of a *chria*," *Religions in Antiquity: Essays in Honor of E. R. Goodenough*, ed. J. Neusner (Leiden: Brill, 1968) 373–411.

derivation or dependence is not ultimate. More important is the comparison between James and other literature. In comparison both similarities and dissimilarities can be observed, leading to a more precise perception of specific literary profiles. The present discussion deals less with lexical resemblances than with broader patterns of comparison: literary shaping, social location and function, and ideological standpoint.[104] The commentary proper will provide many specific points of comparison. At this point it is appropriate to locate James' voice at least generally with respect to (1) Greco-Roman moral exhortation, (2) the OT, (3) Jewish intertestamental literature, (4) canonical, and (5) noncanonical Christian writings.

1. GRECO-ROMAN MORALISTS

The discussion of language and genre showed how James shares formal elements with Hellenistic moral literature. Two questions now present themselves: (1) is similarity to be found only at the formal level or does it extend also to shared material; and (2) do any Hellenistic writings offer themselves for a more extended comparison?

The commentary itself will offer overwhelming evidence that at the level of individual themes, James shares substantially in the moral teaching of the Greco-Roman world. Even the most cursory reading in that tradition uncovers obvious points of resemblance to James. Not surprisingly, many of these concern the status of the wise person (*sophos*), whose true joy is found in virtue (Seneca, *Moral Epistles* 23:2 = James 1:2), whose virtue is proven by testing (Seneca, *On Providence* 2:2, 6; Epictetus, *frag.* 112 = James 1:2), who is, because of virtue, truly free (Epictetus, *Discourse* IV, 1, 13 = James 1:25), wealthy (Plato, *Phaedrus* 279B = James 2:5), kingly (Cicero, *De Finibus* III, 75; Epictetus *Discourse* III, 22, 72 = James 2:8), and even a friend of God (Plato, *Laws* 716D; Epictetus, *Discourse* IV, 3, 9 = James 2:23).

Any number of other statements in James can be matched by those of the philosophers. It is possible to read James 2:10–11 in light of the Stoic principle of the unity of all virtues (Plutarch, *Stoic Self-Contradictions* 27 [*Mor.* 1046F]) and James 1:13 with reference to the frequently stated conviction that God is the cause only of good and not of evil (see Plutarch, *A Pleasant Life Impossible* 22 [*Mor.* 1102F]; Hierocles, *On Duties* 2.9.7). James and these writings also share certain standard images: the mirror as a source of moral self-analysis (Epictetus, *Discourse* II, 14, 21 = James 1:23); the fig tree and its fruit as source of good or evil (Seneca, *Moral Epistles* 87:25; Plutarch *On Tranquillity of Soul* 13 [*Mor.* 472F] = James 3:12); the tongue as venomous (Lucian of Samosata, *The Runaways* 19 = James 3:8); and the charioteer and the pilot as images for

---

[104]The lexical parallels are noted by many commentaries, most fully by Chaine, 41–79, and, above all, Mayor, lxx–cxxvii.

the control of the passions (Plato, *Phaedrus* 254B–D; Dio Chrysostom, *Oration* 12:34 = James 3:3–4).

James shares with Hellenistic moralists some basic convictions concerning the moral life: that principles must be carried out in action to be considered authentic (Plutarch, *Stoic Self-Contradictions* 1 [*Mor.* 1033B]; Seneca, *Moral Epistles* 20:1 = James 1:22–25; 2:17); that control of speech is a fundamental requirement of the virtuous person (Plutarch, *On Garrulousness* 4 [*Mor.* 503E–540C = James 1:19; 3:1–12); that boldness in moral correction is a kindness to others (Dio Chrysostom, *Oration* 77/78:37–45; Hierocles, *On Duties* 4.25.53 = James 5:19–20); that disordered desires and passions create social disorder and wars (Plato, *Phaedo* 66C; Cicero, *De Finibus* 1:43 = James 4:1). The interconnectedness of virtue and vice is suggested by the use of virtue lists and vice lists (e.g., Maximus of Tyre, *Discourse* 36:2; Dio Chrysostom, *Oration* 4:83–96) such as James employs in its contrast of two forms of wisdom in 3:15–17.

James also makes use of certain *topoi* of moral instruction. These are standard treatments of a subject, usually consisting in a loose agglomeration of cliches, propositions, examples, and other statements organized around a central theme and frequently drawn together by a process of association.[105] A great deal of Hellenistic moral instruction was made up of such *topoi*.[106] We can detect their presence already in the classical period. Aristotle's discussion of friendship in the *Nicomachean Ethics* (8–9) is built up on the basis of a handful of proverbial propositions. By the time of James, entire treatises could be constructed on the basis of such collections or *florilegia*, with the author adding individual touches to the standard elements.[107] Knowledge of such *topoi* gathered from wide reading in the primary sources shows them to be flexible and informal examples of associative thinking. They are of considerable value in grasping some of the less obvious connections between ideas in James' argument. The most impressive case is James 3:13–4:10, whose thematic unity is perceptible only in light of the *topoi* on envy (*peri phthonou*) and on friendship (*peri philias*).[108]

James is not a treatise on a virtue, however, nor on the virtues required of the *sophos*. His use of common Hellenistic themes and *topoi* is eclectic and placed in service of his own purposes. No single Hellenistic composition, therefore,

---

[105]See A. J. Malherbe, *Moral Exhortation: A Greco-Roman Sourcebook* (Library of Early Christianity; Philadelphia: Fortress Press, 1986) 144–61.

[106]Such *topoi* are listed under their respective titles in Johannes Stobaeus, *Anthologium*, in four books (ed. C. Wachsmuth and O. Hense, 2nd ed. 1884, reprinted in 1974).

[107]See Malherbe, "Hellenistic Moralists," 320–25; among many examples of essays built on the basis of *topoi* are Plutarch's *On Tranquillity of Soul*, *On Garrulousness*, *On Brotherly Love*, *On Envy and Hatred*, and Cicero's *De Amicitia* and *De Senectute*.

[108]See L. T. Johnson, "James 3:13–4:10 and the *topos PERI PHTHONOU*," *NovT* 25 (1983) 327–47, and ibid., "Friendship with the World and Friendship with God: a Study of Discipleship in James," *Discipleship in the New Testament*, ed. F. Segovia (Philadelphia: Fortress Press, 1985) 166–83.

provides an adequate literary comparison. And there are certain staples of Greco-Roman moral teaching that are completely absent from James. James makes no use, for example, of medical imagery for virtue and vice, a metaphor widely employed by Greco-Roman moral discourse (see, e.g., Plutarch, *On Virtue and Vice* 3–4 [*Mor.* 101B–E]).[109] James' broad agreement concerning moral character, furthermore, cannot conceal an even deeper disagreement on the religious warrants for morality. His measure for valuing worth, for example, directly counters the broad social pattern of the Greco-Roman world based on patronage and on the subtle shades of shame and honor (compare *To Demonicus* 16–17, 26, 33 with James 2:1–5).[110] In James, it is the proud who will be put down and the humble who will be raised up (4:6–10), not by the benevolence of a patron, but by the power of God. In this respect, James is thoroughly at home, not in the classical world of *aretē*, but in the world shaped by the symbols of Torah.

2. THE OLD TESTAMENT

Like all NT writings, James can be regarded as a reinterpretation of the symbolic world of Torah in the light of the confession of Jesus as Messiah and Lord (1:1; 2:1).[111] What marks James as distinctive among NT writings is the way it engages the full range of that symbolic world, in its dimensions of law, of prophecy, and of wisdom. Within the biblical tradition itself, such distinctions are somewhat artificial. Torah is not only law to be observed but also wisdom for instruction: *hautē hē sophia hymōn kai hē synesis enantion pantōn tōn ethnōn*, "This is your wisdom and understanding before all the nations" (Deut 4:6). The prophets call the apostate people back to the covenant and use wisdom motifs (see Isa 11:2; 29:14; Amos 5:13.[112] Specifically, "wisdom" literature not only reinforces covenantal nomism (LXX Pss 1:2; 118:1, 18; Sir 24:23, 2:12–16; Wis 18:9) but often does so with prophetic cadence and urgency (Prov 8:1–36; Sir 5:1–8).[113]

---

[109]See, e.g., A. J. Malherbe, "Medical Imagery in the Pastorals," *Texts and Testaments*, ed. W. E. March (San Antonio, Texas: Trinity University Press, 1980) 19–35.

[110]Despite some overgeneralizations, a valuable contribution has been made on this point by B. J. Malina, *The New Testament World: Insights from Cultural Anthropology* (Louisville: John Knox Press, 1981) 25–50; see also B. J. Malina and J. H. Neyrey, "Honor and Shame in Luke-Acts: Pivotal Values in the Mediterranean World," in *The Social World of Luke-Acts* (Peabody, Massachusetts: Hendrickson, 1991) 25–66.

[111]See L. T. Johnson, *The Writings of the New Testament: An Interpretation* (Philadelphia: Fortress, 1986) 1–20.

[112]See, e.g., J. Crenshaw, "The Influence of the Wise upon Amos," ZAW 79 (1967) 42–51.

[113]The interrelationship of wisdom and law is displayed very fully in E. J. Schnabel, *Law and Wisdom from Ben Sira to Paul* (WUNT 2.16; Tübingen: JCB Mohr [Paul Siebeck] 1985), and with connection to James by C. H. Felder, *Wisdom, Law and Social Concern in the Epistle of James* (Ph.D. diss., Union Theological Seminary, 1982). The influence of wisdom on apocalyptic, in turn, is sketched by G. von Rad, *Wisdom in Israel* (Nashville: Abingdon Press, 1972) 263–83, and is applied to James by R. Wall, "James as Apocalyptic Paraenesis," *ResQ* 32 (1990) 11–22.

a. The Law

The law (*nomos*) is thematic in James. He speaks of the "perfect law of freedom" (*nomon teleion ton tēs eleutherias*) in 1:25, the "law of freedom" (*nomos eleutherias*) in 2:12, and of the "royal law" or "law of the kingdom" (*nomon basilikon*) in 2:8, as something that should not only be "gazed into" (*parakypsas*, 1:25) but also "fulfilled" (*teleioun*, 1:25) and "kept" (*tērein*, 2:10), both in its parts and as a whole (*holon ton nomon*, 2:10). Failure to keep the law means that one is a "transgressor of the law" (*parabatēs nomou*, 2:11). Transgressors slander and judge the law by placing their own authority over it (4:11). By so doing they also place their authority over God's, who is the lawmaker (*nomothetēs*, 4:12) and the judge (*kritēs*, 4:12). Human life, therefore, should be lived in view of judgment carried out by God on the basis of the law of freedom (*dia nomou eleutherias mellontes krinesthai*, 2:12). James' language echoes the perceptions of the law in the biblical wisdom tradition (see LXX Ps 118:55, 105, 109, 142, 153; Sir 21:11; 33:2; 45:5).

But what does James mean by "the law?" To anticipate later discussions, the negative points should be made at once. First, James does not connect language about "works" (*erga*) to his language about law. The expression "works of the law" (*erga tou nomou*), familiar from Paul's polemics (Rom 3:20, 28; Gal 2:16; 3:2, 5, 10), is completely absent in James. Second, James does not use the language of "commandments" (*entolai*) as Paul sometimes does (Rom 7:8; 13:9; 1 Cor 7:19). James recognizes the theoretical divisibility of law into "commandments," but thinks of the commandments as a whole. Breaking any part of the law is like breaking all of it, for obedience is directed not to the *commandment* but to the lawmaker (2:11; see 4:11–12). Third, James does not connect language about law to ritual observance. This point requires emphasis because of the inevitable James/Paul comparison to be discussed later. Circumcision is of no concern to this writing (contrast Gal 5:2–4, 12; 6:12). The text shows no interest in special days or feasts (contrast Gal 4:9–11; Col 2:16). Nor does it advocate any sort of dietary or purity regulations (contrast Col 2:21). In 1:27 James speaks of "pure religion" as being "unstained from the world," but, as we shall show, this involves moral rather than ritual behavior. In short, whatever James means by *nomos*, it cannot be connected with any recognizable program for Jewish ethnic identity, still less any "Judaizing" tendency in early Christianity.

What, then, does *nomos* encompass for James? It obviously includes the decalogue, two commandments of which he cites according to the LXX (whose order differs from that in the MT) in 2:11: *mē moicheusēs, mē phoneusēs* ("do not commit adultery, do not kill," see Exod 20:13, 15; Deut 5:17–18).[114] James'

---

[114]See F. E. Vokes, "The Ten Commandments in the New Testament and in First Century Judaism," *SE* 5 (1968) 146–54.

understanding of law also includes Lev 19:18, *agapēseis ton plēsion sou hōs seauton*, "you shall love your neighbor as yourself." This is what James refers to as the *nomos basilikos*, the "royal law" (2:8). In light of other citations of this commandment in the NT, especially in connection with the pronouncement of Jesus (Mark 12:31; Matt 22:39; Luke 10:27), it is appropriate to designate this as "the law of the kingdom" (see the use of *basileia* in 2:5). The combination of decalogue and Lev 19:18 as a summary of Torah occurs also in Rom 13:9. The language of Gal 5:14 is likewise strikingly similar to that in James: *ho gar pas nomos en heni logō peplērōtai, en tō agapēseis ton plēsion sou hōs seauton*, "for the whole law is fulfilled in one word, namely you shall love your neighbor as yourself." The combined use of the decalogue and Leviticus 19 is found also in *The Sentences of Pseudo-Phocylides*.[115]

The role of the law is not exhausted by these citations. James returns (albeit obliquely) to the combination of murder/adultery in 4:1–4. The use of Leviticus 19 is much more extensive. We notice that James calls for "fulfilling" the royal law "according to the scripture" (*kata tēn graphēn*) in 2:8. Close analysis reveals that James makes use of the original context of Lev 19:18 throughout the letter, in order to articulate the dimensions of this "love of neighbor": Lev 19:12 = James 5:12; Lev 19:13 = James 5:4; Lev 19:15 = James 2:1, 9; Lev 19:16 = James 4:11; Lev 19:17b = James 5:20; Lev 19:18c = James 2:8. Leviticus 19:11 and 19:14 are not verbally echoed but the substance of those commands is covered, respectively, by James 2:14–16 and 3:13–4:10.

It is striking that the allusions to Leviticus 19 occur in close conjunction with elements specific to the Christian tradition, whether the "faith of our glorious Lord Jesus Christ" (2:1), or the "heirs of the kingdom" (2:5), or the dominical commands on judging (4:11; see Matt 7:1) and swearing (5:12; see Matt 5:34–35) and fraternal correction (5:20; see Matt 18:15; Luke 17:3), or the arrival (*parousia*) of the judge (5:9b; see Matt 24:23–33). The integration of specifically legal material and Christian convictions justifies the designation of James as a kind of halachic midrash.[116]

The law is also thematized in James by the use of examples. The image of the mirror of remembrance in 1:22–25 establishes the "perfect law of freedom" as something into which one can "gaze" (*parakypsas*) and "remain in" (*parameinas*) by becoming a "doer of the deed" (*poiētēs ergou*, 1:25). Torah contains the examples that the readers can see and imitate: Abraham and Rahab (2:20–25), Job (5:11), and Elijah (5:17–18). That these examples continue the theme established by the mirror image in 1:22–25 is shown by the specific use of verbs of seeing (*blepeis*, 2:22; *orate*, 2:24; *idou*, *eidete*, 5:11).[117]

In summary, for James the term *nomos* encompasses a set of moral rather

---

[115]See P. van der Horst, *The Sentences of Pseudo-Phocylides* (SVTP 4; Leiden: Brill, 1978) 66–67.

[116]L. T. Johnson, "The Use of Leviticus 19 in the Letter of James," *JBL* 101 (1982) 391–401.

[117]See L. T. Johnson, "The Mirror of Remembrance (James 1:22–25)," *CBQ* 50 (1988) 632–45.

than ritual norms established by divine authority and providing the basis for God's judgment of human behavior. It finds its focus in the love of neighbor, but that love is explicated by specific attitudes and actions prescribed by Torah. Finally, the law provides narrative exemplars for imitation, models precisely of *faith* in several dimensions: the obedient works of faith shown by Abraham and Rahab; the endurance of faith demonstrated by Job, and the prayer of faith exhibited by Elijah.[118]

b. Prophecy

James makes explicit reference to the prophetic tradition in 5:10, where he advises his readers to take as an example (*hypodeigma*) of evil-suffering (*kakopathias*) and long-suffering (*makrothymias*) "the prophets who spoke in the name of the Lord." In the proper place the full implications of this characterization will be examined; for now we can note how speaking in the name of the Lord and suffering for it communicate something of the author's understanding of the community's identity and fate (James 1:12; 2:5–7; 5:1–6), as well as a widely attested conviction in early Christianity that connected prophecy with suffering (Matt 5:12; Luke 6:23; 11:50; 13:34; 1 Thess 2:15; Heb 11:32–34). James appears to include Job among the number of the prophets (5:11), as well as Elijah (5:17–18).

In places, James' language also evokes that of the prophetic tradition, as in his use of *age nyn* ("come now") in 4:13 and 5:1 (compare Isa 43:5–6), in his comparison of earthly wealth to a flower that fades (1:9–11; see Isa 40:6–7), in his condemnation of the oppressive rich (5:1–6; see Amos 2:6–7; 3:10; 4:1; 8:4–6; Isa 3:14–15; 5:8–9), and in his identification of "pure religion" with "visiting orphans and widows in their affliction" (1:27; see Isa 1:17, 23).

Most of all, James shows itself to be a worthy heir of the prophetic voice in its outspoken attack on a "friendship with the world" that is in reality an "enmity with God." The use of "adulteresses" (*moichalides*) in 4:4 is not accidental, for it echoes the prophetic tradition of symbolizing the relationship between Yahweh and the people in terms of a marriage covenant, so that "adultery" becomes equivalent to the idolatrous breaking of covenant (Hos 3:1; Ezek 16:38; 23:45; Isa 57:3; Jer 3:9; 13:27). Although cast in terms of "friendship with God," James' call to conversion in 3:13–4:10 corresponds exactly to the classic prophetic exhortations concerning a return to covenantal loyalty.

---

[118]For further discussion of the law in James, see R. Fabris, *Legge della Liberta in Giacomo* (Supplementi alla Revista Biblica 8; Brescia: Paideia, 1977); H. Frankemölle, "Gesetz im Jakobusbrief: Zur Tradition, contextuellen Verwendung und Rezeption eines belasteten Begriffes," in *Das Gesetz im Neuen Testament*, ed. K. Kertelge (QD 108; Freiburg: Herder, 1986) 175–221; O. J. F. Seitz, "James and the Law," *SE* 2 (1964) 472–86.

c. Wisdom

James' appropriation of the wisdom tradition needs little demonstration.[119] Wisdom (*sophia*) is made thematic in 1:5 and especially in 3:13–18, where a "wisdom from above" is contrasted to a wisdom that is "earthbound, unspiritual, and demonic" (3:15). Such statements correspond to the perception of *ḥokmâ/ sophia* as a measure for human behavior revealed by God that we can find in Proverbs (1:7; 2:6; 22:4), Sirach (1:1, 14, 26; 19:20), and Wisdom (1:6; 7:15). It is important to note, however, that James lacks any personification of *sophia* similar to that in Prov 8:1–36, Wis 7:15–30, or Sir 24:1–34. *Sophia* is implicitly connected to the *pneuma* that God has made to dwell in humans (James 4:5)[120] but never loses its close connection to the realm of human behavior.

In 4:6, James explicitly cites Prov 3:34, "God resists the haughty but gives a gift to the lowly." And as in James' use of Leviticus 19, the influence of the original context of Prov 3:34 can be found throughout James 3:13–4:6 (compare Prov 3:19–35). James also echoes the language of Prov 10:12 in his statement of 5:20, that converting a sinner "will cover a multitude of sins."

James has a number of themes whose language and content bear an unmistakable "wisdom" coloration: the testing of the righteous person's virtue (James 1:2; see Prov 27:21; Sir 2:1; Wis 3:4), of which Job is the obvious paradigm (5:11; see Job 1:21–2:10); the importance of deliberation in speech (James 1:19; see Sir 5:11; Qoh 5:1); the incompatibility of anger and true piety (James 1:20; Qoh 7:9; Prov 15:1); the instability of human life (James 4:14; see Prov 27:1; Qoh 1:1–6); the necessity and difficulty of controlling the tongue (James 1:26; 3:1–12; see LXX Ps 33:14; Sir 5:13; 19:6–12; 23:7–8; 28:12); the importance of helping those in need (James 1:27; 2:14–16; see Prov 19:17; 21:3; 31:9, 20; Sir 4:9; 29:8–9; 34:21–22; 35:2).

Despite all these resemblances to the wisdom tradition, however, James is scarcely defined by it. James' appropriation of the legal and prophetic aspects of the biblical tradition are equally important. And although James shares many wisdom motifs, no biblical wisdom writing offers a genuine literary antecedent for the form of this composition as a whole. James has fewer aphorisms and

---

[119]The wisdom character of James and its multiple connections to the biblical wisdom tradition are recognized by virtually all commentaries, as well as such studies as B. R. Halston, "The Epistle of James: 'Christian Wisdom'?" *SE* 4 (1968) 308–14; W. L. Knox, "The Divine Wisdom," *JTS* 38 (1937) 230–37; J. A. Kirk, "The Meaning of Wisdom in James: Examination of a Hypothesis," *NTS* 16 (1969–70) 24–38; R. Hoppe, *Der theologische Hintergrund des Jakobusbriefes* (FzB28; Würzburg: Echter-Verlag, 1977); H. Frankemölle, "Zum Thema des Jakobusbriefes im Kontext der Rezeption von Sir 2, 1–18 und 15, 11–20," *BN* 48 (1989) 21–49; H. von Lips, *Weisheitliche Traditionen im Neuen Testament* (WMANT 64; München: Neukirchener Verlag, 1990) 409–38; E. Baasland, "Der Jakobusbrief als neutestamentliche Weisheitsschrift," *ST* 36 (1982) 119–39.

[120]See Kirk, "The Meaning of Wisdom in James," 36–38.

more argument than either Proverbs or Sirach. James is less oblique in its exhortation than the Wisdom of Solomon, less introverted than Qoheleth and less dialogical than Job. Above all, James' distinctive moral voice, as we shall see below, cannot be collapsed into any of its biblical predecessors.

3. JEWISH LITERATURE

Judaism in the period between 200 BCE and 200 CE was a highly variegated phenomenon, and its extant literature suggests something of that diversity.[121] What unified Judaism was commitment to a shared story, convictions, symbols, and practice organized around the central symbol of Torah.[122] What diversified Judaism was not simply the geographical, cultural, and linguistic complexity introduced by the centuries-old fact of diaspora, but especially the widely divergent responses made by Jews to the dominant Greco-Roman culture and rule.

The one secure generalization about Judaism during this period is that it was astonishingly prolific in the production of literature, which means that the present survey is necessarily selective. It leaves out compositions whose similarity to James is restricted to a shared use of the Greek language and commitment to Torah, reflected in random designations of Abraham as "Friend of God" (*Testament of Abraham* 1:6; 2:3; *Jubilees* 19:9; *Apocalypse of Abraham* 9:6 = James 2:23), or occurs only at one point, as in the concentration on endurance found both in James 5:11 and *The Testament of Job* 1:5. I therefore set aside all narratives, whether historical (Josephus), fictional (*Joseph and Aseneth*), or broadly targumic (*Jubilees*, Pseudo-Philo's *Biblical Antiquities*). I ignore oracular (*Sibylline Oracles*) and poetic literature (*Pseudo-Ezechiel*). I pass over apologetic writings (Philo, Josephus, Artapanus, Aristobulus) and virtually all apocalyptic and testamentary literature.

What remains is a still substantial and varied assortment of writings, which can legitimately be compared to James because of a shared exhortatory character. The survey will move from compositions whose original language seems to have been Hebrew, and which bear few explicit signs of positive engagement with Hellenistic culture, to those written in Greek, whose use of Hellenistic moral traditions is more explicit, and offer more striking resemblances to James.

a. The Pirke Aboth

The *Pirke Aboth* (Sayings of the Fathers) is a tractate of the *Mishnah*, written in Hebrew, and attributed to Judah the Prince. Although dated ca. 200 CE, it

---

[121]See Johnson, *Writings of the New Testament*, 41–83, and ibid., "The New Testament's Anti-Jewish Slander and the Conventions of Ancient Polemic," *JBL* 108 (1989) 419–41.

[122]See N. T. Wright, *The New Testament and the People of God* (London: SPCK, 1992) 145–338.

contains sayings from the earlier generations of pharisaic sages.[123] It clearly continues the sort of wisdom encouraged (and perhaps even institutionalized) by Sirach (see 24:1–23; 51:23–30), with its ethos joining the study and observance of Torah.

It is not difficult to locate among its sayings a large number of similarities to James. There is the conviction that suffering gains a reward (*PA* 5:23), specifically in the world to come (*PA* 2:16; 4:1, 10, 16; 6:4, 7), conceived of as an inheritance (*PA* 5:19 = James 1:12). As in most wisdom literature, speech commands special attention: students should be "swift to hear" (*PA* 5:12) but not hasty in speech (*PA* 5:7 = James 1:19). Speech should be discerning and appropriate (*PA* 1:5, 9, 11, 17; 3:14 = James 1:19, 26; 3:1–12), but above all, should be translated into deeds (*PA* 1:15 = James 2:14–26). The necessity of translating profession into action is continually stressed (*PA* 1:2; 2:12; 3:10, 18; 4:5; 5:14; 6:5 = James 2:17–18). Such actions include making judgments without partiality (*PA* 1:6; 2:5; 4:5 = James 2:4); being slow to anger (*PA* 4:1 = James 1:19); avoiding false swearing (*PA* 1:9; 4:7, 8 = James 5:12); giving alms to the needy (*PA* 5:13 = James 2:16); praying properly (*PA* 2:13 = James 4:3); working for peace (*PA* 1:12, 18 = James 3:17–18); avoiding the profanation of the divine name (*PA* 4:4; 5:9 = James 2:7); avoiding the vices of jealousy, lust, and avarice (*PA* 4:21 = James 3:16), and especially the vice of envy, expressed in terms of having an "evil eye" as opposed to a "good eye" (*PA* 2:9, 11; 5:19 = James 4:1–5). Also opposed to envy is the desired attitude of lowliness of spirit (*PA* 4:4, 10; 5:9 = James 4:6–10).

Associates are to choose between two "ways" of behavior (*PA* 2:6), which can be expressed in terms of a contrast between the wise man and the clod (*PA* 5:7). In addition to practicing the prescribed virtues oneself, this means avoiding evil neighbors (*PA* 5:18 = James 4:4) and encouraging others to a life of rectitude (*PA* 5:18 = James 5:20). The one who acts according to the commands of Torah is described as a "friend of God" (*PA* 6:1 = James 2:23; 4:4). These "ways" of behavior, in turn, are explicitly attached to religious motivations that also resemble those in James. The observance of the law is taking on the yoke of the kingdom (*PA* 3:5) and gives the one who observes it a sort of kingship (*PA* 6:1 = James 2:8). Humans are created in the image of God (*PA* 3:15 = James 3:9), and God is both their creator and their judge (*PA* 2:21; 4:22 = James 4:12), who judges the world by mercy (*PA* 3:16 = James 2:13). Both "heavy" and "light" commandments must be observed (*PA* 2:1; 4:11; see esp. 4:2 = James 2:10–11). Abraham is called "our father" (*PA* 5:2, 19 = James 2:21) and the ten trials of Abraham—including the binding of Isaac—are listed (*PA* 5:3 = James 2:21).

The fact that *PA* consists largely in maxims provides an obvious resemblance

---

[123]See the introduction provided by H. Danby, *The Mishnah* (London: Oxford University Press, 1933) xiii–xxxii.

to the first chapter of James. For the most part, however, the two compositions are in literary terms more unalike than alike. In *PA*, the sayings are carefully attributed to sages of the past, and the commitment to a chain of tradition is explicit (*PA* 2:8). Each composition contains important themes totally lacking from the other: *PA* has no trace of James' eschatological expectation, and James entirely lacks *PA*'s concern for ritual observance. The context for exhortation is also distinctive in each: James speaks in his own voice to communities, urging them to authenticity in faith and solidarity in love; *PA* gathers the traditional wisdom of the sages for the guidance of students as devoted to the study of Torah as to its practice. What James and the *Pirke Aboth* share is a commitment to the moral life mediated by Torah; what distinguishes them is the framework for reading Torah and, therefore, the primary focus of ethical instruction.

b. Qumran: 1QS, CD

Two of the sectarian writings from Qumran can offer useful comparison to James. Although in literary terms, the *Community Rule* (1QS) and the *Damascus Document* (CD) bear little resemblance to James,[124] each contains exhortation that provides significant parallels. The similarities in *CD* are few: wisdom and understanding are said to come from God (2:3 = James 3:13–17), Abraham is called "friend of God" because he kept the commandments and did not follow his own will (3:2 = James 2:23), and there is a call for the care of the needy, especially orphans and widows (6:16, 21; 14:14 = James 1:27; 2:14–16). The *Community Rule* has a greater number of similarities. It condemns speaking in anger (*1QS* 7:2 = James 1:19) or speaking foolishly (7:9 = James 1:26). It distinguishes between the spirits of haughtiness/pride and humility of spirit (4:9–11; 11:1 = James 4:6–10). The choice between good and evil is spelled out in terms of wisdom and foolishness (4:18, 24 = James 3:13–16). Keeping all the commandments of Moses is required without exception (8:22 = James 2:10–11). Mutual correction within the community is encouraged (5:24–25; 6:1 = James 5:19–29), and forgiveness of sins is available to those with lowliness of spirit (3:8–9 = James 4:6–10; 5:16).

Both writings share with James a strong sense of separation from outsiders. Corresponding to James' definition of "pure religion," in terms of keeping "unstained from the world" (1:27), is the repeated language concerning separation from the impure (*1QS* 5:1–3; 7:24–25; 8:22–24; 9:9). Such separation is undergirded at Qumran also by a spiritual dualism, expressed by a conflict between "spirits" (*1QS* 3:6–8; 3:13–4:26 = James 4:5–8).

---

[124]I obviously disagree with the thesis that James depends on and derives its outline from the *Community Rule*, as argued by D. L. Beck, *The Composition of the Epistle of James* (Ph.D. diss., Princeton Theological Seminary, 1973), esp. 231–55. Even less needs to be said about the hypothesis that Qumran contained fragments of James: see J. O'Callaghan, "Papiros neotestamentarios en la cueva 7 de Qumran?" *Bib* 53 (1972) 99–100, and the response by C. H. Roberts, "On Some Presumed Papyrus Fragments of the New Testament from Qumran," *JTS* n.s. 23 (1972) 446–47.

Despite such points of similarity, the Dead Sea compositions are markedly different from James in literary form and in perspective. In literary terms, they combine narrative (*CD*) and ritual instructions (*1QS*) with moral exhortation. In terms of ideological perspective, they are totally preoccupied with the regulation of the sectarian community and the legitimation of its claims to be the only authentic realization of Israel. The spiritual and ethical dualism corresponds completely to the distinction between insiders and outsiders; the commandments of Moses are to be kept, but above all by the measure of the commandments expressly laid out for *this* community (*1QS* 9:9–10). Apart from the intriguing combination of an ethics derived from Torah wedded to an overall cosmic and ethical dualism, therefore, these writings bear little substantial resemblance to the form, language, or character, of James.

c. *The* Sentences of the Syriac Menander

The *Sentences of the Syriac Menander* are extraordinarily difficult to place. Little is known about its original language or provenance. Does it represent a semitic appropriation of Greek wisdom, or a roughly Hellenized version of Hebrew wisdom?[125] Despite these difficulties, comparisons are valuable, not only for the ways they reveal similarities, but also for the way they expose major differences. *Syriac Menander*, in fact, provides an almost perfect example of what Dibelius considered as the very essence of paraenesis: a loose collection of aphorisms with little evident organization or internal logic. The sentences themselves are preceded by an Epitome that anticipates later themes; in broad terms, the arrangement is analogous to the relationship I have suggested between the aphorisms in James 1:2–27 and the essays in 2:1–5:20.

James shares a range of typical wisdom themes with *Syriac Menander*, which has a number of statements concerning wicked (179), boastful (180), and loquacious speech (301, 304). It considers nothing better than silence (311–13), for the tongue is a source of misery (33, 424). Another classic wisdom theme is the recognition of the fleeting character of human affairs (13). Among the vices rejected by the *Sentences* are quarrelsomeness (176), insolence (35), stealing (145), and adultery (240). As in James 3:13–4:1, jealousy is taken to be the cause of evil and strife (31, 422). On the positive side, humility and kindness are encouraged (355), and there is even a negative formulation of the golden rule (250–251). The reader is told to flee what is hateful (5), and wisdom is said to keep one from wickedness (417).

There are, however, far more dissimilarities than similarities. Apart from the fact that James contains essays of considerable intricacy and rhetorical force, the choice of subject matter and perspective is markedly different in *Pseudo-Menander*. The atmosphere of this writing is almost entirely that of Proverbs,

---

[125]See the discussion by T. Baarda, "The Sentences of Syriac Menander," in *OTP* 2:583–606.

without that composition's poetry: wisdom is a matter of practical adaptation to life in the real world. There is extensive attention paid to sexual ethics and to domestic relations—themes completely absent from James. *Pseudo-Menander* pays particular attention to the respect owed the elderly, especially one's parents. Much of its material is as concerned with manners as with morality. These are located comfortably within an unchallenged honor/shame cultural system. Although *Pseudo-Menander* and James share the broad category of exhortation and some typical wisdom motifs, therefore, they are far different in literary complexity and in voice: *Pseudo-Menander* instructs on how to get along in the world, whereas James prophetically challenges the values of the world in the name of friendship with God (4:4).

d. *The* Letter of Aristeas

The *Letter of Aristeas* is one of a number of Jewish wisdom writings whose combination of devotion to Torah with an affirmative engagement with Greco-Roman culture places them in the broad classification of apologetic literature.[126] *Aristeas* is set in the fictional context of the translation of the Septuagint (3–5; 301–21) and is primarily concerned with several specifically apologetic topics, such as the majesty of the Temple cult (50–210) and the allegorical significance of purity laws (120–71). But the highlight of the work is the symposium discussions between the Hellenistic king and the Jewish translators concerning virtue and true kingship (187–294). This last section contains a number of wisdom/philosophical motifs bearing resemblance to James.

Typical for a Hellenized morality, self-control is highly prized. It is a form of kingship (*Aristeas* 211), indeed the highest form of sovereignty (222 = James 2:8). In contrast, the pursuit of pleasures leads to injustice and greed (277 = James 4:1). *Aristeas* condemns the anger that leads to death (253 = James 1:20), uses the image of the helmsman (251 = James 3:4), recognizes the fleeting character of prosperity (244 = James 4:13–16), and alludes to the *topos* on friendship (228 = James 4:4). In general, *Aristeas* is more decidedly Greek in its sensibilities than is James, as in its praise of moderation (223). In some respects, though, its appropriation of the ideals of Torah brings it closer to James. Notice its repeated prohibition against partiality in judgment (215, 263 = James 2:1, 9), its call for purity of heart (234 = James 4:8), and its insistence on avoiding envy by recognizing the gift of God (224 = James 4:1–6). Most strikingly, *Aristeas* opposes arrogance by declaring that "God destroys the proud and exalts the gentle and humble" (263; see Prov 3:34 and James 4:6).

Although *Aristeas* shows how moral exhortation can be fitted within an (ostensibly) epistolary format and deal with a number of different topics without thereby losing overall coherence, taken as a whole its resemblance to James

---

[126]See the introduction and translation by R. J. H. Shutt, "Letter of Aristeas," in *OTP* 2:5–34.

derives mainly from the shared use of Torah within the context of Greco-Roman moral teaching.

e. 4 Maccabees

4 Maccabees is one of the most distinctive literary productions of Hellenistic Judaism. Taking the form of a speech apparently delivered on the anniversary of the martyrdom of Eleazar and the seven brothers with their mother (1:10; 3:19; 17:8–10), it combines elements of the panegyric with a diatribal argument, in support of the proposition that the life of "devout reason" is demonstrated by the mastery of the passions (1:1, 7).[127] Not unexpectedly, in view of such a statement of purpose, the composition employs a variety of typical Hellenistic moral themes. Pleasures and desires struggle against reason (*4 Macc* 1:22); the pursuit of pleasure can lead to social disruption connected to avarice and jealousy (1:25–26 = James 4:1–3); the mastery of anger is both essential and difficult (2:16 = James 1:20); it is necessary to endure for the sake of virtue (7:22 = James 1:3, 12). Eleazar is compared to a pilot, steering the vessel of piety on the sea of passions (7:1–12 = James 1:6; 3:4)! The diatribal character of the composition is shown also in its use of examples for moral instruction (3:6–17; 7:11; 13:9; 14:20) through imitation (9:23 = James 5:10). Among these examples, Abraham holds a special place (15:28), above all—for obvious reasons—in the offering of his son Isaac (16:20 = James 2:21).

Abraham and other examples are drawn from Torah, and the distinctive character of *4 Maccabees* is found in its combination of a thoroughgoing appropriation of Hellenistic categories with the most unswerving devotion to the ethos of Judaism. Thus, the wisdom necessary for the control of the passions comes by gift from God (1:16) through the law (1:17). It is this that gives sovereignty over the passions (6:35). The composition, therefore, cites Torah directly (2:5; 17:19) and makes "faith in God" an explicit theme (15:24; 16:22 = James 2:1, 5) of what the author terms "religion" (*eusebeia*, 9:7–8, 24).

As in James, God is both creator of the world and establisher of the law (5:25 = James 4:11–12), so that major and minor commandments alike must be observed. Offending against either means being arrogant against the law (5:19–21 = James 2:10–11). Since reason itself is kingly (14:2), demonstrating reason by living according to the law and persevering (15:31) through the testing of faith (17:11–12) means to "reign over a kingdom that is temperate and just and good and true" (2:23), that is, to gain eternal life according to God's word (16:25). As in James, fidelity to God demands a separation from what is impure (5:37 = James 1:27).

This last point, however, also suggests some of the ways this writing differs

---

[127]See the discussion and translation provided by H. Anderson, "Fourth Maccabees," in *OTP* 2:531–73.

from James. In 4 *Maccabees*, separation from the impure connotes loyalty to the ancestral dietary regulations (5:16–18); in James, remaining "unstained from the world" means fidelity to the "noble name invoked" upon the community (2:7) by living according to the measure of the "faith of Jesus Christ" (2:1). In 4 *Maccabees*, there is the memory of persecution; in James, the persecution is present and real (2:6; 5:7–11). Each document, therefore, has its own literary form and focus. In the panegyric of 4 *Maccabees*, moral discourse serves an indirect epideictic function, whereas in James the moral exhortation serves a directly protreptic purpose.

f. The Sentences of Pseudo-Phocylides

The *Sentences of Pseudo-Phocylides* reveal a Jewish wisdom so thoroughly assimilated into the diction and even the outlook of Hellenism (see "the blessed ones" in 75, 163) that for centuries it was not even recognized as a Jewish composition.[128] As with the *Sentences of the Syriac Menander*, the literary form is the simple collection of maxims (in poetic hexameters) loosely organized by theme. *Pseudo-Phocylides* shares with James a number of typical wisdom motifs: the praise of wisdom (88, 130 = James 3:13); the need to control the tongue (20, 123 = James 1:19, 26) and to bridle anger (57, 63 = James 1:20); the observation that prosperity is unstable (27, 110, 116–121 = James 1:9–11; 4:13–16); the conviction that avarice leads to battles, plundering, and murders (44–46 = James 4:1; 5:1–6); and that wealth is connected to arrogance (62 = James 4:16). As in James, human envy is contrasted to the absence of envy in the divine realm (70–75 = James 1:5, 17; 4:5–6). There is even the comment that a tiny spark can set a whole forest ablaze (144 = James 3:5).

The most noteworthy similarity to James, however, is found in the way *Pseudo-Phocylides* combines prohibitions taken from the decalogue (2–8), particularly those against murder and adultery (3–4 = James 2:11), with prohibitions derived from Leviticus 19 (see 9, 15, 17, 19, 39, 230, and the discussion above, p. 31).[129] Given this remarkable similarity to James' method of appropriating Torah, it is more striking that *Pseudo-Phocylides* lacks any allusion to Lev 19:18 ("Love your neighbor as yourself"), which anchors James' appropriation of Lev 19:14–18.

Nevertheless, beneath the Greek poetry, the ethics of Torah are clearly discernible in such features as the insistence on impartiality in judging (9–11, 137 = James 2:1–9), on the payment of laborers for their work (20 = James

---

[128]See the discussion and translation provided by P. W. van der Horst, "Pseudo-Phocylides," in *OTP* 565–82.

[129]See J. Bernays, *Über das Phokylideische Gedicht. Ein Beitrag zur hellenistischen Literatur* (Jahresbuch des juedische-theologischen Seminars 'Franckelschen Stiftung:' Berlin: Hertz, 1856) xxi–xxiv.

5:1–6), and on the necessity of helping the poor at once without delay (22–23, 26, 28–29 = James 1:27; 2:14–16). *Pseudo-Phocylides* makes clear the need to flee the lawless person and speaks of purity of the soul rather than purity of the body (228 = James 1:27).[130]

Such strong points of resemblance, however, must be placed in the context of a document that contains as much material completely foreign to the concerns of James. The Greek emphasis on moderation is one example (36, 69, 98). So is the extensive consideration of sexual morals (175–206) and of domestic arrangements (207–227), as well as the large amount of material devoted to what might be called manners rather than morals (59–69, 89–96, 153–174). These components move *Pseudo-Phocylides* in the direction of a conservative, culturally-adaptive ethics ideologically far removed from James.

g. Philo

Any comparison between James and the (possibly contemporary) writings of Philo Judaeus has an artificial quality. James is a tiny composition of debated provenance and influence; Philo's works are voluminous and of obvious influence in shaping the philosophy of the West. James is directly concerned with exhortation. Philo writes some apologetic works (*Embassy to Gaius, Against Flaccus*), and the overall intention of his interpretive work might be protreptic,[131] but the bulk of his work is, at best, secondarily exhortatory; the imperative is not Philo's characteristic mood. Most of all, Philo's complex intellectual engagement with Hellenistic culture, mediated through his systematic reinterpretation of Torah, is foreign to James' straightforward moralism. Despite these hurdles, however, Philo provides a rich set of parallels to James, at the very least offering an index to the options also available to another contemporary reader of the LXX such as James.

Note, for example, the use of the metaphor of the mirror (*Decalogue* 21; *Migration of Abraham* 34; *Flight and Finding* 38; *Questions on Genesis* 1:57), especially in connection with the theme of memory (*Migration of Abraham* 17 = James 1:22–25). Note also the rhetorical contrast between "slow (*bradys*) and quick (*tachys*)" in *Confusion of Tongues* 12 = James 1:19, as well as the role of imitation in the virtuous life (*Preliminary Studies* 13 = James 5:10–11).

Philo consistently touches on the standard themes of Hellenistic moral discourse. Strikingly similar to James 2:14, for example, is his question *ti gar ophelos* ("for what is the use?") in *Posterity of Cain* 24: "For what good is it to say the best things but to plan and carry out the worst things?" (See also *The*

---

[130]See also P. W. van der Horst, "Pseudo-Phocylides and the New Testament," ZNW 69 (1978) 202.

[131]See the idea, if not the term, in E. R. Goodenough, *An Introduction to Philo Judaeus* 2nd ed. (Oxford: Basil Blackwell, 1962) 33–35.

Worse Attacks the Better 21.) Control of speech is naturally important (*The Worse Attacks the Better* 27; *Change of Names* 42; *On Dreams* 2:40), which is what philosophy can teach people to do (*Preliminary Studies* 14). So Philo condemns the "unbridled tongue" (*The Worse Attacks the Better* 13; *On Dreams* 2:42; *Special Laws* 2:2 = James 1:26). Above all, angry speech is to be avoided (*Allegorical Interpretation* 3:124; 3:131 = James 1:20). Positively, speech is capable of being "perfected" (*teleios*) by being in accord with reason and finding expression in appropriate deeds (*Migration of Abraham* 13; *Posterity of Cain* 24; *Special Laws* 2:14). Speech must be matched by action (*The Worse Attacks the Better* 21; *Preliminary Studies* 13; *Rewards and Punishments* 14 = James 1:22–25; 2:14–16).

Philo agrees with other moralists that the pursuit of pleasures leads to trouble (*On Husbandry* 22); indeed, *epithymia* is like a flame in the forest, destroying everything (*Decalogue* 32 = James 3:5). Uncontrolled pleasures lead to wars (*Decalogue* 28; *On Drunkenness* 18; *On Dreams* 2:21 = James 4:1). Self-control can be compared to the exercise of human control over animals (*On the Creation* 58 = James 3:7). Not surprisingly, then, the metaphors of the bridle and rudder, attached respectively to the examples of the charioteer and the helmsman, are found with great frequency (see *On Creation* 14, 29; *Allegorical Interpretation* 2:26; 3:40; 3:79; *Cherubim* 11; *On Dreams* 1:25 = James 3:3–4).

Philo also uses the various *topoi* on the moral virtues and vices, such as the *topos* "On Friendship" (*On Abraham* 235) and "On Envy" (*On Joseph* 5–12). Finally, Philo makes use of the virtue and vice lists, most extravagantly in *The Sacrifices of Cain and Abel* 32 = James 3:15–17.

Philo regards the foolish person like one tossing in the sea (*Posterity of Cain* 7 = James 1:6–8), but although reason is the law that makes one free (*Every Good Man is Free* 7 = James 1:25), wisdom is more than living according to reason; it means living according to God's law. Philo, indeed, can speak of "earthly wisdom" (*epigeion sophian*) as a copy of the heavenly wisdom (*Allegorical Interpretation* 1:14 = James 3:15). The wise person, therefore, is one who follows the "royal road" (*hodos basilikē*) of God's Word (*Unchangeableness of God* 34–35; *Posterity of Cain* 30), a formulation similar to the "royal law" (*nomos basilikos*) in James 2:8. The wise, consequently, are not only virtuous; they are also God's friends (*philoi*), as the wicked are God's enemies (*echthroi*; see *Allegorical Interpretation* 3:1 = James 4:4). Among such friends are obviously Moses (*Who is the Heir* 5) and Abraham (*Sobriety* 11) = James 2:23.

Philo, in a word, inhabits a world of moral discourse shaped alike by Hellenistic culture and by Torah. Some of his statements provide remarkably close parallels to James. He can use Balaam as exemplifying the paradox of blessing and cursing coming from the same source (*Migration of Abraham* 20 = James 3:10). Humans are created in the image of God (*On Creation* 23 = James 3:9). God is not the creator of evil (*On Creation* 24 = James 1:13); rather, evil desires originate within ourselves (*Decalogue* 28 = James 1:14). God does not change: there is no "turning with the divine" (*Cherubim* 6 = James 1:17). God is the "free giver of all things" (*Cherubim* 34 = James 1:5, 17). God looks after orphans and widows (*Special Laws* 1:57 = James 1:27). Philo even has an image that may throw light on James' use of the *diaspora* in 1:1: he speaks of the wise (*sophoi*) as "sojourners" (*paroikountes*) in God's city; their citizenship is in heaven (*Confusion of Tongues* 17; *On the Cherubim* 34).

h. *The* Testaments of the Twelve Patriarchs

The *Testaments of the Twelve Patriarchs* provide by far the most complex and compelling set of comparisons to James. The comparisons are complex, because the *Testaments* themselves present difficult problems concerning their original language, date, and provenance. Most scholars consider them as Jewish writings to which Christian interpolations have been added,[132] but a vigorous case has also been made that the *Testaments* are entirely Christian compositions.[133] Despite the discovery of an Aramaic fragment of a version of the *Testament of Levi* at Qumran, it seems certain that the *Testaments* in their present form have Greek as their language of original composition.[134] This is certainly the case for the paraenetic materials with which we are primarily concerned.

Although the literary form is classically that of the *testament* or *farewell discourse*,[135] in which the patriarchs at the moment before death predict the future and exhort their descendants, the exhortation in each testament is closely connected to the *narrative* element. Each patriarch recounts some aspect of his life—usually in connection with Joseph—which serves to illustrate the particular virtue or vice that is the subject of that testament. The *exemplary* character of the *Testaments* is, therefore, obvious: for imitation (see *T. Benj.* 4:1), positive models are provided by Levi, Issachar, Zebulon, Naphtali, Asher, Joseph, and Benjamin; for avoidance, negative types are provided by Reuben, Simeon, Judah, Dan, and Gad.

That the distribution of moral themes is not accidental is shown by the subtitles in the Greek manuscripts, which take the form of Greco-Roman moral *topoi*. The *Testament of Simeon*, for example, is entitled *peri phthonou* ("On

---

[132]This view is represented in the discussion and translation provided by H. C. Kee, "Testaments of the Twelve Patriarchs," in *The Old Testament Pseudepigrapha*, ed. J. H. Charlesworth (Garden City: Doubleday, 1983) 1:775–828.

[133]See M. de Jonge, "The Interpretation of the Testaments of the Twelve Patriarchs in Recent Years" and "Christian Influence in the Testaments of the Twelve Patriarchs," in *Studies in the Testaments of the Twelve Patriarchs*, ed. M. de Jonge (SVTP III; Leiden: Brill, 1975) 183–246.

[134]See M. de Jonge, *The Testaments of the Twelve Patriarchs* (PVTG 1.2; Leiden: Brill, 1978), and R. H. Charles, *The Greek Versions of the Testaments of the Twelve Patriarchs* (Oxford: Oxford University Press, 1908).

[135]See J. J. Collins, "Testaments," in *Jewish Writings of the Second Temple Period*, ed. M. E. Stone (CRINT 2.2; Philadelphia: Fortress Press, 1984) 325–55.

Envy"), and the *Testament of Gad* is called *peri misous* ("On Hatred"), whereas the *Testament of Issachar* is called *peri haplotētos* ("On Simplicity"), and the *Testament of Zebulon* is *peri eusplanchias kai eleous* ("On Compassion and Mercy"). In effect, the patriarchs are used to provide biblical examples for the *topoi* of Hellenistic moral exhortation.

The resemblance between James and the *Testaments* in language and outlook has often been noted by commentators.[136] A range of specific points of similarity can be observed. Wisdom and understanding come from the Lord (*T. Zeb.* 6:1 = James 3:13–16). God is the judge (*T. Benj.* 10:8–10) who loves those who keep the law (*T. Levi* 13:1–2; *T. Jos.* 11:1 = James 4:11–12) and who will exalt and glorify those who are virtuous (*T. Jos.* 10:3; 18:1; *T. Benj.* 5:4 = James 4:6, 10). Worship of God involves self-control (*T. Jos.* 6:7 = James 1:26). The virtuous person enjoys a kind of royalty (*T. Levi* 13:9 = James 2:7). God will give a crown of glory to those who do good (*T. Benj.* 4:1 = James 1:12). Humans are created in the image of God (*T. Naph.* 2:5 = James 3:9). Human affairs are transitory and change (*T. Jos.* 10:6 = James 4:13–16). If humans sin, they can repent and confess their sins (*T. Gad* 5:7; 6:13 = James 5:16). Testing proves the disposition of the soul (*T. Jos.* 2:6 = James 1:12).

Desires and passions are very much connected to vice (*T. Jos.* 7:4 = James 1:13–14). Among the passions condemned by the *Testaments* are the love of money (*T. Jud.* 17:1 = James 5:1–6), anger (*T. Dan* 2:2 = James 1:20), hatred (*T. Gad* 3:3; 4:1 = James 4:4), and envy (*T. Sim.* 2:7; 3:3 = James 4:1–3). Envy is especially highlighted, since it plays a central role in the Joseph story (see *T. Dan* 2:5; *T. Gad* 3:3; 4:5; 5:3; *T. Iss.* 4:5–6; *T. Jos.* 4:7). Particularly close to James is the way in which envy (*phthonos*) is connected to social upheaval (*T. Sim.* 4:8 = James 3:16; 4:1) and to murder (*phonos*) (*T. Sim.* 2:7; 3:3; *T. Jos.* 1:3 = James 4:1–2).

Vices of speech are also condemned, specifically being double-tongued in speech (*T. Benj.* 6:5–6 = James 3:1–12), slandering the neighbor (*T. Gad* 3:3; 5:4; *T. Iss.* 3:4 = James 4:11), and boasting (*T. Levi* 14:7; *T. Jud.* 13:2 = James 3:14; 4:16). An overall attitude that is singled out in connection with vice is that of arrogance (*hyperēphania*, see *T. Reub.* 3:5; *T. Levi* 17:11; *T. Jud.* 13:2 = James 4:6).

Among the virtues encouraged are forbearance (*T. Gad* 4:7 = James 5:7), compassion and mercy (*T. Zeb.* 8:1 = James 2:13), and sharing generously with the poor and oppressed (*T. Iss.* 3:8; *T. Zeb.* 7:1–2 = James 2:14–16). The ideal of brotherly love is repeatedly made explicit (*T. Reub.* 6:9; *T. Gad* 6:1; *T. Zeb.* 8:5; *T. Dan* 5:3; *T. Jos.* 17:2 = James 2:8). Offsetting the attitude of *hyperēphania* associated with vice is the attitude of humility (*tapeinōsis*; *T. Gad* 5:3; *T. Benj.* 5:4; *T. Jos.* 10:2–3 = James 4:6, 10).

---

[136]See Cantinat, 22; Laws, 11; Dibelius, 21; J. H. Ropes, 20–21, noted a "special affinity" to James in language, though not in structure or style.

Even more impressive than the points of specific thematic resemblance are the similarities between James and the *Testaments* at the level of symbolism and ideology. They share a powerful dualism at both the moral and cosmic levels. The *Testament of Asher* states it clearly: "Everything is in pairs, the one over against the other" (1:4). There is, therefore, a sharp contrast between "two ways" of behavior (*T. Ash.* 1:3), sponsored respectively by the "two spirits of truth and falsehood" (*T. Jud.* 20:1). Actually, there are any number of *pneumata* (*T. Reub.* 3:5) that go by a number of designations without a great deal of consistency (see *T. Reub.* 2:1; 3:5; *T. Levi* 3:3; 9:9; *T. Jud.* 13:3; 14:3; 16:1–3; *T. Dan* 1:6, 8; *T. Gad* 1:9). The particular "evil spirit" (*T. Levi* 5:6) appears to be named more or less according to the vice that is the target of the particular testament. These spirits empower humans to perform certain actions (*T. Naph.* 2:2) and are given an opening by an upset or disturbed human mind (*T. Dan* 4:6–7).

The spirits are personified by Beliar (*T. Reub.* 4:7; *T. Jud.* 25:3; *T. Dan* 1:7), whose works are "double" (*T. Benj.* 6:2). Beliar can also be called the devil (*diabolos*, *T. Naph.* 8:4 = James 4:7) or Satan (*satanas*, *T. Dan* 6:1–2). Not content with deceiving people, he actually "indwells" them (*T. Naph.* 8:6). In contrast, the person who does good has the Lord "dwelling in" him. The verb used consistently in such passages (*katoikein*) is cognate to that used by James 4:5, when he speaks of the *pneuma* "he made to dwell (*katoikisen*) in us" (*T. Dan* 5:1–3; *T. Jos.* 10:2–3; *T. Benj.* 6:4; *T. Sim.* 3:5).

Despite such cosmic influence, humans are able to choose between allegiance to the Lord or evil, between the "law of the Lord" and the "works of Beliar" (*T. Levi* 19:1). The "conscience of the mind inclines as it will" (*T. Jud.* 20:2). Thus, one can "turn to" Beliar (*T. Iss.* 6:1) or "turn to" evil (*T. Benj.* 7:1). Similarly, one can "flee" (*pheugein*) Beliar and "approach" (*engizein*) God (*T. Iss.* 3:17; *T. Dan* 5:1–3; 6:1–2; *T. Naph.* 8:4; *T. Benj.* 5:2; 7:1 = James 4:7–8). Likewise, Beliar will "flee" from the one who turns to the Lord (*T. Sim.* 3:5; *T. Dan* 5:1; *T. Naph.* 8:4; *T. Benj.* 5:2 = James 4:8).

Language about turning from one spiritual authority to another thus undergirds moral instruction: one also "turns" from evil, envy, and hatred of the brothers (*T. Benj.* 8:1). The rule of good and evil spirits is, therefore, spelled out in terms of vices and virtues. The *Testament of Asher* illustrates both aspects of this doubled dualism. On one side, it emphasizes that God has established "two ways" of good and evil (*T. Ash.* 1:2–5), the latter dominated by Beliar (*T. Ash.* 1:9). Yet there are those who straddle the two ways. They may have good speech but evil deeds (*T. Ash.* 2:1 = James 2:14–16). Or, they do one thing good and another thing evil, making the two aspects as a whole evil (*T. Ash.* 2:5–10 = James 2:10–11). Such a person is "two-faced" (*T. Ash.* 3:1), a term that clearly comes very close in connotation to James' characterization of "double-mindedness" (*dipsychos*, James 1:8; 4:8). The two-faced are "doubly punished because they both practice evil and approve of others who practice it" (*T. Ash.* 6:2).

In contrast, the good person is single-minded (*T. Ash.* 4:1; 6:1) and has integrity of heart (*T. Reub.* 4:1; *T. Jud.* 23:5; *T. Iss.* 3:1; 4:1; *T. Sim.* 4:5; *T. Jos.* 4:6; *T. Gad* 7:7). The repentant should, therefore, "cleanse their minds" (*T. Benj.* 6:7) and gain "singleness of vision" (*T. Iss.* 3:5 = James 4:8). Thus, in a passage strongly reminiscent of James 4:4–8, *T. Ash.* 3:2 advises, "Flee from the evil tendency, destroying the devil by your good works. For those who are two-faced are not of God, but they are enslaved to their evil desires, so that they might be pleasing to Beliar and to persons like themselves." A similar use of conversion language occurs in one of the passages closest to James, the exhortation to turn from "jealousy and envy" in *T. Sim.* 4:4 (see James 4:7–10).[137]

The similarities in theme, language, and ideology are impressive. But more than difference in literary form distinguishes James from the *Testaments*. James lacks many of their important themes, including their highly developed eschatology and priestly ideology (*T. Sim.* 6:1–7:3; *T. Levi* 3:1–4:7; 8:1–19; 14:1–4; 18:1–14; *T. Jud.* 21:1–22:3; *T. Dan* 5:7–13; *T. Jos.* 19:1–12).[138] Above all, James has none of their obsessive concern for sexual morality (*T. Levi* 9:9; 14:5–7; *T. Jud.* 13:2; 14:2; 18:2; *T. Dan* 5:6; *T. Benj.* 8:2; 9:1), with an accompanying misogyny (*T. Reub.* 5:1; *T. Jud.* 15:5; *T. Jos.* 3:9). It would be impossible to demonstrate that James made use of the *Testaments* or that they made use of James; what is clear is that they share a remarkably similar dualistic appropriation of Greco-Roman ethics within the symbolic world of Torah.

BIBLIOGRAPHY

Anderson, H., "Fourth Maccabees," *OTP* 2:531–73.

Baarda, T., "The Sentences of Syriac Menander," *OTP* 2:583–606.

Baasland, E., "Der Jakobusbrief als Neutestamentliche Weisheitsschrift," *ST* 36 (1982) 119–39.

Beck, D. L., *The Composition of the Letter of James* (Ph.D. diss., Princeton Theological Seminary, 1973).

Bernays, J., *Über das Phokylideische Gedicht. Ein Beitrag zur hellenistischen Literatur* (Jahresbuch des juedische-theologischen Seminars 'Franckelschen Stiftung:' Berlin: Hertz, 1856).

---

[137]See L. T. Johnson, "James 3:13–4:10 and the *topos PERI PHTHONOU*," 345.

[138]See also the argument by D. Slingerland that the notion of "law" in the *Testaments* included elements of ritual observance and study, in "The Nature of *NOMOS* (Law) within the *Testaments of the Twelve Patriarchs*," *JBL* 105 (1986) 39–48.

Charles, R. H., *The Greek Versions of The Testaments of the Twelve Patriarchs* (Oxford: Oxford University Press, 1908).

Collins, J. J., "Testaments," in *Jewish Writings of the Second Temple Period,* ed. M. E. Stone (CRINT 2.2; Philadelphia: Fortress Press, 1984) 325–55.

Crenshaw, J., "The Influence of the Wise upon Amos," ZAW 79 (1976) 42–51.

Danby, H., *The Mishnah* (London: Oxford University Press, 1933).

de Jonge, M., ed., *Studies in the Testaments of the Twelve Patriarchs* (SVTP III; Leiden: Brill, 1975).

———, *The Testaments of the Twelve Patriarchs* (PVTG 1.2; Leiden: Brill, 1978).

Fabris, R., *Legge della Liberta in Giacomo* (Supplementi alla Revista Biblica 8; Brescia: Paideia, 1977).

Fischel, H. A., "Story and History: Observations on Greco-Roman Rhetoric and Pharisaism," *American Oriental Society West Branch Semi-Centennial Volume* (Asian Studies Research Institute, *Oriental Studies* 3, Indiana University), ed. D. Sinor (Bloomington, Indiana: 1969) 59–88.

———, "Studies in Cynicism and the Ancient Near East: The History of a *Chria,*" *Religions in Antiquity: Essays in Honor of E. R. Goodenough,* ed. J. Neusner (Leiden: Brill, 1968) 373–411.

Frankemölle, H., "Gesetz im Jakobusbrief: Zur Tradition, contextuellen Verwendung und Rezeption eines belasteten Begriffes," in *Das Gesetz im Neuen Testament,* ed. K. Kertelge (QD 108; Freiburg: Herder, 1986) 175–221.

———, "Zum Thema des Jakobusbriefes im Kontext der Rezeption von Sir 2,1–18 und 15,11–20," *BN* 48 (1989) 21–49.

Goodenough, E. R., *An Introduction to Philo Judaeus* 2nd ed. (Oxford: Basil Blackwell, 1962).

Halston, B. R., "The Epistle of James: 'Christian Wisdom'?" *SE* 4 (1968) 308–14.

Hope, C. H., *Wisdom, Law and Social Concern in the Epistle of James* (Ph.D. diss., Union Theological Seminary, 1982).

Hoppe, R., *Der Theologische Hintergrund des Jakobusbriefes* (FzB28; Wurzburg: Echter-Verlag, 1977).

van der Horst, P. W., *The Sentences of Pseudo-Phocylides* (SVTP 4; Leiden: Brill, 1978).

———, "Pseudo-Phocylides," *OTP* 2:565–82.

———, "Pseudo-Phocylides and the New Testament," *ZNW* 69 (1978) 202.

Johnson, L. T., "Friendship with the World/Friendship with God: A Study of Discipleship in James," *Discipleship in the New Testament,* ed. F. Segovia (Philadelphia: Fortress Press, 1985) 166–83.

———, "James 3:13–4:10 and the *topos PERI PHTHONOU,*" *NovT* 25 (1983) 327–47.

————, "The Use of Leviticus 19 in the Letter of James," *JBL* 101 (1982) 391–401.

Kee, H. C., "Testaments of the Twelve Patriarchs," *OTP* 1:775–828.

Kirk, J. A., "The Meaning of Wisdom in James: Examination of a Hypothesis," *NTS* 16 (1969–70) 24–38.

Knox, W. L., "The Divine Wisdom," *JTS* 38 (1937) 230–37.

von Lips, H., *Weisheitliche Traditionen im Neuen Testament* (WMANT 64; München: Neukirchener Verlag, 1990).

Malherbe, A. J., "Medical Imagery in the Pastorals," *Texts and Testaments*, ed. W. E. March (San Antonio, Texas: Trinity University Press, 1980) 19–35.

————, *Moral Exhortation: A Greco-Roman Sourcebook* (Library of Early Christianity; Philadelphia: Westminster Press, 1986).

O'Callaghan, J., "Papiros neotestamentarios en la cueva 7 de Qumran?" *Bib* 53 (1972) 99–100.

von Rad, G., *Wisdom in Ancient Israel* (Nashville: Abingdon Press, 1972).

Roberts, C. H., "On Some Presumed Papyrus Fragments of the New Testament from Qumran," *JTS* n.s. 23 (1972) 446–47.

Schnabel, E. J., *Law and Wisdom from Ben Sira to Paul* (WUNT 2.16; Tübingen: JCB Mohr [Paul Siebeck], 1985).

Seitz, O. J. F., "James and the Law," *SE* 2 (1964) 472–86.

Shutt, R. J. H., "Letter of Aristeas," *OTP* 2:5–34.

Slingerland, D., "The Nature of *NOMOS* (Law) within the *Testaments of the Twelve Patriarchs*," *JBL* 105 (1986) 39–48.

Vokes, F. E., "The Ten Commandments in the New Testament and in First Century Judaism," *SE* 5 (1968) 146–54.

Wall, R. W., "James as Apocalyptic Paraenesis," *ResQ* 32 (1990) 11–22.

4. NEW TESTAMENT WRITINGS

Before turning to canonical writings that offer the possibility for significant comparison, it is appropriate to consider briefly whether and in what way we can confidently assert that James is Christian literature in the first place. The suggestion has been advanced, after all, that James originated as a Jewish writing "to the twelve tribes of the dispersion" (1:1) and was later lightly baptized by the double interpolation of "Jesus Christ" in 1:1 and 2:1.[139] The interpolation theory has no text-critical basis, since "Jesus Christ" is attested in all extant witnesses. And although some manuscripts are uncertain as to the proper word order in 2:1, the "awkwardness" of this sentence is by no means greater than others in James (see, e.g., 2:8; 2:18; 3:6; 4:2).

---

[139]See L. Massebieau, "L'épître de Jacques: est-elle l'oeuvre d'un chrétien?" *RHR* 31–32 (1895) 249–83; F. Spitta, *Zur Geschichte und Literatur des UrChristentums 2: Der Brief des Jakobus* (Göttingen: Vandenhoeck und Ruprecht, 1896). Their positions will be discussed again in section III of the Introduction.

But even if 1:1 and 2:1 are original, is James nevertheless "mainly Jewish?" This question reveals a premise that needs challenging. First, we need to be reminded that in the first century Judaism itself was an amazingly diverse phenomenon including within its diversity for some decades a nascent messianic movement centered in Jesus.[140] Second, we recall that this messianic movement was itself diverse, with its extant literature showing a variety of ways of negotiating the constitutive elements of the primordial experience of or convictions about Jesus, and the interpretation of the symbols of Torah.[141] It is a mistake in method to isolate any one of these strands in either tradition and establish it as normative for the first century so as to provide a stable basis for comparison. Third, it is clear that reading communities can "construe" texts according to their overall codes of understanding, no matter what the originating code of the composition. Thus, Gnostics were as eager readers of Paul as they were of "gnostic" productions, and read everything within their gnostic code.[142] It was not only the process of adding or subtracting elements that really made the *Testaments of the Twelve Patriarchs* or the *Sibylline Oracles* "Christian" writings, but their appropriation into a code of reading that affected both original and added materials.

Even when all that is said, however, the distinctiveness of James within the NT canon demands attention. Certainly, its *explicitly* messianic character is more muted than any other canonical writing apart from 3 John (which contains no explicit reference to Christ). James makes no *obvious* use of any of the narrative traditions concerning Jesus.[143] Most notably, he makes no mention of the death of Jesus. Those seeking allusion to Jesus' death in 5:6 and 5:11 must strain both the text and their eyesight. Neither is there any clear statement of Jesus' resurrection, although the phrasing of *kyrios tēs doxēs* in 2:1 can be made to support a perception of Jesus Messiah as the exalted one. Nor does James speak of the Holy Spirit, although the *pneuma* in 4:5 might be stretched that way. It follows that we cannot hope to find such explicit Christian elements as the rituals of baptism and eucharist, or the listing of charismatic gifts, or a mystical identification of the church as body of Christ. If "Christian" means "Christocentric," James fails the test.

Despite all that, James not only has multiple parallels to specific and

---

[140]For a variety of perspectives on this question, see the essays in *Jewish and Christian Self-Definition* Vol 2: *Aspects of Judaism in the Greco-Roman Period*, ed. E. P. Sanders et al. (Philadelphia: Fortress Press, 1981).

[141]This position is stated well by G. W. MacRae, "It is now as much a dogma of scholarship as its opposite used to be: orthodoxy is not the presupposition of the church but the result of a process of growth and development," in "Why the Church Rejected Gnosticism," *Jewish and Christian Self Definition* Vol 1: *The Shaping of Christianity in the Second and Third Centuries*, ed. E. P. Sanders (Philadelphia: Fortress Press, 1980) 127.

[142]See especially E. Pagels, *The Gnostic Paul: Gnostic Exegesis of the Pauline Letters* (Philadelphia: Fortress Press, 1975).

[143]For an echo of the healing narratives, see the notes on 5:15.

distinctively Christian writings (which we will trace out, below), but more impressively, uses a language that finds its home only within a developing Christian argot. By this I mean terms and expressions that may be attested occasionally in the LXX or in other Jewish literature, but never with the frequency or intensity or in the same complex combinations as can be found within the NT writings themselves. To demonstrate this point, no single term or expression suffices; only the cumulative effect of evidence is convincing.[144]

We can observe first the use of *kyrios* ("Lord") as a title for Jesus in 1:1 and 2:1. When used titularly, this term is particularly ambiguous. It could refer to Yahweh (and thus, "God and father" for Christians; see James 3:9), who is designated as *kyrios* in the LXX (see, e.g., Isa 40:13; Ps 117:1). It is also, however, a christological title of central importance to the Christian movement.[145] In James, *kyrios* probably refers to God in 1:7; 3:9; 4:10, 15; 5:4, 11, and possibly in 5:10. But in addition to 1:1 and 2:1, the title is probably applied to Jesus in 5:7, 8, 14, 15. Since this title applied to Jesus in the NT refers above all to his exalted status as resurrected messiah (e.g., Rom 1:4; 10:9; 1 Cor 12:3; 2 Cor 4:5) and the term *doxa* ("glory") is also frequently used in that same connection (e.g., John 17:5; Acts 7:55; 22:11; 1 Cor 15:43; 2 Cor 4:4), the combination of *kyrios tēs doxēs* in 2:1 is particularly impressive.[146]

James twice combines the title *kyrios* with *onoma* ("name"). The prophets spoke *en tō onomati tou kyriou* (5:10), and the elders are to anoint the sick *en tō onomati tou kyriou* (5:14). Although the use of *onoma* in the LXX is extensive (see, e.g., Exod 20:7, 24), it appears in earliest Christianity with special reference to the power of the resurrected Jesus (Acts 2:38; 3:6; 4:10; 5:40; 1 Cor 1:2; 1:10; 5:4; Phil 2:10; Col 3:17; 2 Thess 1:12). The absolute use of *onoma* in 2:7, "Do they not blaspheme the noble name invoked over you" (*to kalon onoma epiklēthen eph' hymas*), is, therefore, the more likely to be taken as a specifically Christian self-designation (see Acts 5:41; 9:14–15, 21; Rom 1:5; 3 John 7; 1 Pet 4:14, 16).[147]

Corresponding to the characterization of Jesus as "Lord" in 1:1 is James' self-designation as *doulos*. Again, this term has solid attestation in the LXX for such leaders of the people as Joshua (Josh 24:30), Abraham (Ps 104:42), and David (Ps 88:4), as well as for Jacob as personification of the people (Isa 48:20). But it

---

[144]See the discussion of the "argot" of Pauline churches in W. A. Meeks, *The First Urban Christians: The Social World of the Apostle Paul* (New Haven: Yale University Press, 1983) 93–96, and the early response to Spitta and Massebieau by V. Rose, "L'épître de saint Jacques est-elle un écrit chrétien?" *RB* 5 (1896) 519–34.

[145]See O. Cullmann, *The Christology of the New Testament* rev. ed., trans. S. C. Guthrie and C. Hall (Philadelphia: Westminster Press, 1959) 195–237.

[146]Compare Paul's statement in 1 Cor 2:8, "they crucified the lord of glory" (*ton kyrion tēs doxēs estaurōsan*).

[147]Dibelius, 23, takes this expression as one of the surest signs of James' essentially Christian character.

is used so extensively in the first generations for leaders of the Christian movement that it must be considered part of the messianic argot (Rom 1:1; 2 Cor 4:5; Gal 1:10; Phil 1:1; Col 4:12; 2 Tim 2:24; Titus 1:1; 2 Pet 1:1; Jude 1; Rev 1:1; 22:3; Matt 10:24–25; 20:27; 25:14; Mark 10:44; Luke 12:37, 43; 17:10; Acts 2:18; 4:29; 16:17; John 13:16; 15:20).

James' only terms for officials among his readers are those of teacher (*didaskalos*, 3:1), which appears also as a title for local leaders in Acts 13:1; 1 Cor 12:28–29; Eph 4:11, and "elders" (*presbyteroi*) in 5:14, which is used for local Christian leaders in 3 John 1; 2 John 1; 1 Pet 5:1; Titus 1:5; 1 Tim 5:17, 19; Acts 11:30; 14:23; 15:2–23. Especially striking is Paul's calling *tous presbyterous tēs ekklēsias* ("the elders of the church") in Acts 20:17, which corresponds precisely to James' instruction to call *tous presbyterous tēs ekklēsias* in 5:14.

The use of kinship language is particularly pervasive in Christianity, indeed one of its signatures even for outsiders (see Lucian of Samosata, *Passing of Peregrinus* 13).[148] James' use of this language is distinctive on two counts. First, he uses the term *adelphos* 19 times (1:2, 9, 16, 19; 2:1, 5, 14, 15; 3:1, 10, 12; 4:11 [thrice]; 5:7, 9, 10, 12, 19) and *adelphē* once (2:15). Given James' brevity, this usage is particularly intense (only the 38 instances of 1 Corinthians exceed it and the 19 of Romans equal it, and they are both far longer letters). Second, James uses *only* this egalitarian form of kinship language, lacking entirely the parental imagery adopted, for example, by Paul for his relationship to the communities that he had founded (1 Cor 4:14–15; Gal 4:19; 1 Thess 2:11; 1 Tim 1:2, 18; 2 Tim 1:2; 2:1; Philemon 10). Three times, James accompanies this kinship language with the caritative "beloved" (*agapētoi*) in 1:16; 1:19, and 2:5 (compare 7 instances in 2 Peter, 6 in 1 John and 5 in Romans).

The classic triad of virtues for the nascent messianic movement consisted in faith, hope, and love (1 Thess 1:2–3; 1 Cor 13:13; 1 Pet 1:3–9). That James makes frequent use of "faith" language (*pistis*, 1:3, 6; 2:1, 5, 14 [2], 17, 18 [3], 20, 22 [2], 24, 26; 5:15; *pisteuein*, 2:19, 23) is not by itself therefore surprising. More striking is the connection drawn between faith and being saved (*sōzein*) in 2:14, a combination that is distinctively Christian (Rom 10:9; 1 Cor 1:21; Eph 2:8; Matt 9:2; Mark 5:34; 10:52; Luke 7:50; 8:48–50; 17:19; 18:42; Acts 14:9). Notice the frequency of such language in the Synoptic tradition, which is attested also in James' reference to "saving souls/lives" (*sōsai psychas*, 1:21; 5:20; compare Matt 16:25; Mark 3:4; 8:35; Luke 9:24), as well as in his contrast between "saving and destroying" (*sōsai kai apolesai*, 4:12; see Matt 18:12; Mark 8:35; 9:24). Especially noteworthy is Luke 6:9: *exestin . . . psychēn sōsai ē apolesai* and Luke 9:56: *ouk ēlthen psychas anthrōpōn apolesai alla sōsai* (marginal reading).

James never mentions hope (*elpis*), emphasizing instead endurance (*hypo-*

148Compare Meeks, *First Urban Christians*, 87, 225.

monē, 1:3, 12; 5:11) and patience (*makrothymia*, 5:7, 8, 9, 10). But with other NT writings, James places the commandment to "love the neighbor as yourself" (Lev 19:18) in a central place (2:8). He calls it the "royal law" (*nomos basilikos*). Just as James does, other canonical writings also connect this commandment to the decalogue as a summary of Torah (Rom 13:9; Gal 5:14), and the Gospels specifically connect the privileging of Lev 19:18 to Jesus himself (Matt 5:43; 19:19; 22:39; Mark 12:31; Luke 10:27). That this does not automatically follow from the combination of the decalogue and Leviticus 19 has been demonstrated by the *Sentences of Pseudo-Phocylides*, which in fact makes no use of Lev 19:18 (see above, p. 40).

In the case of James, the designation *nomos basilikos* occurs immediately after the statement that God had chosen the poor to be the heirs of the *basileia*. This statement not only rephrases the expression *basileia tou theou* (see, e.g., Mark 1:15; Luke 4:43; John 3:3; Acts 1:3; Rom 14:7; 1 Cor 4:20; Gal 5:21; 2 Thess 1:5), but the very distinctive Christian interpretation of that *basileia* as being bestowed on the *ptōchoi* (Luke 6:20; Matt 5:3).

When James speaks of the poor as "heirs" (*klēronomoi*) of that kingdom, furthermore (2:5), he makes a connection also found in 1 Cor 6:9–11; Gal 5:21; Eph 5:5. James 2:5 (as well as 1:12) also makes use of the language of "promise" (*epangellomai*), which, while immediately recognizable within the NT argot (see Acts 1:4; 2:33, 39; 7:5, 17; 13:23, 32; 26:6; Rom 4:13, 14, 16, 20–21; 9:4, 8, 9; 15:8; 2 Cor 1:20; 7:1; Gal 3:14, 16, 17, 18, 19, 21, 22, 29; 4:23, 28; Heb 6:13; 10:23; 11:11; 12:26; 1 John 2:25), is found only rarely and insignificantly in the LXX.

In 1:18, James speaks of God giving birth to humans by the *logos tēs alētheias* ("word of truth"). The expression has a loose precedent in passages such as LXX Ps 118:43, 160; Prov 22:21, but in the NT, it appears with special reference to the Christian proclamation (2 Cor 6:7; Eph 1:13; Col 1:5; 2 Tim 2:15). Other terms absent entirely from the LXX but attested in other NT writings include *stephanos tēs zōēs* ("crown of life," 1:12; see also Rev 2:10); "firstfruits" (*aparchē*) with reference to humans (James 1:18; see Rom 8:23; 11:16; 16:5; 1 Cor 15:20–23; 16:15; 2 Thess 2:13; Rev 14:4); *apotithēmi* ("putting off" a quality as a garment, James 1:21; see Rom 13:12; Eph 4:22, 25; Col 3:8; Heb 12:1; 1 Pet 2:1); and the distinctive *prosōpolēmpsia/prosōpolēmteō* (James 2:1, 9), which is based on the LXX *prosōpon labein* (Lev 19:15) but in combined form seems to be a distinctive Christian locution (Rom 2:11; Eph 6:9; Col 3:25; Acts 10:34).

James' eschatological language, especially in combination, also resembles Christian usage elsewhere. Noteworthy in this context is the use of *parousia tou kyriou* ("Coming of the Lord") in James 5:7–8. The term *parousia* is never connected to *kyrios* in the LXX. But in the NT, the expression is a virtual *terminus technicus* for the return of Jesus (Matt 24:3, 27, 37, 39; 1 Cor 15:23; 1 Thess 2:19; 3:13; 4:15; 5:23; 2 Thess 2:1, 8; 2 Pet 1:16; 3:4, 12; 1 John 2:28). Together with this expression, note the use of *eschatais hēmerais* ("in the last days") in James 5:3, which finds exact parallel in Acts 2:17 and 2 Tim 3:1 as well as rough equivalence in other early Christian combinations (Heb 1:2; 1 Pet 1:5, 20; 2 Pet 3:3; Jude 18; John 6:39–40, 44, 54; 7:37; 11:24; 12:48; 1 John 2:18). In the same connection, the distinctive use of the perfect tense of *engizein* (*ēngiken* "is near, has arrived") in James 5:8 is suggestive (see Matt 3:2; 4:17; 10:7; 26:45; Mark 1:15; Luke 10:9, 11; 21:8; Rom 13:12; 1 Pet 4:7).

To evaluate this evidence properly, we must assess not only the incidence of terms but also their combinations and, above all, the density of their use within what is, after all, a very brief composition. When this is done, it is clear that James' language is identifiably "Christian" within the Jewish literature of the first century. This conclusion is only strengthened by more specific comparisons between James and other NT writings.

Once more, we move from writings that have at most a few lexical or thematic resemblances to those for whom more sustained comparisons are appropriate. Thus, the use of *psychichos* in Jude 19 as meaning "those who do not have spirit" (*pneuma*), is useful together with 1 Cor 2:14 in locating the meaning of that term in James 3:15; and the command in Jude 23 to hate "even the garment stained (*espilōmenon*) by the flesh" suggests something of the moral rigor of James 1:27; but even the attribution of the letter to "Jude, a slave of Jesus Christ and brother of James" (Jude 1) does not justify further discussion.

Likewise, the Letter to the Hebrews' use of Abraham (11:8–10, 17–19) and Rahab (11:31) as examples of faith are isolated similarities to James 2:21–25 within an otherwise quite dissimilar composition, with the language used for these examples even put to different ends. The use of such examples does reinforce the point established already by our review of Jewish literature, that Paul and James are scarcely alone in their appeal to Abraham.[149]

a. *Johannine Writings*

The Johannine writings offer at best two significant points of comparison to James, apart from the isolated lexical echo in Rev 3:20, which has Jesus "standing at the door" as does also Matt 24:33 and James 5:9. The first touches on the dualism reflected in the distinction between "friendship with God" and "friendship with the world" in James 4:4. In Jesus' farewell discourse to the disciples, he identifies them as his "friends" (*philoi*) whom he has chosen (John 15:15); they, in turn, are to be hated by the world (*kosmos*) as he has been (15:18): "If you were out of the world, the world would have been friends

---

[149]On this, see R. N. Longenecker, "The 'Faith of Abraham' Theme in Paul, James and Hebrews: A Study in the Circumstantial Nature of New Testament Teaching," *JETS* 20 (1977) 203–12; M. L. Soards, "The Early Christian Interpretation of Abraham and the Place of James within that Context," *IBS* 9 (1987) 18–26; J. S. Siker, *Disinheriting the Jews: Abraham in Early Christian Controversy* (Louisville: Westminster/John Knox Press, 1991) 1–143.

(*ephilei*) with its own; and because you are not out of the world but I have chosen you from the world, on account of this the world hates you" (15:19). In 1 John 2:15, the same dualism is found in an exhortation that provides the closest extant parallel to James 4:4: "Do not love (*agapate*) the world nor the things that are in the world (*kosmos*). If anyone loves the world, the love of the father is not in him. For everything in the world, the desire (*epithymia*) of the flesh, and the desire (*epithymia*) of the eyes, and the arrogance (*alazoneia*) of life, are not from the father but are from the world."

A second example occurs in the exhortation of 1 John 3:17: "Whoever has the world's necessities and sees his brother in need and closes his heart against him, how can the love of God dwell in him?" This matches perfectly the example given by James 2:14–16. And the conclusion in 1 John 3:18 perfectly captures the message of James' example, as well as of James 1:22–25: "Little children, let us not love in word (*logō*) or in speech (*glōssē*) but in deed (*ergō*) and truth (*alētheia*)."

In terms of ideology, the Johannine distinction between a measurement of reality that comes "from above" (*anōthen*) and one that is "from below" (see John 3:2–14) in support of a sectarian ethics over against the dominant cultural norms, is not at all dissimilar from James' contrast between "wisdom from above" and the "earthly wisdom" (3:15–16) that grounds its ethical dualism. These important similarities in perspective, however, gain their impressiveness from being found in literature that is in other respects (such as the Christocentrism of the Johannine literature in contrast to the theocentrism of James) more unalike than alike.

b. First Letter of Peter

The First Letter of Peter contains a range of impressive similarities to James, beginning with the designation of its readers as "elect sojourners of the diaspora" (1:1 = James 1:1)![150] In 1 Pet 1:6–7, the readers are instructed to rejoice if they should experience "various testings" (*poikilois peirasmois*), so that "the provenness of [their] faith" (*to dokimion hymōn tēs pisteōs*) might be found to be "more precious than perishable gold tried in the fire." Particularly in the diction, the resemblance to James is impressive. In contrast to James, however, 1 Peter tends to turn exhortation in a Christological direction. Thus, in this passage he continues, "to praise and honor and glory at the revelation of Jesus Christ" (1:7).

Similarly, 1 Pet 1:23 speaks of Christians "begotten anew not out of a perishable but imperishable seed, the living and enduring word of God," which matches James 1:18 in theme if not precisely in diction. The next verse (1 Pet

---

[150]This is the starting point for the effort by F. Köster to show that both James and 1 Peter were addressed to Christian readers in diverse parts of the "diaspora," in "Ueber die Leser, an welche der Brief des Jakobus und der erste Brief des Petrus gerichtet ist," *TSK* 4 (1831) 581–88.

1:24) continues with a verbatim citation from Isa 40:6–8 ("all flesh is grass"), which is paraphrased also in James 1:10–11 with reference to the passing away of the rich. 1 Peter combines elements found separated and differently applied in James and then concludes with a specifically Christian application: "This is the word that has been proclaimed to you as good news" (1 Pet 1:25).

A similar equivalence in theme, rather than in diction, appears in 1 Pet 2:1–2, which has the same transition from "putting off" (*apotithēmi*) negative qualities and receiving a saving word, as does James 1:21. Much less impressive is the fact that 1 Pet 4:8 cites Prov 10:12 ("love covers a multitude of sins") in an application totally different from the (possible) allusion to the same passage in James 5:20.

A final point of comparison between 1 Peter and James illustrates the greater degree of dissimilarity found within their surface similarity. At first, the resemblances are striking: 1 Pet 5:5 exhorts his readers to submit (*hypotagēte*), as does James 4:8, and to show "lowliness of attitude" (*tapeinophrosynē*), as does James 4:10. Then, 1 Pet 5:5 cites LXX Prov 3:34 ("God resists the proud but gives grace to the lowly") as does James 4:6. Finally, 1 Pet 5:6 commands, *tapeinōthēte oun hypo tēn krataian cheira tou theou hina hymas hypsōsę en kairǫ* ("humble yourselves therefore beneath the powerful hand of God in order that he might exalt you in the appropriate season"), using the same spatial images as James 4:10. A remarkable cluster of ideas and images. But the difference is also great. 1 Peter uses this language in an exhortation to younger people to submit to older people in the community (5:5), a domestic and hierarchical concern totally foreign to the egalitarian ethic of James. The impressive similarities between 1 Peter and James do not rise above the broadly thematic and lexical level. Not only the explicit Christology and ecclesiology of 1 Peter, but also its fundamentally world-affirming stance, make these points of resemblance fade into a fabric of quite another color.

c. Synoptic Tradition

James also has a number of fascinating contacts with the Synoptic Tradition. I have already noted that James makes no use of the standard elements of the kerygma: the death, burial, resurrection of the Messiah, and the sending of the Holy Spirit. Nor does he employ any other of the gospel narrative traditions. The only possible exception is the intriguing echo of gospel healing accounts in James' language about the "saving" of the sick person (5:15): "and the Lord will raise him up" (*kai egeirei auton ho kyrios*; compare Mark 2:11; 4:38; 5:41; 9:27; 10:49 //).

James shows the greatest affinity to the tradition of Jesus' *sayings* rather than to that of Jesus' *stories*.[151] Some of these, indeed, may be attributed to the

---

[151]For a complete listing of the possibilities, see D. B. Deppe, *The Sayings of Jesus in the Epistle of James* (Chelsea, Michigan: Brookcrafters, 1989).

accident of sharing a moral universe that emphasizes the connection between verbal profession and action (Matt 7:21–23; Luke 6:46 = James 2:14–26), as well as the importance not only of *hearing* but also of *doing* (Matt 7:24–27; Luke 6:47–49 = James 1:22–25), and uses agricultural imagery to exemplify the connection between identity and consistent behavior (Matt 7:16; Luke 6:44 = James 3:10–13).[152]

Other gospel sayings have a lexical as well as a thematic resemblance to statements in James. Such is the statement in Matthew's eschatological discourse, which speaks of the *parousia* of the Son of Man (24:27), that when certain signs appear, then *engus estin epi thyrais* ("it is near, at the doors," 24:33), an image that echoes James' *ho kritēs pro tōn thyrōn hestēken* ("the judge is standing before the doors"), equally in connection with the *parousia tou kyriou* (James 5:8–9). Similar is the assurance given by Jesus in Matt 21:21 (// Mark 11:23), that the disciples' prayer would be answered *ean echēte pistin kai mē diakrithēte* ("if you have faith and do not doubt"), which corresponds to James 1:6. Likewise noteworthy is the similarity between James 1:12 and Matt 10:22, *ho de hypomeinas eis telos sōthēsetai* ("the one who has endured to the end will be saved"), as well as the close similarity in thought and diction between James 4:6–10 and Matt 23:12: *hostis hypsōsei heauton tapeinōthēsetai kai hostis tapeinōsei heauton hypsōthēsetai* ("whoever exalts himself shall be humbled and whoever humbles himself shall be exalted"; see also Luke 14:11; Mark 9:35).

Four of the sayings of Jesus that are now located in the beatitudes are particularly close to the language and spirit of James. One can compare *makarioi hoi ptōchoi hoti hymetera estin hē basileia tou theou* ("Blessed are you poor, for yours is the kingdom of God," Luke 6:20; see Matt 5:3) with James 2:5; *makarioi hoi eleēmones hoti autoi eleēthēsontai* ("Blessed are the merciful for they will receive mercy," Matt 5:7) with James 2:13; *makarioi hoi katharoi tȩ kardia* ("Blessed are the pure of heart," Matt 5:8) with James 4:8; and *makarioi hoi eirēnopoioi* ("Blessed are the peacemakers," Matt 5:9) with James 3:18.[153]

Finally, three statements in James appear to have an even more direct connection to the sayings tradition contained in the Synoptics. First, in James 1:5, *aiteitō para tou didontos theou pasin haplōs kai mē oneidizontos kai dothēsetai autȩ* ("Let him ask of God who gives to all simply and without grudging, and it will be given to him"), when relieved of the specifically

---

[152]This point is well made by Dibelius, 28.

[153]See H. D. Betz, *Essays on the Sermon on the Mount*, trans. L. L. Welborn (Philadelphia: Fortress Press, 1985) 156, n. 122: "We can only mention here in passing the completely open problem of the relationship of the SM to the Epistle of James." For studies that pursue that connection more vigorously, see G. Kittel, "Der geschichtliche Ort des Jakobusbriefes," ZNW 41 (1942) 75–105; F. Eleder, *Jakobusbrief und Bergpredigt* (Ph.D. diss., Katholische-theologischen Fakultät der Universität Wien, 1964); P. J. Hartin, "James and the Q Sermon of the Mount/Plain," *SBLSP* 28 (1989) 440–57.

Jacobean designation for God (compare 1:17), yields a lexical and structural correspondence to Matt 7:7: *aiteite kai dothēsetai hymin* ("ask and it shall be given to you"). Second, and somewhat less obviously, language found in two passages of James (4:11–12 and 5:9), when brought together, forms a statement similar to Matt 7:1: *mē krinete hina mē krithēte* ("Do not judge so that you are not judged," see also Luke 6:37). Third, and most obviously, James 5:12: *mē omnuete mēte ton ouranon mēte tēn gēn mēte allon tina orkon. ētō de hymōn to nai nai kai to ou ou* ("Do not take oaths, neither by heaven, nor by earth, nor any other sort of oath. Rather let your 'yes' be 'yes,' and your 'no' be 'no.'") is a simpler version of the same command in Matt 5:34.

These statements in James suggest three conclusions that will be argued more fully in the commentary: 1) James makes use of sayings traditions that are otherwise identified as being from Jesus; 2) although some of his wording resembles Matthew in particular,[154] it is more likely that he makes use of the traditions at a stage of development prior to the synoptic redaction, that is, at a stage roughly that of the gospel sayings source conventionally designated Q;[155] 3) the use of the sayings tradition is James' distinctive way of mediating the "Jesus experience."

BIBLIOGRAPHY

Betz, H. D., *Essays on the Sermon on the Mount*, trans. L. L. Welborn (Philadelphia: Fortress Press, 1985).

Cooper, R., "Prayer: A Study in Matthew and James," *Encounter* 29 (1968) 268–77.

Cullmann, O., *The Christology of the New Testament* rev. ed., trans. S. C. Guthrie and C. Hall (Philadelphia: Westminster Press, 1959).

Davids, P. H., "James and Jesus," in *Gospel Perspectives: The Jesus Tradition outside the Gospels*, ed. D. Wenham (Sheffield: JSOT, 1985) 63–84.

Deppe, D. B., *The Sayings of Jesus in the Epistles of James* (Chelsea, Michigan: Brookcrafters, 1989).

Eleder, F., *Jakobusbrief und Bergpredigt* (Ph.D. diss., Katholische-theologischen Fakultät der Universität Wien, 1964).

---

[154]See F. Gryglewicz, "L'épître de st. Jacques et l'évangile de st. Matthieu," *Roczniki Theologiczno-Kanoniczne* 8 (1961) 33–51; M. H. Shepherd, "The Epistle of James and the Gospel of Matthew," *JBL* 75 (1956) 40–51; R. Cooper, "Prayer: A Study in Matthew and James," *Encounter* 29 (1968) 268–77.

[155]See P. J. Hartin, "James and the Q Sermon on the Mount/Plain," 457; and ibid., *James and the Sayings of Jesus* (JSNT 47; Sheffield: JSOT, 1991); P. H. Davids, "James and Jesus," in *Gospel Perspectives: The Jesus Tradition outside the Gospels*, ed. D. Wenham (Sheffield: JSOT, 1985) 63–84.

Gryglewicz, F., "L'épître de st. Jacques et l'évangile de st. Matthieu," *Roczniki Theologiczno-Kanoniczne* 8 (1961) 33–51.

Hartin, P. J., "James and the Q Sermon on the Mount/Plain," *SBLSP* 28 (1989) 440–57.

———, *James and the Sayings of Jesus* (JSNT 47; Sheffield: JSOT, 1991).

Kittel, G., "Der geschichtliche Ort des Jakobusbriefes," *ZNW* 41 (1942) 75–105.

Köster, F., "Ueber die Leser, an welche der Brief des Jakobus und der erste Brief des Petrus gerichtet ist," *TSK* 4 (1831) 581–88.

Longenecker, R. N., "The 'Faith of Abraham' Theme in Paul, James and Hebrews: A Study in the Circumstantial Nature of New Testament Teaching," *JETS* 20 (1977) 203–12.

Massebieau, L., "L'épître de Jacques: est-elle l'oeuvre d'un chrétien?" *Revue de l'Histoire des Religions* 31–32 (1895) 249–83.

Meeks, W. A., *The First Urban Christians: The Social World of the Apostle Paul* (New Haven: Yale University Press, 1983).

Sanders, E. P., et al., eds., *Jewish and Christian Self-Definition* 3 Vols (Philadelphia: Fortress Press, 1980–82).

Shepherd, M. H., "The Epistle of James and the Gospel of Matthew," *JBL* 75 (1976) 40–51.

Siker, J. S., *Disinheriting the Jews: Abraham in Early Christian Controversy* (Louisville: Westminster/John Knox Press, 1991).

Soards, M. L., "The Early Christian Interpretation of Abraham and the Place of James within that Context," *IBS* 9 (1987) 18–26.

Spitta, F., *Zur Geschichte und Literatur des Urchristentums* 2: *Der Brief des Jakobus* (Göttingen: Vandenhoeck und Ruprecht, 1896).

d. James and Paul

Comparisons between James and Paul are particularly difficult, not least because they have so often been overemphasized and distorted. A great deal of the scholarship devoted to James has focused on this connection. In the History of Interpretation section of this Introduction (III), the several ways that relationship has been understood will be surveyed. The volume of scholarship given to this one point over the past hundred years is overwhelming. Rather than enter into discussion with it, I have decided to simply list the works devoted to this question in the sectional bibliography and in my presentation attempt a broader and more nuanced way of approaching the issue.

Some preliminary considerations may help clear the ground for discussion. First, there are some obvious disparities that complicate comparison. Paul has thirteen letters attributed to him and James only one. Paul writes mainly to specific and named communities and individuals, whereas James addresses a general diaspora readership. Paul is the founder or leader of most of the communities he addresses, whereas James purports only to be a *doulos* of God and Christ and fellow *didaskalos*. Paul addresses Gentile or mixed congregations, whereas the most obvious way to read James is as written to Jewish Messianists. Paul's correspondence is generated by a series of crises in his communities or personal ministry, whereas James' exhortation appears general, rather than specific, and without a personal stake. Paul's teaching is rooted in a Christology fundamentally shaped by his experience of a crucified and raised Messiah who is the source of a transforming Holy Spirit, whereas James' teaching is more theological than Christological and connects more specifically to the sayings of Jesus than to the *kerygma*.

Second, it is obvious in particular that Paul has a range of preoccupations and a richness of thought that do not overlap with James: Paul's concern for his own authority, for example, or for sexual morality, or the ordering of the household, or the structuring of the community's worship—not to mention his need to counter a variety of opposing elitist positions ranging from libertinism to legalism. James, too, has interests not identical to those of Paul, although his range is understandably smaller: modes of speech in the community, for example, relations between rich and poor, the care of the needy, and the ministry of healing and reconciliation. It is equally a mistake in method to reduce James to a comparison to Paul as it is to reduce Paul to a comparison to James.

Third, in addition to the fact that James and Paul share the same messianic argot (as shown above), they share, beyond that, a specific range of language and perception that derives from their role as moral teachers. More than that, they share—and here is where problems of interpretation enter—a narrower range of language revolving around the terms "justification" (*dikaiosynē*), "saving" (*sōzein*), "faith" (*pistis*), "law" (*nomos*), and "works" (*erga*) that is distinctive, if not unique, among the NT writings. Within this narrower range of forensic language (primarily in Galatians and Romans), furthermore, James and Paul appear to many readers to be saying contradictory things. But at the same time these same letters also show the highest degree of *agreement* between James and Paul on several points.

Fourth, a literary comparison between James and Paul inevitably at some point demands consideration of the complex questions concerning the historical Paul (who wrote at least most of the letters attributed to him, and certainly Romans and Galatians) and the historical James (who may or may not have written this letter attributed to him). The relationship between these historical figures can be construed so as to yield a solution to the elements of agreement and disagreement found in the writings. Such a discussion must be deferred to the next part of the Introduction (II) dealing with the question, "Whose Voice?" The present exposition is intended to provide as neutral a review as possible of the data required to be taken into account.

Let us begin with those similarities in the two authors that are largely stylistic, and due to the fact that they both employ a "diatribal" style of moral exhortation. Such tropes as "if anyone thinks" (*ei tis dokei*) to set up a false supposition fall into this category (1 Cor 3:18; Gal 6:3 = James 1:26), as also do such expressions as "do not be deceived" (*mē planasthe* 1 Cor 6:9; 15:33; Gal 6:7 = James 1:16), or "do you not know" (*ouk oidate*, Rom 11:2; 1 Cor 3:16; 5:6; 6:2–3 = James 4:4), or "what is the use" (*ti ophelos*, 1 Cor 15:32 = James 2:14–16; see also the use of *ōpheleia* in Rom 3:1; 1 Cor 13:3; Gal 5:2). Similarly, the expostulation "Oh Man" (*ō anthrōpe*, Rom 2:1, 3; 9:20 = James 2:20) and the transition "but someone will say" (*all' erei tis*, 1 Cor 15:35 = James 2:18) fall into the same category.

Other resemblances can be credited to the fact that James and Paul are both moral teachers. Thus, it should not surprise us to find that both authors use virtue and vice lists with shared elements (e.g., Rom 1:29–31; 13:13; 2 Cor 12:20; Gal 5:19–23 = James 3:14–17), or that both evince a high regard for mutual correction within the community (1 Thess 5:12; Gal 6:1 = James 5:20), or that both employ a similar rhetorical *gradatio* involving endurance and testing (Rom 5:3 = James 1:3).

Above all, it is no shock to find both authors insisting on the need to translate identity into consistent moral behavior. A neutral term to use for such action is *ergon* or "work." James uses the term for such an effect or action in 1:4 and 3:13, and especially applies it to the "working out" of faith (1:25; 2:14, 17–18, 20, 21, 22, 24, 25, 26). As noted earlier (p. 30), James *never* connects *erga* to the term "law" (*nomos*). Rather, like *every* other use of *ergon* in the NT outside of Paul's letters, he uses the term in the moral sense of "deed/effort" (see, e.g., Matt 5:16; 11:19; 26:10; Mark 13:34; Luke 24:19; John 3:19; 10:25; 17:4; Acts 5:38; 9:36; 13:2; 26:20; Heb 3:9; 13:21; 1 Pet 1:17; 2 Pet 3:10; 1 John 3:12; 2 John 11; 3 John 10; Jude 15; Rev 2:2). I underline the point: James' usage concerning "works" is both unconnected to "law" and is entirely consistent with the dominant NT usage concerning moral effort as an expression of convictions.[156]

Of first importance for this discussion is the observation that Paul predominantly uses *ergon* in precisely the same sense! His letters contain some 50 occurrences of the term in this meaning (e.g., Rom 13:3, 12; 14:20; 15:18; 1 Cor 3:13–15; 9:1; 15:58; 16:10; 2 Cor 9:8; 11:15; 1 Thess 1:3; 5:13; 2 Thess 2:17), while only 17 bear the more restricted and polemical sense of "works of the law" (*erga tou nomou*). Paul can speak unembarrassedly about "your work of faith" (*ergon tēs pisteōs*) in 1 Thess 1:3 and of the "work of faith in power" (*ergon pisteōs en dynamei*) in 2 Thess 1:11. Like James, Paul would take it as axiomatic that "each person's work (*ergon*) will become manifest" (1 Cor 3:13) and that "each person should test his own work" (*ergon*, Gal 6:4).

---

[156]See the helpful discussion in U. C. Von Wahlde, "Faith and Works in Jn VI 28–29," *NovT* 22 (1980) 304–15; also, E. Peterson, "*ergon* in der Bedeutung 'Bau' bei Paulus," *Bib* 22 (1941) 439–41.

Since Paul and James were both moral teachers within the symbolic world of Torah, furthermore, it is no surprise to find each of them affirm *ho nomos* ("the law") as the revelation of God's will for humans and therefore as a norm for moral behavior. Paul agrees in principle with James that the "whole law" (*holos ho nomos*) must in some sense be kept (Gal 5:3 = James 2:10). If James can speak of the law positively as "law of liberty" and "perfect law" and "royal law"—meaning, thereby, the law of love in Lev 19:18 (James 1:25; 2:8), Paul can also speak positively of the *nomos* as "spiritual" (*pneumatikos*, Rom 7:14) and "holy and just and good" (Rom 7:12) and "noble" (*kalon*, Rom 7:16).

Both agree, furthermore, that not only knowing but keeping God's law is mandatory. It is Paul, not James, who declares, *ou gar hoi akroatai nomou dikaioi para tǭ theǭ alla hoi poiētai nomou dikaiōthēsontai* ("It is not the hearers of the law who are righteous but the doers of the law who will be considered righteous," Rom 2:13). James has a remarkably similar statement in 1:22–25, using the same distinctive terms of *akroatai* and *poiētai*. Instead of referring to *nomos* ("law"), however, James uses the substantive *logos* ("word") as that which must be heard and practiced.

Likewise, it is Paul rather than James who declares that circumcision "counts" or "profits" (*ōphelei*) if the law is done, but if one is a *parabatēs* ("transgressor") of the law, then circumcision turns into uncircumcision (Rom 2:25–27; see James 2:9–11). In other words, deeds are what count rather than profession or ritual membership. Thus, Paul asserts that neither circumcision or uncircumcision matter, but "keeping the commandments of God" (1 Cor 7:19) and insists that "the righteous requirement of the law" (*to dikaiōma tou nomou*) is fulfilled by those who "walk in the Spirit" (Rom 8:4).

Where does Paul find this "righteous requirement of the law" to be fulfilled? Precisely where James does, in the commandment of love, which, for Paul, "has brought the other law (*heteron nomon*) to fulfillment" and can be expressed, as for James, in the commandment of Lev 19:18, "to love the neighbor as the self" (Rom 13:8). In the Christian community, this involves "bearing one another's burdens and so fulfilling the *nomos Christou*" ("law of Christ," Gal 6:2). It is this understanding, in turn, that allows Paul to repeat in Gal 5:6, "In Christ Jesus neither circumcision matters (*ischuei*) nor uncircumcision, but faith (*pistis*) working itself out (*energoumenē*) through love (*di'agapēs*)."

This already broad range of agreement between James and Paul can be extended further. Both writers have a strong appreciation of God as judge. It is Paul who in Romans 2:6 quotes favorably from LXX Ps 61:13, "he will give to each one according to his deeds (*erga*)," and Paul who declares that the evil are "laying up a treasure of wrath for the day of wrath" (Rom 2:5 = James 5:3!). On the basis of their belief in God as judge, both writers forbid judgment of the neighbor (Rom 14:3, 10, 13). In language remarkably similar to James 4:12, Paul rhetorically asks (14:4), *su tis ei ho krinōn allotrion oiketēn* ("who are you to judge the servant of another?").

Both James and Paul locate "doubting" (*diakrinomenos*) as an antithesis to faithful action (Rom 4:20; 14:23 = James 1:6). Indeed, both recognize a deeper sort of internal dividedness. In James it is "double-mindedness" (*dipsychos*, 1:8; 4:8). In his discussion of the law in Romans 7, Paul speaks of "another law doing battle in my members against the law in my mind" (*en tois melesin mou antistrateuomenon tō nomō tou noos mou* (Rom 7:23), which sounds very much like James' description of wars deriving *ek tōn hēdonōn hymon tōn strateuomenōn en tois melesin hymōn* ("from your desires that are warring among your members," James 4:1). And, lest we think that this sort of moral dividedness for Paul existed only "under the law" or hypothetically, it is interesting to look from the moralist's perspective at his discussion in Gal 5:16–23 of the moral dualism facing his readers. Here there is a battle (*antikeitai*) between the *pneuma* and "the desire of the flesh" (*epithymia*). This desire has as its "works" (*erga*) a variety of vices (5:19–21), in opposition to the "fruits of the spirit" (5:22–23), which so much resemble the "fruit of righteousness" that comes from the "wisdom from above" in James 3:17–18. The choice between the two norms is clear, but for Paul the intense struggle means that sometimes "you are doing those things which you do not wish" (Gal 5:17).

Both James and Paul give primacy to faith, and they agree that being "heirs of the kingdom of God" is a matter of God's promise (Gal 3:29 = James 2:5) and gift (James 1:17; 4:6; Rom 3:24; 5:15). But it is precisely on these points that they have sometimes been thought to diverge. The critical passages are those involving Abraham in Galatians 3 and Romans 4 compared to James 2:18–26. The commentary to follow will dissect the details of the text. For now it can be stated that the perceived contradiction between Paul and James on the question of righteousness or justification (*dikaiosynē*) has little, if any, basis.

A proper sorting through of this question requires first some attention to the context of Paul's discussion. In Galatians, Paul is opposing Gentile believers (abetted by troublemakers) who want to "Judaize," that is, receive circumcision and keep all the commandments of Torah, including the ritual ones (Gal 4:9–10; 5:3, 12). For Paul, the implication of their desire for "more" is the denial of what they have already been given, namely God's gift in Christ. By this Paul means "the faith of the son of God who loved me and gave himself for me" (Gal 2:20).

Paul's polemical attitude toward "works of the law" (*erga tou nomou*) is, therefore, fitted to this specific situation involving circumcision and the keeping of the ritual commandments and is posed in contrast to the *pistis Christou* or "faith of Christ." It is with specific reference to this situation that Paul declares that "a man is made righteous not through *erga nomou* except through the faith of Jesus Christ, and we have believed in Christ Jesus so that we might be justified out of the *pisteōs Iēsou Christou*" (Gal 2:16).

Paul therefore opposes *erga nomou* and *pistis Christou* as principles of justification before God. He denies that right relationship comes through the law (*dia nomou*) apart from faith, but through a free gift from Christ (*dōrean*, Gal 2:21); not from *ergon nomou* but from *akoēs pisteōs* ("hearing of faith" 3:2, 5); not through *nomos* but through *epangelia* ("promise," 3:18). In this argument, Abraham is cited as an example of faith that makes a person righteous in response to God's *epangelia*, and Gen 15:6 is quoted to that effect (Gal 3:6). The principle of faith is thereby established as justifying humans 430 years before the *nomos* was given to Moses (Gal 3:17).

In Romans 4:1–25, Paul's treatment of Abraham is distinctive but broadly consistent. Again, Abraham, "our forefather according to the flesh" (4:1) is cited within the context established by 3:20, *ex ergōn nomou ou dikaiōthēsetai pasa sarx* ("no flesh is made righteous on the basis of the works of the law"). When Paul goes on to speak of *erga* in Rom 4:2, therefore, it is not with respect to moral action broadly considered, but specifically with respect to the commandments of Torah, and most especially the commandment concerning circumcision. This is why the Gen 15:6 citation is used to show that Abraham was declared righteous *before* he was circumcised (4:10). Again, Paul contrasts *nomos* and *epangelia*, *nomos* and *klēronomia*. Abraham, then, is the exemplar of faith for both circumcised and uncircumcised (4:16).

How should the critical passage in James 2:18–26 be read in comparison to the Pauline discussion? The first thing to note is that James' understanding of *nomos*, as I have already twice stated, has nothing whatever to do with the issues Paul is combating. James does not connect *nomos* to any sort of "works," much less those concerning circumcision or the ritual laws. Second, James is entirely in agreement with Paul on placing *pistis*, *epangelia*, and *klēronomia* in the same column (James 2:5). Third, James places in opposition an empty *pistis theou* ("faith in God") or *pistis Christou* ("the faith of Christ"), which consists in profession or claim to membership (2:1, 19), and the living *erga pisteōs* ("works of faith"), which make such profession real. Fourth, Abraham is an example precisely of this "active faith" by his sacrifice of his son Isaac (2:21). Fifth, this *ergon pisteōs* is itself "co-worked by faith" (*synērgei*) and "perfects faith," that is, brings faith to its full realization in deed (2:22). Sixth, the action of Abraham in Gen 22:2–9 is read by James as the textual "fulfillment" of the declaration by God in Gen 15:6 that Abraham's faith made him to be reckoned as righteous (2:23). Finally, James' climactic statement, *ex ergōn dikaioutai anthrōpos kai ouk ek pisteōs monon* ("a person is shown to be righteous on the basis of deeds and not on the basis of faith only," 2:24), which superficially appears to contradict Gal 2:16, does nothing of the sort, for the terms in the respective sentences have quite different referents.

I have tried to suggest that a comparison between James and Paul is distorted when reduced to the single topic of righteousness as found in Galatians/Romans and James 2:18–26. The range of similarities and dissimilarities in the two writers is both broader and more complex than that of a simple agreement or disagreement on one point. Paul's language, furthermore, is consistent within its own context and purposes, just as James' language is consistent within its context and compositional strategy. Despite the remarkable points of resemblance, they appear not to be talking to each other by way of instruction or correction. Rather, they seem to be addressing concerns specific to each author.

The survey of the data provided here leaves open a variety of possibilities for the specific historical relationship between James and Paul, and between Paul's letters and James'. But any such analysis must build on all the data, rather than a predetermined selection taken out of context and thereby misconstrued.

BIBLIOGRAPHY

Bartmann, B., *St. Paulus und St. Jakobus ueber die Rechtfertigung* (BSF 2,1; Freiburg: Herder, 1897).

Bergauer, P., *Der Jakobusbrief bei Augustinus und die damit verbundenen Probleme der Rechtfertigungslehre* (Vienna: Herder, 1962).

Böhmer, J., "Der 'Glaube' im Jakobusbriefe," NKZ 9 (1898) 251–56.

Eichholz, G., *Glaube und Werke bei Paulus und Jakobus* (Theologische Existenz Heute, n.f. 88; München: Kaiser, 1961).

———, *Jakobus und Paulus: Ein Beitrag zum Problem des Kanons* (Theologische Existenze Heute, n.f. 39; München: Kaiser, 1953).

Hamann, H. P., "Faith and Works: Paul and James," *Lutheran Theological Journal* 9 (1975) 33–41.

Hengel, M., "Der Jakobusbrief als antipaulinische Polemik," in *Tradition and Interpretation in the New Testament*, ed. G. F. Hawthorne and O. Betz (Grand Rapids: Eerdmans, 1987) 248–78.

Jeremias, J., "Paul and James," *ExpT* 66 (1955) 368–71.

Johnston, C., "The Controversy between St. Paul and St. James," *Constructive Quarterly* 3 (1915) 603–19.

Kennedy, E., "The Alleged Discrepancy between Paul and James," *Journal of Sacred Literature* 3 (1849) 237–58.

Klopper, A., "Die Erörterung des Verhältnisses von Glauben und Werken im Jakobusbriefe (Cap.2, 14–26)," ZWT 28 (1885) 280–319.

Köhler, A., *Glaube und Werke im Jakobusbrief* (Zittau: Menzel, 1913).

Kübel, R., *Über das Verhältnis von Glauben und Werken bei Jakobus* (Tübingen: Fues, 1880).

Kühl, E., *Die Stellung des Jakobusbriefes zum Alttestamentlichen Gesetz und zum paulinischen Rechtfertigungslehre* (Königsberg: Koch, 1905).

Kuttner, O., "Einzelne Bemerkungen über das Verhältnis des Jakobusbriefes zum paulinische Literatur," ZWT 36 (1893) 481–503.

Lackmann, M., *Sola Fide: Eine exegetische Studie über Jakobus 2 zum reformatischen Rechtfertigungslehre* (BFTh 50; Gütersloh: Bertelsmann, 1949).

Lodge, J. C., "James and Paul at Cross-Purposes? James 2:22," *Bib* 62 (1981) 195–213.

Lohse, E., "Glaube und Werke: zur Theologie des Jakobusbriefes," *ZNW* 48 (1957) 1–22.

Lorenzen, T., "'Faith without Works does not Count before God!' James 2:14–26," *ExpT* 89 (1977–78) 231–35.

Luck, U., "Der Jakobusbrief und die Theologie des Paulus," *Theologie und Glaube* 61 (1971) 161–79.

————, "Weisheit und Leiden: Zum Problem Paulus und Jakobus," *TLZ* 92 (1967) 253–58.

Menegoz, E., "Étude comparative de l'enseignement de saint Paul et de saint Jacques sur la justification par la foi," *Études de Théologie et d'Histoire* (Paris: Fischbacher, 1901) 121–50.

Nicol, W., "Faith and Works in the Letter of James," *Neot* 9 (1975) 7–24.

Noack, B., "Jakobusbrevet som Kanonisk Skrift," *Dansk teologisk tidsskrift* 27 (1964) 163–73.

Schanz, P. "Jakobus und Paulus," *TQ* 62 (1880) 3–46.

Schwartz, G., "Jak. 2, 14–26," *TSK* 64 (1891) 704–37.

Souček, J. B., "Zu dem Problemen des Jk," *EvT* 18 (1958) 460–68.

Stuhlmacher, P., *Gerechtigkeit Gottes bei Paulus* (FRLANT 87; Göttingen: Vandenhoeck und Ruprecht, 1965).

Tielemann, J., "Zum Verständis und zur Würdigung des Jakobusbriefes," *NKZ* 44 (1933) 256–70.

Tielemann, Th., "Versuch einer neuen Auslegung und Unordnung des Jakobusbriefes," *NKZ* 5 (1894) 580–611.

Tobac, E., "Le problème de la justification dans saint Paul et dans saint Jacques," *RHE* 22 (1926) 797–805.

Travis, A. E., "James and Paul: A Comparative Study," *Southwestern Journal of Theology* 12 (1969) 57–69.

Trocmé, E., "Les églises pauliniennes vues du dehors: Jacques 2,1 à 3,13," *SE* 2 (1964) 660–69.

Usteri, L. M., "Glaube, Werke und Rechtfertigung im Jakobusbricf," *TSK* 26 (1889) 211–56.

Via, D. O., "The Right Strawy Epistle Reconsidered: A Study in Biblical Ethics and Hermeneutics," *JR* 49 (1969) 253–67.

Walker, R., "Allein aus Werken: Zur Auslegung von Jakobus 2,14–26," *ZTK* 61 (1964) 155–92.

Ward, R. B., "James and Paul: Critical Review," *ResQ* 7 (1963) 159–64.

Weiffenbach, W. H., *Exegetisch-Theologische Studie über Jacobus cap.II,v. 14–26* (Giessen: J. Ricker'sche, 1871).

Zimmer, M., "Das schriftstellerische Verhältnis des Jakobusbriefes zur paulinischen Literatur," *ZWT* 36 (1893) 481–503.

5. NONCANONICAL CHRISTIAN LITERATURE

The attempt to locate James' voice now takes a new turn. Up to this point our survey was primarily interested in comparison: seeing how James resembles and differs from other moral literature sharpens our perception of James' distinctive profiles. No effort has been made to determine influence or dependence. The sole exception was the OT, whose influence on James is obvious. When we turn to extracanonical Christian literature, however, the question of dependence arises in the opposite direction: did James have any influence on these writings?

The answer to this question has considerable impact on the issue of dating and authorship, as well as on the early history of interpretation. But because the stakes are high, deliberation should be all the more restrained. As we look at the Christian literature produced before the third century, then, we will seek not only comparison (points of similarity and dissimilarity), but also possible traces of literary influence. We do so with considerable trepidation, aware that determining literary dependence in ancient literature is a matter of subtle detection, with few agreed-upon criteria and even fewer agreed-upon results!

The most severe problem facing this sort of inquiry is the literary practice of the first Christians themselves. Before the middle of the second century, when profound conflicts over identity forced the firming up of a canon and with it the desirability of naming one's sources, Christian writers tended to use earlier Christian literature freely, but seldom quoted it explicitly.[157] Their use was characteristically that of allusion and application, of subsumption and expansion.

New Testament scholarship has swung between extremes in evaluating the evidence suggesting literary relationships. Earlier commentators found dependence everywhere; any verbal echo was sufficient to justify claiming that a later writer had read and was using James.[158] On the basis of such literary linkings, attempts were made to establish chains of dependence, which could go either to demonstrate early dating or late and pseudonymous authorship. Thus, 1 Peter could be seen as dependent on James, which was dependent on Ephesians, which was dependent on Colossians.[159]

The opposite tendency has dominated more recent scholarship. Rather than

---

[157]Citations from the OT were usually noted, as in *1 Clem.* 3:1; 4:1; 8:2; 28:3; Ign.*Magn.* 12:1; Pol.*Phil.* 12:1; *Barn.* 4:14; 5:2. *1 Clem.* 23:3 has an otherwise unknown "scripture" concerning the "double-minded," which is also reported by *2 Clem.* 11:2 as a "prophetic word." *Herm.* Vis. 11:3 refers to the Book of Eldad and Modad as "scripture." In contrast, the reference to (apparently) Mark 2:7 as "another scripture" in *2 Clem.* 2:4 is unusual.

[158]The classic instance is Mayor, lxvi–lxxxiv.

[159]See, e.g., O. D. Foster, *The Literary Relations of the "First Epistle of Peter"* (Transactions of the Connecticut Academy of Arts and Sciences 17; 1913) 363–538; the same approach is found in C. L. Mitton, "The Relationship between 1 Peter and Ephesians," *JTS* n.s. 1 (1950) 67–73.

literary dependence, the use of shared traditions is argued.[160] This is a useful corrective to overconfidence about dependence. But it can also become exaggerated when it neglects or downplays the *specific* ways in which even traditional materials can be used. A shared tradition stated in identical language demands consideration of possible influence. Ignoring linguistic echoes as signals of influence flies in the face of the thoroughly and self-consciously *literary* character of the Christian movement. In the case of James, moreover, the denial of dependence has been argued not with reference to specific sources, but with appeals to a vague "common property of primitive Christianity" and the nature of paraenesis.[161]

If it is to be argued that James was known and used by second-century writings, the claims must be matched by evidence. Not everything resembling James came from him. The argument can, however, proceed by the accumulation of probabilities, based on the application of these criteria: a) an overall similarity in outlook and language between the writing and James; b) the presence of distinctive linguistic parallels; c) the incidence of the parallels from more than one part of James and in more than one part of the second-century writing; d) the density and interconnectedness of the parallels sufficient to argue against coincidence. When these criteria are applied, we find that only two writings from the first half of the second century can make a real claim to have been influenced by James, but that their claim is a serious one.

We can begin by narrowing the possibilities. It is striking, for example, that none of the apocryphal literature specifically associated with the name of James reveals any influence. The effort by F. H. Kern to show verbal echoes of James in the Pseudo-Clementine Homilies is unconvincing.[162] The infancy gospel called the *Protevangelium Jacobi* declares at its conclusion, "I, James, who wrote this history in Jerusalem . . . withdrew into the desert until the tumult in Jerusalem ended" (25:1), but nothing in the composition resembles canonical James. The Nag-Hammadi library has brought to light several other works for whom James is the eponymous source. They will be discussed further in the next section of the Introduction (III). The so-called *Apocryphon of James* takes the form of a letter from James and concerns secret books that were revealed to

---

[160]To use the case of 1 Peter again, it appears far less likely that 1 Pet 2:13–3:7 depends on Rom 13:1–7 if both are using a form of *haustafel* widely attested in the culture; see D. L. Balch, *Let Wives be Submissive: The Domestic Code in 1 Peter* (SBLMS 26; Chico, California: Scholars Press, 1981). Likewise, relationships can be explained on the basis of earlier Christian compilations: see A. C. Sundberg, "On Testimonies," *NovT* 3 (1959) 368–81; P. Carrington, *The Primitive Christian Catechism* (Cambridge: Cambridge University Press, 1940).

[161]Dibelius, 34, states: "Virtually nowhere can it be shown that an author is dependent on Jas for the simple reason that the concepts contained in Jas are so unoriginal, and so very much the property of primitive Christianity. In this the essence of paraenesis shows itself once more." One can recognize the circular reasoning here.

[162]See F. H. Kern, *Der Brief Jakobi untersucht und erklärt* (Tübingen: Fues, 1838) 56–60.

James and Peter, which recount secret revelations made by Jesus to these same apostles. The contents of the revelations are a fascinating amalgam of gnostic themes and gospel passages. In no instance, however, is there the slightest echo of the canonical letter of James. The same holds true for *The First Apocalypse of James* and *The Second Apocalypse of James*. Both pay great homage to "James of Jerusalem," who is "James the Just" and "Brother of the Lord," as the privileged recipient of gnostic revelations from the Lord. Neither document contains moral exhortation or any verbal echoes of canonical James.[163]

There is no trace of James in the apologetic literature attributed to Aristeas, Justin, Theophilus, Tatian, and Athenagoras, or in the *Letter to Diognetus*. Among the so-called "Apostolic Fathers," there is no resemblance between James and the *Martyrdom of Polycarp*, nor, despite its exhortatory character, Polycarp's own *Letter to the Philippians*. Ignatius of Antioch's *Letters* share only the most general sorts of themes: the importance of *makrothymia* in the end-times (Ign.*Eph*. 11:1), the value of teaching found in performance (Ign.*Eph*. 15:1), the contrariness of "speaking Jesus Christ yet desiring the world" (Ign.*Rom*. 7:1). Even Ignatius' citation from Prov 3:34 (see James 4:6) is applied, as in 1 Pet 5:5, to submission to bishops (Ign.*Eph*. 5:3)!

In the remaining compositions, there are certain parallels to James that are either isolated or widely attested elsewhere. The expression "double-minded" (*dipsychos*), for example, is distinctive to James 1:8 and 4:8 within the NT canon. But its recurrence in 1 *Clem* 11:2; 23:2–3; 2 *Clem*. 11:2–5; 19:2; *Did*. 2:4; 4:4, and *Barn*. 19:5–7 does not by itself signify a great deal. The incidence in each document is scattered and the possibilities of derivation too uncertain.[164] In some cases, moreover, the term seems to bear a different sense, referring to doubt concerning prophecies of future judgment (1 *Clem*. 23:2; 2 *Clem*. 11:2; *Barn*. 19:5; *Did*. 4:4).

The same caution applies in the designation of Abraham as "a friend of God" (James 2:23) in 1 *Clem*. 10:1; 17:2, or the ideal of impartiality in judgment (James 2:1) in *Did*. 4:3 and *Barn*. 19:4, or the axiom "love covers a multitude of sins" (James 5:20) in 1 *Clem*. 49:5 and 2 *Clem*. 16:4. Other similarities of great interest are too isolated to support influence, such as the striking way 2 *Clem*. 6:3–4 contrasts "friendship with the world and friendship with God"

---

[163]C. M. Tuckett, *Synoptic Tradition in the Nag Hammadi Library* in *Nag Hammadi and the Gospel Tradition*, ed. John Riches (Edinburgh: T & T Clark, 1986) concludes that the *Apocryphon of James* reveals a knowledge of Matthew and Luke (87–96), that the *First Apocalypse* knows Matthew (97–100), and that the *Second Apocalypse* may show awareness of Q traditions (101–7).

[164]For discussion of the antecedents of *dipsychos*, see O. J. F. Seitz, "Antecedents and Significance of the Term *dipsychos*," *JBL* 66 (1947) 211–19; and ibid., "Afterthoughts on the Term *dipsychos*," *NTS* 4 (1957) 327–34; W. I. Wolverton, "The Double-Minded Man in Light of Essene Psychology," *ATR* 38 (1956) 166–75; S. E. Porter, "Is *dipsychos* (James 1,8; 4,8) a 'Christian' Word?" *Bib* 71 (1990) 469–98.

(James 4:4). When all this sorting out is done, then only six early Christian writings deserve closer comparison to James.[165]

a. The Didache

The *Didache* is an anonymous composition that combines moral exhortation (1–6), church order (7–15), and eschatological expectation (16). The moral exhortation is organized according to the "two ways."[166] The "way of life" is sketched in 1–4, and the "way of death" in 5–6. The exhortations themselves combine traditional moral norms with elements from the developing gospel tradition. I have noted above the use of "double-mindedness" in *Did*. 2:4 and 4:4 and the ideal of impartiality in judgment in 4:3. The *Didache* also speaks of being "double-tongued" (2:4) and "double-hearted" (5:1). But apart from the striking exhortation to confess sins within the assembly (4:14), which more likely reflects community practice than a literary dependence on James 5:16, this document otherwise shares with James only the commonplaces of moral exhortation: that speech should be completed in action (2:5) and that jealousy and contentions lead to murder (3:2). The overall resemblance to James is slight. In contrast to James' vivid language, the *Didache* is bland; rather than confrontation and challenge, it calmly transmits "teaching" from the "twelve apostles." In terms of literary form and function, the *Didache* is clearly moving in the direction of formal church orders, with institutional concerns quite other than those of James.

b. The Letter of Barnabas

The *Letter of Barnabas* has some striking points of contact with the *Didache*. Specifically, two instances of *Barnabas* resembling James overlap precisely with the *Didache*: first, the combination of "respecting persons" and "impartiality" in *Barn*. 19:4–5, and second, the use of *dignomōn* ("double-minded," *Barn*. 19:7) and *diplokardia* ("double-hearted," *Barn*. 20:1). Beyond these, the only real similarity to James is found in the exhortation not to be exalted but to be humble in all things (*Barn*. 19:3), and the warning against being unjust judges of the poor (20:2). Both themes are obviously widely attested and they are stated here without compelling linguistic echoes of James. In the case of *Barnabas*, again, the moral exhortation concerning the "two ways" sponsored, respectively, by God and Satan (18:1) is attached to another sort of writing altogether, a treatise concerning the obsolescence of law and the rejection of the Jews. Similarities to James are of the most incidental sort.

---

[165]If, indeed, the *Testaments of the Twelve Patriarchs*, whose multiple and impressive connections with James have already been shown (see above, pp. 43–46), are truly pre-Christian.

[166]This language is found also in the *Testaments of the Twelve Patriarchs*, *Letter of Barnabas*, and from Qumran, *The Community Rule*.

c. *The* Sentences of Sextus

The *Sentences of Sextus* deserves comparison with James at some point, though its precise placement is uncertain. In form, it belongs to the category of *Gnomologia* or *Sententiae*, with one aphorism joined to another with little more by way of organization than some rough topical groupings. The strongest literary affinity is to the *Sentences of Syriac Menander* or the *Sentences of Pseudo-Phocylides*. It may have been composed in Egypt in the second century, and its present form seems to reflect a specifically Christian language. Note, for example, the heavy use of "faith" (*pistis/pistos*; e.g., 6–8; 169–70; 257; 325) and the statement that "a wise man shares in the kingdom of God" (311). One of the sayings, indeed, has a remarkable verbal resemblance to canonical Jude: "Keep spotless your body, the garment of the soul given by God, just as you keep spotless your coat, the garment of the flesh" (449 = Jude 23).

Sentences of Sextus is scarcely explicit in its Christianity. Rather, it mediates a form of "wisdom" (the *sophos* is always the subject, e.g., 143–45) that fits comfortably within the broad "moderate asceticism" of Greco-Roman moral teaching that regards vice as a disease and virtue as a mode of healthy living (207–8).[167] Its individualism and asceticism are sufficiently marked, however, to make the inclusion of this writing in the Nag-Hammadi library logical.[168] Living temperately is the goal (13–14). It involves valuing the soul over the body (55; 101; 346), being chaste (60), and mastering all kinds of bodily appetites (67–74; 108–11), especially the sexual (229–40). Self-control and self-sufficiency are the sage's goals (98; 253b; 264–74; 294; 334; 428–29) and are ideals that shape the composition's concern about speech (82–84; 151–65; 185–87; 253; 366; 432–33).

The *Sentences of Sextus* is exhortation of a different literary type and overall ideology than James. It represents an extreme of individual perfectionism, whereas James represents an extreme of community solidarity. Despite these differences, the *Sentences* do contain a number of points of broadly thematic resemblance to James. It speaks of a "testing of faith" (*dokimē pisteōs*, 7a = James 1:3), for example, and declares that "in the matter of faith, a faithless person is a dead person in a living body" (7b = James 2:26). Sextus calls God "the wise light that has no room for its opposite" (30 = James 1:17) and declares that "God is not the cause of evil" (114 = James 1:13). He says that "The one who judges a person is judged by God" (183; see also 22 = James 4:11–12) and advises that one sin should not be considered greater than another (277 = James 2:10–11).

Demons appear as the opposition to the wise person's soul (348–49), and an

---

[167]See R. A. Edwards and R. Wild, *The Sentences of Sextus* (Chico, California: Scholars Press, 1981).

[168]See F. Wisse, "The Sentences of Sextus," *NHLE*, 454–59.

evil soul "flees" (*pheugein*) from God (313 = James 4:7). The goal of piety for the sage, finally, is "friendship towards God" (*philia pros theon* = James 4:4). Despite its acute individualism, *Sextus* approximates James in its call for mutual correction: "If you release an unrighteous person from his wrongdoing, you punish him according to God [*kata ton theon*]," 63 = James 5:19–20). *Sextus* also demands sharing possessions with the needy: "If you are good to the needy, you will be great in God's sight" (52; see 379 = James 1:27), and, "If when you can you do not give to the needy, you will not receive from God when you are in need" (378 = James 2:13–16).

d. *The* Teachings of Silvanus

Another composition contained in the Nag-Hammadi collection is the *Teachings of Silvanus*.[169] It follows the traditional form of wisdom instruction in its repeated address "my son" (see 85, 88, 91, etc.), in its personification of Wisdom and Folly (89–90), and in its intensely individualistic ethic: everything is directed toward the achieving of discipline over the body and its passions (87, 89, 92, 95). *Silvanus* and James share some motifs that are common to wisdom literature: the importance of controlling speech (97 = James 1:19, 26); immoral behavior as forgetfulness (88 = James 1:24); God as the source of wisdom (89 = James 3:13–16); the images of rudder and reins for self-control (90 = James 3:3–4). There are also themes in *Silvanus* that are much closer to the classical wisdom tradition than to James: advice concerning treatment of friends (97–98) and warnings concerning lust and fornication (105, 108).

Nevertheless, there are some turns in *Silvanus* that strikingly resemble James: the importance of being friends of God (98 = James 2:23); the humbling of the proud and the exalting of the humble (104 = James 4:10); the statement that God "does not need to put any man to the test" (115 = James 1:13); the need to cast away the deceitfulness of the devil and to fear only God (88 = James 4:7–8); the dualism of "indwelling spirit" and "psychic person" (86, 92–93 = James 3:16; 4:5); and most impressively, the characterization of Christ, the unjealous giver of gifts as "the Light of the Father" (101 = James 1:17). The fact that our English translation itself depends on a Coptic translation of the original Greek means that a closer determination of "echo" from James is impossible.

As the last example also indicates, however, *Silvanus* is intensely Christocentric: "live with Christ and he will save you" (98); "Christ is all. He who does not possess all is not able to know Christ" (102); humility of heart is "the gift of Christ" (104); "Know who Christ is and acquire him as a friend, for this is the friend who is faithful" (110). *Silvanus* is also obviously dependent on other Christian writings, such as the Gospels (104),[170] the letters of Paul (108), and

---

[169]See M. L. Peel and J. Zandee, "The Teachings of Silvanus," in *NHLE*, 346–61.
[170]See C. M. Tuckett, *Nag Hammadi and the Gospel Tradition*, 42–46.

perhaps even 2 Peter (111). It is not impossible that James also had some influence on the shaping of this writing that subsequently had influence on the very monks of Egypt who found James so attractive.[171]

e. 1 Clement

Evaluating the relationship between James and *1 Clement* is particularly difficult. At first glance, they are obviously dissimilar. Clement is writing a letter to a specific community (the Corinthians), which is experiencing internal upheaval because of a rebellion of the younger men against the established elders. The persons and situation are explicit and defined. But in response to this crisis, Clement crafts a "letter" that is as much a moral treatise as a personal missive. Furthermore, Clement writes (conventionally, from Rome around 95 CE) with at least two prior Christian compositions (Hebrews and 1 Corinthians) either before his eyes or so much in his memory that he can unmistakably echo them in language and theme, yet never explicitly cite them.[172]

There are places where Clement's use of Hebrews is obvious, because the content and language could come from nowhere else. A prime example is *1 Clem.* 36:2, which clearly alludes to Heb 1:3–4. Indeed, the whole passage derives from Hebrews 1–2.[173] Yet a close comparison of the two texts shows that Clement has used his source with considerable flexibility. He elides phrases, transposes words, adjusts tenses, and all without comment. The language of Hebrews has become, for the moment, his own language. On the basis of such certain appropriations, we can identify other less obvious uses of Hebrews by Clement, such as in *1 Clem.* 9:2–4, where the echoes of Heb 11:5–7 are muted though discernible, and *1 Clem.* 17:1, which recalls Heb 11:37.

The determination that Clement might have used James in similar fashion is complicated by several factors. First, the language of James is not nearly so distinctive as that of Hebrews, nor his themes so immediately recognizable. Second, both James and Clement use the conventions of moral exhortation. Clement uses many of the themes associated with the *topos* "On Envy," just as James does.[174] Likewise, Clement uses the image of the mirror (36:1), which presents to the *sight* of his readers (5:3; 9:2; 19:3; 24:1; 25:1; 36:2) moral exemplars (5:1; 46:1; 60:1; 63:1) for their remembrance (7:1) and imitation (17:1). Third, some of the material in *1 Clement* that is parallel to James is *also* parallel to Hebrews!

---

[171]See Peel and Zandee, "Teaching of Silvanus," 347.

[172]See P. Ellingworth, "Hebrews and 1 Clement: Literary Dependence or Common Tradition?" *BZ* n.s. 23 (1979) 262–69; D. A. Hagner, *The Use of the Old and New Testaments in Clement of Rome* (NovTSup 34; Leiden: Brill, 1973) 179–237.

[173]See Hagner, *Use of Old and New Testaments in Clement*, 179–84.

[174]See Johnson, "James 3:13–4:10 and the *topos peri phthonou*," 338–41.

Despite these difficulties, there are some striking points of similarity. Some of the parallels have little independent value: the care of orphans and widows as a sign of repentance (8:4 = James 1:27), or the single occurrence of the term "double-minded" (*dipsychos*, 23:2–3 = James 1:8; 4:8), or the note that humans are created in the image of God (33:5 = James 3:9). Likewise, little can be made of the appearance of the citation of Prov 10:12 ("love covers a multitude of sins") in *1 Clem.* 49:5 = James 5:20, or the citation of Prov 3:34 ("God resists the proud but gives grace to the humble") in *1 Clem.* 30:2 = James 4:6, for these allusions appear also in 1 Pet 4:8 and 5:5.

Of greater significance is the thematic opposition between arrogance and humility, which is very similar to that in James (e.g., *1 Clem.* 2:1; 13:1; 61:3) and, in at least one instance, takes the form of a strong verbal resemblance. In *1 Clem.* 59:3, we read, "the one who humbles the pride of the arrogant . . . the one who raises the lowly and humbles those on high," which recalls James 4:10: "Humble yourselves before the Lord and he will exalt you."[175] The continuation of the passage in *1 Clem.* 59:3, "the one who kills and who gives life," likewise echoes James 4:12, "the one who is able to save and to destroy."[176]

Other wording in *1 Clement* is very close to that in James. In 46:5, for example, we find, "why are there conflicts and angers and divisions and schisms and war among you," which resembles James 4:1, "whence are the wars and whence the battles among you?"[177] Another striking example: James 3:13 has "Who among you is wise and understanding? By his good manner of life let him demonstrate his deeds in wisdom's meekness," which is matched in form and content by *1 Clem.* 38:2, "Let the wise person demonstrate his wisdom not in words but in good deeds."[178] When taken separately, any one of these points can be dismissed; yet their cumulative effect becomes intriguing.

In tracing *1 Clement*'s use of Hebrews, special value is given to passages containing a high density of verbal and thematic similarities. *1 Clement* has three sections where the use of James seems most likely. The first is Clement's condemnation of the Corinthians' envy (3–4). We find here many points of resemblance to James 3:13–4:10: envy causes social unrest and war (3:2; 6:4); through envy, death came into the world (3:4); envy causes the murder of

---

[175]Compare *1 Clem.* 59:3, *ton tapeinounta hybrin hyperēphanōn . . . ton poiounta tapeinous eis hypsos kai tous hypselous tapeinounta*, with James 4:10, *tapeinōthēte enōpion tou kyriou kai hypsōsei hymas.*

[176]Compare *1 Clem.* 59:3, *ton apokteinonta kai zēn poiounta*, with James 4:12, *ho dynamenos sōsai kai apolesai.*

[177]Compare *1 Clem.* 46:5, *hinati ereis kai thymoi kai dichostasiai kai schismata polemos te en hymin*, with James 4:1, *pothen polemoi kai pothen machai en hymin.*

[178]Compare James 3:13, *tis sophos kai epistēmōn en hymin? deixatō ek tēs kalēs anastrophēs ta erga autou en prautēti sophias*, with *1 Clem.* 38:2, *ho sophos endeiknysthō tēn sophian autou mē en logois all' en ergois agathois.* Dibelius comments (33): "The admonition to the wise in *1 Clem* xxxviii,2 resembles James 3:13 more in form than in content." If one had to choose, one would reach the opposite conclusion.

brethren (4:7). These parallels lose some of their distinctiveness because they are also part of the Hellenistic *topos* on envy. Nevertheless, Clement follows his condemnation of envy with a call to conversion (7:2–8:5), a combination otherwise found only in *T. Sim.* and James.

The second instance is Clement's treatment of Abraham. The more obvious point of comparison here would seem to be Hebrews, for Clement lists Abraham among heroes of faithful obedience, beginning with Enoch and ending with Rahab (1 *Clem.* 9:2–12:8 = Heb 11:5–31). He introduces the list, moreover, with language strongly reminiscent of Hebrews 11. But analysis shows that Clement does not follow Hebrews slavishly. In his presentation of Abraham, Lot, and Rahab, Clement goes into considerably more detail than does Hebrews, and uses the biblical text concerning these characters directly, with multiple citations from Genesis and Joshua.

Why should we think to detect the influence of James? We notice that Clement deviates from Hebrews in the designation of Abraham as "friend of God" (1 *Clem.* 10:1 = James 2:23), which is repeated in 17:2. James and Clement, moreover, both cite Gen 15:6 verbatim, whereas Hebrews cites Gen 15:5 but not 15:6. Finally, Abraham is praised by Clement for his "faith and hospitality" (10:7), which is carried also through the examples of Lot (11) and Rahab (12). The emphasis on hospitality draws Clement's version closer to James than to Hebrews.

All three versions include Abraham's offering of Isaac (James 2:21; 1 *Clem.* 10:7; Heb 11:17). But Clement differs from Hebrews in adding (31:2), "Why was our father Abraham blessed? Was it not because he did righteousness and truth through faith?" Not only does this recall James 2:21, "Was not our father Abraham shown to be righteous on the basis of deeds,"[179] but it follows immediately (and serves as example for) the exhortation of 1 *Clem.* 30:3: "being righteous by deeds not by words" which, in the overall context of James 2:14–26, captures perfectly the sense of James 2:24, "a person is shown to be righteous on the basis of deeds and not on the basis of faith only."[180]

A final passage in 1 *Clement* contains a particularly dense set of parallels to James. It begins in 29:1, with the exhortation to approach God in holiness of soul and with pure hands raised to him (= James 4:7–8). There then follows in 1 *Clem.* 30:1–5, this sequence: his readers are to flee evil speech (*katalalia* = James 4:11), evil desire (*epithymia* = James 4:2), adultery (*moicheia* = James 4:4), and arrogance (*hyperēphania* = James 4:6). Then Clement cites Prov 3:34, "God resists the proud but gives grace to the lowly," as does James 4:6. More

---

[179] Compare 1 *Clem.* 31:2, *tinos charin ēulogēthē ho patēr hēmōn Abraam, ouchi dikaiosynēn kai alētheian dia pisteōs poiēsas*, with James 2:21, *Abraam ho patēr hēmōn ouk ex ergōn edikaiōthē*.

[180] Compare 1 *Clem.* 30:3, *ergois dikaioumenoi mē logois*, with James 2:24, *ex ergōn dikaioutai anthrōpos kai ouk ek pisteōs monon*.

interesting still, Clement then picks up on the theme of "gives more grace," as does James 4:6a, and follows with an exhortation to be "lowly-minded" (*tapeinophronountes* = James 4:10).

Clement then again forbids "evil speech" (*katalalia* = James 4:11), with the statement that they should be justified by deeds and not by words (30:3 = James 2:24). Clement continues with an exhortation to brevity in speech (30:5 = James 1:19) and concludes with the statement that, whereas arrogance is cursed by God (= James 4:16), God blesses gentleness (*epieikeia* = James 3:17), humility (*tapeinophrosynē* = James 4:10), and meekness (*prautēs* = James 3:13). As pointed out above, Clement concludes with the example of Abraham as one who shared in this blessing of God by working righteousness and truth through faith (31:1–2). This is a sequence of thirteen items with the highest degree of thematic and verbal similarity between James and *1 Clement*.[181]

The case is not conclusive, but probability favors the argument that *1 Clement* knew and used James. The parallels are found in concentrated clusters as well as in scattered verbal echoes. They match in outlook as well as theme. They are found in every part of Clement and are drawn from several parts of James. Even taking into account the generic character of paraenesis and the use of a shared *topos*, therefore, the combination of ethical and religious language is remarkable. And in the case of Clement, the fact that he knew and used at least two other canonical writings without naming or citing them verbatim strengthens the argument that he could have used James in the same fashion. If an argument based on this evidence can be made that James used Clement,[182] it is even more convincing for the dependence of Clement on James.[183]

f. The Shepherd of Hermas

The resemblance in outlook, theme, and language, between James and *The Shepherd of Hermas* is remarkable and has often been remarked.[184] Dibelius paid particular attention to the similarities between James and the *Mandates* section.[185] His refusal to acknowledge dependence in this case appears to rest as

---

[181]Dibelius' discussion of this passage (32–33) is so dominated by the false issue of whether Clement was responding to a Pauline teaching, that the real significance of this remarkable sequence of similarities is missed.

[182]See F. W. Young, "The Relation of 1 Clement to the Epistle of James," *JBL* 67 (1948) 339–45.

[183]See Hagner, *The Use of the Old and New Testaments in Clement of Rome*, 248–56.

[184]E.g., on James 3:13–4:10, see Marty, 144; Ropes, 248; Laws, 161–62; Mayor, 128; Cantinat, 31; Dibelius, 213.

[185]For the focus on the *Mandates*, see Dibelius, 3; for his overall appreciation, see: "Here there is found a kinship which goes beyond lexical and conceptual agreement. Extensive and coherent discussions in *Hermas* could be placed alongside isolated admonitions in James and serve as a commentary on the latter" (Dibelius, 31).

much on his presuppositions as on the evidence.[186] The evidence, in fact, is even stronger than Dibelius thought and extends beyond the *Mandates*.[187]

Hermas' use of *dipsychos* (see James 1:8; 4:8) in all its possible permutations— even making a verb of it—is extensive.[188] Opposed to double-mindedness is simplicity (*haplotēs*).[189] In James 1:5, this term is used only for the quality of God's generosity, but it matches perfectly what James understands by being *adiakritos* (3:17) or "pure of heart" (4:8). In Hermas, as well, the terms are interchangeable. Thus, *Herm. Man.* 9:4, "Cleanse your heart of all the foolish things of this world,"[190] is equivalent to *Herm. Man.* 2:7: "found in simplicity, and pure and spotless innocence."[191] As also in James, cleansing the heart signifies repentance (see 4:8), which is the major theme of Hermas as a whole.[192] Thus, "Repent . . . let your hearts become pure and blameless" (*Herm. Vis.* 4,2,5). Conversion means turning from double-mindedness to simplicity and purity of heart.

The pattern of repentance fits within a cosmology that is in substance and expression virtually identical to that in James. Humans are intimately related to the cosmic forces representing, respectively, God and the Devil. As in James, "pneumatology" is focused on these single personified forces. In an exact parallel to James 4:5, *Herm. Man.* 3:1 has, "the spirit that God made to dwell in this flesh."[193] And as in James 4:7, it is the devil who is to be resisted. The devil is responsible for double-mindedness (*Herm. Man.* 9:9) but need not be feared (*Herm. Man.* 12:4,7). If resisted, he will flee (*Herm. Man.* 12:5,2): "If you stand against him, he will flee from you, conquered, shamed."[194]

---

[186]If, as Dibelius, 46, notes, Hermas can be "an expansion of paraenesis, its application to specifically Christian situations, and at least the Christianization of its framework and arrangement of the traditional materials," why could it not do that in dependence on James as much as on the vague "circumstances of the second century," whatever they were?

[187]It is characteristic of O. J. F. Seitz, "Relationship of the Shepherd of Hermas to the Epistle of James," *JBL* 63 (1944) 131–40, to base his rejection of dependence on the analysis of the single term *dipsychos*. For a far fuller analysis of the way Hermas appropriates materials from James, see the discussion on pp. 320–25 in C. Taylor, "The Didache Compared with the Shepherd of Hermas," *Journal of Philology* 18 (1890) 297–325.

[188]See *Herm. Vis.* 3,2,2; 3,3,4; 3,4,3; 3,10,9; 4,1,4; 4,1,7; 4,2,6; *Herm. Man.* 9:1–5; 9:7; 9:9; 9:11; 10:2,2; 11:1; 11:13; 12:4,2; *Herm. Sim.* 1:3; 6:1; 7:1; 8:3–5; 8:9,4; 8:11,3; 9:18,3; 9:21,2.

[189]*Herm. Vis.* 2,3,2; 3,1,9; 3,8,5; 3,9,1; *Herm. Man.* 2:1; 2:4; 2:4,6; 5:2,2; *Herm. Sim.* 9:15,2; 9:24,3; 9:31,4.

[190]*katharison sou tēn kardian apo pantōn tōn mataiōmatōn tou aiōnos toutou*; see also *Herm. Man.* 9:7.

[191]*en haplotēti heurethē kai akakia kathara kai amiantos*; see also *Herm. Vis.* 3,2,2; *Herm. Man.* 4:1; 4:4,3; 12:6,5; *Herm. Sim.* 4:4,7; 5:3,6; 8:11,3.

[192]See, e.g., *Herm. Vis.* 4,2,5; 5,7; *Herm. Man.* 4:1,8–10; 4:2,2–4; 7:6,1.

[193]Compare *to pneuma ho ho theos katōikisen en te sarki tautę* with James 4:5, *to pneuma ho katōikisen en hēmin* ("the spirit he made to dwell in us"); see also *Herm. Sim.* 5:6,5; 5:7,1.

[194]Compare *ean oun antistathēte autǫ nikētheis pheuxetai aph'hymōn kateschymmenos* with James 4:7, *antistēte de tǫ diabolǫ kai pheuxetai aph'hymōn*. See also *Herm. Man.* 4:4; 6:2,7; 12:2; 11:3.

The choice between God and Devil is expressed spatially: "The faith from above is from God and has great power. But double-mindedness is an earthbound spirit from the devil, having no power" (*Herm. Man.* 9:11). This is strikingly close to James 3:15: "this is not the wisdom that comes down from above, but is earthbound, unspiritual, demonic."[195] The choice can also be spelled out in terms of "God" and "this world": "Whoever purify their hearts from the foolish desires of this world (*epithymion tou aionos toutou*) will also live to God" (*Herm. Man.* 12:6,5).

Within this cosmological/religious framework, the ethical concerns of the two writings are unusually close. The problem of wealth and poverty for the Christian community pervades both compositions. In James, three aspects of the subject are emphasized: that wealth and poverty are transvalued in the light of faith (1:9 12; 2:5–7); that those involved with affairs of business lose sight of God's will (4:13–16); and that the luxurious rich have oppressed the poor and can expect to be punished for it in God's judgment (2:6; 5:1–6). Hermas has the same three emphases. First, "The rich person has money but is poor in the things concerning God" (*Herm. Sim.* 2:5). Second, those wrapped up in business and "many other occupations of the world" *Herm. Man.* 10:1,4) "also sin much" (*Herm. Sim.* 4:4, 5; also 9:20; 6:2,2; 6:4,1; 6:5,4). Third, those who live luxuriously must beware "lest those who are lacking groan and their groan rises to the Lord" (*Herm. Vis.* 3,9,6). This statement parallels James 5:4.[196] It is more impressive, then, that it is preceded by "beware of the coming judgment" (*Herm. Vis.* 3,9,5), just as the corresponding passage in James is followed by "the coming of the Lord is near . . . the judge stands before the door (James 5:9). As in James 1:27, furthermore, the proper use of wealth is spelled out in terms of "visiting orphans and widows" (*Herm. Sim.* 1:8; see also *Herm. Man.* 8:10; *Herm. Sim.* 9:26,2; 9:27,2).

Hermas' remarks on speech parallel James' in their severity and pessimism. Slander, or "wicked speech" (*katalalia*) is condemned: "First then do not speak wickedly against anyone, neither gladly listen to wicked speaking" (*Herm. Man.* 2:2 = James 4:11). In James 3:8, the tongue is called a "restless evil" (*akastaton kakon*) and in 3:6 is said to be "enflamed from Gehenna." Compare "wicked speech is evil. It is a restless demon. It never makes peace, but always dwells in divisions" (*Herm. Man.* 2:3). For Hermas also, evil speech is a manifestation of double-mindedness (*Herm. Sim.* 8:7, 21 = James 3:10).

---

[195]Compare *hē pistis anōthen esti para tou kyriou kai echei dynamin megalēn. hē de dipsychia epigeion pneuma estin para tou diabolou, dynamin mē echousa* with James 3:15, *ouk estin hautē hē sophia anōthen katerchomenē, alla epigeios, psychikē, daimoniōdēs.* See also *Herm. Man.* 11:8; 11:11–12; 11:14; 11:21.

[196]Compare *mēpote stenaxousin hoi hysteroumenoi kai ho stenagmos autōn anabēsetai pros ton kyrion* ("lest those in need cry out and their cry arise to the Lord") with James 5:4, *ho misthos . . . ho apesterēmenos aph'hymōn krazei kai hai boai tōn therisantōn eis ta ōta kyriou sabaōth eiselēluthasin* ("the wages of which you have defrauded them are crying out. And the cries of the reapers have reached the ears of the Lord of Armies").

Hermas places the same sort of emphasis on "long-suffering" (*makrothymia*) as does James 5:7–10. In *Herm. Man.* 5:1,2, we read: "For if you are long-suffering, the holy spirit that dwells in you will be pure."[197] And in a statement that echoes the notion of "perfected faith" in James 1:4, we read: "This long-suffering therefore dwells with those who have complete faith" (*Herm. Man.* 5:2,3). The contrast between such perfected faith and double-mindedness, in turn, is expressed by *Herm. Man.* 9:10: "For faith promises all things, perfects all things. But the double-mindedness that has no full faith in itself fails to accomplish all the deeds which it undertakes" (compare James 1:6–8).

We have made the transition from the language characteristic of moral discourse to that characterizing the religious life of the Christian community. Here also we find that Hermas has, if anything, more striking agreements both in emphasis and terminology. James connects effectiveness in prayer directly to faith, with double-mindedness seen as impeding prayer (1:5–8; 4:3; 5:17–18). In a passage that even Dibelius declares "the best interpretation of James 1:5–8 imaginable,"[198] *Herm. Man.* 9:1–4 has: "Keep yourself from double-mindedness, and do not be double-minded at all as you ask for something from God . . . ask from him without doubting . . . but if you doubt in your heart, you will not receive anything of the things you ask for . . . these are the double-minded. . . ."[199] But if it is "an interpretation," does not that suggest the use of James?

When James speaks of rich people oppressing members of the community, he asks, "are they not the very ones blaspheming the noble name that is invoked over you?" (2:7). The expression "noble name" is unusual and taken by Dibelius as one of the distinctively Christian elements in James.[200] It is all the more striking, then, to find Hermas speaking of apostates from the church in this fashion: "and in their sins they have blasphemed the Lord himself. And they have continued to shame the name of the Lord that is invoked over them" (*Herm. Sim.* 8:6,4; also *Herm. Sim.* 9:14,6).[201]

Hermas and James speak about the power to give and destroy life in remarkably similar fashion. James tells his readers: "Receive the implanted word that is able to save your souls" (1:21). Concerning the commandments, (*entolai*),

---

[197]*ean gar makrothymos esē to pneuma to hagion to katoikoun en soi katharon estai*; see also *Herm. Man.* 5:1,1; 5:1,3; 5:1,6; *Herm. Sim.* 8:7,6; 9:15,2.

[198]Dibelius, 31.

[199]*aron apo seautou tēn dipsychian kai mē holōs dipsychēsęs aitēsasthai ti para tou theou . . . aitou par' autou adistaktōs . . . ean de distasęs en tę kardia sou, ouden ou mē lēmpsę tōn aitēmatōn sou . . . houtoi eisin hoi dipsychoi*; see also how *Herm. Sim.* 4:6 provides a parallel to James 4:3.

[200]See Dibelius, 23.

[201]Compare James 2:7, *ouk autoi blasphēmousin to kalon onoma to epiklēthen eph' hymas, to kai blasphēmēsantes en tais hamartiais autōn ton kyrion. eti de kai epaischynthentes to onoma tou kyriou to epiklēthen ep' autous.*

Hermas says, "and they are able to save a man's soul" (*Herm. Sim.* 6:1,1).[202] James forbids judging a neighbor and adds this warrant: "There is one lawgiver and judge who is able to save and to destroy" (James 4:12). In Hermas we read, "Fear the one who is able to save and destroy all things, and keep these commandments, and you will live to God" (*Herm. Man.* 12:6,3).[203]

The most intriguing resemblances are these last ones, because the sentiments expressed in James are otherwise so distinctive, yet are so clearly paralleled in Hermas. James 4:17 condemns sins of omission: "Therefore it counts as a sin for the person who understands the proper thing to do and yet does not do it." In *Herm. Man.* 8:2, we read: "for if you hold back from doing the good thing, you commit a great sin" (see also *Herm. Sim.* 10:4,3).[204] James concludes his letter with the command to mutual correction: "if any among you wanders from the truth and someone turns him back, let him know that the one who turns back a sinner from his erring way will save that one's soul from death" (James 5:19–20). In *Herm. Man.* 8:10, there is a similar command: "do not cast aside those who have been scandalized away from the faith, but turn them back and give them courage; correct sinners."[205]

Hermas meets all the criteria for deciding in favor of a literary dependence. Within a document of manifestly different literary character and purpose, there is an extended sharing in outlook, theme, and language with James. The similarities are found throughout Hermas, although they dominate in the *Mandates*. And they are derived from every part of James.[206] The accumulation of probabilities in the case of Hermas is impressive, indeed, shifting the burden of proof: if James is *not* the source of such distinctive language, then what is?

This survey of noncanonical Christian writings leads to the conclusion, then, that there is little likelihood of James' having influenced the *Letter of Barnabas* or the *Didache*, that there is some possibility that James was known to the authors of the *Sentences of Sextus* and the *Teachings of Silvanus*, that there is strong probability that *1 Clement* knew and used James, and that it is virtually certain that there is a literary dependence on James in *The Shepherd of Hermas*.

---

[202]Compare *dexasthe ton emphyton logon ton dynamenon sōsai tas psychas hymon* to *kai dynamenai sōsai psychēn anthrōpou.*

[203]Compare *heis estin nomothetēs kai kritēs ho dynamenos sōsai kai apolesai* to *phobēthete ton panta dynamenon sōsai kai apolesai kai tēreite tas entolas tautas kai zēsesthe tō theō* (see also *Herm. Sim.* 9:23,4).

[204]Compare *eidoti oun to kalon poiein kai me poiounti hamartia autō estin* to *ean gar enkrateusē to agathon mē poiein hamartian megalēn ergazē.*

[205]Compare *ean tis en hymin planēthē apo tēs alētheias kai epistrepsē tis auton, ginōsketō hoti ho epistrepsas hamartōlon ek planēs hodou autou sōsai psychēn autou ek thanatou* to *eskandalismenous apo tes pisteōs mē apoballesthai all' epistrephein kai euthymous poiein, hamartanountas nouthetein.* (See also *Herm. Sim.* 10:4,3; *Herm. Vis.* 9,10.)

[206]We have cited parallels from James 1:2–4, 5, 6, 8, 10, 21, 27; 2:5, 7; 3:8, 10, 13, 15, 16; 4:4, 5, 7, 8, 11, 12, 13–17; 5:4, 5, 7, 9, 10, 19–20.

BIBLIOGRAPHY

Bacon, B. W., "The Doctrine of Faith in Hebrews, James, and Clement of Rome," *JBL* 19 (1900) 12–21.

Balch, D. L., *Let Wives be Submissive: The Domestic Code in 1 Peter* (SBLMS 26; Chico, California: Scholars Press, 1981).

Carrington, P., *The Primitive Christian Catechism* (Cambridge: Cambridge University Press, 1940).

Edwards, R. A. and R. Wild, *The Sentences of Sextus* (Chico, California: Scholars Press, 1981).

Ellingworth, P., "Hebrews and 1 Clement: Literary Dependence or Common Tradition?" *BZ* n.s. 23 (1979) 262–69.

Foster, O. D., *The Literary Relations of the "First Epistle of Peter"* (Transactions of the Connecticut Academy of Arts and Sciences 17; 1913) 363–538.

Hagner, D. A., *The Use of the Old and New Testaments in Clement of Rome* (NovTSup 34; Leiden: Brill, 1973) 179–237.

Kern, F. H., *Der Brief Jakobi untersucht und erklärt* (Tübingen: Fues, 1838).

Mitton, C. L., "The Relationship between 1 Peter and Ephesians," *JTS* n.s. 1 (1950) 67–73.

Peel, M. L., and J. Zandee, "The Teachings of Silvanus," in *NHLE* 346–61.

Porter, S. E., "Is *dipsychos* (James 1,8; 4,8) a 'Christian' Word," *Bib* 71 (1990) 469–98.

Seitz, O. J. F., "Afterthoughts on the Term *dipsychos*," *NTS* 4 (1957) 327–34.

———, "Antecedents and Significance of the Term *dipsychos*," *JBL* 66 (1947) 211–19.

———, "Relationship of the Shepherd of Hermas to the Epistle of James," *JBL* 63 (1944) 131–40.

Sundberg, A. C., "On Testimonies," *NovT* 3 (1959) 368–81.

Taylor, C., "The Didache Compared with The Shepherd of Hermas," *Journal of Philology* 18 (1890) 297–325.

Tuckett, C. M., *Synoptic Tradition in the Nag Hammadi Library.* In *Nag Hammadi and the Gospel Tradition*, ed. J. Riches (Edinburgh: T & T Clark, 1986).

Wisse, F., "The Sentences of Sextus," *NHLE*, 454–59.

Wolverton, W. I., "The Double-Minded Man in Light of Essene Psychology," *ATR* 38 (1956) 166–75.

Young, F. W., "The Relation of 1 Clement to the Epistle of James," *JBL* 67 (1948) 339–45.

F. MORAL AND RELIGIOUS PERSPECTIVES

The analysis of James' language, structure, and genre suggests that, far from being a haphazard agglomeration of wisdom motifs, James is a carefully crafted composition. Extensive comparison between James and other moral/exhortatory literature from the Greco-Roman world sharpens that perception by revealing how James is similar and dissimilar to roughly contemporary writings of a broadly similar paraenetic/protreptic character.

Building on those observations, we can now move to a more precise description of James' moral and religious voice. We begin with a reminder of the sort of truisms of moral discourse that are virtually universal in James' world: virtue is proven through testing (1:2, 12); riches are unstable (1:9–11); God is not the cause of evil (1:13), but of good (1:17); sin derives from human passions (1:14–15); hearing is better than speaking (1:19) because control of the tongue is, of all things, most difficult (3:1–12), but perfect virtue can be revealed by control of speech (1:26); vices such as anger (1:20) and envy (3:16–4:3) and arrogance (4:6, 13–16) are to be avoided because they lead to social upheaval (1:20; 4:1–2), but virtues such as justice and reasonableness should be pursued because they lead to peace (3:13–18); mutual correction is an appropriate expression of virtue (5:19–20); and in everything, the performance rather than simply the profession of virtue is what counts (1:22–25; 2:14–16).

Despite including so many common themes, James is distinctive within the broad range of Greco-Roman and Jewish moral literature in four notable ways.

1. *James deals with morals, not with manners.* We have seen that virtually all moral exhortation gives substantial attention to getting along in the world as it is traditionally defined, with respect both to its social and symbolic structures. But James lacks any such instruction on the practical wisdom of "knowing and keeping one's place." It has no directives concerning obeisance to rulers, gratitude to benefactors, reverence to the elderly, reciprocal generosity to friends. It has nothing about table manners, courtesy, or conformity.

   Apart from one paradoxical usage (2:5), James entirely lacks language having to do with shame and honor, the motivations that governed so much of the established Greco-Roman (and Jewish) order of things. James is concerned not with behavioral conformity to the customs given by the world, but with moral choices that run into conflict with some of those customs.

2. *James addresses an intentional community, not a household.* This follows from the first point. It is obvious that James does not address behavior within the wider *oikoumenē* of the empire. But it is equally clear that his concerns are not with the natural family or the extended household (*oikos*) that was the basic societal unit of ancient Mediterranean culture, and within which the issues of domestic relations and obligations were paramount.

   Rather, James addresses an *ekklēsia*, an intentional community gathered by certain shared values or goals, in this case summarized by the shorthand of "the faith of Jesus Christ" (2:1). James, therefore, has nothing about *ta kathēkonta* ("obligations") of civic or domestic life. And although this *ekklēsia* has both male and female members (2:15), James shows no interest in marriage (the *moichalides* of 4:4 is metaphorical), or sexual morality, or parental roles, or anything at all to do with children.

3. *James is egalitarian, not authoritarian.* The author does not assume a parental authority over his readers, completely eschewing the traditional "father/son" transferred relationship found so widely in moral literature in Jewish and Hellenistic culture and attested even in Paul (1 Cor 4:14–17; Gal 4:19; 1 Thess 2:11). The author, rather, is merely a *doulos* of the God who alone is "father" of this community (1:17–18, 27). The use of kinship language is entirely egalitarian: the readers are "brothers and sisters" not only of each other but also of the author.

The only community leaders mentioned are reminded of the hazards and obligations of their positions rather than the honor and power: not many should seek to be teachers because they are held to a greater judgment (3:1); elders are to be "summoned" by the sick members of the community (5:14). James does not single out any class within the community: all are alike called to responsible behavior and each can correct the other when in error (5:19–20).

The egalitarian outlook of James is shown as well in its emphatic rejection of *prosōpolēmpsia* or partiality in judging (2:1, 9), as well as all forms of boasting (3:14–15; 4:16) and arrogance (4:6, 10). It finds explicit expression in a hostility shown towards the rich who gain and use their wealth oppressively (1:11; 2:6–7; 5:1–6). It is shown as well in the condemnation of slander and judgment, which imply the superiority of one member over another (4:11–12).

4. *James is communitarian, not individualistic.* Once again, this point builds on the previous one. James is not a teacher of an ethics of individual perfection, which redounds to the honor of its practitioner. In fact, James does not focus on the virtue of the individual, except by calling each person to behavior consonant with the community's profession. James vigorously opposes the sort of individualism that seeks to gain at the expense of the other. Instead, he seeks to create a community of solidarity. For James, the choice is between a life of envy (*phthonos*) that logically tends toward the elimination of the other in murder (*phonos*, 4:2) and a life based on gift (*charis*, 4:6) and mercy (*eleos*, 2:13) expressed in service of the other. Particularly in 5:12–20, James sketches a community whose speech and actions express such a solidarity. In contrast to the logic of envy that leads to oppression and "killing the righteous one" (5:6), James

portrays a community that rallies around the sick and the sinful in order to save/heal them (5:14–16).

These four characteristics of James can be stated with greater confidence because they have been measured against every variation in the extant literature. By revealing James' voice, they also begin to suggest something of James' social location. This is obviously not a writing that represents a ruling elite, or a scribal tradition within a stable, traditional culture. It is rather a voice that stands over against a dominant culture. James' emphasis on group solidarity, egalitarianism, and moral rigor, as opposed to conformity to societal norms, marks his voice as sectarian. James constructs an ethics defined as much by what it opposes as by what it affirms, and what is opposed has specific socioeconomic representation and expression: "Do not the rich people oppress you and themselves drag you into courts? Do not they themselves blaspheme the noble name that is invoked over you?" (2:6–7). This "over against" stance is given great urgency by the eschatological framework of the composition: judgment is coming soon (5:9) when the wicked will be punished (5:1–6) and the righteous rewarded (1:12).

James' probable social location in a sectarian movement that identifies itself with the poor and opposes the wealthy, in turn, is given further support by the dualistic shape of James' moral teaching and theology. Even a cursory survey of this composition shows that James characteristically establishes polar contrasts. At the social level, his most important distinction (apart from the religiously qualified *kyrios/doulos*) is between the rich and the poor (1:9–11; 2:1–6), which is played out morally as a contrast between the "innocent/righteous" (*dikaios*, 5:6) and the oppressor (2:6), between the arrogant and the lowly (4:6).[207]

Other moral contrasts are between "truth" (1:18) and error (1:16); war (4:1–2) and peace (3:17–18); meekness (1:21) and anger (1:20); anger (1:20) and justice (1:20; 3:18); envious craving (3:16; 4:1–3) and generous gift-giving (1:17; 4:6). Still more broadly, James holds in opposition the hearer of the word (1:22) and the doer of the word (1:25); the one who forgets (1:24) and the one who remembers (1:25); perfection or maturity (1:4, 17, 25) and lack or instability (1:4, 6–11).

In philosophical terms, these contrasts express the distance between "wisdom" (1:5; 3:13) and "foolishness" (1:26). In religious terms, the contrasts are expressed as "filthiness" (1:21, 27) and "purity" (1:27; 4:8) or "blessing" and "curse" (3:9). Still more cosmically, James opposes "saving" to "destroying" (4:12), "death" (1:16) to "life" (1:16), the "indwelling spirit" (4:5) to that which is earthbound and unspiritual (3:15).

Such opposites are placed within a spatial imagery of "above and below" and of "rising and lowering." The "wisdom from above" comes from God (1:5, 17;

---

[207]A similar set of polar oppositions in James is presented by T. B. Cargal, *Restoring the Diaspora: Discursive Structure and Purpose in the Epistle of James* (SBLDS 144; Atlanta: Scholars Press, 1993).

3:15). In terms of human behavior, it calls for a "submission" or "lowering/humbling," to which God responds with a "lifting up/exalting" (4:7–10). Opposed to this wisdom is one from below, which James characterizes as "earthbound, unspiritual, demonic" (3:15; 2:19), which is sponsored by the devil (4:7). This "wisdom from below" seeks to elevate the self by boasting and arrogance (4:6). And, just as God raises the lowly (4:10), God resists the arrogant (4:6).

Are such contrasts merely the reflection of a rigid dualism, or are they given structure by means of a coherent principle? James 4:4 offers us the best hope of finding a thematic center for his ethical and religious dualism. Indeed, 4:4 might be taken as thematic for the composition as a whole: "You adulteresses! Do you not know that friendship with the world is enmity with God? Therefore, whoever chooses to be a friend of the world is established as an enemy of God." This short syllogism encapsulates the organizing logic of James' symbolism.

1. The terms God (*theos*) and world (*kosmos*) are opposed as the objects of human allegiance and commitment (friendship).

2. The readers are assumed already to know this (*ouk oidate*, "do you not know").

3. The allegiance is not ontologically defined but is a matter of human choice: "Whoever chooses to be. . . ."

4. The term "world" always has a negative meaning in James. It never has the neutral sense of the arena of human activity or the positive sense of God's creation. In 3:6, James describes the tongue as the "world of wickedness" among the body's members. In 2:5, James contrasts those who are "poor with reference to the world" to those who are "rich in faith." This text is important for signaling the meaning of "world" as a system of value or measurement: those who in the value system of the world are poor are, within the value system of faith, rich. In 1:27, James again speaks of "pure religion in the eyes of God" (*para tō theō*) as one that "keeps oneself unstained from the world." We find, therefore, that "world" stands allied with wickedness and impurity and wealth, but opposed to true religion, faith, and purity. These contrasts are summarized in 4:4 as the opposition between "world" and "God."

5. Humans can choose to be "friends" with this measure of reality (and thus make themselves enemies of God) or can choose to be "friends with God" (and, by implication, be enemies of the world).

As later detailed notes will demonstrate, the language of "friendship" in Hellenistic culture denotes the most serious and pervasive of "free will" relationships, involving both spiritual allegiance and sharing. In the context of the moral *topos* on friendship (*peri philias*), to be "friends of the world" would mean to share completely in its view of reality, to measure things according to its measure, to be of "one mind" with it.

And what, for James, is the measure of the world? It is defined precisely in terms of the logic of envy. Human existence is a zero-sum game in a universe of limited resources, a closed system. Being and worth are dependent on having: having more means being more, and having less means being less. By this logic, therefore, humans are essentially in competition with each other for being and worth, and the surest way to succeed is to eliminate the competition. Such an attitude is expressed perfectly by those who "boast in their arrogance" and seek to ensure their future on the basis of their business ventures as though their lives were in their own control (4:13–16). It is expressed even better by those who defraud their own laborers of their wages in order to increase their own wealth, and thus, in effect, "kill the innocent person."

James' use of the designation "friend of God" for Abraham (2:23) is, in this reading, scarcely accidental. By the offering of his son Isaac, Abraham showed himself to be a "friend of God," because he accepted God's way of viewing reality rather than the world's. By the world's measure, he should have clung to his son in order to ensure the blessing promised him, especially since Isaac had been God's very gift (Gen 18:9; 21:1–2). But Abraham did not view the world as a closed system. He saw reality as one constantly gifted by the "giver of every good and perfect gift" (1:17) and was willing to give back one gift to the one who "gives a greater gift" (4:6).

It is at this point in our discussion that it is appropriate to speak of James' theology. The position taken in this commentary is in sharp opposition to that of Dibelius, who declared flatly that "James has no theology."[208] Dibelius' opinion derived in part from his conviction that James was simply a compendium of typical wisdom motifs with no specific perspective. But it also derived from the tendency to equate theology with a systematic articulation of religious ideas and (especially among Protestant scholars accustomed to working in Paul) with Christology.

In our discussion of James' Christian character, we saw how little explicit Christology James has to offer. And the letter clearly does not present an innovative or complex set of reflections on ultimate reality. Nevertheless, it is not far wrong to consider James one of the most "theological" writings in the NT. Five points support this assertion.

1. James' explicit attention is given to *ho theos* ("God"), as opposed to Jesus or the Holy Spirit. The term occurs 15 times (1:1, 5, 13, 20, 27; 2:5, 19, 23 (2); 3:9; 4:4 (2), 6, 7, 8). In apposition to *ho theos*, James speaks of *patēr* ("father") in 1:17, 27; 3:9. And, as we have seen, at least some of his uses

---

[208]Dibelius, 11.

of *kyrios* ("Lord") must have God as their referent (1:7; 3:9; 4:10; 15; 5:4, 11). In 108 verses, then, James has some 24 explicit references to this "character off stage." James is properly *theo*-logical in its ideology.

2. An analysis of *what* James says about *ho theos* reveals an astonishingly rich set of statements. Like all Jews, James agrees that God is one (2:19), but his understanding of God goes far beyond an assertion of naked monotheism; he portrays God as one who makes "demons tremble" (2:19) as "the Lord of Hosts" (5:4). God can be described negatively as one with whom there is no change or shadow of alteration (1:17), who does not tempt and is untempted by evil (1:13), whose righteousness is unassociated with human anger (1:20). James' positive statements, however, move in the direction of asserting God's powerful presence with creation and humanity. God is not only "light" but the "father of lights," (1:17) who has expressed his will and by a "word of truth" has—in a deeply paradoxical expression— "given birth" to humans as a kind of firstfruits of creatures (1:18) and has created them in his image (3:9). It is God's continuing involvement with humans, however, that is most striking. God has revealed his will in the "perfect law of liberty" (2:8–11) and will judge humans on the basis of that revelation (2:12; 4:12). James states powerfully, "there is one lawgiver (*nomothetēs*) and judge (*kritēs*) who is able to save (*sōsai*) and destroy (*apolesai*)" (4:12). But humans are not left with only a verbal norm. The word of truth is also an "implanted word" able to save souls (1:21), and God has made a "spirit" (*pneuma*) to dwell in humans (4:5). God remains in control of human affairs (4:15) and can declare as righteous and friends those who have faith in him (2:23). Above all, God reveals Godself in mercy and compassion. Indeed, these very terms are defining of God (5:11). Thus, God promises the crown of life to those who love him (1:12; 2:5); has chosen the poor in the world to be rich in faith and heirs of the kingdom (2:5); regards true religion as including the visitation of widows and orphans (1:27), even as he hears the cries of the oppressed (5:4); raises up the sick (5:15); hears the prayers of those who ask in faith (1:5–6) rather than wickedly (4:3); and forgives the sins of those who confess them (5:15).

3. Remarkably, this is a God who approaches those who approach (4:8), raises up the lowly (4:10), and enters into friendship with humans (2:23; 4:4). But this is a God who also resists the proud and the arrogant who exalt themselves by the oppression of others (4:6; 5:6). Above all, however, it is James' characterization of God as gift-giver that is most important. Three times the point is made. In 4:6, James derives from the text of Prov 3:34, "God resists the proud but gives grace to the lowly," the lesson: "but God gives more grace" (*meizona de didōsin charin*). That this is not a random observation is shown by James' first statement about God in 1:5, namely that God "gives to all simply (*haplōs*) and without grudging (*mē*

oneidozontos)." Finally, there is the programmatic statement in 1:17, "every good and perfect gift comes down from above from the father of lights with whom there is no change or shadow of alteration." Taken together, these three statements assert that God's giving is universal, abundant, without envy, and constant.

4. Because God does not exist in isolation from the world, but in active relationship to it, human existence is defined in terms of a story involving as characters both God and humans. The story has a past, defined in terms of what God has already done: created the world and humans, revealed himself in the law and the prophets and in the "faith of Jesus Christ," implanted in humans the "word of truth" and "wisdom from above" and "the spirit." The story also has a future, in terms of what God will do in response to human behavior in the world: reward the innocent and faithful and persevering, who have spoken and acted according to the "royal law of liberty;" punish the wicked oppressors who blaspheme the noble name associated with God's people. James' world, in a word, is not only an "open system" spatially, but also temporally.

5. James uses his theological propositions as warrants and premises for his moral exhortation. This last point will be developed extensively when specific cases are assessed. But it is of immediate importance for understanding the character of this writing. James does not contain a series of statements about God that simply stand in juxtaposition to moral commands. The two sorts of statements, rather, are related, with the theological always functioning as the motivator of the moral. The moral exhortation is *grounded* in James' understanding of the human relationship to God. Precisely this makes his affirmation of the constant, universal, ungrudging, and abundant giving of gifts by God so critical, for it is *this* understanding of reality that enables James to advocate a life of intra-communitarian concern and solidarity rather than one of competitive envy rooted in a view of the "world" that is at enmity with God (4:4).

If James opposes "friendship with the world" to "friendship with God," then, as his most inclusive frame for moral exhortation, the composition's most obvious target is the one referred to as "double-minded" (1:8; 4:8), who wants to be friends with everyone! The incompatibility of friendship with such opposing realms is also suggested by James' castigation of the "adulteresses" in 4:4. The use of such language obviously recalls the prophetic criticism of those who abandoned covenant with Yahweh. If the covenant was like a marriage, then breaking covenant was like adultery (see Hos 3:1; Ezek 16:38; 23:45; Isa 57:3; Jer 3:9; 13:27). So James sees the double-minded person as one who claims to be within the covenanted community but dallies with the values and standards of the outsiders, a spiritual "adulteress."

One of the most intriguing aspects of James' "voice," indeed, is the way it is at once dualistic and "sectarian," yet is also most critical of those inside the community who fail to live up to its standard. In contrast, for example, to the *Wisdom of Solomon*, whose dualism functions entirely for the support and reinforcement of insider status, James challenges insiders concerning the integrity of their lives as insiders. The moral dualism is turned expressly on those who profess "the faith of Jesus Christ," yet whose behavior is governed by the measure of "the world." They pray, but double-mindedly or wickedly for their own gain (1:8; 4:3); they practice partiality in their assemblies (2:1–5); they refuse to help the needy although they use religious language to cover their rejection (2:14–16); they use the same tongue to bless God and curse the brother or sister created in God's image (3:9).

So emphatically does James use polemic against outsiders as a criticism of insiders, that it is difficult to be certain concerning the addressees of some passages and their social location. The problem is acute in the case of the wealthy. Do the attacks on the carelessly affluent in 4:13–16 and the oppressive rich who defraud their workers in 5:1–6 apply to actual members of Christian communities? Or is this a form of rhetoric to be overheard (in the style of the diatribe or the prophetic "woe against the nations") by Christians as a reflection on their own behavior, which, perhaps less severe, is subject to the same norm? It is clear in 2:1–6, in any case, that those in the community who despise the poor *are in effect* adopting the same measure as the oppressive rich who persecute Christians by taking them to court (2:6).

James' challenge to the double-minded person, then, is to become "simple," and to have "purity of heart" (4:8), which means for James, as Kierkegaard saw brilliantly, "to will one thing." The classic Greco-Roman insistence on deeds matching profession is here applied specifically to living consistently according to the measure of reality given by the "wisdom from above" or "faith." For this reason, the "call to conversion" in James 3:13–4:10 can rightly be called the thematic heart of the composition, and 4:4 the most perfect expression of James' "voice."

II. CIRCUMSTANCES OF COMPOSITION: WHOSE VOICE?

◆

The circumstances of the composition of James should be considered only after a comprehensive analysis of its "voice." Too often in NT studies, the reverse is true. Decisions about authorship, readers, dating, and place are used to determine the meaning of a writing.

The procedure is wrong for two reasons. First, it operates with an overly simple understanding of the rhetoric of ancient texts. The meaning of any NT text, leaving aside the question of its significance,[209] is not reducible to its originating circumstances.[210] Romans may indeed have been written as a fund-raising letter, but to suggest that such a function exhausts the meaning of the composition is ludicrous.[211]

Second, the writings of the NT are notoriously difficult to place in historical context. In the NT canon, only a handful of Paul's letters are capable of being dated with some degree of confidence. And even this minimal achievement is due to the happy coincidence of several factors. Paul writes to urban centers about which we have knowledge from other ancient sources and archeology; his movement through these cities can be coordinated with the narrative of Acts that provides some chronological and geographical controls; the letters themselves are filled with incidental detail concerning the addresses and their problems. Only with such convergent lines of evidence is it possible to mount any sort of

---

[209]See the distinction argued in E. D. Hirsch, *Validity in Interpretation* (New Haven: Yale University Press, 1967) 8, 62–7, 140–4.

[210]See L. T. Johnson, "On Finding the Lukan Community: A Cautious Cautionary Essay," *SBLSP* 17 (1979) 87–100.

[211]See L. T. Johnson, *The Writings of the New Testament: An Interpretation* (Philadelphia: Fortress Press, 1986) 315–17.

argument concerning the "social history" of such early Christian communities.[212]

Without such convergent and confirming evidence, "historical reconstruction" or "social location" runs the danger of becoming a paper chase lacking genuine controls except those provided by a variety of theoretical models.[213] Since the mid-nineteenth century, the study of Christian origins has been dominated by two basic sorts of models with many subvariations. The first is a *conflict model*. Christianity is seen as developing through conflict between competing versions. Historical reconstruction involves identifying and allocating these conflicts, and the understanding of the NT writings is determined by their place in these disputes.[214] The second is a *developmental model*. Christianity is seen to move through a progression from simplicity to complexity, or from one social/cultural/ideological matrix to another. Historical reconstruction means reading the sources in the light of such developments. The understanding of the NT compositions is determined by their place in the sequence.[215] Both the

---

[212]It is striking that the most successful work on Paul's social context has derived primarily from the use of the Corinthian correspondence, for there alone do we have such a convergence of evidence sufficient to enable the analysis; see, e.g., W. A. Meeks, *The First Urban Christians: The Social World of the Apostle Paul* (New Haven: Yale University Press, 1983); G. Theissen, *The Social Setting of Pauline Christianity: Essays on Corinth*, trans. J. Schütz (Philadelphia: Fortress Press, 1982); R. Hock, *The Social Context of Paul's Ministry* (Philadelphia: Fortress Press, 1980); the difficulties of social analysis of the Pauline letters lacking such supporting evidence are illustrated by J. Neyrey, *Paul in Other Words: A Cultural Reading of His Letters* (Louisville: Westminster/John Knox Press, 1990) 181–206.

[213]Until very recently, scholars rarely made explicit acknowledgment of their theories or paradigms. They simply considered themselves to be doing history. By no means did that make implicit theory to be less influential on their findings. The awareness of the influence of conceptual paradigms for all research has been influenced by T. S. Kuhn, *Structure of Scientific Revolutions* 2nd ed. (Chicago: University Of Chicago Press, 1977); see the discussion by J. S. Preus, *Explaining Religion: Criticism and Theory from Bodin to Freud* (New Haven: Yale University Press, 1987) x–xii. The work of P. L. Berger and T. Luckmann, *The Social Construction of Reality: A Treatise in the Sociology of Knowledge* (Garden City: Doubleday, 1967), has also helped shape what has come to be called a "postmodern" awareness of the irreducibly perspectival character of social and historical analysis.

[214]The influence of the "Tübingen School" in the development of this model, which has obvious connections with the Hegelian dialectic of history, is clear. The work of F. C. Baur is discussed below. In this century, W. Bauer's *Orthodoxy and Heresy in Earliest Christianity* (1934) 2nd ed., ed. G. Strecker (1964); ed. and trans. R. A. Kraft and G. Krodel (Philadelphia: Fortress Press, 1971), has had fundamental importance. Whereas the Tübingen model read everything through a Jewish Christian/Pauline Christian matrix, more recent work has found a variety of "opponents" for Paul and for the evangelists.

[215]The "conflict model" also sketched a development from Paul to "Catholicism" through the dialectic of opposing theologies. In the twentieth century, developmental models have owed much to the sociological analysis of religion by M. Weber, T. Luckmann, and Peter Berger, and recently, Brian Wilson (for discussion, see M. Y. MacDonald, *The Pauline Churches: A Socio-Historical Study of Institutionalization in the Pauline and Deutero-Pauline Writings* (SNTSMS 60; Cambridge: Cambridge University Press, 1988) 2–28. The Weberian path from "prophet to priest" or

conflict and developmental models have been constructed by scholars who have not always succeeded in keeping their theological convictions concerning "true Christianity" from influencing either the establishment of the model or the reading of the evidence.

Reconstructions that are so heavily reliant on models rather than data should be regarded as interesting speculations rather than certain foundations. Yet such theories too often become the grid for interpreting the very documents that provide the slender basis for the reconstruction itself. The procedure not only uses what is less known as the key to understanding what is better known, but it does so with an obvious circularity.

From the outset, it must be acknowledged that James offers us slender hope of reconstructing its historical situation, beyond the sketchy indicators of its "social location" discussed above (pp. 82 83). The text reveals little about the situation of the implied readers. The Greeting identifies them only as "the twelve tribes in the dispersion" (1:1). While it is natural to take this literally as referring to Jewish Christians in territories outside Palestine, the appropriation of the honorifics of Israel by Gentile Christians (see 1 Pet 2:9–10) gives us pause, as does the possibility of a "spiritual" understanding of the term "dispersion" (see Philo, *Confusion of Tongues* 17; *On the Cherubim* 34).

If the readers were literally "in the dispersion," then we can draw few inferences about their specific social circumstances, since these were bound to vary considerably in different places. In fact, only a handful of social facts about the readers can be asserted, and even these are "the facts" as reported or perceived by the author: they gather in assemblies for decision-making (2:1–4) and prayer (5:13–16); they have leaders called teachers and elders (3:1; 5:14); and they experience persecution and oppression at the hands of those they call "the rich" (2:6; 4:13–5:6). Not only is this a meager set of facts, the author's rhetoric (using *topoi* of moral teaching, posing hypothetical cases) cautions us from moving far beyond them. From the earliest efforts to reconstruct the world of the readers to the most recent, nothing has happened to significantly improve the data.[216]

"routinization of charism" ends up, not surprisingly, with the same category of "early catholicism" as the conflict model. Other presumed progressions include that concerning oral tradition (that it moves from the simple to the complex) or gospel stories (that they move from the Jewish/ eschatological to the Hellenistic), which has recently been reversed (from the cynic to the apocalyptic).

[216]The database remains the same for J. A. Bengel, *Gnomon Novi Testamenti* 7th ed. (Edinburgh: T & T Clark, 1877) 7:14–15; for F. H. Kern, *Der Character und Ursprung des Briefes Jacobi* (Tübingen: Fues, 1835); and for W. Popkes, *Adressaten, Situation und Form des Jakobusbriefes* (Stuttgarter Bibelstudien 125/126; Stuttgart: Katholisches Bibelwerk, 1986). What has changed (besides the size of the books!) is the elaboration of the data and the connections made to other bodies of evidence. For a straightforward recital of the data, see C. Burchard, "Gemeinde in der strohernen Epistel: Mutmassungen ueber Jakobus," *Kirche: Festschrift für Günther Bornkamm*, ed. D. Lührmann and G. Strecker (Tübingen: JCB Mohr [Paul Siebeck] 1980) 315–28.

The best chance of locating James historically would seem to come from the identification of the author. But here we enter one of the most tangled and debated territories in the study of Christian origins. Some patience must be asked of the reader if the threads of the debate are to be disentangled.

Although the evidence is complex, the basic positions are simple.[217] Virtually all critical scholars agree that James the Brother of the Lord is the most likely ascribed author of the letter. If James' authorship is taken as historically accurate, then, in one stroke, we are provided with a place of origin, an approximate dating, and some hope of imagining the circumstances of author and readers. As a not inconsiderable bonus, we are also given valuable evidence for Palestinian Christianity sometime between 35 and 62 CE.

A second position argues that, although James the Brother of the Lord was undoubtedly a critically important figure in the Jerusalem church of the first decades, the preponderance of evidence from the NT and later writings concerning James suggests that he could not have been the real author of this letter. "James" should, therefore, be categorized as pseudonymous literature. This position demands that the composition be dated after the death of James in 62. Most often it is also dated later than Paul's letters, since this position tends also to regard James as responding to Paul or a Pauline tendency. Once a decision for pseudonymity is made, the historical placement of James and the determination of its purpose tend to be dictated by the theoretical model being employed by the investigator.[218]

The evidence used for shaping these divergent positions includes: a) the evidence about James the Brother of the Lord in the NT and extracanonical sources and b) the fit between this construal and the evidence of the letter itself. A careful sifting of this evidence can, I think, move us toward a moral certitude concerning the circumstances of James' composition. It must be emphasized here again, however, that moral certitude is always a matter of the cumulative force of probabilities rather than of mathematical demonstration. Also worth repetition is the conviction that determining the circumstances of the composition ought not in the least affect our appreciation of its voice, such as we have identified it.

A. JAMES THE BROTHER OF THE LORD

1. New Testament Evidence

Before seeking the likeliest candidate for authorship, a word about the name "James" itself is appropriate. Contemporary readers may miss the literary

---

[217]The positions are clearly described in J. Polhill, "The Life-Situation of the Book of James," *Review and Expositor* 66 (1969) 369–78.

[218]In section III (History of Interpretation), some of the variations will be shown.

richness associated with this name in the biblical tradition, since the English "James" gives no automatic clues to its derivation from the Hebrew "Jacob." The English derives from the Old French "Gemmes" or "Jaimes," which equals the Spanish "Jaime," Catalonian "Jaume," and Italian "Giacomo." These, in turn, derived from the late Latin "Jacomus," a softening of the earlier Latin "Jacobus" (see also German "Jakobus"). The Latin is a straight transliteration from the Greek *Iakōbos*, which is itself a transliteration of the Hebrew *ya^caqôb*.[219] This letter from "James," therefore, is in reality a letter from "Jacob," whose role in the biblical story carries with it considerable symbolic weight (see Gen 25:26; Exod 3:6, 15; Isa 40:27; Mic 2:12).

Most scholars agree that the best candidate for "James" in the Greeting (1:1) is James of Jerusalem, called by Paul "the Brother of the Lord" (Gal 1:19). Even this, of course, is a matter of guesswork, only slightly supported by the identification offered by the first Christian writer to explicitly cite this letter, Origen, who refers to the author as "the Brother of the Lord" (*Commentarium in Epistulam ad Romanos* IV, 8).

There are two interrelated reasons for trusting this identification. First, the simplicity and apparent modesty (see the commentary) of the author's self-designation as *doulos*, together with the total lack of other identifying features or protestations of authority, suggests a *Iakōbos* sufficiently well-known so as to be known and accepted as an authority by readers. This is supported by the assumed recognition of James and his position by the Greeting of the letter of Jude, which is simply, "Jude, a servant of God and brother of James" (Jude 1; see Mark 6:3; Matt 13:55).

Second, other candidates either fail to meet that level of recognition or disappear from the scene too quickly. James the son of Zebedee had high recognition value: he appears on all four lists of apostles (Matt 10:2; Mark 3:17; Luke 6:14; Acts 1:13) and appears as one of Jesus' closest followers during his ministry (see Mark 1:19, 29; 5:37; 9:2; 10:35, 41; 13:3; 14:33). But Acts 12:2 reports his death by beheading under Herod Agrippa I. This James would have had to write before ca. 44 CE, which, while not impossible, seems less than likely, since this James' authority is not singled out by any source. Another *Iakōbos* is the "Son of Alphaeus," who also appears on all lists of the apostles (Matt 10:3; Mark 3:18; Luke 6:15; Acts 1:13), but who plays no role in the narratives. Even more obscure is James "The Little" (*ho mikros*) who is briefly identified as a son of Mary and brother of Joses (Mark 15:40 = Matt 27:56; Mark 16:1 = Luke 24:10). Finally, there is the James who is the father (apparently) of Judas, who himself appears in apostolic lists (Luke 6:16; Acts 1:13; but contrast Mark 3:18; Matt 10:3).[220] James "the Brother of the Lord" emerges with impressive clarity from among these candidates.

---

[219]See *A New English Dictionary on Historical Principles*, ed. J. A. H. Murray (Oxford: Clarendon Press, 1901) 5:549.

[220]Ropes, 54–62, devotes a lengthy discussion to the ways in which—in the interest of protecting the virginity of Mary—attempts were made to identify one of these last two obscure Jameses with "the brother of the Lord."

a. Evidence in Paul

In 1 Corinthians (ca. 54), there is one certain and one possible reference to James. In 1 Cor 15:7, Paul includes James in a list of those to whom Jesus appeared after his death: first Cephas, then the Twelve, then to more than five hundred, *epeita ōphthē Iakōbō, eita tois apostolois pasin* ("and then to James, then to all the apostles"). The syntax suggests that Paul here includes James among the rank of apostles but not of the Twelve. This would be consistent with Paul's own criterion for being considered an apostle (1 Cor 9:1). More significant is that Paul concludes the list by asserting the commonality of belief among all those he has listed and himself (1 Cor 15:11).

Earlier in the same letter, Paul makes passing reference to those who travel with a woman/sister, including "the rest of the apostles and *hoi adelphoi tou kyriou* and Cephas" (1 Cor 9:5). James is not mentioned by name, but Paul's language suggests that "the brothers of the Lord" was a recognizable group in the nascent messianic movement. The evidence in 1 Corinthians is of critical importance for assessing the James/Paul relationship. Written well after the events in Jerusalem reported by Galatians 1–2 (Paul's reference to the collection in 1 Cor 16:1–4 assumes the agreement reached in Gal 2:10), it reveals no animus toward James on the part of Paul nor any negative influence of James on Paul's mission (contrast 1 Cor 1:10).

The evidence in Galatians is more complex and difficult to evaluate, not least because of the notorious problems in fixing either the dating or the contours of the controversy Paul faces in the churches of the Galatian region.[221] The three places where Paul mentions James must be analyzed before an overall evaluation is given. First, when speaking of his trip to Jerusalem three years after his call to be an apostle, he says that he went to *historēsai Kēphan* ("inquire of/relate to Cephas," 1:18) and adds, "I did not see another of the apostles except *(ei mē)* James the Brother of the Lord" (1:19). Although he follows this with a declaration before God that he is not lying, he is probably referring to the entire preceding *narratio* rather than to the specific statement about James.[222] What is most important is that Paul here includes James among the leadership in Jerusalem, with his language (as in 1 Corinthians 15) suggesting that Paul considered him to be among the apostles.[223]

---

[221]The elements of the critical discussion are laid out by W. G. Kümmel, *Introduction to the New Testament* rev. ed., trans. H. C. Kee (Nashville: Abingdon Press, 1975) 294–304.

[222]By using the term *narratio*, I acknowledge the rhetorical character of Galatians, as in H. D. Betz, "The Literary Composition and Function of Paul's Letter to the Galatians," NTS 21 (1974–5) 353–73, without subscribing to Betz's classification of Galatians as *apologia*. Galatians is better considered a form of deliberative rhetoric, with the recountal of Paul's experiences functioning as much as *exemplum* as to provide the basis for his self-defense.

[223]The construction *ei mē* can be read in several ways, leading to severe disagreement as to whether Paul did or did not consider James to be an apostle; see, e.g., J. Mader, "Apostel und Herrenbrüder," BZ 6 (1908) 393–406; S. Lyonnet, "Témoignages de Saint Jean Chrysostome et de Saint Jerome sur Jacques le Frère du Seigneur," RSR 29 (1939) 335–51.

The second piece of evidence is found in Gal 2:9, where Paul lists James before Cephas and John as *hoi dokountes styloi einai*. The use of *dokein* ("were considered to be" or "considered themselves to be") indicates some reservation by Paul concerning their reputation. This is made clear also by his reference to those "in repute" *(tous dokousin)* in 2:2 and again in 2:6, where he distinguishes between human reputation and God's impartiality. But although his tone is cool, Paul does not question the authority of the three leaders. Indeed, he comes prepared to submit *(anatithēmi)* for their consideration the gospel he preached among the Gentiles, and specifically states his willingness to defer to their judgment, "lest I am running or have run in vain" (2:2). His claim that they imposed no further obligation on him (2:6), apart from the care for the poor (2:10), and that they recognized the legitimacy of the gift God had given him for his mission to the Gentiles (2:9) is implicit acknowledgment of their authority to discern and judge.

The proper evaluation of the *narratio* to this point is important for the interpretation of the final piece of evidence. Paul has acknowledged James' place in the Jerusalem leadership and, more significantly, joined the "right hand of fellowship" with that leadership (2:9). Nothing in Paul's remarks can be taken as attack or criticism of that leadership. Indeed—and this is most important—in 2:6, Paul carefully *distinguishes* this leadership from the "false brethren" who sneaked in to spy out Paul's "freedom" by requiring circumcision of the Gentile Titus (2:3–5). Paul insists that despite much opposition *neither* he nor the Jerusalem leadership gave way (2:7–9).

The third piece of evidence is Galatians 2:11–14, where Paul recounts his conflict with Cephas in Antioch over the issue of table-fellowship for Jewish and Gentile believers. Paul's complaint is that Cephas (with other Jewish believers, 2:13) ate freely with Gentile believers, until *elthein tinas apo Iakōbou* ("certain people from James arrived," 2:12). Then Peter, out of fear of *tous ek peritomēs* ("those out of the circumcision") withdrew from table-fellowship. Paul accuses Cephas, the other Jewish believers of Antioch, and even Barnabas, of hypocrisy (2:13).

Paul's complaint in this passage is clearly against Peter, whom he confronts "in the presence of all" (2:14). But what role did James play? In Paul's report of the events, "the people from James" clearly acted as a catalyst. Unfortunately, Paul does not inform us how. Were they an official delegation sent out by James? Or were they simply visiting the Antiochean church? Did they represent James' views, or only their own? Did they challenge the Antiochean practice, or did Peter simply (as Paul suggests) cravenly give way of his own accord out of human respect? The *most* that could be said about Paul's own account is that James' representatives posed a challenge to the practice of open table-fellowship. Nothing is implied concerning a difference in understanding the "gospel" (see Gal 1:6).

Because of the extraordinary use to which the evidence of Galatians has been

THE LETTER OF JAMES

put in the history of scholarship, two final interpretive comments are necessary. It is important to remember, first, the rhetorical role of the *narratio* in Galatians. Paul's emphasis on his gift from God, and his defense of that gift in the face of opposition both in Jerusalem and in Antioch, is meant to serve as an *exemplum* to the Galatians, who similarly face those who seek to "enslave them" (Gal 4:3), in order to encourage them to live by the gift that they have received (Gal 3:1–5). Paul explicitly does *not* connect the problems in Galatia to those he had experienced from "false brethren" in Jerusalem. He does *not* make James the cause of the problems in Antioch. He does *not* attribute responsibility for the troubles in Galatia to James or the Jerusalem church. Second, it is important to remember that, apart from these brief references, Paul *nowhere* else in his letters connects any of his opposition either to Peter or to James. Nor does he ever slacken in his devotion to the Jerusalem church for which he had expended such great and frustrating efforts (see Rom 15:25–32). If Paul himself saw James as his enemy, he never said so in his letters.

b. Evidence in the Gospels

The evidence in the Gospels concerning James is sparse. He appears as a member of Jesus' family in Mark 6:3 and Matt 13:55 in a passage that is slighting of Jesus' origins. Mark's Gospel in particular is obviously less than generous toward Jesus' human family as such (see especially Mark 3:20–35). The Fourth Gospel also is negative toward Jesus' "brothers" (John 7:3–5). But although such attitudes are detectable, their evaluation is more difficult. Some scholars appeal to the oblique polemic against opponents in Greco-Roman biographies to legitimate finding such polemic in the Gospels.[224] There have been a number of studies which, from slightly different angles, purport to find in Mark's portrayal of the disciples and/or Jesus' family an allegorical attack on the Christology, eschatology, or ecclesiology of the Jerusalem church, represented above all by James, "the brother of the Lord."[225]

c. Evidence in Acts

The other major source of information about James the Brother of the Lord within the NT is Luke-Acts. Luke omits any specific mention of James in his

---

[224]See esp. C. H. Talbert, *What Is a Gospel? The Genre of the Canonical Gospels* (Philadelphia: Fortress Press, 1977) 8, 94–95. The evidence for *implicit* criticism of the type suggested by Talbert is not, in fact, widespread in ancient biographies; see L. T. Johnson, "On Finding the Lukan Community" 97, n. 22.

[225]See, e.g., W. Kelber, *The Kingdom in Mark: A New Place and a New Time* (Philadelphia: Fortress Press, 1974); T. Weeden, *Mark, Traditions in Conflict* (Philadelphia: Fortress Press, 1971); J. D. Crossan, "Mark and the Relatives of Jesus," *NovT* 15 (1973) 81–113; E. Trocmé, *The Formation of the Gospel according to Mark*, trans. P. Gaughan (Philadelphia: Westminster Press, 1975); a truly extraordinary example of reading a considerable part of the NT in opposition to James is K. L. Carroll, "The Place of James in the Early Church," *BJRL* 44 (1961–62) 49–67.

Gospel. In Acts 1:14, he includes among those waiting with the apostles for the gift of the Holy Spirit "the mother of Jesus and his brothers." James is singled out and named only after the death of James the son of Zebedee under Agrippa I (Acts 12:2) and after Peter's escape from prison (12:3–17). Before "departing to another place," Peter tells the assembly to "inform James and the brothers of these things" (12:17). The language resembles that of Paul in 1 Cor 9:5 and suggests the picture of James standing among a group known as "brothers of the Lord." In Luke's narrative sequence, the statement signals the shift in authority within the Jerusalem community to James and the elders.[226]

James subsequently appears in Acts twice as spokesperson for the Jerusalem *presbyterion*. At the apostolic council, his support for the fundamental freedom of the Gentile mission is decisive (15:12–21). He advocates sending a letter to the churches in Antioch and Syria and Cilicia (15:23–29), rejecting the demand for circumcision and observance of the law that first generated controversy (15:1) and enjoining the minimal requirements for Jewish believers to join Gentile believers in table-fellowship.

Acts does not associate James either with the agitators in Antioch (15:1) or with the Pharisaic party in Jerusalem, who demanded of Gentiles that they be circumcised and observe the law of Moses (15:5). The letter sent out from the Jerusalem council *does* acknowledge that "some from among us" created the controversy in Antioch, a statement that confirms in substance but is even more generalizing than Gal 2:12. There are great problems involved in adjudicating the accounts in Galatians and Acts.[227] But in Acts' version of the events occurring in Antioch and Jerusalem, James is clearly not an opponent of Paul but is, instead, a mediator between Paul and his attackers.

The final appearance of James in Acts is more ambiguous. On Paul's final trip to Jerusalem (which, from Romans 15:25–32 we know involved Paul's collection for the saints, but which Luke curiously does not highlight), Paul is brought into the presence of James and the elders (21:18).[228] He reports on the wonders God was working among the Gentiles (21:19). The elders respond by glorifying God (21:20). In Lukan shorthand, this means they express approval of God's activity through Paul in the Gentile mission (compare Luke 5:26; 7:16; 18:43; Acts 11:18; 13:48).

The essential accord between Paul and the Jerusalem leadership is confirmed also by James' repetition of the "apostolic decree" issued for the Gentiles (21:25). On the one hand, no obligations beyond those sketched in 15:23–29 are imposed. On the other hand, Paul's own fidelity to his Jewish identity is questioned, not by James or the elders, but by some of the Jewish believers

---

[226]See L. T. Johnson, *The Acts of the Apostles* (Sacra Pagina 5; Collegeville: Liturgical Press, 1992) 213–17.

[227]See the discussion and literature in Johnson, *The Acts of the Apostles*, 258–81.

[228]For discussion of the problems, see Johnson, *The Acts of the Apostles*, 373–80.

"zealous for the law" who claim that Paul has told *Jews* to stop circumcising their children or practicing the law (21:20–21).

James and the elders suggest that Paul perform a ritual act in the Temple to show his allegiance to the people (21:24). Several points are worth noting here. First, the entire speech comes from the board of elders as a whole, "they said to him"; James is portrayed simply as one of the group. Second, the charges against Paul come not from the leadership but from the zealous law-observers. Third, the charges have to do not with the validity of the Gentile mission in any fashion, but exclusively with Paul's teaching and practice as a Jew in the diaspora. Fourth, both the narrative of Acts (16:3; 18:18; 20:16) as well as Paul's own letters show the charges to be a canard: Paul *never* advocated Jews' abandoning their ancestral customs; he only resisted the demand that Gentiles adopt them.

In summary, no careful reader of the NT can deny that Acts and Paul's letters resist easy harmonization or even reconciliation. Recent scholarship has, indeed, sharpened the perception of each author's tendencies: if Luke emphasizes Paul's connectedness to Judaism and Jerusalem, Paul no less stresses his independence over against those challenging his authority. Neither source can be taken uncritically; each has its own interest. But research has also tended to confirm that beneath the rhetoric of the separate writings, Paul and the Jerusalem church were in the first generation of the Christian movement more in a cooperative than competitive relationship. In order to derive from these sources a picture of James and Paul as personal or ideological opponents, something more than the evidence offered by the NT is required.

2. Extracanonical Evidence

The evidence concerning James from outside the canonical writings is extensive and far more complex. It requires careful sifting.

a. *Evidence in Josephus*

That James the Brother of the Lord did, in fact, hold an important place in the Jerusalem church of the first decades of the messianic movement is confirmed by the account of his death in the Jewish historian Josephus (*Antiquities of the Jews* 20:200). Critics of an earlier generation tended to dismiss the authenticity of the passage,[229] but it is more widely accepted today.[230]

Josephus is describing events that took place in the interregnum between the procurators Festus and Albinus. The "rash and daring" (20:199) high priest

---

[229]See F. C. Baur, *Paul the Apostle of Jesus Christ* 2nd ed. E. Zeller, trans. A. Menzies (London: Williams & Norgate, 1875) 1:160.

[230]See the discussion and bibliography provided by J. P. Meier, *A Marginal Jew: Rethinking the Historical Jesus* Vol 1 (New York: Doubleday, 1991) 58–9, 72–3.

Ananus took advantage of the absence of Roman oversight to convene "the council of judges" and bring before it "a man named James, the brother of Jesus who was called the Christ, along with certain others." The high priest accused them of being transgressors of the law and delivered them over to be stoned. Having already made the point that Ananus was a Sadducee (20:199), Josephus then describes how the Pharisees (whom we understand as "those in the city strictest in the observance of the law," 20:201) opposed him and protested his action to Albinus (20:200).

The value of Josephus' account lies in confirming the historicity of James, his designation as "Jesus' brother," his place within the Jerusalem community, and the date of his death, ca. 62. Little else about James can be drawn from the account, apart from the observation (consistent with the portrayal in Acts) that he was associated with "certain others." The mode of death by stoning is consistent with the practice of the Sanhedrin for cases of blasphemy (*Mishnah Tractate Sanh* 7:4). The fact that the Pharisees protested the action cannot be read as signifying that they sided or sympathized with James, only that they seized the chance to score against a detested Sadducean opponent (20:201).

b. *Evidence in Christian Writings*

Deciphering the diverse traditions about James in the Christian literature of the first four centuries is a more daunting task.[231] The main reason is that, like other "founding figures" such as Peter and Paul, James was variously appropriated by diverse groups who fitted his figure to their own purposes. In these traditions, James is much more a fictional than a historical character. His presentation is shaped by the ideological standpoint of the tradents, as well as by the hagiographical instinct for pious elaboration.

1. TRADITIONS OF JAMES' DEATH

The hagiographical dimension is demonstrated by the traditions concerning James' death.[232] The church historian Eusebius hands on two versions. In *HE* II,1,5, he quotes from Book 6 of the *Hypotyposes* of Clement of Alexandria (+ca. 215) to the effect that "James the Just"—carefully distinguished from the James who was beheaded—was "thrown down from the pinnacle of the temple and beaten to death with a fuller's club." Then in *HE* III, 23, Eusebius quotes extensively from Hegesippus ("of the generation after the apostles" [III, 23, 3]) concerning James' death. The account is much fuller, including a proclamation of James to all the people from the pinnacle of the Temple on Passover, made at the request of the Jewish leaders who are so concerned at the number of

---

[231]Martin, xli–lxi, provides a good summary of the sources.

[232]The sources dealing specifically with the death of James are displayed by D. H. Little, *The Death of James, the Brother of the Lord* (Ph.D. diss., Rice University, 1971).

converts to Jesus that they want James to dissuade the crowd from such belief (III, 23, 10–11)! James' proclamation naturally has the opposite effect, leading the Scribes and Pharisees to decide to throw him down from the Temple (III, 23, 15–16). But since the fall does not kill James, they decide to stone him (III, 23, 17). And when they are prevented from stoning him by "one of the priests of the sons of Rechab," a laundryman takes a club and hits James on the head (III, 23,18). Hegesippus' version, we see, combines the stoning found in Josephus and the fall/clubbing found in Clement.

The fictionalizing tendency in such accounts is patent. It is doubtful whether either Eusebian account adds anything reliable to our historical knowledge concerning the death of James, even though Eusebius himself claims that Hegesippus' account is "in agreement" with that of Clement.[233] Nor can much more credit be given to the historicity of Hegesippus' rendering of James the Just (or "Oblias") as a Nazirite uniquely allowed into the sanctuary of the Temple, an intimate of Jewish leaders (HE III,23,4–10).

The same conclusion applies to the account of James' being thrown from the steps of the Temple but not killed by "the enemy" in the Pseudo-Clementine Recognitions I, 70–71 (see below), as well as the allusion in the Manichean Psalm Book to "James, his brother also . . . died beneath the storm of stone" (Psalms of Heracleides 192:8–9; see also the more ambiguous reference in the Psalms of Sarakoth 142:25–26). The extensive version of the death of James in the Gnostic tractate The Second Apocalypse of James 61–62 is even more convoluted than that of Hegesippus, with the inclusion of James' prayer before his death drawing the account even more explicitly into the martyrological tradition.[234]

2. JAMES' AUTHORITY AND CHARACTER

Ideological interests are more clearly reflected in traditions concerning James' authority and character. The element that distinguishes James and makes him important differs according to the concerns of the compositions discussing him.[235]

a. Clement/Hegesippus/Eusebius

Clement of Alexandria's testimony is confusing. As reported by Eusebius, Clement states in Book 6 of his Hypotyposes that "Peter and James and John"

---

[233]"It is difficult to understand why a number of scholars have attached any historical value at all to this text with its numerous contradictions," J. Munck, Paul and the Salvation of Mankind, trans. F. Clarke (Richmond: John Knox Press, 1959) 117; also, E. Schwartz, "Zu Eusebius Kirchengeschichte," ZNW 4 (1903) 48–66; see also Dibelius, 15–7; Martin, xlviii–liv.

[234]See Little, The Death of James, 198–234, and A. Böhlig, "Zum Martyrium des Jakobus," NovT 5 (1962) 207–13.

[235]See S. K. Brown, James: A Religio-Historical Study of the Relations between Jewish, Gnostic, and Catholic Christianity in the Early Period through an Investigation of the Traditions about James the Lord's Brother (Ph.D. diss., Brown University, 1972) esp. 278–94.

appointed James the Just as bishop of Jerusalem (*HE* II,1,3). Then in the seventh book, he says that "The Lord gave the tradition of knowledge (*gnōsis*) to James the Just and John and Peter, and these gave it to the other apostles, and the other apostles to the seventy, of whom Barnabas also was one" (*HE* II,1,4). Eusebius tries to clarify the discrepancy by distinguishing between the James who was beheaded and James the Just who was stoned (*HE* II,1,7), but the problem of consistency remains. Was James' authority directly from the Lord, or was it derived? Both versions, it can be noted, differ from the sequence reported by Paul in 1 Cor 15:7. The reports from Clement are also in tension with Eusebius' own statement that James "was first elected to the throne of the bishopric of the church in Jerusalem" (*HE* II,1,2). Add to this the remark from Hegesippus that "the charge of the church passed to James the brother of the Lord *together with the apostles*" (*IIE* II,23,4), and we are left with a hopeless tangle.[236]

b. Gnostic Writings

Clement's report that the resurrected Lord gave "the knowledge" (*gnōsis*) to James (*HE* II,1,4) emphasizes James' authority as receiver of revelation rather than as administrator. Not surprisingly, this aspect is also exploited by the writings from the Nag-Hammadi library discovered in 1946. In the Coptic *Gospel of Thomas*, we find this exchange: " 'We know that you will depart from us. Who is to be our leader?' Jesus said to them, 'Wherever you are, go to James the righteous, for whose sake heaven and earth came into being' " (*Gos. Thom.* 12).

In the same library's *Apocryphon of James*, we find James as author of a letter (the addressee is indecipherable). In it, James says he is sending a "secret book" revealed to him and Peter by the Lord. In fact, this is the second such book; he had been in the process of writing the first when a further revelation occurred, necessitating the composition of another (1–2; compare Jude 3). The *Apocryphon* contains a wealth of revelatory material communicated to Peter and James. When the other disciples heard these revelations, they were displeased: "and so, not wishing to assure their resentment, I sent each one to another place. But I myself went up to Jerusalem, praying that I might obtain a portion among the beloved, who will appear" (16).[237] The *Apocryphon*, then, connects James' authority with that of Peter through divine revelation, locates him in Jerusalem, and has him dispatching the other disciples on mission.

The Nag-Hammadi collection also has a *Second Apocalypse of James*,[238]

---

[236]See also the references to James as "leader and prefect over the church" in *The Teaching of Addai*, trans. G. Howard (SBLTT 16; Early Christian Literature Series 4; Chico, California: Scholars Press, 1981) F.54a (p. 23), F.10a (p. 31), and F.11a (p. 35).

[237]See F. E. Williams, "The Apocryphon of James," in *NHLE* 29–36.

[238]See C. H. Hedrick, "The Second Apocalypse of James," in *NHLE* 249–55.

containing a description of James' death (61–62) similar to that in Hegesippus, but even more developed. The first part of this tractate is a discourse spoken by "James the Just" but transcribed by Mareim, one of the priests. Strikingly, the discourse is delivered from "the fifth flight of steps," a detail that recalls the setting in the *Recognitions* I,55,2. The discourse itself is fragmentary, but is clearly gnostic in sensibility: "I am He who received revelation from the Pleroma of Imperishability" (46). The document is particularly interesting, in fact, for the way in which it combines an account of James' death, which is so close to that found in other sources, and a discourse that is so distinctively different than anything found in those other sources.

The Nag-Hammadi collection also contains *The First Apocalypse of James*.[239] Here the entire focus is on revelation. James addresses questions to Jesus as "Rabbi" and receives back answers from "the Lord." It is fascinating to find in the Nag-Hammadi writings that James finds opposition not in Paul, but with Peter, in the other disciples or the Twelve. In *First Apocalypse of James*, James is told by the Lord to *leave* Jerusalem, "for it is the abiding place of a great number of Archons" (25), and at the end of the tractate, James rebukes the Twelve (42).

The dating of these gnostic writings is difficult. The codices as such were buried ca. 400 CE, so composition had to be earlier than that.[240] The earliest compositions in the collection can be dated to the middle of the second century,[241] with other tractates possibly dating from the third century. But it is abundantly clear that for some of the authors and compilers of this collection, James was esteemed as a Gnostic teacher and recipient of secret revelations from the Lord.

c. *The* Gospel of the Hebrews

The special place of James in the order of revelation also distinguishes the reference to him reported by Jerome (*De Viris Illustribus* 2). Jerome found the passage in the *Gospel of the Hebrews*, which probably originated in the early second century.[242] The passage is intriguing not only because it places James early (perhaps first) in the order of resurrection appearances, or because it has Jesus address him as "My Brother," but also because it suggests that James had been at the last supper with Jesus (thereby suggesting identity with James of Alphaeus?). Where did this text come from? It is apparently one of the "Jewish-Christian Gospels," but the precise delineation of those amorphous entities has

---

[239]See the translation in W. S. Schoedel, "The First Apocalypse of James," in *NHLE* 242–48.

[240]See the discussion in J. M. Robinson, "Introduction," *NHLE* 1–25.

[241]See R. MacL. Wilson, *Studies in the Gospel of Thomas* (London: A. R. Mowbray & Co., 1960) 7–11; G. W. MacRae, "The Gospel of Truth," in *NHLE* 37.

[242]See P. Vielhauer, "Jewish-Christian Gospels," in E. Hennecke, *New Testament Apocrypha*, ed. W. Schneemelcher, trans. R. MacL. Wilson (Philadelphia: Westminster Press, 1963) 1:163.

been difficult for scholars to accomplish.[243] If the fragments now attributed to the *Gospel of the Hebrews* represent "Jewish Christianity," then that phenomenon, as suggested already by the *Second Apocalypse of James*, must be broad enough to contain strong gnosticizing elements (see *frags.* 2, 4a, 4b).

d. Protevangelium of James

Also difficult to locate within the trajectories about James is the document now called the *Protevangelium of James*, dating possibly from the middle of the second century.[244] The "Gospel" concerns the miraculous birth, childhood, marriage, and maternity of Mary, which obsessive attention to her physical purity. It claims to be written by James, who withdrew from Jerusalem after the death of Herod (closer identification is not given) created a tumult (25:1). Nothing is learned from the document about James except that the author found him (as an older "Brother of the Lord" through an earlier marriage of Joseph, 9:2) to be a convenient scribe. Certainly, despite its studiously antiquarian attention to things "Hebrew," it shows little knowledge of a living Judaism, and is best considered a form of Christian encratite Romance.

e. Pseudo-Clementine Literature

The final body of literature in which James plays a role is, by far, also the most difficult to disentangle. A large collection of literature from early Christianity came to be associated with Clement of Rome. His epistle to the Corinthians, which was discussed earlier (*1 Clement*), is usually dated around 96 CE and considered to be authentic. The other writings attributed to him are regarded as inauthentic and are grouped together as *Clementine Literature*.

In the broad sense, the Clementine Literature includes *2 Clement* (a homily) and two *Letters to Virgins*. The designation *Pseudo-Clementines*, however, is usually used for a smaller collection, which includes two lengthy treatises, the *Recognitions* (in ten books) and the *Homilies* (in twenty discourses). The relationship between these two writings is itself complex, since they contain a shared narrative framework and overlapping incidents. Both contain a considerable amount of didactic material as well as narratives that resemble nothing so much as ancient Greco-Roman novels.[245]

Three shorter compositions are also part of the collection: an *Epistle of Peter*

---

[243]See the discussion in Vielhauer, "Jewish-Christian Gospels," *Hennecke-Schneemelcher* 1: 118–39.

[244]See O. Cullmann, "Protevangelium of James," in E. Hennecke, *New Testament Apocrypha*, ed. W. Schneemelcher, trans. R. MacL. Wilson (Philadelphia: Westminster Press, 1963) 1:370–88.

[245]For this characterization, see J. A. Fitzmyer, "The Qumran Scrolls, the Ebionites, and their Literature," *TS* 16 (1955) 345–46, and J. Irmscher, "The Pseudo-Clementines," in E. Hennecke, *New Testament Apocrypha*, ed W. Schneemelcher, trans. R. MacL. Wilson (Philadelphia: Westminster Press, 1963) 2:532.

to James, which exhorts James to keep the books containing Peter's preaching away from those who would misuse them; a *Contestatio* (or "attestation"), which contains the criteria for testing those worthy of being entrusted with Peter's books; and an *Epistle of Clement to James*, which relates how Peter, before his death as a martyr in Rome, had made Clement his successor as bishop.

As a whole, the collection antedates the Latin translation by Rufinus (before 410). The chaotic state of the material has encouraged the supposition that it contains earlier, perhaps considerably earlier, traditions. A great deal of effort has gone into the detection of sources (or the original *Grundschrift*) in this complex collection.[246] The efforts have necessarily had a speculative character and have led to uneven results.[247]

The main impulse for discovering sources within the *Pseudo-Clementines* is to find evidence of earlier traditions, above all concerning the shape of "Jewish-Christianity." The hope is supported by several aspects of the collection beyond its literary disjointedness.

1. Although Clement and his family's misadventures form the narrative thread, much of the material in the *Recognitions* and *Homilies* concerns Peter and James.

2. The form of Christianity reflected by these writings emphasizes continuity between Jesus, the "true prophet," and Torah.

3. The *Letter of Peter*, *Contestatio*, and *Letter of Clement* provide an ideological context in which the authority of Peter and James is asserted over against others who are considered to be in error. Specifically, Peter speaks of "some from among the Gentiles who have rejected my lawful preaching and have preferred a lawless and absurd doctrine of the man who is my enemy" and spells out that Peter does not support the "dissolution of the law." In other words, Peter is presented as the faithful representative of a nomistic "Jewish" Christianity.

4. Some sections of these works appear to oppose—in oblique and camouflaged fashion—Pauline Christianity. Thus, in that part of the *Recognitions* that some consider to have derived from an earlier document called *The Ascents of James*,[248] James stands at the head of the disciples on the

---

[246]For a review, see F. S. Jones, "The Pseudo-Clementines: A History of Research," *SecCent* 2 (1982) 1–33; 63–96.

[247]See J. Irmscher, "The Pseudo-Clementines," and G. Strecker, "The *Kerygmata Petrou*," In E. Hennecke, *New Testament Apocrypha*, ed. W. Schneemelcher, trans. R. MacL. Wilson (Philadelphia: Westminster, 1963) 2:102–27 and 2:532–70.

[248]Now available in a separate translation and analysis in R. E. Van Voorst, *The Ascents of James: History and Theology of a Jewish-Christian Community* (SBLDS 112; Atlanta: Scholars Press, 1989).

steps of the Temple, leading the debate against representative Jewish opponents. His preaching almost wins over the Jewish population (*Recognitions* I,33,3–I,69,8). But then "the hostile man"—which the subsequent narrative identifies as the pre-conversion Paul—disrupts the meeting with violence and almost kills James by throwing him from the steps of the Temple (I,70,1–I,71,6). Likewise, there are sections of the *Homilies* (II,16; XI,35; XVII,13–19) that contain Peter's polemic against "Simon Magus," which is taken by some readers to be a veiled attack on Paul.[249]

5. It has sometimes been assumed that the source material thus uncovered can be traced back to and reflect the outlook of that form of Jewish Christianity that is characterized as heretical and named as "Ebionites" by patristic writers,[250] especially since this group appeared to claim succession from the original Jerusalem church.[251]

It must be said, however, that the Pseudo-Clementine literature is so complex, the determination of its sources so contested, the dating of its evidence even in the best cases so late, and the character of its allegiances so indefinite, that only a series of extrapolations enable one to use this material as evidence for nascent Christianity.[252] More pertinently, what these writings tell us specifically about *James* in particular is remarkably little. What the Pseudo-Clementines illustrates best is how ideological and hagiographical impulses shaped the development of Christianity's eponymous heroes.

In summary, the extracanonical evidence concerning James the Brother of the Lord confirms that later generations perceived him as a leader of the church in Jerusalem, usually in company with others, especially Peter. His character is positively portrayed in terms of piety and righteousness. He is sometimes seen as having received special revelations from the Lord. He is recognized as a spokesperson by non-Christian Jews. The sources are not of such a character or consistency, however, to support notions that James was historically "the first

---

[249]See G. Strecker, *Das Judenchristentum in den Pseudoklementinen* (TU 70/5. 15; Berlin: Akademie Verlag, 1958) 187–96.

[250]See Justin, *Dialogue with Trypho*, 47; Irenaeus, *Against Heresies*, I,26,2; III,21,1; V,1,3; Tertullian, *De Praescriptione*, 33; Hippolytus, *Heresies*, VII,34; IX,13–17; Eusebius, *HE*, III,27; Epiphanius, *Heresies*, XXX.

[251]See G. Lüdemann, "The Successors of Pre-70 Jerusalem Christianity: A Critical Evaluation of the Pella Tradition," in *Jewish and Christian Self-Definition*, ed. E. P. Sanders (Philadelphia: Fortress Press, 1980) 1:161–73; M. Simon, "La Migration à Pella: Légende ou réalité?" *RSR* 60 (1972) 37–54.

[252]See L. Keck, ". . . there is insufficient reason for thinking that the Ebionite Literature, insofar as it is recoverable, reflects a continuous line of connection between the Ebionites and the hypothetical group calling itself 'the Poor' in Primitive Christianity," in "The Poor among the Saints in Jewish Christianity and Qumran," *ZNW* 57 (1966) 64–65.

pope"[253] or "caliph."[254] It is rather his death that receives the most attention and elaboration in the diverse strands of tradition.

It is worth noting as well that James is never said to sponsor any form of ritual observance, certainly not that of circumcision. He is never identified as an active opponent of Paul or Paul's mission. Only one source (the *Recognitions*) brings James into direct contact with Paul, and that is the preconversion "hostile man" who threw James from the steps of the Temple.

BIBLIOGRAPHY

Bauer, W., *Orthodoxy and Heresy in Earliest Christianity* 2nd ed. (1964), ed. G. Strecker; ed. and trans. R. A. Kraft and G. Krodel (Philadelphia: Fortress Press, 1971).

Baur, F. C., *Paul the Apostle of Jesus Christ* 2nd ed., ed E. Zeller, trans. A. Menzies (London: Williams and Norgate, 1875).

Bengel, J. A., *Gnomon Novi Testamenti* 7th ed. (Edinburgh: T & T Clark, 1877).

Betz, H. D., "The Literary Composition and Function of Paul's Letter to the Galatians," *NTS* 21 (1974–75) 353–73.

Böhlig, A., "Zum Martyrium des Jakobus," *NovT* 5 (1962) 207–13.

Burchard, C., "Gemeinde in der strohernen Epistel: Mutmassungen ueber Jakobus," *Kirche: Festschrift für Günther Bornkamm*, ed. D. Lührmann and G. Strecker (Tübingen: JCB Mohr [Paul H. von Siebeck] 1980) 315–28.

von Campenhausen, H., "Die Nachfolge des Jakobus: Zur Frage eines urchristlichen 'Kalifats'," *ZKG* 63 (1950/51) 134–44.

Carroll, K., "The Place of James in the Early Church," *BJRL* 44 (1961/2) 49–67.

Crossan, J. D., "Mark and the Relatives of Jesus," *NovT* 15 (1973) 81–113.

Cullmann, O., "Protevangelium of James," in E. Hennecke, *New Testament Apocrypha*, ed. W. Schneemelcher, trans. R. MacL. Wilson (Philadelphia: Westminster Press, 1963) 1:370–88.

Engelhardt, W., "Zur Frage ueber die Bruder des Herrn," *NKZ* 11 (1900) 833–65.

---

[253]See M. Hengel, "Jakobus der Herrenbruder—der erste 'Papst'?" in *Glaube und Eschatologie*, ed. E. Grässer and O. Merk (Tübingen: JCB Mohr [Paul Siebeck], 1985) 71–104.

[254]H. von Campenhausen, "Die Nachfolge des Jakobus: Zur Frage eines urchristlichen 'Kalifats'," *ZKG* 63 (1950/51) 134–44; E. Stauffer, "Zum Kalifat des Jakobus," *ZRGG* 4 (1952) 193–214; and ibid., "Petrus und Jakobus in Jerusalem," *Begegnung der Christen*, ed. M. Roesle and O. Cullmann (Stuttgart: Evangelische Verlagswerk, 1959) 361–72; P. Gächter, "Jakobus von Jerusalem," *ZKT* 76 (1954) 129–69.

Fitzmyer, J. A., "The Qumran Scrolls, the Ebionites, and their Literature," *TS* 16 (1955) 335–72.

Gächter, P., "Jakobus von Jerusalem," *ZKT* 76 (1954) 129–69.

Geyser, A. S., "The Letter of James and the Social Condition of His Addressees," *Neot* 9 (1975) 25–33.

Hedrick, C. H., "The Second Apocalypse of James," in *NHLE*, 249–55.

Hengel, M., "Jakobus der Herrenbruder—der erste 'Papst'?" in *Glaube und Eschatologie*, ed. E. Grässer and O. Merk (Tübingen: JCB Mohr [Paul Siebeck], 1985) 71–104.

Irmscher, J. "The Pseudo-Clementines," in E. Hennecke, *New Testament Apocrypha*, ed. W. Schneemelcher, trans. R. MacL. Wilson (Philadelphia: Westminster Press, 1963) 2:532–70.

Johnson, L. T., *The Acts of the Apostles* (Sacra Pagina 5; Collegeville: Liturgical Press, 1992).

Jones, F. S., "The Pseudo-Clementines: a History of Research," *SecCent* 2 (1982) 1–33; 63–96.

Keck, L., "The Poor among the Saints in Jewish Christianity and Qumran," *ZNW* 57 (1966) 54–78.

Kelber, W., *The Kingdom in Mark: A New Place and a New Time* (Philadelphia: Fortress Press, 1974).

Kern, F. H., *Der Character und Ursprung des Briefes Jakobi* (Tübingen: Fues, 1835).

Kümmel, W. C., *Introduction to the New Testament* rev. ed., trans. H. C. Kee (Nashville: Abingdon Press, 1975) 294–304.

Little, D. H., *The Death of James, the Brother of the Lord* (Ph.D. diss., Rice University, 1971).

Lüdemann, G., "The Successors of Pre-70 Jerusalem Christianity: A Critical Evaluation of the Pella Tradition," in *Jewish and Christian Self-Definition*, ed. E. P. Sanders (Philadelphia: Fortress Press, 1980) 1:161–73.

Lyonnet, S., "Témoignages de Saint Jean Chrysostome et de Saint Jerome sur Jacques le Frère du Seigneur," *RSR* 29 (1939) 335–51.

MacDonald, M. Y., *The Pauline Churches: A Socio-Historical Study of Institutionalization in the Pauline and Deutero-Pauline Writings* (SNTSMS 60; Cambridge: Cambridge University Press, 1988).

MacRae, G. W., "The Gospel of Truth," in *NHLE*, 37–49.

Mader, J., "Apostel und Herrenbrüder," *BZ* 6 (1908) 393–406.

Meier, J. P., *A Marginal Jew: Rethinking the Historical Jesus* (New York: Doubleday, 1991) 1:58–59, 72–73.

Munck, J., *Paul and the Salvation of Mankind*, trans. F. Clarke (Richmond: John Knox Press, 1959).

Polhill, J. B., "The Life-Situation of the Book of James," *Review and Expositor* 66 (1969) 369–78.

Popkes, W., *Addressaten, Situation und Form des Jakobusbriefes* Stuttgarter Bibelstudien 125/126; Stuttgart: Katholisches Bibelwerk, 1986).

Prentice, W. K., "James the Brother of the Lord," *Studies in Roman Economic and Social History,* ed. P. R. Coleman-Norton (Princeton: Princeton University Press, 1951) 144–51.

Schoedel, W. S., "The First Apocalypse of James," in *NHLE,* 242–48.

Schwartz, E., "Zu Eusebius Kirchengeschichte," *ZNW* 4 (1903) 48–66.

Simon, M., "La migration à Pella: légende ou réalité?" *RSR* 60 (1972) 37–54.

Stauffer, E., "Petrus und Jakobus in Jersualem, *Begegnung der Christen,* ed. M. Roesle and O. Cullmann (Stuttgart: Evangelische Verlagswerk, 1959) 361–72.

Stauffer, E., "Zum Kalifat des Jakobus," *ZRGG* 4 (1952) 193–214.

Strecker, G., *Das Judenchristentum in den Pseudoklementinen* (TU 70/5.15; Berlin: Akademie Verlag, 1958).

Strecker, G., "The *Kerygmatou Petrou,*" in E. Hennecke, *New Testament Apocrypha,* ed. W. Schneemelcher, trans. R. MacL. Wilson (Philadelphia: Westminster Press, 1963) 2: 532–70.

Talbert, C. H., *What Is a Gospel? The Genre of the Canonical Gospels* (Philadelphia: Fortress Press, 1977).

Trocmé, E., *The Formation of the Gospel according to Mark,* trans. P. Gaughan (Philadelphia: Westminster Press, 1975).

Van Voorst, R. E., *The Ascents of James: History and Theology of a Jewish-Christian Community* (SBLDS 112; Atlanta: Scholars Press, 1989).

Vielhauer, P., "Jewish Christian Gospels," in E. Hennecke, *New Testament Apocrypha,* ed. W. Schneemelcher, trans. R. MacL. Wilson (Philadelphia: Westminster Press, 1963) 1:118–39.

Weeden, T., *Mark, Traditions in Conflict* (Philadelphia: Fortress Press, 1971).

Williams, A. L., "The Epistle of James and the Jewish Christians of his Time," *CQR* 123 (1937) 24–32.

Williams, F. E., "The Apocryphon of James," in *NHLE,* 29–36.

Wilson, R. MacL., *Studies in the Gospel of Thomas* (London: A. R. Mowbray & Co., 1960).

B. THEORIES OF AUTHORSHIP

Arguments concerning the authorship of James put together the pieces of evidence in different ways. The strong position taken by the Tübingen School has proven remarkably influential. F. C. Baur's analysis of Christianity's development in terms of theological conflict between Gentile Christianity (represented by Paul) and Jewish Christianity (represented by Peter) was based on a specific judgment concerning sources. The number of Paul's letters viewed as authentic is restricted, which meant that his theological vision can be portrayed in simpler terms. The Acts of the Apostles is dated late and deemed worthless as a historical source except as its tendentiousness, properly assessed, yields a "truer" picture of events concerning Paul.[255] Galatians, 1 Corinthians, and 2 Corinthians are read in terms of a theological battle waged by Paul against a unified opposition. Finally, the *Pseudo-Clementines* are granted considerable historical value.

The effect of dismissing Acts and replacing it with the *Pseudo-Clementines* is dramatic. The hostility shown by (parts of) these writings toward (purportedly) Paul is taken as a faithful representation of the attitudes of the *original* Jewish Christianity of Jerusalem during the time of Paul. Baur declares, "The Ebionites are generally regarded as mere heretics, but their connection with the original Jewish Christianity is unmistakable. Thus, their view of the apostle Paul is no isolated phenomenon."[256]

Actually, the demands of Baur's Hegelian dialectic allows for only two parties standing in opposition. James represents something of an embarrassment to the system. Baur can call the "men from James" in Gal 2:12 Paul's "declared foes and opponents,"[257] but he is very circumspect about attributing Paul's troubles in Galatia directly to James—even though Paul's opponents there do represent the James party.[258] The theory, however, requires folding the party of James into the "party of Peter" for purposes of consistency.[259]

Another embarrassment for the theory is that the canonical Letter of James offers no basis for a direct attack on Paul by James, above all not one in which James is advocating circumcision. Baur seizes on the solution offered by his colleague H. F. Kern[260] and reads James as a pseudonymous production of a "catholicizing" character.[261] Although incompatible with Paul on the teaching of justification by faith,[262] James is not to be taken as a direct reflection of the "Jewish Christianity" that was hostile to Paul.

The overall weaknesses of the Tübingen School have frequently been noted.[263] Its strength, and the clue to its persistent influence long after its

---

[255]F. C. Baur, *Paul, the Apostle of Jesus Christ* 2nd ed., ed. E. Zeller, trans. A. Menzies (London: Williams and Norgate, 1875) 1:110–21; 125–26, n. 1; 129.

[256]F. C. Baur, *The Church History of the First Three Centuries* 3rd ed., trans. A. Menzies (London: Williams and Norgate, 1878) 1:90.

[257]See Baur, *Paul*, 1:203.

[258]Baur, *Paul*, 1:250–57.

[259]Baur, *Paul*, 1:265, 277.

[260]F. H. Kern, *Der Character und Ursprung des Briefes Jakobi* (Tübingen: Fues, 1835) 24–36.

[261]Baur, *Church History*, 1:128–30.

[262]Baur, *Paul*, 2:297–313.

[263]See, e.g., H. Harris, *The Tübingen School* (Oxford: Clarendon Press, 1975) 249–62; S. Neill, *The Interpretation of the New Testament, 1861–1961* (London: Oxford University Press, 1964) 33–60; W. G. Kümmel, *The New Testament: The History of the Investigation of Its Problems*, trans. A. M. Gilmour and H. C. Kee (Nashville: Abingdon Press, 1972) 120–205.

specific theories were disproven, lay in its simplicity. Some scholars continue to read the historical relationship between James and Paul in terms of hostile opposition.[264] Only rarely is this position attached to the actual Letter of James. The position of M. Hengel, who dates the letter early, considers it authentic, and reads it precisely as a sustained (if sometimes indirect) polemic against Paul's theology and missionary practice, is unusual.[265]

The opposite position is represented by J. B. Mayor. He also considers James as early, as authentic, and as in dialogue with Paul. But he reverses the order of the conversation. Instead of seeing James as a response to Paul, Mayor argues that Paul responds to James. Mayor sees James as writing before the apostolic council; his epistle may even inadvertently have created some of the difficulties that erupted in Antioch. Mayor sees Paul's letters to the Romans and Galatians as elaborate responses to James' letter. He argues that it is more likely for Paul—out in the mission field—to have read a circular letter from James, than it was for James to have read a letter Paul wrote to the province of Galatia. Furthermore, given their respective positions of authority in the first generation (fully acknowledged by Paul in Galatians), Paul had more need to clarify his position than James did. Mayor further thinks that Paul does not fundamentally disagree with James, but has a different emphasis within a shared view.[266] One need not agree with Mayor to see that he is persuasive at least on one point. If James and Paul are to be read in light of each other, it is certainly as plausible to have Paul reading James as James (or pseudo-James) reading Paul.

The more consistent tendency in scholarship, however, has been, when the two authors are considered together, to regard Paul as the stimulus and James as the reponse. And since most careful readers correctly fail to see anything resembling a "Judaizing" position in James, they conclude, with Baur, that the letter is pseudonymous and responsive to some later and perhaps distorted version of Paulinism.[267] The letter is, therefore, read not as an attack on Paul but rather as a defense of Paul's real intentions against a libertinist deviation.[268]

The most troublesome aspect of most theories of authorship and provenance,

---

[264]See, e.g., M. Hengel, *Acts and the History of Earliest Christianity*, trans. J. Bowden (Philadelphia: Fortress Press, 1979) 112–26; P. J. Achtemeier, *The Quest for Unity in the New Testament Church* (Philadelphia: Fortress, 1987) 58–61.

[265]See M. Hengel, "Jakobusbrief als antipaulinische Polemik," in *Tradition and Interpretation in the New Testament*, ed. G. F. Hawthorne and O. Betz (Grand Rapids: Eerdmans, 1987) 248–78.

[266]See Mayor, xci–cii, clxxxiii–clxxxviii; for a similar argument for the priority of James to Paul, see C. Powell, " 'Faith' in James and its Bearings on the Problem of the Date of the Epistle," *ExpT* 62 (1950–51) 311–14.

[267]Baur, *The Church History*, 1:128–30; See also H.-J. Schoeps, *Theologie und Geschichte des Judenchristentums* (Tübingen: JCB Mohr [Paul Siebeck], 1949) 343–49; H. Schammberger, *Die Einheitlichkeit des Jakobusbriefes im antignostischen Kampf* (Gotha: Klotz, 1936).

[268]This position is classically and succinctly stated by J. Jeremias, "Paul and James," *ExpT* 66 (1954/55) 368–71; see also G. Eichholz, "Jakobusbrief," *Evangelisches Kirchenlexicon*, ed. H. Brunotte and O. Weber (Göttingen: Vandenhoeck & Ruprecht, 1958) 234–35.

whether conservative or liberal, has been the insistence on reading James and Paul in tandem. Even Dibelius' influential commentary, which rightly seeks to distance itself from the error "of thinking that Paul influenced every branch of Christianity," and does everything possible to portray James as a free-floating pseudonymous repository of wisdom traditions, fails to escape the Pauline connection completely when it declares that James 2:14–26 cannot be understood without presupposing "not only Paul's formulation of the question about the Law but also the resolution of Paul's struggles regarding the Law."[269]

C. Loosening the Pauline Connection

The most unfortunate thing about the continuing influence of the Tübingen model is that it forces a reading of James and Paul solely in relation to each other, to the distortion of both. Some 12 out of James' 108 verses are taken as the key to the composition's meaning and purpose. These twelve verses are measured against an (equally narrow and distorted) construal of Pauline theology. The fixation prevents the appreciation of each author in his own right and clouds the wide range of language and perception that they share beyond the narrow issue of faith and works.

Why then does this continue to be the angle from which James is approached? Partly because of the appeal of simplicity. It is easier to deal with the simplified if distorted version of the evidence than the messiness of all the data. A second reason is the historical and theological bias still very influential in NT scholarship, which sees Paul not only as the first of our extant Christian witnesses but also as the most important. Indeed, Luther's preference for Paul and dismissal of James (to be discussed in section III, below) is still active in those scholars who make Paul the measure of authentic Christianity.[270]

No real progress can be made in the historical reconstruction of earliest Christianity or in the theological appreciation of its diverse canonical witnesses until the Pauline connection is loosened. The time is overdue for the advances of scholarship across a wide range of issues to be brought to bear on this point as

---

[269]Dibelius, 17–18.

[270]The attitude is so pervasive that it scarcely requires demonstration, but it can be observed, e.g., in Bultmann's *Theology of the New Testament* (New York: Charles Scribner's Sons, 1955) 2:131, devoting this single sentence to James: "And can the treatment of the theme 'faith and works' in Jas 2:14–26 be understood in any other way than that it is a debate against misunderstood ideas of Paul?" See also the need for W. G. Kümmel to discuss the "theological problem" presented by the "irreconcilable conflict between James and Paul," in his *Introduction to the New Testament* rev. ed., trans. H. C. Kee (Nashville: Abingdon, 1975) 414–16; also the conclusion by M. Hengel, "Providentia Dei hat die frühe Kirche in Paulus, nicht in Jakobus *den apostolos* gesehen," in "Der Jakobusbrief als antipaulinische Polemik," 264.

well. Here are some of the considerations that invite viewing James in a fresh light:

1. The *Pseudo-Clementine Literature* must definitively be put aside as a source for reconstructing Christian origins. Its late dating and its ideological and hagiographical shaping of characters must be regarded as disqualifying. Above all, the premise that the Ebionites had a "real connection with original Jewish Christianity"[271] should be abandoned. The discovery of the Nag-Hammadi library has shown how the figure of James could be developed in quite a different direction: in those writings, James does not oppose Paul, but the other disciples. Our later sources, in other words, show us diverse trajectories of interpretation concerning James: a) the Orthodox/Hierarchical (Clement/Hegesippus/Eusebius); b) the Gnostic/Revelatory (Clement/Nag-Hammadi/Gospel of the Hebrews); and c) the Ebionite/Hierarchical (the Pseudo-Clementines). None of these has more claim to be historical than the others. None has any claim to greater historical veracity than the canonical writings.

2. Once the legendary character of *all* later traditions is recognized, then the canonical sources also require a more neutral reassessment. Recent research has demonstrated that Acts cannot simply be dismissed as late and tendentious.[272] That Paul's letters are firsthand sources, however, does not guarantee the factual character of their content; his positions are very much shaped by purposeful rhetoric.[273] When these sources are considered dispassionately, they are found to have far more agreement than disagreement concerning the relationship between Paul and the Jerusalem church. The theory of a Hebrew/Hellenist split in the early period, which developed into two separate forms of Christianity—a theory heavily dependent on the construal of the figure of Stephen in Acts 6–7[274]—is not supported by the evidence. Instead, on the basis both of Acts and Galatians, the Jerusalem church is seen as in fundamental agreement with Paul,[275] and James is seen as fundamentally an ally of Paul.[276]

---

[271]Baur, *The Church History* 1:90; Schoeps, *Theologie*, 69.

[272]Among other studies, see C. J. Hemer, *The Book of Acts in the Setting of Hellenistic History* (WUNT 49; Tübingen: JCB Mohr [Paul Siebeck], 1989); G. Lüdemann, *Early Christianity according to the Traditions in Acts: A Commentary* (Minneapolis: Fortress Press, 1989).

[273]See, e.g., the diverse examinations of Paul's rhetoric in 1 Corinthians by E. A. Castelli, *Imitating Paul: A Discourse of Power* (Louisville: Westminster/John Knox Press, 1991); M. M. Mitchell, *Paul and the Rhetoric of Reconciliation* (Louisville: Westminster/John Knox Press, 1991); and A. C. Wire, *The Corinthian Women Prophets: A Reconstruction through Paul's Rhetoric* (Minneapolis: Fortress Press, 1990).

[274]See, e.g., M. Hengel, *Acts and the History of Earliest Christianity*, trans. J. Bowden (Philadelphia: Fortress Press, 1979) 71–80.

[275]See C. C. Hill, *Hellenists and Hebrews: Reappraising Division within the Earliest Church* (Minneapolis: Fortress Press, 1992) 143–47.

[276]Hill, *Hellenists and Hebrews*, 183–92.

3. The overall complexity of Christian origins as reflected in both its canonical and noncanonical writings needs to be taken with full seriousness. It is inappropriate to divide the earliest movement into the (anachronistic and value-laden) categories of orthodox and heretical. Instead, a more comprehensive model is required, one that avoids both the myth of primordial unity and the myth of all-consuming internecine conflict. Just as first-century Judaism had many voices debating claims to represent the authentic version of God's people, and "normative Judaism" is the result of such debates rather than their premise,[277] so earliest Christianity began in a vigorous variety out of which an eventually explicit unity emerged.[278]

4. Scholarship devoted to the religious phenomenon called "Gnosticism" has recognized what a bewildering complexity of literature and outlook that term covers[279] and progressively focuses on different *varieties* of gnostic literature, without measuring the validity of one over another.[280] In the same way, scholarship is increasingly recognizing the complexity hidden beneath the designation "Jewish Christianity." Efforts at definition and classification abound and demonstrate how impossible it is to work any longer with the connections assumed by the Tübingen School.[281] Each segment of "Jewish Christianity" must be analyzed on its own terms.[282]

5. The recognition of diversity does not require a conflict model to make sense of earliest Christianity. That the first Christians fell into frequent conflict is obvious from their writings. But great caution must be exercised in analyzing such signs of conflicts:

---

[277]See L. T. Johnson, "The New Testament's Anti-Jewish Slander and the Conventions of Ancient Polemic," *JBL* 108 (1989) 419–41.

[278]See G. W. MacRae, "Why the Church rejected Gnosticism," in *Jewish and Christian Self-Definition* Vol 1: *The Shaping of Christianity in the Second and Third Century*, ed. E. P. Sanders (Philadelphia: Fortress Press, 1980) 127; also, L. T. Johnson, *The Writings of the New Testament: An Interpretation* (Philadelphia: Fortress Press, 1986) 530–51, and A. Hultgren, *The Rise of Normative Christianity* (Minneapolis: Fortress Press, 1994).

[279]See, e.g., the struggle to find an appropriate protocol for designating various "gnosticoid" tendencies in *Le Origini dello Gnosticismo*, ed. U. Bianchi (Leiden: Brill, 1967).

[280]See, e.g., the essays devoted respectively to "Sethian" and "Valentinian" versions of Gnosticism in *The Rediscovery of Gnosticism* 2 Vols, ed. B. Layton (Leiden: Brill, 1980–81).

[281]In addition to H.-J. Schoeps, *Theologie und Geschichte des Judenchristentums* (Tübingen: JCB Mohr [Paul Siebeck], 1949), and J. Danielou, *Théologie du Judaeo-Christianisme* (Bibliothèque de Théologie; Tournai: Desclée et Cie., 1958), see G. Strecker, *"On the Problem of Jewish Christianity,"* Appendix 1 in W. Bauer, *Orthodoxy and Heresy in Earliest Christianity*, ed. and trans. R. A. Kraft and G. Krodel (Philadelphia: Fortress Press, 1971) 241–85; J. Munck, "Jewish Christianity in Post-Apostolic Times," *NTS* 6 (1959–60) 103–16; A. F. J. Klijn, "The Study of Jewish Christianity," *NTS* 20 (1973–74) 419–31; R. A. Kraft, "In Search of 'Jewish Christianity' and its 'Theology': Problems of Definition and Methodology," *RSR* 60 (1972) 81–92; S. K. Riegel, "Jewish Christianity: Definitions and Terminology," *NTS* 24 (1978) 410–15.

[282]See R. E. Brown, "Not Jewish Christianity and Gentile Christianity but Types of Jewish/Gentile Christianity," *CBQ* 45 (1983) 74–79.

a. Not every difference found in our sources equals a contradiction, nor does every contradiction necessarily play itself out in political struggle. It is in principle important to assert that James could have held a different theology than Paul, without necessarily also asserting that James was against Paul's mission.

b. It is impossible to construct a "unified field theory" adequate to such early Christian conflicts that we find reflected in the texts. They involved a variety of characters and issues and are irreducible to simplistic ideological divisions.

c. Analysis cannot assume that Paul or James knew about each other what subsequent readers of their texts knew about them and their ideas. Earliest Christianity was not the University of Berlin or the University of Tübingen in the nineteenth century, a world in which the ideas were what counted and where every debater read and knew everyone else's positions.

d. Even more, analysis should avoid an anachronistic reading back into such differences and debates later theological position-taking on the basis of those texts. Centuries of Augustinian and Lutheran theology should no more be imported into Paul's letters than the Tridentine understanding of faith and works should be read into James.

6. On the basis of such clarifications, it should be possible to make some real headway. James can be regarded as "Jewish Christian" without imposing on the letter what that "had to mean." Rather, the letter can be taken as an important source for the range of things that designation "might mean." Similarly, the complexity of Paul's letters need not be reduced to a single theological principle that is the standard for all Gentile Christianity. The way is clear to discover aspects of Paul otherwise covered over by presuppositions. Careful literary comparison shows just how wide a range of agreement there is between these two authors (see above, pp. 58–64). Where they appear (from our perspective) to disagree (James 2:14–26), the disagreement is at least partially due to the presupposition we bring that they are debating a single issue. In fact, they are dealing with quite separate issues, but with a language shaped by a shared symbolic world. In other words, it is because both Paul and James derive their symbols from a Palestinian Jewish milieu that their language and examples converge.

7. The most important gain from breaking the Pauline fixation is that it liberates James to be read in terms of 108 verses rather than 12 verses, in terms of its own voice rather than in terms of its supposed muting of Paul's voice.

BIBLIOGRAPHY

Achtemeier, P. J., *The Quest for Unity in the New Testament Church* (Philadelphia: Fortress Press, 1987).

Baur, F. C., *Paul, the Apostle of Jesus Christ* 2nd ed., ed. E. Zeller, trans. A. Menzies (London: Williams and Norgate, 1875).

————, *The Church History of the First Three Centuries* 3rd ed., trans. A. Menzies (London: Williams and Norgate, 1878).

Bianchi, U., *Le Origini dello Gnosticismo* (Leiden: Brill, 1967).

Brown, R. E., "Not Jewish Christianity and Gentile Christianity but Types of Jewish/Gentile Christianity," *CBQ* 45 (1983) 74–79.

Bultmann, R., *Theology of the New Testament* 2 Vols (New York: Charles Scribners' Sons, 1953–55).

Castelli, E., *Imitating Paul: A Discourse of Power* (Louisville: Westminster/John Knox Press, 1991).

Danielou, J., *Théologie du Judaeo-Christianisme* (Bibliothèque de Théologie; Tournai: Desclée et Cie., 1958).

Harris, H., *The Tübingen School* (Oxford: Clarendon Press, 1975).

Hemer, C. J., *The Book of Acts in the Setting of Hellenistic History* (WUNT 49; Tübingen: JCB Mohr [Paul Siebeck], 1989).

Hengel, M., *Acts and the History of Earliest Christianity*, trans. J. Bowden (Philadelphia: Fortress Press, 1979).

————, "Jakobusbrief als antipaulinische Polemik," *Tradition and Interpretation in the New Testament*, ed. G. F. Hawthorne and O. Betz (Grand Rapids: Eerdmans, 1987) 248–78.

Hill, C. C., *Hellenists and Hebrews: Reappraising Division within the Earliest Church* (Minneapolis: Fortress Press, 1992).

Jeremias, J., "Paul and James," *ExpT* 66 (1954–55) 368–71.

Johnson, L. T., "The New Testament's Anti-Jewish Slander and the Conventions of Ancient Polemic," *JBL* 108 (1989) 419–41.

Kern, F. H., *Der Character und Ursprung des Briefes des Jakobi* (Tübingen: Fues, 1835).

Klijn, A. F. J., "The Study of Jewish Christianity," *NTS* 20 (1973–74) 419–31.

Kraft, R. A., "In Search of 'Jewish Christianity' and its 'Theology:' Problems of Definition and Methodology," *RSR* 60 (1972) 81–92.

Kümmel, W. G., *Introduction to the New Testament* rev. ed., trans. H. C. Kee (Nashville: Abingdon, 1975).

————, *The New Testament: The History of the Investigation of its Problems*, trans. A. M. Gilmour and H. C. Kee (Nashville: Abingdon Press, 1972).

Layton, B., ed., *The Rediscovery of Gnosticism* 2 Vols (Leiden: Brill, 1980–81).

Lüdemann, G., *Early Christianity according to the Traditions in Acts: A Commentary* (Minneapolis: Fortress Press, 1989).

Mitchell, M. M., *Paul and the Rhetoric of Reconciliation* (Louisville: Westminster/John Knox Press, 1991).

Munck, J., "Jewish Christianity in Post-Apostolic Times," *NTS* 6 (1959–60) 103–16.

Neill, S., *The Interpretation of the New Testament, 1861–1961* (London: Oxford University Press, 1964).

Powell, C. H., " 'Faith' in James and its Bearings on the Problem of the Date of the Epistle," *ExpT* 62 (1950–51) 311–14.

Riegel, S. K., "Jewish Christianity: Definitions and Terminology," *NTS* 24 (1978) 410–15.

Schoeps, H.-J., *Theologie und Geschichte des Judenchristentums* (Tübingen: JCB Mohr [Paul Siebeck], 1949).

Strecker, G., "On the Problem of Jewish Christianity," in W. Bauer, *Orthodoxy and Heresy in Earliest Christianity*, ed. R. A. Kraft and G. Krodel (Philadelphia: Fortress Press, 1971) 241–85.

Wire, A. C., *The Corinthian Women Prophets: A Reconstruction through Paul's Rhetoric* (Minneapolis: Fortress Press, 1990).

D. THE QUESTION OF LANGUAGE

Before taking up the positive reasons for considering James to be early and quite possibly authentic, a final objection to that theory must be dealt with, namely the issue of language. Our analysis of James' voice in the first part of this introduction began with the recognition that the composition's diction and rhetoric were among the most elevated in the NT. For some, that fact above all has proven decisive in disqualifying James of Jerusalem as the author.[283] A member of Jesus' family from Galilee, it is supposed, could not have been capable of composing the letter.[284]

Even those inclined on other grounds to date the letter early or view it as deriving from James, hesitate on the issue of language. Some adopt a compromise position: James the Brother of the Lord is the source of the traditions in the letter, or even an Aramaic original,[285] but the present Greek version is owed to redaction by a more sophisticated writer, a theory marginally in line with Jerome's characterization in *De Viris Illustribus* 2, that the letter was "edited by someone else under his name."[286]

---

[283]See, e.g., W. G. Kümmel, *Introduction to the New Testament*, 406; Windisch, 3; Ropes, 50.

[284]See Dibelius, 17: "Nor does the language of our text point to an author who spent his life as a Jew in Palestine. The author writes Greek as his mother tongue . . . any hypothesis that the Greek is a translation is untenable." See also Baasland, "Literarische Form," 3676.

[285]The earliest version of this theory appears to be that of Faber (first name not given) in *Observationes in epistolam Jacobi ex Syro* (Coburg, 1770), according to W. G. Schmidt, *Der Lehrgehalt des Jacobus-briefes: Ein Beitrag zur neutestamentlichen Theologie* (Leipzig: Hinrichs, 1869) 10. See also J. Wordsworth, "The Corbey St. James (ff) and its Relation to Other Latin Versions, and to the Original Language of the Epistle," in *Studia Biblica: Essays in Biblical Archeology and Criticism*, ed. S. R. Driver et al. (Oxford: Clarendon Press, 1885) 113–50; S. C. Agourides, "The Origin of the Epistle of St. James: Suggestions for a Fresh Approach," *GOTR* 9 (1963) 67–78.

[286]Even J. B. Mayor, who provides impressive evidence for his own conclusion that James wrote himself in Greek (cclxv), concedes that he could have been helped by a "hellenist brother in revising his epistle" (cclxv). See similarly, G. Kittel, "Der geschichtliche Ort des Jakobusbriefes," *ZNW* 41

There is, however, no need to invoke an amanuensis or deny authenticity on the basis of language. The entire thrust of recent research has been to demonstrate how pervasive and long-standing was the Hellenization of Palestine, shown above all by the use of the Greek language.[287] If this is the case in Judaea,[288] it is even more so in Galilee, with cities such as Sepphoris representing a splendid fusion of Greek and Jewish influences.[289] J. N. Sevenster, in particular, devoted himself to discovering whether the level of Greek found in James could be accounted for in Palestine and answered resoundingly in the affirmative.[290] Galilee, in fact, produced more than its share of distinguished Greek philosophers, rhetoricians, and historians.[291]

Judaism within Palestine, furthermore, produced an extensive literature at once deeply committed to the symbols of Torah yet intensely interactive with Greek culture.[292] Even from the heart of Jewish resistance to Roman rule letters were sent from Bar Kochba, written in Greek and sharing with James the typical Greek epistolary Greeting.[293] There is every reason to think, moreover, that the family of Jesus would have some acquaintance with Greek culture.[294] Finally, there is also the strong likelihood that the first Christian community in Jerusalem

---

(1942) 79; W. Barclay, *The Letters of James and Peter* (Philadelphia: Westminster Press, 1976) 33; Mussner, 8; Mitton, 232; Davids, 22. This approach has been adopted by R. P. Martin, "The Life-Setting of the Epistle of James in the Light of Jewish History," *Biblical and Near Eastern Studies: Essays in Honor of W. S. LaSor*, ed. G. A. Tuttle (Grand Rapids: Eerdmans, 1977) 97–103, and the theory of "two layered stages in the production of the letter" is used in his commentary (Martin, lxx, lxxvii).

[287]See M. Hengel, *Judaism and Hellenism* 2 Vols, trans. J. Bowden (Philadelphia: Fortress Press, 1974) 1:58–106; S. Lieberman, *Greek in Jewish Palestine. Studies in the Life and Manners of Jewish Palestine in the II–IV Centuries CE* (New York: Jewish Theological Seminary of America, 1942); G. Mussies, "Greek in Palestine and the Diaspora," *The Jewish People in the First Century* 2 Vols, ed. S. Safrai et al. (CRINT 1.1; Philadelphia: Fortress Press, 1987) 2:1040–64; J. Barr, "Hebrew, Aramaic and Greek in the Hellenistic Period," in *The Cambridge History of Judaism* Vol 2: *The Hellenistic Age*, ed. W. D. Davies and L. Finkelstein (London: Cambridge University Press, 1989) 79–114.

[288]See M. Hengel, *The "Hellenization" of Judaea in the First Century after Christ*, trans. J. Bowden (London: SCM Press, 1989).

[289]See, e.g., E. Meyers, E. Netzer, C. L. Meyers, "Sepphoris, Ornament of all Galilee," BA 49 (1986) 4–19; S. Freyne, *Galilee from Alexander the Great to Hadrian: A Study in Second Temple Judaism* (Wilmington: Glazier/Notre Dame University Press, 1980) 122–34.

[290]J. N. Sevenster, *Do You Know Greek? How Much Greek Could the First Jewish Christians have Known?* (NovTSup 19; Leiden: Brill, 1968), esp. 3–21.

[291]See Mayor, lx–lxi; G. H. Rendall, *The Epistle of St. James and Judaic Christianity* (Cambridge: Cambridge University Press, 1927) 39.

[292]See N. Walter, "Jewish-Greek Literature of the Greek Period," in *The Cambridge History of Judaism* Vol 2: *The Hellenistic Age*, ed. W. D. Davies and L. Finkelstein (London: Cambridge University Press, 1989) 385–408; and Michael Stone, ed., *Jewish Writings of the Second Temple Period* (CRINT 2.2; Philadelphia: Fortress Press, 1984).

[293]See M. Hengel, "Jakobusbrief als antipaulinische Polemik," 251.

[294]Compare the careful discussion in J. P. Meier, *A Marginal Jew: Rethinking the Historical Jesus* Vol 1: *The Roots of the Problem and the Person* (New York: Doubleday, 1991) 255–68, and A. W. Argyle, "Greek among the Jews of Palestine in New Testament Times," *NTS* 20 (1973–74) 87–89.

was itself at least bilingual if not exclusively Greek-speaking from the beginning.[295] There is, in short, no linguistic reason why James of Jerusalem could not have written this letter.

No support for authenticity is offered, however, by the convergence of language between this letter and the statements attributed to James in Acts 15:13–21 or the letter attributed to the Jerusalem leadership in Acts 15:23–29.[296] The use of *chairein* (James 1:1 = Acts 15:23) is found everywhere, while *agapētoi* (James 1:16, 19, 2:5 = Acts 15:25) and *adelphoi* (James 1:2 = Acts 15:13) are part of the early Christian argot (see above). Both James and Acts draw from the symbolic world of the LXX in their shared use of *episkeptomai* (James 1:27 = Acts 15:14) and *epistrephein* (James 5:19–20 = Acts 15:19). The most striking coincidence is found in the expression *epikeklētai to onoma mou ep' autous* (Acts 15:17) and *to kalon onoma to epiklēthen eph' hymas* (James 2:7), which again may best be explained on the basis of the shared background in the LXX (Amos 9:11–12).

If there is nothing in the composition's language or ideology that prevents its having been written by a Christian leader of the first generation from Jerusalem, are there also positive reasons for arguing its early date and Palestinian provenance?

E. REASONS FOR EARLY DATING

The analysis of James' "voice" in the first part of this introduction authorizes a number of observations that tend to support the hypothesis of an early dating for this letter.

1. James lacks any of the classic signs of late, pseudonymous authorship, according to the criteria used by those interested in placing the NT writings in a developmental line. There is no fictional elaboration either of the author's identity or authority, such as are found in many pseudonymous works.[297] There is no rationalization for the "delay of the parousia," no elaborate doctrinal development, no understanding of tradition as "deposit" rather than process, no attacks on doctrinal deviance, no elaborate institutional structure.[298]

---

[295]See L. Cerfaux's 1939 essay arguing precisely this: "La première communauté en Jérusalem," in *Recueil Lucien Cerfaux* (Biblioteca Ephemeridum Theologicarum Lovaniensium VI–VII; Gembloux: J. Duculot, 1954), 2:125–56, esp. 153–56.

[296]Contra Mayor, iii–v; Adamson, 20; J. A. T. Robinson, *Redating the New Testament* (Philadelphia: Westminster Press, 1976) 130.

[297]See, e.g., L. R. Donelson, *Pseudepigraphy and Ethical Argument in the Pastoral Letters* (Tübingen: JCB Mohr [Paul Siebeck], 1986) 23–54.

[298]By listing these "criteria," I do not mean to imply that I subscribe to them. My argument is simply that, even if these marks of "development" are accepted, James lacks them. For examples of

2. James reflects the social realities and outlooks appropriate to a sect in the early stages of its life.[299] As we have shown, it is entirely concerned with morals rather than the manners of the dominant culture. Its system of values profoundly challenges that of the dominant culture. It reflects a sense of oppression and persecution by outsiders. This is accompanied by an active sense of imminent judgment. The composition shows no interest, furthermore, in sexual morality, or the ethics of marriage, or domestic arrangements. The simple institutional structure (elders and teachers) and activities of the community (judging cases [2:1–4]; assisting the needy [2:14–17]; teaching [3:1–2]; praying and singing [5:13]; anointing the sick [5:14]; practicing mutual confession and correction [5:16, 19]) suggest a face to face *ecclesia* with intense bonds of social solidarity rather than a highly evolved organization

3. Every careful reader of James has noted its proximity to the spirit of Jesus' teaching and its obvious use of the tradition of Jesus' sayings (see above). The fact that the actual shape of the sayings in James is closer to that associated with the hypothetical gospel source called Q than to the redacted versions in the Synoptics has also been observed.[300] The dominant scholarly position that holds James to be late and pseudonymous, however, has delayed taking James into account when analyzing Q and speculating about its role in early Christianity. Yet the very elements that are taken to be distinctive of Q, and therefore of early Palestinian Christianity in close contact with the Jesus movement, namely an emphasis on wisdom and prophecy within the context of eschatological judgment,[301] are also defining aspects of James.

It is somewhat startling, then, to find works emphasizing the wisdom character of Q and its placement within early Palestinian Christianity

---

how such criteria (not always explicitly named) function for the placement of writings, see H. von Campenhausen, *Ecclesiastical Authority and Spiritual Power in the Church of the First Three Centuries*, trans. J. Baker (Stanford: Stanford University Press, 1969); J. Brosch, *Charismen und Ämter in der Urkirche* (Bonn: P. Hanstein, 1951); H. Conzelmann, *History of Primitive Christianity*, trans. J. Steely (Nashville: Abingdon, 1973); and above all, R. Bultmann, *Theology of the New Testament* 2 Vols, trans. K. Grobel (New York: Charles Scribner's Sons, 1953–55) 2:95–236.

[299]For a discussion of the varieties of "sects" according to their views of the outside world and their techniques for group maintenance, see B. R. Wilson, "A Typology of Sects," in *Sociology of Religion: Selected Readings*, ed. R. Robertson (Baltimore: Penguin Books, 1969) 361–83; in his typology, James would most resemble a "utopian" sect.

[300]See Ropes, 39: "James was in religious ideas nearer to the men who collected the sayings of Jesus than to the authors of the Gospels." For a review of scholarship on Q, see F. Neirynck, "Recent Developments in the Study of Q," in *Logia: The Sayings of Jesus*, ed. J. Delobel (Bibliotheca Ephemeridum Theologicarum Lovaniensium 59; Leuven: University Press, 1982) 29–75; J. S. Kloppenburg, ed., *The Shape of Q: Signal Essays on the Sayings Gospel* (Minneapolis: Fortress Press, 1994).

[301]See, e.g., R. A. Edwards, *A Theology of Q: Eschatology, Prophecy, and Wisdom* (Philadelphia: Fortress Press, 1976).

ignoring James completely.[302] Two reasons are apparent. The first is the removal of James from the Palestinian scene by scholarly convention.[303] The second is the conviction that the separation of Q materials into redactional levels can provide a social history of early Christians in Galilee.[304] But there is no positive reason for locating the development of Q materials in Galilee rather than in Jerusalem.[305] The link between the use of the sayings of Jesus in James and those in Q has now been made[306] and strengthens the argument for the Palestinian provenance and early dating of James.[307]

4. As noted earlier, James most resembles—across a broad range of language and perception—our earliest datable Christian writer, Paul. Rather than place Paul and James in direct conversation or polemical conflict, the best way to account for the combination of similarity and difference in their language is to view them both as first generation Jewish Christians deeply affected by Greco-Roman moral traditions yet fundamentally defined by an allegiance to the symbols and story of Torah.

5. In sharp contrast to a writing like *Protevangelium of James*, which purports to be early and come from Palestine, yet betrays its ignorance of local realities, the Letter of James contains a number of incidental details that could be taken as evidence for a Palestinian provenance: the effect of the burning wind on vegetation (1:11); proximity to the dangerous sea (1:6; 4:13); the existence of salt and bitter springs (3:11); the cultivation of figs

---

[302]See J. S. Kloppenburg, *The Formation of Q: Trajectories in Ancient Wisdom Collections* (Studies in Antiquity and Christianity; Philadelphia: Fortress Press, 1987).

[303]It is symptomatic that B. L. Mack, *The Lost Gospel: The Book of Q and Christian Origins* (San Francisco: Harper, 1993), while tracing the "history" of the Q community in Galilee by means of dissecting redactional layers, never mentions James at all, and in a mapping of early Christian literature, lists James with Hebrews, Jude, and Diognetus, under "location uncertain" between the years 120–150!

[304]The choice of Galilee for the origin of Q has as its main appeal, in turn, the fact that we otherwise know next to nothing about the development of Christianity there (making it available), and that a certain stream of scholarship has persisted in regarding the Gospels as critical of "the Jerusalem church" represented by (what we have seen to be) a distorted and legendary portrait of James. For examples of this "community reconstruction" accomplished by asserting that sapiential materials must necessarily be separated from and precede apocalyptic materials, see B. L. Mack, *The Lost Gospel*, and J. S. Kloppenburg, "Literary Convention, Self-Evidence, and the Social History of the Q People," *Semeia* 55 (1992) 77–102; for a criticism of their assumptions and methods, see R. A. Horsley, "Questions about Redactional Strata and the Social Relations Reflected in Q," *SBLSP* 28 (1989) 186–203, and ibid., "Q and Jesus: Assumptions, Approaches, and Analyses," *Semeia* 55 (1992) 175–209.

[305]See the remarkably percipient essay by H. T. Thatcher, "Paul, Q, and the Jerusalem Church," *SBL* 43 (1924) 9–14.

[306]See P. J. Hartin, *James and the Q Sayings of Jesus* JSNTS 47; Sheffield: JSOT, 1991).

[307]See the conclusions of Hartin, *James and the Q Sayings of Jesus*, 220–44.

and olives and grapes (3:12); the distinctive reference to "early and late rain" (5:7); the presence of day laborers on fields deprived of daily wages (5:4); the use of the term "Gehenna" (3:6).[308] The evidence is scarcely straightforward. Many of the images can derive from literary sources, above all from Torah.[309] Yet they need not be literary. The use of *geenna* in 3:6 is instructive. The term does not occur in the LXX, nor in Philo and Josephus. It is not found in other NT writings apart from the Gospels.[310] And its particularly vivid use in 3:6 could support arguing for local knowledge.

6. Finally, despite the danger of circularity in such arguments, if my contention that *1 Clement* knew and used James is correct, then that appropriation by a composition usually dated from Rome ca. 96 argues in favor of a composition of James at a substantially earlier date.[311]

These arguments do not prove that James of Jerusalem, the "Brother of the Lord," wrote the letter. Such proof is unavailable, for the simple reason that, even if early, the document could still have been penned by some other "James" than the one who became famous in the tradition. But the arguments do tend strongly toward the conclusion that James is a very early writing from a Palestinian Jewish Christian source.[312] And James the Brother of the Lord is a reasonable candidate. A letter from *this* James to "the twelve tribes in the dispersion" accords well with the fairest reading of our earliest sources and the self-presentation of the composition itself.

BIBLIOGRAPHY

Agourides, S. C., "The Origin of the Epistle of St. James: Suggestions for a Fresh Approach," *GOTR* 9 (1963) 67–78.

Argyle, A. W., "Greek among the Jews of Palestine in New Testament Times," *NTS* 20 (1973–74) 87–89.

Barr, J., "Hebrew, Aramaic and Greek in the Hellenistic Period," in *The*

---

[308]See Mayor, cxliii; Adamson, 20; D. Y. Hadidian, "Palestinian Pictures in the Epistle of James," *ExpT* 63 (1952) 227–28.

[309]Dibelius, 204–5.

[310]See J. Jeremias, *"geena,"* *TDNT* 1:657–58.

[311]This is conceded by Dibelius, 45–46.

[312]Since I do not place James and Paul in direct conversation, I am not concerned to date the letter more precisely. Those favoring authenticity usually place James *before* Paul's major letters (thus making it one of the very first Christian literary productions), or *after* Galatians and Romans (thus being composed shortly before James' death in 62). For a list of authorities on either side, see Davids, 4.

Cambridge History of Judaism Vol 2: *The Hellenistic Age*, ed. W. D. Davies and L. Finkelstein (London: Cambridge University Press, 1989) 79–114.

Brosch, J., *Charismen und Ämter in der Urkirche* (Bonn: P. Hanstein, 1951).

Bultmann, R., *Theology of the New Testament* 2 Vols, trans. K. Grobel (New York: Charles Scribner's Sons, 1953–55).

von Campenhausen, H., *Ecclesiastical Authority and Spiritual Power in the Church of the First Three Centuries*, trans. J. Baker (Stanford: Stanford University Press, 1969).

Cerfaux, L., "La première communauté en Jérusalem," *Recueil Lucien Cerfaux* (Biblioteca Ephemeridum Theologicarum Lovaniensium VI–VII; Gembloux: J. Duculot, 1954) 2:125–56.

Conzelmann, H., *History of Primitive Christianity*, trans. J. Steely (Nashville: Abingdon, 1973).

Donelson, L. R., *Pseudepigraphy and Ethical Argument in the Pastoral Letters* (Tübingen: JCB Mohr [Paul Siebeck], 1986).

Edwards, R. A., *A Theology of Q: Eschatology, Prophecy, and Wisdom* (Philadelphia: Fortress Press, 1976).

Freyne, S., *Galilee from Alexander the Great to Hadrian: A Study in Second Temple Judaism* (Wilmington: Glazier/Notre Dame University Press, 1980).

Hartin, P. J., *James and the Q Sayings of Jesus* (JSNTS 47; Sheffield: JSOT, 1991).

Hengel, M., *The "Hellenization" of Judaea in the First Century after Christ*, trans. J. Bowden (London: SCM Press, 1989).

———, *Judaism and Hellenism* 2 Vols, trans. J. Bowden (Philadelphia: Fortress Press, 1974).

Horsley, R. A., "Early Christianity, Q and Jesus," *Semeia* 55 (1992) 175–209.

———, "Questions about Redactional Strata and the Social Relations Reflected in Q," *SBLSP* 28 (1989) 186–203.

Jeremias, J., "*Geena*," *TDNT* 1:657–8.

Kittel, G., "Der geschichtliche Ort des Jakobusbriefes," *ZNW* 41 (1942) 71–105.

Kloppenburg, J. S., *The Formation of Q: Trajectories in Ancient Wisdom Collections* (Studies in Antiquity and Christianity; Philadelphia: Fortress, 1987).

———, "Literary Convention, Self-Evidence and the Social History of the Q People," *Semeia* 55 (1992) 77–102.

———, *The Shape of Q: Signal Essays on the Sayings Gospel* (Minneapolis: Fortress Press, 1994).

Lieberman, S., *Greek in Jewish Palestine. Studies in the Life and Manners of Jewish Palestine in the II–IV Centuries* CE (New York: Jewish Theological Seminary of America, 1942).

Mack, B. L., *The Lost Gospel: The Book of Q and Christian Origins* (San Francisco: Harper, 1993).

Martin, R. P., "The Life-Setting of the Epistle of James in the Light of Jewish History," *Biblical and Near Eastern Studies: Essays in Honor of W. S. LaSor*, ed. G. A. Tuttle (Grand Rapids: Eerdmans, 1977) 97–103.

Meier, J. P., *A Marginal Jew: Rethinking the Historical Jesus* Vol 1: *The Roots of the Problem and the Person* (New York: Doubleday, 1991).

Meyers, E., E. Netzer and C. L. Meyers, "Sepphoris, Ornament of all Galilee," *BA* 49 (1986) 4–19.

Mussies, G., "Greek in Palestine and the Diaspora," in *The Jewish People in the First Century* 2 Vols., ed. S. Safrai et al. (CRINT 1.1: Philadelphia: Fortress Press, 1987) 2:1040–64.

Neirynck, F., "Recent Developments in the Study of Q," in *Logia: The Sayings of Jesus*, ed. J. Delobel (Biblioteca Ephemeridum Theologicarum Lovaniensium LIX; Leuven: Leuven University Press, 1982) 29–75.

Rendall, G. H., *The Epistle of St. James and Judaic Christianity* (Cambridge: Cambridge University Press, 1927).

Robinson, J. A. T., *Redating the New Testament* (Philadelphia: Westminster Press, 1976).

Sevenster, J. N., *Do You Know Greek? How Much Greek Could the First Christians Have Known?* (NovTSup 19; Leiden: Brill, 1968).

Stone, M., ed., *Jewish Writings of the Second Temple Period* (CRINT 2.2; Philadelphia: Fortress Press, 1984).

Thatcher, H. T., "Paul, Q, and the Jerusalem Church," *JBL* 43 (1924) 9–14.

Walter, N., "Jewish-Greek Literature of the Greek Period," in *The Cambridge History of Judaism* Vol 2: *The Hellenistic Age*, ed. W. D. Davies and L. Finkelstein (London: Cambridge University Press, 1989) 385–408.

Wilson, B. R., "A Typology of Sects," in *Sociology of Religion: Selected Readings*, ed. R. Robertson (Baltimore: Penguin Books, 1969) 361–83.

Wordsworth, J., "The Corbey St. James (ff) and its Relation to Other Latin Versions, and to the Original Language of the Epistle," *Studia Biblica: Essays in Biblical Archaeology and Criticism*, ed. S. R. Driver, et al. (Oxford: Clarendon Press, 1885) 113–50.

III. HISTORY OF INTERPRETATION: HOW WAS THE VOICE HEARD?

✦

An adequate account of how James was first received and subsequently interpreted has yet to be written. This section of the Introduction can offer only a sketch of what such an account might include. The reason why James, like other writings of the NT, lacks a full history of interpretation is connected to widespread convictions that have influenced the academic study of the Bible. Until recently, the so-called "historical-critical" model dominated biblical scholarship.[313] Regarded by its practitioners as the only "correct" and "critical" way to read the NT, the paradigm viewed its own development in "historical" terms as a liberation from the tyranny of dogma into scientific inquiry.[314]

Not surprisingly, histories of scholarship written from such a perspective treat the centuries of interpretation within the church before the Enlightenment, as well as interpretation carried on outside the guild, as "pre-critical," of interest primarily as examples of error or unwitting anticipations of true critical method.[315] Sources from earlier times given serious attention tend to be the sources most conformable to the paradigm, namely theoretical discussions of hermeneutics, and commentaries. Other sources, such as sermons, letters, and liturgical texts, are rarely read.

---

[313]For a succinct discussion of the differences between "methods" and "models," as well as the goals of the historical model, see L. T. Johnson, *The Writings of the New Testament: An Interpretation* (Philadelphia: Fortress Press, 1986) 1–20.

[314]See the shaping of the discussion in W. G. Kümmel, *The New Testament: The History of the Investigation of its Problems*, trans. S. M. Gilmour and H. C. Kee (Nashville: Abingdon Press, 1972) 13, 31, 39, 51, 74.

[315]Thus, in Kümmel's classic study, *The New Testament*, Part One is called "The Prehistory," with the ancient and medieval periods receiving six pages, and the Reformation period, 20 pages. Fifteen hundred years of interpretation are covered in 26 pages. The fewer than 300 years between Richard Simon and Rudolf Bultmann, on the other hand, receive 364 pages.

The history of the interpretation of James has been particularly affected by the coincidence of two factors. The first is the way in which the historical-critical model, despite its explicit break from dogma, continued to be shaped by the premises and perceptions of the Reformation. The historical project of F. C. Baur, for example, is profoundly, if unconsciously, shaped by the theological predilections of Luther.

The second factor is the hostile attitude taken up toward James by Luther. In "The Babylonian Captivity of the Church" (1520) Luther railed against the letter primarily because James 5:14 was being used as a justification for the sacrament of extreme unction. He raised the question whether James had apostolic authority, but at that point did not declare himself with certainty.[316] Increasingly, however, Luther appropriated Paul's struggle against the Judaizers in Galatia as the template for his struggle for *sola fide* against the Catholic position on "faith and works." The more he privileged Paul, the more scornful he grew towards the writing that he read as contradicting Paul. In his "Preface to the New Testament" of 1522, Luther characterized James as a "strawy epistle" in comparison to those of Paul and Peter and the Gospel of John, which "show thee the Christ."[317] His preface to the letters of James and Jude in that edition of the German Bible provides his most scathing criticism. James had already been rejected by the ancients because it was not written by an apostle,[318] it contradicts Paul and does not show the Christ,[319] and despite containing many fine sayings, it drives one back to the law.[320] Luther's critique is twofold: if James is not apostolic, it is not (by Luther's criteria) properly authoritative as Scripture; and, if it contradicts Paul, then it is theologically unacceptable.

Because of Luther's enormous influence on the form of scholarship that became the historical-critical paradigm, the same judgments on James have continued within a substantial portion of the discipline. The fragmentary patristic references to James are read negatively as evidence for the early marginalization of the writing. James is read as a response to "the first and best apostle," and is placed in the category of "early Catholicism," so that, for many scholars, it becomes impossible to think of James as an early or even the earliest of Christian writings.

The first step toward a more adequate history of biblical interpretation is to recognize the ways in which the dominant paradigm has limited the enterprise. A promising development in recent decades has been the challenge to the hegemony of the historical-critical paradigm, not by denying its impressive

---

[316]*Luther's Works 36: Word and Sacrament II*, ed. A. R. Wentz, (Philadelphia: Fortress Press, 1959) 118–19.

[317]*Luther's Works 35: Word and Sacrament I*, ed. E. T. Bachmann, (Philadelphia: Fortress Press, 1960) 362.

[318]ibid., 395.

[319]ibid., 396

[320]ibid., 396–97.

contributions, but by relativizing its claim to unique legitimacy. While the historical model can do some things well, there are other things it cannot do at all. Other methods and models are no less "critical" even if they are not explicitly "historical."

A positive consequence is liberating the historical-critical model to do the work it does best: inquiring into historical realities and developments, without distorting the practice of history with theological prejudice. Other approaches, in turn, can be recognized as legitimate in their own fashion. The long period of interpretation within the church prior to the Enlightenment—and continuing to this day—can also be read and evaluated more neutrally. Allegorical, typological, and political readings can be evaluated in terms of the rules of discourse that govern them and their readers.

Broadening the understanding of "interpretation," in turn, makes new sources available for the history of interpretation. The historical-critical paradigm privileged commentaries because, like that paradigm, they began with the text and explicated problems raised by the text. But the NT was interpreted as well through all its ecclesial uses in theological tractates, liturgical texts, homilies, letters, poetry, and polemic. Texts were *applied* by way of citation or allusion to some other text, problem, or theme, but such applications contain within them implicit understandings of the text and its possible range of significance. Indeed, the actual *uses* of the Scripture in Christian literature is perhaps the most reliable guide to how these texts were understood within living traditions and a truer indicator of the actual value given to specific writings. There is sometimes considerable distance between canonical acceptance and genuine appreciation or employment of a text.

A. THE RECEPTION OF JAMES IN THE CHURCH

Evidence for the *explicit* recognition of James before the time of Origen (184–254) is inarguably sparse. Jerome opines that James may have been "edited" (*edita*) by someone else under James' name and states that it gained recognition in the church only "little by little."[321] A similar reserve characterizes Eusebius of Caesarea's *Historia Ecclesiastica* (324–325). In his discussion of the NT canon, Eusebius distinguishes the writings (like the Gospels and letters of Paul) that are "recognized" by all (III,25,3) and those (like James, Jude, 2 Peter, 2 and 3 John) that are "disputed" (*antilegomenoi*) by some although they are "known/familiar to" (*gnōrimoi*) to many. These "disputed" books, in turn, are

---

[321]Jerome (ca. 393), *De Viris Illustribus* 2 (*PL* 23, Col. 639).

further distinguished from those (like the Shepherd of Hermas) that are not "genuine" (III,24,4). Finally, Eusebius distinguishes all of the above, "known to most of the writers of the church," from the writings "put forward by the heretics under the name of the apostles" (III,25,6).

Eusebius lists criteria for exclusion from the canon: a) lack of recognition by earlier ecclesiastical writers, b) language different from that of the "apostolic style," c) heretical content and perspective. Such writings are forgeries and to be rejected as "wicked and impious" (III,25,7). By his own criteria, Eusebius includes James in the canonical category *because* it is "recognized by many," has the "apostolic style," and is orthodox in its teaching.

In an earlier passage dealing with the death of James, Eusebius refers to his letter as "the first of the epistles called catholic," and reports that some deny its authenticity since (as in the case of Jude) few of the ancients quote it. Eusebius himself, however, states explicitly, "nevertheless we know that these letters have been used publicly with the rest in most churches *(pleistais ekklēsiais)*" (II,23,25). In his other writings, Eusebius does not quote James frequently, but he does not hesitate to cite James 5:13 under the title "the holy apostle,"[322] or James 4:11 as "scripture,"[323] and in a theological exposition, uses James 5:16 to make a key linguistic point.[324]

Both Jerome's view that James gained its authority incrementally, and Eusebius' acknowledgment that it had been seldom quoted, are confirmed when we scan second-century Christian literature. In part I of this introduction, I showed how few writings before 150 can claim to have been influenced by James (pp. 65–79). Dibelius states flatly that the "earliest incontrovertible citation" from James is in the [Pseudo-] Clementine homily *De Virginitate*.[325] The homily explicitly cites James 3:12 and contains allusions to James 1:5 and 3:15.[326] The difficulty of claiming that this is the earliest citation is connected to the problems in dating the Clementine literature. And is direct citation the only indication of reception and use?

There is, in fact, enough evidence that James was received and used before the third century to suggest the path by which the letter might have gained its authority in the church. The evidence takes the form of allusion and appropriation rather than of direct citation. But James in this respect is scarcely unique: most traces of the NT in second-century writers, before doctrinal controversy forced authors to "name their sources," take the same form. Contemporary scholarship is recovering, under the label of "intertextuality," a sense of how

---

[322]Eusebius, *Commentarium in Psalmos* LVI, 2 (PG 23:505).
[323]Eusebius, *Commentarium in Psalmos* C, 5 (PG 23:1244).
[324]Eusebius, *De Ecclesiastica Theologica* III, 2 (PG 24:976).
[325]Dibelius, 51.
[326]*De Virginitate* (PG 1:404, 406–8).

texts respond to earlier texts by way of echo and allusion.[327] The same appreciation is legitimately extended to the earliest patristic literature.

I argued earlier that two writings in particular can claim some use of James. *1 Clement* and *The Shepherd of Hermas* (see pp. 71–79) appear to appropriate not only the language but also the outlook of James, doing so not with one or another isolated verse, but with material drawn from every part of James. Such an extensive and intensive range of similarities forces the question, "where does this come from if *not* from James?" With such an obvious source available, it seems poor method to invoke instead something so vague as "common traditions," particularly when these specific points of resemblance are precisely "uncommon." The refusal to recognize that James could have been read and used by writers of the Roman church in the early second century appears to be linked to an unwillingness to consider an early dating of the letter.

The recognition that James was read and employed by writers in Rome in the second century is not only appropriate to the evidence but provides a satisfying and logical link in the progression that James must, in any case, have taken for its authority "little by little" to have been acknowledged.

Trying to trace the specific influence of James through other writings of the second and third centuries is less rewarding. The fact that *2 Clement* 6:3–4 uses the phrase "friendship with the world" with the exact diction of James 4:4 is certainly impressive, but it stands isolated. Likewise, Justin Martyr's phrase "at whom even the demons shudder"[328] has sufficiently few antecedents (none in the NT and none obvious in the LXX) to make an allusion to James 2:19 a possibility. Similarly, Irenaeus uses the phrase, "behold the judge is near," which echoes James 5:9.[329] Irenaeus also says twice of Abraham, "he believed God and it was reputed to him as righteousness and he was called friend of God," which echoes James 2:23.[330] The possibility in this last instance that James was being used is muted by the fact that the designation "friend of God" was available elsewhere. But the question remains, where would it most likely have been available to Irenaeus?

A much stronger case—though not a certain one—can be made that Clement of Alexandria (d. ca. 220), Origen's predecessor as the head of the catechetical school, knew and used James. Eusebius reports that Clement composed a work called the *Hypotyposes*, "in which he has set forth his interpretations of the

---

[327]See, e.g., R. B. Hays, *Echoes of Scripture in the Letters of Paul* (New Haven: Yale University Press, 1989), and V. K. Robbins, "The Reversed Contextualization of Ps 22 in the Markan Crucifixion: A Socio-Rhetorical Analysis," *The Four Gospels: Festschrift Frans Neirynck*, ed. F. Van Segbroeck et al. (BETL 100; Leuven: Leuven University Press, 1992) 1161–83.

[328]*hon kai ta daimonia phrissousin* in *Dialogue with Trypho*, 49.

[329]*idou ho kritēs engus* in Irenaeus, *Adversus Haereses* I,13,6.

[330]*credidit Deo et reputatum est illi ad justitiam et amicus Dei vocatus est*, in Irenaeus, *Adversus Haereses* IV,16,2; IV,13,4.

scriptures and his [James'] traditions,"[331] and states further that ". . . in the *Hypotyposes*, to speak briefly, he has given concise explanations of all the canonical scriptures, not passing over even the disputed writings, I mean the epistle of Jude and the remaining catholic epistles. . . ."[332] We have already seen that Eusebius himself considers James the "first of the catholic epistles,"[333] so James would logically appear to have been included in Clement's work. This conclusion is given further support by Cassiodorus (d. ca. 580), who states that Clement's work included James.[334] The extant Latin translation of Clement's work, unfortunately, does not contain James.

Nevertheless, Eusebius' testimony would seem to support the notion that Clement had devoted some commentary to James, for he stated the work to have included Scripture *and* traditions. We have, in fact, seen how Eusebius himself quoted extensively from Clement's traditions concerning James the Just in *Hypotyposes* Books 6 and 7. It would seem logical that these reminiscences would have been attached to Clement's concise explication of the letter itself.

Clement never cites James by name in his other extant writings, even though he does quote explicitly from Jude, 1 Peter, 1 John, and the Apocalypse.[335] Clement possibly alludes to James 4:6,[336] and his use of *basilikos* in connection with righteousness might suggest dependence on James 2:8.[337] Clement refers to the unclean spirits who now "tremble" *(phrissousin)* at the sight of the baptized person (see James 2:19).[338] But other allusions, such as to the "friend of God" need not derive from James 2:23, since Clement certainly could have derived the usage from Philo, whom he uses heavily.[339] The decision concerning Clement remains difficult. But in *Stromateis* IV, 17–18, Clement quotes extensively from *1 Clement*.[340] Could the knowledge of James have reached Alexandria through this medium?

The evidence for the use of James before Origen, therefore, is slender and disputed. But three points can be made. First, the evidence for James is not significantly worse than for some other NT writings, including some of Paul's letters. Second, use of the *letter* (as opposed to the figure of James) appears to have moved through predominantly "orthodox" sources. Third, through some such path as I have tentatively described, James must have made its way through use, little by little, to "recognition" in the wider church.

---

[331]*HE* VI,13,2.

[332]*HE* VI,14,1.

[333]*HE* II,23,25.

[334]Cassiodorus, *De Institutione Divinarum Litterarum* (PL 70:1120).

[335]See N. Nourry, *Dissertatio Secunda de Libris Stromatum* IV,3 (PG 9:1094–95).

[336]Clement, *Stromateis* III,6,52 (PG 8:1152).

[337]*Stromateis* VI,18,13–14 (PG 9:397).

[338]*Excerpta ex Theodoto* 670.

[339]*Paedagogus* III,2,40 (PG 8:573); *Stromateis* II,5,82 (PG 8:952).

[340]PG 8:36–86.

B. THE USE OF JAMES IN THE EASTERN CHURCH

The great teacher who succeeded Clement as head of the Alexandrian catechetical school was acutely sensitive to the distinction between tradition and innovation.[341] Origen's recognition of James therefore argues for the writing having had some earlier use at least in the Alexandrian church. In any case, Origen championed James vigorously, including him in his canon[342] and in his extant writings citing James some 36 times from 24 different verses. Although Origen once refers to it circumspectly as "the letter that circulates under the name of James,"[343] he also calls the author, "the brother of the Lord,"[344] as well as "James the Apostle."[345] He refers to the letter as "scripture."[346]

Under the influence of Origen, the Alexandrian church continued to make heavy use of James. Only a few fragments come down to us from the Alexandrian teachers Dionysius, Peter, and Alexander, but those fragments contain references to James.[347] The first extant commentary on James comes from another head of the catechetical school, Didymus the Blind (313–398),[348] who in his other theological works also quotes some 23 times from 16 verses in James.

The theologians and polemicists Athanasius and Cyril also held James in great favor. Athanasius (296–373) includes James in his influential canonical list found in his Pascal Letter of 364[349] and published a short summary of the letter.[350] He cites James elsewhere some 20 times, using 12 separate verses. Cyril (d. 444) used a number of sobriquets for James, "Disciple of Christ"[351] and "Disciple of the Savior" among his favorites.[352] He uses James more extensively than any other Greek writer, citing from 39 separate verses some 124 times. Cyril's *scholia* on James also contributed heavily to the Greek *Catena* (see below). Among other Alexandrian authors, special mention should be made of Euthalius the Deacon, who issued an edition of the catholic epistles in 459. In the case of James, he included an interpretive summary and an analysis of Scripture citations.[353]

---

[341]See Origen, *De Principiis* I,8 (PG 11:120) and IV,2,4 (PG 11:365).

[342]Origen, *In Librum Jesu Nave* VII,1 (PG 12:857).

[343]Origen, *Commentarium in Johannem* XIX,6 (PG 14:596).

[344]Origen, *Commentarium in Epistulam ad Romanos* IV,8 (PG 14:989).

[345]Origen, *In Exodum Homiliae* III,3 (PG 12:316).

[346]Origen, *In Leviticam Homiliae* II,4 (PG 12:418).

[347]See PG 10:1596 and PG 18:466.

[348]Didymus, *Enarratio in Epistolam Beati Jacobi* (PG 33:1749–54).

[349]Athanasius, *Epistula* XXXIX (PG 26:1177).

[350]Athanasius, *Synopsis Scripturae Sanctae* VI,52 (PG 28:405–8).

[351]Cyril, *De Adoratione in Spiritu et Veritate* XII (PG 68:836).

[352]Cyril, *Commentarium in Amos Prophetam* XXXVII (PG 71:481).

[353]PG 85: 676–77.

The churches of Palestine also favored James. Cyril of Jerusalem (315–386) includes James in his canonical list.[354] Other writers with strong associations with Palestine who make vigorous use of James are Procopius of Gaza (PG 87), Sophronius the Patriarch of Jerusalem (PG 87), John Climacus (PG 88), Zachary the Rhetorician (PG 85), Andrew of Jerusalem (PG 97), Hesychius of Jerusalem (PG 93), Epiphanius of Salamis (PG 41–43), John Damascene (PG 94–96), Antiochus Monachus (PG 89), Zachary, Patriarch of Jerusalem (PG 86), and Dorotheus, Archimandrite of Palestine (PG 88). Hometown pride may have been a factor. Sophronius, Patriarch of Jerusalem from 634, is proprietary: "James, the Brother of the Lord, who was also pastor of this flock."[355] Another reason may be Origen's influence. Pamphilius of Caesarea (240–309) was Origen's ardent student and the teacher, in turn, of Eusebius of Caesarea (260–340), whose own admiration for Origen is clear.[356]

Not every regional church found James equally attractive. The Cappadocians, for example, made scarce use of the letter. There is no trace of any awareness or use of James in the writings of Gregory of Nyssa. Gregory of Nazianzus (329–389) lists James in his canon,[357] but in very few instances does he make even a general reference to James.[358] And in Basil the Great's voluminous works, there are only a handful of references to James,[359] a neglect all the more surprising because Basil was himself a monk (see below), and so many of his sermons developed themes that were virtually identical to the *topoi* in James.[360] Formal canonical recognition does not necessarily mean endearment, and there is often a gap between official canon and working canon.

Some writers, indeed, may have slighted James because he was so popular among the Alexandrians. To appreciate this possibility, we must remember the centuries-long rivalry between the Alexandrian and Antiochean churches, a rivalry that involved politics as well as theology and hermeneutics. In particular, the heavy use of James 1:17 to prove the divinity of Christ[361] may have intensified the problem. The catholic epistles generally had a hard time finding acceptance in the Syriac-speaking church. Although the fifth-century Peshitta includes James and 1 Peter, it excludes other catholic epistles.[362]

---

[354]Cyril of Jerusalem, *Catechesis IV de Decem Dogmaticis* XXXVI (PG 33:499).

[355]Sophronius, *Oratio* I (PG 87:3206–7).

[356]See Eusebius, *HE* VI, which is completely devoted to Origen.

[357]Gregory Nazienzus, *Carminum Liber I Theologica* Sect 1 (PG 37:474); *Carminum Liber II Historica* Sect 2 (PG 37:1597–98).

[358]See, e.g., *Oratio* XXVI (PG 35:1233) and *Oratio* XL (PG 36:425).

[359]See, e.g., *De Baptismo* I,3 (PG 31:1529).

[360]See, e.g., *Quod Deus non est Auctor Malorum* (PG 31:329–54) and *De Invidia* (PG 31:371–85).

[361]See, e.g., Cyril of Alexandria, *Adversus Nestorianum* V,IV (PG 76:229) and *De Recte Fide ad Reginas* (PG 76:1255).

[362]See J. S. Siker, "The Canonical Status of the Catholic Epistles in the Syriac New Testament," *JTS* n.s. 38 (1987) 311–33.

The evidence for use is not extensive.[363] The *Apostolic Constitutions* (fourth century) cites James as a witness to the need for penitence,[364] but verbal allusions to the Letter of James are few and disputable.[365] Theodore of Mopsuestia (350–428) apparently did not like the Letter of James and may have rejected it from his canon. Such at least is the testimony of the sixth-century Leontius of Byzantium,[366] who on this count compares Theodore unfavorably to Marcion. Theodore's view is also reported by the miniscule ninth-century Syriac commentary of Isho'dad of Merv, Bishop of Hadatha. Concerning the catholic epistles, "Theodorus also, the Interpreter, does not even mention them in a single place; nor does he bring an illustration from them in one of the writings he made. . . ."[367] The sparse recognition of James in Syriac-speaking churches is attested also by the slightly more extensive and intelligent commentary by Dionysius Bar Salibi in the twelfth century, who also complains that he had not found prior complete expositions of the catholic epistles on which he was writing.[368]

Monks are always moralists, and for obvious reasons, monks in every region made enthusiastic use of James. John Chrysostom (347–407), for example, is usually thought of as an Antiochene, yet because he is fundamentally a moralist and preacher, he uses James often, quoting the letter some 48 times from 20 separate verses. These citations do not include his *scholia* on James that are found in the *Catena* and are extensive enough to be grouped together as a virtual commentary.[369] Other monks who made significant use of James include the Egyptians Antony, Isaiah, Serapion, Orsiesius (PG 40), as well as Macarius (PG 34), Palladius (PG 65), and Zozimus (PG 78). Monks from other regions writing in Greek include Antiochus Monachus (PG 89), Andrew of Jerusalem (PG 97), Niles the Abbot (PG 79), John Damascene (PG 94), John Climacus (PG 88), and Pachomius (PG 98). In the anonymous collection *Apophthegmata Patrum*, there are citations of James 5:16 attributed to Mark the Egyptian and of James 1:14 attributed to Abba Sisoes. Monks found in James a clear and challenging support for flight from the world of sin and for combat with the devil and self-control.[370]

The Greek commentary tradition is complex, in part because of the natural

---

[363]Siker, "Canonical Status," 331–33, provides a very helpful preliminary survey.

[364]*Apostolic Constitutions* II,55 (PG 1:721).

[365]*Apostolic Constitutions* II,18; VII,5; VIII,44 (PG 1:607, 1001, 1149).

[366]Leontius, *Contra Nestorianos et Eutychianos* III,14 (PG 86:1365).

[367]See *Horae Semiticae* X: *The Commentaries of Isho'dad of Merv*, Vol IV: *Acts of the Apostles and Three Catholic Epistles*, ed. and trans. M. D. Gibson (Cambridge: Cambridge University Press, 1913) 36.

[368]See *Dionysius Bar Salibi in Apocalypsim, Actus, et Epistulas Catholicas*, ed. I. Sedlacek (CSCO 60; Scriptores Syri, 20; Rome, 1910) 88–102.

[369]John Chrysostom, *In Epistolam Sancti Jacobi* (PG 64:1040–52).

[370]See, e.g., Athanasius, *De Virginitate* (PG 28:269); Orsiesius, *Doctrina de Institutione Monachorum* XXXI, XLI, and L (PG 40:883, 887, 891); Antony, *Sermones ad Monachos* 19 (PG 40:975).

tendency of commentaries to borrow from earlier sources without attribution. Research on the *Catena* seems definitively to establish that Didymus the Blind wrote a commentary on James,[371] which also became a source for significant portions of the *Catena* on the catholic epistles.[372] For James, the *Catena* also contains the fifteen fragments from Chrysostom that appear separately as a commentary[373] and the five *scholia* from Hesychius the Elder that also appear separately as fragments of a commentary.[374] But the *Catena* also contains multiple contributions from Cyril (10), Severus of Antioch (4), and the Shepherd of Hermas (2!). Single contributions appear from Apollinaris, Sirach(!), Basil the Great, Dionysius of Alexandria, and Origen. The *Catena*, in short, contains both material known to have been derived from commentaries as well as comments drawn from a variety of other sources.[375]

The *Catena*, in turn, also helps feed the subsequent commentary tradition, including the much fuller expositions attributed to the tenth-century Bishop of Thessaly, Oecumenius of Tricca,[376] and the very similar commentary of the eleventh-century Byzantine exegete, Theophylact the Bulgarian.[377] To this limited number of commentaries should be added the interpretive comments of Euthalius[378] and the encomiastic paraphrase of the letter given by Symeon Theophrastus.[379] Also broadly part of the commentary tradition are the various *scholia* that scribes entered into the margins of manuscripts by way of comment on the text.[380]

As I have already tried to show, however, the commentary tradition by no means suggests the rich use of James in Greek patristic writers. Interpretation of the letter took place in a variety of literary compositions. Among the more fascinating of these, and in which James played a significant role, were the anthologies of Scripture texts to be used as *topoi* for preaching and teaching.[381] Like the commentaries, such collections fed off each other and represented for

---

[371]See K. Staab, "Die griechischen Katenenkommentare zu den katholischen Briefen," *Bib* 5 (1924) 314–20.

[372]See *Catena Graecorum Patrum*, Vol. VIII: *Catena in Epistulas Catholicas*, ed. J. A. Cramer (Oxford: Oxford University Press, 1840) 6–40.

[373]See PG 64:1040–52.

[374]See Hesychius the Elder, *Fragmenta in Epistulam I Sancti Jacobi* [sic] (PG 93:1389–90).

[375]See J. H. Ropes, "The Greek Catena to the Catholic Epistles," *HTR* 19 (1926) 383–88.

[376]See Oecumenius, *Jacobi Apostoli Epistula Catholica* (PG 119:452–509).

[377]See Theophylact, *Accurata Expositio Epistularum Catholicarum* (PG 125:1132–89).

[378]Euthalius, *Elenchus Capitum Septem Epistolarum Catholicarum ad Athanasium Episcopum Alexandrinum* (PG 85:676–77).

[379]Symeon Theophrastus, *Commentarius in Sanctum Jacobum Apostolum et Fratrem Domini* (PG 115:200–17).

[380]These have been gathered by Chr. Ferd. Matthaei, *SS. Apostolorum Septem Epistolae Catholicae* (Riga: J. F. Hartknoch, 1782), and will be cited in the commentary proper as *scholia*.

[381]See, e.g., Maximus the Confessor (mid-seventh century), *Loci Communes* (PG 91); John Damascene (mid-eighth century), *Sacra Parallela* (PG 94); Antonius Melissa (mid-twelfth century), *Loci Communes* (PG 136).

the Christian tradition much the same sort of rhetorical resource provided by the collections of Greek *topoi* by Johannes Stobaeus (early fifth century).

Some of the specific ways James was used will be noted in the commentary proper. In general, the text of James itself was not allegorized, although it was sometimes employed in allegorical interpretations of OT texts.[382] Interpretation tended to be atomistic, with verses often being split and applied to different subjects. James 3:2, "we all fail in many ways," became a frequent tag for human frailty,[383] while "Let not many become teachers" (3:1) was used separately,[384] and James' statement about perfection (3:2) was used in still other connections.[385]

By no means was interpretation entirely uncritical. James 1:13 could be used straightforwardly to place responsibility for sin in human freedom rather than in God,[386] but since James' use of *peirasmos* in 1:2, 12, and 13 seems at least polyvalent, Greek authors had to face the problem of aligning these texts with those describing Jesus being "tested" in the wilderness or before his death. This is a "contradiction in Scripture" taken with full seriousness by writers such as Athanasius[387] and Cyril of Jerusalem.[388] A particularly full treatment is given by Gregory of Palamas.[389]

In contrast, James 2:14–26—the passage that so vexed Western interpreters— offered few problems for these authors. For the most part, they understood James' contrast between "faith and works" in the same way Hellenistic moralists distinguished "words and deeds," as a challenge to turn conviction into consistent behavior. As moralists in the same tradition, they saw James' exhortation as the plainest common sense.[390] When differences between Paul and James were noted, they were harmonized by distinguishing referents: Paul was understood to be talking about the faith that led to baptism, and James about the faith of the baptized.[391] Therefore, as Paul was correct in asserting that no deeds of Torah could lead one to faith in the Messiah, so was James correct in asserting that Christian faith needed to be expressed in deeds.[392]

Far from calling James into question, the discrepancy, if anything, heightens

---

[382]E.g., Origen, *In Leviticam* XII,3 (PG 12:538); Hesychius of Jerusalem, *In Leviticam* (PG 93:819–1090).

[383]E.g., Cyril of Alexandria, *De Adoratione in Spiritu et Veritate* XV (PG 68:949).

[384]Cyril of Alexandria, *De Adoratione in Spiritu et Veritate* V,41 (PG 68:328).

[385]See Cyril of Alexandria, *In Isaiam* V,4 (PG 70:1301).

[386]Didymus of Alexandria, *De Trinitate* II,10 (PG 39:641).

[387]Athanasius, *Epistulae Heorasticae* XIII,6 (PG 26:1417).

[388]Cyril of Jerusalem, *Catechesis Mystagogica* V,17 (PG 33:1121).

[389]Gregory of Palamas, *Homilia* XXXII (PG 151:401–9).

[390]See, e.g., Origen, *In Librum Jesu Nave* X,2 (PG 12:881); Athanasius, *De Virginitate* (PG 28:269).

[391]See, e.g., John Damascene, *De Fide Orthodoxa* IV,IX (PG 94:1121); Euthymius Zigibenus, *Panoplia Dogmatica* XI (PG 130:453).

[392]The distinction is argued particularly well by Isidore of Pelusium (+ca. 450) in his *Epistularum Liber* IV,LXV (PG 78:1121).

James' authority. Both Origen and Cyril, in fact, use James to explicate Paul in their commentaries on Romans![393] In the collection of historical documents gathered by the sixth-century Monophysite bishop Zachary the Rhetorician, there is a fascinating exchange of letters between Julian, Bishop of Halicarnassus (d. after 518), and Severus, the Patriarch of Antioch (ca. 465–538).[394] Julian poses precisely the question of the apparent contradiction between Paul and James. Severus responds with a carefully nuanced argument that takes into account not only the respective contexts of the two letters but also the narrative sequence in Genesis upon which both authors relied. Severus concludes that Paul agrees with James, citing in support Gal 5:6, "Faith working through love." And in strongest contrast to Luther, Severus' governing principle is, "The holy writings and the fathers have always handed on to us a harmonious teaching."[395]

C. JAMES IN THE LATIN CHURCH

The use of James in the West poses another sort of problem. I have argued that on the basis of 1 *Clement* and the *Shepherd of Hermas*, James was known and used in the Roman church by the middle of the second century.[396] But this makes the nonappearance in the *Muratorian Canon* even more puzzling, if the conventional placement of this document in late second-century Rome is correct.[397] Even more dramatic is the absence of any acquaintance with James among the first Latin theologians in Africa.[398] In all of Tertullian (160–215), there is only one possible allusion to James 2:23 in his reference to Abraham as "amicus Dei deputatus."[399] There is even less trace of James in the writings of Cyprian (d. 258). Even a writer as close to Rome as Ambrose of Milan (339–397) could produce a prodigious literature without using James. Apart from the bare possibility of some allusions, there is nothing.[400] The absence is more surprising

---

[393]See Origen, *Commentarium in Epistulam ad Romanos* II,12; II,13; IV,1; IV,3; IV,8; VII,1; IX,24 (PG 14:900, 908, 961, 970, 989–90, 1159, 1226); Cyril of Alexandria, *Epistulam ad Romanos* IV,2; VII,16; VIII,26 (PG 74:781, 812, 825).

[394]Zachary the Rhetorician, *Capita Selecta ex Historicae Ecclesiasticae* Sect IX (PG 85:1176–78).

[395]PG 85:1178.

[396]The Roman connection is sufficiently intriguing to make Laws, 26, date James pseudonymously from that city in the late first century.

[397]See H. Y. Gamble, *The New Testament Canon: Its Making and Meaning* (GBS; Philadelphia: Fortress Press, 1985); for a challenge to the traditional location, see A. C. Sundberg, "Canon Muratori: A Fourth Century List," *HTR* 66 (1973) 1–41.

[398]James is also absent from the African canon called the Cheltenham or Mommsenian (ca. 360); see A. Souter, *The Text and Canon of the New Testament*, rev. C. S. C. Williams (London: Duckworth, 1954) 195.

[399]Tertullian, *Adversos Judaeos* 600:2 (PL 2:638).

[400]Ambrose, *Expositio in Lucam*, has a possible allusion to James 4:8 and 2:5 (PL 15:1669, 1859).

given Ambrose's opportunities for such use, as in his discussion of justification by faith.[401]

So little is James attested in this literature that evidence for some of the earliest knowledge of James in the West is found in the Old Latin translations preceding the production of the Vulgate by Jerome in the late fourth century. The proliferation of such translations stimulated the desire for a uniform version under Damasus I. Examples are found in the fifth-century Codex Bobiensis and in the ninth-century Codex Corbiensis, as well as in passages of the (Pseudo-) Augustinian *Speculum* (eighth or ninth century), and the extant fragments of James from Priscillian (375–386).[402] The Old Latin versions indicate that James was being read and circulated in the West during the fourth century.[403] But James' status among at least some readers may be indicated by the fact that in the Corbey Manuscript, the letter appears not with other NT but with extracanonical writings.[404]

If James was unknown or neglected by some Latin authors, there is no indication that the letter was disliked or rejected. This provides another historical puzzle to ponder: how do we account for the dramatic appearance of James by way of canonical lists and extensive citation in the last two decades of the fourth century? The rapid turnabout may be explained by the convergence of two factors: a) James' previous local usage in the Roman church and b) its sponsorship by scholars aligned in loyalty to that church and to the Alexandrian teacher, Origen.

Evidence for James' early use in the Roman church (apart from *1 Clement* and the *Shepherd of Hermas*) is slender but significant. If attributions of authorship could always be trusted, it would be even more impressive. There is extant, for example, an encyclical letter attributed to Urban I (ca. 230), which begins with an extended mixed citation from James 2:14 and 3:2, introduced as "*Apostolus Jacobus ait.*"[405] Also sometime before 250, Novatian's tractate on the trinity contained a possible allusion to James 1:17 in its reference to God's immutability, "Neither does it turn or change itself in any way into other forms."[406] The possibility is stronger since this is the standard use of James 1:17 in the entire patristic tradition.

Before 257, the Bishop of Rome Stephanus (if the attribution is correct) wrote a series of decretal letters. Among some passages supporting the notion of forgiveness, he says, "judgment will be without mercy to the one who has not

---

[401]See Ambrose, *Epistula* CXXVIII (PL 16:1323–25).

[402]These are displayed in Mayor, 1–27.

[403]Ropes, 83, suggests that they had to have been translated at least by 350 to allow time to circulate before the translation undertaken by Jerome.

[404]Ropes, 83.

[405]Urban I, *Epistola ad Omnen Christianos* (PL 10:135).

[406]"*nec se umquam in aliquas formas vertit aut mutat,*" in Novatian, *De Trinitate* IV,1 (PL 3:919).

done mercy," a possible allusion to James 2:13a.[407] There is no citation of James in the extant works of Hippolytus of Rome (d. ca. 260), but a spurious composition of his has a similar and even clearer allusion to James 2:13.[408] A definite and lengthy citation from James 3:1–8, introduced as "James the Apostle," is found in a letter from Pope Marcellus (Bishop of Rome, 308–309) to the bishops of Antioch.[409] There is also a possible allusion to James 5:9 in an encyclical letter from Liberius, Bishop of Rome between 352 and 366.[410]

Such regular local usage makes less surprising the appearance of James in the canonical list sponsored by Pope Damasus (in 382?)[411] or in that generated by Pope Innocent I (405).[412] Outside this Roman circle, the earliest clear use of James is the citation of 1:17 (in the usual connection concerning divine immutability) by Hilary of Poitier (356–358)[413] and the citation of James 5:20 as coming from "James the Apostle in his epistle" by Ambrosiaster.[414]

James came into general use in the West through the influence of three scholars closely associated with Rome and devoted to Origen: Rufinus, Jerome, and Augustine. Rufinus was Origen's translator and in 401 includes the letter of "James the Brother of the Lord and Apostle" in his canonical list.[415] When he fell into dispute with Jerome, Rufinus pointedly quotes James 3:1, "Let not many become teachers" against him.[416] For his part, Jerome (331–420), whose debt to Origen is explicit,[417] noted, as we have seen, the steady accumulation of authority by James.[418] He obviously subscribed to Origen's esteem for the letter. Speaking of the catholic epistles, Jerome says, "they declared as much mystically as succinctly, and equally shortly and long: short in words, long in sentences."[419] Jerome quotes James frequently,[420] and his observations are often cited by later commentators. Jerome's Vulgate translation, of course, also became the text of James that was subsequently used by commentators up to the time of Erasmus.

It is unquestioningly Augustine's great authority that establishes James' status

---

[407]"*iudicium sine misericordia fuet illi qui non fecerit misericordiam*," in Stephanus, *Epistulae Decretales* (PL 3:1042).

[408][Pseudo-]Hippolytus, *De Consummatione Mundi* XLII (PL 10:949).

[409]Marcellus, *Epistula ad Episcopos Antiochenae Provinciae* (PL 7:1094–95).

[410]Liberius, *Epistula ad Omnes Generaliter Episcopos* (PL 8:1402).

[411]PL 19:787–91.

[412]Innocent I, *Epistula* VI,7,13 (PL 20:501).

[413]Hilary of Poitier, *De Trinitate* IV,8 (PL 10:101).

[414]Ambrosiaster (late fourth century?), *In Galatas* V,10 (PL 17:387).

[415]Rufinus, *Commentarius in Symbolum* 36 (PL 21:374).

[416]Rufinus, *Apologia Contra Hieronymum* I,19,31.

[417]See the discussion in Augustine, *Epistula* 75.

[418]Jerome, *De Viris Illustribus* 2.

[419]"*ediderant tam mysticas quam succinctas, et breves pariter et longas; breves in verbis, longas in sententiis . . .*" Jerome, *Epistula* 53:8 (PL 22:548).

[420]E.g., James 2:10 in *Commentarium in Ecclesiasten* IX,381; James 4:8 in *Commentarium in Isaiam* XV,IV, 6.7; James 2:10–11 in *Dialogos adversus Pelagianos* I,20,1–9.

in the West. Augustine lists James among the canonical writings,[421] and it is no surprise to see the Council of Carthage on 397 also include James in its canonical list.[422] Augustine apparently wrote a short commentary on James, but it is not extant.[423]

His frequent citations suggest some things that may have been in that *expositio*. On numerous occasions, for example, he combines Gal 5:6 and James 2:19–26 to resolve the question of faith and works.[424] Augustine consistently uses James 1:17 to assert the immutability of God[425] and that God is the source of righteousness.[426] He has a full discussion of James 2:10 in relation to the Stoic principle of the unity of virtue and vice[427] and sermonic expositions of James 1:19–22[428] and James 5:12.[429]

By the early years of the fifth century, James is everywhere known and used. Chromatius of Aquila (d. 449) cites James 1:12 and 1:15.[430] Eucherius of Lyons (d. 449) takes up the question whether God "tests" by discussing the tension between Deut 13:3 ("for the Lord your God is testing you") and James 1:13 ("God is not tempted by evils and He himself tempts no one").[431] And John Cassian (360–435), whose contacts in the East were extensive, makes frequent use of James in his writings for monks.[432]

The Latin commentary tradition before the Reformation is as literarily complex yet substantively simple as the Greek. Cassiodorus (485–580) composed essentially an interpretive paraphrase with a couple of interesting perspectives.[433] As with so many things medieval, one important starting point was Gregory the Great (540–604). His voluminous *Moralia*, based on the Book of Job, commented in passing on virtually all other things as well.[434] It contains some 46 citations and comments on James from 27 different verses. He comments on James in other writings as well. Gregory's younger contemporary and secretary, Paterius, drew some of these comments (seven passages on 1:17, 19, 20, 26;

---

[421]Augustine, *De Doctrina Christiana* II,13 (PL 34:41).

[422]Council of Carthage, Canon 39 (see Souter, *Text and Canon*, 204).

[423]Augustine lists it among his *opuscula* in *Retractiones* II,32 (PL 32:643–44).

[424]See *De Fide et Operibus* XIV,23 (PL 40:212); *De Trinitate* XV,18 (PL 42:1083); *De Gratia et Libero Arbitrio* VII,18; *Discourse 2 on Psalm 31* 1–26; and the newly discovered *Epistula* *2:6.

[425]See *De Trinitate* I,1 (PL 42:821).

[426]See *De Spiritu et Littera* 11, 22, and 63 (PL 44:207, 214, and 242); *Epistula* 147:46 (PL 33:617); *Epistula* 214:4 (PL 33:970); *De Gratia et Libero Arbitrio* VI,15 (PL 44:890).

[427]*Epistula* 167 (PL 33:733–42).

[428]*Sermo* 179 (PL 38:966–72).

[429]*Sermo* 180 (PL 38:972–79).

[430]Chromatius, *Tractatus in Evangelium S. Matthaei* XVI,7 (PL 20:362) and IX,1 (PL 20:349).

[431]Eucherius, *Instructionum Liber* I,2 (PL 50:810).

[432]John Cassian, *Institutes* VII,15,2; XII,10; VIII,1,2; XII,6,2 (PL 49:53–477), and *Conferences* III,16; V,4; IX,22–23; VII,8; XIII,3–9; XV,3; XVI,16; XVIII,13; XX,8 (PL 49:477–1328).

[433]Cassiodorus, *Epistola S. Jacobi ad Dispersos*, in his *Complexiones in Epistolas Apostolorum* (PL 70:1377–80).

[434]Gregory the Great, *Expositio in Librum Job, sive Moralium Libri XXV* (PL 75–76).

2:10, 11; 3:8) into a Gregorian *Catena*.[435] Three of the passages deal with 1:17. Paterius' work is puzzling in that it neither exhausts the resources of the *Moralia*, nor ventures outside it.

In the twelfth century, the monk Alulfus (d. 1143) made a second redaction of the Gregorian *Catena*.[436] The section on James is considerably more ambitious than Paterius' effort. Although it has only one comment on James 1:17 (in contrast to Paterius' three), it also includes a wider range of verses from every chapter in James and draws as well from other places in Gregory, specifically the *Homiliae in Evangelia* and the *Librum Regulae Pastoralis*. Alulfus obviously seeks to provide a commentary on James as a whole, even if it is drawn completely from Gregory.

Deservedly the most influential commentary in the West was that of the Venerable Bede (673–735).[437] Bede provides a very full treatment of James, characterized by close attention to the literal meaning and the liberal use of other scriptural passages. He also makes use of earlier authors, such as Jerome, Augustine's Letter 167, Gregory the Great, and Innocent I. The straightforward, sober, and intelligent character of Bede's commentary still recommends it.

Heavily dependent on Bede is the *Glossa Ordinaria* on James, composed by the middle of the twelfth century. It is sometimes attributed to Wilfred Strabo but probably was composed under the direction of Anselm of Laon (d. 1117).[438] Also indebted to Bede is a considerably larger commentary on James attributed to a certain Martin, Priest of Legio in Spain (d. 1021).[439] Martin uses Bede cleverly, sometimes contracting his source, sometimes expanding it. At certain points, his commentary takes Bede's text as its subject. Bede, for example, drops a casual reference to "Scylla and Charybdis" without explanation,[440] but Martin is compelled to devote a section to explaining that allusion![441]

In the fourteenth century, Nicholas of Lyre (1270–1340) also made heavy use of Bede and earlier sources, such as Jerome, in his notes on the Letter of James.[442] In contrast, a Carthusian named Dionysius (1402–71) produced a full commentary on James in the fifteenth century that shows considerable independence.[443] It does make use of Bede and Augustine, but now the opinions

---

[435]Paterius, *De Testimoniis in Epistolas Catholicas* (PL 79:1095–98).

[436]Alulfus, *Expositio Novi Testamenti* (PL 79:1381–86).

[437]Bede, *Super Epistolas Catholicas Expositio* (PL 93:9–42).

[438]PL 114:671–80.

[439]Martin of Legio, *Expositio in Epistolam B. Jacobi Apostoli* (PL 209:183–216). The "special relationship" between Spain and James is celebrated by Isidore of Seville (530–636) in *De Ortu et Obitu Patrum*, which not only makes James the Apostle the author of this letter, but specifies that it was written "to the twelve tribes dispersed among the nations, including Spain"! (PL 83:151).

[440]PL 93:26.

[441]PL 209:193.

[442]See Nicolas of Lyre, *Postilla super Totam Bibliam* IV (Strassburg, 1492; reprint, Frankfurt: Minerva, 1971).

[443]*Enarratio in Epistolam Catholicam Beati Jacobi* in *Doctoris Ecstatici D. Dionysii Cartusiani Opera Omnia* (Monstrolii, 1901).

of Thomas Aquinas and a considerable amount of scholastic sensibility come to light. The commentary is particularly full in its discussion of James 2:14–26.

As in the East, however, commentaries do not exhaust the range of interpretation. When lections from James appeared in the liturgy, sermons were devoted to the exposition of the text. In the ninth century, Haymo preached on James 1:17–18 and 1:22–27,[444] and Abbot Smaragdus commented on James 1:20–27 and James 5.[445] In the twelfth century, Radulphus Ardens preached on James 1:2–12 and James 1:17–18.[446] In the thirteenth century Abbot Godfridus devoted homilies to James 1:17–20 and 1:22–27.[447] And James' influence was not absent from such medieval spiritual writers as Bernard of Clairvaux (1090–1153),[448] Albert the Great (1200–80),[449] Meister Eckhardt (1260–1327),[450] and Thomas à Kempis (1380–1471),[451] nor from medieval theologians, such as Thomas Aquinas.[452]

D. THE SIXTEENTH CENTURY

The long history of harmonious (and harmonizing) interpretation of James changed at the beginning of the sixteenth century. As a result, James became one of the most disputed of NT compositions. Luther's antagonism was not the only factor. Equally significant was the spirit of critical inquiry associated with the Renaissance: the rediscovery of Greek, the questioning of historical attributions of authorship, the beginnings of textual criticism, the awareness of the NT as a collection of writings whose language and rhetoric were shaped by a world utterly different than that of Christendom.

All of these are present already in the notes of Erasmus of Rotterdam on the Letter of James.[453] Erasmus questions the apostolic authorship of the letter and anticipates Luther's position with his comment that the letter lacked "apostolic

---

[444]Haymo, *Homiliae de Tempore* 86 (PL 118:514) and 88 (PL 118:520).

[445]Abbot Smaragdus, *Collectiones in Epistulas et Evangelia* (PL 102:299–307).

[446]Radulphus Ardens, *Homiliae de Sanctis* 9 (PL 155:1521–26) and *Homiliae in Epistolas et Evangelia Dominicales* 60 (PL 155:1884–88).

[447]Abbot Godfridus, *Homiliae Dominicales* 52 (PL 154:347–52) and 55 (PL 174:359–64).

[448]See, e.g., Bernard, *Sermons on the Song of Songs* 64:8; 85:4–7.

[449]See *The Paradise of the Soul* (attributed to Albert), 9, 14, 20, 24, 26, 28, 30, 31, 37, 40.

[450]Meister Eckhardt's *Sermon* 19 is based on James 1:17.

[451]Thomas à Kempis, *The Imitation of Christ* I, 7, 10, 13; II, 8, 12, 15; III, 30; IV, 18.

[452]It is noteworthy that the very first line of (Pseudo-) Dionysius [the Aereopagite], *De Coelestia Hierarchia* I,1 (PG 3:119), is an unacknowledged but clear citation of James 1:17, providing the scriptural starting point for his neo-platonic theology, which had such a profound effect on the mysticism and theology of the West. For points of influence on Aquinas in particular, see J. F. Ben M. de Rubies, O.P., *Dissertatio* in PG 3:88–90.

[453]Erasmus, *Annotationes in Epistolam Jacobi* (1516) in *Opera Omnia* 6 (Leiden: Vanden, 1705) 1025–38.

majesty and gravity."[454] He offers linguistic parallels from Pliny and Suetonius (see 1:6 and 1:12), seeks to establish the Greek text on the basis of manuscript evidence (see 4:6), pays attention to the logic of the argument (see 2:24), and, when he cannot make sense of the text, suggests an emendation (see 4:2). But Erasmus does not decisively break with the prior tradition, quoting Bede, Augustine, and Jerome (see 1:18, 2:13). And on the issue of faith and works, Erasmus harmonizes: "truly Paul in that place speaks of the observance of the law of Moses, here [James] is concerned with the offices of piety and charity" (2:23).[455] Nevertheless, he challenges the medieval church's stand that the sacraments of extreme unction and confession could be supported by James 5:14–16.[456]

A similar independence characterizes Cardinal Thomas de Vio (Cajetan), who in 1518 was Luther's disputant.[457] Quoting Jerome, he questions the apostolic authorship of James. Cajetan calls the Greeting of the letter "a secular sort of greeting" *(profane more salutem)*. He explicitly denies that 5:14 supports extreme unction: "Neither from the words nor from the conjunction do these words speak about the sacrament of extreme unction."[458] But he also agrees that a faith that is not "prepared to work *(parata operari)*" is dead.

It will be remembered that Martin Luther's complaint against James began with the same issue of extreme unction and led to the questioning of the letter's apostolic authorship—which for Luther determined its authority. On these points, he shared the views of Erasmus and Cajetan. But Luther pushed the principle of *sachkritik* ("content criticism") to the extreme of rejecting James entirely because of its (perceived) contradiction to Luther's fundamental principle of *sola fide*.[459] This position was adopted also by Luther's temporary ally Andreas Bodenstein of Carlstadt, who placed James, on the basis of its teaching and its lack of apostolic authorship, in what he termed "the third and weakest rank of divine authority" together with 2 Peter, 2 and 3 John, Jude, Hebrews, and the Apocalypse.[460]

Lutheran insistence on this point generated equally extreme reactions from the Catholic party. The Council of Trent (1546) not only simultaneously asserted James' canonicity and apostolic authorship[461] but also used James as

---

[454]*Annotationes*, 1038.

[455]*Annotationes*, 1031.

[456]*Annotationes*, 1038.

[457]Thomas de Vio, *Epistulae Pauli et aliorum Apostolorum ad Graecam Castigate* (Paris: Badius Ascensius et J. Parvus et J. Roigny, 1529).

[458]*Nec ex verbis nec ex effectu verba haec loquuntur de sacramentali unctione extreme unctionis.*

[459]His formal views were more than adequately expressed as well by his marginal annotations on James, as reported by W. Walther, "Zu Luthers Ansicht über den Jakobusbrief," *TSK* 66 (1893) 595–98.

[460]Andreas Bodenstein, *De Canonicis Scripturis Libellus D. Andreae Bodenstein Carolstadii* (Wittemberg, 1520).

[461]See *Enchiridion Symbolorum Definitionum et Declarationum de rebus Fidei et Moribus* 33rd ed., eds. H. Denziger and A. Schönmetzer (Rome: Herder, 1965) 1503.

explicit warrant for the sacrament of extreme unction[462] and the traditional teaching on faith and works.[463] The Catholic Counter-Reformation also provided the Letter of James with an able intellectual defender in the controversialist Robert Bellarmine (1542–1621), who took up eight separate arguments made against James and systematically responded to them.[464]

On the other side of Reformation debates, the position of Luther and Carlstadt on the Letter of James was not shared by all reformers. William Tyndale followed many of Luther's theological positions, but in his 1525 translation of the NT declared, "I think it [James] ought rightly to be regarded as Holy Scripture."[465] Philip Melanchthon extensively compares James and Paul on good works, concluding "Paul talks about one kind of faith, James another,"[466] and "James therefore does not fight with Paul, but speaks about another reality. He refutes the error of those who think themselves to be righteous on account of a profession of doctrines."[467] Ulrich Zwingli also quotes James favorably[468] and argues that the letter is misunderstood when read in the "papist" fashion.[469] He says to those whose faith is "languid," ". . . we have already urged them, as have Christ, Paul, and James, that, if they are to be faithful, they must prove themselves faithful with works, for faith without works is dead."[470] The Westminster Confession of 1646 explicitly included James in the canon, as the Thirty-Nine Articles (1553) did implicitly. Even the Anabaptist Dordrecht Confession (1632) explicitly cites James 5:12 in support of the prohibition of taking oaths and 5:19 in support of fraternal correction in the community.[471]

Luther's position, indeed, was to be of greater influence on later scholars in the German Lutheran tradition than it was on his fellow reformers. John Calvin (1509–64) clearly has Luther in mind when he says, "There are also some at this day who do not think it entitled to authority. I, however, am inclined to receive it without controversy, because I see no just cause for rejecting it."[472] Calvin's commentary combines a close reading of the Greek text (including positive and negative responses to Erasmian textual decisions), together with

---

[462]*Enchiridion*, 1699.

[463]*Enchiridion*, 1535.

[464]Robert Bellarmine, *Prima Controversiae Generalis: De Verbo Dei Quatuor Libris Explicata* I,18.

[465]See R. V. G. Tasker, *The General Epistle of James* (Tyndale NT Commentaries; London: Tyndale Press, 1956) 15.

[466]"*de alia fide Paulus, de alia Jacobus loquitur*," in *Loci Communes Theologici* (1559) IX,V,2.

[467]"*non igitur pugnat Jacobus cum Paulo, sed de alia re loquitur, refutat errorem eorum qui fingebant re justum esse propter professionem dogmatum*," in *Loci Communes* IX,V,12.

[468]U. Zwingli, *Defense of the Reformed Faith* (1523), Art. 10, 15, 16, 22.

[469]*Defense of the Faith*, Art. 18, 27, 52.

[470]U. Zwingli, *Expositio Fidei*, (1531) fol. 14v.

[471]See *Creeds of the Churches* rev. ed., ed. J. H. Leith (Atlanta: John Knox Press, 1973) 194, 269, 305, 306.

[472]John Calvin, *Commentaries on the Epistle of James* (1551), trans. J. Owen (Grand Rapids: Eerdmans, 1948) 276.

attention to the religious message of the composition. Calvin makes several attacks on "sophists and papists" for their misreadings of James (see on 1:15; 2:10; 5:14–16). As might be expected, that critique is fiercest in the discussion of James 2:14–26. But Calvin insists that James and Paul themselves are not in disagreement. On 2:21, he notes, "when, therefore, the sophists set up James against Paul, they go astray through the ambiguous meaning of a term."[473] This last statement points to another quality in Calvin's commentary: in addition to using Greco-Roman sources to explicate the language of James (Plato, Pythagoras, Aesop, the Stoics, Horace, Pliny), Calvin shows himself particularly attuned to the conventions of classical rhetoric, and in several passages he evokes such conventions to make sense out of the sequence of James' argument (see on 2:14; 2:18; 2:19–20; 3:16; 4:6).

Before turning to the directions taken by later Protestant commentaries, it is appropriate to pause appreciatively over a monument of learning in many ways still unsurpassed. The Flemish Jesuit Cornelius à Lapide (1567–1637) produced a commentary on the entire Bible that is extraordinarily impressive not only for its sheer magnitude but its depth of scholarship. The commentary on James alone is equivalent to 500 pages of close print."[474] For every verse, not only the minutiae of language (Hebrew, Syriac, Greek, Latin), but a whole range of literary allusion is brought into the discussion. For James 3:14, for example, citations are provided from Statius, Ovid, Pliny, Antonius, Aristotle, and Martial, not to mention Isidore of Pelusium and Belesarius. Not only the number but the appositeness of the citations is impressive. Comment on individual verses is arranged in a series of scholastic-like observations, providing a selection of approaches to the passage. If there is a deficiency, it is that the amount of attention to the individual verse precludes the sort of rhetorically subtle reading that Calvin provided. But the wide range of learning stands as vivid testimony to the marriage of Renaissance scholarship with patristic and scholastic traditions that marks the Catholic Counter-Reformation. Also impressive from the Catholic side is the commentary of G. Estius, composed in 1564–66, which displays less learning from antiquity but is closely attentive to the language and enters into vigorous dispute with the "heretics" (i.e., Protestants).[475]

E. THE SEVENTEENTH AND EIGHTEENTH CENTURIES

Protestant interpretation of James after the Reformation tended to follow one of the paths laid out by the great sixteenth-century figures. Some picked up on

---

[473]Calvin, *Commentaries on James*, 314.

[474]Cornelius à Lapide, *Commentaria in Scripturam Sanctam* (Paris: Ludovicus Vives, 1868), Vol 20: *Commentarius in Epistolas Catholicas*.

[475]G. Estius, *Commentariorum in Epistulas Apostolicas* (Paris: Fr. Leonard, 1659).

the historical criticism implicit in Luther's position and pursued the placement of James in early Christianity. Others built on the work of Erasmus to construct ever more elaborate parallels from the ancient world. Still others followed the lead of Calvin, combining linguistic analysis with particular attention to the religious message of James.

It is precisely at this point, however, that the present exposition must be recognized for the sketch that it is. Biblical scholarship of every sort explodes in the seventeenth and eighteenth centuries, and no survey can take account of it all. In the mid-nineteenth century, for example, James Darling listed from the seventeenth and eighteenth centuries some twelve commentaries on the catholic epistles and eleven commentaries on James in addition to the ones I mention here.[476] And commentaries are only one mode of interpretation. Darling also has sixteen closely printed columns of sermons and tracts devoted to specific passages in James.[477] James 5:14–16 was put to particularly heavy use in heated debates among Protestant divines concerning the anointing of the sick.[478] The following remarks, therefore, can do little more than indicate some typical approaches and some turning points.

The approach of Calvin is ably carried forward by Thomas Manton, whose interpretation of James originated in weekly lectures to his congregation.[479] Manton is well acquainted with earlier traditions of interpretation, cognizant of controversies concerning the letter, and capable, like Calvin, of combining in one paragraph an astute rhetorical point with an attack on the "papists" (see on 1:27). His work, however, is above all "practical," that is, directed to the religious life and practices of his listeners; all his learning tends to this end. Similar in purpose, although much more modest in scope, are the annotations of John Wesley.[480] Wesley relies heavily on the scholarship of Bengel (see below), but succinctly turns everything to the uses of piety: thus, on 1:16, "It is a grievous thing to ascribe the evil and not the good we receive to God."

The approach of Hugo Grotius is closer to Erasmus in spirit.[481] Grotius speculates on the historical circumstances eliciting James 4:1, but for the most part, his concerns are almost entirely linguistic. He cites a number of Greek and Latin parallels to James. But his distinctive contribution is to bring in extensive

---

[476]See J. Darling, *Cyclopaedia Bibliographica* (London: James Darling, 1859). In addition to the commentaries on James treated here, he lists: Rungius (1600), Turnbull (1606), Stvartius (1610), Paez (1617), Mayer (1629), Laurentius (1653), Brochmand (1658), Benson (1746), Semler (1781), and Morus (1794).

[477]Darling, *Cyclopaedia Bibliographica*, 2:1642–58.

[478]See, e.g., Jeremy Taylor, *The Rule and Exercise of Holy Dying* (1651), and Christopher Love, *The Penitent Pardoned* (1657).

[479]Thomas Manton, *A Practical Commentary or an Exposition with Notes on the Epistle of James* (1640; reprint, Banner of Trust, 1962).

[480]John Wesley, *Explanatory Notes on the New Testament* (1754; London: Epworth, 1950).

[481]H. Grotius, *Annotationes in Epistulam Jacobi* (1642); El. Chr. Ern de Windheim, II,2 (Erlangen and Leipzig: Tetzschner, 1757).

references to the Hebrew, specifically that found in rabbinic sources (see on 1:6 and 2:21). Grotius shows the influence of John Lightfoot's "Christian Hebraism" (1602–75). Grotius and Erasmus are included in the magnificent British combined commentary called *Critici Sacri*.[482] The section entitled *Annotationes in Epistolam Jacobi* contains as well the comments of Valla, Vatablus, L. and J. Capellus, and many others. The range of learning is once more most impressive, with Pricaeus (Pricc) in particular educing a vast range of Hellenistic parallels to the text of James, and L. Capellus using Talmudic Hebrew to explicate passages like James 2:13. The comments of J. Cameron on James 2 and the opinions of the "Pontiffs" are also valuable. Another commentary in the Erasmian spirit is by J. J. Wettstein,[483] who contributed an improved critical text with a fuller display of manuscript variants and, in his notes, pulled together a rich collection of Greco-Roman parallels. The advance on Cornelius à Lapide is that the parallels, though still diffuse and unsorted, are more focused on the Hellenistic period and include Plutarch and Philo. These commentaries, however, never address the question of the text's meaning or argument, much less its religious import.

The approach of Luther is perhaps best seen in J. A. Bengel.[484] In addition to notes on James' language (in this case drawn primarily from other biblical sources), Bengel shows some concern with understanding the letter's historical circumstances, suggesting what "rich and poor" might mean in first-century Jerusalem (on 2:5–6). Most of all, Bengel identifies those addressed by James on the issue of faith and works explicitly as those who had known Paul's teaching on justification by faith and had distorted it: ". . . already pretended Christians had abused this doctrine . . . and had employed Paul's words in a sense opposite to what he intended" (on 2:14). Bengel thus anticipates a position that later becomes dominant. Although Lutheran, Bengel resisted opposing Paul and James themselves: "Both wrote the truth, and appropriately, but in different ways, as having to deal with different kinds of men" (on 2:14).

An even more decisive step was taken toward historical analysis by J. G. Herder (1744–1803).[485] His monograph consists in a lengthy examination of the figure of James and a series of conjectures intended to resolve textual difficulties. Herder's originality lay in his complete focus on the historical setting of the letter. He attributes it to James the Brother of the Lord and insists that he and Paul knew each other and each other's views on justification. But Herder places

---

[482]*Critici Sacri* (1660), ed. J. Pearson, A. Scatterfield, et al. (Amsterdam: H. Boom et al., 1698).

[483]J. J. Wettstein, *Novum Testamentum Graecum* 2 Vols (Amsterdam: Ex Officiana Dommeriana, 1752).

[484]J. A. Bengel, *Gnomon Novi Testamenti*, 3d ed. (Stuttgartiae: J. F. Steinkopf, 1891; originally published in 1773). Bengel is used heavily, in turn, by G. C. Storr, *Dissertatio Exegetica in Epistolam Jacobi* (Tübingen: Fues, 1784).

[485]J. G. Herder, *Briefe zweener Brüder Jesu im unserem Kanon* (1775); in *Herders sämmtliche Werke*, ed. B. Suphan, Vol 7 (Berlin: Weidmann, 1884) 471–573.

them within two primordial streams of early Christianity. For the first time, so far as I have discovered, James is explicitly seen as the basis for the Jewish Christianity that became Ebionitism. Herder not only anticipates the later position of Kern and Baur, but for the first time, the historical setting and "historical standpoint" of James become decisive for interpretation. Rather than a text that is to be heard and apprehended in the present, James is the object of historical inquiry to be "explained" in terms of the past.

In this period, Roman Catholic scholarship remained fundamentally conservative in spirit and purpose. Augustin Calmet (1672–1757), for example, wrote a literal commentary on the entire Bible based on the Vulgate rather than the Greek text.[486] The comments on James make references to the Greek text but they are relegated to footnotes. The commentary pays some attention to Protestant objections to 2:14–26 and 5:14–16, but it aligns it with the patristic and medieval traditions of interpretation, with some appropriation of the literary parallels uncovered by the great commentaries of the Renaissance and Catholic Counter-Reformation.

F. NINETEENTH-CENTURY BATTLE LINES

The shape of the historical-critical paradigm began to emerge in the nineteenth century. The early part of the century still saw thoroughly traditional commentaries, such as those of Hottinger[487] and Schulthess,[488] the very learned effort of Theile,[489] and Gebser.[490] Gebser provides very full citations from patristic and medieval interpreters, as well as a selection of Greco-Roman parallels. He also represents a survival of the earlier premise that the text's self-presentation was to be taken on its own terms to be explicated or appropriated. An even stronger note of continuity with church tradition is sounded by B. Jacobi, whose commentary consists in nineteen sermons preached on James![491]

Most commentators, however, began to follow the direction established by historians like J. G. Herder. The writings of the NT are to be apprehended in terms of their historical circumstances. This approach was abetted by the development of the genre of "Introduction to the New Testament," which took

---

[486]A. Calmet, *Commentarius Litteralis in Omnes Libros Veteris et Novi Testamenti* 3rd ed., trans. J. Mansi (Venice: S. Colet, 1767–75); the comments on James are found in 8:499–520.

[487]J. J. Hottinger, *Epistolae B. Jacobi atque Petri I* (Leipzig: Dyck, 1815).

[488]J. Schultess, *Epistola Jacobi Commentario Copiossisimo et verborum et sententiarum explanata* (Turici: F. Schulthess, 1824), a commentary that relies very heavily on Zwingli.

[489]C. G. G. Theile, *Commentarius in Epistolam Jacobi* (Leipzig: Baumgärtner, 1833). He follows an earlier commentator named Rauch in thinking that James 5:12–20 is a later interpolation.

[490]A. R. Gebser, *Der Brief des Jakobus* (Berlin: A. Rüker, 1828).

[491]B. Jacobi, *Der Brief des Jakobus* (Berlin: Keimer, 1835).

as its goal the historical placement (and by implication) the explanation of the various canonical writings. J. D. Michaelis (1717–91) was the pioneer.[492] His introduction was historically conservative: James was written by an apostle and does not contradict Paul on justification.[493] It is also theologically perceptive; regarding Luther's dismissal of James as a "letter of straw," Michaelis sardonically notes that the Sermon on the Mount could be dismissed on the same grounds![494] But Michaelis explains James from within its historical context and makes its interpretation depend on the determination of that context. Indeed, for Michaelis, its very canonicity depends on the historical determination that it *was* an apostle who wrote it.[495]

Like Michaelis, the German scholars A. Neander and M. Schneckenberger used the historical method to reach traditional conclusions. In his influential history of the church, Neander regards James as one of the three pivotal figures (together with Paul and John) in earliest Christianity but sees no real conflict among them.[496] And in Neander's popular commentary, he argued that James was both authentic and very early—before the Antiochean controversy—with its teaching on faith and works to be understood as a response to converted Jews who had carried with them an attitude that membership and proper belief were sufficient, without observance. Neander rejects the possibility that James could have been responding to Paul, for it was unlikely for any Jacobean churches to have extensive contacts with Paul's thought so early.[497] M. Schneckenberger similarly argues that James is written to counteract the "faith alone" attitudes of recent Jewish converts, quoting Philo to show that there were such views in Judaism.[498] Like Neander, Schneckenberger attributes the letter to James the Brother of the Lord, written before the controversy at Antioch.[499] What is noteworthy about these works is not their conclusions, but the effort they expend in making specifically *historical* arguments to *explain* the text.

The work of F. H. Kern is literally epochal. By taking the historical-critical approach in the opposite direction, he began a century-long debate.[500] Kern combined an analysis of James' place in early Christianity with that of the "inner character" of the letter into an elaborate historical argument. He emphasized the incompatibility of Paul and James on the issue of justification, declaring

---

[492]J. D. Michaelis, *Introduction to the New Testament* (1750; English translation, London: 1823).

[493]Michaelis, *Introduction*, 4:281, 302.

[494]Michaelis, *Introduction*, 4:296.

[495]Michaelis, *Introduction*, 4:314.

[496]A. Neander, *Geschichte der Pflanzung und Leitung den christlichen Kirche* 2 Vols (Hamburg: Perthes, 1832–33).

[497]A. Neander, *Epistle of James Practically Explained* (1850), trans. H. C. Conant (New York: Sheldon, 1852) 30, 33–35.

[498]M. Schneckenberger, *Annotatio ad Epistolam Jacobi Perpetua cum Brevi Tractatione Isagogica* (Stuttgart: F. L. Löflund, 1832) 128, 135.

[499]Schneckenberger, *Annotatio*, 140–48.

[500]F. H. Kern, *Der Character und Ursprung des Briefes Jacobi* (Tübingen: Fues, 1835).

that in this matter, Luther's view was correct.[501] He also connected James' language and outlook to that of the "Ebionite" Jewish Christianity of the *Pseudo-Clementine Literature*. Then Kern determined the *Tendenz* of the letter to be one that combined: a) hostility between rich and poor with b) evidence of conflict and persecution and c) the theological controversy concerning justification. But it is not the historical James and Paul who are at odds, but later streams of Christianity: James must be seen in the context of hostility between marginalized Jewish-Christian communities and dominant Gentile churches.[502] James is then to be dated in the second century as part of catholizing (antignostic) Christianity.[503] In this work, Kern established the second major way to account for James within the historical-critical approach. This approach is clearly devoted to history but is equally determined by a Lutheran perception of Christianity.

Remarkably, Kern himself abandoned this radical solution. Three years after his ingenious historical argument, he published a commentary that came to quite different conclusions. The evidence now pointed to the exact opposite conclusion concerning the *Ursprung* of the letter: it was written by James the Brother of the Lord shortly before the fall of Jerusalem.[504] It is Kern's radical reading, however, that gets adopted by the most influential church historian of the nineteenth century. F. C. Baur explicitly appropriate's Kern's earlier explanation as his own.[505]

Kern had already quoted W. M. L. De Wette's introduction to support the rejection of James' authorship on the basis of language.[506] Now, Kern's radical reading is taken up in turn by De Wette's fifth edition[507] and by the 1847 edition of De Wette's commentary,[508] although the third edition of the commentary (under B. Brueckner, 1865) moved from Kern's strong reading to a more generalized characterization: James is late, pseudonymous, and catholicizing, with no literary coherence or theological perspective, entirely devoted to moralizing).[509] Kern's earlier position is also taken up and extensively developed by Baur's student and colleague, A. Schwegler.[510]

---

[501]Kern, *Character*, 18–20, 44.

[502]Kern, *Character*, 25–36.

[503]Kern, *Character*, 86, 101–8.

[504]See F. H. Kern, *Der Brief Jakobi Untersucht und Erklaert* (Tübingen: Fues, 1838) 85.

[505]F. C. Baur, *Paul, The Apostle of Jesus Christ* 2nd ed., (London: Williams & Norgate, 1875) 2:297–313; and ibid., *The Church History of the First Three Centuries* (1853–62) 1:128–30.

[506]W. M. L. De Wette, *Lehrbuch der historisch-kritischen Einleitung in die kanonischen Bücher des Neuen Testaments* 2nd ed. (Berlin: 1830).

[507]W. M. L. De Wette, *Historical-Critical Introduction to the Canonical Books of the New Testament*, trans. F. Frothingham (Boston: Crosby, Nichols, 1858) 330–33.

[508]W. M. L. De Wette, *Kurze Erklärung der Briefe des Petrus, Judas, und Jakobus* (Leipzig: Hirzel, 1847).

[509]De Wette, *Kurz Eklärung* 3rd ed., ed. B. Brückner (1865) 192–206.

[510]A. Schwegler, *Das nachapostolische Zeitalter in den Hauptmomentum seiner Entwicklung* (Tübingen: Fues, 1846) 413–48.

The middle of the nineteenth century, therefore, saw the battle lines drawn between those who favored an early date for James and read it in terms of its traditional attribution and those who read it as a pseudonymous production witnessing to historical currents within Christianity. For the remainder of the century, the battle itself was uneven. By far the greatest number of scholars working on James preferred the traditional conclusions. I have already noted Kern's change of mind in his 1838 commentary. One can add those of H. Boumann,[511] H. Ewald,[512] J. Hofmann,[513] J. G. Rosenmüller,[514] D. Erdmann,[515] and W. G. Schmidt.[516] Writing in the first edition of the Meyer commentary series, J. E. Huther could claim that the majority of scholars agreed with his traditional position on the critical questions.[517] Immediately after him, the commentaries of Carr[518] and Beyschlag[519] were just as conservative, as was that of P. Feine.[520] Finally, J. B. Mayor's great commentary, with its argument that James could well be our first extant Christian writing, had its first publication in 1892.[521]

Major critical introductions, moreover, also subscribed to the same views, including those of J. L. Hug,[522] K. A. Credner,[523] and G. Salmon, who declared ". . . to a disciple of Baur there is no more disappointing document than this Epistle of James."[524] At the end of the century, the conservative view was also given the support of the great historian Theodore Zahn.[525]

---

[511]H. Boumann, *Commentarius Perpetuus in Jacobi Epistolam* (Utrecht: Kennick, 1865).

[512]H. Ewald, *Die Sendschreiben aus der Hebräer und Jakobus' Rundschreiben* (Göttingen: Dieterich, 1870).

[513]J. Hofmann, *Der Brief Jacobi* (Nördingen: Beck, 1875).

[514]J. G. Rosenmüller, *Scholia in Novum Testamentum* 6th ed. (Nürnberg: Felkser, 1881).

[515]D. Erdmann, *Der Brief des Jakobus* (Berlin: Wiegand und Grieber, 1857).

[516]W. G. Schmidt, *Der Lehrgehalt des Jacobus-Briefes: Ein Beitrag zur neutestamentlichen Theologie* (Leipzig: Hinrichs, 1869).

[517]J. E. Huther, *Critical and Exegetical Commentary on the General Epistles of James, Peter, John and Jude* (1857), trans. P. J. Golag (New York: Funk and Wagnalls, 1887).

[518]A. Carr, *The General Epistle of St. James* (Cambridge: Cambridge University Press, 1896).

[519]W. Beyschlag, *Der Brief des Jakobus* (1882) 3rd ed. (Göttingen: Vandenhoeck & Ruprecht, 1897).

[520]P. Feine, *Der Jakobusbrief: Nach Lehranschauungen und Enstehungsverhältnissen* (Eisenach: M. Wilckens, 1893).

[521]J. B. Mayor, *The Epistle of St. James* 3rd ed. (London: MacMillan and Co., 1910).

[522]J. L. Hug, *Introduction to the New Testament* 3rd ed., trans. D. Fosdick (Andover: Gould and Newman, 1836).

[523]K. A. Credner, *Einleitung in das Neue Testament* (Halle: Waisenhaus, 1836).

[524]G. Salmon, *A Historical Introduction to the Books of the New Testament* 3rd ed. (London: John Murray, 1888) 485–86.

[525]Th. Zahn, *Introduction to the New Testament* (1897) 3rd ed., trans. M. W. Jacobus (Edinburgh: T & T Clark, 1909). One can add these articles of the nineteenth century that favor authenticity and early dating: G. Jäger, "Der Verfasser des Jakobusbriefes," *Zeitschrift für die gesammte lutherische Theologie und Kirche* 33 (1878) 420–426; K. Werner, "Ueber den Brief Jacobi, *Theologische Quartalschrift* 54 (1872) 246–79; P. Feine, "Über literarische Abhängigkeit und

In contrast, among major commentators De Wette appeared to be joined only by H. Von Soden, who espouses pseudonymity and dates James in the time of the Domitian persecution.[526] It is not by means of commentaries that the position concerning James' late and pseudonymous character is disseminated, but by German histories of early Christianity, introductions, and theologies of the NT. After Kern's early conclusions were taken up by the fifth edition of De Wette's influential introduction (1848), it appears also in H. J. Holtzmann's history[527] and his handbook on NT theology.[528] The historian C. von Weizsaecker attributes the letter to a "spiritual successor to James" within an Ebionite Christianity.[529] A. C. McGiffert places James in the late first century as a sermon addressed to "the church at large."[530] The influence of Th. Zahn on the conservative side was more than matched by that of Adolf von Harnack, who considered James to be complex in composition, not to be dated earlier than 120–140, and perhaps gaining its title as late as the end of the second or the beginning of the third century.[531]

At the close of the century, therefore, the radical position was widely adopted and disseminated. It was adopted wholeheartedly by A. Jülicher,[532] whose discussion of James anticipates the work of Dibelius on most key points: James has no definite train of thought, but only ideas connected by association;[533] it has no consistent thesis;[534] it could only have been written after the Pauline question had been formulated and resolved;[535] it uses 1 Clement;[536] and it is "the least Christian book of the New Testament."[537]

Zeitverhältnisse des Jakobusbriefes," *Neue Jahrbuch für deutsche Theologie* 3 (1894) 322–34; Th. Zahn, "Die sociale Frage und die Innere Mission nach dem Brief des Jakobus," *Zeitschrift für kirchliche Wissenschaft und kirchliches Leben* 60 (1889) 295–307.

[526]H. von Soden, *Hebräerbrief, Briefe des Petrus, Jakobus, Judas* (1890) (Handkommentar zum Neuen Testament 2.3; 1899); see also von Soden's "Der Jakobusbrief," *Jahrbücher für Protestantische Theologie* 10 (1884) 137–92, as well as W. Brückner, "Zur Kritik des Jakobusbriefs," *Zeitschrift für wissenschaftliche Theologie* 17 (1874) 530–41, and the reviews of Erdmann and Beyschlag by E. Haupt, *Theologische Studies und Kritiken* 65 (1883) 177–94.

[527]H. J. Holtzmann, *Lehrbuch der historischen-kritischen Einleitung in das Neuen Testament* 3rd ed. (Freiburg: JCB Mohr, 1892).

[528]H. J. Holtzmann, *Lehrbuch der neutestamentlichen Theologie* (Freiburg: JCB Mohr, 1897) 2:349–50; see also his article arguing that James was written from Rome in the late first century, "Die Zeitlage des Jakobusbriefes," *Zeitschrift für wissenschaftliche Theologie* 25 (1882) 292–310.

[529]C. von Weizsäcker, *The Apostolic Age of the Christian Church* 2nd ed., trans. J. Miller (London: Williams and Norgate, 1899) 30–32.

[530]A. C. McGiffert, *A History of Christianity in the Apostolic Age* (New York: Charles Scribner's Sons, 1897) 579–85.

[531]A. von Harnack, *Geschichte der altchristliche Literatur bis Eusebius* Teil 2: *Die Chronologie* (Leipzig: Hinrichs'che Buchhandlung, 1897) 2:486–91.

[532]A. Jülicher, *An Introduction to the New Testament* (1st ed., 1894); trans. from 1900 edition by J. P. Ward (New York: Putnam, 1904).

[533]Jülicher, *Introduction*, 216.

[534]Jülicher, *Introduction*, 218.

[535]Jülicher, *Introduction*, 222.

[536]Jülicher, *Introduction*, 224.

[537]Jülicher, *Introduction*, 225.

By the end of the nineteenth century, the battles within the historical-critical approach had reached a stalemate. Using the same methods and identical evidence, scholars came to diametrically opposed conclusions. No one convinced anyone else. Criticism was less a matter of incremental progress than of proclaiming allegiance. Commentaries became more and more self-referential, citing strings of earlier commentators agreeing with the author's position on debated points.

What is perhaps most dismaying about this state of affairs is how little light was thrown on the actual text of James. Since there was little or no attention paid to James' rhetoric of argumentation, it was an easy step to conclude that James was "formless." The commentary genre itself abetted this conclusion, since each verse was isolated and loaded down with its own weight of information. What the debates made most clear, however, was what happened when James became mainly a matter of historical inquiry and "explanation," rather than of passionate engagement or appropriation. The scholars were almost all churchmen, but interpretation increasingly became the property of the academy.

It is against the backdrop of Jülicher's statement that James was the "least Christian book of the New Testament" that the boldest critical stroke of the late nineteenth century can be appreciated. Almost simultaneously, two scholars took the marginalization of James to its logical extreme. L. Massebieau asked whether James was even a Christian composition and answered his own question in the negative: James was originally a Jewish composition of Essene coloration composed in the first century BCE and known to Paul. Only later were the two mentions of Jesus (1:1; 2:1) added to make this a "Christian" writing.[538] Virtually the same position was argued by F. Spitta, who devotes three lengthy chapters to "the problem and its solution." He tries to demonstrate that this was a pre-Christian Jewish writing only lightly baptized by the interpolation of 1:1 and 2:1, as well as some judicious emendations.[539] Although vigorously rebutted by Zahn and others, this most radical of solutions to the "problem" represented by James was not to disappear completely.[540] The enduring contribution of Spitta was to bring a wealth of Hellenistic Jewish parallels to bear on the text.

What the thesis of Massebieau and Spitta most vividly illustrates is the way in which the logic of the scholarly discussion in some circles had led to the removal of James from serious consideration as properly "Christian" literature at all, whether early or late!

In sharpest contrast to this enveloping scholasticism, S. Kierkegaard showed how, outside the academy, biblical interpretation continued to thrive in the service of meaning. His Edifying Discourse of September 10, 1851, "For Self-

---

[538]L. Massebieau, "L'epître de Jacques: est-elle l'oeuvre d'un chrétien?" *RHR* 31–32 (1895) 249–83.

[539]F. Spitta, *Zur Geschichte und Literatur des Urchristentums 2: Der Brief des Jakobus* (Göttingen: Vandenhoeck & Ruprecht, 1896).

[540]See the reviews of Spitta by E. Haupt in *TSK* 69 (1896) 747–77, and R. Steck, "Die Konfession des Jakobusbriefes," *TZ* 15 (1898) 169–88.

Examination Proposed to this Age," takes as the text for its first section James 1:22–27 and is entitled "How to Derive True Benediction from Beholding Oneself in the Mirror of the Word." This brilliant reflection calls on James in support of the understanding of James held by Luther, against the official Lutheranism of his own day! And in the process, Kierkegaard excoriates those whose hearing of the word stops short at the consultation of dictionaries and commentaries rather than allowing true "self-examination." Likewise, in the sermon entitled "The Unchangeableness of God," dedicated to his father and dated May 18, 1851, Kierkegaard placed himself in the tradition of patristic and medieval interpretation by invoking as his text James 1:17 in support of God's immutability and, therefore, God's constancy in giving.[541]

Commentaries also continued to be produced that bypassed the debates over historical placement and directed themselves expressly to the life of the church, such as that by J. P. Lange and J. J. Oosterzee, which, in addition to its conservative views on authorship, appended to the "exegetical/critical" discussion of each passage also a "doctrinal/ethical" and finally a "homiletical/practical" section, the last made up primarily of citations from notable sermons preached on these passages.[542] And the commentary by R. W. Dale consisted entirely of ten sermons written on James 1:1–4:6.[543]

G. TWENTIETH-CENTURY DEVELOPMENTS

Two factors make a survey of the twentieth century problematic as part of a "history of interpretation." The first is the impossibility of surveying so much scholarship in so small a space: the universe of critical literature is an ever-expanding one and ever less capable of being circumscribed. The second is the fact that the present commentary interacts with twentieth century scholarship as part of a continuing conversation and is incapable of defining its contours as though it were a distant object. The present section contents itself, therefore, with showing how some of the trends of the nineteenth century continued through the twentieth and indicating some of the more noteworthy contributions that shape the present discussion of James as a whole.

---

[541]See T. Polk, "Heart Enough to be Confident: Kierkegaard on Reading James," in *The Grammar of the Heart*, ed. R. Bell (San Francisco: Harper and Row, 1988) 206–33.

[542]J. P. Lange and J. J. Oosterzee, *The Epistle of James* 2nd ed., trans. J. I. Momsert (New York: Charles Scribners, 1867).

[543]R. W. Dale, *The Epistle of James and Other Discourses* (London: Hodder and Stoughton, 1895); see also C. F. Deems, *The Gospel of Common Sense as Contained in the Canonical Epistle of James* (New York: Ketcham, 1888), and R. Johnstone, *Lectures Exegetical and Practical on the Epistle of James* 2nd ed. (Edinburgh: Oliphant Anderson and Ferrier, 1889).

1. THE PLACE OF JAMES IN CHRISTIAN HISTORY

The historical-critical debate concerning date and authorship continued with little progress. In 1903, R. St. John Parry concluded that James was written by the Brother of the Lord around 62 CE.[544] A year later, E. Grafe, using the same evidence, came to diametrically opposed conclusions: James was a pseudonymous production of the second century![545] Grafe, in turn, was immediately answered by a pamphlet published by B. Weiss, in which, after a lengthy rebuttal of the "non-traditional" critical position, he sagely observed, "The newer critics also have their unshakeable dogmas and their tenacious traditions."[546] Little new was offered either by way of evidence or argument some forty years later when the conservative position was argued by G. Kittel[547] and immediately answered by K. Aland.[548] The conservative position was also argued masterfully by G. H. Rendall[549] and, fifty years later, by J. A. T. Robinson.[550] But in the meantime the relative popularity of the respective positions had moved steadily away from the position advocating authenticity and early dating.

Into the 1920s, the majority of commentaries remained conservative on these points: see J. E. Belser,[551] R. J. Knowling,[552] A. Schlatter,[553] F. J. A. Hort,[554] A. Plummer,[555] Fr. Hauck,[556] J. Chaine,[557] L. Gaugusch,[558] as well as the two-stage theory of W. E. Oesterly.[559] Apart from the pivotal commentaries to be

---

[544]R. St. John Parry, *A Discussion of the General Epistle of St. James* (London: C. J. Clay and Sons, 1903).

[545]E. Grafe, *Die Stellung und Bedeutung des Jakobusbriefes in der Entwicklung des Urchristentums* (Tübingen: JCB Mohr, 1904).

[546]B. Weiss, *Der Jakobusbrief und die Neuere Kritik* (Leipzig: Dieckert'sche, 1904) 50.

[547]G. Kittel, "Die geschichtliche Ort des Jakobusbriefes," ZNW 41 (1942) 71–105; see also his review of Dibelius' commentary in *Theologisches Literaturblatt* 44 (1923) 3–7.

[548]K. Aland, "Der Herrenbruder Jakobus und der Jakobusbrief: Zur Frage eines urchristlichen Kalifats," TLZ 69 (1944) 97–104; see also, ten years earlier, H. Preisker, "Der Eigenwert des Jakobusbriefes in der Geschichte des Urchristentums," *TBl* 13 (1934) 229–36, which, while arguing for inauthenticity, dated the letter between 70–100.

[549]G. H. Rendall, *The Epistle of James and Judaic Christianity* (Cambridge: Cambridge University Press, 1927).

[550]J. A. T. Robinson, *Redating the New Testament* (Philadelphia: Westminster Press, 1976).

[551]J. E. Belser, *Die Epistel des Heiligen Jakobus* (Freiberg in Breisgau: Herder, 1909).

[552]R. J. Knowling, *The Epistle of James* 2nd ed. (London: Methuen, 1922).

[553]A. Schlatter, *Die Briefe des Petrus, Judas, Jakobus, der Brief an die Hebräer* (Stuttgart: Calwer Verlag, 1900).

[554]F. J. A. Hort, *The Epistle of St. James* (London: Macmillan and Co., 1909).

[555]A. Plummer, *The General Epistles of St. James and St. Jude* (New York: George H. Doran, 1920).

[556]Fr. Hauck, *Der Brief des Jakobus* (Leipzig: A Dichertsche, 1926).

[557]J. Chaine, *L'Épître de Saint Jacques* 2nd ed. (Paris: J. Gabalda, 1927).

[558]L. Gaugusch, *Der Lehrgehalt des Jakobusepistel: Eine exegetische Studie* (Freiburger theologische Studien 16; Freiburg: Herder, 1914).

[559]W. E. Oesterley, *The Greek Epistle of James* (Expositor's Greek Testament; New York: Hodder and Stoughton, 1910); later commentaries espousing authenticity include P. de Ambroggi, *Le*

mentioned below, the position in favor of pseudonymity was represented among major commentators mainly by G. Hollmann[560] and J. Moffatt.[561]

As in the late nineteenth century, however, commentaries had less influence than histories and introductions, most of which now began to reflect the critical position represented by Jülicher. Among early twentieth-century introductions, B. W. Bacon explicitly sponsored the German "higher criticism" and dated James ca. 90 CE.[562] O. Cone dated James in the early years of the second century.[563] Similar views were found in the introductions by A. S. Peake,[564] J. Moffatt,[565] and E. F. Scott.[566] These perceptions were supported by historians such as A. Loisy,[567] E. Meyer,[568] and J. Weiss.[569]

As the century progressed, this position—without much additional argument or evidence[570]—grew progressively stronger. The eighth edition of P. Feine and D. J. Behm's introduction, for example, still held to a conservative position on dating and authorship.[571] But the thirteenth edition, by W. G. Kümmel, not only stated emphatically that James was written at the end of the first century but devoted a short discussion to the "theological problem" presented by having James in the canon at all.[572]

By the second half of the century, it was still possible to find critical introductions favoring the traditional authorship and dating, for example those

---

Epistole Cattoliche di Giacomo, Pietro, Giovanni E Guida (La Sacra Biblia: Turin and Rome: Marietti, 1947); R. V. G. Tasker, *The General Epistle of James* (Tyndale New Testament Commentaries; London: Tyndale Press, 1956); F. Grünzweig, *Der Brief des Jakobus* (Wuppertaler Studienbibel; Wuppertal: Brockhaus, 1973); P. A. Deiros, *Santiago y Judas* (Commentario Biblico Hispanoamericano; Miami: Editorial Caribe, 1992).

[560]G. Hollmann, *Der Jakobusbrief* (Göttingen: Vandenhoeck & Ruprecht, 1908).

[561]J. Moffatt, *The General Epistles: James, Peter, and Jude* (London: Hodder and Stoughton, 1928); among later commentaries holding this view, see R. R. Williams, *The Letters of John and James* (Cambridge: Cambridge University Press, 1965).

[562]B. W. Bacon, *An Introduction to the New Testament* (New York: Macmillan and Co., 1900).

[563]O. Cone, *International Handbooks to the New Testament* III (New York: G. P. Putnam's Sons, 1901); see also his article "Letter of James" in the *Encyclopedia Biblica* (1914) 2321–26.

[564]A. S. Peake, *A Critical Introduction to the New Testament* (London: Duckworth and Co., 1909).

[565]J. Moffatt, *An Introduction to the Writings of the New Testament* 2nd ed. (Edinburgh: T & T Clark, 1918).

[566]E. F. Scott, *The Literature of the New Testament* (New York: Columbia, 1933).

[567]A. Loisy, *Les livres des Nouveau Testament* (Paris: Émile Nourry, 1922).

[568]E. Meyer, *Ursprung und Anfänge des Christentums* 3 Vols (Stuttgart: J. G. Cotta'sche, 1923).

[569]J. Weiss, *The History of Primitive Christianity* 2 Vols, trans. F. C. Grant (New York: Wilson-Erickson, 1937).

[570]One can note K. Aland, "Jakobusbrief," *RGG* (1959) 3:526–28; L. E. Elliott-Binns, "James," *Peake's Commentary on the Bible* (1962) 1022–25; E. Lohse, review of Mussner's commentary in *TLZ* 91 (1966) 112–14.

[571]P. Feine, J. Behm, *Einleitung in das Neue Testament* (Leipzig: Quelle & Meyer, 1936).

[572]W. G. Kümmel, *Einleitung in das Neue Testament* 13th ed. (Heidelberg: Quelle & Meyer, 1964) 301–2.

by W. Michaelis,[573] A. Wikenhauser,[574] B. M. Metzger,[575] A. F. J. Klijn,[576] and D. Guthrie.[577] But together with the widely used introduction of W. G. Kümmel, even more introductions and histories proposed a late dating and pseudonymity: C. F. D. Moule,[578] W. Marxsen,[579] E. Lohse,[580] H. von Campenhausen,[581] and H. Köster.[582] What is most remarkable is that this position no longer seems to need argument: it is simply asserted.

Three commentaries helped establish what was to be the dominant position for the rest of the twentieth century. In America, J. H. Ropes' impressive learning and judicious argumentation made his decision for James' pseudonymity and dating between 75–125 persuasive.[583] In France, J. Marty provided a similar argument for dating James between 75–80.[584] But it was M. Dibelius in Germany who established the framework for subsequent discussion. He had begun work on James before 1910, but his commentary did not appear until 1921.[585] Dibelius reversed the conservative position of the Meyer series. Dibelius did not really advance any novel theory concerning James: his critical positions were essentially those of A. Jülicher in 1897. But coming as it did after the Great War and from one of the pioneering figures of *Formgeschichte*, Dibelius' definition of James, as paraenesis that demanded a placement after Paul but otherwise responded only to general situations to be found in a moralizing church of the late first century, proved to be persuasive for many readers.

As in the nineteenth century, the debate concerning James' place in early Christianity has largely consisted in "talking past each other," which continues with little new evidence or insight. The growth of the more radical position owes as much to the politics and fashion of scholarship as it does to argumenta-

---

[573]W. Michaelis, *Einleitung in das Neue Testament* (Bern: BEG-Verlag, 1946).

[574]A. Wikenhauser, *New Testament Introduction* 2nd ed. (New York: Herder and Herder, 1956).

[575]B. M. Metzger, *The New Testament: Its Background, Growth, and Content* (Nashville: Abingdon, 1965).

[576]A. F. J. Klijn, *An Introduction to the New Testament* (Leiden: Brill, 1967).

[577]D. Guthrie, *New Testament Introduction* (Downer's Grove, Illinois: Intervarsity Press, 1970).

[578]C. F. D. Moule, *The Birth of the New Testament* (London: Adam and Charles Black, 1966).

[579]W. Marxsen, *Introduction to the New Testament*, trans. G. Buswell (Philadelphia: Fortress Press, 1968).

[580]E. Lohse, *The Formation of the New Testament* 3rd ed., trans. E. Boring (Nashville: Abingdon Press, 1981).

[581]H. von Campenhausen, *The Formation of the Christian Bible*, trans. J. Baker (Philadelphia: Fortress Press, 1972).

[582]H. Köster, *Introduction to the New Testament 2: History and Literature of Early Christianity* (New York: Walter de Gruyter, 1982).

[583]J. H. Ropes, *A Critical and Exegetical Commentary on the Epistle of St. James* (ICC; Edinburgh: T & T Clark, 1916).

[584]J. Marty, *L'Epitre de Jacques: Etude Critique* (Paris: Felix Alcan, 1935).

[585]M. Dibelius, *Der Brief des Jakobus* (Kritisch-exegetischer Kommentar ueber das Neue Testament 15; Göttingen: Vandenhoeck & Ruprecht, 1921); see also "Jakobusbrief," *RGG* 2nd ed. (1929) 3:18–21.

tion. But the establishment of that view has had two major consequences. First, as James is cut loose from any historical moorings, ever fuzzier theories about its place can be entertained. Thus, W. Popkes can account for the remarkable linkage between James and the Sermon on the Mount by invoking a "school" that reworked James' "traditions" around a decade after the death of Paul.[586] Second, since James is effectively removed from its Palestinian location, ever more elaborate theories about Palestinian Christianity can be developed, without adversion to what might be our earliest evidence for such Christianity. B. Mack can hypothesize a history of the Q community in Galilee without taking into account the similarities between James and that hypothetical document because, without argument, he places James around the year 150, "location uncertain."[587]

2. JAMES AND PAUL

An obviously enduring fascination for readers of James throughout the history of scholarship is the relationship between James and Paul. The analysis of that relationship played a key role in the studies devoted to James' place in early Christianity. The past century has also seen a steady stream of works trying to adjudicate the theological differences between James and Paul. The obvious sticking points are the writers' respective understandings of justification, faith, and the role of "works" in salvation. A listing of such efforts is found in the bibliography given above in section I.E.4. (pp. 64–65). It must be said that most of these efforts do not much improve on the earlier discussions in the history of interpretation. That the topic continues to generate such constant, if not obsessive, attention suggests something about the angle from which James has been approached within the historical-critical paradigm, as well as the theological preoccupations that have dominated a purportedly "scientific" study of the Bible.[588]

3. LITERARY ASPECTS OF JAMES

This introduction has already discussed in some detail the question of the literary genre of James, considering in turn the diatribal, paraenetic, protreptic,

---

[586]W. Popkes, *Addressaten, Situation und Form des Jakobusbriefes* (Stuttgart: Katholisches Bibelwerk, 1986) 187.

[587]B. L. Mack, *The Lost Gospel: The Book of Q and Christian Origins* (San Francisco: Harper, 1993) 259. There is no indication that Mack is aware of the thesis of L. E. Elliott-Binns, *Galilean Christianity* (Studies in Biblical Theology; London: SCM Press, 1956) 43–53, that because James fit so well what we otherwise knew (!) of Galilean Christianity and was so primitive in its tone, yet its "whole atmosphere is different from that which we should associate with James and the church at Jerusalem" (47), this letter should stand as the best evidence for Galilean Christianity!

[588]The same tendency is found in theological discourse; see, e.g., K. Barth, *Church Dogmatics*, ed. G. W. Bromiley, T. F. Torrance (Edinburgh: T & T Clark, 1957) II, 2, 588–94.

rhetorical, and epistolary dimensions of the composition, and in the process indicating seminal scholarly contributions (see I.A–D, pp. 16–26). The discussion focused on the literary categories of Greco-Roman culture. I am convinced that these give us our best access to James' literary voice.

At the same time, I also stressed James' involvement in the symbolic world of Torah. One of the important developments in twentieth-century scholarship on James has been the investigation of the letter's literary and social connections to Judaism, particularly Palestinian Judaism.

The most obvious point of entry is through James' use of Torah. A number of studies have uncovered the subtle ways in which James appropriates the language of Scripture. S. Laws analyzed some possibilities for James' scriptural allusion in 4:5;[589] L. T. Johnson detected the influence of Leviticus 19;[590] and K. F. Morris examined the echoes of Isaiah in James.[591] Some scholars have, in fact, read James as a sort of proto-rabbinic midrash on one set of scriptural verses or another.[592]

The discovery of the scrolls from Qumran in 1947 naturally stimulated a rash of investigations seeking a connection between the literature and life of these first-century sectarians with the nascent Christian community.[593] Certain broad areas of similarity between James and the sectarian writings are obvious,[594] but studies have sought an even closer connection in specific areas having to do with James' understanding of the law,[595] his dualistic psychology,[596] and his imagery.[597]

---

[589]S. Laws, " 'Does Scripture Speak in Vain?' A Reconsideration of James IV,5," *NTS* 20 (1974) 210–15.

[590]L. T. Johnson, "The Use of Leviticus 19 in the Letter of James," *JBL* 101 (1982) 391–401.

[591]K. F. Morris, *An Investigation of Several Linguistic Affinities between the Epistle of James and the Book of Isaiah* (Ph.D. diss., Union Theological Seminary in Virginia, 1964).

[592]See A. Hanson, "Report on the Working Group 'On the Use of the Old Testament in the Epistle of James,' " *NTS* 25 (1979) 526–27; M. Gertner, "Midrashic Terms and Techniques in the New Testament," *SE* 3 (1964) 463; and ibid., "Midrashim in the New Testament," *JSS* 7 (1962) 267–92; P. Sigal, "The Halakah of James," *Intergerimi Parietis Septum (Eph 2:14): Essays Presented to Markus Barth*, ed. D. Y. Hadidian (Pittsburgh: Pickwick Press, 1984) 337–53; L. F. Rivera, "La Epistola de Santiago, Modelo de halaka cristiana," *RevistB* 21 (1969) 69.

[593]For a review of the first generation of scholarship after the discoveries, when most of these connections were drawn, see H. Braun, *Qumran und das Neue Testament* (Tübingen: JCB Mohr [Paul Siebeck], 1966); P. Benoit, "Qumran et le Nouveau Testament," *NTS* 7 (1967) 276–96.

[594]See, e.g., D. Flusser, "The Dead Sea Sect and Pre-Pauline Christianity," *Scripta Hierosolymitana* IV *Aspects of the Dead Sea Scrolls*, ed. C. Rabin and Y. Yadin (Jerusalem: Magnes, 1965) 215–66; D. L. Bartlett, "The Epistle of James as a Jewish Christian Document," *SBLSP* 17 (1979) 2:173–86.

[595]E. Stauffer, "Das 'Gesetz der Freiheit' in der Ordensregel von Jericho," *TLZ* 77 (1952) 520–32.

[596]See W. Wolverton, "The Double-Minded Man in the Light of Essene Psychology," *ATR* 38 (1956) 166–75; O. J. F. Seitz, "Afterthoughts on the Term 'Dipsychos'," *NTS* 4 (1957–58) 327–34; ibid., "Two Spirits in Man: An Essay in Biblical Exegesis," *NTS* 6 (1959–60) 82–95; J. Marcus, "The Evil Inclination in the Epistle of James," *CBQ* 44 (1982) 606–21.

[597]See R. Eisenman, "Eschatological 'Rain' Imagery in the War Scroll from Qumran and in the Letter of James," *JNES* 49 (1990) 173–84.

The Qumran community's self-designating language of "the poor" in particular suggested similarities to early Palestinian Christianity,[598] and in particular to the Letter of James.[599] The best of these studies, by R. B. Ward, did not focus exclusively on Qumran but included a range of rabbinic literature in its fruitful attempt to locate the symbolic world within which James' communal concerns—especially in 2:1–26—made most sense.[600]

The Jewish connection has also been exploited to account for the distinctive literary shape of the work as a whole. Before the discoveries at Qumran, W. L. Knox suggested that James may have been based on a collection of Genizah fragments preserved from the church at Pella or Jerusalem.[601] D. L. Beck argued that James' order could be explained on the basis that it used as a source the Community Rule (1QS) from Qumran.[602] M. Gertner finds the hidden structure of James in a midrash on Psalm 12.[603]

By far the most elaborate effort to explain James in terms of a Jewish *Grundschrift*, however, was A. Meyer's.[604] He took as his framework the suggestion of Massebieau and Spitta (see above) that James was a Christianized adaptation of a first-century BCE Essene composition and provided what he considered to be the literary character of the *Grundschrift*, which would help account for the apparent lack of literary coherence in the present letter. Meyer argued that the original composition was a sermon written for delivery in the Hellenistic synagogue, which based itself on a tradition of *allegorizing* the names of the patriarchs for the purposes of moral instruction. In effect, then, James is not to be read as a linear argument, but as a subtly coded collection of allusions to Jacob and his sons ("the twelve tribes"). Meyer's study is impressively erudite, but his thesis fails to convince because it fails to make better sense out of James. His thesis has not been without influence, however, on those studies that continue to approach James as a form of homily.[605]

---

[598]See L. Keck, "The Poor among the Saints in the New Testament," ZNW 56 (1965) 109–29.

[599]See F. X. Kelly, *Poor and Rich in the Epistle of James* (Ph.D. diss., Temple University, 1973); C. H. Felder, *Wisdom, Law and Social Concern in the Epistle of James* (Ph.D. diss., Columbia University, 1982); C. W. Boggan, *Wealth in the Epistle of James* (Ph.D. diss., Southern Baptist Theological Seminary, 1982).

[600]R. B. Ward, *The Communal Concern of the Epistle of James* (Ph.D. diss., Harvard University, 1966); ibid., "Partiality in the Assembly," HTR 62 (1969) 87–97; ibid., "The Works of Abraham: James 2:14–16," HTR 61 (1968) 283–90.

[601]W. L. Knox, "The Epistle of James," JTS 46 (1945) 10–17.

[602]D. L. Beck, *The Composition of the Epistle of James* (Ph.D. diss., Princeton Theological Seminary, 1973).

[603]M. Gertner, "Midrashic Terms in the New Testament," JSS 7 (1962) 267–92, esp. 283–91.

[604]A. Meyer, *Das Rätsel des Jakobusbriefes* (BZNW 10; Giessen: Töpelmann, 1930). I was unable to obtain a copy of K. Kürzdorfer, *Der Character des Jakobusbriefes: Eine Auseinandersetzung mit den Theses von A. Meyer und M. Dibelius* (Ph.D. diss., Tübingen University, 1966).

[605]See, e.g., H. Thyen, *Der Stil des jüdisch-hellenistischen Homilie* (FRLANT 47; Göttingen:

The effect of such close attention to the Jewish side of James has been to confirm the judgments that guide this commentary: in literary terms, James is best understood as a form of protreptic discourse in epistolary form; in terms of symbols and values, James is best understood as a form of Jewish Christian literature of the first Palestinian generation.

4. JAMES' THEOLOGICAL AND MORAL VOICE

The study of James has moved beyond the classic position represented by Dibelius in its willingness to consider the distinctive theological dimensions of the composition. Dibelius' argument that James lacked theology could be taken to the absurd reduction found in J. T. Sanders, who argues not only that there is "no consistent principle or set of principles upon which James relies for his paraenesis," but that the closest he comes to such a sustaining principle is a sort of vague humanism![606] In contrast to such a simplistic view are studies that argue that James does have a consistent set of ethical principles,[607] but that they tend to have a communitarian, rather than an individualistic focus,[608] which is expressed, above all, in its concern for the plight of the poor.[609]

James' ethical teaching, in fact, is closely connected to his theology and finds its basis in his theological perceptions.[610] Among the attempts to characterize the theological framework more completely are those that focus on its grounding

---

Vandenhoeck & Ruprecht, 1955) 14–16; G. Hartmann, "Der Aufbau des Jakobusbriefes," *ZTK* 66 (1942) 63–70; A. Cabaniss, "A Note on Jacob's Homily," *EvQ* 47 (1975) 219–22.

[606]J. T. Sanders, *Ethics in the New Testament* (Philadelphia: Fortress Press, 1975) 126–28.

[607]See, e.g., W. Bieder, "Christliches Existenz nach dem Zeugnis des Jakobusbriefes," *TZ* 5 (1949) 93–113; R. B. Brown, "The Message of the Book of James for Today," *Review and Expositor* 66 (1966) 415–27; T. B. Maston, "Ethical Dimensions of James," *Southwestern Journal of Theology* 12 (1969) 23–29.

[608]See J. B. Souček, "Zu den Problemen des Jakobusbriefes," *EvT* 18 (1958) 460–68; R. B. Ward, *The Communal Concern of the Epistle of James* (Ph.D. diss., Harvard University, 1966); L. T. Johnson, "Friendship with the World and Friendship with God: a Study of Discipleship in James," *Discipleship in the New Testament*, ed. F. Segovia (Philadelphia: Fortress Press, 1985) 166–83.

[609]See, e.g., A. M. Charue, "Quelques avis aux riches et aux pauvres dans l'épître de St. Jacques," *Collationes Namurences* 30 (1936) 177–87; B. Noack, "Jakobus wider die Reichen," *ST* 18 (1964) 10–25; A. S. Geyser, "The Letter of James and the Social Condition of his Addressees," *Neot* 9 (1975) 25–33; P. U. Maynard-Reid, *Poverty and Wealth in James* (New York: Orbis Books, 1987).

[610]See C. E. B. Cranfield, "The Message of James," *SJT* 18 (1965) 182–93; 338–45; S. Laws, "The Doctrinal Basis for the Ethics of James," *SE* 7 (1982) 299–305; J. B. Adamson, *James: the Man and his Message* (Grand Rapids: Eerdmans, 1989) 259–471; H. Rusche, "Standhaben in Gott: Einführung in die Grundgedanken des Jakobusbriefes (1:1–27)," *BibLeb* 5 (1964) 153–63; ibid., "Der Erbarmer hält Gericht: Einführung in die Grundgedanken des Jakobusbriefes (2:1–13a)," *BibLeb* 5 (1964) 236–47; J. Zmijewski, "Christliche 'Vollkommenheit': Erwägungen zur Theologie des Jakobusbriefes," *Studien Neuen Testament und seiner Umwelt* 5 (1980) 50–78.

in the cult,[611] in the word of God,[612] in wisdom,[613] or even in Christology.[614] All of these investigations agree that James' moral discourse is deeply embedded in the theological convictions of Judaism and the nascent Christian community.

Finally, this sketch of a history of the interpretation of James can conclude by taking note of the fact that although the gap between scholarly and pastoral publications has perhaps never been greater, the tradition of interpretation within and for the life of the church has not altogether disappeared in the twentieth century, as shown by commentaries that seriously engage the text from the perspective of faith,[615] or that incorporate the dimension of preaching,[616] or that deal pastorally with themes in James.[617]

BIBLIOGRAPHY

Bergauer, P., *Der Jakobusbrief bei Augustinus und die damit verbundenen Probleme der Rechfertigungslehre* (Wien: Herder, 1962).

Brooks, J. A., "The Place of James in the New Testament Canon," *Southwestern Journal of Theology* 12 (1969) 41–55.

Davids, P. H., "The Epistle of James in Modern Discussion," ANRW II, 25.5 (1988) 3621–45.

Hilgenfeld, A., "Der Brief Des Jakobus," ZWT 16 (1873) 1–33.

Kawerau, G., "Die Schicksale des Jakobusbriefes im 16 Jahrhundert," ZKWKL 10 (1889) 359–70.

Kittel, G., "Der Jakobusbrief und die apostolischen Väter," ZNW 43 (1950–51) 54–112.

---

[611]See G. Braumann, "Der theologische Hintergrund des Jakobusbriefes," TZ 18 (1962) 401–10; A. Hamann, "Prière et culte dans la lettre de saint Jacques," ETL 34 (1958) 35–47.

[612]See J. Sanchez Bosch, "Llei I Papaula de Deu en la Carta de Jaume," *Revista Catalana de Teologia* I (1976) 51–78.

[613]R. Hoppe, *Der theologische Hintergrund des Jakobusbriefes* (FzB 28; Wurzburg: Echter-Verlag, 1977); L. Simon, *Une Ethique de la Sagesse: Commentaire de l'Epitre de Jacques* (Geneve: Editions Labor et Fides, 1961).

[614]R. Obermüller, "Hermeneutische Themen im Jakobusbrief," Bib 53 (1972) 234–44; M. Karrer, "Christus der Herr und die Welt als Stätte der Prüfung," KD 35 (1989) 166–68; F. Mussner, " 'Direkte' und 'Indirekte' Christologie im Jakobusbrief," *Catholica* 24 (1970) 111–17.

[615]See, e.g., S. Zodhiates, *The Epistle of James and the Life of Faith*: Vol 1: *The Work of Faith: An Exposition of James 1:1–2:13*; Vol 2: *The Labor of Love: An Exposition of James 2:14–4:12*; Vol 3: *The Patience of Hope: An Exposition of James 5:13–5:20* (Grand Rapids: Eerdmans, 1959–60); A. von Speyr, *Die Katholischen Briefe* Vol 1 (Einsiedeln: Johannes, 1961).

[616]Ed. Thurneyson, *Der Brief des Jakobus* (Basel: Fr. Reinhardt, 1941); J. Haar, *Der Jakobusbrief: Praktische Schriftauslegung für Predigt* (Bibelarbeit 9; Stuttgart and Göttingen: Klotz, 1971).

[617]A. T. Robertson, *Practical and Social Aspects of Christianity: The Wisdom of James* (New York: Doran, 1915); H. Rendtorff, *Hörer und Täter: Eine Einführung in dem Jakobusbrief* (Hamburg: Furche-Verlag, 1953); W. Stringfellow, *Count it all Joy: Reflections on Faith, Doubt and Temptation through the Letter of James* (Grand Rapids: Eerdmans, 1967).

Kubo, S., "The Catholic Epistles in the Greek Lectionary: A Preliminary Investigation," *AUSS* 1 (1963) 65–70.

Kümmel, W. G., *The New Testament: The History of the Investigation of its Problems*, trans. S. M. Gilmour and H. C. Kee (Nashville: Abingdon Press, 1972).

Matthaei, Chr. Ferd., *SS. Apostolorum Septem Epistolae Catholicae* (Riga: J. F. Hartknoch, 1782).

Meinertz, M., *Der Jakobusbrief und sein Verfasser im Schrift und Überlieferung* (BSF 10, 1–3; Freiburg: Herder, 1905).

Meyer, A., *Das Rätsel des Jakobusbriefes* (BZNW 10; Giessen: Töplemann, 1930).

Noret, J., "Une scholie de l'épître de Jacques tirée de Syméon Métaphraste," *Bib* 55 (1974) 74–75.

Pearson, B., "James, 1–2 Peter, Jude," in *The New Testament and its Modern Interpreters*, ed. E. J. Epp and G. W. MacRae (Philadelphia: Fortress Press, 1989) 371–406.

Ropes, J. H., "The Greek Catena on the Catholic Epistles," *HTR* 19 (1926) 383–88.

Schmidt, W. G., *Der Lehrgehalt des Jakobus-Briefes: Ein Beitrag zur neutestamentlichen Theologie* (Leipzig: Hinrichs, 1869).

Schmidt-Clausing, F., "Die unterschiedliche Stellung Luthers und Zwinglis zum Jakobusbrief," *Reformatio* 18 (1969) 568–85.

Siker, J. S., "The Canonical Status of the Catholic Epistles in the Syriac New Testament," *JTS* n.s. 38 (1987) 311–33.

Staab, K., "Die griechischen Katenenkommentare zu den katholischen Briefen," *Bib* 5 (1924) 296–353.

Walther, W., "Zu Luthers Ansicht ueber den Jakobusbrief," *TSK* 66 (1893) 595–98.

IV. EXPLANATION AND INTERPRETATION: ON HEARING JAMES' VOICE

✦

Up to this point, our introduction to James has been of a descriptive character: we have examined the literary and religious aspects of the composition, theories concerning its historical circumstances, and the history of its reception and interpretation. This sort of discussion will continue throughout the commentary on the text proper. Every attempt will be made to *explain* the composition in terms of its language and logic, as well as the shape and sources of its symbols. Such explanation, however, does not yet constitute interpretation in the fullest sense. Interpretation demands not only that the text be described but that its message be engaged.

My distinction may become clearer by analogy. The text of Plato's *Republic* can be approached and analyzed from several perspectives. It can be connected to events in the author's career or to historical events in Athens; it can be placed within the development of political philosophy by other writers; it can be compared to other Platonic dialogues in terms of its language and logic. Yet most students of philosophy would agree that, however valuable and even necessary such analyses are, they still only occupy the foyer in the house of hermeneutics. Unless the reader is willing to move beyond description to engagement with Plato's ideas, the reader cannot claim truly to have read Plato. The *Republic* demands not only that the reader be able to state what Plato thinks Justice is, but that the reader ask with Plato what Justice is. The *Republic* is a text that resists being treated simply as an object to be explained. It poses a question that the serious reader needs to engage with Plato, even if the reader's conclusions turn out to be quite different from Plato's.

The Letter of James particularly calls for such engagement because it presents itself as a form of wisdom and consists in exhortations. The reader is, therefore, invited to test its statements not simply according to their appropriateness to ancient circumstances or ideas, nor simply according to a theoretical self-

162

consistency. The exhortations ask to be tested against human experience and our understanding of reality itself. When James asks readers, "Do you not know that friendship with the world is enmity with God" (4:4), interpretation is not finished when the meaning of the terms is determined within the context of ancient *topoi* or when the question is situated within the rhetoric of the letter as a whole. The reader is asked directly to test the *truth* and not only the *meaning* of the proposition. The question is not simply whether the statement makes sense given the author's worldview, but also whether it is true within the reader's worldview.

When James declares, again, that "human anger does not accomplish God's righteousness," it makes a statement of considerably provocative force. It can be dismissed or trivialized by being categorized as an "aphorism." But when the statement has thus been distanced, it can rightly be asked whether it has truly been read. Such engagement, such interpretation, is particularly difficult for contemporary readers precisely because the "understanding of the world" held by James and by us is so different. When James commands "approach God and God will approach you," the contemporary reader is challenged not only in terms of presumptions concerning spatial-temporal coordinates, or the relationship between the disposition of human freedom and the divine, but—more than at any other time since James was written—concerning the very meaningfulness of language about God.

No commentary can accomplish everything, but often commentaries, by seeking to *explain*, avoid the one thing necessary, which is to *interpret*. Although the present commentary will give due attention to all the mechanics of explanation, it also seeks at least to point in the direction of passionate engagement and what it might entail to take seriously such "wisdom from above" concerning an "implanted word able to save your lives."

For Christian readers the need to read James in something more than a purely descriptive fashion is also rooted in its authority as part of the canon of Scripture. As the history of interpretation has shown, James' inclusion in the canon has been a source of discomfort for a significant minority within the Christian tradition, primarily because of that tradition's tendency to define as essentially Christian what is simply distinctively Christian. Protestant scholars deeply influenced by Luther found the apparent tension between James and Paul on one issue to be so threatening that it needed to be eliminated, either by marginalizing or harmonizing James. But James' canonical status has not proven problematic either to the Orthodox or to the Roman Catholic tradition, nor for that matter to the largest portion of the Protestant tradition.

A proper appreciation of canonical authority for the life of the church and its theological reflection refuses the options of suppressing witnesses (based on some sort of "canon within the canon") or of precipitously harmonizing them, or of managing their diversity by means of an all-encompassing theological principle. It rather seeks to allow the diverse witnesses within the canon to speak as clearly as possible in their distinctive voices, understanding that only within such an open conversation can a historical community that spans generations and exists in multiple circumstances continue to be challenged and enlivened by these texts.

Within such an understanding, James offers positive and powerful contributions to the conversation concerning the right relationship of humans to God and to each other that we call theology. James' grounding of its exhortations in *theological* rather than *Christological* principles, for example, provides a genuine bridge between Christians and others (such as Jews and Muslims) who share belief in one God who is creator and lawgiver and judge, but who do not share the specific gift given in Jesus. Rather than an embarrassment to a Christianity that defines itself as much as possible in terms of its *difference* from Judaism, James is a gift (particularly in a post-Holocaust generation) to the Christian community to examine how the "faith of Jesus Christ" can positively be affirmed as much in continuity with "the perfect law of freedom" as in discontinuity.

And because James mediates to the Christian community the wisdom traditions both of the Greco-Roman and Jewish cultures, it also provides a bridge for the discussion of issues and values between Christians and non-Christians within that shared context, without demanding, first, a commitment to the specifically Christian understanding of those issues and values. It is striking, for example, that alone of the NT writings, James provides some sort of basis for a social ethics. The most obvious example is its prophetic condemnation of the oppression of the poor by the exploitive rich. But equally important are the outspoken criticism of discrimination between humans on the basis of appearance; the portrayal of the power and perils of speech; the analysis of the roots of social conflict, war, and murder in the logic of envy. No other text of the ancient world offers as rich a set of reflections on the grounds for violence and peace in the world as does James.

For the Christian community itself, James not only speaks with extraordinary clarity concerning the gift and the mandate of life before God, it provides an unparalleled portrait of a community constituted by gift-giving and solidarity in the face of a dominant culture defined by envy and acquisitiveness. Christians who read James, then, as something more than a classic of moral exhortation, find themselves questioned not only as individuals but, above all, as a community concerning the coherence and consistency of their profession and practice.

TRANSLATION
AND
COMMENTARY
ON THE
LETTER OF JAMES

◆

GREETING 1:1

1:1 James, slave of God and of the Lord Jesus Christ, sends greetings to the twelve tribes in the dispersion.

NOTES

1. *James:* For questions concerning the identity of the implied author, see Introduction IIA–B. The combination of simplicity and authority found in the superscription suggests that it is James, the "Brother of the Lord," who could assume such immediate recognition. The Greek *Iakōbos* transcribes the Hebrew *yaᶜaqôb*, a name with obvious resonances in the symbolic world of Torah. The fact that Jacob was the progenitor of the "twelve tribes of Israel" (see Acts 7:8) provides what little basis there is for theories that this composition allegorizes patriarchal characteristics (A. Meyer). Decisive points making such theories unnecessary are: a) the canonical and extracanonical evidence for a James with a widely recognized authority in the Jerusalem church and b) the fact that this composition does not place "James" in a filial relationship with the readers. There is no "father/son" language such as is found in, e.g., *The Testaments of the Twelve Patriarchs.*

slave of God: The term *doulos* denotes literal bondage to the authority of another (Plato, *Rep.* 395E). Thus, the Israelites were "slaves in the land of Egypt in the house of Pharaoh" (1 Sam 2:27 LXX). Religiously, it connotes the special relationship between God and humans defined in terms of possession (by God) and service (by humans). Thus, the declaration in Euripides, *Ion* 309, "I call myself the slave of God" (*doulos tou theou*); thus the recognition of Paul and companions as "slaves of the most high God" in Acts 16:17. In the Hebrew

Bible, the term *ebed* is used to define such a religious relationship. The people Israel is called "slave of the Lord" in LXX Pss 134:1; 135:22; Isa 49:3; and Ezek 28:25. The religious expression of slavery as dedication to God permeates the piety of the Psalms (see, e.g., LXX Pss 118:38, 76; 122:2; 133:1; 135:1; 142:12). In Isa 42:19, the Hebrew "servant of the Lord" is rendered by the LXX in the plural as *douloi tou theou* ("slaves of God"), the only instance of this phrase in the LXX. The term *doulos* is, in turn, often attributed to those leaders who mediate between God and humans, such as Joshua (Josh 14:7; 24:30; Judg 2:8), David (2 Sam 7:8, 25, 29; 1 Chr 17:4; LXX Pss 77:70; 88:4, 21; 131:10; 143:10; Ezek 34:23; 1 Macc 4:30), and Moses (LXX Ps 104:26, 42; Mal 3:24). Only once is the term applied to Isaac (Dan 3:35) or to the patriarchs as a group (2 Macc 1:2). More often, it is used of the prophets as messengers of Yahweh (Amos 3:7; Joel 3:2; Jonah 1:9; Zech 1:6; Jer 7:25; 25:4; Ezek 38:17). In the NT likewise, the term can be applied to Jesus (Phil 2:7) or to Christians generally (1 Pet 2:16; Acts 2:18; 4:29; Rev 10:7; 19:5; 22:3, 6). But it also appears as a title for Christian leaders, either in the form "slave of Jesus Christ" (Rom 1:1; Phil 1:1; 2 Pet 1:1) or "slave of Christ" (Gal 1:10). Only in Titus 1:1 is the title *doulos theou* also applied to Paul. According to one analysis (Sahlin, 1947), the odd designation of James as *OBLIAS* by Hegesippus (in Eusebius, *HE* II,23,7) is due to a scribal error, mistaking the Greek Δ for the Λ, thus yielding *OBLIAS* rather than the original *OBDIAS*. The name Obadiah, furthermore, means "slave of Yahweh" in Hebrew. Such an explanation would make sense of Eusebius' otherwise inexplicable supplying of the "Greek meaning" of *OBLIAS* as "rampart (*perioche*) of the people and righteousness," for the beginning of the prophecy of Obadiah ("slave of Yahweh") in the LXX says that the Lord set out a "rampart" (*perioche*) for the nations (*ethne*). The link to this author's self-designation is tenuous but possible.

and of the Lord Jesus Christ: Particularly since both *theos* and *kyrios* are anarthous, it is possible to read "slave" as having only one referent rather than two: thus, Vouga, 35, has: "slave of Jesus Christ, God and Lord." He justifies this from what he regards as parallel usage in James 1:27 and 3:9 and a reference in the patristic writer Pseudo-Andrew of Crete. But the reading is forced. James is ambiguous in his use of *kyrios*, having it apply both to God and to Jesus, but he is not careless elsewhere about his designation *theos*, referring it clearly to *ho pater* (1:27; 3:9). The textual variant *patros*, added in the present verse by some MSS, is probably not original but represents an accurate interpretation. Both Oecumenius (PG 119:456) and Theophylact (PG 125:1136) make the point that by calling himself slave of both God and Lord, James acknowledges equality of essence and dignity among the divine persons but does so by establishing a distinction between them: "Slave of God, namely the father, but of the Lord, Jesus Christ."

sends greetings: The infinitive *chairein* ("to rejoice") is a conventional epistolary greeting (White). The translation seeks to supply the (understood) verb of speaking, as in "speak greetings" (*legei chairein*; see 2 John 10, 11). Cajetan was correct to call James' greeting "*more profano*" ("in the profane mode"), for it is found everywhere in Greco-Roman (see Plutarch, *Sayings of Spartans* 59 [Mor. 213 A]) and in Jewish letters (see Josephus, *Life* 217, 365; 1 Macc 10:18, 25; 11:30, 32; 12:6, 20; 13:36; 14:20; 15:2, 16; 2 Macc 1:1; 9:19; 11:16, 22, 34; 3 Macc 3:12; 7:1; *Ep.Arist.* 41). In the NT, this simple form of greeting is found also in Acts 15:23 and 23:26.

to the twelve tribes: The *dōdeka phylai* ("twelve tribes") traditionally designated the fullness of the Israelite people descended from "Jacob and the twelve patriarchs" (Acts 7:8; see Exod 24:4; 28:21; 36:21; Josh 4:5; Sir 44:23; Ezek 47:13). It is found as a designation for Israel also in *Pss.Sol.* 17:26–28; the *Syb. Or.* 3:249; 2 *Apoc. Bar.* 77:2; 78:4; and Josephus, *Ant.* 1:221. Given the historical experiences of exile and loss, the very term suggests also an idealized restoration of Israel (see 1QS 8:1). Such is certainly the case in the logion of the "twelve thrones" (Matt 19:28; Luke 22:29–30), when the twelve apostles are promised a role judging "the twelve tribes of Israel." Such also is the vision of the heavenly roll called from the twelve tribes in Rev 7:5–8, as well as the city on which are engraved "the names that are the twelve tribes of Israel" (Rev 21:12). The term occurs as well in the *Prot. Jas.* 1:1, 3 and some MSS of 1 *Clem.* 55:6. The designation clearly locates the composition within the symbolic world of Torah.

in the dispersion: Translating a number of Hebrew verbs, the Greek *diaspeirein* ("scatter") is used by the LXX for the dispersal of Israel by the Lord among the nations as a punishment (Lev 26:33; Deut 4:27; 28:64; 32:26; LXX Ps 43:12; Jdt 5:19; Tob 13:3), only to be gathered back from the places they were scattered (Isa 11:12; 56:8). The noun form *diaspora* likewise translates a number of different Hebrew words—often ones denoting punishment or tribulation (see Deut 28:25; 30:4; LXX Ps 146:2; Jer 15:7; 41:17). It can, therefore, refer both to the population dispersed (see 2 Macc 1:27; *Pss. Sol.* 8:28; John 7:35) and to the geographical territories where they were scattered (Philo, *Rewards and Punishments* 115; Jdt 5:19; *T. Ash.* 7:3). In Acts, the verb *diaspeirein* is used for the scattering of the church beyond Jerusalem (8:1, 4; 11:19). And in 1 Pet 1:1, the substantive *diaspora* is used for the readers of that letter located throughout Asia Minor.

COMMENT

The character of the Greeting is important for setting the character of the writing. In literary terms, the Greeting establishes the composition that follows as a letter. Whatever its original literary form may have been, it *becomes* a letter by being given such a praescript. In the context of ancient epistolary theory and practice, moreover, a personal connection (Malherbe) and social relationship (Stowers) are established between sender and recipients. The terms of the conversation are suggested already by the form of the Greeting.

In this case the Greeting is remarkably simple and "secular" in character. It resembles the sort of letter samples reported by the Books of Maccabees and the Acts of the Apostles, rather than the more elaborate greeting formulas found in Paul's letters. Does this suggest anything about the early date of the letter? Not necessarily. But despite the contention that the word-linkage between the Greeting and v.2 argues for a literary self-consciousness appropriate to a later date (Dibelius, 68), nothing in this unadorned salutation demands seeing it as a pseudonymous production.

The Greeting has most often been read as the source for clues as to the composition's circumstances. Some have seen the lack of elaboration of James' position as a sign of authenticity, the mention of the twelve tribes as an indication of Jewish-Christian readership, and the reference to the diaspora as indicating not only the location of the readers outside Palestine but the location of the writer within Palestine. There is nothing intrinsically improbable about any of these deductions. We have evidence from the Talmud and Tosefta of encyclical letters being written from rabbinic leadership in Palestine to "the residents of the exile of Babylon, and residents of the exile of Media, and of all other exiles of Israel," including one from Judah the Prince that uses the title "slave" in the praescript (Pardee, 186, 199–202). As the usage in Acts suggests, the spread of communities beyond Jerusalem early on could be regarded as a kind of Christian "diaspora" (Bede). As Galatians 2:12 shows, James would have had considerable recognition and influence among communities in Syria. And Acts 15:23–29 describes a letter of instruction sent from the Jerusalem leadership to churches "in Antioch and Syria and Cilicia" already in the late forties or early fifties.

Other readers, as we have seen, construe the clues quite differently. The reason "James" requires no elaborate self-presentation is because he is already—as the traditions about him proliferate—a legendary figure by the time this letter is composed in the second century. The designation "twelve tribes" does not suggest a Jewish readership but the opposite, the appropriation by Gentile churches of the titles of Israel, a process evident already in Gal 4:26; 6:16; 1 Pet 2:9. And the reference to the diaspora, far from indicating a geographical location, designates a place of spiritual exile. The basis for this symbolic appropriation is found already in Philo. Commenting on Lev 25:23, he describes humans as "sojourners on earth as though in a foreign city" (*Cherubim* 120; see also *Rewards and Punishments* 115–18). Paul's language about the Jerusalem above (Gal 4:26) and the commonwealth in heaven (Phil 3:20) are seen as fitting within such a dualistic understanding of Christian identity. Even more emphatically, the language of sojourn and exile is applied to Christians by 1 Pet 1:17; 2:11; Heb 11:8–16; 13:14. Such texts picture

Christians on earth as being on pilgrimage toward their heavenly home. In such a framework, the "diaspora" of James 1:1 should be understood like the "diaspora" of 1 Pet 1:1, as a statement about spiritual distance from the structures of society, rather than as a geographical designation. And because the language of "sojourning" also occurs with some frequency in early second-century Christian texts such as *Herm. Sim.* 1:1; *1 Clement* 1, and Pol. *Phil.* 1, this reading would tend to support the placement of James among the pseudonymous literature of the second century, addressed not to Jewish Christians but to Gentile Christians who had assumed the garments of Torah as their own (Dibelius 66–67).

In fact, however, these are false alternatives. The texts surveyed above themselves show that language about a "spiritual diaspora" began very early on: if it could be used by Philo, it could be used by a first generation Christian! Any use of the designation "the twelve tribes" by a messianic sect, furthermore, would obviously connote a spiritual restoration within a remnant of historic Judaism. Such "spiritualization" is available already to such Jewish Christians as Paul and the editors of Q (see Matt 19:28; Luke 22:29–30). It could equally have been available to James, who speaks of the readers as a kind of *aparchē* ("firstfruits") of God's creatures in a manner remarkably similar to Paul's designation for the remnant of Israel within the church (Rom 11:16; compare Martin, 8).

However ambiguously the Greeting works to locate the text in the real world, it works effectively to construct a *compositional* world. First, it delineates the character of the implied author. The self-designation of *doulos*, as the notes demonstrate, carries with it a powerful twofold connotation in the religious world of the Mediterranean and specifically within the symbolism of Torah. If James is *doulos* of "God and of the Lord Jesus Christ," then he is certified to readers as one who is himself defined by the measure he applies to them. His life is one of service to God and to Jesus as Lord. By implication, then, by the standards of that world, he is a reliable spokesperson for God and the Lord Jesus Christ, since he lives out what he preaches. The term *doulos* also has the (paradoxical) connotation of religious leader. Particularly in the framework of Torah, the term designates the prophetic spokespersons for the Lord: the one who best serves is the one who best represents. Thus the designation supports both the implied author's genuine personal commitment and his authoritative role within the messianic movement (see D. B. Martin, 50–61).

The Greeting also deftly sketches the symbolic world shared by the implied readers and author. It is the world of Torah. Whether intended literally or figuratively, the "twelve tribes in the dispersion" is a designation that makes sense only within the framework of one specific set of texts and one shared story in the Mediterranean world. Readers who accept their status as recipients of this letter—in whatever age they are readers, it should be noted—accept also this designation and a place within that symbolic world: they *become*, for the purposes of this composition, the hoped-for restored Israel among the nations. Whoever receives the author's "greetings" welcomes as well a self-definition as part of a spiritual Israel normed by the texts of Torah and living in service to God and the Lord Jesus Christ.

BIBLIOGRAPHY

Baltzer, K., "Die Bezeichnung des Jakobus als OBLIAS," ZNW 46 (1955) 141–42.

Gerhard, G. A., "Untersuchungen zur Geschichte des griechischen Briefes," Philologus 64 (1905) 27–65.

Köster, F., "Ueber die Leser, an welche der Brief des Jakobus ist und der erste Brief des Petrus gerichtet is," TSK 4 (1831) 581–88.

Lieu, J. M., " 'Grace be to you and Peace': The Apostolic Blessing," BJRL 68 (1985) 161–78.

Malherbe, A. J., "Ancient Epistolary Theorists," Ohio Journal of Religious Studies 5/2 (1977) 1–77.

Martin, D. B., Slavery as Salvation: The Metaphor of Slavery in Pauline Christianity (New Haven: Yale University Press, 1990).

Pardee, D., Handbook of Ancient Hebrew Letters (SBL Sources for Biblical Study 15; Chico, California: Scholars Press, 1982).

Sahlin, H., "Noch Einmal Jacobus 'Oblias'," Bib 28 (1947) 152–53.

Schoeps, H.-J., "Jacobus Ho Dikaios kai Oblias," Bib 24 (1943) 398–403.

Stowers, S. K., "Social Typification and the Classification of Ancient Letters," The Social World of Formative Christianity and Judaism, ed. J. Neusner et al. (Philadelphia: Fortress, 1988) 78–90.

Torrey, C. C., "James the Just, and his Name 'Oblias'," JBL 63 (1944) 93–98.

White, J. L., Light from Ancient Letters (Philadelphia: Fortress, 1986) 189–200.

II. EPITOME OF
EXHORTATION 1:2–27

✦

1:2. My brothers, consider it entirely as joy whenever you encounter various testings, 3. since you know that the testing of your faith produces endurance. 4. And let endurance yield a perfect product, in order that you might be perfect and complete, lacking in nothing. 5. But if any of you is lacking wisdom, let him ask of God, who gives to all simply and without grudging, and it will be given to him. 6. But let him ask in faith, without doubting. For the one who doubts is like a wave of the sea that is tossed and turned by the wind. 7. That sort of person should not think that he will receive anything from the Lord. 8. He is a double-minded man. He is unstable in all his ways. 9. Let the lowly brother boast in his exalted position. 10. But let the rich person boast in his humbling, because like a wild flower he will pass away. 11. For the sun rises with its burning heat and dries up the grass, and its flower falls, and the beauty of its appearance is lost. Thus also the rich person will disappear in the midst of his activities. 12. Blessed is the man who endures testing, because when he has been proven sound, he will receive the crown of life which [God] has promised to those who love him. 13. Let no one when tested say, "I am being tempted by God." For God is not tempted by evils. Nor does he himself tempt anyone. 14. Instead, each person, by being drawn away and lured, is tempted by his own desire. 15. Then the desire, once it has conceived, brings forth sin. And when sin is brought to term, it gives birth to death. 16. Do not be deceived, my beloved brothers. 17. Every good giving and every perfect gift is from above, coming down from the father of lights. With him there is no alteration or shadow of change. 18. By his decision, he gave us birth through a word of truth, in order that we might be a kind of firstfruits of his creatures. 19. You know this, my beloved brothers. Then let every person be quick to hear, slow to speak, slow to anger. 20. For a man's anger does not accomplish God's righteousness. 21. Put aside, therefore, all filthiness and excess of evil. With meekness receive the implanted word that is able to save your souls. 22. But become doers of the word, and not simply hearers. That would be to deceive yourselves. 23. Because if anyone is simply a hearer of the word and not a doer, this person is like a man noticing his natural face in a mirror. 24. For he glances at himself, and he leaves, and immediately he forgets what he looks like. 25. But the one who has gazed into the perfect law of freedom and has remained there has become, not a forgetful hearer, but a doer of the deed. This person will be blessed in everything he does. 26. If anyone considers himself religious without bridling his tongue and while indulging his heart, this person's religion is worthless. 27. This is pure and undefiled religion before the God who is also father: to assist orphans and widows in their trouble, and to keep oneself unstained from the world.

THE SECTION AS A WHOLE

In many ways, the first chapter of James presents the most challenging questions to interpreters and provides a test of interpretive strategies. The challenges center on the question of internal coherence. Every careful reader of the Greek recognizes that the individual sentences are linked by a series of word-linkages: the *chairein* of the greeting is picked up immediately by the *charan* of 1:2. 1:3–4 are joined by the repetition of *hypomonē*, as well as by *ergazomai/ergon*; 1:4a and 4b are connected by *teleion/teleios*, while 1:4 and 1:5 are joined by *leipomenoi* and *leipetai*. The command *aiteitō* in 1:5 is repeated in 1:6 and *diakrinomenos* is repeated in the two parts of 1:6. The parts of 1:12–13 are connected by the repetition of *peirasmos, peirazetai, peirazomai,* and *apeirastos.* Likewise, 1:14–15 are linked by the repetition of *epithymia,* 1:19–20 by *orge,* 1:21–22 by *logos,* and 1:26–27 by *thrēskos/thrēskeia.* At the very least, then, the sentences are joined by word-linkage.

But does such an arrangement suggest anything more than the mechanics of mnemonics? It is not easy to find internal coherence in this chapter. Dibelius at least has boldness and consistency on his side in choosing to regard each statement in isolation (Dibelius, 69–116). Most efforts to find structure in the chapter amount to an outline of its themes (see Martin, cii). More recently, the argument has been made that James 1:2–18 should be regarded as the *exordium* of his discourse, with 5:7–20 functioning as its *peroratio* (Baasland, "Form," 3656; Frankemölle, "Semantische," 175–93). Although I am fundamentally sympathetic to a rhetorical reading of James (as the subsequent remarks make clear), I am unconvinced that 1:2–18 by itself stands off as the *exordium* of the entire composition, especially since such a demarcation does not yet account for the apparently fragmentary state of 1:19–27.

As stated in the introduction, therefore, I take chapter one as something of an *epitome* of the work as a whole. If the term *exordium* appeals, I have no objection. What is more important is to recognize the ways in which chapter one functions within the larger letter to anticipate themes developed more fully by way of essays. The theme of enduring testing in 1:2–4 and 1:12 is developed further by 5:7–11; the prayer of faith in 1:5–8 is elaborated by 4:3 and 5:13–18; the reversal of the fortunes of rich and lowly in 1:9–11 is found also in 2:1–7 and 4:13–5:6; the contrast between wicked desire and God's gift-giving in 1:13–18 is argued more extensively by 3:13–4:10; the use of the tongue in 1:19–20 is picked up by the essay in 3:1–12; the necessity of acting out religious convictions in 1:22–27 is elaborated by the essay in 2:14–26.

But it is equally important to recognize that 1:2–27 has its own distinctive character. The establishment of the polar oppositions that James works with throughout the composition is accomplished in these opening verses (Cargal, 56–105). First is the contrast between two measures, that which comes from God and that which comes from the world opposed to God. The outlook of the world is duplicitous and envious. In contrast, God gives to all with simplicity and without rebuke (1:5); God can even be defined as the giver of every good and perfect gift (1:17). Worldly desire conceives sin, and sin, when it reaches term, gives birth to death (1:15). In contrast, God gives genuine birth to humans by a word of truth and makes them the firstfruits of his creatures (1:18).

The second set of contrasts is between the attitudes and behaviors consistent with each measure. To live by God's word of truth means to put aside anger in favor of meekness, because "anger does not accomplish God's righteousness" (1:20). It means regarding wealth and poverty in ways shocking to the world, which uses them as a means of testing worth; before God "the poor brother boasts in his exaltation, and the rich person in his humiliation" (1:9). It means being driven not by evil desires (1:14) but by the wisdom that comes from God in response to the prayer of faith (1:5–6). Most paradoxically, it means counting trials "entirely as joy" (1:2), an attitude possible to those who view the world as an open system created by God, in which God will give the crown of life to those who love him (1:12).

The third contrast is between the sham religiosity of speech or appearance and a true devotion "pure and undefiled before God," which is expressed in honest speech and in care for the dispossessed in society (1:26–27). These are the attitudes and actions that keep oneself "unstained from the world" (1:27). Mere learning without doing is a form of self-deception (1:8, 16) and "worthless" (1:26).

The feature of chapter one that most sets it apart within the exhortation as a whole, however, is its emphasis on proper *understanding*. Notice that the very first exhortation to the readers is cognitive in character: they are to "reckon/calculate/consider" the reality of trials in one way rather than in another (1:2). Prior to speech or action, in other words, is the proper apprehension of reality. This concern for right perception runs through the chapter: in the first 27 verses, there are some 17 terms touching on one aspect of knowing or another. In the remaining 81 verses, terms of knowledge occur only 7 more times (2:20; 3:1; 4:4; 4:5; 4:14; 4:17; 5:20). The first chapter works through the connections between right perception, right speech, and right action. The notes and comments to follow will trace the connections as they are developed.

1:2–8

2. My brothers, consider it entirely as joy whenever you encounter various testings, 3. since you know that the testing of your faith produces endurance. 4. And let endurance produce a perfect product, in order that you might be perfect and complete, lacking in nothing. 5. But if any of you is lacking wisdom, let him ask of God, who gives to all simply and without grudging, and it will be given to him. 6. But let him ask with faith, without doubting. For the one who doubts is like a wave of the sea that is tossed and turned by the wind. 7. That sort of person should not think that he will receive anything from the Lord. 8. He is a double-minded man. He is unstable in all his ways.

NOTES

2. *brothers*: In the Greek, the vocative is postpositive, but it is appropriately placed first in English. James resists a completely inclusive translation, above all where he uses *anēr* (see 1:8). The inclusion of "sister" in 2:15 shows that the author thought of women as part of his readership. For the use of kinship language in earliest Christianity, see the Introduction, I.E.4. The personal pronoun *mou* ("my") has the effect of placing the implied author at the same level as the readers.

consider it entirely as joy: The noun *charan* picks up the *chairein* of the Greeting (Mayor, 33). For the way a letter can artfully begin its exposition by such echoing of the Greeting, compare Pseudo-Plato's play on *prattein* in *Letter* 8 (352A–B). The Greek of James 1:2 poses two translation problems. First, the verb *hēgēsasthai*, the first command in the composition, is particularly difficult to render. As used in the NT, the verb always denotes some sort of mental judgment, such as "regarding" (Acts 15:22; 1 Thess 5:13; 2 Thess 3:15); "considering" (Acts 26:2; 2 Cor 9:5); and "calculating" or "reckoning" (Phil 2:3, 6, 25; 3:7, 8; Heb 10:29; 11:26). In every usage, there is an element of value judgment. Second, the phrase *pasan charan* (literally "all joy" or "entire joy") demands being treated adverbially. The calculation or consideration of testings is to be unequivocal concerning what it represents, namely "joy." This simple moral judgment stands in contrast to the equivocation of the "double-minded" person (1:7–8). The term *joy* (*chara*) not only echoes *chairein* (compare Plutarch, *A Pleasant Life Impossible* 8 [*Mor.* 1091 E]), but corresponds to a pervasive characteristic of early Christian experience (see Acts 13:52; Rom 14:17; 15:13; 2 Cor 1:15; 2:3; Gal 5:22; Phil 1:4; Col 1:11; 1 Pet 1:8; 1 John 1:4; 2 John 12). A distinctive aspect of such joy is its compatibility with suffering (see John 16:20–22; 2 Cor 7:4; 1 Thess 1:6; Heb 10:34). Clearly, something other is meant by this joy than simple pleasure (*hēdonē*) or happiness (*eudaimonia*); see Nauck, "Freude im Leiden," 68–80.

whenever you encounter various testings: The triple alliteration with *p* in *peirasmois*, *peripesēte*, and *poikilois* is striking. The conjunction "whenever" and the adjective "various" generalize: *every kind* of testing is to be regarded in terms of joy. For "various" (*poikilos*), see 3 Macc 2:6. The verb *peripiptein* literally means to "fall in with," as ships coming together at sea (Herodotus, *Persian War* 6:41). It frequently has the sense of "falling into" unfortunate circumstances (Herodotus, *Persian War* 1:96) or events (Philostratus, Vit. Apol. I, 33), as "to fall among thieves" (Luke 10:30). These are not, therefore, circumstances that are chosen or sought out. They are encountered. The term *peirasmos* ("testing") can mean either a trial from without (see 1 Pet 1:6; 4:12) or a "temptation" from within (see Luke 4:13; 1 Tim 6:9). Either sense is possible here, although in 1:13, the "internal" sense is demanded.

3. *since you know*: The circumstantial participle grounds their perception: the ability to perceive testings as joy derives from a more fundamental construal of reality, in this case the conviction that adversity strengthens character. The appeal to shared knowledge is a common feature of paraenesis (Introduction I.D). The participle also introduces the rhetorical figure known as a *gradatio* or *sorites*, in which one clause builds on another (Dibelius, 74–76). In this case, 1 Pet 1:6–7 and Rom 5:2b–5 provide impressive parallels.

the testing: The majority of MSS read *dokimion*, which is undoubtedly to be preferred to the reading *dokimon* ("approved character") found in a few MSS, or the omission of the phrase altogether (as in the Harclean Syriac). Not only is it the best attested, but its similarity to (the best reading of) 1 Pet 1:7 also makes it the harder rather than the easier reading. In 1 Pet 1:7, the phrase *to dokimion tes pisteōs hymōn* uses the neutral singular of the adjective *dokimios* ("genuineness") in order to state, "the genuineness of your faith." In the present passage, *to dokimion* is the substantive that is elsewhere attested in the sense of "means of testing" (see, e.g., Plutarch, *Sayings of Spartans* {Namurtes} [*Mor.* 230 B], and Prov 27:21). It must be admitted that Oecumenius, whose sense of the Greek was better than ours, read it as "that which has been proven," but he may have been harmonizing with 1 Pet 1:7. Certainly the translation "testing" better accords with James' thought in this passage, since "means of testing" picks up naturally from "testings." It is harder to see how "genuineness of your faith" fits the logic.

of your faith: Notice the plural pronoun: not only the virtue of the individual, but the character of the entire community is at stake. Nor is it *aretē* ("virtue") that is proven, but rather *pistis* ("faith"). This is the first of fourteen instances of the term *pistis* in James. In the present case, it denotes, at least, a human attitude or commitment that both can be threatened and can grow. In the broadest terms, this can be understood as a kind of *aretē*, but one that also defines the community of readers' *ēthos*.

produces endurance: This is James' only use of *katergazesthai* ("to bring about/produce"), although he uses *ergazesthai* in 1:20 and 2:9. The term sets up the use of *ergon* (literally "work," but translated as "product") in the next line. More significantly, the construction shows from the start of the composition how James characteristically connects "faith" and its "work/deed/product," namely as the effective development and expression of faith itself. For the use of *katergazesthai*, see Herodotus, *Persian War* 7:102; Philo, *Noah's Work as a Planter*, 50. The most striking parallel is provided by Rom 5:3, *hypomonēn katergazetai*, which is discussed in the Comment. For "endurance" (*hypomonē*) as a quality particularly important for those belonging to a religious movement that is subject to trial/testing, see Luke 8:15; 21:19; Rom 2:7; 8:25; 15:4–5; 2 Cor 1:6; Col 1:11; 1 Thess 1:3; Heb 12:1. In James, it will recur in the example provided by Job (5:11), as well as in the statements (using the verb form *hypomenein*) in 1:12 and 5:11. The cultivation of *hypomonē* is a major theme also in 4 Macc 1:11; 7:22; 9:30; 17:4; 17:12. The general principle that virtue must be tested to prove itself is widely attested in the moral literature of antiquity (see, e.g., Seneca, *On Providence* 2:1–6; Epictetus, *frag.* 28b; Prov 27:21; Sir 2:1; Wis 3:5–6; PA 5:3; 4 Macc 7:22; 1QH 5:16; *T. Job.* 4:2–11; *T. Jos.* 2:6–7; *Jub.* 17:17–18; 19:8–9; *Sentences of Sextus* 7a; *Herm. Man.* 5.1,1–6).

4. *yield a perfect product*: the *gradatio* becomes more evident in the repetition of *hypomonē*: as testing leads to endurance, endurance is to "have" (*echetō*) or "yield" a "perfect product"—more literally, "work" (*ergon*). The adjective *teleios* is a favorite of James (see 1:17, 25; 3:2) and denotes that which is finished, complete, or mature (see, e.g., "perfect virtue" and "perfect friendship" in Aristotle, *Nicomachean Ethics* 1129b, 1156b, and "perfect love" in 1 John 4:18). In the present instance, it is the deed or effect of endurance that is "perfect." The thought corresponds exactly to James' statement concerning Abraham in 2:22: "from deeds (*ergon*) the faith (*pistis*) was perfected (*eteleiōthē*)."

you might be perfect and complete: The term "perfect" now shifts from the action to the person: "*you* are the perfect work" (Dibelius, 74). The deed perfects the person (see 1 Cor 2:6; Eph 4:13; Phil 3:15; Col 1:28; 4:12; Matt 5:48; 19:21; also Wis 9:6; Sir 44:17; Philo, *Allegorical Laws* 3:45–49). The adjective *holoklēros* ("complete") derives from the verb *holoklērein*, which means to be in good health, and has the nuance of "wholeness" or "soundness" in contrast to disease (Acts 3:16). See the LXX usage with respect to "intact" stones (Deut 27:6; Josh 9:2), translating *šlm*. In moral discourse, see Plato, *Laws*, 759C; see also "complete piety" in 4 Macc 15:17. The idea of perfection here is similar to that in Matt 5:48.

lacking in nothing: The participial phrase may at first glance appear redundant, since it only makes explicit what is implicit in *holoklēros*: to be whole means to lack nothing. But it actually provides the moral edge to the exhortation, since the "lacking" here has nothing to do with material realities (as in Prov 19:4; Titus 1:5; 3:13; and later in James 2:15) but rather moral or spiritual realities: "lacking" means "falling short." Compare the use in Epictetus, *Discourses* II, 22, 5, and Luke 18:22.

5. *lacking wisdom*: As the use of the indefinite *tis* and the conditional *ei* suggests, the exhortation is directed at any who are not able to share the community's perception (*hēgēsasthai*) rooted in a common knowledge (*ginōskontes*). The word-linkage of *leipomenoi/leipetai* is obvious. Of more importance is the implication that *sophia* ("wisdom") is the lack most critical to remedy. The early occurrence of this term signals the character of James as a wisdom writing (see Introduction I.E.2.c). This wisdom is practical rather than theoretical, enabling not only true perception, but also proper action in the world. The nature of this wisdom as a measure for behavior is spelled out in 3:13–18, as noted already by the *scholia*.

ask of God: That wisdom finds its source in God is axiomatic for the Jewish tradition: "The fear of the Lord is the beginning of wisdom" (Prov 9:10), for wisdom was with God from the beginning (Prov 8:22–31). This cosmic wisdom "from above" found its expression also in "the law which Moses commanded us" (Sir 24:23), so that God can declare of his commandments and statutes, "keep them and do them, for that will be your wisdom and your understanding in the sight of the peoples" (Deut 4:6). It was natural, then, to "ask God" for wisdom, but no figure more exemplified this instinct than Solomon, whose "asking" (*aitein*) for a discerning heart was answered generously by the Lord (1 Kgs 3:5–15). In Wis 7:7, Solomon is made to say, "Therefore I prayed, and understanding was given to me; I called upon God and the spirit of wisdom came to me." Bede gets the logic of James' exhortation perfectly: "How am I to see trials in this light . . . it needs a higher wisdom."

who gives to all: The attributive participle is so arranged as to emphasize the very *identity* of God as giver: *tou didontos theou pasin*. The present participle can be read as describing present progressive action: God continually gives. Most startling is the assertion that God does not restrict giving only to those who make request, but simply gives "to all." In 1:17, James will again identify gift-giving as the essential attribute of God.

simply and without grudging: The adverb *haplōs* signifies simplicity as opposed to complexity; by extension it suggests a lack of calculation and openness. In connection with the verb "giving," the adverb probably should be seen in the light of the use of *haplotēs* in such contexts to mean "generosity/ liberality" (see *T. Iss.* 3:3, 8; Josephus, *Ant.* 7:332; Rom 12:8; 2 Cor 8:2;

9:11–13). The basic meaning of *oneidizein*, in turn, is to rebuke or reproach (see Prov 25:8–9; Sir 22:20; Matt 5:11; Rom 15:3; 1 Pet 4:14). The verb sometimes occurs in contexts of giving, when a reproach accompanying a gift means a lack of generosity (see Plutarch, *How to Tell a Flatterer* 22 [*Mor* 64A]; *Sentences of Sextus* 339: "The one who gives with reproaching is insulting"; also Sir 20:15; 41:25). This is undoubtedly the sense here as well. The giving of God, in other words, is universal, unequivocal, and generous.

it will be given: The bracketed description of God's generosity assures the realization of the response to prayer. If that description is removed, the resulting sentence, "Let him ask from God and it will be given to him" (*aiteitō para tou theou kai dothēsetai autǭ*), unmistakably echoes the saying of Jesus in Matt 7:7, *aiteite kai dothēsetai hymin* ("ask and it will be given to you"). See the variants also in Matt 7:11; 21:22; Luke 11:9; John 16:23.

6. *ask with faith*: Literally "in faith" (*en pistei*). *Pistis* here suggests the trust and "simplicity" appropriate to requests made to a God who gives simply and without grudging.

without doubting: In contrast, the attitude of "doubting" disables prayer. The verb *diakrinein* is used in the NT for judgment of persons (1 Cor 4:7; 11:31), distinguishing between various foods (Rom 14:23), and of internal debate or doubt revealing a divided consciousness or motivation (see Acts 10:20; Rom 4:20). Once more, the words of Jesus can be detected underneath James' exhortation. In Mark 11:23, the one who "doubts in his heart" in prayer is contrasted with the one who has faith. And in Matt 21:21, Jesus says, "Amen I say to you, if you have faith and do not doubt (*diekrithēte*) . . . it will happen." See also the contrast between faith and doubting in Rom 4:20. Several textual variants appear in this verse, either filling out the notion of unbelief, or anticipating the element of "receiving" in v.8. They are clearly secondary.

like a wave of the sea: The verb *eoika* ("be like") is perfect in form, present in meaning, and found in the NT only here and in 1:23. The comparison itself is perfectly fitted to the doubting person. What could be more unstable than a wave of the sea, responding to every wind? The translation supplies the word "wind," although it is implicit in both participles: the passive of *anemizein* literally means to be driven by the wind, and the passive of *rhipizein* likewise means to be blown about. By itself, the phrase *klydon thalassēs* can connote "rough seas" (see Philo, *On the Creation*, 58; Josephus, *Ant.* 9:210). For the comparison of the doubting person to a ship on a storm-tossed sea, see Philo, *Migration of Abraham*, 148; and for mental anguish as the tossing of waves, see also Philo, *On the Giants*, 51.

7. *that sort of person*: Since *anēr* is used in the next line, the translation takes the liberty of rendering *anthrōpos* as "person" and the demonstrative pronoun *ekeinos* in a generalizing direction. The Greek text shows some uncertainty concerning the logical status of the sentence. The text used here has *gar* ("for") as a connective, but none in the next verse. Some MSS supply *gar* at the

beginning of v.8, making it a separate explanatory clause. The present translation drops the connective altogether and allows the resulting asyndetic character of the separate sentence to carry the burden of signaling explanatory clauses.

should not think: The imperative *oiesthō* (from *oiomai*) forms a parachesis with *eoiken* in the previous verse. And like it, the verb is widely attested in Hellenistic literature but is used only rarely by the LXX (14 times) and the NT (John 21:25; Phil 1:17).

receive anything from the Lord: The neuter indefinite pronoun *ti* is lacking from some MSS but is understood in any case. The basic sense of "something" can, in statements such as this one, be generalized to "anything" (see Matt 5:23; Mark 8:23; John 16:23). The verb *lambanein* ("receive") echoes another part of Jesus' saying on prayer found in Q material, "for everyone who asks, receives" (Matt 7:8; Luke 11:10). The phrase "from the Lord" (*para tou kyriou*) matches "from God" (*para tou theou*) in 1:5.

8. *a double-minded man*: The term *dipsychos* is unattested before James. But despite the flat assertion, "it is not at all likely to be the coinage of the author" (Ropes, 143), the roots of the term resist discovery in literature antecedent to James (despite the efforts of O. J. F. Seitz). Certainly, the basic notion of a divided person is known as early as Plato's "twofold man" (*diplous anēr*) in *Rep.* 397E; 554D. In Jewish literature, see the phrase *en kardia dissē* in Sir 1:28, and the use of *diprosōpos* in *T. Ash.* 2:5. Nevertheless, the specific use of *dipsychos* is not found, and it well *may* be the coinage of James (Porter), especially since it appears everywhere in literature after and dependent on James. See the use of the verb *dipsychein* (*1 Clem.* 23:2; *2 Clem.* 11:5; *Herm. Vis.* 2,2,7), the noun *dipsychia* (*Herm. Vis.* 3,10,9; *Herm. Man.* 9:7,9; *2 Clem.* 19:2), and the adjective *dipsychos* (*Herm. Man.* 9:6; *1 Clem.* 11:2; *2 Clem.* 11:2). Other such constructions also abound: "double-hearted" (*diplokardia*) in *Barn.* 20; "double-tongued" (*diglōssa*) in *Did.* 2:4; *Barn.* 19:7, and "double-minded" (*dignōmōn*) in *Did.* 2:4; *Barn.* 19:7, and noted as a synonym for *dipsychos* here by the *scholia*. In the present verse, the sense of "double-minded" is clearly connected to "doubting" in prayer (as in *Did.* 4:4; *Barn.* 19:5; *Herm. Man.* 9:1). When the term recurs in 4:8, some of the broader dimensions of "living by two measures" will be evident.

unstable in all his ways: The adjective *akatastatos* here has the sense of fickle and unsteady (compare Epictetus, *Discourses* II, 1, 12; Polybius, *Histories* 7,4,6). In James 3:8 and 3:16, "instability" takes on a more active and malign character. The term "way" (*hodos*) is used of behavior or way of life (see LXX Pss 1:1, 6; 15:11; 118:1, 32; Prov 1:15; Wis 5:6). In James 5:20, James speaks of turning a brother from "the way (*hodos*) of error." Such language naturally suggests the ethics of "the two ways" found in other Jewish moral literature (e.g., *4 Ezra* 7:12–18; *1 Enoch* 91:18; *2 Enoch* 30:15; 42:10; *Sib. Or.* 8:399–403; *T. Ash.* 1:3–5; *1QS* 3–4, though this passing allusion does not make that framework explicit.

COMMENT

The opening lines of James demand immediate decisions. Is James going to be heard in its own voice or not? Is James' challenge to the readers' understanding of the world going to be taken seriously or not?

The first decision is of a more technical sort. At the level of form, the internal logic of James' statement can be ignored by concentrating only on the rhetorical effect of word-linkage or the rhetorical figure of the *sorites*. At the level of literary analysis, the opening sentences can be regarded as an isolated aphorism, with no internal connection to the rest of the chapter or to the rest of the composition. At the level of content, James' statement can be reduced without remainder to a broad moral tradition. As the notes demonstrate, it is something of a commonplace that the testing of virtue leads to strength of character. It is possible, then, to render James' exhortation in the manner of an anodyne: "Cheer up, trials are good for you." More specifically, this particular *sorites* can be compared to the similar constructions in Romans 5:2–4 and 1 Pet 1:6–7 and categorized as an "early Christian *topos* on suffering."

On every count, the interpretation here decides in the other direction. In terms of form, the significant thing to note in these verses is not the word-linkage and formation of a rhetorical *climax*, but the fact that there is a tight logic joining the parts of the statements together. There is not only affirmation, but also argument here. The opening command concerning perception (1:2) is grounded in a warrant (1:3). The second command concerning perfection (1:4a) builds on the same warrant and leads to a purpose clause (1:4b). A conditional clause (1:5a) introduces an exception to the perception first commanded, which is answered by a further command to prayer for the proper perception (1:5b), accompanied by a second warrant in the form of assurance concerning the prayer's answer (1:5c). The command is then repeated with a qualification concerning its manner (1:6a). The contrary of that recommended manner is then examined (1:6b) together with a warning of nonresponse to prayer of that sort (1:7). The initial section ends with a characterization of the person whose double-mindedness marks him as the exception to the recommended perceptions of the community.

At the level of literary context, the opening exhortation should be taken as stating the basic thesis that is worked out both in this chapter and in the rest of the composition. The theme is faith and its reaching a fullness or perfection through a variety of "testings" presented by an alternative understanding of the world. The rest of the composition will elaborate a series of such "testings" that challenge faith's perception of reality: testings that arise not only from human cravings and passions but from a measurement of reality that is actively hostile toward that offered by faith. The composition will unfold as well the way faith is "perfected" by proper modes of speech and behavior, especially in the obedience and hospitality of faith shown by the "works" of Abraham and Rahab (2:20–25); in the "endurance of faith" demonstrated by Job (5:10–11); in the "prayer of faith" offered by Elijah (5:17–18). This opening exhortation contains in compressed form each one of these themes: faith's perfect "work/product," endurance, and prayer. It remains to the rest of the chapter to work out the conceptual understanding of this thesis more fully.

The content of James' first exhortation, furthermore, is scarcely reducible to a moral truism. The testing of the community's *faith*, after all, cannot simply be equated with the perfection of an individual's *virtue*. Nor is prayer in faith to God for the wisdom to have a faithful perception of trials the same as the self-sufficiency of a sage's wisdom.

The resemblance between the *gradatio* in James 1:2–4 and those in Rom 5:2–4 and 1 Pet 1:6–7 is more apparent than real. Between James and 1 Peter there is mainly the sharing of the phrases "various trials" (*poikilois peirasmois*) and "provenness of faith" (*dokimion hymōn tēs pisteōs*) within the general context of suffering. But the internal connections are entirely different. In Romans, in contrast, we also find the structure of the *sorites* as in James, but with a different set of verbal correspondences: the "accomplishing of endurance" (*hypomonēn katergazetai*) and the "proven endurance" (*hypomonē dokimē*). Once more, however, the logic of the passage moves in another direction. In short, James' voice in these verses cannot without loss be reduced to the common chorus of Greco-Roman philosophy or Christian paraenetic tradition.

These considerations bring us to the second sort of decision concerning James 1:2–8: if its voice is distinctive, how will it be heard? By isolating it as a discrete aphorism, by focusing only on mechanical connections, by reducing its content to a commonplace or truism, readers stave off the conceptual challenge posed by this exhortation and its threat to the structure of the world assumed by its readers.

James' call for a perception of testing as a chance to grow in a commitment is certainly at odds with a world that conceives of life solely in terms of gratification and self-aggrandizement. In that worldview, anything interfering with pleasure is a source of "suffering," which must at all costs be avoided. The ideal of "endurance" is not attractive to hedonism, for it assumes an understanding of human character based on something more profound than pleasure, possession, or power. James' understanding on this point would not, as the notes have shown, be greatly at odds with philosophical traditions such as Stoicism, which understood the close connection between *mathein* ("learning") and *pathein* ("suffering") and recognized that "progress in virtue" inevitably involved some sort of suffering.

James' real distinctiveness comes in the breathtaking assertion—grounded in the symbolic world of Torah shared by every form of Judaism including the nascent movement rooted in the "faith of Jesus Christ"—that human existence is not located within a closed system of competition (even for virtue or excellence) but rather within an open system ordered to a God who gives gifts to humanity. This is the theological perspective of "faith." And it is this under-standing of reality that grounds the positive perception of testing. The "endur-ance" here is not the demonstration of a human being's moral character, but of a community's fidelity to God as the source of its being and worth. The "perfect product" of endurance is not a finished moral paragon, but a community that has become what 1:18 calls "a certain firstfruits of God's creatures." This theological construal of reality is what makes the turn to prayer something other than an arbitrary piece of pious advice. Prayer is the essential conversion for one unable to "perceive" or "calculate" life's testings in the appropriate way. It is surely not by accident that James' composition begins and ends on the topic of prayer, since prayer is the activity that most fundamentally defines and expresses that construal of reality called "faith."

Since this "measure of reality" (or "wisdom") is one that is essentially ordered to God, it follows that only God can bestow it when it is lacking. Yet, even to make this turn toward God means at some deep level that one does, in some fashion, participate in the overall construal called "faith." Otherwise, one would not pray. When James opposes the *manner* of praying "in faith" and "in doubting," therefore, he identifies from the start the reason for his entire exhortatory composition: it is addressed to those who share the community's ethos of "faith" but do so with a divided mind; they seek to live by two measures at once. These "double-minded persons" are the particular target of warning. When James suggests that "they should not think that they will receive anything from the Lord," he suggests something about the dynamics of community life: those who share the group's ethos with only half a mind are already half out of the community.

1:9–12

9. Let the lowly brother boast in his exalted position. 10. But let the rich person boast in his humbling, because like a wild flower he will pass away. 11. For the sun rises with its burning heat and dries up the grass, and its flower falls, and the beauty of its appearance is lost. Thus also the rich person will disappear in the midst of his activities. 12. Blessed is the man who endures testing, because when he has been proven sound, he will receive the crown of life, which [God] has promised to those who love him.

NOTES

9. *the lowly brother*: The term *tapeinos* is here opposed to "rich," but connotes "lowliness" of any sort, whether of position, privilege, or stature. In

the biblical tradition, the *tapeinoi* are the special recipients of God's saving activity (see LXX Pss 9:39; 17:28; 33:19; 81:3; 101:18; Isa 11:4; 14:32). The term recurs in James 4:6, where the principle is generated from Prov 3:34: God resists the arrogant, but gives a gift to the lowly (*tapeinois*)."

boast: The verb *kauchasthai* is straightforward enough, meaning to vaunt oneself or one's claims (Herodotus, *Persian War* 7:39), especially against another (Aristotle, *Politics* 1311b). In the biblical wisdom tradition, the human tendency to boast is recognized as legitimate: the issue concerns the grounds of boasting. Thus, in a lengthy addition to the Hebrew of 1 Sam 2:1–10, the instruction of v.3, "Do not boast and speak high things" is amplified by the LXX to: "let not the cunning boast in his cunning; let not the mighty boast in his might; let not the rich boast in his riches, but let the one who boasts, boast in this, understanding and knowing the Lord, and doing judgment and righteousness in the midst of the earth." The addition has an obvious resemblance to Jeremiah 9:23–24. And in Sir 24:1–2, Wisdom herself "boasts in the midst of the people." In the NT, the language of boasting is found, outside of James and Heb 3:6, exclusively in the Pauline literature. In Paul, also, the issue is the ground for boasting, either something of one's own (Rom 2:7, 23; 1 Cor 3:21; 4:7; 2 Cor 5:12; 11:18; Gal 6:13; Eph 2:9) or what comes from the Lord (Rom 5:2–3, 11; 1 Cor 1:29–31; 4:7; 2 Cor 10:13–15; 10:17; Gal 6:14; Phil 3:3). James will return to a form of *inappropriate* boasting in 3:14 and 4:16.

his exalted position: *ho hypsos* provides an obvious spatial contrast with *tapeinos*. The term can denote any kind of "height," whether of stature (Herodotus, *Persian War* 1:50) or rank (1 Macc 1:40; 10:24). Three questions immediately arise from this oxymoronic command: what *is* the exalted position, where is it to be found, and when is it given? The exaltation can be read as including the future reward of the one who endures, which is promised by 1:12, and therefore be seen as eschatological (Dibelius, 84). But it also has already been realized in God's election of the poor to be "rich in faith" in the kingdom (2:5): "Not any future elevation in this or the other world, but the present spiritual height conferred by his outward lowliness, the blessing pronounced on the poor, the possession of the kingdom of God" (Hort, 15).

10. *the rich person*: This is a very difficult verse. The meaning of the term *plousios* is not in doubt: in contrast to the polyvalent *tapeinos*, it refers specifically to material wealth. In the Mediterranean as in other cultures, wealth itself commanded certain privileges (see James 2:1–4). In the sayings of Jesus, the rich are uniformly treated harshly (see Matt 19:23–24; Mark 10:25; 12:41; Luke 6:24; 12:16; 14:12; 16:19; 18:25). James continues that tradition in 2:5–6 and 5:1–6. But is the present statement to be read as harsh (Dibelius, 85) and ironic (Bede, Calvin)? Or is it to be read more straightforwardly? Much hinges on the decision whether the "rich person" is to be considered as a "brother," as the symmetrical structure of the sentence would seem to demand; (see Martin,

25, for the options, and for the view that the statement refers to a fellow Christian, see Ropes, 146, and Mayor, 45–46).

in his humbling: The structure of the sentence demands that we supply "should boast" before "in his humbling." Taken together, the two statements provide still another echo of Jesus' saying found in Q: "Whoever exalts the self will be humbled (*tapeinōthēsetai*), and the one who humbles self will be exalted (*hypsōthēsetai*)" (Matt 23:12; Luke 14:11; 18:14). Hort, 15, perceptively notes that the rich man will "suffer the loss not of wealth only, but of the consideration which wealth brings."

because like a wild flower: The *hoti* clause is meant to explain why the rich person [brother] should [boast] in his humiliation. But how does it? The Comment will take up the overall problem in logic. The comparison suggests fragility and transience. *Chortos* is generally used of field plants such as hay and *anthos* of a flower or bloom. Taken together, the terms suggest the fragile wild flowers of the field that are exposed to the sun.

he will pass away: Or possibly, "it will pass away," referring to the wealth rather than to the person. The *anthos* is also the image for the transient quality of human life in LXX Job 14:2; Ps 102:15; Zeph 2:2. The phrase *anthos chortou* provides an allusion to LXX Isa 40:7, which will be spelled out in the next verse: *pasa sarx chortos kai pasa doxa anthrōpou hōs anthos chortou. exaranthē ho chortos kai ho anthos exepesen. to de rhēma tou theou hēmōn menei eis ton aiōna* ("All flesh is grass and all human glory is like the wild flower [blossom of the grass]. The grass has dried up and the blossom has fallen. But the word of our God remains forever"). The Isaiah passage is explicitly cited by 1 Pet 1:24.

11. *for the sun rises*: The aorist tense of the verbs poses a problem for translation. They can be regarded simply as gnomic aorists, such as are frequently used in aphorisms (Mayor, 46; Hort, 16; Dibelius, 86), and be translated, as here, with the present tense: such is the way of things (compare 1:24). But it is also possible to see James (and the LXX) as having taken over the force of the Hebrew perfect in the prophetic literature (Moule, *Idiom Book*, 12), so that the aorist has something of a "proleptic" sense (*Zerwick/Grosvener* 2:692): this is the way it is going to be.

the grass and its flower: Some MSS have the pronoun *autou* ("its"), which has the effect of separating *anthos* and *chortou* into parts of the same plant. That text makes explicit what the present translation in any case supplies.

the beauty of its appearance is lost: The noun *euprepeia* can be used of "propriety," as in style (Plato, *Phaedrus* 274B). It can also connote speciousness or mere plausibility (Plato, *Euthydemus* 305E). In this detailed appropriation of the Isaian metaphor, it is difficult not to conclude that James is anticipating the *visual* impact made by the rich person in 2:1–4.

the rich person will disappear: Although the statement in v. 10 that "it will pass away" did not make clear whether the wealth or the person was intended, the application (*houtōs* = thus) attaches the comparison to its intended referent.

The verb *marainein* originally referred to the slow failing of a fire and came to be used for a variety of cessations (see LXX Job 15:30; 24:24). But what is meant by "will pass away?" Is this a reference to the parousia (Dibelius, 87)? Such a conclusion would fit 5:1–6. Or does James intend simply to indicate the perennial transitoriness of life and its possessions, as he does also in 4:13–16 (compare Luke 12:16–21, especially with its moral, *houtōs ho thēsaurizōn heautǭ kai mē eis theon ploutōn*, "thus is the one who piles up treasure for himself and is not rich toward God").

in the midst of his activities: The noun *poreia* derives from the verb *poreuesthai* ("to go") and ranges in meaning from literal journeys (Num 33:2; Luke 13:22) to a "way of life" (Prov 2:7; Jer 10:23). In the present case, *poreia* could mean "ways of behaving" and thus echo the use of *hodos* in v.8. By way of anticipating the development of the theme of transience in 4:13–16, the translation "journeys" would be apt. The translation aims at capturing something of each nuance. If the passage is eschatological, it fits the theme of the *suddenness* of the parousia and the way it intersects the daily round of business (see Mark 13:33–36; Luke 17:28–37; 1 Thess 5:2–3); if it is sapiential, it fits the truth that death with its loss of possessions can happen at any moment (see Luke 12:16–20). Oecumenius takes "the ways" as referring to the rich person's business dealings, which will face vicissitudes; Theophylact takes it as referring to "the course of the present life."

12. *blessed is the man*: The term "man" (*anēr*) is explicit here as also in 1:8, 20, 23; 2:2; 3:2, and it is the best reading. Some MSS, perhaps sensitive to the exclusive connotations of *anēr*, have *anthrōpos* ("human person") instead. The nonexclusive intent of James' language should be clear, however, from the fact that he states a universal premise for human life before God. The blessing formula begins with *makarios*. Although the translation "happy" is certainly possible (Hort, 19; see Plato, *Rep*. 354A; Gen 30:13), "blessed" is preferable not only because it can be distinguished from "happiness" (*eudaimonia*; see Aristotle, *Nicomachean Ethics*, 1101A), but also because of its consistent use within the biblical tradition to describe the result of right relatedness of humans to God (Deut 33:29; LXX Pss 1:1; 2:12; 31:1; 39:5; 83:5; 111:1; 143:15; Prov 3:13; Sir 34:15). In the gospel tradition (especially in the material found in Q), the macarism is especially associated with the speech of Jesus (Matt 5:3–11; 11:6; 13:16; 16:17; 24:46; Luke 6:20–22; 7:23; 10:23; 11:27–28; 12:37–38, 43; 14:14; 23:29; John 13:17; 20:29).

who endures testing: A textual variant here has "will endure"; some of the most important witnesses, however, have the present tense, "endures"; but they also leave out the object of the endurance, namely, "testing." It may have been thought by some scribes that *peirasmon* was an expansion, perhaps by attraction from James 5:11. It is, however, more likely that *peirasmon* is original, tying this statement to that in 1:2 and, in turn, anticipating 5:11: "behold we call blessed (*makarizomen*) those who have endured (*hypomeinantas*)." The verb *hypomenein* with the accusative has the sense of "being patient under something" or "standing one's ground in the face of something" (see Xenophon, *Mem* 2,1,3; Herodotus, *Persian War* 6:12). It can also bear the meaning of "wait for patiently" (LXX Pss 24:3, 5, 21; 26:14; 32:20; Prov 20:9c), as the Vulgate translation "*patientes*" suggests. In the Gospels, "endurance to the end" is attached to the expectation of salvation (Matt 10:22; 24:13; Mark 13:13; Luke 21:19). The wording of the present macarism does not explicitly resonate any attributed to Jesus, although the theme of being blessed even in circumstances of persecution and rejection is certainly found in Matt 5:10–11; 10:22; Luke 6:22. The closest parallel to this macarism is found in Dan 12:12 (Th): *makarios ho hypomenon* . . . "blessed is the one who endures . . ."

when he has been proven sound: The occurrence of *dokimos* ("approved by test/genuine," see *T. Jos.* 2:7) here helps account for its appearance as a textual variant in 1:3. The difference is between "means of testing" (*dokimion*) and "being tested and shown worthy" (*dokimos*).

will receive the crown of life: The *stephanos* was, in Greek culture, the wreath or chaplet that was used to award victors in games (Herodotus *Persian War* 8:26; see 1 Cor 9:25; 2 Tim 2:5), to honor public service (Plato, *Laws* 943C; see Heb 2:7–9), and to signify rank (Aristotle, *Athenian Constitution* 57:4; see 2 Sam 12:30; Isa 22:21). It can also be used generally for any sort of reward (Prov 17:6; Sir 25:6). Its metaphorical force can be seen in passages such as Isa 28:1–5. Given the widespread use of *zōē* or *zōē aiōnios* as shorthand for the goal of Christian existence (see Matt 7:14; 19:16–17; 25:46; Mark 9:45; 10:17; Luke 10:25; 18:18, 30; John 3:15–16; 5:29; 20:31; Acts 3:15; 13:46–48; Rom 5:21; 6:22–23; Gal 6:8; Jude 21), the "crown of life" could be understood as "the crown that signifies elevation into future life with God," which finds an exact parallel in Rev 2:10; or better, "the crown that is life with God" (compare "crown of righteousness" in 2 Tim 4:8 and "crown of glory" in 1 Pet 5:4).

[God] has promised: The translation supplies in brackets the understood subject of the verb. A large number of MSS also reflect a concern for supplying the subject, either "Lord" or "God." Although the translation is forced to compensate, the shorter Greek text is the harder and to be preferred. Given the importance of the language of "promise" in the NT (see, e.g., Luke 24:49; Acts 2:33; 7:17; 13:23; 23:21; 26:6; Rom 4:13–21; 9:4; 15:8; 2 Cor 1:20; Gal 3:14–29; 4:28; Eph 1:13; Heb 4:1; 6:13), it is remarkable how little role it plays in the LXX (see only Ps 55:9; 2 Macc 2:18). The "promise of life" is found in the NT otherwise only in the Pastorals (1 Tim 4:8; 2 Tim 1:1; Titus 1:2). Note that the structure of the clause is remarkably similar to that in James 2:5, with the term *basileia* ("kingdom") occurring there instead of "crown of life."

to those who love him: In Exod 20:5–6, the expression "those who love me" is equivalent to "those who keep my commandments" (see likewise Deut 7:9 and 30:20). To "love the Lord your God" is also the commitment expressed by the *shema 'Israel* (Deut 6:4). Those who love God are, therefore, those in proper covenantal relationship with God (see LXX Pss 5:12; 17:1–2; 30:24; 68:37; 96:10; Sir 34:16; 47:8), which implies always that they also "love his commandments" (see LXX Ps 118:47, 48, 97, 113, 159; Sir 2:15). LXX Ps 5:12–13 nicely combines the elements of James' statement: "and they will boast in you, all those who love your name, because you have blessed the righteous one. Lord, as with a crown of good pleasure you have crowned (*estephanōsas*) us." In the Synoptics, "loving God" is found only in the context of the *shema* (Matt 22:37; Mark 12:30; Luke 10:27). In both John and Paul, the main emphasis is on the love God has shown humans (John 14–16; 1 John 4:7–10; Rom 8:37; Eph 2:4; 5:2; 1 Thess 1:4; 2 Thess 2:16). Nevertheless, 1 John 5:2 contains the traditional Jewish combination: "In this we know that we love the children of God when we love God and keep the commandments." Paul also uses the traditional language in Rom 8:28; 1 Cor 2:9; 8:3. James will use the expression again in 2:5.

COMMENT

The arrangement of these sentences once more forces decisions on the interpreter. How should the verses be joined or separated? The lack of connectives in the Greek makes the decision difficult. Verses 9–11 must obviously be read together, but do they stand as a separate unit? Likewise, should 1:12 stand alone? If it does not, should it be connected to what follows in 1:13 or (as here) with what precedes in 1:9–11?

If Dibelius is followed, and the segments of chapter one are regarded as a loose collection with no connections in thought, the decisions are easier. Then 1:9–11 can be taken as a single unit, 1:12 as a solitary aphorism, and 1:13–15 as still another segment whose placement is due entirely to the word-linkage with 1:12 (Dibelius, 69–71).

The interpretation here goes in the opposite direction. Although the word-linkage between 1:12 and 1:13 is obvious, there are better reasons for taking 1:12 together with 1:9–11 as a single thought, and then regarding 1:13–15 as a clarification of the principle enunciated in 1:9–12.

The first reason for reading 1:12 with 1:9–11 is that they have a loose similarity in form: 1:9 begins with "boasting" and 1:12 with "blessing." Furthermore, each is concerned with the *end* of respective persons: the rich man disappears, while the one who endures gains a crown of life. We observe also in these verses a contrast between transience and permanence. Most of all, it seems clear that 1:12 draws to a close the argument begun by 1:3: the means of testing accomplishes endurance. And if 1:12 responds to that thesis, then—if we grant any coherence to this chapter at all, which the present interpretation assumes—then 1:9–11 must also play some role in the argument.

If, then, 1:9–12 are taken as a unit, what do they say, and what is their

189

function within the argument of chapter one? It seems clear that the content and the function of the verses go together. In 1:2–3, James had called his readers to a certain perception or calculation of "testings," based on a prior construal of reality. The present verses sketch in shorthand precisely that understanding of things assumed to have been known (*ginōskontes*) in 1:3. *This* is the understanding of reality that the readers are presumed to share with the author.

Once more, we see that the world is viewed as open to God and human existence as ordered by relationship to God. This measure, therefore, affects the perception of every circumstance of life. Most especially, it affects the perception of human destiny. 1:12 makes this explicit: God rewards with life those whose endurance of testing has proven them worthy. They have shown by this faithful patience that they "love God." And by crowning them with life, God shows himself faithful to his promises. The entire premise underlying 1:2 is thus made clear.

If 1:9–11 makes the same point, it does it so obliquely and allusively. Few interpreters have been able to make sense of it as part of a logical argument. The main problem has to do with the identification of the rich person, and the point of what is being said about him. We can approach the problem by moving from what is more certain to what is less so. The "boasting of the lowly brother" in the present context makes obvious sense, especially when correlated with 1:12. The "lowliness" can be seen as a form of "testing" from the side of the world's evaluation and as a "blessing" from the side of God's election. 2:5 will make precisely this contrast explicit. Therefore, the "exalted position" can be seen to correspond to the "crown of life"/"kingdom" promised by God to those who love him (1:12; 2:5). The lowly can boast in this exalted position both now, in terms of their election and inclusion in the people that "loves God," and in terms of their future gaining of the "crown of life."

But what about the rich person? The main difficulty is whether or not James intends this to be a rich person among his readers, that is, within the Christian community. Following that determination, the next difficulty is whether the tone is that of savage irony or of gentle encouragement.

If the rich person were to be understood as someone outside the community and among the "rich oppressors" attacked by 5:1–6, then it would be appropriate to see James' tone as one of irony. Such as those could "boast" even though God's reversal of status will lead to their disappearance together with their riches!

The difficulty with this reading is that the structure of James' sentence in 1:9–10 seems to demand seeing the "rich person" also as a "brother." If this is the case, then the character of his "boasting" and the point of his "passing away" are less clear. One possibility is to take the saying more prophetically (in line with 2:5–6 and 5:1–6) and see James' language as sarcastic: the brothers who are among the rich are not truly among the brothers. They are of the world, whose value-system is incompatible with that of faith. Therefore, there really is no reason for the rich person to "boast" at all. His humbling will be punishment for giving in to the "testing" of wealth and placing his reliance on it.

Another possibility is to read the sentence more sapientially, as an implied exhortation to the brother who has wealth: he should "exalt" in the humbling that inclusion within a community that does not honor him for the status wealth ordinarily brings with it and even condemns wealth altogether. His "boasting" then would not be entirely ironic: the rich brother is reminded of the transitoriness of wealth in order to realize the better status he has among "the lowly" who are blessed by God. Such a reading corresponds better with the tone of 4:13–16.

Either reading is possible and can reasonably be argued. What is important for James' argument, however, is that in neither reading does 1:9–12 appear as direct exhortation. It is, rather, *the stating of basic principles* concerning the human condition before God. In the light of this, the harsher reading seems more likely, for it is important that the contrast between conditions and destinies be made as sharply as possible.

This position is strengthened by the way in which James sets out the destiny of the rich. The comparison to the wildflower is obviously based on an allusion to Isaiah 40:7 (Morris, 145–49). But why did James so extend the allusion? In order to make its point unmistakable. Such NT allusions to Scripture often bear within them an implied reference to the larger context of the passage quoted (Dodd, 127). The allusion carries with it, as Hays has shown in the case of Paul, an "echo" of the larger scriptural context (Hays, 1–33). This is surely also the case here. An allusion to the "wildflower" with a stress on its impermanence obviously calls for the contrast to be made with what *is* permanent. The contrast is provided by Isaiah 40:8: "The Word of our God remains forever." The reader of James who catches this allusion (spelled out by 1 Pet 1:24) is prepared for the stress on "the word of truth" in 1:18 and "the implanted word able to save your souls" in 1:21. Once more, then, the contrast between the rich, on one hand, and the lowly/tested ones on the other, turns out also to be a contrast between the two measures of reality, one given by the "world" and the other given by the "wisdom from above." The subsequent development in chapter one will demonstrate whether this attempt to identify in James 1:9–12 a fundamental statement of principle concerning the two measures is correct.

1:13–21

13. Let no one when tested say, "I am being tempted by God." For God is not tempted by evils. Nor does he himself tempt anyone. 14. Instead, each person, by being drawn away and lured, is tempted by his own desire. 15. Then the desire, once it has conceived, brings forth sin. And when sin is brought to term, it gives birth to death. 16. Do not be deceived, my beloved brothers.

17. Every good giving and every perfect gift is from above, coming down from the father of lights. With him there is no alteration or shadow of change. 18. By his decision he gave us birth through a word of truth, in order that we might be a kind of firstfruits of his creatures. 19. You know this, my beloved brothers. Then let every person be quick to hear, slow to speak, slow to anger. 20. For a man's anger does not accomplish God's righteousness. 21. Put aside, therefore, all filthiness and excess of evil. With meekness receive the implanted word that is able to save your souls.

NOTES

13. *let no one when tested*: The ambiguity rooted in the concept of "testing" is now more clearly revealed. In 1:2 and 1:12, the translation "testing" was appropriate for *peirasmos*, for the structure of those sentences emphasized the outer source of the threat. In 13a, the verb *peirazein* begins a transition to the other aspect of "testing," namely the internal dividedness that outward trial creates (see Bede; Calvin). Even in 1:6–8, this side of things was reflected in the language about "doubting" in prayer and "double-mindedness." The translater must make a decision somewhere in this sequence. "Testing" could work for both instances in 13a, but v.14 so emphasizes the psychological dimension of temptation—its being rooted in human desire—that the reading of *peirazomenos* as "being tempted" virtually is demanded.

"I am being tempted by God": Some MSS read *hypo* ("by") rather than *apo* ("from"). But the prepositions are less severely distinguished in the koine (Moule, *Idiom Book*, 48–49). This is the first case of direct speech in James and, like those that follow, it expresses a mistaken view that requires correction. The view here enunciated was broadly repudiated by ancient moralists, beginning with Homer (*Od.* 1.30–35; see also Hierocles, *On Duties* 2,9,7; Sir 15:11; Philo, *On Creation* 24; *Allegorical Laws* 2:19; *The Worse Attacks the Better* 32; *Teachings of Silvanus* 115). But for those shaped by the narratives of Torah, the complaint might seem more justified. Did not God "test" (*peirazein*) Abraham by commanding him to sacrifice his son Isaac (Gen 22:1; see James 2:21–23!)? Did not God "test" (*peirazein*) the people in the wilderness (Deut 8:2; 13:4)? In light of the clarification that follows, it is critical that such testings not be regarded as "tempting to evil."

for God is not tempted by evils: The connective *gar* ("for") indicates the premise for the previous statement. The reason God cannot be charged with tempting someone to evil is countered with respect to both terms. The first is taken up here: God is not tempted by evils. The translation depends almost entirely on what is demanded by the argument, for *apeirastos* is otherwise unattested before the NT. By etymology, the expression *apeirastos kakōn* could equally mean "inexperienced in evils," or "untested by evil people," or "incapable of being tempted by evils," or even "ought not to be tested" (Davids, "The Meaning," 391). The basic point is clear enough: God has nothing to do with evil. The sentiment here is crisply stated by *Sentences of Sextus*, 30: God is "the wise light that has no room for its opposite."

nor does he himself tempt anyone: The active character of this clause makes the passive reading in the previous clause more likely. The point of this affirmation is to counter the second aspect of the charge that God tempts anyone to evil. He not only has nothing to do with evil; he does not tempt anyone. This flat statement obviously creates a "contradiction in Scripture" with those statements (such as Gen 22:1) that clearly declare that God *did* test some humans! See the Comment for discussion.

14. *instead, each person*: The conjunction *de* is given its maximum adversative force in the translation to capture the sharp opposition between the wrong opinion and its clarification. The adjective *hekastos* does not mean simply "everyone," but as the subsequent use of *idios* shows, each individual person.

by being drawn away: The literal meaning of *exelkein* is to physically drag someone away (see Plato, *Rep.* 515E; Gen 37:28; Judg 20:31), but it can also be used in a moral sense: see "desire (*epithymia*) drew me away" (Plato, *Letter* 7 [325B]).

and lured: The image is very graphic. The noun *delear* is literally "bait," and the verb *deleazein* has the sense of "hooking with bait," that is, to entice or seduce. Compare Philo, *Every Good Man is Free* 159: ". . . if the soul is driven by desire (*epithymia*) or enticed (*deleazetai*) by pleasure. . . ." It is used of the lure of food by Xenophon, *Mem.* 2,1,4; of money and pleasure by Lucian of Samosata, *Apology* 9 and Julian the Apostate, *Or.* 6:185A. See the combination of *deleazein* and *epithymia* in 2 Pet 2:18.

by one's own desire: The noun *epithymia* basically means desire, and by itself is neutral, gaining its moral connotation from the worth of the object desired (see Luke 22:15; Phil 1:23; 1 Thess 2:17). Its use for sexual desire or appetite, however, enables the term easily to slide into the sense of "lust" (Plato, *Phaedo* 83B; *Phaedrus* 232B). In the LXX, *epithymia* and *epithymein* continue to be defined by their object. Thus, the decalogue forbids *epithymia* of neighbor's wife or property (Exod 20:17; Deut 5:21). Yet the *epithymia* of the righteous person is acceptable (Prov 10:24). In Hellenistic moral discourse, especially that dominated by Stoicism, *epithymia* tends to take on a negative connotation without regard to object (see, e.g., Epictetus, *Discourses* II, 16, 45; II, 18, 8; III, 9, 21;). This tendency is found also in Hellenistic Jewish literature (see Wis 4:12; 4 Macc 1:22; 3:2; Philo, *Special Laws* 4:93–94; *Contemplative Life* 74). It can appear absolutely in vice lists (Philo, *Preliminary Studies* 172; *Migration of Abraham* 60; *Contemplative Life* 2). The negative sense predominates in the NT (see Mark 4:19; Rom 1:24; 6:12; 7:7–8; 13:14; Gal 5:24; Col 3:5; 1 Tim 6:9; 2 Tim 3:6; 4:3; Titus 3:3; 1 Pet 1:14; 2 Pet 2:10; 1 John 2:16–17; Jude 18). In this and the next verse, therefore, it would be legitimate to translate *epithymia* as "evil desire," since James is making a moral, even more than a psychological, judgment. He will return to it in 4:2. It should be noted, however, in light of the role given to Satan later, that James shows no real trace here of a psychology of the "two inclinations" (*yetzer ha ra* = the evil inclination; *yetzer ha tob* = the good inclination) found inchoately at Qumran and in the *Testaments of the Twelve Patriarchs*, and fully developed in later rabbinic literature (contra Davids 79–83; Martin 30, 36; Marcus, 620–21).

15. *then the desire, once it has conceived*: The transitional adverb *eita* ("then") establishes a strong link between the previous statement and this one. The form of v. 15 is once more that of the *sorites*, with the linked phrases forming a chain that leads to a rhetorical *climax* (see Dibelius, 94–99; Marty, 35–36; Davids, 85). For other examples, see Demosthenes, *De Corona* 179; Cicero, *Pro Roscio Amerino* XXVII,75; Wis 6:17–19; Rom 8:28–30; 2 Pet 1:5–7; *Herm. Vis.* 3,8,7). The two parts of this verse are perfectly balanced with each containing a subject, predicative participle, verb, and object: *hamartia* is the object of the first clause and the subject of the second. The progression moves from desire to death and passes through sin. The sexual connotation of *epithymia* (see above) is exploited by the vivid sexual imagery of the present verse. *Epithymia* is personified as a female who becomes pregnant (for *syllambanein* in this sense, see Plutarch, *On Borrowing* 4 [*Mor.* 829B]; *Ep. Arist.* 165; LXX Gen 4:1, 17; Luke 1:24). For the basic connection between passion and vice, see 4 Macc 1:25–26; Philo, *On Husbandry* 22–25; *T. Jos.* 7:1–8; *Teachings of Silvanus* 87, 89, 92, 95.

brings forth sin: The verb *tiktein* literally means to give birth (Matt 1:21; John 16:21; Rev 12:4). It is used metaphorically by Plato, *Symp.* 212A; *Syb. Or.* 3:235; Prov 10:23). In this verse sin (*hamartia*) is in the singular, continuing the rhetorical figure of *personification*: sin is the singular child of evil desire (see also 2:9; 4:17). The use of the singular resembles that of John 1:29; 16:8; Rom 5:12–13; 1 Cor 15:56. James uses the plural with reference to specific acts in 5:15, 16, 20 (compare Rom 7:5; 1 Cor 15:3; Gal 1:4).

and when sin is brought to term: The predicative participle *apoteleisthai* ("brought to term") balances the phrase "when it has conceived" in the previous clause. The verb *apotelein* means to bring to completion and, in the passive, "to be fully formed." The sense here, therefore, could be "completed in action" (see Plato, *Laws* 823D), but the context of sexual imagery virtually demands the translation given, "brought to term."

gives birth to death: Some MSS have the future tense, "will give birth," but the present tense better suits the gnomic quality of the sentence. The imagery is obviously shocking. The verb *apokuein* means literally to bear young (Lucian of Samosata, *Dialogues of the Sea Gods* 10:1) but can also be used metaphorically, as in 4 Macc 15:17: "O Unique woman who has given birth to perfect piety." For the relationship between sin and death, see John 8:21; Rom 5:12, 21; 1 Cor 15:56. The verb *apokuein* will be used again immediately of God in 1:18.

16. *do not be deceived*: The basic meaning of *planan* is to wander or to go astray (see Matt 18:12–13), and it is used in that sense in James 5:19. In the passive, it can mean "to be led astray" (Deut 11:28) or "to be deceived/in error" (Deut 4:19; Luke 21:8). The negative imperative *mē planasthe* is a diatribal feature in Epictetus, *Discourses* IV, 6, 23, and is used by Paul (1 Cor 6:9; 15:33; Gal 6:7; see also LXX Isa 44:20).

my beloved brothers: For the use of *adelphos* ("brother"), see 1:2. James uses the caritative *agapētoi* ("beloved") also in 1:19 and 2:5. The verbal adjective (from *agapan*) is used frequently of children (Gen 22:2; Philo, *On Drunkenness* 30) and also of other close relationships (Tob 10:13; Josephus, *JW* 1:240; *Ant.* 15:15). It is frequently used by Christian writers for fellow members of the community (Acts 15:25; Rom 1:7; 16:5, 8, 9, 12; 1 Cor 4:14, 17; 2 Cor 12:19; Phil 2:12; 4:1; Col 1:7; Philemon 1; Heb 6:9; 1 Pet 2:11; 2 Pet 3:1; 1 John 2:7; Jude 3) and undoubtedly reflects an element in early Christian *argot*.

17. *every good giving and every perfect gift*: This well balanced sentence takes the form of an imperfect hexameter (Ropes, 159). For opinions as to whether it is a quotation (particularly since it is introduced by *mē planasthe*), see Fischer, 377–79; Mussner, 90; Ropes, 159; Mayor, 57; Dibelius, 99). Since in any case we do not have the source, the question is both moot and unhelpful. The conceptual difference between "giving" (*dosis*) and "gift" (*dōrēma*) should not be overdone (Marty, 39). *Dosis* is used of the ordinary human exchanges of giving and receiving (Epictetus, *Discourses* II, 9, 12; Phil 4:15), but it can also refer to gift-giving by God (Plato, *Philebus* 16C; *Ep. Arist.* 229; see the *dosis agathē* from God in *T. Zeb.* 1:3; Sir 26:14). *Dōrēma* is less frequently attested in prose and has a more solemn tone (see Aristotle, *Nicomachean Ethics* 1099B). It occurs in the LXX only as a marginal reading at Sir 34:18, and in the NT, it is used at Rom 5:16, where it has the sense of "free gift." Although it is tempting to render one as "endowment" or "bequest" (see RSV, Reicke) or to distinguish "giving" and "gift" (NAB and the present translation), the main reason for doing so is to capture the difference in sound between *dosis* and *dōrēma*. The point of using both is the rhetorical force of repetition with variation and to place emphasis on the unequivocal goodness and perfection (*teleios*) of whatever comes from God. The term *teleios* echoes 1:4. For God as the source of goodness and good gifts, see, e.g., Plutarch, *A Pleasant Life Impossible* 22 [Mor 1102D–F]; Hierocles, *On Duties* 2,9,7; Philo, *On the Cherubim* 34; *Teachings of Silvanus* 101.

is from above: The word order supports taking *anōthen estin* together and treating *katabainon apo* as a dependent participial clause (with Hort, 290; Mussner, 91; Ropes, 160; and the Vulgate). Alternatively one could take *estin* as governing the entire sentence and render it: "is coming down from above" (with Marty, 40; Dibelius, 100). The textual variants in this part of the verse do not affect the meaning. The MSS that read *para* rather than *apo* could be seeking agreement with 1:5 (*para tou theou*) and 1:7 (*para tou kyriou*). The use of the adverb *anōthen* ("from above") is scarcely incidental. Its depiction of gifts moving downwards "from above" corresponds to the spatial imagery of 3:15–17, which speaks of the *anōthen sophia* ("wisdom from above"). See particularly the phrase *hē sophia anōthen katerchomenē* in 3:15, which may account for the textual variant *katerchomenon* in the present verse.

coming down: Not surprisingly, some Greek patristic writers connected this verse to John 3:31, "The one who is coming from above is above all" to make trinitarian and christological arguments (see, e.g., Cyril of Alexandria, *In Epistolam II ad Corinthios* III,4–6 [PG 74:929]; *Adversus Nestorianum* V,IV [PG 76:229]; *In Johannis Evangelium* II,II [PG 73:268]; John Chrysostom, *In Matthaeum* Homilia XXXIX [PG 56:847]).

from the father of lights: James uses *pater* ("father") for God also in 1:27 and 3:9. In combination with the genitive "of lights" (*tōn phōtōn*), the image suggested is that of the creator: God is the source of the lights. But what does James intend by these? The suggestions that they are "the angels or enlightened persons" (*scholia*) or the "spiritual charisms" (Bede) clearly reveal the canonical code of reading. The plural suggests the "heavenly lights" of sun and moon or perhaps the planets (see, e.g., Dio Chrysostom, *Or.* 40:38; *T. Abr.* 7:1–7; Jer 4:23; LXX Pss 135:7; 148:3). To call God "Father of Lights" would then mean simply that God was their creator, as Genesis 1:3, 14–17 states.

with him there is: The prepositional phrase *par'hō* ("with whom") is, in contrast to 1:27, a dative of respect or reference. The verb *enestin* is here in the short form of *eni*, used in the NT in such negative constructions as this one (see 1 Cor 6:5; Gal 3:28; Col 3:11; compare Job 28:14). Some MSS have the more common *estin*. The negation establishes a contrast between the creator and what is created.

no alteration or shadow of change: The phrase contains considerable textual confusion. The translation is based on the Nestle-Aland text, which decides for the reading given by $\aleph^2$, A, C, P, Ψ, and the majority of minuscules, as well as the Vulgate and Syriac. A second reading is attested by the original hand of $\aleph$, and B: *parallagē hē tropēs aposkiasmatos* (literally, "no alteration of changing shadow"). A third reading is found in a number of minuscules: *parallagē ē tropē aposkiasmatos* ("alteration or change of shadow"). A fourth option is read by only two late MSS: *parallagē ē tropē ē tropēs aposkiasma* ("alteration or change or shadow of change"). A fifth version is attested by a Latin MS and Augustine: *parallagē ē ropē aposkiasma* ("alteration of shadow of turn"). A sixth reading is found in 𝔓23: *parallagēs ē tropēs aposkiasmatos*, which is virtually untranslatable, unless a conjecture (like that of Hauck) helps out by supplying *ti* ("something"): "there is not anything of change or of shadow of turning." Dibelius, 102, also offers a conjecture: *parallagē tropēs ē aposkiasmatos*: "alteration of change or shadow." Despite all this confusion, several points can be made decisively: 1) the phrase seemed strange to scribes—all its terms are NT *hapax legomena*—and, therefore, seemed to call out for "correction"; 2) the variations provide virtually every possible combination; 3) the basic meaning remains clear despite all the variations. The text opposes the steadfastness of God to the changeableness of creation, exemplified by the heavenly bodies. The noun *parallagē* means generally "change/alteration" (see LXX 2 Kgs 9:20; *Ep. Arist.* 75). It also appears as an astrological term (see LSM, s.v.). The noun *tropē* also occurs frequently in astrological contexts, usually for solstices (see Herodotus, *Persian War* 2:19; Plato, *Laws* 767C; see also Deut 33:14; Job 38:33, and especially Wis 7:18). Finally, the noun *aposkiasma* literally means "shadow" (Plutarch, *Pericles* VI,4). Here, it is the shadow cast by the alteration of a heavenly light.

by his decision: Although the verb *boulomai* ("to will/desire") is sometimes used in the NT for the divine plan or decision (see Luke 10:22; 22:42; 1 Cor 12:11; Heb 6:17), a participial construction such as this is not found. Yet its position at the beginning of the sentence with no transition (the *gar* is found only in a few Greek MSS and the Clementine Vulgate) demands that it be given considerable weight. God's creation of humans is taken to be the great demonstration of the conviction that he is the source of all good gifts. The *boulētheis* also points decisively toward the following purpose clause: God has a plan for humans. For *boulētheis* in connection with creation, see Philo, *On Creation* 16, 44, 77, 138.

gave us birth: The sexual imagery corresponds to its negative use in 1:15, with the same verb *apokuein* in both places. This is a "father" (*patēr*) who "brings forth/gives birth," one of the most striking female images for God in the NT. As in v.15, the language is densely metaphorical rather than literal. The *scholia* says that he gave birth, not out of passion, but out of love (*agapē*). Bede takes the birth here to be that of regeneration by baptism. Some MSS, perhaps offended by possible implications, change *apokuein* ("give birth") to *poiein* ("make"). There is no reason to suppose that James is influenced by the language of the Mysteries (Marty, 44–45). There is a splendid parallel in Philo, *On Drunkenness* 30.

through a word of truth: The instrumental dative indicates the means by which they were given birth. Should the anarthous genitive construction *logos alētheias* be translated as "word of truth" or as "truthful word"? The translation "truthful word" would have the advantage, first, of contrasting God's truth-speaking to human "falsification of the truth" (3:14), and, second, of connecting God's word to the LXX language about *alētheia* as fidelity/faith (e.g., Pss 24:5; 30:6; 39:11; see also *T. Gad* 3:1; *Odes Sol.* 8:8; *Pss Sol.* 16:10)—thus contrasting God's covenantal loyalty to human disloyalty (4:4). The translation "word of truth" = "word about truth" could be taken the same way but also suggests being understood as a particular expression of God's "Word." Three obvious options suggest themselves. First, the word by which God created humans (Gen 1:26–30; see also James 3:9 and Rom 1:25; see Edsman, "Schöpferwille," 11–44; Elliott-Binns, 159–61). Second, the creation of the people Israel by the giving of Torah—the law *is* designated as *logos alētheias* in the LXX (Ps 118:43, 142, 151; Mal 2:6). Finally, the creation of the Christian community by the word of the Gospel—in several NT passages, the expression *logos alētheias* has precisely that connotation (see esp. 2 Cor 6:7; Eph 1:13; Col 1:5; 2 Tim 2:15; also Acts 26:25; Gal 2:5, 14; 1 Tim 3:15); see Edsman, "Schöpfung,"). In this final case, the entire clause would remind us of the language about regeneration or rebirth through the Gospel found in passages such as John 1:13; 3:3–5; 1 Cor 4:15; Gal 4:19; Philemon 10, and especially 1 Pet 1:23–25. Both Oecumenius and Theophylact were careful enough readers to recognize a tension between the statement that God was without alteration and this act of giving birth; they resolve the tension through taking the "word of truth" Christologically, that is, as the "word through whom all things were made."

in order that we might be: The *eis to* + infinitive construction expresses a strong sense of purpose: the precise reason for "our" generation by God is a goal that is consonant with God's "design/decision" (*boulētheis*).

a kind of firstfruits: The indefinite adjective *tina* has the effect of making the substantive less definite and heightening its metaphorical character: thus, the translation "a kind of" (see RSV). The noun *aparchē* is widely attested for "beginning sacrifice" or for the "first part of a sacrifice" (see, e.g., Herodotus, *Persian War* 1:92; 4:71). In the LXX, it translates a number of Hebrew terms for the offering to God of the first products of field or flock (Exod 22:28; 25:2–3; Lev 2:12; Num 15:20–21; Deut 18:4). In Exod 23:19, it is defined as the "first products of the earth." It can also be used metaphorically for first results, or pledge (Euripides, *Ion* 402; Dio, *Or.* 71:2; Plato, *Protagoras* 343B), that is, the part that represents the whole. In the LXX, the term never takes on a metaphorical sense. In the NT, however, the term is used metynomically: for the pledge of the Spirit (Rom 8:23); for the first to rise from the dead (1 Cor 15:20, 23); for the founding of Christian communities (Rom 16:5; 1 Cor 16:15; possibly 2 Thess 2:13), the elect community in heaven (Rev 14:4), and, most strikingly, the remnant of Israel (Rom 11:16).

of his creatures: From *ktizein* ("to create"), the noun *ktisma* is roughly equivalent to *ktisis* ("creation"). It is seldom used in the LXX (Wis 9:2; 13:5; 14:11; Sir 36:14; 38:34; see also *Ep. Arist.* 17; 3 Macc 5:11), but always with respect to "that which is created by God" (see 1 Tim 4:4). The use of the plural (only here and Rev 8:9) is important, identifying the readers as representative of "God's creatures," not simply of "creation." Some MSS strengthen the possessive by reading *heautou* ("of his own creatures").

19. *you know this*: The short statement contains several interconnected difficulties. First, the state of the text is uncertain (Amphoux, "relecture," 154–55). The witnesses containing *iste* (sometimes with the connective *de* added) are probably correct, with those reading *hōste* to be understood as "corrections" in service of a smoother transition. Second, it is uncertain whether *iste* should be read as an imperative or indicative form of *oida*. The present

translation takes it as indicative (with Bede; Mayor, 64–65; Chaine, 27; Reicke, 19–20; and against Cantinat, 100; Mussner, 99; Dibelius, 108–9). Third, how does it connect with what goes before and comes after? If we supply the required implied object "this," to what does it refer? Since the present commentary works with the presumption of a coherent argument, it takes the indicative as referring back to the principle just enunciated in 1:17–18, thus providing the warrant for the command that follows concerning hearing and speaking. The *adelphoi agapētoi* is, therefore, not to be taken simply as a transition but, above all, as an *inclusio* with 1:16 for the sake of emphasis.

then let every person: The translation "then" creates perhaps a stronger impression of connection than given by the Greek, where once again, the textual evidence is mixed between a simple *estō* and *estō* preceded by *kai* or followed by *de*. The sense of the imperative following v.18, however, allows "then" as the natural English transition.

quick to hear: The threefold saying (compare *PA* 1:2; 2:10) is perfectly balanced in its first two members. The adverbs "quick" (*tachys*) and "slow" (*bradys*) are both followed by the same sort of *eis to* + infinitive construction as in 1:18, but here with the sense of "with respect to" (compare 1 Thess 4:19). For the play on *tachys/bradys* see Pseudo-Isocrates, *To Demonicus* 34; Aristotle, *Nicomachean Ethics* 1142B; Philo, *Confusion of Tongues* 12. In an oral/aural culture, the association of wisdom with "hearing" is obvious: see Sir 5:11; 6:33, 35; 21:15; *PA* 5:12; Diogenes Laertius, *Lives of Eminent Philosophers* (Zeno) VII, 23; Lucian of Samosata, *Demonax* 51; Plutarch, *On Garrulousness* 2 (*Mor* 502E). Theophylact takes "quick to hear" as expressing also "quick to do."

slow to speak: deliberation in speech is associated in rhetoric with strength (Demetrius, *On Style* I,7; I,9; V,241; Seneca, *Moral Epistles* 40:14) and in ordinary speech with sagacity (see Diogenes Laertius, *Lives of Eminent Philosophers* I,70; I,104; VII,24; Philostratus, *Vit. Apol.* VI,11; Epictetus, *Enchir.* 33, 1–2; Plutarch, *On Garrulousness* 3 [*Mor* 503C]; Philo, *Special Laws* 2:14; *Sentences of Sextus* 253b; 294; 429–430. Thus, parallels to this passage are plentiful (see, e.g., Prov 29:20; Sir 4:29; 5:13; 19:6–12; Qoh 5:1; 1QS 7:2; 7:9; *Sentences of Syriac Menander* 310, 314; *Sentences of Pseudo-Phocylides* 20, 123; *PA* 1:15; Philo, *The Worse Attacks the Better* 13, 27; *On Dreams* 2:42. Bede notes that it is foolish for anyone to presume to teach what he himself has not learned.

slow to anger: The third part of the commandment breaks the grammatical pattern, perhaps for rhetorical effect. The dangers of anger (*orgē*) are extensively catalogued in ancient moral discourse: see Plutarch, *On Rage* (*frag.* 148); Qoh 7:9; LXX Prov 15:1; 16:32; Sir 1:22; *PA* 2:10; 4:1; *Ep. Arist.* 253; 4 Macc 2:16; *Sentences of Pseudo-Phocylides* 57, 63; *T. Dan* 2:2; compare also Col 3:8; Eph 4:26, 31; *Did.* 3:2. Despite the claim of Dibelius, 110, that anger and speech need not go together, it is striking how often in fact they are connected in the moral literature: see, e.g., Prov 29:11; Qoh 7:9; Sir 1:22–24; Diogenes Laertius,

Lives of Eminent Philosophers I,70; VIII,23; Plutarch, *How to Profit by One's Enemies* 8 (*Mor* 90C); *On Anger* 3, 7, 16 (*Mor*. 454F; 461C; 464B–C); *On the Education of Children* 14 (*Mor*. 10B); Philo, *Allegorical Laws* 3:42–44; 123–28.

20. *for a man's anger*: The connective *gar* indicates the reason why a person should be "slow to anger." Once more, there is the contrast between a negative form of human behavior and the divine measure of reality (1:13–18). The Greek *anēr* cannot be translated except as "man." Although in antiquity, anger was associated more with men than with women (see Longinus, *On the Sublime*, 32), the maxim obviously applies to all humans.

does not accomplish: Literally, "does not work" (*ergazesthai*), the second occurrence of language connected to "deed/action/result" (see *ergon teleion/ katergazetai* in 1:3–4). As in the first instance, the language focuses on moral behavior in the broad sense. Some MSS, perhaps affected by 1:3, read *ou katergazetai* rather than *ouk ergazetai*. The meaning is much the same in either case (compare, e.g., Rom 2:9–10; 4:5, 15; 2 Cor 7:10).

God's righteousness: This is James' first use of *dikaiosynē* (see also 2:23; 3:18). Together with the use of the verb *dikaioun* in 2:21, 24, 25, the language invites comparison with Paul, whose use of these terms is the most prominent in the NT (see especially *dikaiosynē tou theou* in Rom 1:17; 3:5, 22; 10:3; 1 Cor 1:30; 2 Cor 5:21). Discourse about righteousness extends far beyond the Pauline literature, both in the NT (see Matt 5:6; John 16:8–10; Acts 24:25; Heb 5:13; 11:7, 33; 1 Pet 2:24; 2 Pet 2:5; 1 John 3:10; Rev 22:11; see Descamps, *Les Justes*) and in other Jewish literature (see, e.g., 1QS 1:5; 8:2; 11:9–15; 1QH 4:30; 4 Macc 1:4, 18; 2:6). Behind these is the rich and complex use of *dikaiosynē* in the LXX (translating most of the variations of the radical *sedeq*, but also at times *ḥesed* (see Gen 21:23), or even *'emet* (Josh 24:14). The range of meaning in the LXX itself, furthermore, precludes contraction into a single "theological concept" (compare, e.g., Gen 15:6; Exod 15:13; Deut 33:19; Pss 4:2; 9:5; 118:62, 121; Prov 11:21; Wis 1:1, 15; 8:7; 12:16; Sir 16:22; Isa 5:7; 60:17). Each composition's context, rather than a general concept, governs meaning. In the present case, the elliptical construction itself enables two possibilities: 1) human anger is not acceptable before God the righteous judge, that is, does not match God's measure of righteousness and, therefore, cannot win God's approval. This meaning would accord with the designation of the one declared righteous as "friend of God" in 2:21–24. 2) Human anger is not a legitimate instrument for effecting those right relationships God desires for creatures. This reading would go well with the use of *dikaiosynē* in 3:18. The meanings need not be exclusive. In a religious framework, "righteous human behavior" is always measured by God's norm for righteousness (see Diogenes Laertius, *Lives of Eminent Philosophers* [Plato] III, 79 and III, 83). Moral analyses, especially of angry speech, emphasize its disruptive and hurtful character; see esp. Plutarch, *On Anger* 9 (*Mor*. 457D); 14 (*Mor*. 462C); 16 (*Mor*. 464B–D), and *On the Delays of Divine Vengeance* 5 (*Mor*. 551A).

21. *put aside therefore*: The connective *dio* ("therefore") is very strong (see Rom 1:24; 2:1; Gal 4:31; Phil 2:9; 1 Pet 1:13) and provides transition to the concluding admonition of this section of James' exhortation: the rejection of one measure for another. The verb *apotithēmi* ("put aside") can be used literally of taking off clothes and laying them aside (Herodotus, *Persian War* 4:78; 2 Macc 8:35; Josephus, *Ant.* 8:266). Metaphorically, it signifies a "putting away from oneself." The early Christian use of such expressions (sometimes with the participle functioning imperatively, as here) may owe something to baptismal catechesis attached to the ritual of taking off and putting on clothing (Braumann, "Hintergrund" 401–409; Meeks, "Myth of the Androgyne"): see, e.g., Rom 13:12; Eph 4:22, 25; Col 3:8; Heb 12:1; 1 Pet 2:1; *1 Clem.* 13:1; *2 Clem.* 1:6.

all filthiness: The use of alliteration with *p* is impressive in the first part of the verse *apothemenoi/pasan/perisseia/prautēti*. The term *ryparia* literally means physical dirt or filth (Plutarch, *Advice to Bride and Groom* 28 [*Mor.* 142A]); in moral discourse, it means that which is base or ignoble (Plutarch, *How to Tell a Flatterer* 19 [*Mor* 60E]); see Epictetus' reference to "filthy impressions" (*Discourses* II, 18, 25). Although the noun is a NT hapax, James uses the adjective *rypara* in 2:2 for the poor man's "filthy clothing." Two literary connections should be noted. The first is to the striking language in Zech 3:3–4, in which Joshua is stripped of his "filthy garments" and clothed in rich apparel by an angel. The second is James' statement in 1:27 that true religion means keeping oneself "unstained from the world" (*aspilon heauton tērein apo tou kosmou*).

and excess of evil: As parallel uses of *perisseia* (literally "abundance/overflowing") suggest, its main function here is rhetorical: with *pasa* it extends the negative admonition to every form of wickedness (see Rom 5:17; 2 Cor 8:2; 10:15). There is no need to tease out more subtle significance (contra Mayor, 67–68). The generalizing effect is furthered by the use of *kakia*, which can stand generically as the opposite of *aretē* (virtue); see Aristotle, *Rhetoric* 1383B; Plato, *Meno* 72A; Xenophon, *Mem.* 2,1,26. The sense, then, is of morally bad behavior, not the abstract sense of "evil" (see Gen 6:5; Prov 1:16; Wis 16:14). James also uses *kakos* in 1:13 and 3:8, as well as the adverb *kakōs* in 4:3. The noun *kakia* frequently appears in NT vice lists (Rom 1:29; 1 Cor 5:8; Col 3:8; Titus 3:3; 1 Pet 2:1). A case can be made that the element of "malice" might be stressed in the term here, because of its proximity to "anger" and its contrast to "meekness" (Mayor, 68), but the statement is inclusive of all forms of vice.

with meekness: The noun *prautēs* means "mildness" or "gentleness." It is explicitly opposed to anger (*orgē*) in Aristotle, *Nicomachean Ethics*, 1125B; *Rhetoric*, 1380A. In the LXX, both the noun and the adjective *praus* are used to translate terms cognate with the Hebrew *anaw*, that is, "lowly/humble" (see Num 12:3; Pss 33:2; 146:6; Zeph 3:12). "Meekness," in other words, is in this tradition very close to the meaning of *tapeinos* (see James 1:9). This sense comes through clearly in the Beatitudes of Matt 5:3–5 and in Matthew's portrayal of Jesus (Matt 11:29; 21:5). The term occurs in NT virtue lists as often as "anger" does in vice lists: see, e.g., 1 Cor 4:21; Gal 5:23; Eph 4:2; Col 3:12; 2 Tim 2:25; Titus 3:2; 1 Pet 3:4, 15. In combination with "quick to hear" and "receive the word," the term suggests an attitude of receptivity and docility in contrast to angry aggressiveness and self-assertiveness. The textual variant "meekness of wisdom" can be accounted for by assimilation to 3:13. The scribes who supplied that reading can at least be credited with literary sensitivity, for the passages definitely illumine each other.

receive the implanted word: The positive command corresponds to the negative one. Rather than speak of "putting on" certain qualities in contrast to those "put off" (as in Rom 13:14; Eph 4:24; Col 3:10), however, James counsels them to ("receive") that which comes to them from another. The verb *dechesthai* ("receive") has a rich range of applications in the NT, including the reception of Jesus (Matt 10:40) and of the apostles (Luke 10:8–10; Gal 4:14); the things of the Spirit (1 Cor 2:14); and the grace of God (2 Cor 6:1). Most striking, however, is the use of this verb with respect to "receiving the word of God/Gospel" (see Luke 8:13; Acts 8:14; 11:1; 17:11; 2 Cor 11:4; 1 Thess 1:6; 2:13). In the light of James' use of *logos alētheias* in 1:18, there can be little doubt that the "implanted word" here also refers to the Gospel (see the *scholia*). But how is it "implanted?" The verbal adjective *emphytos* has the basic sense of "natural" or "innate" (see Herodotus, *Persian War* 9:94; Plato, *Symposium* 191D; *Phaedrus* 237D). Such is the sense in the only LXX use of the word, Wis 12:10: "natural wickedness" (*emphytos kakia*). Since it is a NT hapax, little help is offered on the meaning here. "Innate/natural" seems inappropriate, since it is to be "received." But we are undoubtedly to understand the "implanted word" as that "word of truth" by which God gave them birth. For those who are Christians, that word is now already *emphytos* ("implanted"). But James now exhorts them to be "quick to hear" and to "receive with meekness." The point is to accept the word by which they were gifted as the norm for their lives. Rather oddly, Oecumenius and Theophylact take it to mean the ability to discern between that which is better and that which is worse.

that is able to save your souls: Some MSS read "our souls." At the most obvious level, the association of "power" (*to dynamenon*) with the word reminds us of Paul's claim concerning the "power of the Gospel", particularly in connection with "saving" (see Rom 1:16; 1 Cor 1:18). See especially 2 Cor 6:7; "in the word of truth, in the power of God." More important is to notice James' use of "power" language elsewhere in the letter. He will contrast the human inability to achieve desires (4:2) and the inability of naked faith to "save" humans (2:14) with the "power" of this implanted word to save souls (1:21), and in 4:12, the portrayal of God as "lawgiver and judge" who is "powerful to save and destroy." These passages emphatically assert the *extra nos* character of salvation in James and that human moral effort is based on a gift given freely by God (1:17–18). This should be kept in mind especially when reading 5:20, which promises that one correcting a brother will "save his soul from death."

What James means by "saving souls" (*psychas*) is less clear, although it definitely seems to have an eschatological aspect (see 1:12; 2:12–13; 3:1; 5:5, 7).

COMMENT

The argument of chapter one now enters its climactic stage. James' readers were told to perceive testing from a certain perspective in 1:2–8: testing is a matter not for sorrow but for joy, since it enables faith to reach perfection. In 1:9–12, the premise for that view of things was enunciated by showing how God is deeply involved in human destiny. But precisely that principle now requires clarification. If God is an active agent in the process by which humans are proven worthy of the crown of life, is it not fair to place responsibility for every sort of testing and temptation on God?

The declaration of the imagined interlocutor in 1:13, therefore, "I am being tempted by God," is not trivial. It exposes a fundamental problem—or mystery—at the heart of covenantal theology. Within the framework of a polytheistic religious system, the problems of theodicy are less severe. This god or that might prove mischievous to humans, but the divine system itself cannot be held to blame. Indeed, it tends to be self-adjusting. The gods have problems of their own, just like humans. It makes no sense to blame them for human failings.

The biblical tradition, however, establishes humans in relationship with a single, personal, all-powerful God who is Master of the Universe and source of all that is. This relationship, furthermore, is portrayed in narrative and prophecy as intensely interactive, with—as James himself has suggested—God intimately involved in the destiny of individual humans. More than that, the normative texts of this tradition declare outright that this God did in fact "test" the patriarch Abraham and the people Israel in the wilderness!

Patristic readers of James were more alert to the problems posed by his assertion "God does not tempt anyone," possibly because they shared more deeply and unequivocally in the worldview shaped by the Scriptures than did later commentators. It was not James' teaching on faith and works that appeared most problematic to them, but this passage. So while it could be used straightforwardly as a proof that God tests for good rather than evil (Dionysius of Alexandria, *Commentarium in Lucam* XXII, 46 [PG 10:1596]), it also demanded explication as a "contradiction in Scripture," not only with OT passages, but with such NT passages as the Lord's Prayer. Some of this discussion is indicated in the Introduction III.B. In general, commentators like Oecumenius and Bede distinguished between tempting to evil, which they attributed to the devil (see also the *Catena* and the *scholia*), and the "testing for virtue" that can be attributed to God. As the *scholia* puts it: "God by testing does not provide the opportunity for evil, but through patience, the opportunity for a crown."

Once the point has been raised by the interlocutor, James' argument takes on a more diatribal character. The first response is by way of aphorism: God is neither tested by evils nor himself tests anyone (1:13). The clarity and decisiveness of this statement deserve attention. Part of it simply removes God from the realm of evil: God has nothing to do with it. But the other part also removes God from the "testing game" entirely. And here is where the conceptual difficulty appears. Does James suggest, then, that God is not the source of all that is? Are the "various testings" that the readers encounter (1:2) within God's control, or not? If they are, then it must be God who "tests"; if they are not, then God does not control the universe. Or, do they come from some cosmic forces (such as demons) who are fighting God for control? None of the options is entirely satisfactory. The patristic resolution, furthermore, that God does not "tempt" to evil but does "test" for virtue, may not truly solve the problem, but at least it has the virtue of taking the problem (and the text) seriously.

As often in the diatribe, the objection and first abrupt response to it only prepare the way for a more elaborate discussion. In 1:14–1:19a, James responds to the wrong perception with the correct understanding of the roots of temptation and of God's relationship to humans. Then, in 19b–21, James sketches the wrong and right responses of humans to this relationship.

Critical to James' argument is the semantic shift in the meaning of *peirasmos/ peirazein* from "testing" to "tempting." The shift is from external circumstance to internal measurement. It is human *epithymia* ("desire"), here personified, that leads humans to sin and eventually to death. As the notes make clear, James uses *epithymia* in the manner already widely attested in Hellenistic moral discourse. It refers, not to legitimate human desire, but to desire disordered by sinful passion. The Vulgate's translation, *concupiscientia* ("concupiscence") is appropriate. James will later show more fully how such distorted desire leads to the death of others, in murder (4:1–4; 5:1–6)!

In 1:17–18, James removes God completely from this realm of human passion and destructiveness. First, he defines God in terms of complete and generous goodness. God is not only associated with light rather than darkness, with stability and consistency rather than with change and alteration, but (as in 1:5) with the giving of every good and perfect gift, rather than with the attitude of grasping that is characteristic of *epithymia*.

James' declaration in 1:17 is rightly perceived as one of the noblest *theologoumena* in the NT. Patristic writers recognized its extraordinarily rich and foundational quality. They use it in discussions of God's nature and attributes but also in discussions of human transformation (John Chrysostom, *In Psalmum CXVIII*, 33 (PG 55:683). It was such a favored text through the entire Eastern tradition that one is not surprised to find that in the *Liturgy of St. John*

Chrysostom as it is celebrated to this day, James 1:17 is the last citation from Scripture heard by the worshipers before leaving the liturgical assembly.

In 1:18, James turns to the expression of God's generosity most pertinent to humans. In a daring appropriation of the language of sexual generation he has used of desire/sin/death in 1:15, James speaks of how "by his decision," God "gave birth" to humans by a "word of truth." The reversal is complete in every respect, countering the deceptiveness, the drivenness, and the destructiveness of *epithymia*.

There is legitimate debate concerning what James might have meant specifically by "word of truth." Is it the word of creation, of Torah, or of the Gospel? In the context, the most likely referent would be the Gospel. But no hard and fast distinction need be drawn among creation, covenant, and grace, for each builds on the other, and each is an expression of the "good and perfect gifts that come down from above." More significant for interpreting James' argument is the purpose clause with which 1:18 concludes. God's giving birth by a word was not only intentional, but it has a specific intention: that the humans thus given life might represent all creatures before God. In short, the gift (*datum*) bears within it also a mandate (*mandatum*).

It is to that mandate that James turns in 1:19–21. The first requirement of those who have been given birth by a word (that is, had it "implanted" in them) is to "receive" that word and allow it to become the norm for their existence, just as it is the basis of their existence and of their future, with its power to "save their souls." The proper stance for such reception, of course, is "hearing." James exhorts his readers to be "quick to hear and slow to speak." Such advice is universal in wisdom traditions that understand how the one who is too quick to speak can never learn what is important.

Such hearing, in turn, can only be effective when it is accompanied by meekness. As the notes suggest, the qualities of "meekness" and "lowliness" are closely associated in the biblical tradition (see 1:9–11). They are equally opposed to the attitude that James declares is incompatible with the "righteousness of God," namely human anger (*orgē*). Human wrath does not work God's righteousness because it is associated precisely with *epithymia*, the self-aggrandizing drive to acquire pleasure and possessions and power, because when such *epithymia* is thwarted, it generates *orgē* and *orgē* leads to murder (see 4:1–4).

Once more, therefore, the argument advances mainly by deepening. The contrast remains between two ways of life based on two measures of reality. James' readers are being prepared for the fundamental choice between being friends with God or friends with the world (4:4).

1:22–27

22. But become doers of the word and not simply hearers. That would be to deceive yourselves. 23. Because if anyone is simply a hearer of the word and not

a doer, this person is like a man noticing his natural face in a mirror. 24. For he glances at himself, and he leaves, and he immediately forgets what he looks like. 25. But the one who has gazed into the perfect law of freedom and has remained there has become, not a forgetful hearer, but a doer of the deed. This person will be blessed in everything he does. 26. If anyone considers himself religious without bridling his tongue and while indulging his heart, this person's religion is worthless. 27. This is pure and undefiled religion before the God who is also father: to assist orphans and widows in their trouble, and to keep oneself unstained from the world.

NOTES

22. *become doers of the word*: The verb *ginomai* needs to be translated as "become" (with Mayor, 69) rather than simply as "be" (Ropes, 174; Dibelius, 114), in line with James' use elsewhere (1:12, 25; 2:4, 10, 11; 3:1) and other NT constructions with the imperative *ginesthe* (Rom 12:16; 1 Cor 4:16; 7:23; 11:1; 2 Cor 6:14; Gal 4:12; 5:26; Eph 4:32; 5:1, 7, 17) for it is *becoming* rather than *being* that is at issue, namely, turning profession into action. The phrase "doers of the word" is clearly a Semitism, for the phrase in classical Greek would mean a wordsmith or poet (Plato, *Phaedo* 61A; *Ep. Arist.* 31). The textual variant, "doers of the law" (*poiētai tou nomou*) is undoubtedly to be attributed to the influence of 4:11 (*poiētēs nomou*), but also to the remarkably similar construction in Rom 2:13: *ou gar hoi akroatai nomou dikaioi para tǭ theǭ, all' hoi poiētai nomou dikaiouthēsontai* ("not the hearers of the law are righteous before God but the doers of the law will be declared righteous"). In the present verse, however, especially with the contrastive *de*, the "word" can only refer back to the "word of truth" that was the theme of 1:18–21.

and not simply hearers: The contrast here is highly illuminating for several reasons. First, the use of the adverb *monon* ("alone") alerts us to the exact parallel construction concerning "faith and deeds" in 2:24. Second, the present contrast shows that the basic issue is "living out" profession in practice, with the language of "doer" here exactly matching that of "deed" in 2:24 and of "demonstrating" in 3:13. Third, that which is to be done has nothing to do with the ritual demands of Torah but rather with the "word of truth" by which God has engendered the community and whose "reception with meekness" is equivalent to "faith" (1:3, 6). Finally, the contrast of hearing/doing (or speech/practice) is one of the most widespread in ancient moral instruction. For the sense of *akroatēs* as a "listener to moral instruction," see Plato, *Rep.* 536C, and as a "disciple/learner," see Aristotle, *Nicomachean Ethics* 1095A. And for the need to translate theory into practice, see Seneca, *Moral Epistles* 20:1; Plutarch, *Stoic Self-Contradictions* 1 (Mor. 1033B); *Progress in Virtue* 14 (Mor. 84B);

Diogenes Laertius, *Lives of Eminent Philosophers* I,53; IX,37; Philo, *Life of Moses* 1:6, 19; 2:8, 48; *Special Laws* 2:14, 53; *Preliminary Studies* 67; *The Sentences of Sextus* 177; *Did.* 2:5; Epictetus, *Discourses* II, 1, 31; II, 9, 21; III, 22, 9; Julian the Apostate, *Or.* 7:255A; Dio Chrysostom, *Or.* 35:2, 3, 11.

that would be to deceive yourselves: The translation makes an independent sentence out of the predicate participle *paralogizomenoi heautous*, partly for reasons of style and partly to emphasize its importance in the exhortation. As the parts of the verb suggest, *paralogizomai* denotes a kind of "miscalculation" (Aristotle, *Poetics* 1460A; *Rhetoric* 1408A), but it is frequently used also in the moral sense of "deceive" or "defraud" (see Epictetus, *Discourses* II, 20,7; Dio, *Or* 11:108; Gen 29:25; 31:41; Josh 9:22). Most striking is the use in Col 2:4, where the "fraudulent deception" persuades the Colossians to accept the false coinage of human philosophy instead of the "treasures of Christ." The same sense is present here: those who learn but don't do are both "deceiving themselves" (into thinking that passive profession is enough) and "defrauding themselves" (by missing out on the path to perfection through the doing of the word).

23. *if anyone is simply a hearer*: The repetition from v.22 is for emphasis; the translation supplies "simply" to capture the sense. A fairly wide spread of witnesses omits the explanatory *hoti*, but the omission could well have resulted from the failure to recognize *how* the sentence functions as explanation. The text variant *nomou* ("law") for *logou* ("word") seems to continue the judgment made on the same terms in the previous verse.

this person is like a man: Once more, the *anēr* in the Greek demands the translation as "man." The comparison that follows is somewhat convoluted, but grasping the cultural associations of mirror-gazing in antiquity helps sort it out. For the construction "is like" (*eoiken*), see the note on 1:6.

noticing his natural face: The participle is anarthous, so can be translated attributively (as "a man who") or circumstantially. The fact that the character of the action is what anticipates the point of contrast supports the adverbial translation here. The verb *katanoein* can mean either to "perceive" (Plato, *Timaeus* 90D; Exod 2:11; Num 32:8; Luke 6:41) or to "apprehend/understand" (Herodotus, *Persian War* 2:28; LXX Pss 9:35; 118:15; Luke 12:24; Rom 4:19). In the present case, the repetition of the verb with "leaving and immediately forgetting" (1:24) obviously puts the stress on the sensory and transitory character of the glance: hence, "noticing." The phrase *tēs geneseōs autou* is literally "of his origin," which here probably means, "of his birth" = "natural" (see LXX Gen 31:13; Ruth 2:11; Wis 3:12; 12:10; Matt 1:18). The point of contrast is to the face presented by the perfect law. Patristic commentators tended to read this more theologically, taking the "face of birth" as the face of "rebirth" into the *eikona tou theou* (*scholia*). In 3:6, James uses the phrase in a somewhat more technical sense.

in a mirror: Although the phrase *en esoptrō* is tiny, it governs the entire trope.

In the Hellenistic world the mirror (usually made of polished metal) was chiefly used for purposes of personal inspection and adornment (Aristotle, *On Dreams* 459B–460A; Josephus, *Ant.* 12:81; Sir 12:11; Seneca, *Natural Questions* I,17,2–3). But the fact that the mirror provided a reflection of the self obviously gave it metaphorical potential. In one direction, an epistemological distinction was developed, in which the mirror signified the distance between reality and image (see Plato, *Timaeus* 33B; *Hermetica* 17; Wis 7:26); this seems to be the sense in 1 Cor 13:12 and possibly 2 Cor 3:18. In another direction, the mirror is used in paraenetic literature for the image of "moral self-examination/ reflection" (see, e.g., Epictetus, *Discourses* II, 14, 17–23; Seneca, *Natural Questions* I,17,4; *On Anger* 36:1–3; Plutarch, *Advice to Bride and Groom* 14 and 25 [*Mor.* 139F and 141D]). The analogy is worked out especially by Plutarch, *On Listening to Lectures* 8 (*Mor.* 42A–B), who employs the theme of *memory* in a manner similar to James. See also Plutarch, *The Education of Children* 13–20 (*Mor.* 9F–14A); *Progress in Virtue* 14–15 (*Mor.* 84B–85A); Seneca, *On Clemency* I,1,1; I,1,7; I,6,1; I,7,1; I,15,3; Philo, *Contemplative Life* 25, 29, 75, 85, 88. There is no reason to connect the metaphor here to any notion of the "image of God" (against Martin 50, 55). Above all, it is certainly erroneous to assert that "James is not relying on any fixed tradition or previous literature" (Davids, 98), for his allusion makes sense only within the intertextual field here described.

24. *for he glances at himself*: The *gar* shows this to be the explanation for the previous clause: thus, the emphasis on the momentary and fleeting "glance/ noticing" of the face (with *katanoein* used in both clauses). The gnomic aorist is often used in comparisons (see 1:11) and is equivalent to the present.

and he leaves: The perfect tense emphasizes the suddenness of his action (Moule, *Idiom Book* 12–13): "just a glance and he is off" (Mayor, 72). Everything in the description stresses haste and casualness.

immediately forgets what he looks like: The *euthus* ("immediately") further stresses the haste of glance and departure. The verb *epilanthanō* in its aorist form makes a parechesis with "leaves" (*apelēlythen/apelatheto*). Although the verb is not used frequently in the NT (Matt 16:5; Mark 8:14; Phil 3:13; Heb 6:10; 13:2, 16), its use in the LXX sometimes bears the sense of moral failure (see Deut 4:9, 23, 31; 6:12; 8:14; Prov 2:17). The theme of *memory* is a staple in paraenesis. See, e.g., Pseudo-Isocrates, *Demonicus* 9; Lucian of Samosata, *Demonax* 2; *Nigrinus* 6–7; Seneca, *Moral Epistles* 94:21, 25; Dio Chrysostom, *Or.* 17:2. In the NT, see above all 2 Tim 1:3, 4, 5, 6; 2:8, and (for forgetting) see 2 Pet 1:9; 3:5, 8. The phrase "what he looked like" is literally "what sort he was (*hopoios ēn*)." The construction is an indirect question; more vividly: "what were you like?" "I forget."

25. *but the one who has gazed*: The three aorist participles in this clause set up the future tense in the next. In effect, the participles form the protasis of a conditional sentence to which the future responds as apodosis. The choice not

to treat the aorists as gnomic can be debated, but the sense of progression seems significant. In contrast to the "glance" into the mirror (*katanoein*) is the "gaze" (*parakyptein*). The term is a bit strange, having as its original meaning "to bend over" (see John 20:11). The sense here is attested also by Philo, *Embassy to Gaius* 56; Sir 14:23; Gen 26:8. It is not the term itself that establishes the meaning "gaze into," however, but the note of stability given by the participle *parameinas* ("has remained there"). The *scholia* takes the "remaining" to mean "doing what is demanded (*ta kathēkonta*)."

into the perfect law of freedom: The law (*nomos*) has now replaced the mirror as that into which the person gazes. This is the first mention of *nomos* in James. In 2:9, 10, 11, and 4:11, it appears absolutely. In 2:8, it is called "the royal law" and in 2:12, the "law of freedom." Here, James combines two terms: *teleios* ("perfect") must obviously be associated with the use of the same word in 1:4 and 1:17. God is the source of "every perfect gift," and the law, for James, is certainly among them. The praise of God's law is frequent both in Torah itself and in later Jewish literature. LXX Ps 18:8 calls the law *amōmos*, i.e., without fault/perfect. LXX Ps 118 elaborates the ways the law mediates the qualities of God: it is a source of mercy (118:29), a light (118:105; see Prov 6:23), and truth (118:43). The *Ep. Arist.* 31 declares the law "full of wisdom and free from all blemish." That the observance of the law is, in turn, to be associated with freedom (*eleutheria*) is emphasized by Philo, *That Every Good Man is Free* 45, 4 Macc 5:22–26; 14:2; PA 3:5; 6:2. It will be remembered that Paul also can characterize *nomos* as "spiritual" (Rom 7:14) and "good" (Rom 7:16; see 1 Tim 1:8) and the *entolē* ("commandment") as "holy and righteous and good" (Rom 7:12). The position that obedience to the law renders a person free reminds some commentators (e.g., Dibelius, 116–18; Mayor, 73–74) of the Stoic principle that only obeying the law of nature makes a person truly free and that, therefore, only the sage is truly free (see Diogenes Laertius, *Lives of Eminent Philosophers* [Zeno] VII,121; Epictetus, *Discourses* IV, 1, 1; Seneca, *On the Blessed Life* 15:7; Plutarch, *To an Uneducated Ruler* 3 [*Mor.* 780C]), but the idea is widespread enough—as the examples from Jewish literature attest—to make any direct dependence on Stoic ideas unnecessary. Of more pertinence is the question of what James includes within the concept of *nomos*. At the very least, the use of the figure of the mirror suggests that he saw it as containing *exempla* of moral behavior (see 2:20–26; 5:10–11; 5:16–18), as was seen by Oecumenius. Bede takes the "law of liberty" to mean the grace of the Gospel, and Theophylact identifies it with the "Law of Christ."

has become not a forgetful hearer: Some MSS place the demonstrative pronoun "this" (*houtos*) here rather than in the next clause. The participle *genomenos* is read as "becoming" rather than "is" and as governing both phrases. The "forgetful hearer" is literally "hearer of forgetfulness," an example of the genitive of quality (compare 2:4; 3:6). The noun *epilēsmonē* is extremely rare in literary texts (otherwise only in Sir 11:27) but is found in some inscriptions. The phrase *poiētēs ergou* ("doer of the deed") has a textual variant, "doer of the law," that is less well attested.

this person will be blessed: For the form and meaning of the macarism, see the note on 1:12. James' thought here accords with the statement of Seneca (*Moral Epistles* 75:7) that "the blessed one is not he who knows these things but the one who does them," but even closer to hand is Jesus' declaration, "Blessed are those who hear the word of God and keep it" (Luke 11:28) and Jesus' lesson concerning the *phronimos*, namely, "the one who hears these words of mine and does them" (Matt 7:24; Luke 6:47).

26. *if anyone considers himself religious*: Textual variants offer a number of "corrections" by supplying *de* ("but") at the beginning and *en hymin* ("among you") at the end of this phrase. The corrections are secondary. The verb *dokein* ("think/consider") is frequently used in the NT for false opinion, as it is here (see Matt 3:9; 6:7; 26:53; Mark 6:49; Luke 8:18; 12:51; 13:2; 19:11; 24:37; Acts 12:9; John 5:39). Of special interest is the way James' posing of the question (*ei tis dokei*) also is found frequently in Paul (1 Cor 3:18; 8:2; 11:16; 14:37; Gal 6:3; Phil 3:4). The adjective *thrēskos* is a hapax legomenon, but its meaning is easily derived from the common term *thrēskeia* in this verse and the next: it denotes a relationship with the divine.

without bridling his tongue: A vivid image to be picked up again in 3:3, "bridling the tongue" is doubly metaphorical: the tongue stands metonymically for speech, and the bridle metonymically as a means of control. One important MS (B) reads *chalinōn*, which has more the sense of "putting a bit in the mouth of a horse" but is also used with reference to controlling emotions like anger (*Sentences of Pseudo-Phocylides* 57). The verb read by the majority of MSS is *chalinagōgein*, "leading about by a bit or bridle," also used in the moral sense of controlling passions by Lucian of Samosata, *The Dance* 70, and *Tyrannicide* 4, as well as for controlling speech (see Philo, *On Dreams* 2:165). In the Greek tradition, the *religious* connotations of speech were complex. Silence was associated especially with the observance of the Mysteries (see Plutarch, *On Garrulousness* 17 [*Mor.* 501E]; Philostratus, *Vit. Ap.* III,20; Plutarch, *On Progress in Virtue* 10 [*Mor.* 81E]; *Education of Children* 14 [*Mor.* 10F]), and brevity was associated with the Delphic Oracle (see Philostratus, *Vit. Ap.* I,17; III,42).

and while indulging his heart: This phrase is usually translated, "but deceiving his heart," which everyone recognizes as problematic. The structure of the sentence is unexpected. As Mayor, 76, correctly notes, we would expect this phrase to be in the apodosis, thus: "If he does not control the tongue, then he deceives himself and his religion is vain." It is possible to make sense of the sentence as presently construed, especially since the theme of self-deception has run through the chapter (1:6–7, 14, 16, 22). We are not surprised to find it here. But what if something else is being said? A way is opened to a new reading by the possibility of reading *apatan* not as "deceiving" but as "giving pleasure to." The noun *apatē* frequently has the sense of a kind of pleasure that leads to vice (see Philo, *Decalogue* 55), and it is used in that way by *Herm. Sim.* 6,2,1; 6,4,4; 6,5,1; *Herm. Man.* 11:12. This is quite possibly the meaning in 2 Pet 2:13 as well. But can the verb, which most often means "deceive" (see *T. Naph.* 3:1; Josephus, *Life* 302; Eph 5:6) also mean "give pleasure to?" There is a reading in LXX Sir 14:16 that offers some support for this suggestion: "Give and take and give pleasure to your soul (*apatēson tēn psychēn sou*) because in Hades there is no indulgence (*tryphēn*)." The parallelism of *apatan/tryphē* suggests synonymous meaning. See also Sir 30:23: *apata tēn psychēn sou kai parakalei tēn kardian sou* ("indulge your soul and comfort your heart"). In this verse, the meaning "deceive" is simply impossible. In light of these instances, a number of other Septuagintal passages can be reexamined, such as Jdt 9:3; 12:16; 13:16. If the translation of *apatan* is possible—and it almost appears necessary—then the clause can be translated: "without controlling his tongue and while indulging his heart." The gain would be to eliminate the awkwardness of this phrase in the protasis. Furthermore, it would anticipate the condemnation of those seeking the fulfillment of their *hēdonai* and *epithymiai* in 4:1–3, as well as that of the oppressive rich who have lived in luxury and pleasure and have "fattened the heart" for a day of slaughter (5:5). Finally, this reading would provide a fuller contrast to 1:27, which emphasizes the sharing of possessions with the needy.

this person's religion is worthless: With *thrēskeia*, James chooses a term that stresses the cultic aspects of religion (see Wis 14:18, 27; 4 Macc 5:7, 13; Philo, *Special Laws* 1:315; Josephus, *Ant.* 1:222; 12:271). In the NT, it is used neutrally of Judaism in Acts 26:5 and of "worship with/of angels" in Col 2:18. The term *mataios* denotes vain, empty, worthless (Exod 20:7; LXX Ps 59:13; Prov 21:6; Titus 3:9; 1 Cor 3:20; 15:17). Two specific connotations can be noted: first, in wisdom contexts, *mataios* can mean "foolish" as opposed to "wise" (see LXX Pss 5:10; 11:3; Wis 13:1); second, such foolishness is particularly associated with idolatry (Wis 13:1; Esth 4:17; 3 Macc 6:11; Acts 14:15; Rom 1:21; 8:20; Eph 4:17). It is not too much to think, therefore, that James sketches a supposed religion of uncontrolled speech and self-gratification (or deception) as idolatry.

27. *pure and undefiled religion*: Many MSS try to supply a connective, either *de* or *gar*, in order to make clearer the explanatory character of this sentence. The translation attempts the same thing by moving the emphatic *hautē* ("this") to first position in the sentence. James now picks up *thrēskeia* from the previous verse and gives it positive definition in terms of ethical behavior. What gives the definition particular point, however, is the adjectives James uses for "authentic religion." The term *katharos* is associated in Judaism with cultic objects and persons in a condition fit to approach God (Gen 7:3; 8:20; Lev 4:12; 7:19; 11:32; 15:13; Num 8:7; Deut 12:15; see Luke 11:41; Rom 14:20; Titus 1:15; Heb 10:22) but can also, as here, be taken in terms of sincere moral behavior (see LXX Ps 50:12; Prov 12:27; Plato, *Rep.* 496E; *T. Ben.* 8:2; 1 Pet 1:22; 2 Tim 2:22). The

adjective *amiantos* has similar connotations, since *miainein* is repeatedly used in the LXX for rendering someone or something ritually impure (see Lev 5:3; 11:24; 18:24; Num 5:3; Deut 21:23) and also has the figurative sense of moral or religious purity in Plato, *Laws* 777E; Wis 4:2; 8:20; Heb 7:26; 13:4; 1 Pet 1:4.

before the God who is also father: The construction *para tō theō* means "in God's eyes" or "with reference to God's scale of measurement" (compare Rom 2:13, *dikaioi para tō theō*; 9:14; 1 Cor 3:19; Gal 3:11; 2 Thess 1:6; 1 Pet 2:4, 20; and especially James 1:17). It is also possible to translate "God and father," but the construction suggests the translation given, especially in the context of 1:17.

assist orphans and widows: The verb *episkeptesthai* becomes in the LXX virtually a technical term for the "visiting" of God to rescue or save the people (Gen 21:1; 50:24; Exod 3:16; 4:31; Josh 8:10; Ruth 1:6; 1 Sam 2:21; Judith 8:33; Sir 46:14; Zech 10:3; see also Luke 1:68, 78; 7:16; Acts 7:23; 15:14). James here makes it a covenantal obligation of *humans* toward each other. And the ones he singles out for such "assistance" are the classic recipients of God's help and the object of Israel's care, those who were, in a landed and patriarchal society, the endemically impoverished: the orphans and widows. By singling them out as the special targets of covenantal obligation, James continues the emphasis of the law (see Exod 22:20–21; 23:9; Lev 19:9–10; 19:33; 23:22; Deut 10:17–19; 14:28–29; 16:9–15; 24:17–18; 26:12–15), the prophets (Amos 2:6–8; 3:2; Hos 12:8–9; Mic 3:1–4; Zeph 1:9; Zech 7:8–10; Mal 3:5; Isa 3:5, 14–15; 5:7–10; Jer 22:3), and writings (Prov 19:17; 21:3; 31:9; Sir 4:9; 29:8; 34:21–22; 35:13–15). By placing the assistance of the poor at the heart of true religion, James not only prepares for his rebuke of those who favor the rich over the poor in 2:1–7, his insistence on helping the needy in 2:14–16, and his condemnation of the oppressive rich in 5:1–6, but also places himself in the context of Jewish piety as reflected, for example, in PA 1:1; 1:2; 5:13; CD 6:16, 21; 14:4; *Sentences of Pseudo-Phocylides* 22–23, 26, 28–29; *Exodus Rabbah* mish. 31:13; *b*T Ber. 5b; 8a; *b*T Suk. 49b; T. Iss. 3:8; T. Zeb. 7:1–2; Philo, *Special Laws* 1:57; see also 1 Clem. 8:4 and *Sentences of Sextus* 52 and 379: "If you are good to the needy, you will be great in God's sight."

in their trouble: The term *thlipsis* means to be under pressure or stress caused by circumstances, either of oppression and persecution (Exod 4:31; Deut 4:29; Matt 13:21; 24:9; Acts 7:10; 11:19; Rom 8:35) or simply from the circumstances attendant upon such inevitable situations as childbirth (John 16:21) or poverty (Gen 42:21; Pss 4:2; 24:17; Acts 7:11). There is no need to look beyond the chronic condition of the orphans and widows for a suitable definition of *thlipsis*.

keep oneself unstained: The verb *tērein* with a double predicate means to maintain a certain condition or stance (see 1 Cor 7:37; 2 Cor 11:9; 1 Tim 5:22; 6:14). Compare Marcus Aurelius, *Meditations* VI, 30: "Keep oneself simple," and Wis 10:5, "I kept myself blameless." The adjective *aspilos* means to be spotless or without blemish. 1 Tim 6:14 speaks of "keeping the commandment unblemished" (see also 2 Pet 3:14, and possibly Jude 25). There is an interesting textual variant in $\mathfrak{P}^{74}$, *hyperaspizein autous* "protecting them from the world" (see Black, 45).

from the world: This is James' first use of the term *kosmos*, and it appears in climactic position in opposition to the measure of God (*para tǭ theǭ/apo tou kosmou*), as it does elsewhere in the letter (2:5; 3:6; 4:4). It is clear that "keeping oneself unstained from the world" has nothing to do with ritual or cultic observance and everything to do with moral attitude and action.

COMMENT

This last part of James' argument in chapter one is perfectly clear, with only its mode of expression somewhat obscure because it is embedded in a trope familiar to ancient readers but strange to us. The basic point is the one that has been implicit from the beginning, when James noted that the testing of faith produced endurance and endurance could produce a perfect product: for "faith" to be real, it must be translated into "works"; for identity to be authentic, it must be enacted in deeds: it is not enough for one to be a "hearer of the word" only; one must also become a "doer of the word."

As the notes show, James here agrees with the most widespread ancient conviction concerning the philosophical life and picks up one of the main themes of protreptic literature. Theoretical correctness counts for little if one's life does not conform to the truth one espouses. The notion that some sort of profession/confession of belief or conviction could be significant if it were not demonstrated by a consistent pattern of behavior is not, in James' world, to be taken seriously.

To make his point, James employs a *topos* commonly used in paraenetic literature. As the notes suggest, the use of the mirror for personal inspection and improvement lent itself to an obvious metaphorical appropriation. The mirror could stand for a moral exemplar held up for one's contemplation, remembrance, and—most significantly—imitation or emulation. It was an image perfect for paraenesis, which tended to combine models, memory, and mimesis. Moral discourse elaborated diverse aspects of this rich metaphor. And although James makes only the most passing allusion to it by the phrase *en esoptrǭ* ("in a mirror"), the metaphor governs the passage. The ancient reader could supply the missing pieces automatically. We need to do so more carefully.

First, then, James begins with a person's catching sight of his "natural face" in a mirror, going away, and forgetting what he looks like. Only the recognition that James is playing off an instantly recognizable *topos* enables us to perceive that the "forgetting what he looks like" represents a negative moral judgment. He is like a man who heard moral teaching but failed to put it into practice (i.e., "remember it") in his behavior. James is thereby restating his proposition that it is necessary to be a doer of the word and not merely a hearer.

Second, James shifts the metaphor slightly. Not only is there a contrast between the "glance" and the "gaze"—which again stresses the theme of memory—but there is something different seen in the mirror. Now it is not one's "natural face" but the "perfect law of freedom." James here makes deliberate connection to "the word of truth" in 1:18. The word of God received with meekness is "able to save souls," but it also provides guidance for behavior. It is guidance given not by "birth" but by the "implanted word" with which God "birthed" this community.

Notice that the logic of this passage makes "the word of truth" and "the perfect law of freedom" virtually synonymous. When discussing 1:18, the point was made that the most obvious way to understand the phrase "word of truth" was in reference to the Gospel, that is, the Christian proclamation. But I also argued that too great a distinction should not be made between Gospel, Torah and the word of creation, since for James they all represent gifts of God.

The same point needs to be emphasized here. As James' argument develops, we will see that his understanding of faith/word/law is inclusive. The "faith of Jesus Christ" and the "law of freedom" are not in opposition, but represent different moments of the same revelation. Indeed, we shall see that Torah as law is given perfect expression by the "law of the kingdom," which is the commandment of love found both in Leviticus and in the words of Jesus.

Having so briefly sketched the metaphor of the mirror, James leaves it. But not entirely. Three times he will return to the image, as he presents models from Torah for his readers to imitate: in the stories of Abraham and Rahab, they will "see" the exemplification of the obedient works of faith (2:20–26). In the story of Job, they will "see" the exemplification of faith's patient endurance (5:10–11). And in the story of Elijah, they will "see" the power of the prayer of faith (5:16–18). And all of these examples make the same point that James has been developing from the start; that faith, to be perfected, must be enacted.

In 1:26–27, then, James concludes this opening argument that sets the stage for the essays that will develop these basic points. Once more, we see the emphasis placed upon proper understanding that has run through this whole chapter. The person who "thinks/considers" himself religious without the corresponding behavior has a religion that is "foolish/vain" and perhaps even—if we take the associations of *mataios* in the LXX seriously—idolatrous. Such a person wants the profession without the performance. This person wants to talk rather than to listen, wants to "indulge the heart" (see notes) rather than look to the needs of others. In James' view, this is the very essence of "double-mindedness" (1:8). The "religion" espoused by James is not about cultic purity or ritual separation, but precisely *about* caring for the needy in their affliction! Thus, James closes with the fundamental contrast between the measurement of the world and God's measurement that has run through the entire chapter. The "religion" that is "the faith of Jesus Christ" (2:1) is one that is measured "in God's eyes," which means precisely to be "unstained from the world" (1:27).

BIBLIOGRAPHY

Amphoux, C. B., "À propos de Jacques 1, 17," *RHPR* 50 (1970) 127–36.

———, "Une relecture du chapitre I de l'épître de Jacques," *Bib* 59 (1978) 554–61.

Baasland, E., "Literarische Form, Thematik und geschichtliche Einordnung des Jakobusbriefes," ANRW II, II, 25.5 (1988) 3656–59.

Black, M., "Critical and Exegetical Notes on Three New Testament Texts: Heb xi.11; Jude 5; James 1:27," *Apophoreta: Festschrift für E. Haenchen* (Berlin: Töpelmann, 1964) 39–45.

Braumann, G., "Der theologisches Hintergrund des Jakobusbriefes," *TZ* 18 (1962) 401–10.

Cargal, T. B., *Restoring the Diaspora* (SBLDS 144; Atlanta: Scholars Press, 1993) 57–105.

Davids, P. H., "The Meaning of APEIRASTOS in James I.13," *NTS* 24 (1977–78) 386–92.

Descamps, A., *Les justes et la justice dans les évangiles et le christianisme primitive hormis la doctrine proprement paulinienne* (Gembloux: J. Duculot, 1950).

Dodd, C. H., *According to the Scriptures: The Substructure of New Testament Theology* (London: Nisbet, 1952).

Edsman, C. M., "Schöpferwille und Geburt Jac 1:18," *ZNW* 38 (1939) 11–44.

———, "Schöpfung und Wiedergeburt: nochmals Jac 1:18," *Spiritus et Veritas* (Eutin: Ozolins Buchdruckerei, 1953) 43–55.

Elliott-Binns, L. E., "James 1:18: Creation or Redemption?" *NTS* 3 (1956–57) 148–61.

Fischer, H., "Ein Spruchvers im Jakobusbrief," *Philologus* 50 (1891) 377–99.

Frankemölle, H., "Das semantische Netz des Jakobusbriefes: Zur Einheit eines umstrittenen Briefes," *BZ* 34 (1990) 161–97.

Greeven, H., "Jede Gabe ist gut, Jak.1,17," *TZ* 14 (1958) 1–13.

Hays, R. B., *Echoes of Scripture in the Letters of Paul* (New Haven: Yale University Press, 1989).

Johanson, B. C., "The Definition of 'Pure Religion' in James 1:27 Reconsidered," *ExpT* 84 (1972–73) 118–19.

Johnson, L. T., "Taciturnity and True Religion (James 1:26–27)," *Greeks, Romans, and Christians: Essays in Honor of A. J. Malherbe*, ed. D. Balch et al. (Minneapolis: Fortress Press, 1990) 329–39.

———, "The Mirror of Remembrance (James 1:22–25)," *CBQ* 50 (1988) 632–45.

Manns, F., "Une tradition liturgique Juive sous-jacente à Jacques 1,21b," *RSR* 62 (1988) 85–89.

Marconi, G., "Una nota sullo specchio di Gc 1,23," *Bib* 70 (1989) 396–402.

Marcus, J., "The Evil Inclination in the Epistle of James," *CBQ* 44 (1982) 606–21.

Marshall, S., "*Dipsychos*: a local term?" *SE* 6 (1973) 348–51.

Meeks, W. A., "The Image of the Androgyne: Some Uses of a Symbol in Earliest Christianity," *HR* 13 (1974) 165–208.

Morris, K. F., *An Investigation of Several Linguistic Affinities between the Epistle of James and the Book of Isaiah* (Ph.D. diss., Union Theological Seminary in Virginia, 1964) 145–49.

Nauck, W., "Freude im Leiden: Zum Problem einer urchristlichen Verfolgungstradition," *ZNW* 46 (1955) 68–80.

Palmer, F. H., "James 1:18 and the Offering of First-Fruits," *TynB* 3 (1957) 1–2.

Porter, S. E., "Is *dipsychos* (James 1,8; 4,8) a 'Christian' Word?" *Bib* 71 (1990) 469–98.

Riesenfeld, H., "*HAPLOS*: zu Jak. 1,5," *Coniectanea Neotestamentica* 9 (1944) 33–41.

Roberts, D. J., "The Definition of 'Pure Religion' in James 1:27," *ExpT* 83 (1971–72) 215–16.

Rusche, H., "Standhaben in Gott: Einführung in die Grundgedanken des Jakobusbriefes (1, 1–27)," *BibLeb* 5 (1964) 153–63.

Schökel, L. A., "Culto y justicia en Sant 1,26–27," *Bib* 56 (1975) 537–44.

Seitz, O. J. F., "Afterthoughts on the Term 'Dipsychos'," *NTS* 4 (1957–58) 327–34.

———, "Antecedents and Significance of the term *Dipsychos*," *JBL* 66 (1947) 211–19.

Sigal, P., "The Halakah of James," *Intergerini Parietis Septum (Eph 2:14): Essays Presented to Markus Barth*, ed. D. Y. Hadidian (Pittsburgh: Pickwick Press, 1981) 337–53.

Stagg, F., "Exegetical Themes in James 1 and 2," *Review and Expositor* 66 (1969) 391–402.

Thomas, J., "Anfechtung und Vorfreude," *KD* 14 (1968) 183–206.

Wolverton, W. I., "The Double-Minded Man in the Light of Essene Psychology," *ATR* 37 (1956) 166–75.

Wuellner, W. H., "Der Jakobusbrief im Licht der Rhetorik und Textpragmatik," *LB* 43 (1978) 5–65.

Zeller, E., "Ueber Jak. 1,12," *ZWT* 6 (1863) 93–96.

III. THE DEEDS OF FAITH 2:1–26

✦

2:1. My brothers, do not hold the faith of Jesus Christ our glorious Lord together with acts of favoritism. 2. For if a man with gold rings and splendid clothing enters your assembly, and also a poor man dressed in filthy clothing, 3. and you look favorably on the one wearing the splendid clothing and say to him, "you sit here in a fine place," while you also say to the poor person, "you stand there, or sit below my footrest," 4. are you not divided within yourselves, and have you not become judges with evil designs? 5. Listen, my beloved brothers! Has not God chosen the poor in the world to be rich in faith and heirs of the kingdom which he has promised to those who love him? 6. But you have dishonored the poor person! Is it not the rich who oppress you and are they not the very ones who are dragging you into courts? 7. Are they not the very ones blaspheming the noble name which has been invoked over you? 8. If you actually fulfill the royal law according to the Scripture, "you shall love your neighbor as yourself," you are doing well. 9. But if you are practicing favoritism, you are committing a sin. You are convicted by the law as transgressors. 10. For whoever undertakes keeping the entire law, yet fails in one thing, has become accountable for them all. 11. For the one who has said, "Do not commit adultery," also said, "Do not kill." Now if you do not commit adultery but do kill, you have become a transgressor of the law. 12. So speak and so act, as people who are going to be judged by the law of freedom. 13. For judgment is merciless to one who has not shown mercy. Mercy triumphs over judgment. 14. What use is it, my brothers, if someone says he has faith but does not have deeds? Is the faith able to save him? 15. If a brother or sister is going naked and lacking daily food, 16. and if one of you should say to them, "Go in peace! Be warmed and filled," but does not give to them what is necessary for the body, what is the use? 17. So also faith, if it does not have deeds, is by itself dead. 18. But someone will say, "you have faith, and I have deeds." Show me your faith apart from deeds, and by my deeds I will show you my faith. 19. You believe that God is one. You do well! Even the demons believe, and they shudder! 20. Do you wish to know, you empty fellow, that faith apart from deeds is useless? 21. Was not our father Abraham shown to be righteous on the basis of deeds when he offered his son Isaac on the altar? 22. You see that faith was working together with his deeds, and by the deeds faith was brought to perfection. 23. And the Scripture was fulfilled that declared, "And Abraham believed God and it was reckoned to him as righteousness," and he was called a friend of God. 24. You see that a person is shown to be righteous on the basis of deeds and not on the basis of faith only. 25. And likewise also Rahab the prostitute: was she not shown to be righteous on the basis of deeds when she received the scouts and sent them out by another route? 26. For just as the body apart from the spirit is dead, so also faith apart from deeds is dead.

THE SECTION AS A WHOLE

It is easy to see why some readers could take 1:26–27 not as the ending of a discussion but as the start of another (Chaine, 39; Vouga, 70), for the basic contrasts between true and specious religion, between the measure of the world and God's measure, dominate this next section of the letter. Yet the solemn prohibition in 2:1, with its formal invocation of the "faith of Jesus Christ our glorious Lord," clearly marks the beginning of a section that just as obviously comes to a satisfying end in 2:26 with the conclusion that faith without deeds is dead. Of all the parts of James, this one appears to the majority of readers as the most unified and coherent.

It is also the section in which the characteristic features of the Greco-Roman diatribe most abound: the direct address of the implied reader (2:1, 5, 14), the use of apostrophe (2:20), of rhetorical questions (2:4, 5, 7, 14, 20), of hypothetical examples (2:2–3; 2:15–16), of *exempla* cited from Torah (2:8–11; 21–25), and of paronomasia (2:4, 13, 20).

More obviously than in chapter one, moreover, James is clearly putting such stylistic features in the service of an argument. Examples, citations, questions, and commands are instruments of persuasion. James 2 is a splendid example of deliberative rhetoric that seeks to move the readers from one mode of behavior to another.

The major interpretive issue is whether the chapter contains a single argument or several. It is certainly possible to detect transitions. There is no mistaking the internal coherence of 2:1–7, dealing with discrimination against the poor in the assembly. But is 2:8–13, which no longer speaks of the poor but takes up the subject of the royal law, a continuation of the same argument, or is it the beginning of a new one? And is the discussion of faith and works in 2:14–26 the separate sort of discussion that scholarship has so often considered it, or is it actually the third stage of the same argument that began in 2:1? The decision involves the proper identification of the "real topic." Does James move from one topic to another, from discrimination to the keeping of the law of love, to the necessity of performing works? Or does he elaborate one topic through three interrelated stages?

The position taken here is that in chapter two James develops a single argument. From beginning to end, it concerns faith and its deeds. The faith is that associated with the Messiah Jesus and given summary expression in the royal law of love for the neighbor as the self. Each stage of the argument is intricately connected to the next. Thus, the "royal law" in 2:8 picks up from the promise of "the kingdom" to the poor in 2:5; the "mercy that overcomes judgment" in 2:13 anticipates by way of pun the example of "merciless" behavior toward the poor that begins the third part of the argument, concerning the "uselessness" of faith without deeds; the sin of partiality, which is taken as the transgression of the law of love in 2:9, obviously corresponds to the prohibition of partiality in 2:1; the negative example of favoring the rich man over the poor man in 2:2–3, which is used to illustrate "partiality," matches perfectly the negative example of the rejection of the poor by members of the community in 2:15–16, and these refusals of hospitality are answered in turn by the positive examples of Abraham and Rahab in 2:21–25.

The argument from beginning to end, then, concerns the necessity of living out the faith of Jesus in appropriate deeds. In this sense, the final part of the discussion in 2:14–26 only provides the broadest formal framework for the specifics argued in 2:1–13. Likewise, the point of the discussion in 2:14–26 is not to be found by way of engagement with a Pauline position, but rather by the specific points argued in 2:1–13.

James seeks to hold the community to its professed ideals. Do the readers claim as their own the "faith of Jesus" that announced to the poor an elect place in the kingdom? Then they cannot adopt the standards of the world that scorns the poor and treats them with contempt. Do the readers claim as their own the "law of love" associated with Jesus' preaching of the kingdom? Then they must live out that love consistently and not practice the sort of discrimination against the poor that the very law quoted by Jesus itself condemns. Do they profess to live in a community that shares its possessions? Then they cannot, in the face of dreadful human need, cover up neglect with the camouflage of pious language.

This is the context for James' argument that "faith without deeds is dead." His implied audience is not like Paul's readers in Galatia, who were proposing to do more by seeking circumcision and observance of law. James portrays his implied audience as one that avoids even the minimum required by its profession of the faith of Jesus.

2:1–7

1. My brothers, do not hold the faith of Jesus Christ our glorious Lord together with acts of favoritism. 2. For if a man with gold rings and splendid clothing enters your assembly, and also a poor man dressed in filthy clothing, 3. and you look favorably on the one wearing splendid clothing and say to him, "you sit here in a fine place," while you also say to the poor person, "you stand there, or sit below my footrest," 4. are you not divided within yourselves and have you not become judges with evil designs? 5. Listen, my beloved brothers! Has not God chosen the poor in the world to be rich in faith and heirs of the kingdom which he has promised to those who love him? 6. But you have dishonored the poor person! Is it not the rich who oppress you and are they not the very ones who are dragging you into courts? 7. Are they not the very ones blaspheming the noble name which has been invoked over you?

NOTES

1. *Do not hold*: The negation (*mē*) of a present imperative can mean to cease an ongoing activity. But it can also stand as a general prohibition. Given the typical rather than specific character of the example that follows, the translation provided is probably better. Ropes, 46, and Chaine, 40, suggest that the verse might be read as a question demanding a negative answer.

the faith of Jesus Christ: Two major problems are posed by the text. The first is the proper word order. Some MSS place "of glory" (*tēs doxēs*) immediately after "faith," which would then yield the natural translation, "glorious faith" (so Reicke, 27). The position after "our Lord Jesus Christ," however, is to be preferred. The second problem concerns the meaning of the genitival phrase *pistis tou kyriou hēmōn Iēsou Christou*. Many commentators choose the objective genitive, "faith in Our Lord Jesus Christ" (so Chaine, 40; Marty, 70; Ropes, 187; Cantinat, 120). The subjective "faith of Jesus Christ" is more likely for two reasons: First, the Christology of the letter is not such as to make "faith in Christ" natural; elsewhere faith is clearly directed to "God who is father" (2:19, 23). Second, the use of Jesus' sayings throughout the composition suggests a meaning like "the faith of Jesus in God as reflected in his teaching," or perhaps "the faith that is from Jesus Christ," in the sense "declared by Jesus." Such an understanding connects 2:1 to the explicit use of Jesus' saying in 2:5 as well as to the "royal law" of 2:8.

our glorious Lord: The extraordinary separation of the phrases *tou kyriou* and *tēs doxēs* helped generate theories of interpolation (see Introduction, p. 151, and Windisch, 13–14), even though no MS evidence supports such theories. A variety of translations has been suggested. Erasmus made the fascinating suggestion (followed by Calvin and Michaelis) that *doxa* should be taken in the sense of "opinion," which would connect directly to "acts of favoritism." For the translation "Lord Jesus Christ of glory," see Vouga, 70, and Mussner, 114. Less likely are the options "who is the glory" (Hort, 47–48; Mayor, 80–82; Laws, 95–97) or "our glory" (Adamson, 103–4; Cantinat, 120–21). The translation "glorious Lord" is read by Ropes, 187; Mussner, 116; Davids, 106; Chaine, 41; Marty, 70; Dibelius, 126; and Martin, 60. It is difficult, though supported by 1 Cor 2:8. The term *doxa* is frequently found as shorthand for the resurrection of Jesus (see Luke 24:26; Acts 22:11; John 17:5; 1 Cor 2:8; 15:43; 2 Cor 4:6; Phil 2:11; 3:21; Col 1:11; Heb 2:7; 1 Pet 1:11). To define faith as that proclaimed by Jesus does not preclude James also from confessing Jesus as the resurrected one.

together with acts of favoritism: the Greek phrase *en prosōpolēmpsiais* is critical to the entire argument. The prepositional phrase sharpens the dative of accompanying circumstances. The phrase suggests not simply a general attitude but specific and repeated acts, an implication the translation makes explicit. The term *prosōpolēmpsia* is a Christian neologism, based on the Hebrew *naśa panîm*, translated in the LXX by *lambanein prosōpon*, literally "to lift up the face/appearance" (see Lev 19:15 and, similarly, Mal 1:8), in the sense of "respecting persons" or showing favoritism (see Luke 20:21; Gal 2:6; also *Did.* 4:3; *Barn.* 19:4). The usage in Lev 19:15 makes it clear that the original context of the language was that of judging cases in the community: unjust judgment was that based on appearances rather than on the merits of the case. Elsewhere in the NT, *aprosōpolēmpsia* is a *theologoumenon* expressive of God's righteousness: God does not show favoritism in judging humans (see Acts 10:34; Rom 2:11; Eph 6:9; Col 3:25). Only in James 2:1 and 2:9 is the term associated with human attitudes and practices. The connection with the citation of Lev 19:18 is critical to James' argument. The practice of favoritism in judging is vigorously condemned by Sir 7:6–7, and the impartiality of the Lord is praised in Sir 35:10–18. Leviticus 19:15 is alluded to as well in *The Sentences of Pseudo-Phocylides* 10. The thematic link between 1:27 and the essay beginning in 2:1 is noted by Chaine, 39, and Vouga, 70.

2. *a man with gold rings and splendid clothing*: The connective *gar* links the example to the preceding prohibition and builds to the climactic question in v.4. The description makes the wealth of the person obvious even though the term *plousios* is not used. The "splendid clothing" catches the radiant, brilliant connotations of *lampros*; compare Homer, *Od.* 19:234; Luke 23:11; Acts 10:30. The wearing of gold rings (*chrysodaktylios*) suggests not only display but also power and arrogance (compare Epictetus *Discourses* I, 22, 18; Seneca, *Natural Questions* VII, 31, 2; Lucian of Samosata, *Timon* 20; Philo, *On Joseph* 149). Although the wearing of a gold ring was the mark of equestrian rank (Reicke, 27; Laws, 27), the broad contrast between rich and poor here does not demand such a literal identification of parties (Vouga, 72).

enters your assembly: The textual evidence divides between the presence or absence of the definite article with *synagōgē*. With it, the emphasis would fall more on the synagogue as building; without it, on the synagogue as an assembly of people. The difference is slight in either case. James uses the term only here. It seems roughly synonymous with *ekklēsia* in 5:14. Although some later Christian compositions use the terms antithetically for Jewish and Christian meetings, respectively (e.g., Justin, *Dialogue with Trypho* 134:3), other compositions reflect greater flexibility in usage (see, e.g., Ign. *Pol.* 4:2; *Tral.* 3:1; *Herm. Man.* 11:9, 13–14; *Dialogue with Trypho* 63:5). For the use of both terms in Greco-Roman associations of various sorts, see Dibelius, 133. Throughout the diaspora, the synagogue was the institutional locus for Jewish identity (Philo, *Against Flaccus* 48; *Embassy to Gaius*, 312), as it was indeed within Palestine itself (*y.meg.* 73d). As shown by Acts, the synagogue functioned as a place of worship (thus, *proseuchē* = house of prayer, Acts 16:13; 3 Macc 7:20; Philo, *Against Flaccus* 45, 47; Josephus, *Ap.* 2:10; *Life* 277) and—as *beth hammidrash*—as place of reading and study (see Acts 15:21; Philo, *On the Creation* 128, Josephus, *Ant.* 16:43; *Ap.* 2:175). Other activities included—in connection with the *gerousia*, or board of elders—the settling of community disputes (see Philo, *Embassy to Gaius* 229; 2 Macc 1:10; 11:27) and the distribution of community funds in almsgiving (see Josephus, *Ant.* 4:211; *Life* 294–302; Philo, *Life of Moses* 2:216; *Special Laws* 2:62; *b.Ber.* 6a; 64a; *b.Ket.* 5a; *b.B.M.* 28b; *b.Pes.* 101a); for the evidence concerning Jewish local courts, see Mitchell, 151–91.

a poor man dressed in filthy clothing: Throughout this passage, James uses *ptōchos* rather than the *tapeinos* ("lowly") of 1:9. It refers to literal material poverty in contrast to material wealth (Plato, *Thaetetus* 175A). In the LXX, such poverty is often seen as resulting from human wickedness and oppression (Pss 9:19, 30; 34:10; 36:14; 39:18; 108:16; Sir 4:1, 4; 13:3; Amos 4:1; 8:4; Isa 3:14–15; 10:1–2; see also Matt 26:11). The degree of poverty is expressed by the characterization of the clothing as *rypara* ("filthy"; see 1:21; for the same contrast between "splendid" and "filthy" clothing, see Philo, *On Joseph* 20). The contemporary equivalent would be the street person whose lack of access to facilities leads to being clothed in filthy and stinking rags. The sharp contrast between the two characters reminds us of the Lukan parable of Lazarus and Dives (Luke 16:19–31). The wealthy (*plousios*) man there dined "splendidly (*lamprōs*)" every day as he ignored the poor man (*ptōchos*) lying at his gate (see the notes on 2:13, below).

3. *and you look favorably*: The use of the verb *epiblepein* makes a subtle point. Although literally it means simply to "look upon," it is used in the LXX in the sense of "look upon with favor" (see LXX Pss 12:4; 24:16; 32:13; 68:17; 73:20; also, Josephus, *Ant.* 1:20). Furthermore, this "favorable look" is here based entirely on appearance: all they seem to know about the rich man is that he is "wearing" (*phorein*) splendid clothing.

you sit here in a fine place: The short sentence says everything necessary about flattery and obsequiousness. The rich person is invited to sit rather than to stand, to proximity rather than distance, to comfort or prestige rather than to discomfort and dishonor. Arguing from later Greek usage, Ropes, 190, proposes that *kalōs* could mean here something like "please." For a remarkable parallel in public behavior, see Plutarch's description of the flatterer's response to being interrupted by a wealthy person (Plutarch, *How to Tell a Flatterer* 15 [*Mor.* 58C–D]).

you stand there: The textual variants reflect confusion on what these directions might signify. One variation has "you stand or sit there beneath my footrest"; another, "stand here or sit there"; another, "stand there or sit here." The reading adopted here best accounts for the variations (Metzger, 680). This first command reverses the concern shown toward the wealthy: rather than being invited to sit in honorable proximity, the poor man is distanced and made to stand.

sit below my footrest: Once more the variants show scribes' attempts at understanding a situation that eluded them. One variant replaces "below" (*hypo*) with "upon" (*epi*). Some scribes recognized an allusion to LXX Ps 109:1, "Until I place your enemies beneath the footrest of your feet" (see Acts 2:35; Heb 1:13; 10:13) and add the words "of your feet" (*tōn podōn sou*). The use of the image in Ps 109:1, as well as in other NT and LXX passages (Ps 98:5; Isa 66:1; Matt 5:35), subordinates one person to another. In contrast to the proximity of the rich person ("sit here in a fine place"), the closeness here is even more humbling than being made to stand at a distance; it is a form of mockery.

4. *divided within yourselves*: After such a complex protasis, James turns on his readers with a powerful apodosis in the form of two interrelated questions. The phrase *diekrithēte en heautois* has a rich ambiguity. At the literal level, the passive of *diakrinō* demands being taken as internal dividedness (see Mayor, 85; Chaine, 44; Ropes, 192; Mussner, 119; Martin, 63): they are trying to live by two measures at once and are "divided in consciousness" (see Matt 21:21; Mark 11:23; Acts 10:20; Rom 4:20; 14:23; and esp. James 1:6). At the same time, something of the active sense of *diakrinō* ("to make distinctions/discriminate," as in Matt 16:3; Acts 11:12; 15:9) is retained (as in Dibelius, 136; Laws, 102; Cantinat, 125; Davids, 110; Marty, 68; Mussner, 119).

become judges with evil designs: The genitive is one of quality (Ropes, 193); compare *kritēs tes adikias* in Luke 18:6. James' question is critical for determining the specific context of the example: deciding cases within the community. R. B. Ward ("Partiality in the Assembly," 87–97; "Communal Concern," 78–107) has assembled the comparative material from rabbinic texts that describes the situation in terms identical to those sketched by James: *Deuteronomy Rabbah*, Shof. V,6; *b.Sheb.* 31a; *Sifra*, Ked.Pireh 40,4; *PA* 1:4; *Aboth de Rabbi Nathan* 1:10). Evidence for such procedures in the synagogue is provided by the note on 2:2; for the same in Christian communities, see Matt 18:15–20; 1 Cor 5:3–5; 6:1–8; 1 Tim 5:19–24. The judicial context of Lev 19:15, which forbids "favoritism," continues here. It says, "In righteousness you will judge your neighbor." In contrast, these are judges with "evil designs" since they do what Leviticus forbids: "Do not practice favoritism in judgment." For the translation "evil designs," compare Matt 15:19; the strong translation is justified on two counts: a) *dialogismos* has a negative connotation throughout the NT (Matt 15:19; Mark 7:21; Luke 5:22; 6:8; 9:46–47; 24:38; Rom 1:21; 14:1; 1 Cor 3:20; Phil 2:14; 1 Tim 2:8); b) the *calculation* that is built into favoritism toward the rich; in the ancient system of patronage there would have been a *quid pro quo*. The prohibition of partiality is retained by ancient church orders (see *Didascalia Apostolorum* 12; *Apostolic Constitutions* II, 58).

5. *listen, my beloved brothers*: The imperative of *akouein* ("listen") emphatically marks the importance of what follows in the law (Deut 6:3–4; 9:1), the prophets (Amos 3:1; 5:1; Mic 1:2; 6:1; Joel 1:2; Isa 1:10; 7:13; 48:1), and wisdom (Ps 118:149; Prov 1:8; 4:1; 19:20; Wis 6:1; Sir 6:23); see also Matt 13:18; Mark 7:14; Luke 18:6; Acts 1:22; 15:13; 22:1. A principle of fundamental importance is to follow.

Has not God chosen the poor in the world: James reminds his readers of the basic principle of their existence: God's paradoxical and surprising choice. The words echo the biblical election (*eklegein*) of Israel as God's people (Num 16:5; Deut 4:37; 7:7; LXX Pss 32:12; 134:4; Isa 14:1; 43:10), which also carries over to the NT (Acts 13:17) and is applied specifically to the messianic community (Mark 13:20; John 15:16; Eph 1:4). Whom has God chosen? The textual variants show some uncertainty as to how to read *ptōchous tọ kosmọ*. As it stands, it is a dative of reference or respect (Hort, 51; Windisch, 15; Mayor, 85; Ropes, 193; Dibelius, 138): "those who are poor in the world's eyes." The reader must supply the content of the term "world." In the light of James' overall conception (see 1:27; 3:6; 4:4), the "world's" measurement of value is directly opposed to God's. Some MSS, however, read it in local terms, and add the preposition *en* to yield, "those in the world who are poor." Others, possibly under the influence of the parallel Pauline passage, read "poor of the world (*tou kosmou*)." The decision to go with the harder reading here is critical for properly apprehending James' ethical dualism. It is not simply a question of fact but a matter of value, not only an issue of location, but of meaning. Those who are economically poor are thereby *regarded* by "the world" as inferior to others. The most striking parallel to James' language is found in the series of affirmations by Paul to the Corinthians: "God chose (*exelexato*) the foolish of the world . . . God chose the weak (*asthenē*) of the world . . . God chose the ignoble (*agenē*) of the world and the things that are rejected (*exouthenēmena*)" (1 Cor 1:27–28). It is unlikely that there is literary dependence; rather, James and Paul build on a shared understanding of God's election that derives from Jesus' own proclamation.

to be rich in faith: The translation supplies "to be." The reading "as rich in faith" is also acceptable. Here the text does supply the preposition *en* before faith. But it is still to be read as a dative of respect: they are rich from the perspective of faith (Ropes, 194); or, in the context of the community of faith, they are regarded as rich. The text cannot be taken to mean that the poor have more faith; that would not only reverse the point of God's election, but also the flow of the argument (Marty, 77).

and heirs of the kingdom: The language of inheritance is rooted in the biblical tradition. The first "inheritance" (*klēronomia*) promised to Abraham was the land (Gen 28:4; Deut 1:8; 2:12; 4:1; see Acts 7:5). The deeper dimension of inheritance is suggested by LXX Ps 15:5, which speaks of the Lord as one's inheritance, and Ps 36:18, which speaks of an eternal inheritance. This is the only time "heir" occurs in James, but it is found with reference to Christian identity in Paul (Rom 8:17; Gal 3:29; 4:7; Titus 3:7; Eph 1:14, 18) and Hebrews (11:7). This is also the only time James uses *basileia*, but Paul uses it rather frequently in connection with inheritance (Gal 5:21; 1 Cor 6:9–10; 15:50; Eph 5:5). The image of the "kingdom" puts an ironic twist on the image of "footrest" in Ps 109:1. In the kingdom of the risen Christ, the poor are meant to be heirs, but James' implied readers put the poor "under their footrest."

which he has promised: The language here clearly echoes that of 1:12: "He will receive the crown of life which He [God] promised to those who love him," with the term "kingdom" here taking the place of "the crown of life." For the biblical background to "promise" see the note on 1:12. Notice also that "promise" is connected to "inheritance" in Gal 3:18, 29; Heb 6:12, 17; 11:9. James is clearly employing common features of the primitive Christian *argot* (see Introduction I.E.4). If we ask the source of this promise, we can find it in the proclamation of Jesus, *makarioi hoi ptōchoi hoti hymetera estin hē basileia tou theou* ("Blessed are you poor, for yours is the kingdom of God"), as found in Luke 6:20; see also Matt 5:3; Gos. Thom. 54 (Wachob, 236–66).

6. *dishonored the poor person*: James gives a distinctive turn to the honor/shame axis of values characteristic of the Greco-Roman world. The term *atimazein* means "to shame/hold in dishonor" (Plato, *Phaedo* 107B; Xenophon, *Cyropaedia* 1,6,20; see Mark 12:4; Luke 20:11; John 8:49; Acts 5:41). The favoritism shown toward the rich has turned out to be a rejection of the honor God has shown to the poor. As a result, these wicked judges have rejected God's measure of what is truly honorable. James continues the outlook of Prov 14:21: "The one who dishonors the poor commits sin" (see also Prov 22:22). Once more, Paul shares the same outlook, although he uses different language. With reference to the inequities practiced at the Lord's Supper in Corinth, he accuses those who have eaten while others have gone hungry, "you have despised the assembly of God and you have shamed those who have nothing" (1 Cor 11:22).

who oppress you: The verb *katadynasteuein* means to oppress or exploit someone (Xenophon, *Symposium* 5:8). It is used in the LXX for the oppression of the Israelites by the Egyptians (Exod 1:13) and of the righteous by the unjust (Wis 2:10; 15:14; Hab 1:4), and especially of the poor by the wealthy (Amos 4:1; 8:4; Zech 7:10; Jer 7:6; 22:3; Ezek 18:12; 22:7, 29). James shifts to the third person to speak of these oppressors (Vouga, 75). With the identification of the "rich" as "those who oppress you," James has tapped into a rich vein of the

Jewish tradition (Dibelius, 39–45). Already in the prophets and the psalms, the division between the righteous and the sinners tended to be aligned with that between the powerless poor and powerful wealthy (Johnson, *Sharing Possessions*, 79–116). In the intertestamental literature the polarity, if anything, became sharper (see, e.g., *1 Enoch* 94:6–77; 96:8; 97:8–10; 98:1–16; 100:6; *Pss. Sol.* 1:4–8; 5:2; 10:6; 15:1; *1QH* 1:36; 2:32, 34; 3:25; 5:13; 14:3; 17:22; *1QM* 11:9; 13:14; *1QS* 2:24; 3:8; 4:3; 5:3; 5:25; 11:1; *CD* 6:16; 14:14; *4QpH* 8:8–12; 9:4–5; 12:3–10; *4QpPs37* 2:8–9; 3:10–11) and is reflected also in the sayings of Jesus (see note on 2:5).

the very ones who drag you into courts: The translation "very ones" seeks to capture the force of the intensive *autoi* (contra Ropes, 195). The verb *elkein* denotes violence, whether physical or legal (see Josephus, *JW* 1:591; Acts 21:30). The *Kritērion* is a court of law (Plato, *Laws* 767B; Philo, *On the Virtues* 66; 1 Cor 6:2, 4). In Acts 16:19, Paul and Silas are, for financial reasons, "dragged" into the forum to be tried before the rulers. There is no need to postulate a formal persecution (contra Reicke, 28; Cantinat, 131). It is universal enough a characteristic of the world's rich to oppress and humiliate the poor by "legal" means. James is outraged because the "evil judges" of this community are doing the same thing!

7. *blaspheming the noble name*: The term *blasphēmein* literally means to speak harshly or slanderously against someone (Philo, *Special Laws* 4:197; Josephus, *Life* 232). When directed against the divine, such reviling becomes "blasphemy" in the religious sense (Vouga, 79; see Matt 9:3; 26:65; Luke 12:10; John 10:36). In the present case, it is the "noble name" (*kalon onoma*) borne by the community, whether that of God or Christ. For blaspheming the name of God (called *kalos* in LXX Ps 134:3), see 1 Tim 6:1; Rev 13:6; 16:9; 2 *Clem.* 13:1; in the case of Rom 2:24, 2 *Clem.* 13:2a, and Ign. *Tral.* 8:2, the text of Isa 52:5 lies in the background: "Because of you, my name is blasphemed among the nations." For blasphemy explicitly directed toward Christians, see Acts 26:11; 1 Tim 1:13; Justin, *Dialogue with Trypho* 117.

invoked over you: The verb *epikalein* means to "call upon" someone (Gen 12:8; Acts 2:21; Rom 10:13). When a "name is invoked" over someone, it constitutes a statement of ownership (see Gen 48:16; Deut 12:11). In the case of Israel's relationship with Yahweh, the expression designates the special relationship between the Lord and the people (see Amos 9:12; 2 Macc 8:15). In the present case, the most obvious "name" invoked is that of "Jesus Christ our glorious Lord" mentioned in 2:1 (compare *Herm. Sim.* 8,6,4: *to onoma kyriou to epiklēthen ep' autous*).

COMMENT

James' reputation for vividness owes not a little to this passage. Suddenly, the reader is transported from the realm of general axioms to the most specific sort of social situation in which those maxims are put to the test. Now, the contrast between the pure religion in God's eyes and the world (1:26–27) is spelled out by the behavior of the messianic community with respect to its poorer members. The opening prohibition simply states the incompatibility of "the faith of Jesus"—meaning here the measure of life as preached and taught by Jesus—with attitudes of partiality toward the rich. It is the explication of that prohibition that draws readers into a deeper realization of the absolute divide between the two measures.

With remarkable concision, James sketches a situation in which the "dividedness" of the community is revealed. He pictures them in the assembly (2:2–3). The portrayal raises a number of critical questions. Does the use of *synagōgē* demand a conclusion concerning the Jewish-Christian character of the community? No, but neither does it argue against it. Does James refer to the *synagōgē* primarily as the building where the community assembles, or as the assembly itself? The evidence does not enable us to decide. Is the rich person who enters the assembly so ostentatiously garbed a member of the community, or an outsider? If 2:4 is taken to mean "making distinctions among yourselves," then he would seem to be a member of the community, but we cannot be certain.

Is the community assembled for the purposes of worship and study, or for the specific purpose of reaching a judicial decision? Here the parallel passages adduced from the rabbinic tradition by R. B. Ward are extremely helpful. At the very least they make clear that Lev 19:15, which forbade favoritism in judging, was spelled out by the rabbis in a manner strikingly similar to James. As the notes suggest, there is every reason to think that early Christians took over from the synagogue the practice of settling disputes in such a community setting. It is at least possible that any occurrence of favoritism, even in the course of the liturgy, could generate the use of the judicial *topos* from Leviticus.

This consideration leads to the final critical question: is James generalizing from specific instances of which he has heard, or is he constructing the scene for its rhetorical effect? Once more, it is impossible, on the basis of the evidence offered here, to decide. Nor does the decision on any of these points really matter, for the force of James' example does not derive from its historical referentiality, but from its rhetorical function.

That function is to provide his readers with an example of behavior so egregious and so clearly contrary to their community ethos that the rhetorical question posed in 2:4 is unanswerable. Yet it gains its force only from an assumption concerning that shared ethos that is made explicit in 2:5–7. The scene, therefore, is intended to stir among the readers a growing sense of inappropriateness, which James' subsequent questions will reveal to be the dissonance between their behavior and the measure by which they claim to live.

Although the social setting may seem exotic, the dynamics of the scene are instantaneously recognizable: James sketches human behavior that is virtually universal. The rich and powerful are the ones who can benefit us, and the favor shown them, it is assumed, will come back to us. No great grasp of cultural comparisons is required to make this example come alive: it is enacted daily in countless ways. But James does provide us a glimpse of the ordinary way in which honor and shame worked in the patronage system of the ancient Mediterranean world. In the "way of the world" those who have possessions and power and prestige are shown honor, whereas none is due those lacking such signs of status.

James' perception of such behavior is strongly negative. In this respect, James shares the perspective of Hellenistic philosophers who challenged the dominant system of honor and shame by appealing to a higher sort of honor won by virtue. It is not difficult to imagine Lucian of Samosata employing just such a vignette as this to lampoon the inconsistency of would-be philosophers who claimed virtue yet who curried favor with the rich (see, in fact, his *Dialogues of the Dead* 20).

James' language, however, invokes the world of Torah more than that of Hellenistic moral philosophy. The very term *prosōpolēmpsia* (2:1) is unintelligible apart from the frame of reference provided by Scripture. It is a word choice that deliberately echoes Lev 19:15, so that the question "have you not become judges with evil designs" (2:4) finds its explicit significance in the ancient norms for exercising righteous judgment among the people. It is in this respect that Ward's application of rabbinic texts to this passage helps illuminate what otherwise might appear to be a harsh or unexpected indictment in 2:4 and uncover the assumptions shared by James and those other readers of Torah: "Rabbi Meir used to say, 'Why does the verse say, Ye shall hear the small and great alike (Deut 1:17)? So that one of the litigants shall not be kept standing and the other sit . . .'" (*Aboth de Rabbi Nathan* 1:10). Such passages show that placing one person in an advantageous position while placing another in a disadvantageous one simply on the basis of their appearance is, by the measure of Torah, *already* to have become "respecters of persons" and, therefore, to have become "unrighteous judges." James' allusion to the law in Lev 19:15 is particularly important for understanding the transition to the discussion that follows in 2:8, concerning the "royal law."

Even more than the measure of Leviticus, however, those who show favoritism in the assembly offend against the measure of "the faith of Jesus." In 2:5–6a, James contrasts the way God has treated the poor and the way James' implied readers are treating them. By the measure of faith, the poor are "rich" because God has chosen them to be heirs of the kingdom. As the notes suggest, James' language here seems clearly to echo the beatitudes (Luke 6:20; Matt 5:3). God, in a word, has chosen to *honor* the poor by elevating their status: they are rich, they are heirs of the kingdom. One hearing this text read aloud would surely have caught the allusion back to the contrast in 1:9–11 between the wealthy who disappeared in the midst of their affairs and the lowly who were exalted, as well as the clear correspondence between the "lovers of God" in 1:12 and the "lovers of God" here in 2:5.

In the sharpest possible contrast to God's honoring of the poor, however, the readers are said to have "dishonored the poor person." Those who claim to live by the measure of the faith of Jesus are not truly doing so; instead, in the clearest manner possible, they are actually living by the measure of the world.

The absurdity of such behavior for *this* community in particular is now made explicit by James in a series of three questions, the answers to which, we assume, are all too obvious. The questions appeal to the readers' own experience as members of a marginalized community, with the form of the questions in Greek demanding the emphatic answer "yes." James asks whether it is not the rich people who oppress *them*, and whether it is not the rich themselves who drag *them* into law courts for the purposes of oppressing them, and whether it is not the rich who blaspheme the noble name invoked over *them* (2:6b–7).

In regard to the rich and powerful of the world, in other words, the community as a whole has suffered from those "acts of favoritism" by which the wheels of the world are greased: they have suffered at the hands of "judges with evil designs" instigated by the powerful machinations of the rich. The passion in James' words fairly leaps off the page as he asks these questions, for their point is all too clear: they have adopted the attitudes of the oppressors against their own members! Although they claim to live in a community shaped by the honor of the poor, in their actual assemblies they practice just the same favoritism toward the rich that has been turned against them. The attitudes of "the world" have infected the assembly. This is indeed "double-mindedness."

Because the final part of this chapter (2:14–26) has so often been read with reference to Paul rather than with respect to its own concerns, it is important before leaving this section to highlight the comparison to 1 Cor 11:22 mentioned in the notes. It is not simply that Paul, like James, speaks of "shaming those who have nothing" (*kataischynete tous mē echontas*); more significantly, this charge is placed in the context of disunity and favoritism in the assembly. The community gathers to celebrate the Lord's Supper, but that symbol of unity is broken by people looking to their own satisfaction. The result is that "one goes hungry, another gets drunk" (1 Cor 11:21). The careful analysis of the social realities of fellowship meals in the Hellenistic world (see Theissen, 145–74) has suggested that similar tensions were present in the Pauline churches as are suggested by the present passage in James: the wealthy members of communities expected to be granted the same privileges *en ekklēsia* that they enjoyed *en kosmō* (see Countryman), and great effort was required to shape a community ethos that was genuinely egalitarian in character and based on the Good News concerning the poor (see 1 Cor 1:10–31).

2:8–13

8. If you actually fulfill the royal law according to the Scripture, "you shall love your neighbor as yourself," you are doing well. 9. But if you practice

favoritism, you are committing a sin. You are convicted by the law as transgressors. 10. For whoever undertakes keeping the entire law, yet fails in one thing, has become accountable for them all. 11. For the one who said, "Do not commit adultery," also said, "Do not kill." Now if you do not commit adultery but do kill, you have become a transgressor of the law. 12. So speak and so act, as people who are going to be judged by the law of freedom. 13. For judgment is merciless to the one who has not shown mercy. Mercy triumphs over judgment.

NOTES

8. *if you actually fulfill*: Verses 8 and 9 are two simple conditional sentences that state two contrasting performances of the "royal law" of love. For reading *mentoi* itself as adversative, see Mayor, 89, and Davids, 114. Most commentators agree with the position here, that *mentoi* has the sense of "really" (see Ropes, 198; Marty, 81; Adamson, 113; Dibelius, 141; Martin, 67; Hort, 53; Laws, 107). The particles *mentoi . . . de*, however, should be taken together and placed in strong opposition: "If you *really* fulfill . . . if *however*. . . ." The verb *telein* in the present tense clearly has the sense of "perform completely or wholly," since at issue is leaving out a critical aspect of the law.

the royal law: The adjective *basilikos* can refer to that which is "kingly" in character or excellence (Plato, *Minos* 317C; Epictetus, *Discourses* IV, 6, 20; Philo, *The Posterity and Exile of Cain* 101–2; 4 Macc 14:2) or simply because the "king" does it, as in the "royal custom" (Xenophon, *Cyropaedia* 1,3,18). The adjective can also be attached to that which *belongs* to the king in any fashion, such as the road used by the king (Num 20:17), or the king's country (Acts 12:20), or the king's officers (John 4:46, 49), or clothing (Esth 8:15; Acts 12:21), or commandments (see *entolai basilikai* in 2 Macc 3:13; 4:25). In the present case, the close proximity to *basileia* in 2:5 suggests a reading like "law of the kingdom" (contra Ropes, 199; with Windisch, 15; see Xenophon, *Oec.* 14,7), meaning the law articulated or ratified by Jesus "the glorious Lord," whose name "is invoked over them" (2:7). Although a number of commentators think that James restricts the "royal law" to Lev 19:18 (Hort, 54; Martin, 67; Laws, 108–9; Mussner, 124), those who think that James means all of the law (given explicit expression by Lev 19:18) are probably correct (Davids, 114; Marty, 82; Dibelius, 144; Cantinat, 132).

according to the Scripture: Especially because of its placement, the phrase is ambiguous. Although it precedes a citation of Lev 19:18b, it is not really a formula of introduction. In James' other explicit citations, he uses variations of *legein* ("says"): *ho eipōn . . . eipen* (2:11); *hē graphē legousa* (2:23); *hē graphē legei* (4:5); *dio legei* (4:6). In these modes of introduction, James most resembles

Paul (see *hē graphē legei* in Rom 4:3; 9:17; 10:11; 11:2; Gal 4:20; 1 Tim 5:18). In contrast, when James uses *kata*, he means "according to," in the sense of "in correspondence with" (see 2:17; 3:9). Furthermore, James obviously wants to place Lev 19:18b in its full context, which includes Lev 19:15 (with Spitta, 67; contra Davids, 115; Dibelius, 142). To capture the sense of the passage, one must almost render it, "If you actually keep the royal law 'love your neighbor as yourself' *according to the Scripture,* you are doing well." The meaning then would be "in accordance with the Scripture" as in 1 Cor 15:3, 4.

you shall love your neighbor as yourself: This is a verbatim citation from LXX Lev 19:18c. There will follow in 2:9 an allusion also to Lev 19:15. Other allusions to Leviticus 19 in James are found in 4:11 (Lev 19:16); 5:4 (Lev 19:13); 5:9 (Lev 19:18b); 5:12 (Lev 19:12) and 5:20 (Lev 19:17b) (Johnson, "Use of Leviticus 19"). This commandment is, above all, "royal" because it is identified with Jesus as his distinctive summation of Torah (see Matt 19:19; 22:39; Mark 12:31; Luke 10:27; Rom 13:9; Gal 5:14).

you are doing well: The adverb *kalōs* ("well/nobly") asserts the author's genuine opinion, in contrast to the ironic use of the expression in 2:3 and 2:19 (compare Dio, *Or.* 47:25).

9. *but if you practice favoritism:* The second conditional is introduced by *de* to provide a contrast with the perfect fulfillment of the law of love. See the note on 2:1 for discussion of the neologism *prosōpolēmptein.* The allusion to Lev 19:15 is even more obvious than in 2:1. In the immediate context of the "law of love," Leviticus also says "do not practice wickedness in judgment. Do not accept the appearance of the poor man nor be astounded at the appearance of the powerful man. In justice you will judge your neighbor" (see Windisch, 16).

committing a sin: James' two uses of the verb *ergazesthai* ("to work") are both negative: in 1:20, he declared that anger does not "work" the righteousness of God, and here the "working" of a sin opposes righteous judgment. Note that sin (*hamartia*) does not have here the personified sense it had in 1:15, but rather points to the "transgression of the law" as disobedience to the lawgiver.

you are convicted by the law: The participial clause is here translated as an independent sentence for emphasis. The verb *elenchein* means to reprove someone (Luke 3:19) or to expose (John 3:20) or convict someone of something (John 8:46). Here the passive with *hypo* indicates the thing by which they are convicted (compare Philo, *On Joseph* 48; *Special laws* 3:54; 1 Cor 14:24). Since breaking Lev 19:15 clearly reveals that Lev 19:18c is not being kept, the law itself exposes and convicts the sinner.

as transgressors: The noun *parabatēs* is related to *parabasis* (an "overstepping" or "transgression"): see "transgression of the oaths" in 2 Macc 15:10 and "transgression of the laws" in Philo, *On Dreams* 2:123; Josephus, *Ant.* 8:129; Rom 2:23. The term *parabates*, however, is found in the NT outside of Paul (Gal 2:18; Rom 2:25, 27) only in James 2:9, 11.

10. *whoever undertakes keeping the entire law:* The textual variants reveal the

grammatical oddity of the first clause. In form, it appears as a relative conditional clause (*hostis* + aorist subjunctive), although one would ordinarily expect the particle *an* as well. The lack of this sequel perhaps led some scribes to change the tense to the simple future either of *tērein* or *telein* or *plērein*. The translation of the aorist as conative is made necessary by the logic of the entire sentence. It must be that someone *tries to keep* the whole law, since the condition of not keeping each part individually shows that the translation "whoever keeps the whole law" is impossible. One certainly need not, with Reicke, 29, suppose a problem of legalism in the community. The point of reference is whether the "royal law" of Lev 19:18 is kept in its entirety. Thus, the *Catena*, Oecumenius, Theophylact, and Bede all assume that the "whole law" means the law of love, the law of Christ.

yet fails in one thing: The verb *ptaiein* literally means to "stumble" and lends itself readily to moral application (see Philo, *Allegorical Laws* 3:66). James uses it again in 3:2 (see also Rom 11:11 and 2 Pet 1:10). More difficult is deciding what is meant by "one thing" (*heni*). Does it refer to a commandment? Notice that this selection of "one among many" explains the shift in the apodosis from the collective noun "law" to the plural "them all."

accountable for them all: The adjective *enochos* is difficult. Basically, it means "subject to/liable to," but it has a wide range of applications: responsible to laws (Plato, *Laws* 869B) or bound to slavery (Heb 2:15) or responsible for the body and blood of the Lord (1 Cor 11:27). It can also mean to be liable to a legal charge (Plato, *Thaetetus* 148B) or liable to a penalty (Aristotle, *Rhetoric* 1380A; Matt 26:66) and, thus, "guilty." Which meaning best applies here? Ropes, 200, suggests that the phrase is "a rhetorical way of saying that he is a transgressor of 'the law as a whole,'" and this must surely be correct. Although it is tempting to appeal to Paul's statement in Gal 5:3, "I testify again to any person who is being circumcised that he is obliged (*opheiletēs*) to do (*poiēsai*) the whole law (*holon ton nomon*)," it would be misleading, for Paul is referring to the choice between allegiance to Christ and a commitment to the law that would exclude the crucified messiah (Gal 5:4). James' focus is on the genuine fulfillment of the law of love in its scriptural context. Yet Paul's statement as well as James' points to a widespread conviction that since the commandments all came from God, all require obedience. For similar passages, see *b.Hor.* 8b; *b.Shab.* 70b; *b.Yeb.* 47b; *T.Ash* 2:5–10; *1QS* 8:16; Philo, *Allegorical Laws* 3:241; 4 Macc 5:20; Matt 5:18–19; 23:23. In his *Epistula* 167 (PL 33:733–42), Augustine discusses the apparent similarity of James' statement to the Stoic principle on the unity of virtue and vice (see Marty, 85; Boyle, 611–17).

11. *for the one who has said*: The *gar* identifies this as a clause that explains why a person failing in one thing is responsible for the whole law. Critical to the argument is that the commandment is not just a text but "someone speaking," namely the lawgiver, God (4:11–12). See the note on 2:8.

do not commit adultery: James quotes two of the "ten words" that form the decalogue. The order of the commandments is that of the LXX. In Exod 20:13–15, adultery is followed by stealing, then killing; in Deut 5:17–18, the order is precisely the same as here. In each case, the LXX reverses the order of the MT's killing/adultery. The textual variants here seek to conform James' aorist subjunctive to the future indicative found in the LXX.

do not kill: For the combination of murder and adultery as exemplifying the central commandments of God, see Matt 5:21 and 5:27; Matt 19:18 and Mark 10:19. In those cases, however, the order follows that of the MT. In Luke 18:20 and Rom 13:9, the two commandments are found in the same sequence as in James and the LXX. Note further that in 4:4, James charges those who are killing with being "adulteresses" and in 5:6 refers to the killing of the righteous person. Against Martin, 70, however, there is no need to take these as opposing zealot activity in the Palestine of the sixties. Bede is extremely bold, stating that if one practices partiality, then it is the same as if one had committed murder or adultery.

transgressor of the law: Some MSS read "apostate from the law" (*apostatēs*) rather than "transgressor" (*parabatēs*), but that reading seems to be both secondary and drawing a conclusion beyond that being argued (against Kilpatrick, 433). James argues that obedience or disobedience of the commandments is unified by the fact that they express the will of the lawgiver (a point only made clear in 4:11–12 but anticipated here). Since the same authority issued both commands, breaking any of them makes one a "transgressor of the law" (as a whole), that is, a "lawbreaker." The example uses the cases of adultery and killing, but James has in mind the necessary connection between love and the refusal to practice favoritism in judging (2:8–9).

12. *so speak and so act*: The *houtōs/hōs* construction is rhetorically effective. The combination of speaking/acting encompasses all the behavior described in 2:1–4, as well as the principles enunciated in 1:26–27. Laws, 116, renders it, "Speak and act in every respect."

going to be judged: That God is judge is implicit in James' language about reward in 1:12 and 2:5. The theme of judgment is made more explicit as the composition progresses (3:1; 4:11–12; 5:5; 5:9; 5:12). The participle *mellontes* ("going to be/about to be") provides an eschatological edge; there is certainly nothing in James that suggests judgment will be far distant (compare 5:9). But whenever the judgment takes place, James reminds his readers that those who have carried out judgment on others (2:1–4) are themselves held to account, not by the rules of the world, but by the rules revealed by God in the "perfect law."

by the law of freedom: It is understood that judgment is by God alone (4:11–12). The *dia* here expresses the *means* used by God for judgment. God judges on the basis of the measure that has been revealed to humans. For "law of freedom," see the note on 1:25. One MS ($\mathfrak{P}^{74}$) has "word of freedom," but this represents a harmonization with 1:18.

13. *for judgment is merciless*: The *gar* again signals that this sentence grounds

the previous one: the "law of freedom" is once more identified as essentially about love and mercy. Failure to live by it (as when practicing favoritism toward the rich and powerful) means one will be judged on that basis. The adjective *aneleos* is a *hapax* in the LXX and NT.

the one who has not shown mercy: The noun *eleos* responds to the negative *aneleos*. James here states negatively the principle found positively in the words of Jesus, "blessed are the merciful, for they shall receive mercy" (*makarioi hoi eleēmones hoti autoi eleēthēsontai*; see also Matt 18:23–35; 25:34–46). The importance of mercy as a moral principle is widely attested in Jewish wisdom writings (Sir 27:30–28:7; Tob 14:9; *b.Shab.* 15b; *T. Zeb.* 5:3; 8:1–3; *Sentences of Pseudo-Phocylides* 11). In the LXX, *eleos* translates the Hebrew *ḥesed*, the expression of God's loving kindness toward humans (e.g., Pss 5:8; 6:5; 39:11; 47:10). In Sirach, the expression "show mercy" (*poiein eleos*) becomes linked to the sharing of possessions with the poor (Sir 29:1; see also 18:13), thus creating a bridge to the concept of almsgiving (*eleēmosyne*, which translates either *ḥesed* or, more often, *ṣedāqâ*). For the theme of almsgiving, see, in particular, the *Book of Tobit*. In Greco-Roman writings, we also see cases where *eleos* is directly connected to the helping of the poor (see Hands, 77–88). It is perhaps not surprising, therefore, that the *scholia* on this passage interprets it in terms of almsgiving, as do John Chrysostom, Oecumenius, and Theophylact. And in patristic interpretation, James 2:13 was a standard proof-text for the efficacy of almsgiving (see, e.g., Athanasius, *De Titulis Psalmorum* XL, 2 (PG 27:810); Caesarius of Cappadocia, *Dialogus* III, 140 (PG 38:1061); Cyril of Alexandria, *De Adoratione in Spiritu et Veritate* VII (PG 68:528). The connection is not arbitrary, for the sequence in 2:14–16 obviously picks up that theme.

mercy triumphs over judgment: The translation masks the obscurity and difficulty of the statement. There are many textual variants, reflecting widespread dissatisfaction with the text as it stands: a) some MSS alter the verb, either by making it a third person imperative ("let mercy triumph over judgment") or a second person indicative ("you boast—of mercy?—over judgment"); b) some MSS add the particle *de* to relieve the severe asyndeton between sentences ("but/yet let mercy triumph over judgment"). These variants appear to be "improvements" of the harder reading correctly adopted by Nestle-Aland. In its present form, the statement stands as an aphorism whose point is derived from how one understands the verb. *Katakauchasthai* combines the sense of boasting with the prefix *kata* to express "boasting over" (see LXX Zech 10:12; Jer 27:11, 38). This aggressive sense is clearly present in Rom 11:18, where Paul warns the Gentiles not to "boast against" the Jews. In James 3:14, furthermore, the verb occurs in a negative context with "lying against the truth." In the present context, it is best understood as the way in which mercy (in contrast to the lack of mercy) "wins out" in judgment. Once more, patristic writers exploit this part of the text with reference to almsgiving and the efficacy of almsgiving for future judgment. In particular, this text is used in the interpretation of the parable of

Lazarus and Dives in Luke 16:19–31. The rich man could have "triumphed over judgment" if he had given alms (*eleos*) to the poor man at his gate (see John Chrysostom, *De Lazaro et Divite* 2 [PG 59:595]; *Homilia de Eleemosyna* IX [PG 64:441]; Nilus the Abbot, *Peristeria* IV, XV [PG 79:845]; Johannes Xiphilinus, *Orationes Post Ascensionem* [PG 120:1228]).

COMMENT

Although James mentions "law" (*nomos*) here for the first time since 1:25, it is clear that 2:8–13 is not in the least a transition to another topic than that pursued in 2:1–7. His argument still concerns consistency in living out professed convictions. There are, furthermore, multiple rhetorical links between 2:8–13 and 2:1–7. The double conditional sentences in 2:8–9 echo the pattern of 2:2–4. The example of "favoritism" in the second of these conditionals (2:9) obviously points back to the opening prohibition in 2:1. And the designation of the law as "royal" (*basilikos*) follows naturally from the characterization of the inheritance as a "kingdom" (*basileia*) in 2:5. Finally, the citation of Lev 19:18c in 2:8, "you shall love your neighbor as yourself," naturally follows from the mention of those who "love God" in 2:5, filling out the dominical summary of the law as found in Matt 22:37–39, which combines the commandment of the *Shemaᶜ*, "You shall love the Lord your God with all your heart and all your soul and all your mind," with that in Lev 19:18c, "You shall love your neighbor as yourself."

James, in fact, began this argument with the measure of the law as consonant with the "faith of Jesus" and continued it with reference to Jesus' proclamation of the kingdom to the poor. Now James returns to the full understanding of God's measure as expressed in the law of love enunciated both by Torah and by the words of Jesus. It is of the first importance for the proper appreciation of this section that it be read, not as a separate and abstract deliberation on the law and the terms of its observance, nor a philosophical engagement with Stoic arguments concerning the unitary character of virtue and vice—still less as a shift from faith to law as the measure for Christian existence—but as a continuation of an argument about the consonance of profession and practice within the community.

The subject, then, is not law but consistency in practice. In the previous section, James condemned those living within a kingdom promised to the poor who, in their turn, shamed the poor. Now he insists that those who claim to live within a kingdom defined by the "royal law" of love cannot, at the same time, practice partiality. His reasons are not vague. They are rooted in the text of Torah itself. As the notes demonstrate, the prohibition of partiality in judgment in Lev 19:15 provides part of the context of the commandment of love of neighbor in Lev 19:18c. James understands this law of love to be articulated by its context. Thus his odd turn of phrase, "if you really keep the royal law *according to the scripture* (2:8)." And it is this understanding that illuminates his insistence that anyone undertaking to keep the law must observe it entirely. In this case, he means precisely the law of love as articulated by its scriptural context. One cannot claim to love while practicing favoritism in judging, for the prohibition of such favoritism is part of the law of love.

The contrast here, then, is between "really" keeping the law of love (2:8) and the mere pretense of doing so while, in fact, disobeying one of its provisions. This would be the same as claiming that one kept the ten commandments if one avoided adultery . . . even while one committed murder (2:11)! The law, in other words, is not simply a collection of commandments; rather it reflects the will of the lawgiver (a point that James will not make entirely clear until 4:11–12). Thus, James emphasizes the *speaking* of the commandments: the same one who "says" not to kill is the one who "says" not to commit adultery.

It must be admitted that James himself obscures this point by the virtual personification of *nomos* in this section. Thus, the law "convicts" someone as a transgressor (2:9), one who fails in one matter is "accountable for them all" (2:10). And in 2:12, James' readers are to speak and act as those "who are going to be judged by the law of freedom." But in view of his overall argument, it is quite clear that the one who convicts and judges is God "the one lawgiver and judge" (4:12), and despite the vividness of James' language, *nomos* here remains the measure by which God makes judgment.

Just as 1:26–27 could be seen as a transitional statement that both recapitulated the development in 1:2–25 and looked forward to the argument of 2:1–26, so can 2:12–13 be regarded as a sort of bridge between parts of James' argument. At first, 2:12 seems completely resumptive as James exhorts his readers to speak and act as those who will be judged by the law of freedom—which we recognize from the content and from 1:25 to mean the teaching of Torah as given perfect expression by the "faith of Jesus." But the notion of being judged inevitably raises the issue of being "righteous" or "unrighteous." Verse 12 also therefore anticipates the discussion in 2:14–26 in which "righteousness" appears. Likewise, v.13, which speaks of merciless judgment of the unmerciful and of mercy triumphing over judgment, points forward to the example of "mercilessness" that James will recount immediately in 2:14–16. But at the same time, it connects that "neglect of the poor" to the merciless "shaming of the poor" in 2:2–4.

2:14–26

14. What use is it, my brothers, if someone says he has faith but does not have deeds? Is the faith able to save him? 15. If a brother or sister is going naked

and lacking daily food, 16. and if one of you should say to them, "Go in peace! Be warmed and filled," but does not give to them what is necessary for the body, what is the use? 17. So also faith, if it does not have deeds, is by itself dead. 18. But someone will say, "you have faith and I have deeds." Show me your faith apart from deeds, and by my deeds I will show you my faith. 19. You believe that God is one. You do well! Even the demons believe, and they shudder! 20. Do you wish to know, you empty fellow, that faith apart from deeds is useless? 21. Was not our father Abraham shown to be righteous on the basis of deeds when he offered his son Isaac on the altar? 22. You see that faith was working together with his deeds, and by the deeds faith was brought to perfection. 23. And the Scripture was fulfilled that declared, "And Abraham believed God and it was reckoned to him as righteousness," and he was called a friend of God. 24. You see that a person is shown to be righteous on the basis of deeds and not on the basis of faith only. 25. And likewise also Rahab the prostitute: was she not shown to be righteous on the basis of deeds when she received the scouts and sent them out by another route? 26. For just as the body apart from spirit is dead, so also faith apart from deeds is dead.

NOTES

14. *what use is it*: The noun *to ophelos* means "advantage/benefit/use." Not surprisingly, James' question is a common one for moralists, who are above all concerned with behavior that shapes character, rather than simple profession of ideals (see, e.g., Plato, *Gorgias* 504E; 513E; Epictetus *Discourses* I, 4, 16; I, 6, 33; III, 24, 51; LXX Job 15:3; Sir 20:30; 41:14; Josephus, *Ant.* 17:154; Philo, *Migration of Abraham* 55; *Posterity and Exile of Cain* 86; 1 Cor 15:32). See also the similar question, using *ophelein* in Matt 16:26; Mark 8:36; Luke 9:25; 1 Cor 14:6. In contemporary terms, the question might be put, "What difference does it make?"

says he has faith but does not have deeds: The logic of the argument suggests that this "saying" is actually a claim to possess faith. The term *pistis* picks up the theme begun in 2:1. Most MSS have the present or aorist subjunctive *echē/ schē*, which has the effect of making the second clause "but does not have deeds" a part of the author's observation, rather than the person's declaration. A few MSS have the infinitive *echein*, which would make the second clause, as well, part of the person's statement: he says that he has faith but not deeds. Perhaps this reading attempts to establish some consistency with the problematic v.18, below. The translation of *erga* as "deeds" attempts to represent more accurately the point as well as to avoid precipitous or inaccurate comparisons with Paul.

is the faith able to save him: The form of the question demands a negative response: "No, the faith is not able to save him." The reader who has followed James' argument to this point already knows the answer. It is the "word of truth" implanted by God that is "able to save their souls" (1:18), but only, as 1:22–25 argues, if they are "doers of the word and not hearers only." The contrast between faith and deeds here, in other words, is the same as that between hearing and deeds earlier. It is God who saves humans (4:12) but the person who has received the word from God that saves and puts it into action in deeds of mercy (2:18–26) and prayer (5:15) and mutual correction (5:20) "saves his soul from death." The context here is not dissimilar to the language concerning faith and deeds (*erga*) in the 2 *Apoc. Bar.* 14:12; 24:1; 51:7; 4 *Ezra* 7:77; 8:32–36; 9:7; 13:23). As in the debate between Jesus and his Jewish opponents in John's Gospel, such discussions consistently deal with the grounds for considering oneself truly a member of God's people. Is it simply ethnic lineage, or a claim to share that heritage's "faith," or is it a matter of living in a certain fashion? As John has Jesus declare: "If you are children of Abraham, do the deeds (*erga*) of Abraham" (John 8:39).

15. *if a brother or sister*: Some MSS provide a *de* or *gar* to provide a smoother transition. James poses the same sort of long and complex hypothetical question (*ean* + subjunctive), followed by a devastating question in the apodosis, that he did in 2:2–4. This is one of the remarkably few instances in the NT where the female equivalent of *adelphos*, designating a member of the community, appears (see also Philemon 2; 1 Tim 5:2; 1 Cor 7:15; 9:5; Rom 16:1).

going naked and lacking daily food: A few witnesses replace the *kai* ("and") with *ē* ("or"). As in the example of 2:2–4, the situation is sketched in vivid and unambiguous terms. The circumstances of the needy are not in doubt. They are dramatic and immediate. Nothing could express vulnerability more than nakedness. It is associated with poverty (Rev 3:17) and shame (Gen 3:10; Ezek 16:7; Rev 3:18). The naked are, therefore, those most obviously in need of assistance (see Tob 1:17; 4:16). The designation echoes the statement in Matt 25:36: "I was naked and you clothed me." For the expression "necessary things," which is roughly equivalent to "daily food," see Dionysius of Halicarnassus, *Roman Antiquities* VI, 23, 3; VIII, 41, 5; Philo, *Against Flaccus* 143. James is describing those whose need is so immediate and obvious that to refuse them is to betray the very nature of covenant (see Sir 4:1–6; 34:20–22). It was for just such as these that every local Jewish synagogue designed the "pauper's dish" to meet emergency needs with no questions asked (see *m.Peah* 5:4; 8:7; 10:1; *m.Demai* 3:1; PA 5:9).

if one of you should say: Literally, "someone (*tis*) from among you (*ex hymōn*)." The translation "should say" aims at the hypothetical sense of the subjunctive. Notice here, that in contrast to 2:2–4, it is an individual's speech that is singled out. As in the former case, however, the speech gives expression to the lack of correspondence between professed ideals and behavior.

go in peace: The greeting "peace" (*eirēnē*) or "go in peace" (*poreuou en eirēnē*) is a staple of the biblical tradition (Judg 6:23; 18:6; 19:20; 1 Sam 20:22; 29:7; 2 Sam 15:27; 2 Kgs 5:19; Jdt 8:35) and enters into Christian usage, found in the stories about Jesus (Mk 5:34; Luke 7:50; 8:48; 24:36; John 20:19), in the exchanges between Christians (Acts 16:36; Eph 6:23; Phil 4:9; 1 Thess 5:23; 3 John 15), and as a standard element in letter-greetings (Rom 1:7; 1 Cor 1:3; 2 Cor 1:2; Gal 1:3; Phil 1:2; Col 1:2; 1 Thess 1:1; 2 Thess 1:2; 1 Tim 1:2; 2 Tim 1:2; Titus 1:4; 1 Pet 1:2; 2 Pet 1:2; Rev 1:4). It is not the form of the statement that is reprehensible, but its functioning as a religious cover for the failure to act. Here is the example of the person who "thinks himself religious" but who shows both a failure to "control the tongue" and refuses to feed "orphans and widows in their trial" (1:26–27).

be warmed and filled· The exhortations correspond to the conditions of nakedness and hunger, revealing that the speaker *knows* the needs but refuses to meet them. The point, once more, is the emptiness of such speech when unaccompanied by effective action (see 1:22–25).

what is necessary for the body: The adjective *epitēdeios* can have the general meaning of "what is suitable, appropriate, or convenient" (see Plato, *Rep.* 390B; 1 Chr 28:2; 1 Macc 4:46), but also what is needed (Herodotus, *Persian War* 2:174; 1 Macc 10:19). The plural substantive here has the stronger meaning: the things *necessary* for the body, that is, the minimal covering and food to sustain life.

what is the use: The apodosis is as harsh a question as that posed in 2:4. It is as if the sketching of the situation itself in such dramatic terms ought to convince the readers of the inappropriateness of their position.

17. *faith if it does not have deeds*: For *houtōs kai* ("thus also"), see 1:11; 2:26; 3:5. The phrase "does not have deeds" picks up 2:14, and as in that place, the term *erga* is translated as "deeds" rather than "works."

is by itself dead: The phrase *kath'heautēn* is literally "according to itself" or "considered alone" (compare Acts 28:16; Rom 14:22). As Mayor, 99, astutely observes, this is not simply reporting "if it has no deeds" but rather points to the essential deadness of a faith that does not yield fruit. The image of death is particularly striking because of the example provided. If the verbal profession of faith does not come to life in acts applicable to those naked and hungry and living on the margin, *they* will die! The exhortation here is very close to that in 1 John 3:17–18.

18. *but someone will say*: Although textually secure, this verse is one of the most difficult in James, or, as Dibelius, 154, claims, in the entire NT. Who is the interlocutor? Is he an opponent or an ally, real or implied? The best solution here is to recognize the diatribal character of this section and see the interlocutor as the imaginary conversation partner who poses an objection that is used by the primary speaker to advance the argument (Dibelius, 154; Ropes, 218; Hort, 60; Marty, 96). That the statement should be taken as an objection is supported by two considerations: a) the *tis* picks up from the earlier uses in 2:14; b) the *alla*

plainly identifies what follows as an objection (compare 1 Cor 15:35; *Barn.* 9:6), against Chaine, 61, and Mussner, 137, who see *alla* as emphatic.

you have faith and I have deeds: The second problem posed by the verse is determining the extent, punctuation, and meaning of the objection. Given the scarcity of punctuation in MSS, there are a number of possibilities. 1) The interlocutor could *ask* "do you have faith?" to which the author could respond, "*and* I have deeds!" 2) The interlocutor could state, "you have faith," and the author could reply, "and I have deeds," etc. 3) The interlocutor could ask, "Do you have faith? And do I have deeds?" 4) The interlocutor could make a statement, "you have faith," followed by a question, "and do I have deeds?" 5) Finally, the interlocutor's statement could, in principle, run all the way through the verse, with all the permutations already given! If, as seems likely, the interlocutor is an imaginary opponent, then it is also most likely that his statement ends at "and I have deeds," since the rest of the statement clearly reflects the author's own position. But this poses the biggest difficulty of all: the interlocutor now appears to hold a position that should be James' own! The positions appear illogically reversed: the interlocutor should claim to have faith rather than deeds, as the *tis* in 2:14 had. But if the position agreed with James, then why would it be placed in an opponent's mouth (this is why some take *alla* as nonadversative). The best solution has been offered by Ropes, 209, (followed by Dibelius, 156), who cites a passage from Teles (Stobaeus, *Anthologium Graecum* III, 1, 98) in which the terms *sy/egō* appear to function as here, that is, to make a statement about the divisibility of the two concepts being discussed. The interlocutor, therefore, would be saying something like, "this person has faith, another has deeds," as though they could stand separately (Laws, 122–24; Davids, 123; Ropes, 208–9). The solution is not entirely satisfactory, but it enables the passage to be read intelligibly without recourse to emendations.

show me: The author responds to the interlocutor in diatribal fashion with an abrupt command: show me! The verse plays on two related meanings of the verb *deiknymi*. James asks him to "show/reveal" what faith without deeds is like (compare Plato, *Thaetetus* 200E; Herodotus *Persian War* 4:150; see also Matt 4:8; Mark 1:44; Luke 24:40; Rev 1:1), whereas he will "prove/demonstrate" faith on the basis of his deeds (compare Plato, *Laws* 896B; Epictetus, *Discourses* I, 6, 43; 1 Cor 12:31). James' other use of *deiknymi* fits this second sense: "Let him demonstrate his deeds out of a good manner of living" (3:13).

19. *you believe that God is one*: There are many textual variants, which have to do mainly with a) the order of the words and b) the presence or absence of the definite article. If the article is lacking, then the content of belief is "that there is one God," namely, a general confession of monotheism. The definite article, in turn, would lead to the translation, "that God is one," which is the specific confession of the Jewish *Shema*ᶜ (see Deut 6:4; *Ep. Arist.* 132; Josephus, *Ant.* 3:91; Philo, *On the Creation* 171; *Decalogue* 65). As to the word-order, the sequence *heis (ho) theos estin* is closer to the characteristic Christian

240

confession (see 1 Cor 8:6; Eph 4:6; 1 Tim 2:5), whereas the sequence *heis estin ho theos* is closer to the normal Jewish version (Deut 6:4; Matt 19:7; Mark 12:29). In any form, the statement makes merely a cognitive assent: *pistis* is reduced to mere belief. The patristic commentators picked up on exactly this point: James is referring to "simple assent," which is not the fullness of faith as response to God in action (Oecumenius, Theophylact).

you do well: The phrase *kalōs poieis* is here clearly meant to be sarcastic, perhaps in direct contrast to the *kalōs poieite* in 2:8.

even the demons believe: The position of the *kai* demands its being read as "even" rather than "also." The sentence needs to be filled out; even the demons believe "that God is one." Although *ta daimonia* could in the Greek world denote a positive divine entity (see Euripides, *Bacchae* 894; Plato, *Apology* 26B; Acts 17:18), here the designation is shaped by the world of Torah. In the LXX *ta daimonia* are identified with false gods (Deut 32:17; Pss 95:5; 105:37; Isa 65:3; also 1 Cor 10:20–21; 1 Tim 4:1; Rev 9:20). In the gospel tradition, *ta daimonia* are identified with the "unclean spirits" who torment humans as the minions of Satan or Beelzebul (see Matt 7:22; 9:32–34; 10:8; 11:18; 12:24–28; 17:18; Luke 4:33; 8:2, 26–39). A remarkable feature of the portrayal of these spirits/demons is that they recognize the visitation of God in Jesus (see Mark 1:24; 5:7).

and they shudder: A wonderful choice of words: *phrissein* is the involuntary reaction of the body in shaking, as in a fever, and is frequently used for reactions of fear (Plato, *Phaedrus* 251A; Philo, *The Worse Attacks the Better* 140). It can be used of a "holy awe" (Plutarch, *How to Study Poetry* 8 [*Mor.* 26B]; Julian the Apostate, *Or.* 7:212B). Magical papyri attest to demons shuddering in response to spells, and similar language is used in later Christian texts (Clement of Alexandria, *Stromateis* V, 125, 1; Justin, *Dialogue with Trypho* 49:8; Pseudo-Clementine *Homilies* V, 5). Whether the response is that of terror or awe, the "faith" of demons plainly shows that one can confess God without doing the deeds that God commands. Bede takes the reaction of demons to Jesus in the gospel tradition as evidence for James' statement.

20. *do you wish to know*: The use of this sort of question is common in the diatribe; compare *ouk oidate* in 4:4 (see also Rom 6:16; 11:2; 1 Cor 3:16; 5:6; 6:2–3, 9, 15, 16, 19; 9:13, 24).

you empty fellow: Literally, "O empty man." Again, such use of apostrophe (direct address to an imaginary interlocutor) is a common feature of the diatribe (see Epictetus, *Discourses* I, 21, 2; II, 6, 17; Plutarch *On Tranquillity of Soul* 8 [*Mor* 469B]; Seneca, *On Anger* III, 28, 1; and compare Rom 2:1, 3; 9:20; Gal 3:1). The choice of *kenos* is also typical (see Epictetus, *Discourses* II, 19, 8; IV, 4, 35; Philo, *Special Laws* 1:311). It denotes empty-headedness or foolishness. It is particularly effective here because of the way the term *kenos* is used to mean "without result/without profit" in passages like Acts 4:25; 1 Cor 15:10, 58; 1 Thess 2:1; and 2 Cor 6:1; and the way in which it sets up the use of *argē* ("without effect/work").

faith apart from deeds is useless: As in 2:18, it is important to recognize that *chōris* simply means "apart from" or "without." James is not asserting *anything* about the value of deeds "apart from" faith. It is precisely the disjunction that he challenges. Above all, there is no reason to read this statement as a response to such Pauline passages as Rom 3:28: "We maintain that a human being is made righteous by faith apart from (*chōris*) the works of the law (*erga tou nomou*)," because that contrast is simply not at issue here. Rather, James' contrast is between mere faith as belief and faith as a full response to God. This makes James' choice of words particularly telling: the adjective *argos* means to be without profit/idle/giving no yield (Xenophon, *Cyropaedia* 3, 2, 19; Philo, *Special laws* 2:86; Wis 14:5; Matt 20:3) because it is *a* + *ergos* = without deed. The textual variants supplying *kenē* ($\mathfrak{P}^{74}$) and *nekra* (the majority of MSS) apparently do not recognize the pun.

21. *our father Abraham*: James unequivocally claims the heritage of Judaism that comes from Abraham. The promise to Abraham in Gen 17:4–5 was that he would be *patēr*; for the designation, see Isa 51:2; Sir 44:19, 22; *Pirke Aboth* 5:2, 19; and in the NT, Matt 3:9; Luke 1:73; 3:8; 16:30; John 8:39, 56; Acts 7:2; Rom 4:1.

shown to be righteous on the basis of deeds: The hardest term to translate here is *dikaioun*, primarily because of its frequent use by Paul in contexts opposing righteousness by faith and "works of the law" (Rom 2:13; 3:4, 20, 24, 26, 28, 30; 4:2, 5; 5:1, 9; 8:30, 33; Gal 2:16–17; 3:8, 11, 24) and the complex use of the verb and its cognates in the OT (e.g., LXX Gen 38:26; Exod 23:7; Deut 25:1; Pss 50:6; 81:3; 142:2; Sir 1:22). The precise meaning in each case must be determined by context, not some general theological concept. Given the previous statement demanding the *demonstration* of faith, the translation here as "shown to be righteous" seems appropriate (see Hort, 63, "appear righteous in God's sight," and Marty, 104, "God sanctions his righteousness"). The meaning would be similar to such NT passages as Matt 11:19; 12:37; and 1 Cor 4:4. The phrase *ex ergōn* (literally, "out of works") has the sense of "on the basis of deeds," meaning that the deeds make his righteousness manifest. At first glance, the sentence appears flatly to contradict Paul's argument concerning the righteousness of Abraham on the basis of faith rather than works (Gal 2:16; 3:5–6; 3:24; Rom 4:2), until we remember that in Paul's case, the contrast is with "works of the law" (including circumcision), whereas in James it is with a *pistis argē* (ineffectual faith).

offered his son Isaac on the altar: James makes explicit reference to the *Akedah* ("the binding of Isaac"), which is recounted in Gen 22:1–18. From Gen 22:9, James draws the term *thysiastērion* ("altar"), but he uses *anapherein* ("offer") from Gen 22:2, 13 rather than the LXX's *epitithēmi* ("place") for the critical moment in 22:9. For the offering of Isaac as one of the trials by which Abraham's faith in God was tested (see James 1:2–4), compare 1 Macc 2:52; Sir 44:20; PA 5:3; *Aboth de Rabbi Nathan* 32; *Jub.* 17:17; 18:15–16; 4 Macc 16:20.

Especially striking is Heb 11:17–19, which declares it was "*pistei* ('by faith') that Abraham *when he was tested* brought forth Isaac and offered his only son." This is James' idea exactly, as the next verse will make clear.

22. *you see*: The verb is singular, catching the intimate demonstration to the supposed interlocutor. This may be only a vivid way to catch attention, or it may pick up the image of the mirror from 1:22–25: the readers can see in the *perfect law* of freedom how faith is *perfected* by deeds.

faith was working together with his deeds: A few MSS have the present tense *synergei*, but the imperfect is better and fits well with the aorist in the next clause. This is, however, one instance where the practice of translating *erga* as "deeds" misses an important nuance in James' statement, which reads literally "faith was co-working with his works."

by the deeds faith was brought to perfection: The verb *teleioun* clearly picks up from 1:4, "let endurance have a perfect product (*teleion ergon*)." In the tradition, Abraham is equally celebrated with Job as one who "endured testing" (1:12; see PA 5:3). Note above all that it is *faith* that is the subject of both clauses. Faith makes possible (co-works) the deeds, and the deeds bring the faith to its mature expression. It is no wonder that patristic commentators found here the same point being made by Paul in Gal 5:6, "in Christ Jesus, neither circumcision matters nor lack of circumcision, but faith working itself out through love (*pistis di'agapēs energoumenē*)." See the discussion of Julian of Halicarnassus in Zachary the Rhetorician's *Capita Selecta ex Historiae Ecclesiasticae* XIX (PG 85:1178).

23. *Scripture was fulfilled*: The use of *plēroun* for designating the way in which texts of Scripture were considered to be "completed" in subsequent events is frequent in the NT (see Matt 1:22; 2:15, 17, 23; 4:14; 8:17; 12:17; 13:14; 21:4; 26:54, 56; 27:9; Mark 14:49; 15:28; Luke 4:21; 24:44; John 13:18; 15:25; 17:12; 19:24; Acts 1:16; Rom 13:8). This is the only such usage in James, and it is distinctive. He states that the *graphē* declaring Abraham righteous in Gen 15:6 was fulfilled by the *deed* that Abraham performed by offering his son Isaac. This is finding a prophecy/fulfillment pattern within Torah itself (see Marty, 105; Davids, 129).

Abraham believed God: James cites the LXX of Gen 15:6 verbatim, except for the connective *de* ("and/but") added by many MSS. For the same citation, see Gal 3:6 and Rom 4:3, 9. Note that James sees the offering of Isaac as the *demonstration* of this faith rather than its replacement.

called a friend of God: This is obviously not part of the citation from Gen 15:6. What, then, is its origin? Two streams come together in this pregnant expression, revealing James' rootedness in both the worlds of Torah and Greco-Roman moral discourse. 1) There was a full-fledged *topos* in Hellenistic moral teaching concerning friendship (*peri philias*). It stressed in various ways the essential equality and unity of friends. They are "one soul" (Euripides, *Orestes* 1046); they "share all things in common" (Aristotle, *Nicomachean Ethics* 9, 8,

2; Plutarch, *On Having Many Friends* 8 [*Mor.* 96F]); a friend is "another self" (*Nicomachean Ethics* 1166A; Cicero, *On Friendship* 21:80). Such proverbs stressed the sharing of outlook between friends. Friends "saw things the same way" because friendship was "equality" (Plato, *Laws* 757A; 744B; *Nicomachean Ethics* 1157B; Iamblichus, *Life of Pythagoras* 29:162; 30:167; Plutarch, *On Brotherly Love* 12 [*Mor.* 484B–C]; Plato, *Lysis* 214B). 2) As part of this same outlook, those who were sages could see themselves as "friends of God" (see Xenophon, *Memorabilia* 2, 1, 33; Plato, *Laws* 716D; Epictetus, *Discourses* IV, 3, 9; Cicero, *On the Nature of the Gods* I, 121–22). 3) Although there are discussions of friendship in Jewish wisdom literature (e.g., Sir 5:15–6:17; 37:1–6), they lack this distinctive Hellenistic coloring. 4) In the Hellenistic Jewish writing *Wisdom of Solomon*, the gift of wisdom (7:14) is seen as enabling friendship with God (*philia pros theon*, 7:14) since it enters into souls and creates "friends of God and prophets" (*philous theou kai prophētas*, 7:27). 5) The only individual called "friend of God" in Torah is Moses, since God spoke with him face to face as to his friend (*philos*, Exod 33:11, translating the Hebrew *rᶜhw*). 6) Abraham is never directly called "God's friend." In 2 Chr 20:7 and Isa 41:8, the LXX renders the Hebrew *'hb* with forms of "to love" (*agapan*), rather than "friend" (*philos*). 7) The passage that above all would give rise to the designation of Abraham as God's friend in the Hellenistic sense is Gen 18:17, "shall I hide from Abraham my servant what I am about to do?" 8) Philo rendered this text *mē epikalypsō egō apo Abraam tou philou mou* ("shall I hide this from Abraham my friend?" [*on Sobriety* 56]). Philo undoubtedly saw God's resolve to share his insights with Abraham as an example of how "friends hold all things in common." He also designates Abraham as *theophilēs* in *On Abraham* 19. 9) The designation of Abraham as "friend" occurs repeatedly in the *T. Abr.* (Recension A; 1:7; 2:3; 2:6). Such is the background of the expression. More significant is the way that James 2:23 connects to the key verse in 4:4. Abraham stands for James as the supreme example of what it means to have "friendship with God" rather than "friendship with the world."

24. *you see*: For the possible connection to the mirror image in 1:22–25, see above on v.22. Now, however, the verb is once more plural. The private instruction over, the author addresses all the readers.

is shown to be righteous on the basis of deeds: For this translation of *dikaioun*, see the note on 2:21. The entire argument rests on the concept of "demonstration." Patristic readers saw the potential for conflict with Paul on this point, but resolved it simply by two distinctions: a) that between faith as "simple assent" and faith as full response in action, and b) that between faith leading to baptism and faith after baptism. They take Paul to be referring to faith before baptism, which is an assent to the Gospel and therefore "saves," using Abraham to make this point. They take James to be referring to faith after baptism that needs to be expressed in deeds like those of Abraham, citing Gal 5:6

to show Paul's fundamental agreement on this point (see *Catena*, Oecumenius, Theophylact, Bede).

on the basis of faith only: The use of the adverb *monon* ("only") corresponds exactly to that in 1:22, where it involved the contrast between "hearing only" and "doing the word" (see Mussner, 127). Here, the contrast has been between "faith only" and "doing the faith." The *monon* is also equivalent to the *pistis kath'heautēn* in 2:17.

25. *Likewise also Rahab the prostitute*: The use of a female *exemplum* is striking. Is it accidental that the figures of Abraham and Rahab correspond to the needy "brother and sister" in 2:15? In Jewish tradition, Rahab was celebrated as a proselyte and as a model of hospitality (see, e.g., *b.Meg.* 14b–15a; *Mekilta* on Exod. par. Jith. Amal. 18:1; *Exodus Rabbah* 27:4; *Numbers Rabbah* 3:2; 8:9; 16:1; *Deuteronomy Rabbah* 2:26–27; *Ruth Rabbah* 2:1; *Song of Songs Rabbah* I, 3, 3; I, 15, 2; IV, 1, 2; VI, 2, 3; *Ecclesiastes Rabbah* V, 6, 1; V, 11, 1; VIII, 10, 1; Josephus, *Ant.* 5:5–30). The story of Rahab in Josh 2:1–21 already makes clear that Rahab's deeds were an expression of *faith*. She reports to the scouts all the works of God that she had heard and concludes with this confession: "For the Lord your God is he who is God in heaven above and on earth beneath" (Josh 2:11). She then acts on this faith by hiding the scouts from those seeking them and sending them back to their people by another route (2:16). In turn, this faith acts for her "salvation" (2:13–14), when Joshua did not destroy her or her family together with the rest of Jericho but "saved her alive" (Josh 6:25). Rahab thereby fits James' paradigm of faith perfectly (see Hort, 66, and Vouga, 90). Rahab's faith is also singled out by Heb 11:31, and the examples of Abraham and Rahab are combined by *1 Clem.* 10 and 12.

just as the body apart from spirit is dead: The *hōsper/houtōs* construction in this sentence corresponds to but reverses the *houtōs/hōs* pattern used earlier. The *pneuma* (without definite article) here means simply "spirit" in the sense of life-principle, that which animates the body (see Pseudo-Aristotle, *On the Soul* 415B; Euripides, *Supplicants* 533; *Sib. Or.* 4:46; LXX Judg 15:19; Ps 30:6; Ezek 37:10; Luke 8:55; 23:46; 1 Cor 7:34).

faith apart from works is dead: The adjective *nekra* picks up the same term from 2:17. The point is not that deeds give life, but that they express life, "demonstrate" that life is present. The obvious assumption is that whatever is living also acts. The ultimate expression of the harmonizing tendency of the patristic tradition can be found in the Pauline/Jacobean tag, "as faith without works is dead, so are works without faith dead," found as early as John Chrysostom, *In Genesin* I, *Homilia* II,5 (PG 53:31), and used frequently thereafter.

COMMENT

For the reader who has followed James' argument to this point, 2:14–26 presents no great puzzle. The theme implicit from the first, namely the necessity of acting out one's faith in consistent deeds, now becomes explicit. And for the reader uncommitted to theories of literary fragmentation, the connection between this section and chapter one is equally obvious. In 1:22–25, James had insisted on being "not only a hearer of the word" but also a doer; now, the contrast is between "faith alone" and the doing of faith (2:18–26). Likewise, in 1:27, James had identified the "visiting of orphans and widows in their distress" as the mark of genuine rather than counterfeit religion. Now, he provides the negative example of the one whose religious language camouflages a failure to respond to the needs of the poor (2:14–17).

The essential connection between this section and the first part of chapter two is also fairly obvious. After the opening rhetorical question in 2:14 that poses the same sort of opposition as did 2:1, James provides a similar lively hypothetical case (2:15–16; see 2:2–3), ending in a rhetorical question (2:16; see 2:4). In 2:5–7, the readers were shown the logical inconsistency of their behavior; now in 2:18–19, the claim that faith and deeds are separable is refuted by a *reductio ad absurdum*. As 2:8–11 argued *halachically* for the unitary character of obedience to the law of love, so 2:20–25 argues *hagadically* from the examples of Abraham and Rahab, given by the narratives of Torah, for the unitary character of faith and faith's deeds. Finally, as the first section ended aphoristically with a *houtōs/hōs* construction (2:12), so does 2:26 conclude this section with an aphorism in *hōsper/houtōs* form. The main difference between the two sections is the appearance of the interlocutor in 2:18, whom James uses, in typical diatribal style, to advance his argument.

Insistence on these internal literary connections and on James' internal logic is all the more necessary because of the disproportionate and distorting attention these verses have received in the history of interpretation. Disproportion and distortion go hand in hand. These verses have received disproportionate attention because they have been seen in relationship to Paul's teaching on righteousness by faith and have, in fact, been primarily read with a view to that point of reference. The verses have therefore also been distorted, for their meaning must be determined not with reference to another author, but from their place in this composition's argument. But by having been taken out of James' context and read over against Paul, James' argument has been lost and these verses distorted.

Responsible interpretation of this part of the composition cannot entirely dismiss or slight such a long history of interpretation. But any attempt to deal with it inevitably makes that "misreading" central and perpetuates its force, precisely when all the interpreter's energies are required to keep focus on James' text on its own literary terms. The strategy adopted in the present commentary has been to discuss the several aspects of the Pauline connection extensively in the Introduction under three rubrics: the literary connections between James and Paul (see I.E.4.d, which provides the extensive bibliography dealing with these verses from that perspective), the historical connections between James and Paul (see II.A–C), and the ways in which this passage has figured in the history of interpretation (see III). These discussions will be assumed here rather than repeated.

Despite the very knotty exegetical problems posed especially by 2:18, the basic points made by James are clear enough and entirely consistent with his overall argument. He opens with the question of *usefulness* but ends with the question of *living* or *dead*. Both questions are actually addressed to the authenticity of faith that is professed but is not demonstrated in deeds (= *erga* = works). As the notes demonstrate, the issue is one typical for moralists both in Greco-Roman and Jewish cultures. The necessary unity between attitude and action was the fundamental assumption of all ancient moral discourse. It enabled polemicists to connect bad morals to bad convictions. It enabled parodists to mock the hypocrisy of those who said one thing and did another. Such an understanding is crystallized in the later scholastic dictum, *agens sequitur esse*: the way something acts follows on its being. The point is never that the deeds substitute for the attitude, but that the deeds *reveal* the attitude; and if there are no deeds, then the attitude is simply "empty" or "profitless" or "dead."

It is within such a moral framework that this part of James must be understood. His opening illustration provides the perfect negative example: the brothers and sisters obviously and desperately in need of food and clothing are dismissed with fond wishes and religious language (2:15–16)! Here indeed is a case of false religion as defined by James 1:26–27, combining self-indulgence, careless use of speech, and a refusal to visit orphans and widows. It is, therefore, not "unstained from the world" and not "pure and undefiled before God."

However the exchange in 2:18 is rendered, the rhetorical function of 2:19 is obviously by means of parody to refute any attempt to sever the assumed connection between faith and deeds. The faith that declares "God is One" is obviously not the "faith" that James sees as adequate. It is, rather, a mockery of true faith, a matter of cognition or confession but not of genuine "love of God" (see 2:5), a fact obvious from the recognition given by demons to the true God even while they shudder in fear.

James' own understanding of genuine ("perfect") faith is revealed in the examples he cites from Torah. Both Abraham and Rahab had faith that was *demonstrated* by their actions. The example of Abraham is much more elaborated. James' choice of the "testing of Abraham" (in God's call to sacrifice his son Isaac) is particularly appropriate, for that act of fidelity by Abraham serves precisely to make James' point: the *Akedah* was not a replacement of faith by deeds but was itself a deed worked by faith: "You see that faith was working together with his deeds" (2:22). And the point of the example is that "*faith* was brought to perfection" (2:22; see 1:4).

For James, the significance of Abraham begins and ends with his faith. The issue is only how that faith is expressed and brought to its fulfillment. And this is why James makes such an interesting use of the citation of Gen 15:6. He says that this text was itself "fulfilled" by the later text of Genesis 22, just as the "faith" of Abraham in response to God's call in Genesis 12 and 15 was brought to its fullest expression in Abraham's obedient offering of his son. It is in this light that the present translation renders the Greek as "shown to be righteous" (2:21, 24), for the entire line of argument here has involved *demonstration*: "show me your faith apart from deeds, and by my deeds I will show you my faith" (2:18).

The distinctive element in James' treatment of Abraham is his designation of the patriarch as "friend of God" (2:23). The notes discuss the background of the term. It is important to emphasize here, however, that this small addition to the citation from Gen 15:6 is hardly accidental. It is, in fact, the most revealing aspect of James' understanding of Abraham within the dualistic framework of his own composition. As we have seen, James has been opposing the measure of the world to the measure of God. Earlier in this chapter, he explicitly opposed the measures of world/God with respect to the honor/shame shown to the rich/poor. This ethical dualism will become fully explicit in 4:4, when James will pose an absolute distinction between "friendship with the world" and "friendship with God."

Abraham, then, represents above all the person of faith who is *not* double-minded, who truly thinks and acts according to the measure of God. If Abraham had been a "friend of the world," he would not have been willing to offer his son in sacrifice, for he would have viewed life as a closed system in which his future was determined by what he possessed. Even though Isaac was a gift from God, he was now Abraham's possession and his hope for the future possession of the land. Thinking in worldly terms, then, killing his son when he had no human hope for another was foolishness.

But Abraham was a "friend of God" because he measured by God's measure. He viewed the world as an open system in which God gives generously to all without grudging (1:5) and is the giver of every good and perfect gift (1:17) and to the humble gives a greater gift (4:6). If God gave Isaac, then God could give another gift. Abraham's willingness to give back to God what God had given demonstrated and perfected his faith and revealed what "friendship with God" might mean.

The example of Rahab is sketched in only one verse, but her presence here raises an intriguing question concerning James' overall point. We notice that in her case, James—in contrast to Heb 11:31—makes no mention of her faith, although the fact that her reception and concealment of the Israelite spies was motivated by her faith is made clear in the narrative in Joshua that recounts the story. But James makes no real point of the connection between faith and action here. As in other Jewish traditions concerning Rahab, it is above all her act of hospitality that is singled out for attention.

Why does James include Rahab at all if he does not develop her significance more fully? This question, together with James' odd use of the plural "works" (*erga*) with reference to Abraham in 2:21–22—odd, because only one "work," the offering of Isaac, is mentioned—caused R. B. Ward ("Works of Abraham," 283–90) to ponder the more complex midrashic implications of James' use of Abraham and Rahab. Ward notes that Abraham is one of the figures from Torah (together with Job) who are, in the Rabbinic tradition, most highly praised for their hospitality (see, e.g., Philo, *On Abraham* 167; *Aboth de Rabbi Nathan* 7; *T. Abr.* 1:3; 4:1–11; *Genesis Rabbah* XLIX, 4; LV, 4; LXI, 5).

He asks, therefore, if by implication James means to include Abraham's deeds of hospitality among those "works" that demonstrate his faith. This would certainly make sense of the inclusion of Rahab as his partner in illustration. It would also provide a male/female model of hospitality to match the "brother or sister" in need (2:15). Even more pertinently, the examples of Abraham and Rahab together then fit the overall argument of chapter two, which concerns at the general level the translation of faith into appropriate deeds, but which at the particular level concerns the way in which the poor are treated within the community. In the examples of Abraham and Rahab, who received all the needy, the community finds models for its own reception of the poor without discrimination and with effective and not simply verbal care.

If James' argument is carefully followed throughout chapter two (and indeed as flowing from chapter one), this final section appears less as a "special topic" than as a natural progression. There is absolutely no reason to read this section as particularly responsive to Paul. But if that is the case, two questions linger.

First, is it really plausible that James could find it necessary to remind Jewish Christians of the first generation on such a fundamental point as this? Second, if James' point is so different from Paul's, then why does he use a language that is found elsewhere mainly in Paul?

The answer to the first question is straightforwardly, "Yes, messianic Jews in the first generation could need such reminders." The assumption that first-century Jews, either in Palestine or in the Diaspora, were all "Pharisaic" in their devotion to Torah is a distortion caused by reading earlier realities through the lens of a later normative Judaism. Judaism in the first century was widely diverse, and "Jewish Christianity" was also in all likelihood a diverse phenomenon. The evidence of the Gospels suggests that the Jesus movement in Palestine succeeded most among those who were not particularly devoted to Torah. The range of extant moral literature from Judaism, furthermore, suggests that there were any number of those calling themselves Jews who were in need of vigorous reminding that "true Judaism" meant obedience to the commandments (see only Matt 3:8–9; Rom 2:17–29).

It is certainly possible for there to have been converts from among ordinary Jewish folk to the messianic movement, both in Palestine and the Diaspora, who had an equally "technical" commitment to "the faith" and who needed strong reminders of the need to translate identity into action. Passages such as Matt 7:21, after all, had some target: "Not everyone who says to me, 'Lord, Lord,' shall enter the kingdom of heaven, but he who does the will of my father who is in heaven" (see also Matt 25:31–46). The writer of 1 John 3:17–18, which is almost a perfect parallel to our passage, also had some intended audience: "If anyone has the world's goods and sees his brother in need, yet closes his heart against him, how does God's love abide in him? Little children, let us not love in word or speech but in deed and truth."

The answer to the second question, "why does James use language so associated with Paul," is more difficult to answer, because to be convincing it requires a review of literature more extensive than this commentary can provide in its limited space. But the basic point can be stated clearly enough. It is not that discussions of "faith and works" are absent elsewhere in Jewish and Christian literature; as the notes demonstrate, these combinations do occur. It is not that "faith and righteousness" do not occur in combination, for they do, nowhere more impressively than in the Qumran writings. And Abraham certainly is used as an example elsewhere; the notes show how omnipresent Abraham is in this literature.

The problem, rather, is that James and Paul bring these elements together in unusual concentration. It, therefore, *appears* that they are discussing the same topic. In fact, as I tried to show earlier, they are not. They use the same words but in different ways. The direction of James' argument is different from the direction of Paul's.

But then why is the language so close? The best answer is probably to be found not in a hypothetical power struggle between early Christian leaders, or in a subtle literary polemic, but in the simple fact that both James and Paul were first generation members of a messianic movement that defined itself in terms of the "faith of Jesus." And because both Paul and James were Jewish and interacted primarily with Palestinian Judaism, they both instinctively turned to Torah for that explication and found—as did the Christian movement generally—the figure Abraham as open to midrashic exploitation. From within their separate concerns, they developed separate midrashic arguments that converge at the semantic level in intriguing (yet obvious) ways, yet diverge at the level of meaning in still more important ways.

BIBLIOGRAPHY

Bacon, B. W., "The Doctrine of Faith in Hebrews, James and Clement of Rome," *JBL* 19 (1900) 12–21.

Baird, W., "Abraham in the New Testament," *Int* 42 (1988) 367–79.

Barton, G., "The Meaning of the 'Royal Law,' Matt. 5:21–48," *JBL* 37 (1918) 54–65.

Boyle, M. O'Rourke, "The Stoic Paradox of James 2:10," *NTS* 31 (1985) 611–17.

Brinktrine, J., "Zu Jak. 2, 1," *Bib* 35 (1954) 40–42.

Countryman, L. Wm., *The Rich Christian in the Church of the Early Empire: Contradictions and Accommodations* (Texts and Studies in Religion 7; New York: Edwin Mellen, 1980).

Donker, C. E., "Der Verfasser und sein Gegner: Zum Problem des Einwandes in Jak 2:18–19," *ZNW* 72 (1981) 227–40.

Dyrness, W., "Mercy Triumphs over Justice: James 2:13 and the Theology of Faith and Works," *Themelios* 6 (1981) 11–16.

Eckart, K.-G., "Zur Terminologie des Jakobusbriefes," *TLZ* 89 (1964) 522–26.

Fabris, R., *Legge della Liberta in Giacomo* (Supplementi alla Revista Biblica 8; Brescia: Paideai, 1977).

Frankemölle, H., "Gesetz im Jakobusbrief: Zur Tradition, kontextuellen Verwendung und Rezeption eines belasteten Begriffes," in *Das Gesetz im Neuen Testament*, ed. K. Kertelge (QD 108; Freiburg: Herder, 1986) 175–221.

Hands, A. R., *Charities and Social Aid in Greece and Rome* (Ithaca: Cornell University Press, 1968) 77–88.

Hanson, A. T., "Rahab the Harlot in Early Christian Tradition," *JSNT* 1 (1978) 53–60.

Hodges, Z. C., "Light on James 2 from Textual Criticism," *Bibliotheca Sacra* 120 (1963) 341–50.

Jacobs, I., "The Midrashic Background for James II, 21–23," *NTS* 22 (1975–76) 457–62.

Johnson, L. T., *Sharing Possessions: Mandate and Symbol of Faith* (Overtures to Biblical Theology; Philadelphia: Fortress Press, 1981).

———, "The Use of Leviticus 19 in the Letter of James," *JBL* 101 (1982) 391–401.

Karo, G., "Versuch Über Jac. 2,18," *Protestantlische Monatshefte* 4 (1900) 159–60.

Kilpatrick, G. D., "Übertreter des Gesetzes, Jak. 2,11," *TZ* 23 (1967) 433.

Longenecker, R., "The 'Faith of Abraham' Theme in Paul, James, and Hebrews: A Study in the Circumstantial Nature of New Testament Teaching," *JETS* 20 (1977) 203–12.

McKnight, S., "James 2:18a: The Unidentifiable Interlocutor," *WTJ* 52 (1990) 355–64.

Marconi, G., "La struttura di Giacomo 2," *Bib* 68 (1987) 250–57.

Mehlhorn, P., "Noch ein Erklärungsversuch zu Jac 2,18," *Protestantische Monatshefte* 4 (1900) 192–94.

Mitchell, A. C., *1 Corinthians 6:1–11: Group Boundaries and the Courts of Corinth* (Ph.D. diss., Yale University, 1986).

Nötscher, F., " 'Gesetz der Freiheit' im NT und der Mönchsgemeinde am Toten Meer," *Bib* 34 (1953) 193–94.

Peterson, E., "Der Gottesfreund: Beiträge zur Geschichte eines religiösen Terminus," *ZKG* 42 (1923) 161–202.

Quecke, H., "Ein altes bohairisches Fragment des Jakobusbriefes," *Orientalia* 43 (1974) 382–92.

Rönsch, H., "Abraham der Freund Gottes," *ZWT* 16 (1873) 583–90.

Ropes, J. H., " 'Thou hast Faith and I have Works,' (James II.18," *The Expositor* seventh series 5 (1908) 547–57.

Rusche, H., "Vom lebendigen Glauben und vom rechten Beten: Einführung in die Grundgedanken des Jakobusbriefes (2, 14–26; 4, 1–10)," *BibLeb* 6 (1965) 26–37.

———, "Der Erbarmer hält Gericht: Einführung in die Grundgedanken des Jakobusbriefes (2:1–13a)," *BibLeb* 5 (1964) 236–46.

Seitz, O. J. F., "James and the Law," *SE* 2 (1964) 472–86.

Siker, J. S., *Disinheriting the Jews: Abraham in Early Christian Controversy* (Louisville; Westminster/John Knox Press, 1991).

Soards, M. L., "The Early Christian Interpretation of Abraham and the Place of James within that Context," *IBS* 9 (1987) 18–26.

Theissen, G., *The Social Setting of Pauline Christianity: Essays on Corinth*, ed. and trans. J. H. Schütz (Philadelphia: Fortress Press, 1982) 145–74.

Van der Westhuizen, J. D. N., "Stylistic Techniques and their Functions in James 2:14–26," *Neot* 25 (1991) 89–107.

Vokes, F. E., "The Ten Commandments in the New Testament and in First Century Judaism," *SE* 5 (1968) 146–54.

Wachob, W. H., *"The Rich in Faith and the Poor in Spirit": The Socio-Rhetorical Function of a Saying of Jesus in the Epistle of James* (Ph.D. diss., Emory University, 1993).

Ward, R. B., *The Communal Concern of the Epistle of James* (Ph.D. diss., Harvard University, 1966).

———, "Partiality in the Assembly: James 2:2–4," *HTR* 62 (1969) 87–97.

———, "The Works of Abraham: James 2:14–26," *HTR* 61 (1968) 283–90.

Watson, D. F., "James 2 in Light of Greco-Roman Schemes of Argumentation," *NTS* 39 (1993) 94–121.

Wiersma, S., "Enige Opmerkingen over de Betekenis van de Woorden Diakrinesthai en Pistis in de Brief van Jacobus," *Gereformeerd theologisch tijdschrift* 56 (1956) 177–79.

Windisch, H., "Zur Rahabsgeschichte," *ZAW* 35 (1917–18) 188–98.

IV. THE POWER AND PERIL OF SPEECH
3:1–12

◆

3:1. Not many of you, my brothers, should become teachers, since you know that we will receive a more severe judgment. 2. For we all fail in many ways. If someone does not fail in speech, this person is perfect, powerful enough to guide the whole body as well. 3. And if we place bits in the mouths of horses in order to make them obey us, we lead their whole bodies around as well. 4. See also how great ships buffeted by severe winds are guided by the tiniest rudder wherever the will of the steersman desires. 5. So also the tongue is a small member, and it boasts of great things. See how small a flame sets such a large forest ablaze! 6. And the tongue is a fire. The tongue is the world of wickedness established among our members. It pollutes the entire body. And even as it is inflamed from Gehenna, it sets aflame the cycle of life. 7. For every kind of beast and bird, of snake and sea-creature, is being tamed, indeed has been tamed, by humankind. 8. But no human can tame the tongue. It is a restless evil. It is full of death-dealing poison. 9. With it, we bless the Lord and Father. And with it we curse the people who have been made according to God's likeness. 10. Blessing and curse come out of the same mouth! My brothers, things like this should not happen! 11. Does the spring gush forth both sweet and bitter water from the same opening? 12. Is it possible, my brothers, for a fig tree to produce olives, or for the grapevine to produce figs? Neither does a salty source produce sweet water.

THE SECTION
AS A WHOLE

This is one of the more obviously self-contained sections in the letter. Like 2:1, it begins with a prohibition of a general character and, like 2:26, concludes with a short aphorism. It can be argued that 3:13–18 continues the same line of thought, with "the one who is wise" being taken as equivalent to the "teacher" (see Ropes, 226). But as the later analysis will show, the language of 3:13–18 turns more obviously toward 4:1–10, and 3:13–4:10 forms a single rhetorical unit.

At the same time, 3:1–12 stands as an intelligible discourse on its own. It is bracketed by the opening *adelphoi mou* in 3:1 and the closing *adelphoi mou* of 3:12. The section opens with a negative commandment (*mē*) and accompanying maxims (3:1–2). It closes with two rhetorical questions (*mēti . . . mē*) and a final aphorism (3:11–12). The essay shows signs of careful composition. There is a high incidence of alliteration: *polla ptaiomen . . . hapantes* (3:2); *mikros melos . . . megalē* (3:5); *phlogizousa . . . phlogizomenē* (3:6); *damazetai . . . dedamastai* (3:7); *damasai dynatai* (3:8). There is the repeated use of *idou* (in 3:4–5) and the balanced clauses, *hēlikēn pyr hēliken hylēn* in 3:5 and *en autē . . . en autē* in 3:9. The use of particles, furthermore, demonstrates that something more than a loose collection of aphorisms have been brought together; James is constructing an argument.

Already in 3:1–2, the direction of his argument is announced: on the one hand, 3:2 seems to agree that human perfection is possible and that control of speech represents the height of that perfection. On the other hand, the prohibition in 3:1 seems to state a harsher perception: that the business of being a speaker is a perilous one. Following this opening ambiguous set of statements, 3:3–4 develop the optimistic side according to the typical Hellenistic *topos* on the control of speech. But 3:5–6 move in a far more pessimistic direction, by emphasizing both the power of the tongue and its fundamentally destructive character. This pessimism is given most explicit statement in 3:7–8, which contrasts the control of humans over beasts to the human failure in controlling "savage speech." The *exemplum* provided by 3:9–10 is explicitly theological and draws the discussion of speech into the ethical and religious dualism that dominates the composition as a whole: nothing could more dramatically reveal the destructiveness of the tongue than the cursing of another human person; nothing could more harshly reveal the human attempt to live by two measures simultaneously than to have such cursing emerge from a mouth that also blessed God. The theme of "doubleness" is then developed by the rapid series of contrasts in 3:11–12, all of which have the simple point: this ought not to be so.

We have seen that James tends to announce themes in chapter one that are developed in later essays. 3:1–2 obviously elaborate the statements found in 1:19, "Let every person be quick to hear, slow to speak, slow to anger," and 1:26, "If anyone considers himself religious without bridling his tongue and while indulging his heart, then this person's religion is worthless." But this essay on the power and perils of the tongue also provides an explicit discussion of a theme that runs throughout the composition. The proper and improper uses of speech are of central concern to James. Before this essay, we have seen as negative modes of speech the self-justifying claim that one is tempted by God (1:13), the flattering speech that reveals partiality toward the rich and shames the poor (2:3–6), the careless speech of those who wish well toward the poor but do not help them (2:16), the superficial speech of the one claiming to have faith even without deeds (2:18). After this essay, we shall see these other examples of improper speech: judging and slandering a brother (4:11), boasting of one's future plans without regard for God's will (4:13), grumbling against a brother (5:9). And in 5:12–20, James will develop the proper modes of speech within the community of faith.

NOTES

1. *not many . . . teachers*: The designation "teacher" (*didaskalos*) is attributed to Jesus in the gospel tradition (see Matt 8:19; 23:8; Mark 4:38; Luke 9:38; John 13:13–14) and is attested as a title for ministers within the messianic movement (Acts 13:1; 1 Cor 12:28–29; Eph 4:11). As in 2:1, the negative command using the present tense has a gnomic quality and serves to highlight the moral discussion that follows. The prohibition is not meant to check an unwelcome development. There is no reason to think that too many were becoming teachers (Adamson, 146) and even less to think (against Trocmé, "églises paulinienne," 665; Vouga, 94–95) that James intends here an anti-Pauline polemic (with Laws, 141; Marty, 117; Dibelius, 183). Chrysostom, it is true, understands the prohibition to be against those who taught that it was not necessary to combine deeds with faith, but he does not connect this with Paul. The Old Latin *Speculum* reads *multiloqui* ("speakers of many things"). Mussner, 159, comes close to this by reading *polla* adverbially and translating, "do not teach at great length."

since you know: Although the adverbial participle *eidotes* could go either with the second person or third person plural, it is more naturally placed with the second person: knowledge of their peril grounds the readers' avoidance of this dangerous office (compare the use of *ginōskō* in 1:3).

receive a more severe judgment: The shift to the first person plural is surprising since the implied association of the author with *didaskaloi* provides the first personal note since the greeting in 1:1. The precise meaning of *krima* here is difficult. Does it mean (so Laws, 144) that they are to be judged by a higher standard (compare Epictetus, *Discourses* II, 15, 8; Rom 5:16), or does it mean (so Ropes, 226; Dibelius, 182) that they will be punished more severely (see Rom 2:2; 3:8; 1 Cor 11:34; 2 Pet 2:3)? The English "judgment" allows both construals. For the construction, see Rom 13:2; for the idea that teachers receive a harsher sentence, see the condemnation of the Scribes by Jesus in Mark 12:38–40: *houtoi lēpsontai perissoteran krima* ("these shall receive a greater judgment"; compare Matt 23:13; Luke 20:47). Once more, James' allusion to "what they should know" includes an awareness of the Jesus tradition.

2. *we all fail in many ways*: The connective *gar* indicates that this is explanatory of the previous sentence. By itself, however, the statement does not completely clarify why teachers should receive more severe judgment; that must be teased out from the conviction that errors in speech are most pervasive and destructive and are virtually unavoidable by teachers: "Teachers being men of words *par excellence* are particularly exposed to the danger of sins of speech" (Laws, 140). The verb *ptaiein* (see also 2:10) does not by itself suggest moral failure but can cover a variety of "stumblings" and "trippings" (see Josephus, *JW* 6:64; Rom 11:11). The adage "we all fail in many ways" is a Hellenistic commonplace (see, e.g., Thucydides, *Peloponnesian War* III, 45, 3; Seneca, *On Clemency* I, 6, 3; Epictetus, *Discourses* I, 11, 7; Philo, *On the Unchangeableness of God* 75). In Greek patristic literature following James, his version of the truism enters moral discourse (see, e.g., Origen, *Selecta in Psalmos*, Hom. IV in Ps, XXXVI, 2 [PG 12: 1351]; Cyril of Alexandria, *De Adoratione in Spiritu et Veritate* XV [PG 68: 949]; Procopius of Gaza, *Commentarius in Leviticum* XI, 2 [PG 87: 727]).

this person is perfect: The use of *teleios* ("perfect") is somewhat startling in the light of 1:4, 17, 25; 2:8, 22. These passages all emphasized that speech was perfected by deeds. Can James seriously think that "perfection in speech" can make a person perfect? Two premises seem to be at work. First, for James, speech *is* an "act" or "work," a manifestation of the inner self and its dispositions. Second, James assumes that speech directs other actions, as the metaphors that follow demonstrate. Once more, there was widespread agreement in Hellenistic moral teaching that speech was dangerous and, in order to avoid error, either silence or brevity was best (see Diogenes Laertius, *Lives of Eminent Philosophers* VII, 26; Apollonius of Tyana, *Letters* 81–82; Plutarch, *On the Education of Children* 14 [Mor 10F]; *On Hearing Lectures* 4 [Mor 39C]; *On Garrulousness* 23 [Mor 515A]), a bias that was shared as well by Jewish wisdom (Prov 12:13; 13:3; 21:23; Sir 14:1; 19:6; 20:18; 22:27; 25:8; 28:12–16; Philo, *On Flight and Finding* 136). The closest parallel to James on the perfection of the one who has perfected speech is found in Philo, *The Posterity and Exile of Cain* 88 and *The Migration of Abraham* 73.

powerful enough to guide: The adjective *dynatos* is here roughly equivalent to *dynamenos* ("to be able"), which in fact is contained in some MSS. The translation "powerful enough" helps establish the comparisons that follow. For the use of *chalinagōgein* ("control with a bit of bridle"), see the discussion on 1:26. The verb serves to set up the following comparison.

the whole body as well: Perhaps the *kai* can be taken as intensive: "even the whole body." This would emphasize the disparity between the tongue and that which it controls. The "whole body" here obviously means a person's physical movements and, specifically, the person's moral actions. In 1:26, it was the tongue that was to be controlled; here it controls the body.

3. *and if we place bits*: The textual problem here is severe. There is substantial manuscript support either for *idou* ("behold") or *ide* ("see"), and one of those readings is accepted by such commentators as Windisch, 22; Chaine, 77–78; Mayor, 108–9; Ropes, 229; Adamson, 141; and Laws, 146. In addition to the manuscript support, this reading would match the use of *idou* in 3:4, which is followed by a *kai* ("also"). The reading followed here is *ei de* ("and if"), which could well, through itacism, have been mistaken for either *idou* or *ide*. This is the harder reading, since it creates a very awkward conditional, but it is probably correct. It is adopted by the 26th edition of Nestle-Aland and such commentators as Hort, 69; Marty, 119; Dibelius, 184–85; Cantinat, 168; Mussner, 158; Vouga, 93; Davids, 138; and Martin, 102–3.

in order to make them obey us: The use of *chalinagōgein* in 3:2 prepared for the image of the bit or bridle (*chalinon*) being placed in the mouths of horses to control them (see Xenophon, *Cyropaedia* IV, 3, 9). The image of the charioteer as one who controls powerful beasts is widespread (see, e.g., Dio, *Or.* 36:50; Philo, *Decalogue* 60; *On Special Laws* 1:14) and, especially following Plato's appropriation of the image for reason's control of the passions (see *Phaedrus* 246B–247C), found in moral discourse (see, e.g., Aristippus [in Stobaeus, *Anthologium* III, 17, 17]; Pseudo-Aristotle, *On the World* 400B; Plutarch, *How to Study Poetry* 12 [*Mor.* 33F]; Philo, *On Husbandry* 69; *On the Creation* 86–88; *Allegorical Laws* 3:223; *On Husbandry* 69; *The Confusion of Tongues* 115; *Against Flaccus* 26; *On Joseph* 149.

4. *see also how great ships*: Literally, "behold" (*idou*), which is repeated in 5b. The first of two textual problems in this verse concerns the placement of a second definite article *ta* before *tēlikauta*, which would make the participle more obviously attributive. The present translation glosses the difficulty by translating "how great ships" rather than by the more literal "behold also the ships, being so great. . . ." For *tēlikautos*, see 2 Cor 1:10; Heb 2:3; Rev 16:18.

buffeted by violent winds: The verb *elaunein* basically means "to drive" (see Luke 8:29) and is used in sailing for the propulsion given by the wind (Josephus, *Ant.* 5:205; Mark 6:48; 2 Pet 2:17). In the present case, the winds are "severe" or "violent" (*sklēros*; compare LXX Prov 27:16), so "buffeted" is an appropriate translation. The emphasis is on the difficulties for control posed by the combination of mass and force. The reader is reminded of the unfavorable nautical comparison made in 1:6 concerning the double-minded person.

guidance of the tiniest rudder: The elative superlative *elachistos* (Zerwick/ Grosvener, 696) could be rendered simply by "very small" (RSV; NB), but the exaggerated contrast is best captured by the translation given. The verb *metagein* ("guide") is the same used in v. 3 for the direction given horses.

wherever the will of the steersman desires: A number of MSS have an alternative construction, using *an* (*ean*) + the subjunctive; the meaning is not affected. The noun *hormē* ("will") can be taken as mere "impulse" (see Plutarch, *On Moral Virtue* 12 [*Mor* 452C]). Once more, the image of the pilot or steersman guiding a huge ship by means of a rudder is both ancient (found as early as *The Sayings of Amen-Em-Opet* 8) and widely used in moral discourse (see Dio, *Oration* 12:34; Cicero, *On the Nature of the Gods* II, 34, 89; Lucian of Samosata, *The Double Indictment* 2; Philo, *On the Cherubim* 36; *On Abraham* 70; *Confusion of Tongues* 115). In this case, James makes all three components explicit: the guiding desire (the steersman), the means of control (the rudder), and that which is controlled (the ship), corresponding in turn to human desire, the tongue, and the body.

5. *so also*: The phrase *houtōs kai* draws the previous comparisons (bit/horse; rudder/ship) to their specific application; compare James' use of the same construction in 1:11, 2:17, and 2:26. Some MSS read *hōsautōs* ("similarly").

is a small member: James' fondness for alliteration is shown by the threefold repetition of *m* (*mikron/melos/megala*; see Laws, 147). The noun *melos* here and in the next verse has its ordinary meaning of a part of the body (see Josephus, *JW* 1:656; Philo, *Against Flaccus* 176; 1 Cor 12:12). The usage in 4:1 is more problematic.

and boasts of great things: James uses the verb *auchein* (here with the accusative), which, while widely enough attested in Hellenistic literature (see Herodotus, *Persian War* 7:103; Lucian of Samosata, *Dialogues of the Dead* 2:2), is otherwise unattested in the LXX or NT. Perhaps scribal unfamiliarity helps account for the textual variant *megalauchei*, which *is* attested in the LXX (see Ps 9:39; Sir 48:18; Zeph 3:11). Similar to its conflated reading in 3:1, the Old Latin Speculum here has *magniloqua*. James does not denounce such boasting for, in fact, the tongue's claims are correct (see Hort, 70; Mayor, 112).

how small a flame: James plays on the two possible meanings of the adjective *hēlikos*. With regard to the forest (*hylē*), the term means "how great" (compare Josephus, *Ant.* 8:208; Col 2:1); and with regard to the flame (*pyr*), the same term means "how small" (compare Lucian, *Hermotimus* 5; Epictetus, *Discourses* I, 12, 26). The textual variant *oligos* ("little") must be seen as a "correction" made by a scribe who did not recognize this polyvalence. Bede is aware of the textual variant and provides an interpretation for each version. For *hylē* as "forest," see Josephus, *Ant.* 18:357; Sir 28:10; *Sentences of Pseudo-Phocylides* 144; Philo, *Decalogue* 173; and for the capacity of fire to destroy the forest, see *Sentences of Pseudo-Phocylides* 144; 1QH 5:13–14. The most striking parallel is provided by Philo, *On the Decalogue* 173: "For nothing escapes desire . . . like a flame in the forest, it spreads abroad and consumes and destroys everything."

6. *and the tongue is a fire*: This makes a natural stopping point for concluding the previous statement (Mayor, 113). The structure of 5b–6b is chiastic: the tongue is a member/fire burns a forest/the tongue is a fire/it is the world of wickedness among our members. The metaphor is carried by metonymy: the physical organ of the tongue = speech, and fire = speech's destructive effects.

The following statements play out the metaphorical possibilities. For the image of the tongue as a fire, see LXX Prov 16:26–27; Sir 28:11, 22; *Pss. Sol.* 12:2; *Leviticus Rabbah* 16:4; Plutarch, *On Garrulousness* 10 (*Mor* 507B).

the world of wickedness established among our members: This verse is notoriously difficult. Ropes, 233–34, declares that no satisfactory interpretation is possible in the present form of the text, while Windisch, 23, and Dibelius, 194–95, consider it a gloss. The problems revolve mainly around how to understand the phrase *ho kosmos tēs adikias*, especially since it has a definite article, and how to understand it syntactically in relation to the substantive "the tongue" and the attributive participles that follow it (*he spilousa . . . phlogizousa . . . phlogizomenē*). Inadequate solutions include translating *kosmos* as "ornament" (Oecumenius; Chaine, 81) or following the Vulgate's "sum total of wickedness (*universitas iniquitatis*) or the Peshitta's allegorical, "The tongue is fire, the sinful world, wood" (followed by Adamson, 143). Some MSS have tried to lessen the problem by adding *houtōs* and turning the statement into a simile. But James is working with metaphor, not simile. He is not simply stating that the tongue is *like* "a world of wickedness" (Marty, 126). Syntactically, the phrase is best understood as the predicate of *kathistēmi* (Hort, 7; Ropes, 234; Dibelius, 194) or at least as in apposition to "the tongue" (so Mussner, 163; Martin, 114). James' meaning is only to be grasped in the light of 1:27 and 2:5, where *kosmos* and God are opposed, and in light of 4:4, where the same verb (*kathistēmi*) is used for those whose choice of "friendship with the world" has "established" them as an enemy of God (see Mayor, 115–16; Marty, 126). As Mayor, 115, observes, "in our microcosm, the tongue represents or constitutes the unrighteous world." The expression "among our members" means our physical bodies, but the metaphor extends naturally to the power of speech in the assembly of believers. Although Reicke's elaborate allegory of the body standing for the community is not convincing (37; see also Vouga, 97; Martin, 104; Davids, 139), there is no reason to think that such a natural extension of ideas would be foreign to James.

it pollutes the entire body: For emphasis, the translation makes the attributive participle into an independent sentence. The use of the verb *spiloun* ("pollute/stain"; see also *T. Ash.* 2:7; Jude 23) is particularly appropriate here, for it corresponds to the directive in 1:27 to "Keep oneself unstained (*aspilon*) from the world (*apo tou kosmou*)." But now the "world of wickedness" dwells in the very body! Once more, the term *sōma* here means first the individual's body, but it can be extended—especially in the light of James' covenantal interest—to the communal body as well (see the previous note).

even as it is inflamed from Gehenna: The translation reverses the order of the Greek participial phrases in order to place the *effect* of speech in the prominent final position. The verb *phlogizein* ("to set afire;" see Exod 9:24; Num 21:14; Ps 96:3) is used in both phrases, a repetition the translation seeks to capture by "enflamed/sets aflame." The noun *geena* does not occur as such in the LXX, although *gaienna* appears in Josh 18:16. It is the Grecized form of *gê ben-hinnōm* or *gê'-hinnōm* ("Valley of Hinnom"; see Josh 15:8; Neh 11:30). It appears in some Jewish and Christian apocalyptic literature (see "fiery gehenna" in *Apoc. Abr.* 15:6; *Apoc. Ezra* 1:9; *Ascension of Isaiah* 1:3; 4:14; *Sib. Or.* 1:100–105, and 2 *Clem.* 5:4. In the NT it occurs only in the Gospels as a place of punishment (Matt 5:22, 29, 30; 10:28; 18:9; 23:15, 33; Mark 9:45, 47; Luke 12:5). It is associated with *fire* in Matt 5:22; 18:9. The usage by James would seem to indicate a close connection either to Jewish usage or the developing gospel tradition. Note also how the consuming fire in *1QH* 5:13 is connected to the "torrents of Satan." Bede understands by Gehenna "the devil and his angels."

sets aflame the cycle of life: Depending on how it is accented, *trochos* means either "wheel" (*Iliad* 6:42) or "course." It can refer to any number of literally wheel-shaped things (LXX 2 Sam 24:22; Ps 76:19; Prov 20:26). Metaphorically, it can easily be applied to fortune, which now favors one person and now another. Such usage was as pervasive in Jewish as in Greco-Roman literature (see, e.g., *Sentences of Pseudo-Phocylides* 27; *Syb. Or.* 2:295; *Exodus Rabbah* 31:3; *Leviticus Rabbah* 34:3; *b.Shab.* 151b; Philo, *On Dreams* 2:44). The modifier *geneseōs* provides an obvious balance to *geena* in the previous phrase. But how should it be taken? The noun *genesis* can mean beginnings and origin (see Luke 1:14; Matt 1:1) or simply "existence" (Plato, *Phaedrus* 252D; Jdt 12:18; Wis 7:5). In James' other usage (1:23), it refers to origin: when the person glances at *to prosōpon tēs geneseōs autou*, it is equivalent to "his natural face." Commentators give considerable attention to this phrase in James because of its possible connections with ancient Orphism, where the expression seemed to have been a technical one (see Dibelius, 196–98). As Ropes notes, "The interest of the phrase lies not so much in its exact meaning as in the fact that it cannot be accounted for from Jewish modes of expression and implies contact with (though not understanding of) Greek thought" (236). In fact, however, as our references show, the image of the wheel as symbol for life's cyclic circumstances was widely diffused in Hellenistic as well as Rabbinic Judaism. Although Theophylact is aware of a textual variant that reads "wheel of Gehenna," he prefers "wheel of becoming" and, like Bede, Oecumenius, and the *scholia* takes it to mean the round of human life with its temporal changes. The point of the image in James is that the tongue is not only influenced by cosmic evil but affects all of life. A thoroughly pessimistic view.

7. *for every kind of beast and bird*: The noun *physis* ("nature") here and later in the verse is rendered as "kind," for the point is obviously how the human species has controlled all other species of creatures: "every kind of animal is *naturally* subject to man" (Mayor, 119). The connective *gar* indicates that this sentence explains the previous one: how do we know that the tongue is lit by a cosmic force? Because humans have tamed everything else but it! The submission of nature to humans is a commonplace of Hellenistic moral teaching

(Cicero, *Nat. Deor* II, 60, 151; *De Officiis* I, 22; Seneca, *On Benefits* II, 29, 4; Philo, *On Dreams* 2:152; *On the Creation* 88 and 148; *Decalogue* 113).

of snake and sea-creature: James anticipates the creation of humans in God's image in 3:9 by this allusion to Gen 1:26–28. The list also resembles that in Gen 9:2. After the flood, God blesses Noah and repeats the instruction of Gen 1:28 to be fruitful: "The fear of you and the dread of you shall be upon every beast of the earth and upon every bird of the air and everything that creeps on the ground and all the fish of the sea." The catalogue is obviously intended to be inclusive. The vocabulary is standard except for *enalioi* ("sea-creatures"), which is *hapax* for the LXX and NT (but see Philo, *Decalogue* 54).

is being tamed: James' delight in language is clear throughout this section and nowhere more emphatically than in this assonant redundancy (*damazetai/dedamastai*). For obvious reasons, some MSS reverse the order of the verbs, so that the perfect tense would precede the present tense. The verb *damazein* can be used of taming animals (Xenophon, *Memorabilia* 4, 3, 10), or of subduing anything (see LXX Dan 2:40; Mark 5:4).

8. *no human can tame*: Some MSS change the order of the words, with no impact on the meaning. The adversative *de* needs to be taken at full force. In contrast to the human ability to control everything else, the incapacity to subdue (same verb = *damasai*) the tongue is all the more shocking.

a restless evil: The translation breaks two appositional phrases into separate English sentences. James uses *kakos* only here and in 1:13. Notice that, typical of the contrasts he has consistently employed, there God is "untempted by evils," whereas here the tongue is "the world of wickedness" and a restless evil. For "restless" (*akatastatos*), see 1:8, where it is translated as "unstable," and see also *akatastasia* in 3:16, below. The element of restlessness fits both the sense of being untamed and the image of a raging fire. Some MSS have the variant *akatascheton* ("unruly/uncontrollable").

full of death-dealing poison: The noun *ios* can mean either an arrow, or rust, or poison. In 5:3, it clearly means rust, and in the present case, poison (see Philo, *Embassy to Gaius* 166; Rom 3:13). In the *T. Reub.* 5:3, *ios* is used for female seductiveness, but in LXX Pss 13:3 and 139:4, as here, it refers to the "poison on the lips" that leads to violence between humans. The adjective *thanatēphoros* means literally "death-bearing" (Plato, *Rep.* 617D) and in LXX Num 18:22 is used to modify "sin" (*hamartia*). The translation "death-dealing" seeks to capture the aggressive quality of speech in James' portrayal.

9. *we bless the Lord and Father*: The shift to the first person plural here is again striking, as James associates himself with the readers (see 3:1). Many Greek MSS, as well as versions, have "God" (*theos*) rather than "Lord" (*kyrios*). But "Lord" is clearly the harder reading: "God" would fit better with "likeness of God" later in the verse and would match James' reference to God and Father in 1:27. But some basis for James' locution might be found in Jewish prayer. The blessing formulary begins: "Blessed are you Lord God" (*eulogētos kyrios ho*

261

theos; see Gen 9:26; 24:27; Exod 18:10; Ruth 2:20; 4:14; 1 Sam 25:32; 2 Sam 6:21; 18:28; 1 Kgs 1:48; 8:15; 1 Chr 29:10; 2 Chr 2:11; Tob 3:11; Pss 40:14; 67:19–20; 71:18; 88:53; 118:12). For "Lord Father" elsewhere, see Isa 63:16; Sir 23:1, 4. To "pronounce blessing" is, of course, the fundamental form of prayer in Judaism (see LXX Pss 15:7; 25:12; 33:2).

we curse the people: The verb *katarasthai* means to "call curses down on someone" (Herodotus, *Persian War* 2:39; Philo, *The Worse Attacks the Better* 103) and is found frequently in the LXX (Gen 12:3; 27:29; Lev 24:15; Num 22:6; Deut 21:23; Ps 36:22). For the contrast between "cursing and blessing," see Philo, *Who is the Heir* 177; Luke 6:28; Rom 12:14; *1 Clem.* 15:3.

made according to God's likeness: Rather than the second perfect participle *gegonotas*, some MSS have the more usual first perfect *gegenemenous* or the second aorist *genomenous*; there is no great difference in meaning. James is clearly alluding to Gen 1:26–28, which has God making the human *kat' eikona hemēteran kai kath' homoiosin* ("according to our image and likeness"), so that the human could rule over "the fish of the sea and the birds of the air and the creatures of all the earth and the serpents crawling on the earth" (1:26). The allusion anticipated by 3:7 is here made explicit.

10. *blessing and curse*: For the grammatical construction, compare Sir 28:12; Eph 4:29. The most famous example of "blessing and curse" coming from the same source is Moses in Deut 11:26. There, however, it was the choice placed before the people. Here it is the inconsistency of speech that is the problem, when one blesses God but curses humans (compare Sir 5:13; 28:12; *T. Ben.* 6:5).

should not happen: Literally, "My brothers, these things ought not to happen thus." James uses the impersonal verb *chrē* with the accusative + infinitive construction (*Od.* 6:207; *Ep. Arist.* 231; Xenophon, *Symposium* 4:47). This is the only example of the usage in the NT and wonderfully captures the moralist's sense of outrage at "what ought not to be." For the theme of inconsistency in speech, see, e.g., Plato, *Laws* 659A; Philo, *Decalogue* 93; Prov 18:21; Sir 5:9–13; 28:12. Here "double-mindedness" (1:8) is revealed in being "double-tongued" (see *Did.* 2:4; *Barn.* 19:7).

11. *does the spring*: The interrogative particle *mēti* indicates that the question expects a negative answer (see Epictetus, *Discourses* II, 11, 21; IV, 1, 133). The noun *pēgē* means literally a spring of water or a fountain (Josephus, *Ant.* 2:294; Gen 24:13; Exod 15:27; John 4:6). The definite article is somewhat surprising.

gush forth both sweet and bitter water: The verb *bryein* has the sense of being full to overflowing, especially with reference to plants budding (see Mayor, 124); thus, the "gushing" spring. James again chooses a term unknown to the LXX or other NT writings. It can be found, e.g., in Josephus, *Ant.* 13:66; *Syb. Or.* 6:8). The noun "water" is understood as that which is modified by "sweet" (*glykys*; see Rev 10:9–10) and "bitter" (*pikron*, in the NT only here and in 3:14, below).

from the same opening: The noun *opē* refers to any sort of hole in rock or ground (see Exod 33:22; Judg 15:11; Ezek 8:7; Heb 11:38). The comparison of blessing and curse to sweet and bitter waters is particularly powerful in the context of Israel's desert experience.

12. *is it possible*: Once more, the form of the question demands a negative answer. It is striking that James has repeated "my brothers" so frequently in this section (3:1; 3:10; 3:12).

fig tree to produce olives: James' assertions are commonplace; plants produce according to kind; failure to produce according to kind is "unnatural." In Greco-Roman literature, very similar statements can be found in Plutarch, *On Tranquillity of Soul* 13 (*Mor* 472B–473B); Epictetus, *Discourses* II, 20, 18; Marcus Aurelius, *Meditations* 8:46; Seneca, *On Anger* II, 10; see also Seneca, *Moral Epistles* 87:25: "Good does not spring from evil any more than figs grow from olive trees." Closer to home, see the statement in Sir 27:6 and especially that in Matt 7:16–17: "You will know them by their fruits. Are grapes gathered from thorns, or figs from thistles? So every sound tree bears good fruit, but the bad tree bears evil fruit. A sound tree cannot bear evil fruit, nor can a bad tree bear good fruit." James' sense of outrage is that those who claim to be "good" and "bless God" are also speaking evil of each other.

neither does a salty source: We would expect *oude* rather than *oute*, but the terms were frequently exchanged in MSS (BAGD, 596) and, in fact, in the *koinē* were sometimes used interchangeably (Hort, 80; Ropes, 243). The shift back to "water" after the plant metaphors is also disconcerting. The compressed character of the statement has given rise to a number of variants that attempt to make it read more smoothly. The anarthous adjective *alykēs* in the neuter must be taken as a substantive meaning "salty source" (compare Gen 14:3; Num 34:3; Deut 3:17; Josh 15:2).

COMMENT

As the detailed notes suggest, James' discourse on the power and peril of the tongue would, in many ways, recommend itself to any Hellenistic moralist. Indeed, itself a model of the *brachylogia*, or "brevity"—so frequently associated with wisdom literature—this essay contains a variety of the conventional motifs concerning the use of the tongue. First among these is the importance of controlled speech for the sage (*didaskalos*, 3:1). Teachers particularly are vulnerable to failures in speech, not only because their profession demands of them that they speak more than others, and they must do so in public and before a frequently captive audience, but because such a setting provides temptations to virtually every form of evil speech: arrogance and domination over students; anger and pettiness at contradiction or inattention; slander and meanness toward absent opponents; flattery of students for the sake of vainglory. Such failures were even graver in a cultural context in which the fundamental perception of teaching was as a modeling of virtue. The failure to control speech would indeed bring "a greater judgment" (3:1).

But James also adopts from the commonplaces of Greco-Roman moral discourse the image of the bridle that controls the horse by controlling the horse's mouth (3:3), the image of the mighty ship controlled by the will of the pilot by means of a tiny rudder (3:4), even the image of controlling wild animals (3:7). Equally familiar is the recognition of the tongue's impressive power to effect both good and bad (3:5–6).

In several important ways, however, James' discourse deviates from the standard *topos* on taciturnity (Johnson, "Taciturnity," 336–39). For one thing, James is far more pessimistic in his evaluation of human speech. Hellenistic moralists are quick to recognize the difficulty in controlling speech, but they think it is possible. In contrast, James flatly asserts that no one can truly control speech (3:8). Following the logic demanded by 3:2, therefore ("if any does not fail in speech, this is a perfect person"), James does not regard human perfection to be possible.

James also heightens the tongue's capacity for doing evil. He personifies it, as though indeed it were completely independent of anyone's control: "it boasts of great things" (3:5)! More than that, he portrays the tongue as a cosmic force. It is a "world of wickedness established among our members," a fire that is "inflamed from Gehenna" that also "sets aflame the cycle of life" (3:6).

James' treatment of speech is also more fundamentally and pervasively religious than that found in Hellenistic moral discourse. In the Greek world, the value of silence was attached primarily to the ethical ideal of the philosopher whose virtue was expressed by the ways in which reason controlled the passions. Silence or brevity was of religious significance primarily in connection with the Mysteries and with the prophetic oracles at shrines such as Delphi (see Notes). In contrast, James makes failure to control speech the very antithesis of authentic religion (1:26), and his religious framework is that of Torah. Speech is evaluated in relational, indeed, covenantal terms: human speech and action should be normed by the speech and action of the God who has involved himself with humans.

The essay of 3:1–12 provides three important insights into this perspective. First, the theme of human "double-mindedness" (1:8; 4:8) is here located in behavior that is "double-tongued." But we notice that this is not simply a matter of saying one thing and meaning another. When one uses the same tongue to bless God, yet curse the human person who is created according to the likeness of God (3:9), one betrays in a fundamental way the allegiance by which one claims to live. This is not a matter of error or fault, but of sin. The theological warrant, that humans "are created according to God's likeness," in turn, does not derive from the observation of human behavior but is rooted in the tradition and teaching of Torah. Something more than the perfection of the human sage is at stake, here. What is at issue is the proper mode of perceiving and responding to God's creation.

Second, when James says that the tongue is "inflamed by Gehenna" (3:6), he does more than evoke the symbolic world of Judaism. He points to the cosmic dualism underlying the "two ways" of disposing human freedom. The rule of God in the world is opposed by the work of the devil. This theme is developed more fully in the call to conversion that will immediately follow this discourse on speech (3:13–4:10). The central religious polarity in James is between the "wisdom from above" that leads humans into "friendship with God" and the "wisdom from below" that manifests itself in a "friendship with the world" that is also enmity with God (3:13–16; 4:4). All human activity, including speech, is defined in terms of these two allegiances. This understanding shapes all of James' sayings on speech. The command to be "quick to hear, slow to speak, slow to anger" (1:19) is classically Hellenistic, as the notes on that verse indicate. So also is the connection between rash speech, anger, and the doing of injustice. But for James, there is this difference, which would startle Plutarch: for James, it is *human* anger that does not work *God's* righteousness. The two levels of activity are densely interwoven within James' covenantal schema.

Third, James places human speech within the context of God's word. The readers are reminded in 1:18 that they have been given birth as a kind of "firstfruits of creation" (note again the creation imagery as in 3:7–10) by "the word of truth" (*logos tēs alētheias*). And in 1:21, they are told to "receive with meekness the implanted word that is able to save [their] souls." Human speech is qualified by reference to the creative and saving word of God. God's word shapes a form of identity and behavior not measurable by the world and its "wisdom." When James in 3:1 speaks of teachers receiving "greater judgment," therefore, he does not mean in the eyes of fellow humans. He means before the eyes of God: "so speak and so act, as people who are going to be judged by the law of freedom" (2:12).

BIBLIOGRAPHY

Bratcher, R. G., "Exegetical Themes in James 3 and 5," *Review and Expositor* 66 (1969) 403–13.

Carr, A., "The Meaning of *kosmos* in James III,6," *The Expositor* seventh series 8 (1909) 318–25.

Charue, A., "La maîtrise de la langue dans l'épître de saint Jacques," *Collationes Namurcenses* 29 (1935) 395–407.

Elliott-Binns, L. E., "The Meaning of HYLE in James III,5," NTS 2 (1955–56) 48–50.

Filson, F. V., "The Christian Teacher in the First Century," *JBL* 60 (1941) 317–28.

Johnson, L. T., "Taciturnity and True Religion (James 1:26–27)," *Greeks, Romans, and Christians*, ed. D. Balch et al. (Minneapolis: Fortress Press, 1990) 329–39.

Milikowsky, C., "Which Gehenna? Retribution and Eschatology in the Synoptic Gospels and in Early Jewish Texts," *NTS* 34 (1988) 238–49.

Schnayder, G., *De Antiquorum Hominum Taciturnitate et Tacendo* (Traveaux de la societé des sciences de Wroclaw 56: Wroclaw, 1956).

Trocmé, E., "Les églises paulinienne vues du dehors: Jac 2,1 à 3,12," *SE* 2 (1964) 660–69.

Wandel, G., "Zur Auslegung der Stelle Jak 3, 1–8," *TSK* 66 (1893) 679–707.

Wanke, J., "Zur urchristlichen Lehrer nach dem Zeugnis des Jakobusbriefes," *Kirche des Anfanges: Festschrift H. Schürmann*, ed. R. Schnackenburg (Erfurter theologische Studien 38; Leipzig: St. Benno Verlag, 1977) 489–511.

Watson, D. F., "The Rhetoric of James 3:1–12 and a Classical Pattern of Argumentation," *NovT* 35 (1993) 48–64.

Wolmarans, J. L. P., "The Tongue Guiding the Body: The Anthropological Presuppositions of James 3:1–12," *Neot* 26 (1992) 523–30.

V. CALL TO CONVERSION
3:13–4:10

✦

3.13. Who among you is wise and understanding? By his good manner of life let him demonstrate his deeds in wisdom's meekness. 14. But if you have bitter jealousy and selfish ambition in your heart, do not boast and lie against the truth. 15. This is not the wisdom that comes down from above, but one that is earthbound, unspiritual, demonic. 16. For where there is jealousy and selfish ambition, there is disorder and every kind of mean practice. 17. But the wisdom from above is first of all pure, then it is peaceable, gentle, open to persuasion. It is filled with mercy and with good fruits. It is not divided. It is not insincere. 18. But the fruit that is righteousness is sown in peace by the makers of peace. 4:1. From where do wars, and from where do battles among you come? Is it not from your desires that are at war among your members? 2. You desire and you do not have: so you kill. And you are jealous and cannot obtain: so you do battle and wage war. You do not have because you do not ask. 3. You ask and you do not receive because you ask evilly, so that you might spend it on your desires. 4. You adulteresses! Do you not know that friendship with the world is enmity with God? Therefore, whoever chooses to be a friend of the world is established as an enemy of God. 5. Or do you suppose that the Scripture speaks in vain? Does the spirit which he made to dwell in us crave enviously? 6. Rather, he gives a greater gift. Therefore it says: "God resists the arrogant, but he gives a gift to the lowly." 7. Submit therefore to God. But resist the devil and he will flee from you. 8. Approach God and he will approach you. Cleanse your hands, you sinners! And purify your hearts, you double-minded! 9. Be wretched and mourn and weep. Let your laughter be turned into mourning and your joy into dejection. 10. Humble yourselves before the Lord and he will exalt you.

267

THE SECTION AS A WHOLE

The approach taken by the present commentary to this part of James can perhaps best be shown by contrast to that of M. Dibelius. Consistent with his generally atomistic reading of James, Dibelius sees this section of text as nothing more than loosely arranged independent units. 3:13–17 deals with one topic, but 3:18 is completely independent in origin and function. 4:1–6, in turn, takes up still another subject. Dibelius can acknowledge some "uniformity of tendency," but no train of thought or formal unity (207–8). Dibelius sees 4:7–10, in turn, as a contrast, both formally and thematically, to the preceding verses (208–9). Other commentators tend to break up the pieces in much the same way (see, e.g., Laws, 158; Marty, 141), although some argue that 3:13–18 continues the theme of 3:1–12 (Hort, 80; Adamson, 149; Mussner, 168–69).

It is, indeed, possible to find multiple links between 3:1–12 and 3:13–4:10—certainly more than there are between 3:13–4:10 and the text following. There is the word-linkage between *pikros* ("bitter") in 3:11 and 3:14; the phrase "in your members" both in 3:6 and 4:1; a form of *akatastasia* in 3:8 as well as in 3:16. One can acknowledge a natural transition between the two sources of water and their fruits in 3:11–12 and the two sources of wisdom and their fruits in 3:13–18. Likewise, the cursing of one's fellow human (3:9) is not less antisocial than wars and battles (4:1). Most of all, there is the natural link between the *didaskalos* of 3:1 and the *sophos* of 3:13. No case is being made here that James does not connect parts of his argument! Just the opposite: all of these natural ties and progressions only serve to highlight just how distinctive the literary structuring of 3:13–4:10 is when taken as a whole.

The section is, first, intensely sermonic in character, with all of those stylistic quirks characteristic of the diatribe: rhetorical questions (3:13; 4:1, 4, 5), virtue and vice lists (3:14–15, 17), abusive epithets (4:4, 8), vivid imagery (4:1, 9), sharp contrasts (3:14–17; 4:4, 6, 10), the citation of authoritative texts (4:6). But the sermon also appears to have a coherent structure that falls into two parts: 3:13–4:6 sets up an indictment, to which 4:7–10 responds.

The connective *oun* ("therefore") in 4:7 indicates that the series of imperatives and assurances in 4:7–10 is indeed based on what preceded it. The language of the exhortation, furthermore, mirrors that of the indictment. Thus, the "purifying of the heart" in 4:8 corresponds to the "selfish ambition in the heart" in 3:14, as well as the "purity" of the wisdom from above in 3:17; the "dejection" (*katēpheia*) of 4:9 matches the *hyperēphania* ("arrogance") of 4:6; the "double-minded persons" (*dipsychoi*) correspond to the "undivided" (*adiakritos*) of 3:17. Most obviously the final command and promise, "humble yourselves (*tapeinō-thēte*) before God and he will exalt you" (4:10), picks up from the "lowly" (*tapeinoi*) in 4:6, as well as the above/below pattern found both there and in 3:13–17. As for the content of the exhortation, in addition to submission (4:7,

10) and the movement toward God and away from the devil (4:7–8), the commands demand ethical purification and mourning (4:8–9). This is, in short, a call to conversion.

The indictment in 3:13–4:6 that sets up that call is more complex. We can notice first how it moves primarily by means of a series of rhetorical questions in 3:13, 4:1 (2), 4:4, and 4:5 (2). The first and second of these are joined: 3:13 asks about the wise and understanding *en hymin* ("among you"), and 4:1 asks about the source of wars *en hymin* ("among you"). The rhetorical questions are each followed by exposition or accusation. In 3:13–14, an initial contrast between wisdom from above and bitter jealousy is explained by a second set of antithetical statements in 3:15–16 (*ouk estin . . . alla* and *hopou . . . ekei*). 3:17–18 then resumes, with an emphasis on *eirēnē* ("peace"), the thematic opposition established by 3:13: true wisdom is manifested in mild and peaceful behavior.

The second set of rhetorical questions forms an antithesis to 3:17–18, returning to the bitter jealousy of 3:14–15, spelled out now not simply in terms of social unrest (*akatastasia*) but in terms of wars and battles (4:1). Accusations rather than exposition follow these questions: "you desire . . . you kill . . . you are jealous . . . you do battle . . . you wage war" (4:2). These are followed by a short explanation why their requests do not get fulfilled (4:3) and still another rhetorical question, which reminds them of a traditional understanding of the irreconcilability of friendship with God and friendship with the world (4:4).

The climax of the indictment is reached in 4:5–6. However difficult it is to translate precisely, its rhetorical intent is clear. The whole exposition comes down to the validity of the scriptural witness to the way God works in the world. Is all that the Scripture says in vain? Is envy really the proper sort of longing for the spirit God placed in humans? The citation of Prov 3:34, finally, sets up the exhortation in 4:7–10.

Viewed in this fashion, the thematic importance of envy appears obvious, for the climactic rhetorical question concerns precisely the compatibility between *phthonos* ("envy") and the spirit God gave humans. However obvious the contrast between war and peace in this discussion, it is dependent on the still more fundamental theme of envy as reflecting "enmity with God" (see *zēlos pikros* in 3:14; *zēlos kai eritheia* in 3:16; *zēloute* in 4:2; and *phthonos* in 4:5).

NOTES

13. *who among you is wise and understanding*: Some MSS read *ei tis*, which would make *tis* an indefinite demonstrative pronoun rather than an interrogative and would match the *ei* in the next verse. The evidence supports the reading adopted here. The phrase "among you" (*en hymin*) reminds us of similar

expressions in 2:4, 16; see also 4:1; 5:14, 19. For the form of the question, compare LXX Isa 50:10; Ps 33:13; Deut 20:5–8; Judg 7:3; Jer 9:11; Sir 6:34. The adjective *sophos* can be used anarthrously as a substantive for a "wise person" in the sense of being practically skilled (Herodotus, *Persian War* 3:85) or generally learned (Plato, *Phaedrus* 278D). It was the designation applied to the legendary sages of Greece (Diogenes Laertius, *Lives of Eminent Philosophers* I, 40) and Israel (see LXX Prov 9:8–12; 13:10; 19:20; Wis 7:15; Sir 1:8; 9:17; 21:13). In the NT the term is used more often negatively for those with "worldly wisdom" who are blind to God's revelation (Matt 11:25; Luke 10:21; Rom 1:22; 1 Cor 1:19–20, 25–27; 3:18–19, 20), but it can also be used as a designation for leaders (Matt 23:34) and as a desirable quality in the community (Rom 16:19; 1 Cor 3:10; 6:5; Eph 5:15). The adjective *epistēmōn* has much the same range of meaning, from skilled or knowledgeable (Plato, *Gorgias* 448B) to being "wise/prudent" (*Od.* 16:374), although it places somewhat greater emphasis on knowledge. In the LXX, for example, *sophos* is used repeatedly to translate *ḥākām*, whereas *epistēmōn* is used to translate *bîn* or *yādaᶜ*. More significantly, the combination *sophos kai epistēmōn* itself becomes stereotypical (see Deut 1:13, 15; 4:6; Sir 21:15; Dan 1:4; see also Philo, *Migration of Abraham* 58). James' very choice of words, in short, suggests the context of Torah: who is wise according to God's measure of reality? (See also Davids, 150.)

by his good manner of life: Literally "out of" (*ek*). James uses the same verb (*deiknymi*) that he did in 2:18 when calling for the "demonstration" of faith "out of" deeds (*erga*). The basic thought remains the same beneath the variation: perception must be translated into practice. The noun *anastrophē* denotes an entire manner of life (see the Vulgate's translation as *conversatio*): compare Diogenes Laertius, *Lives of Eminent Philosophers* IX, 64; Epictetus, *Discourses* I, 9, 24; I, 22, 13; Tob 4:14. Paul uses it to characterize his life before his conversion (Gal 1:13). See also Eph 4:22; 1 Tim 4:12; Heb 13:7; 1 Pet 1:15, 18; 2:12; 3:1–2, 16; 2 Pet 2:7; 3:11. The adjective *kalos* is only partially rendered by "good," since it also connotes excellence and beauty (compare James 2:7; 4:17), but here the moral aspect obviously dominates.

in wisdom's meekness: The phrase echoes two previous passages: the reference to the prayer for wisdom from God in 1:5 and the exhortation to "receive with meekness" the implanted word in 1:21. The term *praus* is not accidental: the entire passage takes up the contrast between the qualities of mildness associated with God's wisdom and the harshness of a worldly wisdom based on envy. Meekness is a special theme in Matthew (5:5; 11:29; 21:5), but it is claimed as a moral virtue also in 1 Cor 4:21; 2 Cor 10:1; Gal 5:23; 6:1; Eph 4:2; Col 3:12; 2 Tim 2:25; Titus 3:2; 1 Pet 3:15. There is a striking parallel in Sir 3:17, *teknon, en prautēti erga sou diexage* ("child, perform your deeds with meekness").

14. *but if you have bitter jealousy*: James here begins a series of antithetical statements. This first simple conditional has an imperative as its apodosis. The adversative *de* should be given its full strength, as the addition of *ara* by some

MSS suggests (with Mussner, 170; Davids, 151; against Ropes, 245). James calls *zēlos* "bitter" (*pikros*), establishing a verbal link with 3:11. But it is, above all, the meaning of *zēlos* that is important for determining the theme of the section as a whole. In *Rhetoric* 1387B–1388A, Aristotle defines *zēlos* as a certain sorrow (*lupē*) that one experiences because someone else is in possession of what one is not. Positively, the term can be used for the desire to emulate a quality and thus attain it. Negatively, however, the term denotes the desire to acquire by taking something away from another. In this sense, "jealousy" is equivalent to envy (*phthonos*), and Hellenistic moralists tend to use the terms interchangeably, as James does (see, e.g., Plutarch, *On Brotherly Love* 14 [*Mor.* 485D–E]; *How to Profit by One's Enemies* 1 [*Mor.* 86C]; 9 [*Mor.* 91B]; *On Tranquillity of Soul* 10 [*Mor.* 470C]; 11 [*Mor.* 171A], Plato, *Symposium* 213D; *Laws* 679C; Epictetus, *Discourses* III, 22, 61; see also Hort, 81). It appears as a vice with this sense in Acts 5:17; 13:45; Rom 13:13; 1 Cor 3:3; 2 Cor 12:20. Compare the statement in Wis 6:23, which says that *phthonos . . . ou koinōnēsei sophią* ("envy . . . will have nothing in common with wisdom"). The translation "bitter zeal" in the sense of fanaticism is clearly wrong (against Ropes, 245; Marty, 142; Vouga, 105; Martin, 130). The discussion of this section of James by Didymus Alexandrinus, *De Trinitate* III,1 (PG 39:776) is worth remarking.

and selfish ambition in your heart: The "heart" (*kardia*) is the seat of affections and intentions in the biblical tradition (Gen 6:5; Exod 4:21; Deut 6:6; Ps 11:2; see James 1:26 and esp. 4:8, below). James has a singular noun with a plural possessive pronoun; some MSS therefore seek to improve by putting "hearts" in the plural. The noun *eritheia* does not have much of a history before the NT. It is unattested in the LXX. Aristotle uses it for "party spirit" in the political sense (*Politics* 1302B; 1303A). In the NT it is closely associated with antisocial attitudes destructive of community (Rom 2:8; Gal 5:20; Phil 1:17; 2:3). James will use it again in 3:16.

do not boast: In this case, *mē* with the present imperative could mean "stop boasting" (so Adamson, 151). The verb *katakauchesthai* presents the same problems here as in 2:13. The prefix suggests aggressiveness against another— "stop asserting yourselves at the expense of others" (compare Rom 11:18)—but here such an object is lacking. Some MSS understandably correct to the simple *kauchesthai*.

and lie against the truth: The verb *pseudesthai* means simply to speak falsely; for "speaking falsely against someone" see Plato, *Euthd.* 284A; Matt 5:11. And the expression "lie against the truth" is attested in *T. Gad* 5:1; 4 Macc 5:34. But what can the phrase mean here? Is it a redundancy? Some MSS change the word order, to yield, "boast against the truth and lie." The best parallel may be that in Acts 5:3, where "lying against the Holy Spirit" means something like "falsifying the Holy Spirit," that is, counterfeiting the life guided by the Spirit. In the present case, then, "lying against the truth" must mean living in a manner contrary to the "word of truth" (1:18) that was implanted in them and

271

that they were to receive "with meekness" (1:21). Such an existential, rather than conceptual, understanding of truth is supported as well by James' last use of the term in 5:19.

15. *this is not the wisdom*: Some MSS alter the word order of this first phrase in order to put *hautē* ("this") in what seems a more appropriate position. The statement on *sophia* ("wisdom") follows naturally on the question concerning who was wise (*sophos*, 3:13).

that comes down from above: The phrase *anōthen katerchomenē* unmistakably echoes 1:17, which refers to every good and perfect gift "coming down from above" (*anōthen estin katabainon*). Considered together with 1:5, it is clear that James regards genuine wisdom as a divine gift, a perception deeply rooted in the world of Torah (see, e.g., Ps 50:8; Jer 9:11; Prov 2:6; 8:30–36; Wis 7:15–22; 9:13–18; Job 28:20–23; 1QS 4:3; 1QH 11:7–10; 14:8; Philo, *Rewards and Punishments* 51).

earthbound: James uses three adjectives that are relatively rare and that gain their specific sense from the context in which he uses them. They move in a negative progression (Ropes, 248). The term *epigeios* is the most widely attested. It generally means "earthly" (Plato, *Rep.* 546A; Philo, *Rewards and Punishments* 51). It is not found in the LXX but is used by Philo (*On the Cherubim* 101) in contrast to "heavenly" realities, a meaning that predominates in NT usage as well (John 3:12; 1 Cor 15:40; 2 Cor 5:1; Phil 2:10). As Hort, 84, notes, Phil 3:19 provides a parallel moral application: "their minds are set on earthly things (*ta epigeia*)." The translation "earthbound" tries to capture the perspective of James, that a wisdom that excludes consideration of God is, in fact, not simply "earthly" in a neutral sense, but represents a kind of closure.

unspiritual: The adjective *psychikos* is more difficult. It means generally "of the soul," and in normal usage it tends to denote human mental activity, as opposed to that which is physical (*sōmatikos*) as in 4 Macc 1:32. Plutarch can combine it with *pneuma* ("spirit") with reference to the "breath of life" (*On Common Conceptions* 46 [*Mor.* 1084E]). In the NT, however, it is consistently used to oppose *pneuma* (see 1 Cor 2:14; 15:44, 46; and esp. Jude 19: *houtoi eisin . . . psychikoi, pneuma mē echontes* ["these are . . . the psychics, not having the spirit"]). Such a contrast seems to be at work here, since in 4:5 James speaks of the *pneuma* God made to dwell in humans. As Hort, 84, notes, "It is simply 'of the mind' rather than 'of the Spirit.'" James' characterization is consonant with Paul's language about a "wisdom of the world" (*sophia tou kosmou*) in 1 Cor 1:20 and 2:6 (see Davids, 152) and a "fleshly wisdom" (*sophia sarkikē*) in 2 Cor 1:12 (see Cantinat, 190).

demonic: The adjective *daimoniōdēs* is a NT hapax and unattested before Christian literature. The construction with *ōdēs* may suggest "demon-like" (Hort, 84), but in context it seems to imply "having its origin in demons" (Adamson, 152). For the role of "demons" in opposing God's work, see 1 Cor 10:20–21; 1 Tim 4:1. James has already spoken of *ta daimonia*, who assent intellectually to the reality of God but do not work God's righteousness (2:19). The use of "demonic" here, however, gains richness from the reference in 3:6 to the evil force of the tongue as "inflamed from gehenna," and the exhortation in 4:7 to "flee the devil." The strikingly similar language in *Herm. Man.* 9:11 ("double-mindedness is an earthly spirit from the devil") may well be dependent on James (see Introduction IE5f).

16. *there is disorder*: The *gar* indicates that this sentence provides the basis for the previous one (Ropes, 248): antisocial behavior reveals the character of a wisdom rooted in envy as "earthbound, unspiritual, demonic." The link between deed and attitude is now being worked the opposite way. Some MSS insert *kai* before "disorder," creating a "both/and" conclusion. In 1:8 James called the double-minded person "unstable" (*akataotatoo*) and in 3:8 called the tongue a "restless (*akatastatos*) evil." Now *zēlos* and *eritheia* are associated with "social unrest" (*akatastasia*; compare Dionysius of Halicarnassus, *Roman Antiquities* VI,31,1; Prov 26:28; 1 Cor 14:33). Aristotle calls envy a *lupē tarachōdēs* ("an agitating sorrow," *Rhetoric* 1386B). Note that *akatastasia* is linked, as here, with *polemoi* ("wars") in Luke 21:9 and with *eris* ("strife/discord," which some MSS read here in place of *eritheia*) in 2 Cor 12:20. Likewise, *zēlos* is placed in NT vice lists with *eris* and *pthonos* ("envy") and *echthra* ("enmity," see James 4:4): Rom 1:29; 13:13; 1 Cor 3:3; 2 Cor 12:20; Phil 1:15; 1 Tim 6:4; 1 Pet 2:1; Titus 3:3, and esp. Gal 5:20–21.

every kind of mean practice: The *pas* ("all") is inclusive; thus, "every kind." The noun *pragma* is used for any deed or thing (see Josephus, *Ant.* 16:376; Matt 18:19; Acts 5:4), but it can be used specifically also for a "lawsuit" (Xenophon, *Memorabilia* 2, 9, 1; Josephus, *Apion* 2:177; 1 Cor 6:1). In the light of James 2:6, which depicts the rich dragging the poor into *kritēria*, such an understanding is just possible here. Certainly, lawsuits are among the clearest demonstrations of envy and causes of *akatastasia*. The adjective *phaulos* does not argue against this, for when it is used negatively, it tends to connote lowliness, cheapness, and meanness even more than moral wickedness (see Plato, *Rep.* 519A; Xenophon, *Symposium* 4:47; Prov 5:3; 22:8). As Hort, 85, observes, it "expresses not so much moral evil as worthlessness." Yet it is also true that the NT literature otherwise emphasizes the moral aspect of the term (John 3:20; 5:29; Rom 9:11; 2 Cor 5:10; Titus 2:8; see Davids, 153).

17. *first of all pure*: The adjective *hagnos* ("pure") is used especially of things or persons dedicated to the gods (see *Od.* 21:259; Euripides, *Ion* 243; Pss 11:7; 18:10), but is also used of moral innocence (Plato, *Laws* 759C; Prov 21:8; 4 Macc 18:7; 2 Cor 7:11; Phil 4:8; 1 Tim 5:22; Titus 2:5; 1 Pet 1:22). Note particularly 1 Pet 3:2, "your pure manner of life" (*hagnen anastrophēn hymōn*). James places this term first because of the thematic importance of being "unstained from the world" for what he calls "pure (*katharos*) religion before God" (1:27). Living according to the wisdom that comes from God demands a

separation from the evil qualities just listed (Hort, 86). This will be made explicit in 4:8, when James exhorts them to "purify your hearts (*hagnisate kardias*)."

then it is peaceable, gentle, open to persuasion: The three adjectives are set off by the conjunction *epeita* ("and then"). Although the use of alliteration is striking (all of them beginning with *e*), they are joined by more than mere rhetorical considerations (against Chaine, 93); they amount in combination to a definition of the "meekness" enjoined by 3:13 (see also Ropes, 250). The adjective *eirēnikos* ("peaceable/peaceful") provides a direct contrast to the social unrest provoked by jealousy/envy. Likewise, *epieikēs* means primarily to be reasonable and fair-minded (see Aristotle, *Nicomachean Ethics* 1137B; Plato, *Symposium* 210B; 1 Pet 2:18). In LXX Ps 85:5 it combines with *chrēstos* ("sweet") as a divine attribute. The term has the quality of "gentleness" suggested also by its use in Phil 4:5 and in particular 1 Tim 3:3 and Titus 3:2, where it is matched with *amachos* ("not battling/peaceful"). Similarly, *eupeithēs* derives from the nouns *eupeitheia* ("ready obedience"), suggesting the quality of docility and willingness to get along with others (see Plato, *Phaedrus* 254A; Epictetus, *Discourses* III, 12, 13; 4 Macc 8:6; 12:6). This is the only use of the term in the NT. Although it is good method not to overemphasize the elements in any virtue or vice list, the combination that James has here provided obviously has more than a rhetorical effect: these are precisely the qualities required for the ethics of cooperation, rather than competition, that characterize his teaching.

it is filled with mercy and with good fruits: The translation breaks phrases into separate sentences, since they express distinct, if related, ideas. James now shifts to the results of the peaceable attitudes he associates with the wisdom from above. The phrase *mestē eleous* reminds us first of the aphorism concerning mercy (*eleos*) in 2:13 and even more of the characterization of the tongue as *mestē iou thanatēphorou* ("full of death-dealing poison") in 3:8. The phrase "good fruits," in turn, anticipates the agricultural imagery of 5:17–18, but even more the immediate turn to the "fruit of righteousness" in 3:18. The language of "fruit-bearing" in moral discourse clearly refers to the results of deeds (see 3:12 and Matt 7:16–20). Conscious of this, some scribes inserted *ergon* in order to create the expression "the fruits that are good deeds."

it is not divided: The last two terms have the alpha-privative form found so frequently in such lists (compare Rom 1:31). The adjective *adiakritos* is a NT hapax and rarely found elsewhere outside medical discussions (see the LXX only at Prov 25:1). It derives from *diakrinō* ("to divide/judge") and in normal usage we would expect it to mean "mixed," that is, "not divided up" (compare Aristotle, *On Sleep and Waking* 458A). A decision about its precise meaning here is complicated by James' other uses of *diakrinō* in 1:6 and 2:4, both of which are connected to the concept of "double-mindedness." The best clue to its meaning here is provided by the exhortation to purity of heart among the "double-minded" in 4:8, below (compare *T. Zeb.* 7:2; Ign.*Magn.* 15:2; Ign.*Tral.* 1:1; Ign.*Eph.* 3:2). To be *adiakritos* here, therefore, means to be "simple" rather than double in consciousness (see Hort, 86; Marty, 150; Dibelius, 214). It does not bear the sense of "not making distinctions" or "being impartial" (against Laws, 164; Vouga, 108; Martin, 134).

it is not insincere: The term *anupokritos* provides assonance with *adiakritos*. In Pseudo-Demetrius, *On Style* 194, the term means simply "undramatic," but in moral discourse it takes on the meaning of "insincere" (see Wis 5:18; 18:15; Rom 12:9; 1 Tim 1:5; 2 Tim 1:5; 1 Pet 1:22). For the condemnation of "hypocrisy" in the sayings of Jesus, see Matt 6:2, 5, 16; 7:5; 15:7; Mark 12:15; Luke 12:56; 13:15. These final two terms both tend in the direction of the simplicity and honesty that James will call for as "purity of heart" in 4:8.

18. *the fruit that is righteousness*: As the connective *de* suggests, James returns to the necessity of *acting* on the positive qualities associated with the wisdom from above. This is certainly not a separate and isolated statement (against Marty, 152; Dibelius, 214) but is part of James' argument in 3:13–4:10. An exegetical decision is demanded by *karpos dikaiosynēs*, which some MSS try to assist by adding the definite article to the word *dikaiosynē*. Is the genitive simply adjectival = "righteous fruit"? Is it subjective = the reward for righteousness (Ropes, 250)? More probably, the genitive is epexegetical = that fruit which is righteousness (Hort, 87; Adamson, 156). This is supported by James' insistence that righteousness be revealed or demonstrated in deeds (2:20–23) and the logic of the aphorism itself: the *deed* is the doing of peaceful acts; the *result* is justice or righteousness. This appears to reverse the order of Isaiah 32:17, *kai estai ta erga tēs dikaiosynēs eirēnē* ("and peace will be the works of righteousness"; see Cantinat, 194), but clearly operates in the same framework.

is sown in peace: The phrase *en eirenę* is instrumental, "by means of peace," that is, peaceful acts. The image of "sowing" for moral activity is naturally connected to the image of "fruit" and is found, e.g., in Prov 11:21; 22:8; Sir 7:3; Hos 10:12; 1 Cor 9:11; 2 Cor 9:6; Gal 6:7–8.

the makers of peace: The dative is ambiguous, suggesting not simply pure agency but also advantage (Hort, 87). Indeed, many commentators prefer to take it entirely as a dative of advantage: "for those who are makers of peace" (see Chaine, 95; Mayor, 133; Laws, 165; Dibelius, 215; Martin, 135; and compare *karpon eirēnikon* as that which is yielded by discipline in Heb 12:11). The sense of agency, however, seems stronger. It is, once more, difficult to avoid the impression that Jesus' macarism has had some influence on James' language: *makarioi hoi eirēnopoioi hoti autoi huioi theou klēthēsontai* ("Blessed are the peacemakers, for they shall be called children of God," Matt 5:9).

4:1: *from where do wars*: The question follows directly from the statement concerning the making of peace in 3:18. This is not the start of a new section (against, among many others, Laws, 166) but the continuation of the same argument. Wars (*polemoi*) and battles (*machai*) are the standard activities of armies (see the terms in combination in *Il.* 1:177; Epictetus, *Discourses* III, 13, 9). But why should James pose this question to his readers? Is he responding to present (Reicke, 46; Townsend, 211–13) or former (Martin, 144) zealot activity among his readers? Is he using language about wars hyperbolically for the private disputes among his readers (Chaine, 96; Hort, 88; Cantinat, 195; Mussner, 176–77; Davids, 156; Ropes, 252–53)? When the passage is considered out of context, such hypotheses are appropriate if unanswerable. But if the question posed is part of James' argument that is using the Hellenistic *topos* on envy, then it should be seen as one of the standard features of that *topos*, based less on the supposed activities of his readers than the logic of the argument. This was seen clearly by Bede, who connects the question about wars to the "zeal and contentiousness" discussed in the previous verses; it is also seen partially by Windisch, 26. The phrase *en hymin* thus has the same sort of rhetorical force as in 3:13. In fact, envy is constantly associated with wars and battles, as it is with social upheaval: see Anacharsis, *Letter* 9:10–25; Plutarch, *On Tranquillity of Soul* 13 (*Mor.* 473B); *On Brotherly Love* 17 (*Mor.* 487E–488C); Epictetus, *Discourses*, III, 22, 61; Dio, *Or.* 77/78:17–29; *T. Gad* 5:1–6; *T. Jos.* 1:2–7; *T. Sim.* 3:1–5; 4:8–9; *Sentences of Pseudo-Phocylides* 70–75; Philo, *On Joseph* 5.

your desires that are at war among your members: The term *hēdonē* usually means simply "pleasure," particularly sensual pleasure (Herodotus, *Persian War* 1:24) but it can also be used in the sense of "desire for pleasure" (see Xenophon, *Memorabilia* 1, 2, 23; Dio, *Or.* 49:9; 4 Macc 5:23; Philo, *On Husbandry* 83). The fact that James follows immediately with *epithymein* suggests that this is also the meaning here (compare Luke 8:14; Titus 3:3; 2 Pet 2:13; and see Cantinat, 196; Adamson, 166). The "warring" of these desires can be taken both internally and externally, and they are logically connected: desires for pleasure tend to come into conflict within the human person, and the insensate drive for such pleasures creates tensions between people (Hort, 89). Since "desiring/ craving" is so integral an aspect of envy, it is not surprising to find the same connection to social unrest connected to *hēdonē* in Hellenistic moral discourse: Plato, *Laws* 862D; *Phaedo* 66C; Xenophon, *Memorabilia* 1, 2, 24; Anacharsis, *Letter* 9:10–25; Cicero, *De Finibus* 1, 13, 43–46; Seneca, *On Anger* II, 35, 1–6; Lucian, *The Cynic* 15; 4 Macc 1:20–29; 6:35; *Ep. Arist.* 277–78; Philo, *On the Decalogue* 153; *On Joseph* 10–11; *The Posterity and Exile of Cain* 116–19; *Migration of Abraham* 44–48.

2. *you desire and you do not have*: In 1:14–15, James stated aphoristically that *epithymia* could lead to death (*thanatos*). Now he shows the readers the logic behind that connection, moving from desire to "the serious and inevitable consequences of this emotion" (Laws, 172). The staccato and asyndetic character of these lines, however, raises two difficult and interrelated problems. The textual tradition is stable, with no significant variations. But it is difficult to know how to punctuate these lines (see the extensive discussion in Mayor, 134–36). The second problem is how to understand the harsh statement "you kill," which seems intolerably strong when written to Christian readers. Oecumenius offered the solution of spiritualizing: they died a spiritual death.

Erasmus offered the solution of emendation, and read *phthoneuete* ("you envy") here rather than *phoneuete* ("you kill"). The suggestion is reasonable for two reasons: first, NT MSS frequently confuse the two terms, as the critical apparatus for some NT vice lists attest (see in particular 1 Pet 2:1 and Gal 5:21). Second, the emendation recognizes that the real theme being developed here is that of envy (*phthonos*). The sentences then could be punctuated and read this way: "You desire and you do not have. You envy and are jealous and are not able to obtain. You fight and do battle." This makes sense to many commentators (Chaine, 98; Marty, 156; Adamson, 168; Windisch, 27; Mayor, 136–39). Dibelius, 217, calls it ". . . really a rather obvious solution." But it is a faulty solution. Appeals to emendation should always be a last resort, and there is really no basis for it here (Hort, 89; Cantinat, 198; Laws, 171). The solution fails to recognize, further, that "killing" (*phonos*) is a common element in the *topos* on envy (see below) and, for a Hellenistic reader, would have been expected in this context. It is better, therefore, to go with the text as it is (with Ropes, 254; Laws, 169; Hort, 89; Mussner, 178; Cantinat, 199; Davids, 158). The translation follows the punctuation provided first by Hort, 89, and followed by Mayor, 136, and Ropes, 254: thus the two statements, "you kill" and "you do battle and wage war" follow as the result of "you desire and do not have" and "you are jealous and cannot obtain." In order to capture the sequential character of the clauses, the present translation adds "so" to each final clause.

so you kill: As noted above, there is no textual variant offered for *phoneueite* ("you kill"). But it fits the context perfectly, because in the *topos* on envy, murder is regarded as a logical concomitant of envy. The logic of competition moves in the direction of elimination. See Plato, *Laws* 869E–870A, but the connection is particularly strong in the Septuagintal tradition (Wis 2:24; Josephus, *Ant.* 2:10–18; Philo, *On Joseph* 5–12; *T. Gad* 4:5–6; *T. Jos.* 1:3; *T. Ben.* 7:1–2, 5; *T. Sim.* 3:2–3; see also Acts 5:17; 7:9; 13:45; 17:5; Mark 15:10; Matt 27:18). The connection between envy and murder is made also by *1 Clem.* 4:9–5:2 and Basil the Great, *Homilia* XI,4 (PG 21:377).

and you are jealous: The double *kai* in this clause is all the more surprising after the previous asyndeton. The translation of *zēloute* as "you are jealous" deliberately picks up the theme established by 3:14–16 and leading to 4:5. The translation "you covet" (RSV) is acceptable, but the more literal rendering is used here to make the development of the theme more transparent.

and cannot obtain: James is simply tracing out the logic of envy. It is the failure to "obtain" (*epitynchanein*) and "have" (*echein*) that generates the rage that leads eventually to murder and war.

because you do not ask: James is not thinking of persons asking each other for things, as though good manners could assuage envy by supplying what it craves. No, his option comes from another view of the world. One can "obtain," but only by recourse to God the giver of gifts. The use of *aitein* ("ask") here deliberately echoes 1:5. If persons do not already live within the "wisdom from above," however, they are not likely to turn to God with their requests.

3. *because you ask evilly*: James now turns to the ultimate perversion of envy: it is possible to turn to God in prayer, yet do so "wickedly" or "evilly" (*kakōs*). The term is stronger and more pointed than the translation "wrongly" (RSV; NAB) would suggest; it is not merely a matter of using the wrong formulae but of approaching God with evil motives. Their prayer itself is "evil" in the way that the tongue is characterized as a "world of wickedness." For "speaking evilly," see 1 Macc 7:42 and Josephus, *Ant*. 6:299, and for the thought, compare Wis 14:30, which condemns idolators for "thinking evilly (*kakōs*) about God."

spend it on your desires: The verb *dapanan* means simply to spend any resource (Xenophon, *Memorabilia* 1, 3, 11; Herodotus, *Persian War* 2:37) but can also imply extravagance (see esp. Luke 15:14). Here the dative *en hēdonais* is cryptic: they ask to acquire the resources to enable them to obtain the objects of their desire and craving. The key to understanding why this is "evil" is the purpose clause and the negative valuation of *hēdonē*. The gift-giving God is here manipulated as a kind of vending machine precisely for purposes of self-gratification (see 1:26, *apatōn kardian*). In this case, "prayer" is a form of idolatry and, as we shall see, expressive of "friendship with the world."

4. *you adulteresses*: The harsh condemnation of the audience is not an uncommon feature of the diatribe (see 2:20 and the references given there). Some scribes were surprised by the exclusive use of the female gender for this charge here, just as many contemporary readers are likely to be offended (Schmitt, 331). The scribes therefore amended to *moichoi kai moichailides* ("adulterers and adulteresses"). The shorter text, however, is both harder and better attested and therefore to be preferred. Although James also connected murder and adultery in his statement concerning the decalogue in 2:11, such a thematic link is not present here. Despite Hort's conviction that James was addressing the literal problem of adultery in the community (Hort, 91), virtually all major commentators otherwise agree that James is using the symbolism found in Torah for the covenantal relationship between Yahweh as groom and Israel as bride. The covenant was like a marriage (Isa 54:4–8) in which Israel's frequent infidelities could be considered as adultery (see LXX Ps 72:27; Jer 3:6–10; 13:27; Isa 57:3; Hos 3:1; 9:1; Ezek 16:38; 23:45). In symbolic shorthand, James' epithet accuses the readers of idolatry, which is precisely what their manner of prayer (4:3) revealed (see also Ropes, 260; Cantinat, 201; Chaine, 99; Davids, 160; Mayor, 139; Laws, 174; Vouga, 115; Marty, 157).

do you not know: This is the clearest example in James of the diatribal rebuke for not acting upon an assumed store of shared knowledge (compare Epictetus, *Discourses* I, 12, 24–26; III, 24, 9–10; Dio, *Or*. 21:8; Seneca, *Moral Epistles* 7:5; 1 Cor 3:16; 5:6; 6:2; 9:13; Rom 6:16; 11:2). Their behavior implies a rejection of what they know but refuse to live by.

friendship with the world: For the Hellenistic understanding of *philia* ("friendship"), which enables us to understand the strength of this statement, see the note on James 2:23. It must be remembered above all that "friendship" involved "sharing all things" in a unity both spiritual and physical. Thus, friends are *mia psychē* ("one soul"; see Euripides, *Orestes* 1046; Aristotle, *Nicomachean Ethics* 1168B). The *scholia* therefore understands the phrase to be equivalent to "the world's lustful desires." Both genitives here are objective: it is a matter of being friends "towards" the world and enemies "towards" God (so Ropes, 160).

is enmity with God: Nowhere is James' thematic opposition between "the world" and "God" more explicit than here. For *echthra tou theou* ("enmity with God"), compare Rom 8:7, *to phronēma tēs sarkos echthra eis theon* ("the tendency of the flesh is enmity towards God"). As we would expect, *echthra* is the opposite of *philia* (see LXX Sir 6:19; 37:2; Luke 23:12). The more difficult question is why James should assume his readers would know this. There is no such proverb in the Greco-Roman moral literature, or in Hellenistic Jewish writings. Only a very partial parallel is offered by phrases like that in *T. Iss.* 4:6, *apo tēs planēs tou kosmou*. Mayor's conclusion that "the reference is to our Lord's words, Matt 6:24" (p. 139), is surely wrong, for although the sayings are compatible as to substance, both the phrasing and sense are different. Nor is a true parallel offered by 2 Tim 3:4, which refers to false teachers as *philēdonai mallon ē philotheoi* ("friends of pleasure more than friends of God"). The closest parallel is found in 1 John 2:15: "Do not love the world or the things in the world. If anyone loves the world, love for the father is not in him." The passage is close enough to suggest the existence of a shared Christian tradition to which both John and James could appeal. The fact that John uses the language of "love" rather than "friendship," however, only heightens the perception of "friendship" language as distinctively James' own and fitted to his thematic concerns.

therefore, whoever chooses to be a friend of the world: For the first time in the composition, James uses the inferential *oun* ("therefore"; see after this 4:7, 17; 5:7, 16). The relative conditional sentence posits a general premise = "everyone who." The verb *boulesthai* is deponent. It has the general sense of "willing/wishing" but, as here, often with the nuance of "choosing/preferring" (see Plato, *Gorgias* 522E; *Rep.* 347B; Epictetus, *Discourses* I, 12, 13; LXX Gen 24:5; Deut 25:7; Ps 39:9; Matt 1:19; Luke 10:22; 1 Cor 12:11). The strength of James' own use can be gauged from its appearance in 3:4 and above all in 1:18. The phrase "friend of the world" (*philos tou kosmou*) exactly opposes the description of Abraham in 2:23 as "friend of God" (*philos tou theou*). James means by this something stronger than simply being agreeable to the general culture (against Ropes, 260); he means rather a more fundamental compromise with "the values of human society as against those of God" (Laws, 174; see also Chaine, 100; Hort, 92). Bede notes accurately: "All lovers of the world, all seekers after trifles, are enemies of God . . . they may enter churches, they may not enter churches, they are enemies of God."

is established as an enemy of God: For the translation of *kathistēmi*, see the discussion of 3:6. The *echthros* is the opposite of the *philos* (see Prov 15:28; Sir 5:15; 6:9). The expression "enemy of God" is extremely harsh (compare Aeschylus, *Prometheus Bound* 119; Xenophon, *Cyropaedia* V, 4, 35; Philo, *Special Laws* 3:88; LXX Pss 88:52; 91:10; Rom 5:10; 11:28).

or do you suppose: The problem of punctuation appears again in this verse in perhaps an even more acute form and has generated more discussion than virtually any section of James. This translation takes the sentence as ending with *legei* and takes it as a rhetorical question that matches the one in 4:4, "do you not know." For *dokein* ("think/suppose") as introducing a false opinion, compare 1 Cor 3:18; 8:2; 10:12; 14:37; Mark 6:49; Luke 12:51; 24:37; and, above all, James' own earlier use in 1:26.

that the Scripture speaks in vain: For James' understanding of the "Scripture (*graphē*) speaking," see the note on 2:8. The main issue here has to do with what James might be referring to. Does he mean "Scripture as a whole" (see 2:8) or a specific passage (see 2:23)? If a specific passage, which one? There certainly is no passage in the OT, as we now have it, containing any such verse as we find here in 4:5 (Windisch, 27; Cantinat, 202–3). Is James, then, referring to a lost passage or one otherwise unknown to us (Marty, 159; Davids, 162; Mussner, 184)? Or is he making a broad allusion to the "sense" of Scripture (Bede; Mayor, 140–41; Ropes, 262; Dibelius, 222)? The key is punctuation. If, with Nestle-Aland 26th edition, we place a colon after "says/speaks," then this verb serves to introduce the next clause, which must logically be understood both as a quotation and as an affirmation. It is better to take the two parts of this verse as two rhetorical questions, as in 4:1. Then, *legei* is taken to mean not "says," but "speaks" (compare Rom 3:5; 4:3; 11:4; Phil 4:11). Finally, the referent for this speaking is taken to be the explicit quotation in 4:6 from Prov 3:34 (as seen by Oecumenius). The adverb *kenos* means empty/vain/useless/to no purpose (compare Epictetus, *Discourses* II, 17, 6). This is its only occurrence in the NT, but see the use of the adjective in Isa 49:4 and earlier in James 2:20. In the present case, it asks whether Scripture speaks to no effect (Laws, 174) or without meaning what it says (Ropes, 261).

does the spirit which he made to dwell in us: The textual problem is one of choosing between the intransitive verb *katoikein* ("which dwelt," so Adamson, 165) or the transitive verb *katoikizein* ("made to dwell," see Gen 3:24; Josh 6:25). The evidence strongly supports the adoption of *katoikizein*. The implied subject of the transitive verb in this case can be only God (*theos*), who is the implied subject of 4a and explicitly identified as subject in 4b. But what does James mean by *pneuma* here? It is probable that a contrast with *psychikos* in 3:15 is intended. But James' only other use of *pneuma* in 2:26 is unhelpful. There is no reason to suppose that James is thinking of the Holy Spirit. Two possibilities are the *pneuma* that God gave to humans as their life-breath in creation (see Gen 7:15; 45:27) or the *pneuma* that God gives as a gift to humans by way of prophecy or wisdom (see esp. LXX Exod 31:3; 35:31; Deut 34:9; Isa 11:2). A third possibility is that James is using a psychology similar to that in some Jewish circles. In rabbinic texts, the notion of *yēṣer hārāᶜ* and the *yēṣer haṭṭôb* refer to an "impulse" not entirely to be identified with individual psychology but equally with cosmic powers. Similar language about "The Spirit of Truth" and the "Spirit of Falsehood" is found also in the Qumran literature (see, e.g., *1QS* 4:9–26). But it is in the *Testaments of the Twelve Patriarchs* that we find the most parallels to James' usage. There we find the "spirit of truth" and "spirit of falsehood" (*T. Jud.* 20:1) and many other "spirits." In the *Testaments*, the spirits seem to sponsor the various vices or virtues by which the eponymous heroes live (see, e.g., *T. Reub.* 3:5; *T. Dan* 1:6), but these spirits in turn seem to derive from some central source such as the devil (*T. Naph.* 8:4) or Satan (*T. Dan* 6:1–2), who is said to "dwell" (*katoikein*) in a person. Conversely, the one doing good has the Lord "dwelling" (*katoikein*) in him (*T. Dan* 5:1–3; *T. Jos.* 10:2–3; *T. Ben.* 6:4). These texts seem to share a symbolic framework with this passage in James. James places on one side the "earthbound, unspiritual, demonic" wisdom from below (3:15) sponsored by the devil (4:7), which operates on the basis of envy and makes those who choose it enemies of God. On the other side, James places those who live by the "wisdom from above" (3:17), which derives from "the spirit God made to dwell" in humans (4:5) and operates on the basis of purity of heart and peace (3:17–18). Human freedom, then, is seen as operating in allegiance to one or the other of these "spirits" (see Marcus, "Evil Inclination").

crave enviously: The proper understanding of this phrase determines the interpretation of the entire passage. But it has been subject to quite different readings. Many commentators take the subject of *epipothein* to be God (Hort, 93; Mussner, 176; Davids, 164; Reicke, 46; Mayor, 142; Ropes, 264; Vouga, 117; Marty, 159; Dibelius, 224; Martin, 151) and render it softly as "yearn for." The phrase *pros phthonon*—itself rare in construction and usually taken to be adverbial—they understand as "jealously." Thus the sentence is understood as Yahweh's "jealous love" for the human spirit he created. There are severe and perhaps fatal problems with this understanding. The LXX passages that use *epipothein* do so with reference to the human spirit's longing for God, rather than the opposite (Pss 41:2; 118:20, 131, 174). Most of all, this reading must accept that *phthonos* can be applied to God. Some recognize the difficulty but simply accept it as an anomaly (Hort, 94; Davids, 164; Mayor, 145; Marty, 159; Cantinat, 204). But the lexical problem is more substantial than that. As we have seen, *zēlos* is capable of being understood both positively and negatively, but in Greek usage, *phthonos* is *always* a vice; it cannot be used positively (so correctly, Laws, 177–78). Martin's claim that the term is used with reference to God is simply erroneous; the passages he adduces do not refer to God but to humans as having *phthonos* (Martin, 150). Part of the *topos* on envy, indeed, is that the divine realm cannot be associated with envy (see Plato, *Phaedrus* 247A;

Timaeus 29E; *Sentences of Pseudo-Phocylides* 70–75). Note that in the LXX, *zēlos* is applied frequently to God (Deut 29:19; 32:19; Ps 78:5; 2 Kgs 19:31), but the translators reveal their Hellenistic sensibilities by restricting the term *phthonos* to humans (Tob 4:7, 16; Sir 14:10; Wis 2:24 [the devil]; 6:23; 1 Macc 8:16; 3 Macc 6:7). It is virtually impossible, therefore, for James to use *phthonos* for God. And while it is true that *epipothein* tends to be used positively in other NT texts (e.g., Rom 1:11; 2 Cor 5:2; 9:14; Phil 1:8; 2:26; 1 Thess 3:6; 2 Tim 1:4; 1 Pet 2:2), it can easily bear the more negative connotation of "crave" (see Herodotus, *Persian War* 5:93; Plato, *Laws* 855E; Deut 13:9; Ps 61:11; Wis 15:19; Sir 25:21). In the light of these considerations, it is not God who should be taken as the subject, but the *pneuma* within humans (Adamson, 170–72; Laws, 177–78). The rhetorical question, therefore, expects a negative response; as Laws paraphrases: "Does the Scripture mean nothing? Is this (according to Scripture) the way the human spirit's longing is directed, by envy?" (Laws, 178). The major objection to this reading is the absence of the particle *mē*, which usually introduces questions expecting a negative response. But the solution offered has fewer problems than any other and fits the argument James is making in the passage. Bede read it as: "Does the spirit that dwells in you have a desire for envy," and he declares that this question must be understood as a rebuke. As Nilus the Abbot also noted, "Scripture speaks against all passions, but especially against envy" (*Epist.* I, CXLV; [PG 79:141]).

6. *rather, he gives a greater gift*: The translation renders the adversative *de* with maximum strength in an attempt to capture the abrupt turn. God's way of acting (that is, God's *aphthonia*) is contrasted with the "craving enviously" of the human spirit dominated by earthly/demonic wisdom. The term *charis* can naturally be translated as "favor" (Hort, 96), but the use of the verb *didōmi* and the theme of God as gift-giver, already established by James in 1:5 and 1:17, support the translation given here (compare Ropes, 265). The meaning of "favor" in this case is that it *is* a gift, rather than something grasped (see Tob 7:17; Ps 83:12; 1 Cor 1:4; 3:10; 15:10; Gal 2:9; Eph 2:8; see esp. Paul's language about his collection for Jerusalem in 1 Cor 16:3; 2 Cor 8:4, 6, 7). James does not use *charis* elsewhere in the letter, and the phrase *didōsin charin* derives from the citation from Prov 3:34, which follows immediately. What, then, is meant by *meizona* ("greater")? It emphasizes once more the note of God's generosity: "he gives to all simply and without grudging" (1:5). In contrast to the human envy, which seeks to compete with others in order to secure for oneself what they have, God's *aphthonia* is demonstrated by his abundant giving.

therefore it says: The verb *legei* connects with the rhetorical question "does the Scripture speak in vain?" in 4:5. The connective *dio* ("therefore") is equivalent to "because it says," introducing the *graphē* on which James bases his argumentation.

God resists the arrogant: James quotes Prov 3:34 from the LXX but has *theos* ("God") instead of the LXX's *kyrios* ("Lord"); the MT lacks either designation.

Remarkably, no manuscript "corrects" back to the LXX. The same citation appears in the same form in 1 Pet 5:5, but in quite a different context: Peter uses it to encourage mutual submission in the community. The selection of this text is not arbitrary, but in fact grounds James' argument. We can notice first how "arrogance" (*hyperēphania*) is found consistently in Hellenistic discussions of envy (see, e.g., *Epistle of Heraclitus* 2:7; *T. Reub.* 3:5; *T. Levi* 17:11; *T. Jud.* 13:2; 18:3; *T. Gad* 3:3; *T. Dan* 5:6; LXX Exod 18:21; Pss 30:19; 100:7; Prov 8:13; Tob 4:13; Wis 5:8, and esp. Sir 10:7: "Hateful to God and humans is arrogance"; see also Rom 1:30; 2 Tim 3:2; Luke 1:51). Note the citation of James 4:6 in Isidore of Pelusium's letter "On Arrogance" (*peri hyperēphanias* [PG 78:292]). Second, the *context* of Prov 3:34 finds a number of intriguing echoes in James 3:13–4:10: God's wisdom is the basis of reality (Prov 3:19), and following this wisdom is the way to receive God's favor (*charis*; 3:22). This means walking in peace, *en eirēnē* (3:23), not taking away from the needy or saying to them that they will be helped on the morrow (3:27–28; see James 2:15–16); not envying (*zēloun*) the ways of the wicked (3:31; noticed by Hort, 96) because their way is "unclean (*akathartos*) before the Lord" (3:32). The curse (*katara*) of God is on the household of the impious, but the dealings of the righteous will be blessed (*eulogein*; 3:33; compare James 3:9). Then there is the present verse, quoted by James (3:34). Finally, "the wise (*sophoi*) will inherit (*klēronomēsousin*) glory (*doxan*; see James 1:12), but the impious will raise up shame" (3:35). The parallels are sufficiently dense and striking to suggest that James had more of this passage from Proverbs than simply 3:34 in mind. As in his use of Leviticus 19 and Isaiah 40, James assumes among his readers the capacity to catch allusions to the context of the *graphē* he explicitly cites.

7. *submit therefore to God*: The *oun* ("therefore") provides the essential hinge to the second part of James' call to conversion. He has charged his readers with infidelity and now calls them to a return to covenant. All the imperatives are second person plural. The change James calls for begins with the reversal of that arrogance resisted by God. They must begin by "submitting" (*hypotassein*; see Epictetus, *Discourses* III, 24, 65; IV, 12, 11; LXX 1 Chr 22:18; Pss 36:7; 61:2, 6; 2 Macc 9:12). James' use is particularly close to that in Rom 10:3 and Eph 5:24. It is noteworthy, however, that while James demands submission to God (see also 4:10), he does not share other NT writings' interest in submission to ruling authorities (Rom 13:1; Titus 3:1; 1 Pet 2:13, 18) or authorities in the church (1 Cor 14:34; 16:16; 1 Pet 5:5) or slaves to their masters (Titus 2:9) or women to their husbands (Eph 5:22; Col 3:18; Titus 2:5; 1 Pet 3:1).

but resist the devil: Some MSS omit the connective *de*, probably because of the asyndeton throughout the rest of this section. The verb *anthistēmi* has a definite military nuance (see Herodotus, *Persian War* 5:72; LXX Lev 26:37; Deut 9:2; *Epistle of Jeremiah* 56; Wis 10:16; 11:3; 1 Macc 14:29; see the expressions "resist God," "resist the Lord" in Hos 14:1; Mal 3:15; Jer 27:24). The devil personifies the negative side of James' cosmic dualism, the force that influences the *kosmos* resistant to God's kingdom (see notes on 2:19; 3:6). In particular, the mention of the *diabolos* here corresponds to the characterization of earthbound wisdom as *daimoniōdēs* in 3:15. For the *diabolos* as the agent of mischief, see the LXX Job 1:6–12; 2:1–7; Wis 2:24 (it was his *phthonos* that brought death into the world); Matt 4:1–11; 13:39; 25:41; Luke 4:2–13; 8:12; John 6:70; 8:44 (in connection with murder); 13:2; Heb 2:14 (in connection with death). For "resisting the devil" in Christian exhortation, compare Eph 4:27; 6:11; 1 Tim 3:6–7; and above all, 1 Pet 5:8–9 (using *anthistēmi* as here).

he will flee from you: A remarkably positive understanding of the cosmic battle. The expression is all the more remarkable in that there are parallels for humans "fleeing" (in the sense of avoiding) various vices (see 4 Macc 8:19; *T. Reub.* 5:5; 1 Cor 6:18; 10:14; 1 Tim 6:11), but James' statement of the evil itself "fleeing" finds no parallel except in *Herm. Man.* 12:4, 7; 12:5, 2 (probably in dependence on James).

8. *approach God and he will approach you*: As in the previous statement, this exhortation reveals a powerful optimism. The use of the verb *engizein* taps into a complex imagery employed by the LXX, by which the human relationship with God is expressed spatially in terms of "approaching." At Sinai, the people are told not to "approach" God (Exod 19:21), whereas the priests could "approach" (Exod 19:22), as also could Moses (Exod 24:2). The fact that Israel's God was one who "approached" people, in contrast, was regarded as exceptional (Deut 4:7): "what great nation is there to whom their god approaches (*engizein*) as the Lord our God does for all those who call upon him" (see also Hos 12:7). In the NT, only James and Heb 7:19 have this sense of "approaching God," although the idea of fleeing Beliar and approaching God can also be found in *T. Iss.* 3:17; *T. Dan* 5:1–3; 6:1–2; *T. Naph.* 8:4; *T. Ben.* 5:2; 7:1. See also LXX Zech 1:3: "Turn to me and I will turn to you, says the Lord." Bede notes, "not everyone is far from God by distances, but by dispositions."

cleanse your hands, you sinners: In the symbolic world of Torah, the notion of "approaching God" inevitably has ritual overtones (see the references to Mt. Sinai in the previous note). God dwells in a realm of purity. Approaching God demands self-purification. See the uses of the verb *katharizein* for priestly purifications in Lev 16:19–20 and with specific reference to sins (*hamartiai*) in Lev 16:30; Sir 23:10; see also Heb 9:14, 22, 23; 1 John 1:7, 9; 2 Cor 7:1. But why purify the hands? It is through the hands that gifts are offered, objects are declared clean, and others are ordained (Lev 4:4; 14:15, 26, 32). In Pharisaic Judaism, the cleansing of the hands was an important method of ensuring separation from realms of impurity (see the discussions in *m. Yad.* 1:1–4:8, and Matt 15:2; Mark 7:2–5). If, in the biblical idiom, the heart is the symbol of intention, then the hands are the symbol of action (Gen 3:22; 4:11; Exod 3:20; Deut 2:7; Ps 89:17). It is therefore also appropriate for *moral* purity to be symbolized by the "cleansing of the hands" as it is in Pss 17:21, 25; 23:4; 25:6;

72:13. Notice that James speaks of the "sinner" (*hamartōlos*) once more in 5:20 as one who needs to be turned from his way.

purify your hearts, you double-minded: As in the case of *katharizein*, James here uses language associated with cultic purity (see *hagnizein* in Exod 19:10; Num 8:21; 19:12; 31:23; and the combination in Isa 66:17) for a context dealing with moral intention. The heart is the seat of affection and decision (Gen 6:5; Deut 8:2). The "pure heart," therefore, is the symbol for one in right relationship with God (see above all LXX Ps 50:1–12). The expression *katharoi tē kardia* is found in Matt 5:8 and 1 Tim 1:5. The command given here by James corresponds perfectly with the indictment leading up to it: 1) As the wisdom from above is "pure" (*hagnē*), so must the double-minded "purify (*hagnizein*) their hearts" to live by it. 2) It is their hearts (*kardiai*) that need purification, for it is the heart that is in 3:14 filled with "bitter jealousy and rivalry." 3) The result of this purification will be the removal of the condition of being *dipsychos* ("double-minded") and living within the wisdom that is *adiakritos* ("undivided," 3:17).

9. *be wretched*: The verb *talaiporein* is intransitive and means to endure hard labor, distress, or hardship (Thucydides, *Peloponnesian War* I, 99, 1; V, 74, 2; Josephus, *Apion* 1:237). The verb is a hapax in the NT. The noun is found with reference to the calamity facing the rich in James 5:1 (see also Rom 3:16). In the LXX, the term appears constantly in the prophets with reference to the sort of catastrophe visited upon the people by the Lord because of their apostasy and idolatry (see Hos 10:2; Mic 2:4; Joel 1:10; Zech 11:2–3; Jer 4:13, 20; 9:18; 10:20; 12:12). Here, however, rather than threaten his readers with such a calamity from without, James calls on them to induce such distress in an act of conversion. It is not easy to find an English equivalent, but the RSV's "be wretched" comes close (compare also the use of the adjective in Rev 3:17; Rom 7:24).

and mourn: The verb *penthein* is used for mourning the dead (Herodotus, *Persian War* 4:95; Plato, *Phaedrus* 258B). It is used that way as well in the LXX (Gen 50:3; Num 14:39; Sir 7:34). But once more, the verb also appears in prophetic speech for the punishment that comes upon Israel for apostasy from the covenant with Yahweh (Amos 1:2; 8:8; Joel 1:9–10; Isa 24:4; 33:9; Jer 4:28; 14:2; Lam 1:4; Ezek 7:27). The most striking parallel in the NT is Matt 5:4, "Blessed are those who mourn, for they shall be comforted" (*makarioi hoi penthountes, hoti autoi paraklēthēsontai*).

and weep: Again, the verb *klaiein* means to give expression to sorrow and mourning by weeping (see Gen 37:35; Num 11:10; Deut 1:45). As with the other terms, it appears in prophetic discourse concerning the experience of sorrow at Yahweh's punishment (Hos 12:5; Joel 1:5; 2:17; Isa 22:4; 30:19; Jer 8:23; 13:17; Lam 1:1). Note the combination of "sorrow and weeping" in Rev 18:11, 15, 19.

laughter be turned into mourning: The language of reversal once more:

laughter (*gelōs*) is the opposite of weeping. In the LXX, the term is associated again with prophetic discourse about disasters befalling Israel because of apostasy (see Amos 7:9; Mic 1:10; Jer 20:7; Lam 1:7; 3:14). The use of the substantive is a hapax in the NT, but the verb *gelan* is used by Luke in a remarkable set of parallel statements. In Luke 6:21, Jesus says, "Blessed are you who are weeping (*klaiountes*), because you will laugh (*gelasate*)"; and in 6:25, "Woe to you who are laughing now, because you will mourn (*penthesate*) and weep (*klausete*)."

your joy into dejection: Here is a reversal from 1:2: those who were experiencing testing were to regard it "entirely as joy" (*chara*). But those who are friends of the world must abandon the *chara* associated with the pursuit of desires. The removal of *chara* is again a theme of the prophets (Joel 1:5, 12, 16; Jer 16:9; 25:10; Lam 5:15). The noun *katēpheia* refers to the literal casting down of the eyes, the physical sign of dejection or gloom (see Chariton of Aphrodisas, *Chaereas and Callirhoe* 6, 8, 3). It is found neither in the LXX nor elsewhere in the NT. It provides a neat contrast to the "elevation" found in the arrogant. (*hyperēphania*).

10. *humble yourselves before the Lord*: Literally, "be humbled." The verb *tapeinoun* recalls the "lowly person" (*tapeinos*) who is exalted in 1:9, as well as the lowly ones (*tapeinois*) to whom God gives greater gifts in 4:6. For the "lowly" as those specially favored by God, see LXX Pss 9:39; 17:28; 33:19; 81:3; Zeph 3:12. The prophets with some frequency speak of the Lord "lowering" or "humbling" the arrogant (Hos 5:5; 7:10; 14:9; Isa 2:11; 3:17; 5:15; 10:33; 13:11; 25:11; Lam 1:5; Ezek 17:24; 21:31). Here, the "lowering" is to be taken on oneself.

and he will exalt you: Again, the note of exaltation (*hypsoun*) recalls the elevation of the lowly in 1:9, which fits within the biblical theme of God "raising the lowly" (LXX Esth 1:1; 1 Sam 2:7; Job 5:11; Ezek 17:24; 21:31; Luke 1:52). The most striking parallel is found in the words of Jesus reported by Luke and Matthew: "everyone who exalts oneself (*hypsōn heauton*) will be humbled (*tapeinōthēsetai*), and the one who humbles the self will be exalted (*hypsōthēsetai*)" (Luke 18:14; Matt 18:4; 23:12). The final exhortation matches the spatial imagery of the passage as a whole: the wisdom from below seeks self-assertion but will be lowered. The wisdom from on high lifts up those who make themselves lowly.

COMMENT

This middle portion of James, when treated as a disjointed series of observations, has presented exegetical problems of the severest sort. The apparently intractable character of these problems has, in turn, served to heighten the perception of James' composition as fragmented and lacking in coherence. But when 3:13–4:10 is taken as a literary unit, not separate from its context but distinct within it, a powerful call to conversion reveals itself in the heart of this composition. It is a prophetic indictment and challenge, which in its structure and its themes provides the fullest statement of James' theological convictions and their moral implications.

In the comment on the section as a whole, I showed how 3:13–4:6 forms an indictment and 4:7–10 responds with a call to change. I also indicated how the entire passage contains a contrast between above and below, and between exaltation and humbling. There is first the contrast between a "wisdom from below" (earthly, unspiritual, demonic) and a "wisdom from above" (3:15–17). From 1:5 and 1:17, the reader recognizes this "wisdom from above" as the wisdom that comes from God, indeed as the "word of truth" that comes from God (1:18) and, as "implanted word," is to be received in "meekness" (1:21).

Second, there is the contrast between the "arrogant" whom God resists and the "lowly" to whom God gives gifts (4:6). Such language clearly suggests, in the first case, a movement from below upward in self-assertion and self-aggrandizement and, in the second, a posture of meekness ready and able to "receive gifts."

Third, there is the double command (in 4:7 and 4:10) to "submit" and to "humble" oneself before God, together with the assurance in 4:10 that the Lord will respond: "he will raise you up."

These spatial contrasts between lower and higher, between rising up and putting down, help define the religious framework for James' moral exhortation. Human behavior derives from and is measured by some overall perception of reality that can be designated as "wisdom," whether or not it takes God into account. But the only wisdom that is "true" is that which measures reality by the God who is the giver of all gifts (1:5, 17; 4:6) and who is able to "save and destroy" (1:21; 4:12). This is the God who made a spirit (*pneuma*) to dwell in humans (4:5). Will the human spirit live by the wisdom that comes from God, or will it live according to an earthbound, unspiritual, demonic spirit, sponsored by the devil (3:15; 4:7)? Ethical dualism—reflecting the choices made by human freedom—is placed by James within this cosmic, religious dualism.

In order to describe life lived by the measure of a wisdom that is "from below," James employs the Hellenistic *topos* on envy (*phthonos*). This means more than the fact that cognates of *zēlos* occur throughout 3:13–4:6; realizing that an author is employing a *topos* enables us to recognize, in what at first appear to be disparate remarks, the commonplace connections drawn by ancient moralists concerning a specific subject. In a culture that regarded virtue as health and vice as sickness, the vice of envy was regarded as particularly loathsome. In a saying attributed to Socrates, envy was termed an "ulcer of the soul" (Stobaeus, *Anthologium* III, 38, 48). The term "ulcer" nicely captures the gnawing pain of what Aristotle called "a certain sorrow" experienced simply because someone has something that we do not (*Rhetoric* 1387B).

Why such sorrow? It derives from the premise that being depends on having, that identity and worth derive from what is possessed. In such a view, to have less is to be less: less worthy, real, or important. To have more is to be more. Fundamental to envy also is the conviction that humans exist in a closed system, a finite world of limited resources. There is only so much to go around. The world is a zero sum game: for one to have more means for another to have less. To become more, therefore, one must somehow possess more. The logic of envy moves toward competition for scarce resources.

The ancient moralists were precise in their dissection of vices and virtues. When they considered the logic of envy as it was displayed in real human behavior, they saw that it lay behind every sort of rivalry, party spirit, and competition. In the moral literature, envy is consistently associated with hatred, boorishness, faithlessness, tyranny, malice, hybris, ill will, ambition, and above all, arrogance (*hyperēphania*). It is envy that creates desires to have and possess (see 4:2). And envy recognizes no bounds to its ambition. The result? Social upheaval and unrest, battles and wars (3:16; 4:1). And ultimately, murder (4:2). Killing the competition is the ultimate expression of envy. This is the true face of arrogance (*hyperēphania*) that God resists (4:6). And this is the wisdom of the world that sees reality as a closed system, so that even prayer to God is carried out for the purpose of achieving desires (4:3).

In 4:4 James draws his sharpest contrast between two measures of reality and two paths of life. His readers are not those who live completely by the measure of the world. But they are those who are "double-minded" (4:8). They want to live within God's measure but also to act by another measure. Using the language of biblical prophecy, James charges them with "adultery" from their covenant with God (4:4). James rebukes them for failing to live by what he clearly regards as a shared understanding: that friendship with the world means enmity with God (4:4). To appreciate the full force of his language, we must appreciate the richness of friendship language in the Greco-Roman world. To be friends meant above all to share: to have the same mind, the same outlook, the same view of reality. To be "friends of the world," then, means to live by the logic of envy, rivalry, competition, and murder. James' language is particularly shocking since, in Hellenistic moral discourse, vice and true friendship are considered to be polar opposites (see, e.g., Cicero, *On Friendship* 5:18; 18:65; 22:83).

James' ethical and religious dualism here is complete. Even someone who "chooses" to be a friend of the world is already established as an enemy of God (4:4). We see once more how consistently James has opposed "world" and "God." In 1:27 the religion that was "pure and acceptable to God" meant being "unstained from the world." In 2:5, those who are poor in the world's view are chosen by God to be heirs of the kingdom. In 3:6, the tongue is "established as the world of wickedness in our members." James' call to conversion, then, is directed at those double-minded people who want to be "friends with everyone," who do not want to have to choose, who want to live by God's measure and the world's measure simultaneously. This James will not allow. The one who is "wise and understanding" must "demonstrate his deeds in wisdom's meekness" (3:13), not by the violence inherent in the logic of envy.

By calling these double-minded people "adulteresses" (4:4) James has used the language of the prophets, who imaged the people's relationship with Yahweh in terms of marriage and, therefore, considered apostasy from covenant as an adultery. James concludes the indictment with thundering rhetorical questions. One opposes "the spirit God made to dwell in humans" and "envy." The other points to the evidence in Prov 3:34 that "Scripture does not speak in vain" (4:5), for there we read that God opposes the arrogant and gives gifts to the lowly (4:6).

James then returns to prophetic language for his call to repentance (4:7–10). The terms of repentance are breathtakingly simple. Submitting oneself to God, humbling oneself before God, "approaching God," are all gestures that effect "friendship with God," for they depend on a construal of reality opposed to that given by the world governed by envy. This construal regards human life as placed within an open system, one drenched by gifts from God, one that bestows being and identity and worth not from what humans can seize and control but by simple "reception in meekness" of what God implants in us.

And although James employs the elaborate symbols for repentance in the prophetic tradition (4:9), the act of repentance is itself quite straightforward. It is a matter of "purifying the heart" from its double-mindedness (4:8), of seeing reality as the "wisdom from above" enables us to see it and as the Shaker hymn rendered it truly: " 'tis a gift to be simple." The gift of simplicity is enabled by the God who gives to all simply and without grudging.

BIBLIOGRAPHY

Bohnenblust, G., *Beiträge zum Topos PERI PHILIAS* (Berlin Universitäts Buchdruckerei von Gustave Schade, 1905).

Cantinat, J., "Sagesse, justice, plaisirs. Jac 3,16–4,3," *Assemblées du Seigneur* 56 (1974) 36–40.

Cargal, T. B., *Restoring the Diaspora: Discursive Structure and Purpose in the Epistle of James* (SBLDS 144: Atlanta: Scholars Press, 1993) 137–67.

Coppieters, H., "La signification et la provenance de la citation Jac IV,5," *RB* 12 (1915) 35–58.

Dugas, L., *L'Amitié Antique* (Paris: Felix Alcan, 1914).

Eglinger, R., *Der Begriff der Freundschaft in der Philosophie* (Ph.D. diss., University of Basel, 1916).

Engelhardt, E., "Bemerkungen zu Jac. 4,V u.6," *Zeitschrift für die gesammte lutherische Theologie und Kirche* 3 (1869) 232–43.

Findlay, J. A., "James IV. 5,6," *ExpT* 37 (1926) 381–82.

Grimm, W., "Über die Stelle Br. Jakobi IV, v. 5 und 6," *TSK* 27 (1854) 934–56.

Hoppe, R., *Der theologische Hintergrund des Jakobusbriefes* (FzB 28; Wurzburg: Echter-Verlag, 1977) 44–71.

Jeremias, J., "Jac 4:5: *epipothei*," *ZNW* 50 (1959) 137–38.

Johnson, L. T., "Friendship with the World/Friendship with God: A Study of Discipleship in James," *Discipleship in the New Testament*, ed. F. Segovia (Philadelphia: Fortress Press, 1985) 166–83.

———, "James 3:13–4:10 and the *Topos* PERI PHTHONOU," *NovT* 25 (1983) 327–47.

Kirk, J. A., "The Meaning of Wisdom in James: Examination of a Hypothesis," *NTS* 16 (1969–70) 24–38.

Kirn, O., "Ein Vorschlag zu Jakobus 4,5," *TSK* 77 (1904) 127–33.

———, "Noch einmal Jakobus 4,5," *TSK* 77 (1904) 593–604.

Laws, S., "Does Scripture Speak in Vain? A Reconsideration of James IV.5," *NTS* 20 (1973–74) 210–15.

von Lips, H., *Weisheitliche Traditionen im Neuen Testament* (WMANT 64; Neukirchen: Neukirchener-Verlag, 1990) 427–38.

Marconi, G., "La 'Sapienza' nell'esegesi di Gc 3,13–18," *RevistB* 36 (1988) 239–54.

Marcus, J., "The Evil Inclination in the Epistle of James," *CBQ* 44 (1982) 606–21.

Michl, J., "Der Spruch Jakobusbrief 4.5," *Neutestamentliche Aufsätze: Festschrift J. Schmid*, ed. J. Blinzler, et al. (Regensburg: Verlag Friedrich Pustet, 1963) 167–74.

Milobenski, E., *Der Neid in der griechischen Philosophie* (Klassisch-Philologische Studien 29; Wiesbaden: Otto Harassowitz, 1964).

Paret, E., "Noch ein Wort über 4,5 nebst 1Mos 4,7a," *TSK* 36 (1863) 113–18.

———, "Nochmals das Zitat in Jak. 4,5," *TSK* 80 (1907) 234–46.

Perkins, P., "James 3:16–4:3," *Int* 36 (1982) 283–87.

Prockter, L. J., "James 4:4–6: A Midrash on Noah," *NTS* 35 (1989) 625–27.

Schmitt, J. J., "You Adulteresses! The Image in James 4:4," *NovT* 28 (1986) 327–37.

Schökel, L. A., "James 5,2 [sic] and 4,6," *Bib* 54 (1973) 73–76.

Spicq, C., "*Epipothein*: désirer ou chérir," *RB* 64 (1957) 184–95.

Townsend, M. J., "James 4:1–4: A Warning against Zealotry?" *ExpT* 87 (1978–79) 211–13.

van Unnik, W. C., *APHTHONOS METADIDOMI* (Brussel: Paleis der Academien, 1971).

———, *De APHTHONIA van God in de Oudchristelijke Literatuur* (Amsterdam: Noord-Hollandsche Uitgevers Maatschapij, 1973).

Zyro, F. F., "Ist es mit Jakbus 4, 5 nun im Reinen?" *TSK* 45 (1872) 716–29.

———, "Noch einmal Jakob. 4,5.6," *TSK* 34 (1861) 765–74.

———, "Zur Erklärung von Jakob. 4,5.6," *TSK* 30 (1840) 432–50.

VI. EXAMPLES
OF ARROGANCE
4:11–5:6

$$\blacklozenge$$

11. Do not slander each other, brothers. The person who slanders a brother or judges his brother slanders the law and judges the law. But if you are judging the law, then you are not a doer of the law but its judge. 12. There is One who is the lawgiver and judge, the one who is able to save and to destroy. But you who are judging your neighbor, who are you? 13. Come now, you who are saying, "Today or tomorrow we will go to a certain city and we will spend a year there and will make sales and a profit." 14. You are people who do not know about tomorrow, what your life will be like. For you are a mist which appears only for a moment and then disappears. 15. Instead, you should say, "If the Lord wills it, we will both live and will do this thing or that thing." 16. But now in your pretentiousness you are boasting. Every boast of this sort is evil. 17. Therefore it counts as a sin for the person who understands the proper thing to do and yet does not do it. 5:1. Come now, you rich people! Weep and wail over the miseries that are coming to you! 2. Your wealth has rotted, and your clothes have become moth-eaten! 3. Your gold and your silver have rusted, and their rust will be testimony against you and will eat your flesh like fire. You have built up a treasure in the last days. 4. Behold! The wages of the laborers who have harvested your fields—the wages of which you have defrauded them—are crying out. And the cries of the reapers have reached the ears of the Lord of Armies. 5. You have lived luxuriously upon the earth, and you have taken your pleasure. You have stuffed your hearts for a day of slaughter! 6. You have condemned, you have murdered the righteous one. Does [God] not oppose you?

THE SECTION AS A WHOLE

Defining the limits and logic of this section of James is difficult. That 4:11 represents some sort of starting point seems clear: 4:10 rounds off the call to

291

conversion that began in 3:13, and 4:11 takes the form of a negative commandment (using *mē*) such as we find at the start of other discrete sections in James
(see 2:1; 3:1; 5:12; against Marty, 303; Ropes, 5; Mussner, 175–93; Reicke,
44–50; and Davids, 28). But should 4:11–12 be read simply as a discrete unit,
one more fragment in James' compositional pastiche?

At first glance, it would seem so, for 4:13 has its own distinctive opening (*age
nyn*), which is found a second time in 5:1. On this basis, many commentators
divide the section into three discrete units: 4:11–12, 4:13–17, and 5:1–6 (see
Vouga, 119–31; Dibelius, 228–40; Cantinat, 11; Adamson, 175–82). Since
4:13–17 and 5:1–6 have identical introductions and deal in some fashion with
the getting and use of wealth, however, it could also be argued that they form a
separate section of their own (Chaine, 107–9).

This part of the text appears to end in 5:6, for 5:7 makes another distinctive
though not totally disconnected turn, signaled by the connective "therefore"
(*oun*) and the positive focus on community attitudes in contrast to those sketched
in 4:13–5:6 (against Laws, 186–95, who extends the third unit to 5:11).

The present commentary takes 4:11–5:6 as a single unit, primarily because an
identifiable thematic thread can be seen to run through it. Whether those
addressed are "brothers" (4:11), or are "those who say" (4:13), or are "the rich"
(5:1), their behavior is attacked by the author. More significantly, the kinds of
behavior condemned are clearly identifiable as manifestations of arrogance, or
hyperēphania. Slandering and judging a neighbor (4:11), pretentious boasting
(*alazoneia/kauchēsis*) that tomorrow's activities can be secured without reference
to God (4:13), living luxuriously upon the earth while simultaneously condemn-
ing, and murdering the innocent (5:5–6), are all activities that demonstrate the
arrogance that 4:6 declares God as opposing. The section, therefore, follows the
call to conversion in 3:13–4:10 with three specific examples of arrogance, which
are connected to that earlier section by James' final rhetorical question in 5:6:
"Does [God] not oppose you?"

NOTES

4:11. *Do not slander*: The shift in greeting from "adulteresses" in 4:4 to
"brothers" here is dramatic (Chaine, 108). Although the verb *katalalein* means
simply to "speak against" someone (e.g., LXX Num 12:8; 21:5, 7; Job 19:3; Ps
77:19; Mic 3:7; Mal 3:13), it can also be used in the particular sense of
"slander," that is, speaking against someone secretly and with malice. Thus, in
Ps 49:20, "speaking against your brother" is in the context of guile and
deception. See also Ps 100:5: *katalounta lathra tou plēsion autou* ("speaking
secretly against his neighbor"). Likewise, see Ps 49:20; Prov 20:13; Hos 7:13; and
katalalia in Wis 1:11. In the NT, *katalalia* has a position in vice lists that

supports understanding it as slander (2 Cor 12:20; Rom 1:30; 1 Pet 2:1; and *katalalein* in 1 Pet 2:12; 3:16). See also the usage in *1 Clem.* 30:3; 35:5; *Herm. Man.* 2:2–3; *Herm. Sim.* 9, 26, 7. The form of this prohibition and its close connection to the notions of law and judgment make it likely that James is again making an allusion to the context of the commandment of love in Lev 19:18c (Marty, 165; Mitton, 166; Johnson, 395; against Dibelius, 228). There is a thematic, though not verbal, resemblance to Lev 19:16: *ou poreusę dolǫ en tę ethnei sou, ouk episustēsę eph' haima tou plēsion sou* (see Mussner, 187; Windisch, 28). This can be translated as: "You shall not walk deceitfully among your people, you shall not stand forth against the life of your neighbor." The phrase *ou poreusę en dolǫ* translates the Hebrew *lō'-tēlēk rākîl*, which means, "do not go about as a slanderer," and is elsewhere similarly translated (see LXX Jer 9:3).

slanders . . . or judges his brother: The way in which James places these terms as virtually synonymous is a key to his meaning. For one human being to slander another means that the status of a *judge* has been assumed. The other is measured, found wanting, and is condemned—all in secret. The deadly effect of such vicious speech is well cataloged (see, e.g., Plutarch, *On the Control of Anger* 9 [*Mor.* 457D–458B]; 14 [*Mor.* 462C]; Pss 49:20; 100:5; Prov 18:8; 20:13; 26:22; Wis 1:11; *T. Gad* 3:3; 4:3; 5:4; *T. Iss.* 3:3–4; *PA* 2:4; *Deuteronomy Rabbah* 6:8; *Midrash on Psalms* on Ps 12:2). For the rabbinic tradition of judging others in their favor, see *b.Shab* 127a–b. What is most pertinent for James is that such judgment is a form of arrogance (*hyperēphania*), in which one asserts superiority over another. In effect, we find here the hidden form of the same sort of discrimination described in 2:1–4. James' language here and in 5:9 recalls the saying of Jesus in Matt 7:1: *mē krinete hina mē krithēte* ("Do not judge so that you are not judged").

slanders . . . and judges the law: This forms the apodosis of a proposition that is conditional in meaning if not in form, a fact recognized by the MSS that add *gar*. The logic of this conclusion, however, remains obscure unless one grants that James has in mind precisely an allusion to Lev 19:16. Why is slander against a neighbor also a judging of the law? Because the law of love forbids such slander (see Bede)! To practice slander and judgment against a neighbor is, therefore, to assume not only an arrogant superiority toward an equal but also to assume an arrogant superiority toward the law that forbids such behavior: one assumes the right to decide which laws apply and which ones don't.

not a doer of the law but its judge: An interesting textual variant is found in some MSS, which have *ouketi* ("you are no longer a doer") rather than *ouk ei* ("you are not a doer"). The person who determines which laws to keep and which to disregard has assumed the role of a judge (*kritēs*). Note here the application of the principle stated in 2:8–11 concerning the obligation to obey all the law. James' use of *poiētēs nomou* (which in classical Greek would be taken to mean "lawmaker" [Mayor, 148; Ropes, 274]) matches *poiētēs logou* "doer of the word" in 1:22–23 and helps account for the textual variant in that passage.

12. *One who is the lawgiver and judge*: The emphatic position of *heis* ("one") recalls the declaration "God is one" in 2:9 and echoes familiar statements of faith in Judaism (compare Deut 32:39; 1 Sam 2:6; *1QS* 10:18; *PA* 4:8; see Windisch, 29; Vouga, 120). Some MSS omit the definite article before *nomothetēs*, which is a NT hapax. It can be used for any legislator (Plato, *Rep.* 429C). In the LXX, the noun form is found only in Ps 9:21, but the verb form (*nomothetein*) is applied frequently to God (Exod 24:12; Ps 24:8, 12; 26:11; 83:7; 118:33, 102, 104). God is designated as "lawgiver" also in 4 Macc 5:25; Philo, *The Sacrifices of Cain and Abel* 131; see Heb 7:11; 8:6. Hellenistic Jewish authors followed Greek custom by referring to Moses as *nomothetēs* (Philo, *Life of Moses* 2:9; Josephus, *Ant.* 1:19), but James clearly refers to God. That God is also judge (*kritēs*) is axiomatic in the tradition of Torah (see LXX Ps 7:12; 49:6; 67:6; 74:8; Sir 35:12; Isa 30:18; 33:22; 63:7; see also 2 Tim 4:8; Heb 12:23). The designation *kritēs* is missing in some MSS, but in this case the longer reading seems to be the better.

able to save and to destroy: Although this specific epithet is lacking in the OT, it is everywhere stated that God is one who saves (*sōzein*) the people (see LXX Deut 33:29; Judg 2:16; 3:9; 6:14; 1 Sam 4:3; Pss 3:8; 7:11; 16:7; 21:22; 27:9; 68:2; 71:13; 105:8; Sir 2:11; Mic 6:9; Zeph 3:17; Zech 9:16; 12:7; Isa 19:20; 33:2; 60:16; Jer 15:20; 26:27; Dan 6:21, 23) and also one who is capable of destroying (*apolluein*) them (Exod 19:24; Lev 17:10; 20:3; 26:41; Num 14:12; Deut 2:12, 21; 8:20; 11:4; Josh 24:10; Pss 5:7; 9:6; 91:10; 142:12; 145:4; Wis 18:5; Obad 1:8; Zeph 2:5; Isa 1:25; 13:11; 29:14; Jer 25:10; 26:8; Ezek 25:7, 16; 29:8). Among the NT passages that oppose "saving" and "destroying," see 1 Cor 1:18; Matt 8:25; 16:25; Luke 6:9; 19:10. Closest to James' language and meaning is Matt 10:28 (missing in the Lukan parallel, 12:4): "fear rather the one who is able to destroy your body and soul in Gehenna." The corresponding notion is found emphatically in James' characterization in 1:21 of God's implanted word as "able to save your souls."

you who are judging your neighbor: In good diatribal style (Cantinat, 214), the question picks up directly from v.11. Some MSS have the relative clause *hos krineis* rather than the participial construction, *ho krinōn*, while others replace "neighbor" with "another." Still another reading is "who judge another, because it is not for a man but for God to guide a man's steps." This expansion is found also in 1 *Clem.* 60:2 and appears to derive from LXX Ps 36:23. In the form given here, James' question finds its closest parallel in Rom 14:4, "You who judge another's servant, who are you?"

13. *come now, you who are saying*: The same Greek phrase will be used again in 5:1, directed to the rich. The present singular imperative of *agein* is found, as here, with the plural as early as Homer (*Il.* 3:441; *Od.* 3:332) as well as in drama (Aristophanes, *The Knights* 1011; Aeschylus, *The Persians* 140;

Eumenides 307) and prose (Herodotus, *Persian War* 7:103; Xenophon, *Cyropaedia* V,5,15; *Apology* 14); in the diatribe, see Epictetus, *Discourses* III, 24, 40; see also LXX Judg 19:6; Isa 43:6; *Syb. Or.* 3:562). As so often in James, it is speech as revealing the orientation of the heart that is the special target (2:3, 14, 16, 18; 3:9, 14).

today or tomorrow we will go to a certain city: Some MSS have "today *and* tomorrow," rather than the disjunctive. More critical to the sense, some MSS correct the mood of the verb throughout from the indicative to the subjunctive in order to express intention: "Let us go . . . let us spend . . . let us make sales . . . let us make a profit." In each case, the simple future indicative is the better attested. And since the subjunctive appears as an obvious correction, the future is also the harder reading. One could also argue that the future indicative better expresses the fatuous sense of certainty implied by the speech. The translation "a certain city" derives from James' use of the demonstrative pronoun *tēnde* ("this one"), which generally denotes the definite rather than the general (Ropes, 276) but fits the hypothetical character of the example (compare the usage in Plutarch, *Table Talk* 1, 6 [*Mor.* 623E]).

we will spend a year there: With the accusative (*eniauton* = a year), the verb *poiein* can mean to "spend time" (compare Prov 13:23; Tob 10:7; Josephus, *Ant.* 6:18; as well as Acts 15:33; 18:23; 20:3; 2 Cor 11:25). Some MSS eliminate the adverb of place (*ekei*), and still others add the qualifier *hena* ("one") to *eniauton*.

make sales and a profit: Literally, "we will do business" (*emporeuesthai*) and "we will gain" (*kerdainein*). The first term includes both buying and selling and, as the etymology suggests, often connotes travel for the sake of trade (see Plato, *Laws* 952E). The only other NT use associates the verb with avarice (*pleonexia*; see 2 Pet 2:3). The verb *kerdainein*, on the other hand, refers not to the doing of business but its positive results (see Herodotus, *Persian War* 4:152; Matt 25:16, 17, 20, 22).

14. *you are people who do not know*: The translation reflects a textual decision in favor of the second person plural verb (*epistasthe*) following the relative adjective *hoitines*, rather than the alternative reading, which has the third person plural *epistantai* ("they are people who do not know"). This is only the first of the textual difficulties presented by this verse, whose overall sense is plain enough but whose syntax is obscure. How much the obscurity caused the multiple textual corrections, and how much resulted from them, is impossible to determine. In any case, this is the only use of *epistasthai* in James, but it fits his constant attention to true knowledge rather than false (see 1:2, 3, 6, 7, 13, 14, 16, 19, 22, 26; 2:20; 3:1, 13; 4:4, 5).

about tomorrow, what your life will be like: Another textual difficulty: MSS disagree concerning the presence or absence of the definite article before *tēs aurion*. Some have *to tēs aurion* ("that concerning tomorrow") and others the plural *ta tēs aurion* ("the things concerning tomorrow"), while still others omit any article. In addition, some excellent witnesses provide a *gar* after the interrogative adjective *poia*. If this version is read, then it would be logical to separate the clauses in this fashion: "You do not know the things concerning tomorrow. For what is your (*hymōn*) life?" Or, as in still other MSS, "For what is our (*hēmōn*) life?" The short rhetorical question would fit the diatribal character of the passage. On the whole, however, it seems better to follow the text and punctuation of the 26th edition of Nestle-Aland, as in the translation given here, despite its awkwardness. The sentiment concerning the fragility and uncertainty of life is a commonplace in moral literature (see, e.g., Plutarch, *A Letter to Apollonius* 11 [*Mor.* 107A–C]; Marcus Aurelius, *Meditations* II, 17; Seneca, *To Marcia on Consolation* 10:1–5; *On the Shortness of Life* 1:1–4; 9:1–10:1; *The Sayings of Amen-em-ope* 18; Prov 27:1; Sir 11:18; Ps 38:6; *The Sentences of Pseudo-Phocylides* 116).

for you are a mist: The translation takes the noun *atmis* as the first word in the sentence, followed by the explanatory *gar*, and with a definite article (*hē*) in the secondary position in order to create an attributive participial phrase. The second person plural verb (*este*) is read rather than the third person singular (*estin*/*estai*) found in some MSS. Although "vapor of smoke" appears as evidence for the Lord's presence in Lev 16:13; Wis 7:25; Acts 2:19, the term *atmis* itself suggests transitoriness and lack of solidity. In *1 Clem.* 17:6, it refers to steam rising from a pot as a symbol of nothingness. In Jewish apocalyptic literature, the wicked are compared to a mist or smoke that will disappear (see *4 Ezra* 7:61; *2 Bar.* 82:3; *1 Enoch* 97:8–10; *1QM* 15:10). Note also the similar characterization of the life of the wealthy in James 1:10–11 (Mussner, 190–91).

appears only for a moment and then disappears: The phrase *pros oligon* expresses temporal duration. The two participles (*phainomenē*/*aphanizomenē*) have the same relationship as the two terms used to translate them ("appears"/ "disappears"). Some MSS seek to strengthen the adversative character of the last phrase by adding *de*: "but then also disappears."

15. *instead, you should say*: The phrase *anti tou legein hymas* means "in place of your saying" and attaches syntactically to the *legontes* in the previous verse (Mussner, 191; Ropes, 278). The structure of vv. 13–15 should, therefore, be "come, now, you who are saying . . . instead of saying." The complexity of v. 14 obscures this simple structure, making it necessary to translate *anti tou legein hymas* as an exhortation.

if the Lord wills it: Some MSS have the present subjunctive of *thelein* rather than the aorist, but the difference in meaning is slight. The phrase has come to be called the *conditio Jacobaea*. Although the notion of God's "will" (*thelēma*) is found pervasively in the LXX (e.g., Pss 1:2; 15:3; 39:9; 142:10; Isa 44:28; Wis 9:13; Hos 6:6), the actual expression "the will of God" (*to thelēma tou theou*) or "the will of the Lord" (*to thelēma tou kyriou*) is not attested. The practice of deferring to the will of the gods is, in contrast, widely witnessed in Greco-Roman literature (see, e.g., Plato, *Alcibiades* 135D; *Phaedo* 80D; *Thaetetus* 151B; Epictetus, *Discourses* I, 1, 17; III, 21, 12; III, 22, 2). And it is found with remarkable frequency in the NT, as "the will of God" (Rom 12:2; 1 Cor 1:1; Heb 10:36) or (in the words of Jesus) the "will of the father" (Matt 7:21; 12:50; 18:14; 21:31) or "the will of the one who sent me" (John 4:34; 5:30) or "the will of God" (Mark 3:35). It is striking that the expression "your will be done" is attributed to Jesus as his prayer before death (Matt 26:42; Luke 22:42) and is found also in Matthew's version of the Lord's Prayer (*genēthētō to thelēma sou*, 6:10). James' language, therefore, is thoroughly at home in the early Christian usage (Chaine, 111). Indeed, James' recommended expression is put in the mouth of Paul when he promises to return to the Ephesians "if God wills (*tou theou thelontos*)" in Acts 18:21. Likewise, in Acts 21:14 the believers accede to Paul's plan to go to Jerusalem by saying, "the Lord's will be done (*tou kyriou to thelēma genēthētō*)." 1 Peter 3:17 refers to possible oppression as *oi theloi to thelēma tou theou* ("if the will of God should will it"). Paul also uses similar expressions in his letters (Rom 1:10; 15:32).

we will both live and will do: The two future tenses are again replaced in some MSS by cohortative subjunctives, following the lead of the corrections made in v.13. The subjunctive makes even less sense here. The phrase "this thing or that thing" corresponds in its vagueness to "a certain city" in v.13. James' exhortation applies to every circumstance. Notice also that James has "life" precede "doing." This is the first gift that comes "from the will of God" (see James 1:18).

16. *but now in your pretentiousness you are boasting*: For understandable reasons, some MSS have *katakauchasthai* rather than the simple *kauchasthai*; see the discussion on 1:9, 2:13, and 3:14. In the present case, *kauchasthai* is the better attested. James is here exposing the foolishness of such heedless speech by calling it "pretension" (*alazoneia*). In the Greek philosophical tradition, the *alazōn* ("braggart") is a stock character, expressing empty arrogance (see Xenophon, *Cyropaedia* II, 2, 12; Plato, *Rep.* 560C; *Philebus* 65C; *Phaedo* 253E; *Gorgias* 525A; Aristotle, *Nicomachean Ethics* 1108A; 1127A; Plutarch, *On Listening to Lectures* 10 [*Mor.* 43B]; *On Love of Wealth* 1 [*Mor.* 523E]; Epictctus, *Discourses* II, 19, 19; III, 24, 43; IV, 8, 27. In the LXX, the characterization is found in Job 28:8; Prov 21:24; Hab 2:5; Wis 2:16; 5:8; 17:7). Not surprisingly, it is found frequently in Hellenistic Jewish moral discourse (4 Macc 1:26; 2:15; 8:19; *T. Jos.* 17:8; *T. Dan* 1:6; Philo, *On the Virtues* 162; Josephus, *Ant.* 6:179; 14:111). As Oecumenius states, and as Ropes, 281, correctly notes, *alazoneia* is essentially connected with *hyperēphania* ("arrogance"); note its placement in Rom 1:30 (*hyperēphanous, alazonas*). For other Christian literature, see 1 John 2:16; 2 Tim 3:2; *1 Clem.* 13:1; 14:1; 16:2 (with *hyperēphania*); 21:5; 35:5; *Herm. Man.* 6:2, 5; 8:5; *Did.* 5:1. The connection with *hyperēphania* in James 4:6 is not accidental.

every boast of this sort is evil: The correlative adjective *toiautē* specifies the sort of boasting that is meant: that which arrogantly presumes on the future without consideration of God's will. That some sort of "boasting" can be good is shown by James' own recommendation in 1:9 and 2:13. The *alazoneia* here is not, however, simply foolishness; it is "evil" (*ponēra*).

17. *therefore it counts as a sin*: The form of this verse is that of a *sententia* or maxim (Chaine, 112; Adamson, 181; Ropes, 281), shifting from the second to the third person and from the specific to the general. Some commentators speculate that it may not have originated with James (Mussner, 192), and some emphasize its independence from its present context (Cantinat, 219; Marty, 176; Martin, 168). Nevertheless, it flows intelligibly from the previous section (Adamson, 181; Mayor, 152; Ropes, 281; Laws, 194). It is best seen as serving the same function as 2:13 and 3:18 (see Vouga, 125), that is, as providing a hinge between the example provided in 4:13–16 and that in 5:1–6. Although the thought is clear enough, the sentence is not easy to translate. The present translation places the final emphatic phrase (literally, "it is a sin to that one") into an emphatic first position, supplying the English "counts" in an attempt to capture the force of the Greek dative (*autǭ, eidoti*). The inferential *oun* ("therefore") shows that, at least in James' mind, this thought flows from the foregoing (Davids, 174). The "sin" (*hamartia*) must refer back to the *ponēra* in the previous verse, which is in turn connected to "every such boasting." Compare the use of *hamartia* in 1:15 and 2:9.

understands the proper thing to do and yet does not do it: The Greek sentence begins, "for the one who understands" (*eidoti*). Here is still another situation in which knowledge is not matched by appropriate action (see 1:22–27; 2:14–26). In this case, the person understands the "proper" thing to do (*kalos* rather than *agathos*). What does James mean by "proper thing" in the present context? Presumably he means that one should preface one's endeavors with prayer and place one's projects within the will of God (4:15). That is the only omission to which the *oun* ("therefore") could refer. Another instance of omission, however, will follow, and it is again the case of those who know what they are supposed to do (pay their laborers) but fail to do it.

5:1. *come now, you rich people*: For *age nyn*, see the note on 4:13. Once more, the rich (*hoi plousioi*) take center stage (see 1:10–11; 2:5–6). Now, the tone of straightforward hostility is remarkable, matched only by some strands within the Jewish tradition (see 1 Enoch 94:6–9; 97:1–10; 98:1–16; 99:11–16; 100:7–9; 102:1–11) and within the gospel tradition (Mark 10:25; Matt 19:23–24; Luke 1:53; 6:24; 12:16–21; 14:12–14; 16:19–31; 18:23–25; 21:1–4). On this count, as on others, James seems close to the sensibility of some sectarian Jews in Palestine.

weep and wail: For the use of *klaiein* ("weep") in prophetic laments, see the note on 4:9. The participle *ololyzontes* ("wailing") has the force of an imperative (Mussner, 193). It is onomatopoeic. From Homer on, it is used for women crying out to the gods, usually in joy (*Od.* 4:767; 22:408; Aeschylus, *Eumenides* 1043; Euripides, *Bacchae* 689). The LXX, in contrast, uses the verb exclusively in the context of laments in response to the disasters visited on the people by

Yahweh for their apostasy (see Hos 7:14; Amos 8:3; Zech 11:2; Isa 10:10; 13:6; 14:31; 15:2–3; 16:7; 23:1, 6, 14; 24:11; 52:5; 65:14). Its use here reinforces the strongly prophetic character of James' discourse in this section.

miseries that are coming to you: Literally, your miseries that are coming upon (*eperchomenais*), with some MSS adding *hymin* ("to you") to make the implied indirect object explicit. In the note to 4:9, it was shown how the verb *talaipōrein* was associated with prophetic laments. The noun form used here (*talaipōria*) can be used of miseries in general, such as those connected to poverty or mockery (Job 5:21; Pss 11:6; 39:3; 68:21; 87:19), but it is used predominantly in connection with the miseries suffered by those who have resisted God (Pss 13:3; 139:6; Hos 9:6; Amos 3:10; 5:9; Mic 2:4; Joel 1:15; Hab 1:3; Zeph 1:15; Isa 16:4; 47:11; 59:7; 60:18; Jer 4:20; 6:7).

2. *your wealth has rotted*: The noun *ploutos* is used for any sort of wealth or treasure (Herodotus, *Persian War* 2:121; Plato, *Laws* 801B). The tendency of wealth to offer false security, and thus alienate humans from themselves, is targeted by such NT passages as Mark 4:19; Matt 13:22; Luke 8:14; 12:21; 1 Tim 6:9. James ruthlessly exposes how fragile both wealth and its manifestations are. The verb *sēpein* in the active means "to cause to rot," but the perfect tense is sometimes used as equivalent to the passive (see *Il.* 2:135). For its use in the LXX, see Job 19:20; 33:21; Ps 37:6; Sir 14:19. The use of the perfect tense would seem to have less to do with the fact that these miseries have already started (Chaine, 114), than to create a vivid sense of their imminence (Ropes, 284), perhaps by the deliberate use of prophetic diction (see the note on 1:11 and Mussner, 194; Cantinat, 222; Adamson, 185; Mayor, 154).

clothes have become moth-eaten: The construction *sētobrōta* seems to echo Job 13:28, where humans are *hōsper himation sētobrōton* ("like a moth-eaten garment"), since the construction (*sēs* = moth + *bibraskō* = to eat) is found only in these two texts. The image itself is widespread (see LXX Prov 25:20; Sir 42:13; Isa 33:1; 50:9; and above all, 51:8). The closest parallel to this passage in James is again found in the words of Jesus recommending "treasure in heaven" that is impervious to moth, worm, or thief (Matt 6:19–20; Luke 12:33). Clothing is frequently singled out in ancient texts as a sign of wealth (Ropes, 285) and is so frequently also in NT texts (see Matt 6:28–31; Luke 7:25; 12:27–28; 16:19; 20:46; Acts 12:21). Does James also intend his readers to catch a deliberate reversal of the "splendid clothing" (*esthēs lampra*) worn by the rich person in 2:2–3?

3. *your gold and your silver have rusted*: James uses the singular perfect passive of *katioomai* ("to cause to rust") for both nouns. It is found in this sense also in Strabo, *Geography* 16, 2, 42; Epictetus, *Discourses* IV, 6, 14, but is a hapax in the LXX and NT (except for a variant reading in Sir 12:11). The image is all the more striking because the reason gold and silver are "precious" is their resistance to "rust" in the proper sense (Chaine, 115; Vouga, 128). This is surely a realization shared by ancients (see Philo, *Who is the Heir* 217), but the same

image is found also in *The Epistle of Jeremiah* (Bar 6:24) and Sir 29:10. Again, it is possible that James is deliberately reversing the portrayal of the rich as wearing "gold rings" in 2:2.

their rust will be testimony against you: In this part of the verse, the noun *ios* has its meaning of "rust," whose visible disfiguring of the precious metals stands as a "witness." The construction *eis martyrion hymin* could be taken as "witness to you" in the sense of a warning to the rich to repent (Cantinat, 223; Vouga, 129). But the meaning "against you" accords better with the dominant sense of this idiom in the gospel tradition (see Matt 8:4; 10:18; 24:14; Mark 1:44; 6:11; 13:9; Luke 5:14; 9:5; 21:13) and is more likely in this context, which is a condemnation rather than a call to conversion (so Vouga, 129; Adamson, 184; Davids, 176; Laws, 199; Dibelius, 237). The use of the image is striking on two counts. First, James uses it to establish another courtroom setting, which reverses that in 2:6 where the rich dragged the poor into courts in order to oppress them; now the rich are the ones in the dock. Second, the very corruption (rust) of their wealth is personified (Mussner, 195) in order to bear testimony against them.

will eat your flesh like fire: Some MSS unnecessarily add *ho ios* ("the rust") before the phrase "like fire." A more difficult problem concerns punctuation. Should "like fire" go with the next clause or with this one? Ropes, 287, followed by Reicke, 50–51, argued that the verb *thēsaurizein* cannot be used absolutely and needed an object; therefore, following the precedent of passages such as Prov 16:27, he read, "like fire have you built up treasure in the last days." In fact, *thēsaurizein* does appear absolutely (see Luke 12:21). And it is far more likely that "like fire" should modify the effect of rust (so Windisch, 31; Chaine, 116; Marty, 284; Laws, 200; Dibelius, 237). Now, however, *ios* seems to assume some of its other meaning of "poison" that it had in 3:8. One could argue that rust and fire are simply different points on the continuum of oxidation. For "fire eating flesh," see LXX Jdt 16:17 and esp. Ps 20:10, *kataphagetai autous pyr*. There may also be a play on the dictum that "gold is tested by fire" (*en pyri dokimazetai chrysos*, Sir 2:5; see 1 Pet 1:7). Since the rich have placed their trust and their very sense of worth in their gold and silver, the same poison/rust that destroys the metals destroys them as well. Neither they nor the metals are refined, only destroyed. The *pyr* is the punishing fire (see James 3:6).

you have built up a treasure in the last days: This sentence is not difficult to translate, but it seems to have several possible meanings. The verb *thēsaurizein* is straightforward: it means to accumulate wealth and keep it secure (Herodotus, *Persian War* 2:121; Xenophon, *Cyropaedia* VIII, 2, 24; 2 Kgs 20:17; 2 Cor 12:14). At the simplest level, we can read this sapientially. The rich are people saving up in order to provide security for themselves "in the last days," which they understand to be their retirement years. In this respect, they resemble Luke's "Rich Fool," who sought to secure his life by his possessions (Luke 12:19). In Luke's parable, however, the end came suddenly when the man's life was required of him (12:20). He was revealed as a fool, and his possessions went to others. Here, likewise, the rusted metals of the treasure trove are a "witness against" the rich of their foolishness in placing their hope in transitory wealth. The lesson would be like that in Luke: "Thus is the one who builds treasure for himself but is not rich towards God" (Luke 12:21). This reading would also fit a sapiential reading of 1:11, which declared that the rich would pass away in the midst of all their affairs. But we can also read it prophetically. Now, "the last days" (*eschatais hēmerais*) are not the anticipated retirement years of the rich, but the time of God's judgment (Hos 3:5; Mic 4:1; Isa 2:2; Jer 23:20; Ezek 38:16; Dan 2:28; 10:14). Among early Christian readers, such an understanding virtually would be demanded, so widely did these words trigger eschatological associations (John 6·39–44; 11:24; Acts 2:17; 2 Tim 3:1; Heb 1:2; 1 Pet 1:5, 20; 2 Pet 3:3; 1 John 2:18; Jude 18). Now the displaced hopes of the wealthy are seen as a heedless disregard of God's judgment. Read this way, the notion of "treasuring up" may be used metaphorically (see Prov 1:18; Amos 3:10; Mic 6:10) and bear another level of irony, of the sort Paul had in mind when he spoke of the wicked "storing up" wrath (*orgē*) for God's judgment (Rom 2:5). This added twist would fit the sharp sarcasm embedded also in 5:5.

4. *the wages of the laborers*: The use of the imperative *idou* ("behold"; see 3:4, 5; 5:7, 9, 11) heightens the drama of this charge. Just as the rich were to contemplate the miseries coming on them, now they are to gaze on the cause of those miseries. The money that they have piled up and allowed to rust stands as witness against them, precisely because it should have been given out in wages. Here, above all, is the "proper thing to do" (4:17), which has not been done. The *misthos* is what is owed to another either by way of reward (see Matt 5:12) or by way of earned payment. It is an obvious principle of social ethics that "the laborer deserves his pay" (Luke 10:7; 1 Tim 5:18), not as a matter of grace but as a matter of justice (Rom 4:4). The term *ergatēs* ("laborer") emerges from the world of great landowners (frequently absentee) whose practices concerning their tenant farmers and day laborers (see Herodotus, *Persian War* 4:109; Philo, *On Husbandry* 5) was in first-century Palestine, as reflected in the parables of Jesus, often cruel and capricious (see Matt 18:23–34; 20:1–15; 21:33–43; Luke 12:16–21; 12:42–48; 16:1–8; 19:12–27; 20:9–18).

who have harvested your fields: The verb *aman* means to "mow" or "cut down," but refers specifically to the act of cutting grain (Hesiod, *Works and Days* 480; LXX Lev 25:11; Deut 24:19; Mic 6:15; Isa 17:5). Several things about the language here are significant. First, James uses the aorist participle: the laborers *have* harvested and are, therefore, now owed their wages. Second, this labor has been done for "your" (the rich owners') fields. Third, James' entire characterization echoes the biblical laws regulating the payment of agricultural laborers. It is possible once more to detect an allusion to Leviticus 19, which, as we have seen, plays an important role in this letter as an explication of the demands of the "law of love" (2:8). Specifically, Lev 19:13 reads, "You shall not oppress (*adikēseis*) your neighbor or rob (*harpaseis*) him. You shall not keep by you overnight until morning the wages of a hired servant (*ho misthos tou misthōtou*)." This allusion has been recognized by several commentators (Dibelius, 238; Mussner, 196; Mayor, 158; Ropes, 288; Mitton, 179; Adamson, 186). James' language is also close to that in Mal 3:5: "I will come to you for judgment and I will bear witness quickly against the magicians and adulterers and those who are swearing in my name falsely, and those who have held back the wage of the hired laborer . . . (*aposterountas misthon misthōtou*)." For the concern for such social justice in the Jewish tradition, see also Exod 23:9–11; Lev 6:4; 19:35; Deut 24:10–16; *T. Job* 12:1–4; *Syb. Or.* 2:74; *Sentences of Pseudo-Phocylides* 19.

of which you have defrauded them: The textual problem here affects the tone of the translation. Some MSS read *aphysterēmenos* for what was done to the wages. The verb is rare, but appears in LXX Neh 9:20 and Sir 14:14 in the straightforward sense of "holding back." The majority of MSS, however, read *apesterēmenos*. This also means "to hold back," but with the added nuance of deliberate fraud. It is the verb found in such legal passages as LXX Exod 21:10; Deut 24:14 (with *misthos*); as well as Sir 4:1 (the life of the poor man); 29:6 (of a borrower robbing a lender); 34:22 (with *misthos*); and finally, Mal 3:5 (see previous note). In the NT, the verb is used absolutely in the sense of "defraud" (see Mark 10:19; 1 Cor 6:7–8). It might be argued that scribes would seek to conform James' usage to that of the LXX (Laws, 201). But in this case, James' allusion seems so deliberate as to make the argument *for* the best-attested reading, *apesterēmenos* (Metzger, 684–85). And if this is the best reading, then James can be understood as implying that the withholding of wages was deliberate fraud.

are crying out: The use of *krazein* continues the personification of the wealth. In v.3, its rust bore witness against the hoarders. Now, as wealth gained by oppression and fraud, it "cries out." The verb echoes the "crying out" of Israel to the Lord when in distress (Exod 5:8; 22:22; 32:17; Num 11:2; Judg 1:14; 3:9; 4:3; 6:7; Pss 3:5; 17:42; 21:3; 27:1; 64:14; Mic 3:4; Isa 19:20).

the cries of the reapers: The use of *therisantes* ("those who have harvested") is synonymous with *amēsantes* in the previous clause. The use of the aorist participle is again significant: they have completed the task and now are owed. They join their cries to those of the expropriated wages. James again chooses a particularly evocative term (*boai*). The blood of the innocent Abel "cried out" (*boan*) to God and led to the punishment of Cain (Gen 4:10). Likewise, the "cries" (*boai*) of the defrauded Israelites in Egypt reached God (Exod 2:23).

have reached the ears of the Lord of Armies: The use of the perfect tense is especially powerful here: God has already heard of these things. Once more, James is clearly evoking the experience of Israel in Egypt. At the burning bush, Yahweh says to Moses, "I have seen the affliction of my people in Egypt and *I have heard their shouts* (*tēs kraugēs autōn akēkoa*, Exod 3:7). The language resembles also LXX Ps 17:7: "In my affliction I called on the Lord and I cried out (*ekekraxa*) to my God. From his holy temple he heard my voice and my shout (*kraugē*) before him will come to his ears (*eiseleusontai eis ta ōta autou*)." The final phrase recalls Isa 5:9: "These things have been heard in the ears of the lord of Armies (*ēkousthē gar eis ta ōta kyriou sabaōth tauta*)" (see Morris, *An Investigation*). The phrase "Lord of Armies/Hosts (*kyrios Sabaōth*)" is a transliteration of the Hebrew and is used titularly in LXX Josh 6:17; 1 Sam 1:3; Zech 13:2; Isa 1:9; 5:7; 19:4; Jer 26:10. It emphasizes Yahweh's *power* to act. That the cries of the oppressed do reach God is stated also by Exod 22:21–27; *I Enoch* 47:1; 97:5.

5. *you have lived luxuriously upon the earth*: James shifts back again to the heedless behavior of the wealthy. The verb *tryphan*, like its cognate *tryphē*, can have both a positive and negative sense. Positively, it means to take pleasure or delight in something. Thus, Eden is called the "garden of delight (*tryphēs*)" in Gen 2:15; 3:24; Joel 2:3. And one can "delight" in goodness or good things (Neh 9:25; Sir 14:4). Negatively, it means to live luxuriously and, as a result, to be soft or wanton. And in the rigorous outlook of Hellenistic moral discourse, shaped by Cynicism and Stoicism, such "pleasure-taking" would always be regarded as a vice (see, e.g., Plato, *Laws* 901A; Aristotle, *Politics* 1266B [large estates promote luxury]; *Sentences of Sextus* 73; Josephus, *Ant.* 4:167; Philo, *Special Laws* 2:240; *On Dreams* 1:123; *T. Jos.* 9:2). James is the only NT text to use the verb, but the negative implications of the noun are found in Luke 7:25 and 2 Pet 2:13. The qualification "upon the earth" may mean something like "merely earthly" in contrast to "heavenly," but more likely it has a straightforward literal sense: they have lived well "off the land."

taken your pleasure: The verb *spatalan* has much the same range of meaning as *tryphan*, except that it tends automatically to suggest excessive comfort and overindulgence (see, e.g., Sir 21:15; 27:13; Ezek 16:49; 1 Tim 5:6). Taken together, the two terms suggest conspicuous consumption and heedless pleasure-seeking; thus, the arrogance implied by the translation, "taken your pleasure."

stuffed your hearts for a day of slaughter: The verb *trephein* means basically to feed (see Matt 6:26; 25:37; Acts 12:20) and, by extension, to raise or educate (Luke 4:16). But what does it mean to "feed the heart"? The oddity of this expression may account for the textual variant in some MSS of "feed your flesh." But the reading "hearts" is better attested. What, then, is the connection between this peculiar "nourishment" and "in a day of slaughter (*en hēmera sphagēs*)"? We are clearly in the realm of specifically biblical imagery, and the interpretation can proceed by tracing out sometimes obscure intertextual connections. It is clear, first of all, that *kardia* ("heart") is being used here in its frequent sense as the seat of human intentionality, the self (compare James 1:26; 3:14; 4:8; 5:8). Second, it is also clear that the "day of slaughter" echoes Jer 12:3, a prophetic logion that threatens evildoers in this fashion: "pull them out like sheep for the slaughter and set them apart for the day of slaughter." This image is itself complex. It builds on the ordinary method of providing food in an agricultural context, namely by slaughtering animals (see Ps. 43:23; Prov 7:22; Isa 53:7). But in the prophets, this quotidian and ritual activity became the image for divine judgment on evildoers (see Zech 11:4, 7; Isa 34:2, 6; 65:12; Jer 15:3; 19:6; 32:34). James therefore uses this "end-time" image to shape the significance of the "feeding" image. Now "feeding the hearts" becomes, by implication, equivalent to "stuffing" or force-feeding an animal to fatten it for the slaughter. The rich oppressors' self-indulgence is perceived ironically as preparation for self-destruction "in the last days." This reading corresponds nicely to the interpretation given in 1:26 for *apatōn tēn kardian* ("indulging the heart"). For the certainty of a day of judgment for evil oppressors, see *I Enoch* 94:9; 97:8–10; 99:15; *Jub.* 36:9–10; *1QH* 15:17–18; *1QS* 10:19.

6. *you have condemned*: The verb *katadikazein* derives from forensic contexts: a sentence of condemnation is given against someone for a crime (see Herodotus, *Persian War* 1:45; Job 34:29; Josephus, *Ant.* 7:271; Matt 12:37; Acts 25:15). James' use of the courtroom image reminds us forcefully of 2:6, where the rich have dragged the poor into court for the purpose of oppressing them (Davids, 179). Such "legal" oppression—or judicial murder (Laws, 205)—was recognized already in Torah under the rubric of the "perversion of justice" by moving landmarks (Deut 19:14; 27:17), by refusing to return what was taken in pledge from the poor (Lev 5:23–24; Deut 24:12–13), by the use of false weights and scales (Lev 19:35; Deut 25:13–16), or by the taking of bribes in making decisions (Exod 23:7–8; Lev 19:15; Deut 10:17–19; 16:18–20; 24:17; 27:19).

you have murdered the righteous one: Despite the view of Oecumenius, Bede, and Cassiodorus (and more recently, Feuillet, 276–77), there is no reason to see "the righteous one" (*ho dikaios*) as Jesus (see Luke 23:47; Acts 3:14) and even less to identify him with James (Mayor, 160 [possibly: Martin, 182; Dibelius, 240]). The reference is rather more general. Any laborer defrauded in this manner is "innocent" with respect to the oppressive action of the rich. James' language appears to echo that of *The Book of Wisdom*, which portrays evildoers plotting against the righteous one (*ton dikaion*, 2:12) and planning for him a shameful death (*thanatō aschēmoni katadikasōmen auton*, 2:20). That such was the common fate of the innocent poor is found also in *I Enoch* 95:7; 96:8; 99:15; and this collective understanding of the righteous is probably correct (Marty, 189–90; Davids, 180; Laws, 206; Martin, 182; Dibelius, 239). James continues to develop what we have called "the logic of envy," which seeks to eliminate any competition. In 3:13–4:10, envy was connected to idolatry, that "friendship with the world" that identifies being with having, so that oppression and murder follow as a matter of course (4:1–2). The specific link among idolatry, oppression, and murder is established already by Scripture (see, e.g., Deut 12:30–31; Amos 5:4–6; Hab 1:16; Jer 2:27, 34; 22:3; Ezek 16:49, 52; Isa 1:21–23), but nowhere is it more powerfully stated than in Sir 34:21–22: "The bread of the needy is the life of the poor. Whoever deprives them of it is a man of blood. To take away a neighbor's living is to murder him. To deprive an employee of his wages is to shed blood."

does [God] not oppose you: The more common way to read this final clause in 5:6 is as a statement, rather than as a question, with the subject continuing to be *ho dikaios* ("the righteous one") (see Mussner, 193; Windisch, 30; Chaine, 119; Cantinat, 228; Vouga, 131; Marty, 189–90; Reicke, 51; Adamson, 188; Mayor, 160; Dibelius, 240; Martin, 182). Such seemed to have been the understanding also of the scribes who added *kai* to the beginning of the clause, yielding, "you have murdered the righteous one and he does not oppose you." Alternative translations, including the one given here, are discussed by Vouga, 131; Laws, 207; and Martin, 172; but are then rejected. Feuillet (275–76) takes it as a question but refers it to Christ, with the support of NT passages that stress his suffering without retaliation (Acts 8:32–35; 1 Pet 2:21–25); Bede, Oecumenius, and Theophylact also refer it to Christ. Ropes, 292, and Davids, 180, take seriously the possibility that it is a question but refer it to "the righteous one," by which they mean that the righteous one opposes the rich in the time of judgment. The translation given here, which provides "God" (*ho theos*) not as a textual emendation but as the implied subject of the verb, is difficult but can be supported on the following grounds: 1) the passage 5:1–6 moves alternatively from the behavior of the rich to their prospective fate, and the reading given here forms the logical response to their final murderous act; 2) the use of a rhetorical question fits James' diatribal style; 3) if we grant James' compositional unity, the use of *antitassetai* in such close proximity to 4:6 cannot be accidental. There, God is said to *oppose the arrogant*. James has now given three examples of arrogance, climaxing with the act of judicial murder. That God *opposes them* makes a fitting conclusion. 4) If 5:6 concludes not with a statement about the righteous person's lack of opposition, but an assurance of God's opposition in judging the arrogant, then the *oun* ("therefore") in 5:7 makes much more sense. Much of this same argument is found in Schökel, "James 5,6," 73–76.

COMMENT

Consistent with the ethical and religious dualism that has structured his entire composition, James here opposes three forms of arrogance (*hyperēphania*) that illustrate "friendship with the world," operating within the logic of envy, to the reality of the living God who "opposes" such human arrogance (4:6). As I noted above in the discussion of the section as a whole, the three examples do not appear, on the surface, to have much in common. But a closer look reveals that in each case, James opposes a form of human pretension with a reminder of God's claim on creation.

In 4:11–12, the "brothers" who slander each other are accused of placing themselves in the position of being judges, even of the law given by God! James reminds them that the one who gave the law is alone able to "save and destroy." The reminder deflates their pretensions: "who are you?" In 4:13–17, the entrepreneurs who assume the security and predictability of their projects for gaining wealth are directly accused of a boasting that is "evil." Their pretension is countered by the reminder that they cannot secure their very existence: "you are a mist that appears only for a moment and then disappears" (4:14). In 5:1–6, the heedless luxury of the rich that is won by the oppression of the laborers and ultimately by the condemnation and murder of the innocent is countered by the reminder that God hears the cry of the oppressed and is preparing a day of slaughter in which the wealth of the rich will stand in testimony against them.

Reading 4:11–5:6 in this fashion reveals its thematic unity and the logic of its literary placement. In the middle of James' call to conversion from "friendship with the world" to "friendship with God," he asserts that "God opposes the arrogant." These three examples build on that declaration and demonstrate it so that the final question, "Does he [God] not oppose you?" provides an appropriate closure.

The examples move progressively from "the brothers," whom we assume to be within the community, to "the rich" who are quintessentially the outsiders for this community (2:2–7). There is also a progression in the demonstration of arrogance, from the secret speech (slander) that judges another, to the public boasting that launches public projects, to the systemic corruption of the society and the destruction of the innocent. Corresponding to these degrees of influence is the weight of condemnation, from the reminder of who is the judge and lawgiver, to the declaration of behavior as evil and sin, to the threat of condemnation in the day of judgment.

Beneath these obvious differences, however, a single argument is working, which reflection on each example reveals. The shape of the argument is laid out by James himself in 4:11–12. He begins with a straightforward prohibition of slander (*katalalia*). At first, this might appear to be simply one more fault of speech singled out for attention (see 3:1–12). But James then draws a fascinating conclusion, "the person who slanders a brother or judges his brother slanders the law and judges the law" (4:11). The conclusion is based on several unstated premises. The first is that slander by its very nature involves a secret judging (and condemnation) of an associate. In the most obvious way, to presume the right to judge and condemn another is to claim a privileged position of superiority over them. But the superiority is not real: no one has appointed me as judge of my brother! Why do I assume that position? Here is where the logic of envy (*phthonos*) helps make sense of slander. Slander serves the double function of lowering my neighbor and elevating me; it takes away status from another and gives it to me. It is the perfect example of life as competition. Slander is, therefore, a form of *hyperēphania* (arrogance) that seeks to assert oneself by destroying another. It is a form of arrogance that can exist between those calling themselves "brothers" because slander is evil speech done in secret.

James' conclusion that such judging is also a "judging of the law" is more difficult to understand, until we remember the way in which he has used Lev 19:13–18 thematically throughout the composition. Leviticus 19:16 prohibits such speech against a neighbor. To disobey this law against slander is, therefore, also to place oneself in a position of superiority to the law: it is for me to pick and choose which of the commandments I will take seriously. I can claim to be a "brother" and to live by the royal law of love (2:8), while still engaging in secret speech against my associates. James identifies this form of arrogance precisely: "you are not a doer of the law but its judge." And he counters such staggering arrogance by the crisp reminder that the One who gave the law is also the judge of all humans. The final contrast in 4:12 serves to state the truth of the matter that slander serves to camouflage: the God who gave the law and who judges according to the law (2:12–13) is "able to save and to destroy." In comparison with this, "who are you?" As always in James, the theological statement serves as warrant for moral exhortation: it is because God alone has power of life and death that God alone has the right to reveal the law and judge by the law. Any human seizure of that right—especially in secret—is revealed as pitiful pretension.

There is nothing subtle about the form of arrogance displayed in 4:13–17. James characterizes it as *alazoneia*, universally recognizable in the Greco-Roman world as the quality of the boaster, the braggart, the pretentious person. At the most obvious level, the traders are criticized for their arrogant assumption that they can depend on the future. But at a deeper level they share the outlook of "the world" expressed by envy: that having is the same as being and that "selling and getting a profit" is a way of securing their *own* future. James' first response to them is a common one in the wisdom tradition; as Qoheleth so eloquently demonstrated, a reminder of the evanescent quality of life is an effective deflater of pomposity: how can these entrepreneurs plan their selling campaign for a year, when they cannot even guarantee they will see tomorrow? The awareness of human existence as a "mist that is here and gone" encourages an appropriate modesty concerning human projects and plans.

James' critique cuts deeper than that, however, for he challenges the very view of reality assumed by such "friends of the world." Their speech betrays a perception of the world as a closed system of limited resources, available to their control and manipulation, yielding to their market analysis and sales campaign. When James recommends that they say "If the Lord wills it, we will both live and do this thing or that thing," he is not recommending an empty piety, but a profoundly different understanding of reality. He challenges their construal with the perception given by faith and friendship with God: that the world is an open system, created by God at every moment, and infinitely rich in the resources provided by God for humans to exist and prosper in cooperation, rather than in competition. And within *this* understanding, their pretension and boasting is not the symptom simply of foolish heedlessness. It is the symptom of something evil (*ponēra*; 4:16).

In 1:9–12, James spelled out the basic principles governing faith's perceptions of wealth and poverty, of suffering and success. It spelled them out in terms of paradox and reversal. The lowly were to boast in their exaltation, the rich in their humiliation. Those who endured trials would find reward with God. And those who lived by their wealth, rather than God's word, would pass away in the midst of their affairs. The failure so to think about one's life and the failure so to speak with reference to God's will is, for one living in the community of faith, "to understand the proper thing to do and not do it." James does not consider this in simple moral terms as failure, but in specifically religious terms as sin (*hamartia*; 4:17). This statement, couched in the third person as a general maxim, serves as a hinge between the examples. It applies to the "sin of omission" of the entrepreneurs who refuse to take God into account when they plan their futures. Even more profoundly, it will apply to the case of the rich, who refuse to take God into account as they omit to do what the law plainly demands, namely providing wages for their workers.

The final example of arrogance is the most blatant and evil (5:1–6). James devotes to it some of his most vivid language, adopting once again the rhythms of the great social prophets of Israel, who also had railed against the oppressive rich. He goes into much greater detail concerning their behavior and the consequences they must face because of their behavior. What makes this attack so distinctive is the way in which the two realities are artfully interwoven, providing a harshly ironic dimension to virtually every statement.

The reader is startled by the energy and force of the opening: the rich are to "weep and wail" over the miseries that are coming upon them (5:1). But rather than move to a depiction of those miseries, James describes the fate of their *wealth* itself: it has become rotted, moth-eaten, rusted (5:2). They had, according to the logic of envy, identified themselves with their possessions. They have been willing to do anything to get more possessions, including fraud, violence, and murder (5:6). They thought that by so doing they were building a nest egg for "their last days." And with bitter irony, James agrees: they have laid up a treasure for these last days (5:3), but they are to be days of judgment, indeed of slaughter (5:5). And the very possessions in which the rich had sought security most eloquently symbolize their own fate: their precious metals have rusted, and "their rust will be a testimony against [them] and eat [their] flesh like fire" (5:3)!

The attitudes and actions of the rich perfectly exemplify the logic of envy and arrogance as James sketched them in 3:13–4:6. We see that the rich devoted themselves to an exploitive relationship to the earth, living to fulfill their own desires for pleasure (5:5; compare 4:1). And to enable this, they have been willing, in complete disregard for the law (see Lev 19:13), to deprive their hired laborers of the wages that were owed them (5:4). Indeed, James' language in 5:6

suggests the sort of judicial procedure mentioned in 2:6: the rich use the law courts to perpetuate their fraud and "condemn" the poor. And consistent with the biblical tradition, James recognizes that such fraud is a form of violence and murder: to deprive the poor of their wages is truly to deprive them of the means of life: "to deprive an employee of his wages is to shed blood" (Sir 34:22).

Here is the logic of envy worked out in action, as James sketched it in 4:2: "you desire and you do not have: you kill." Here also is the ultimate arrogance: the rich assume the divine prerogative to judge and do so unjustly ("you have condemned the righteous person"). They arrogate to themselves the divine power to "save and destroy" and use it to destroy ("you have killed the righteous person").

Here then, also, James matches violence for violence, not from the side of the oppressed, but from the side of the God who has "heard the cries of the laborers" (5:4). It is the willful denial of this God's power and authority that has enabled the rich to make "friends of the world" and exploit its systems to their own pleasure. But from the perspective of faith, James asserts, even in the face of experience, that God's power is more real. The world is not a closed system available to human control. It is an open system answerable to the God who creates it. And in contrast to those who are "judges with evil designs" (2:4), this God judges without partiality and on the basis of human deeds (2:12). The rich who have oppressed the poor will experience in their own flesh how God opposes them (5:3, 6). They will discover indeed how "judgment is merciless to the one who has not shown mercy" (2:13).

BIBLIOGRAPHY

Adamson, J. B., *James: The Man and His Message* (Grand Rapids: Eerdmans, 1989) 228–65.

Boggan, C. W., *Wealth in the Epistle of James* (Ph.D. diss., Southern Baptist Theological Seminary, 1982).

Bottini, G. V., "Uno Solo E'll Legislatore e Giudice (Gc 4, 11–12)," *Liber Annuus* 37 (1987) 99–112.

Charue, A. M., "Quelques avis aux riches et aux pauvres dans l'épître de Jacques," *Collationes Namurcenses* 30 (1936) 177–87.

Felder, C. H., *Wisdom, Law and Social Concern in the Epistle of James* (Ph.D. diss., Columbia University, 1982).

Feuillet, A., "Le sense du mot parousie dans l'évangile de Matthieu: comparaison entre Matth XXIV et Jac V, 1–11," *The Background of the New Testament and its Eschatology*, eds. W. D. Davies and D. Daube (Cambridge: Cambridge University Press, 1964) 261–80.

Frankemölle, H., "Gesetz im Jakobusbrief: Zur Tradition, kontextuellen Verwendung und Rezeption eines belasteten Begriffes," in *Das Gesetz im Neuen Testament*, ed. K. Kertelge (QD 108; Freiburg: Herder, 1986) 175–221.

Geyser, A. S., "The Letter of James and the Social Condition of his Addressees," *Neot* 9 (1975) 25–33.

Johnson, L. T., *Sharing Possessions: Mandate and Symbol of Faith* (Overtures to Biblical Theology; Philadelphia: Fortress Press, 1981).

Kelly, F. X., *Poor and Rich in the Epistle of James* (Ph.D. diss., Temple University, 1973).

Maynard-Reid, P. U., *Poverty and Wealth in James* (New York: Maryknoll, 1987).

Mayordomo-Marin, M., "Jak 5,2.3a: Zukünftiges Gericht oder gegenwärtiger Zustand?" ZNW 83 (1992) 132–37.

Morris, K. F., *An Investigation of Several Linguistic Affinities between the Epistle of James and the Book of Isaiah* (Ph.D. diss., Union Theological Seminary in Virginia, 1964).

Noack, B., "Jakobus wider die Reichen," *ST* 18 (1964) 10–25.

Schökel, L. A., "James 5,2 [sic] and 4,6," *Bib* 54 (1973) 73–76.

Ward, R. B., *The Communal Concern of the Epistle of James* (Ph.D. diss., Harvard University, 1966).

VII. PATIENCE IN TIME OF TESTING
5:7–11

✦

7. Therefore be patient, brothers, until the coming of the Lord. Look! The farmer waits for the precious fruit of the earth, being patient with it until it receives the early and late rain. 8. You also be patient! Strengthen your hearts, because the coming of the Lord is near. 9. Brothers, do not grumble against each other, so that you are not judged. Look! The judge stands at the gate. 10. Brothers, take as an example of suffering and of patience the prophets who spoke in the name of the Lord. 11. Look! We call blessed those who have endured. You have heard about the endurance of Job. And you have seen the result accomplished by the Lord, for the Lord is rich in compassion and is merciful.

THE SECTION AS A WHOLE

These verses stand as something of a hinge between 4:11–5:6 and the final exhortations in 5:12–20. The exhortation responds to James' depiction and denunciation of the three modes of arrogance and, in particular, his attack on the oppressive rich. This is shown not only by the connective *oun* ("therefore"), which joins 5:6 and 5:7, but also by the continuation of the theme of God's judgment, which began in 4:11.

But it is equally clear that this section begins an explicit turn to the community of readers that continues in 5:12–20. This is shown not only by the threefold repetition of *adelphoi* ("brothers") in 5:7, 9, and 10, but also by the fundamentally positive and reassuring character of the exhortations.

As the notes will indicate, there are other small stylistic touches that justify isolating this section, such as the threefold repetition of *idou* ("look") in 5:7, 9, 11 and the *inclusio* formed by 5:7 and 11. But it is, above all, its transitional

311

character that makes the section distinct, for it is defined as much by what precedes it as by what follows it. In terms of the overall composition, these verses bring to explicit expression two themes. First, just as 4:13–5:6 filled out the negative side of the reversal sketched in 1:9–11, so do these verses fill out the positive side as sketched in 1:12: those who endure to the end are blessed. Second, the theme of God's judgment, which underlay so much of James' exhortation (1:12; 2:12; 3:1; 4:12) is here brought to clear expression in terms of a vivid expectation of the *parousia* of the Lord. The two themes are interrelated.

In terms of the immediate context, the exhortation in these verses takes its character above all from the atmosphere of crisis established by the attack on the rich in 5:1–6. The affirmation that God hears the cries of the laborers and is preparing a day of slaughter and is opposing the oppressors naturally raises the questions of when and how. And the characterization of the rich as oppressing the community of the poor and righteous through judicial violence raises with even greater force the question, "how should we respond?" This eschatological setting then frames the remainder of the community exhortations in 5:12–20.

NOTES

7. *therefore . . . brothers*: The designation *adelphoi* ("brothers") occurs three times in this short segment (5:7, 9, 10), marking an emphatic turn from the rich (*plousioi*) who are the community's oppressors and foil (Ropes, 293). The connective *oun* ("therefore") signals that this exhortation follows closely from the previous section (Mussner, 199; Davids, 181) where the rich were reminded of "the miseries coming upon them" (5:1) in the "last days" (5:3), which for them will be a "day of slaughter" (5:5). Above all, if the reading here is correct, the rich are reminded that God opposes them (5:6; see 4:6). The *oun* marks the transition to the attitude that the community itself should have in the light of these circumstances.

be patient: James' choice of words is puzzling. He had advocated *hypomonē* ("endurance") in 1:2–3 and had used the verb *hypomenein* ("endure") in 1:12, as he also will again in 5:11. But in vv.7–8, he uses the verb *makrothymein* three times and the noun form *makrothymia* in 5:10. Is there something more than stylistic variation at work here? If so, it must reside in the nuances of the terms. The verb *hypomenein* is fundamentally passive, meaning simply "to wait" (Xenophon, *Anabasis* IV, 1, 21) or "remain" (Josephus, *Ant.* 18:328) or "endure" through some circumstance or trouble (Plato, *Thaetetus* 177B). In the LXX, the verb is used primarily for a literal "waiting" (Exod 12:39; Num 22:19; Tob 5:7) and for the religious "waiting upon the Lord" (Pss 24:3; 26:14; 32:20; 36:9, 34; 39:2; 129:5; Prov 20:9c; Mic 7:7; Nah 1:7; Hab 2:3; Zeph 3:8; Zech 6:14; Isa 40:31; 49:23). In Job, it appears with some frequency in the sense of

312

"enduring" (6:11; 9:4; 14:14; 15:31; 17:13; 22:21). The noun *hypomonē*, likewise, can be used of endurance (Job 14:19) or of hope (Jer 14:8). But again, the relationship is one of passivity toward the activity of another. The verb *makrothymein* (literally, "to be long-tempered," Mayor, 161) likewise can be used in the sense of waiting (Plutarch, *The Sign of Socrates* 24 [*Mor.* 593F]), and the noun *makrothymia* can mean to have patience or endure (*T. Dan* 2:1; *T. Jos.* 2:7). In the LXX, however, these terms are used only rarely of relations between equals or of humans at all (see only Job 7:16; Sir 2:4; Baruch 4:25; Isa 57:15). Mostly, they are used of the attitudes of a superiority to an inferior (Prov 16:32; 19:11; 25:15; Sir 29:8; 1 Macc 8:4). Against Ropes, 293, then, who claims that these terms have "more the meaning of patience and submission," the evidence seems to suggest that *makrothymein/makrothymia* means the active adoption of an attitude of "forbearance" and "putting up with" another. The power relationship suggested is opposite that of *hypomenein*. This is supported by the predominant usage in the LXX in connection with the attitude of God as judge toward humans (Sir 18:11; 35:19; 2 Macc 6:14; Jer 15:15). The adjective *makrothymos* is joined to *polueleos* ("rich in mercy") as a constant epithet of the Lord (Exod 34:6; Num 14:18; Neh 9:17; Pss 85:15; Wis 15:1; Sir 2:11; 5:4; Joel 2:13; Jonah 4:2; Nah 1:3). In the NT, *hypomenein/hypomonē* are used mostly for "enduring" (Matt 10:22; 24:13; Mark 13:13; Luke 8:15; 21:19; Rom 2:7; 5:3; 8:25; 12:12; 15:4; 1 Cor 13:7; 2 Cor 1:6; 6:4; 1 Thess 1:3; 2 Thess 1:4; 2 Tim 2:10, 12; Heb 10:32; 12:2; 1 Pet 2:20). And whereas *makrothymia/makrothymein* can also bear this meaning (see 1 Cor 13:4; Gal 5:22; Col 1:11; 3:12; Eph 4:2; Heb 6:15; 2 Tim 3:10), they also can refer to the attitude of a judge (see Matt 18:26, 29; Luke 18:7). The other terms never do. *Makrothymia* is used of the attitude of God as judge toward humans in Rom 2:4; 9:22; 1 Tim 1:16; 1 Pet 3:20; 2 Pet 3:9, 15. James' use of *makrothymein* here was noted by John Chrysostom (PG 64:1049) and developed further by Oecumenius and Theophylact: before the time of judgment, God shows *makrothymia*; so should the community also share that outlook. They need more than simple "endurance"; they require "patience and long-suffering."

until the coming of the Lord: The noun *parousia* means first of all simply "presence" (Plato, *Gorgias* 497E; 2 Macc 15:21). It came to be used of the "arrival" of eminent personages, such as kings (Euripides, *Alcestis* 209; Thucydides, *Peloponnesian War* I, 128, 5; 3 Macc 3:17; Judg 10:18), or the "appearance" of a divinity (Diodorus Siculus, *History* III, 65, 1; IV, 3, 3; Josephus, *Ant.* 3:80; 9:55). The four certain uses in the LXX (Judg 10:18; 2 Macc 8:12; 15:21; 3 Macc 3:17) are all secular. In no case is the term applied to God, and the expression *parousia tou kyriou* ("coming of the Lord") is unattested. The term is found in intertestamental Jewish literature with reference to God (Cantinat, 232), as in *T. Jud.* 22:2; *T. Levi* 8:11; *T. Abr.* 13:4; 2 *Baruch* 55:6; Josephus, *Ant.* 3:80; 9:55, although the text in some cases has been disputed (see Marty, 192). Against this background, the NT usage is fascinating.

The term *parousia* can be used in a straightforward sense of the "arrival" or "presence" of persons (1 Cor 16:17; 2 Cor 7:6–7; 10:10; Phil 1:26; 2:12) and of Satan (2 Thess 2:9) and once of God (2 Pet 3:12). But the predominant use is with reference to the future coming of Jesus (1 Cor 15:23; 2 Pet 3:4, 12; 1 John 2:28) as Son of Man (Matt 24:3, 27, 37, 39) or, above all, as "Lord" (*kyrios*): 1 Thess 2:19; 3:13; 4:15; 5:23; 2 Thess 2:1; 2 Pet 1:16. It is certainly the case, then, that James' double use of *parousia tou kyriou* in 5:7–8 reflects a virtually technical Christian usage (Mussner, 201; Chaine, 120; Cantinat, 232; Mayor, 161; Ropes, 293; Marty, 192; Laws, 208; Martin, 190) and, in all likelihood, refers to the coming of Jesus as judge (Davids, 182; Dibelius, 242–43; Mussner, 201; Laws, 208–9). If this is so, then the case is strengthened for the position that the one "opposing" the rich in 5:6 is also Jesus, but that connection, though possible, is not necessary.

the farmer waits for the precious fruit: The use of *idou* ("look") is the first of three in this section (see 5:9, 11) and, as in 3:4, focuses the readers' attention on the analogy. The *geōrgos* is one who works the land by cultivation (Herodotus, *Persian War* 4:18; Plato, *Phaedrus* 276B; LXX Gen 9:20; 49:15). In the NT, the term appears primarily in the parable of the "wicked husbandmen" (*geōrgoi*), who would correspond to the *ergatai* in James 5:4 (see Mark 12:1–9; Matt 21:33–41; Luke 20:9–16). In the LXX, the *geōrgos* is not used as a model for anything. But in John 15:1, God is imaged as a *geōrgos* who tends the vine that is the community. A striking parallel to the present passage occurs in 1 Cor 9:7, 10, where, using different language, Paul engages in an agricultural comparison to apostolic labor: ". . . who plants a vineyard without eating of its fruit? Who tends a flock without getting some of the milk? . . . the plowman should plow in hope, and the thresher thresh in hope of a share in the crop." Even closer is the language in 2 Tim 2:6, which says, "the hardworking farmer (*geōrgos*) ought to have the first share of the crops (*karpon*)." Although the main point is the desired attitude of patience, the characterization of the fruit as "precious" (*timion*) is noteworthy. This is certainly the only time in the biblical literature that something so lowly as produce has been given a designation usually associated with jewels and crowns. James identified with the specific anxiety and joy of the farmer in a hard land, for whom a crop is never to be taken for granted and is, therefore, "precious." See Mayor (161): ". . . the preciousness of the fruit justifies the waiting."

until it receives the early and late rain: A number of small textual variants reflect some uncertainty about the meaning of the image, with an accompanying eagerness to "correct." Some MSS have, as the object of *makrothymein*, the phrase *ep'auton* ("over it") rather than *ep'autō* ("concerning it"). Others add *hou* to the particle *heōs* in an understandable attempt to create a more recognizable form. Still other MSS add either the noun *hueton* ("rain") before "early and late"—a modest clarification—or, in a more dramatic alteration, add *karpon*, with the effect that the farmer receives the early and late fruit! The scribal corrections reveal ignorance of the implied substantive signaled by the adjectives "early" (*proimion*) and "late" (*opsimon*). In the LXX, the combination appears in Deut 11:14; Hos 6:3; Joel 2:23; Zech 10:1; Jer 5:24; see also *m. Taan.* 1:2. In the light of this understanding, it is certainly the fruit that receives the rain rather than the farmer who receives the fruit (Windisch, 31; Chaine, 121; Mayor, 162). It is also the case that the image contains no real reference to the duration of time before the *parousia* (Laws, 210–11). The image does reflect the climatic conditions specific to Palestine, where fall rains in October are followed by those in mid-November (Chaine, 121; Ropes, 296). James, at the very least, provides a touch of genuine local color (Marty, 193). But does this derive from an actual Palestinian provenance (as Ropes, 296; Adamson, 191; Davids, 184)? Or, since the phrase occurs in Torah, can it be another instance of literary allusion (as Laws, 212; Dibelius, 244)? Either or both are possible, with a resolution—if one can be gained at all—dependent on an assessment of all the other evidence in James. Theophylact provides a wonderful example of a "spiritual reading": the rains refer to the tears of repentance in youth and in old age!

8. *you also be patient*: Several excellent MSS add the inferential particle *oun* ("therefore"), which makes so much sense that its absence is the harder and, therefore, the preferred reading. The emphatic *kai hymeis*, in any case, does the job of *oun*: the analogy is driven home by means of the vivid imperative.

strengthen your hearts: The verb *stērizein* with a direct object means to "set firmly" or "establish" first of all in the physical sense (LXX Gen 28:12; Luke 16:26; *I Clem.* 33:3). It is used for "strengthening" the self through the ingestion of food (Gen 27:37). Figuratively, it is used for "strengthening one's hands" (Exod 17:12) or "strengthening" others in their commitment (see Luke 22:32; Acts 18:23; Rom 1:11; 16:25; 1 Thess 3:2; 2 Thess 2:17; 3:3). In the prophetic literature, the "setting of the face" denotes steadfastness of purpose (Amos 9:4; Jer 3:12; 21:10; 24:6; Ezek 6:2; 13:17; 14:8), a meaning carried over in Luke 9:51. But James' language evokes a Septuagintal idiom, "strengthening the heart," which, depending on context, can mean to gain physical strength, as for a journey (Judg 19:5, 8; Ps 103:15), or courage that comes from trust in the Lord (Ps 111:8), or firmness of intention (Sir 6:37; 22:16; see also 1 Thess 3:13). It is undoubtedly one of these latter two meanings James intends. He does not want his readers to remain simply passive in their waiting (Vouga, 133); they are to focus themselves: ". . . make your courage and purpose firm" (Ropes, 297; see Cantinat, 235). Note the similarity to the call for "purity of heart" in 4:8. These exhortations stand in contrast to the "deception/indulgence of the heart" in 1:26 and the "stuffing of the heart" in 5:5.

because the coming of the Lord is near: The exhortation to strengthen the heart is followed by a *hoti* clause, creating the possibility of two distinct readings. If *stērizein* is taken in the sense of "fix one's attention/be certain of," then the *hoti* clause can be understood as a noun clause, yielding "be established (certain) in your hearts *that* the Lord's coming is near." More probable, however, is that *hoti* introduces an explanatory clause: the readers should strengthen their purpose/commitment, *because* of the Lord's proximity. Some MSS add *hēmōn*, to create the phrase "Our Lord," which heightens what is already probably a Christological reference. The verb *engizein* means "to approach/draw near," whether in terms of space (Gen 18:23; 27:27) or time (Ezek 12:23). James uses the perfect tense (*ēngiken*), whose employment in other NT passages dealing with the kingdom of God has often been understood as pointing to a "realized eschatology" (Dodd, "The Kingdom of God," 138–41): see, e.g., Mark 1:15; Matt 3:2; 4:17; 10:7; Luke 10:9, 11. It is found with reference to an eschatological moment also in Luke 21:8; Rom 13:12; 1 Pet 4:7. Here, however, the sense may be as much spatial as temporal, for James notes at once that "the judge stands at the gate," and in 4:8 James has said, "approach (*engizein*) God and he will approach (*engizein*) you." The use of spatial and temporal categories with reference to God is always, in any case, necessarily metaphorical.

9. *do not grumble against each other*: The verb *stenazein* means simply to "sigh" or "groan" in response to situations to distress (Euripides, *Alcestis* 199; *T. Jos.* 7:1). Two aspects of the present construction are odd. First, they are "groaning against" each other (*kat'allēlōn*). The verb *katastenazein* occurs in the LXX (Exod 2:23; Jer 22:23; Lam 1:11), but here the *kata* definitely increases the confrontational character of the "groaning" (Chaine, 122; Cantinat, 236; Adamson, 191; Martin, 192). Some MSS make this even more obvious by arranging the word order so that "against each other" follows immediately after "do not grumble." The second odd aspect of this verse is the sanction *hina mē krithēte* ("that you not be judged"). As in other places we have noted, a prohibition is connected either to the law or to judgment or both (see notes on 2:1; 3:1; 4:11; 5:12). And as in several of such passages, it is possible here as well that James is making a thematic (not verbal) allusion to Leviticus 19. Immediately preceding the "law of love" in Lev 19:18b, the LXX reads, *kai ouk ekdikatai sou hē cheir kai ou mēnieis tois huiois tou laou sou* ("your hand shall not avenge you and you shall not be angry with the children of your people," Lev. 19:18a; see Johnson, "Use of Leviticus," 396–97). Despite Dibelius' usual rejection of any contextual connection (244) it is precisely the context that provides the point of the prohibition. The readers have been told to have the attitude of the long-suffering judge (*makrothymia*) until the coming of the Lord. But in the meantime, they are suffering oppression. The predominant use of *stenazein* in the LXX is in such situations of oppression (Job 30:25; Isa 59:10; Lam 1:21; Neh 3:7; Ezek 26:15; 1 Macc 1:26). The classic case is the complaint of the people in Egypt: *katastenaxen hoi huoi Israēl . . . kai eisēkousen ho theos ton stenagmon autōn* ("the children of Israel complained . . . and God heard their complaint"; Exod 2:23–24; 6:5). The "complaint of the people," therefore, is properly directed to the Lord, not to their fellows. Such situations, however, always tempt the oppressed to turn on each other and "grumble against each

other." As always, James advocates solidarity. The force of his statement is nicely captured by Laws, 213: "do not keep complaining." The refusal to turn against each other in revenge or anger becomes a fulfillment "according to the Scripture" of the royal law, "Love your neighbor as yourself" (Lev 19:18; James 2:8).

so that you are not judged: That is, by God. The sanction resembles those in 2:12–13; 3:1; 4:11–12; and 5:12. The "law of freedom," which is also the "law of love," is the measure by which they are to act and by which they are to be measured. The phrasing, in fact, resembles that in Matt 7:1: *mē krinete hina mē krithēte* ("do not judge so that you are not judged").

the judge is standing before the gate: The noun *thyra* means simply a door or gate, with the plural form (as here) having the equivalent meaning (see *Od.* 17:267; Aristotle, *Rhetoric* 1391A; Josephus, *Against Apion* 2:119). There is an obvious sense in which being "at the gate" suggests proximity (see Acts 5:9; 12:6). The image here, however, strongly resembles that in the eschatological discourse in Mark 13:28–29. The disciples are told that when the fig tree puts forth its leaves, *ginōskete hoti engus to theros estin. houtōs kai hymeis hotan idēte tauta ginomena ginōskete hoti engus estin epi thyrais* ("know that the harvest is near. Likewise when you see these things happening, know that he is near, at the gate/door"). Note the combination of harvest (*theros*), being near (*engus*), and door/gate (*thyrai*). The saying is repeated virtually verbatim by Matt 24:32–33, whereas Luke omits the wordplay, having instead *engus estin hē basileia tou theou* ("the kingdom of God is near"). Luke does retain the language of the door/gate (*thyra*) in his saying concerning entering the kingdom through the "narrow door" in 13:24–25. In John, Jesus is himself imaged as a door (*thyra*) through which the sheep are to pass (John 10:1–9). Finally, in Rev 3:20, the risen Lord declares in a letter to the church at Laodicaea, "Behold I am standing at the door and knocking" (*idou hestēka epi tēn thyran kai krouō*). James' statement that the judge is at the gate fits within this complex of images in early Christian eschatology in the same way that the comparison of the end-time to a "thief in the night" can be found in a logion of the risen Lord in Rev 3:3, in a letter of Paul (1 Thess 5:2), and as a logion of Jesus in the Gospels (Matt 24:43//Luke 12:39). The play of *theros/thyra* in Mark 13:28–29 is found here also (*therizantes*, 5:4; *thyrais*, 5:9) in combination with the specifically Christian language concerning the *parousia tou kyriou* and its location as "near" (*ēngiken*). Such a clustering makes it difficult not to see (as in Acts 10:42; 2 Tim 4:8) the *kritēs* ("judge") as Jesus (so Mussner, 205; Marty, 195), although James' usage in 4:12 should again make that conclusion a cautious one.

10. *take as an example*: Like the noun *paradeigma* (see Herodotus, *Persian War* 5:62; Plato, *Rep.* 500E; *Meno* 77B), the noun *hypodeigma* can mean either a "sample/illustration" or, more specifically, a "pattern/model" presented for imitation (see Sir 44:16; 2 Macc 6:28, 31; Josephus, *JW* 6:103; Philo, *Who is the Heir* 256; John 13:15; 2 Pet 2:6). Thus, in 4 Macc 17:23, the Tyrant Antiochus,

when he had seen the courage and endurance of the Maccabean martyrs, proclaimed them to his soldiers as an example for their own endurance (*eis hypodeigma tēn eikeinōn hypomonēn*). Although this is the first time James has used the explicit language of "example," we have noted how he follows the ancient practice of presenting a series of moral exemplars to his readers for their consideration and emulation (see 1:22–25; 2:20–25; 5:17–18; Johnson, "Mirror," 632–45). The verb *lambanein*, therefore, means "to receive" in the sense of "consider/imitate." This reading is surely better than that of some MSS, which contain *echete* ("you have").

of suffering and of patience: Although the substantives are joined by *kai* ("and"), it is clear that James means: "an example of suffering *with* patience" (or: "patience in hardship," Ropes, 298). The term *makrothymia* ("long-suffering/patience") was discussed in the note on 5:7. James' presentation of the model rounds off the exhortation that began with that verse. The noun *kakopathia* (or *kakopatheia*) is found only here in the NT. It means literally distress or misery (Aristotle, *Politics* 1278B; Thucydides, *Peloponnesian War* VII, 77, 1; *Ep. Arist.* 208; Philo, *On Joseph* 223). It is used sometimes actively for expending a strenuous effort (see 2 Macc 2:26), but the meaning here is clearly that of passive suffering accompanied by endurance (compare 4 Macc 9:8: *dia tēsde kakopatheias kai hypomonēs*), as the use of *kakopathein* in 5:13 also shows (compare 2 Tim 2:9; 4:5).

the prophets who spoke in the name of the Lord: Some MSS add *andras* to make "men who were prophets." Speaking in the name of the Lord is biblical idiom for speaking as a prophet in behalf of Yahweh and with the authority of Yahweh (see LXX 2 Kgs 2:24; 5:11), therefore, a sign of being a "prophet of Yahweh" (see 1 Kgs 18:32; 1 Chr 21:19; Ezek 5:1; Jer 44:17; Dan 9:6). Yet false prophets could also claim to "speak in the name of the Lord" (2 Chr 33:18; Zech 13:3; Jer 14:14–15; 20:6; 34:14–15), making it necessary to devise ways of distinguishing the true from the false prophet. An *a posteriori* method was proposed by Deut 18:15–22: if something a prophet predicted did not come true, then one knew that the prophecy was not spoken in the name of the Lord. The phrase here in James reflects the development of another kind of norm: like Jeremiah, whose struggle with false prophets of good cheer spoken in "the name of the Lord" was most intense, the true prophets came to be perceived as those who suffered hardship, especially that of not being heard and of being rejected by those to whom they spoke. This tradition is rooted in the careers of the prophets Jeremiah and Ezekiel, is continued explicitly in figures such as Daniel (see Dan 9:6; 2 Chr 36:16), is carried forward in such apocalyptic productions as *The Martyrdom and Ascension of Isaiah*, and is found extensively displayed in the NT (Matt 5:12; 23:34–37; Luke 6:23; 11:49–51; 13:33; 24:25; Acts 7:52; Heb 11:32–38; 1 Thess 2:15). James' use of such language continues the separation between "friendship with the world" and "friendship with God," by reaffirming this community's tradition as one of being gathered "in the name of the Lord"

(5:14) and as being persecuted by the rich who "blaspheme the noble name invoked over them" (2:7). The very experience of such persecution helps solidify the community's sense of being in the line of the true prophets who also so suffered (see esp. Luke 6:23, 26).

11. *we call blessed those who have endured*: Some MSS have the present participle *hypomenontes*, rather than the aorist *hypomeinantas*, an interesting reversal of the scribal tendency to replace the present with the future tense in 1:12. The present statement is closely related to that in 1:12: "Blessed is the person who endures testing," and is one of the strongest pieces of evidence for the literary interconnectedness of this composition (Fry, "Testing," 434–35). For the discussion of the terms of the macarism and their internal relationships, see the note on 1:12. Some commentators observe the semantic shift from *makrothymein* to *hypomenein* but regard the terms as synonymous (Cantinat, 239) or the shift as merely stylistic (Davids, 182). More probably, the shift is one of meaning along the lines sketched in the note on 5:7. The persecution/ oppression is one that they must endure; the attitude they take towards their oppressors and their brethren is to be one of long-suffering and patience (see Chrysostom).

you have heard about the endurance of Job: The first striking thing about this statement is the implied position of Job among the prophets. Job is designated as a "righteous man" together with Noah and Daniel in Ezek 14:14, but he does not appear as one of the prophets. Second, what does James mean by "you have heard"? Does he mean from the reading of Scripture? This is not likely, since the portrayal of Job in the canonical book is scarcely that of the "patient Job" presumed here. Perhaps James is referring to apocryphal traditions transmitted in assemblies such as the synagogue (Marty, 197; Ropes, 299)? Such traditions might have been based on the prose framing of the dialogues in the canonical Job (1:20–21; 2:9–10; 42:7–12). But the complaining Job of the dialogues does not seem to fit this picture (Cantinat, 239). In the LXX, the noun *hypomonē* occurs only once, and that is in reference to the destruction of endurance (Job 14:19)! The verb *hypomenein* occurs 14 times. In 8 of these instances, it translates 6 different verbs in the Hebrew MT (see 3:9; 6:11; 8:15; 14:14; 17:13; 20:26; 32:4; 32:16). Oddly, none of these uses pertains to Job's endurance. Five occurrences of the verb appear only in the LXX (7:3; 9:14; 15:31; 22:21; 33:5), and 3 of these *are* applied to Job himself (7:3; 22:21; 33:5). It can be said, therefore, that the LXX increases the perception of Job as "enduring" but not very extensively. Nor is Job's patience celebrated in the rabbinic tradition, where his hospitality receives most attention (see *Tanchuma* 29:4; *Aboth de Rabbi Nathan* 1:7), or in the early Christian literature, where his faith is celebrated (*1 Clem.* 17:3–4; *2 Clem.* 6:8). It would seem that James has considerable responsibility for shaping the perception of "endurance/patience" as the most memorable feature of Job. James' emphasis, however, is emphatically shared by the *Testament of Job*, probably a Jewish composition roughly within the same period of James and loosely based on the LXX version of the canonical writing (Spittler, "Testament of Job" 829–38"). Job is a man of hospitality (9:1–13:6) but is, above all, one whose patience has remained steadfast (1:5; see Haas, "Job's Perseverance," 117–54). Throughout his trials, he endures (26:4–5), and he declares that *makrothymia* is above everything (27:6–7)! Furthermore, he confounds his accusers, who are astonished at his degradation, by pointing to the heavenly wealth that he has (34:4; 36:3; compare James 1:12). Whatever the date of the *Testament of Job,* or any possible dependence between these compositions, its understanding of Job is remarkably similar to that sketched here so briefly by James (Davids, 187). It is all the more puzzling, therefore, that in his discussion of this theme in *T. Job,* Haas ("Job's Perseverance") does not make the connection.

and you have seen the result accomplished by the Lord: The difficulties with this statement begin with textual variants. Some MSS replace "you have seen" (*eidete*) with the imperative "see" (*idete*) or the indicative "you know" (*oidate*). The variants reflect uncertainty about the meaning of the phrase *telos kyriou,* an uncertainty that continues through the history of interpretation. The ambiguity rests upon the multiple possibilities of meaning for each word in the phrase. To take the genitive first, *kyrios* can refer to God (either as a character in the Book of Job or in history) or to Jesus. The substantive *telos* has the same range of possibilities as in Rom 10:4, when Paul declares that Christ is *telos nomou.* The noun can mean simply "end" as termination (see Luke 1:33; 1 Pet 4:7) or it can mean "end" in the sense of purpose or result (see Dio, *Oration* 17:3; Epictetus, *Discourses* I, 30, 4; Matt 26:58). Mussner (206) lists three possible understandings: a) the end of Jesus' life; b) the parousia; c) the fate of Job, as shown in the canonical book. If we accept the tense of *eidete,* the parousia is not a real possibility, since that is clearly future for James' readers (against Gordon, "*kai to telos*," 94–95). The Christological interpretation was held by Augustine (PL 40: 634) and offered as a possibility by Bede. It is possible to speak of the "end of a man" with respect to his death (see *T. Ash.* 6:4), and James could so point to the vindication of Jesus' death in his resurrection, thus filling out the "reward" side of the macarism in 1:12, which has again been stated here. The "seeing" in this case could be an appeal to the readers' own experience. But the reference would be extraordinarily cryptic and unexpected in a document that has made no other clear reference to Jesus' life (unless one take the Christological reading of 5:6). It is more likely that the *kyrios* intended by James is not Jesus, but God (Windisch, 32; Chaine, 124). In this case, the genitive would point to agency (BAGD 811): the readers are reminded of the purpose/result worked out by God. In this case, the most obvious referent would be the ending of the book of Job itself (42:7–12), where Job is vindicated and restored (Dibelius, 246); there is no need to suggest an emendation from *telos* to *eleos* (Fitzmyer, "Wandering Aramean," 176–77). This is a happy outcome that would fit the macarism of 1:12 and that the readers could "see" in the text of Job. Bede perceives this, as does the *Catena*, which notes that the end of Job shows "the sycophancy of the devil and the true witness of God." Only the precise nuance of *telos* remains unresolved in such a reading. Some commentators emphasize the element of *purpose*: "you have seen the purpose/intention/design of the Lord" (Cantinat, 240; Martin, 195; Mayor, 164; Ropes, 299). Others stress the element of *result*: "you have seen what the Lord brought about" (Laws, 216; Reicke, 53; Adamson, 193). It is perhaps best to recognize that the phrase contains elements of both (Davids, 188). How then do we account for the variation between "hearing" and "seeing"? Possibly there is nothing more to it than a stylistic variation found in other places (see 1:19; 2:5, 22, 24).

for the Lord is rich in compassion and is merciful: This is one of the *theologoumena* so richly employed by James (1:5, 13, 17, 18, 20, 27; 2:5, 11, 13; 3:9; 4:4, 12; 5:6). Its precise relation to the previous statement is not, however, certain. As a *hoti* clause, it could function as a noun clause in apposition to the preceding phrase: "you have seen the purpose/result accomplished by the Lord, that he is rich in compassion and merciful." In this case, both phrases would be the object of "you have seen." It seems better, however, to take the *hoti* clause as explanatory: the good result accomplished by the Lord reveals his attributes of compassion and mercy. Such an understanding would also enable us to regard this *hoti* clause as the warrant for the entire exhortation of 5:7–11. God's *makrothymia* with Job certainly matched Job's *hypomonē*—in imitation not only of Job but also of the Lord, this community is exhorted not only to *hypomonē* but also *makrothymia*. This connection is suggested because James employs a standard way of designating the Lord in Torah, beginning in Exod 34:6, where the qualities *oiktirmōn* ("merciful") and *eleōn* ("compassionate") are joined to *makrothymos* ("long-suffering") and *alēthinos* ("faithful"). Variations of the combination appear also in Num 14:18; Neh 9:17; Pss 7:12; 85:15; 102:8; 110:4; 144:8; Sir 2:7–11; *Pss. Sol.* 10:7; *T. Zeb.* 9:7). For *oiktirmos/oiktirmōn* in the NT, see Rom 12:1; 2 Cor 1:3; Luke 6:36. Oddly, the term *polysplanchnē* ("rich in compassion") is unattested in the LXX or elsewhere in Greek literature before James, but it appears both in noun and adjectival forms in a writing almost certainly dependent on James, the Shepherd of Hermas (*Herm. Vis.* 1, 3, 2; 2, 2, 8; 4, 2, 3; *Herm. Man.* 1:3, 5; 9:2; *Herm. Sim.* 5, 7, 4).

COMMENT

James' ringing affirmation that God opposes the arrogant and has prepared a day of slaughter for the oppressive rich in order to respond to the cries of the laborers (5:4–5) makes explicit the eschatological character of James' composition. When he began the letter with an assertion that trials served to test the endurance of faith (1:3) and stated also that, although the rich pass away in the midst of their activities, those who endure inherit a crown of life (1:12), he could have been understood in a purely sapiential sense: such is the fixed cosmological order.

But 4:13–5:6 has made clear that James understands the role of God as judge not simply in terms of being the one who keeps score fairly, but as being the one who "does justice" on the side of the oppressed and the poor. James' understanding of judgment is not simply sapiential, it is prophetic, and deals with the living God who is active in human history.

Neither is his idea of God's judgment abstract; it is particularized in the expectation of the *parousia* of the Lord Jesus (5:7). As the notes indicate, James' language concerning *kyrios* ("Lord") is ambiguous, in some places seeming to apply to God and sometimes possibly to Jesus. But in this section, there seems to be no doubt that "the Lord" whose arrival is awaited is Jesus.

Finally, James' expectation of the judgment appears to be imminent rather than distant. The exhortation to be patient is even more pertinent for those expecting an event to happen soon as it is for those who know it is delayed. James' language about the farmer waiting over the crop until it receives the early and late rain (5:7) need not be taken as a caution against intense eschatological expectation; it could, indeed, be taken the opposite way, as suggesting the relatively short time before the divine judgment. The assertions, furthermore, that the *parousia tou kyriou* is "near" (*ēngiken*, 5:8) and that "the judge stands at the gate" (5:9) should be taken as straightforward statements of conviction rather than as compensatory reassurances.

In short, James gives every indication of sharing in an eschatological expectation that is intense and focused on the return of Jesus as judging Lord. It is not possible to move directly from this conclusion to one concerning James' historical placement. It is conceivable, after all, that a document written well into the second century could imaginatively construct an eschatological scenario with this degree of internal coherence. But it must be said that nothing in James' language itself would lead to such a conclusion. Far from appearing as an archaizing expression of "primitive eschatology" in the face of diminishing expectations, his language seems a direct and fresh expression of genuine convictions concerning an imminent intervention.

It is also possible that a new outbreak of expectation (such as that witnessed by Montanism) could invigorate earlier language and give it fresh life. But when the language here is taken together with all the other evidence (positive and negative) within James, it must be said that the most sensible conclusion is that it reflects a genuinely first generation Christian sensibility.

Whether James is responding to an actual life-setting of persecution that generated a hope for a sudden and soon liberation for the oppressed and punishment for the wicked or he is in quite different circumstances constructing this scenario as a literary exercise, the more important point is what significance he attaches to the moment and what moral conclusions he draws for the community inhabiting such a stressful situation.

The hope is real that God will oppose the wicked and reward the righteous. The first part of that hope is expressed in 5:4–6; the second is asserted in 5:11, "we call blessed those who have endured," a statement that obviously recalls the macarism of 1:12: "blessed is the man who endures testing because when he has been proven sound he will receive the crown of life that [God] has promised to those who love him." But before that hope is realized, the condition of the community of faith remains one of suffering, a suffering more intense, it should be said, because of the cognitive dissonance between the conviction that "God opposes the arrogant" and the experience that the arrogant condemn and murder the righteous ones. God will take care of the future; but how should the community act in this in-between time?

James' fundamental exhortation is placed in 5:8: "strengthen your hearts, for the coming of the Lord is near." As we have seen throughout, the language of the "heart" expresses human disposition: "indulging the heart" (1:26) was the opposite of pure religion acceptable to God; "stuffing the heart" was the expression of self-indulgence leading to oppression and murder (5:5); "bitter jealousy in the heart" was symptomatic of friendship with the world opposed to God (3:14); therefore, "purifying the heart" was the necessary gesture of conversion to cease from double-mindedness (4:8). Now James enjoins on the entire community that they "establish/strengthen" their hearts in the proper perception of reality—the Lord is approaching to judge—and the proper behavior that follows from that perception.

Positively, they are to "be patient" (5:7). Considerable space was given in the notes to the precise nuance attached to this expression: they are not simply to endure their suffering; they are to adopt the same attitude toward their oppressor that the judge does, who waits for the proper time of intervention. The readers, in a word, are not to usurp God's functions in violent retaliation for the violence done them. Nor are they to "grumble against each other" (5:9). The classic ploy of oppressors is to divide in order to conquer; the constant temptation of those oppressed is to turn on each other in abuse. James does not excuse such (psychologically understandable) behavior. Oppression done to us does not justify oppression done to each other. James reminds the readers, indeed, that they can also "fall under judgment," which lies so close at hand (5:9). They are to strive, rather, as the succeeding instructions will make clear, to create a community of solidarity that alone can effectively resist, with its peaceful cooperation, the insidious effects of oppression from outside.

Finally, James commands them to "take as an example" the prophets who spoke in the name of the Lord (5:10). By so doing, he not only taps into a pervasive self-understanding of early Christianity, but also strengthens his readers' understanding of themselves as a prophetic community whose "friendship with God," expressed by solidarity with each other, stands as a witness—and often a suffering witness—against those "friends of the world" who seek to eliminate the other through competition and violence.

Somewhat surprisingly, given the picture of him that emerges from the dialogues of the canonical book, James proposes as his last model for imitation from Scripture the "prophet" Job (5:11). As the notes suggest, James may have drawn his view of "patient Job" from extracanonical tradition, such as is reflected in *The Testament of Job*. But although part of what the readers are to take as an example is the "endurance" they have heard about in Job, the most important lesson is to be learned from the way the book of Job turned out: God rewarded the one who, despite his suffering, stayed loyal to God. The exact translation of *telos kyriou* in 5:11 is difficult, but certainly the phrase at least contains the sense that in the suffering of the righteous one, God is working purposefully. In the context established by James, the readers are to grasp that the judgment so to be dreaded by the wicked as a day of slaughter is to be one anticipated by the righteous as a day of "blessedness" (5:11), when the "crown of life" will be given to those who love God (1:12), because the God who creates, sustains, reveals, saves, and, yes, judges, is "rich in compassion and is merciful" (5:11).

BIBLIOGRAPHY

Bischoff, A., "*to telos kyriou*," ZNW 7 (1906) 274–79.

Dodd, C. H., "The Kingdom of God has Come," *ExpT* 48 (1936) 138–41.

Feuillet, A., "Le sense du mot parousie dans l'évangile de Matthieu: comparaison entre Matt xxiv et Jac v, 1–11," *The Background of the New Testament and Its Eschatology*, ed. W. D. Davies and D. Daube (Cambridge: Cambridge University Press, 1964) 261–80.

Fine, H., "The Tradition of a Patient Job," *JBL* 74 (1955) 28–32.

Fitzmyer, J. A., A *Wandering Aramean: Collected Aramaic Essays* (SBLMS 25; Missoula: Scholars Press, 1979) 176–77.

Fry, E., "The Testing of Faith: A Study of the Structure of the Book of James," *BT* 29 (1978) 427–35.

Gard, D. H., "The Concept of Job's Character according to the Greek Translator of the Hebrew Text," *JBL* 72 (1953) 182–86.

Gordon, R. P., "*KAI TO TELOS KYRIOU EIDETE* (Jas.v.11)," *JTS* n.s. 26 (1975) 91–95.

Haas, C., "Job's Perseverance in the Testament of Job," *Studies on the Testament of Job*, ed. M. A. Knibb and P. W. van der Horst (SNTSMS 66; Cambridge: Cambridge University Press, 1989) 117–54.

Johnson, L. T., "The Mirror of Remembrance (James 1:22–25)," *CBQ* 50 (1988) 632–45.

———, "The Use of Leviticus 19 in the Letter of James," *JBL* 101 (1982) 391–401.

Preuschen, E., "Jac. 5:11," ZNW 17 (1916) 79.

Spittler, R. P., "The Testament of Job," in *OTP* 1:829–68.

VIII. SPEECH IN THE ASSEMBLY OF FAITH
5:12–20

◆

12. But above all, my brothers, do not take oaths, neither by heaven, nor by earth, nor any other sort of oath. Rather, let your "yes" be "yes," and your "no," "no," so that you do not fall under judgment. 13. Is anyone among you suffering? Let that person pray. Is anyone feeling good? Let that person sing. 14. Is anyone among you ill? Let that person call the elders of the assembly, and let them, after anointing him with oil in the name of the Lord, pray over the person. 15. And the prayer of faith will save the sick person, and the Lord will raise him up. And if the person has committed sins, he will be forgiven. 16. Therefore, confess sins to each other and pray for each other so that you may be healed. A righteous person's prayer is able to have a strong effect. 17. Elijah was a human like us in nature. Yet he prayed fervently for it not to rain. And it did not rain upon the earth for three years and six months. 18. And he prayed again, and the heaven gave rain. And the earth produced its fruit. 19. My brothers, if any among you wanders from the truth, and someone turns him back, 20. let him know that the one who has turned back a sinner from his erring way will save that one's soul from death and will cover a multitude of sins.

THE SECTION AS A WHOLE

In discussing 5:7–11, I pointed out how that section already began a series of positive instructions to the community of readers even though it appeared to respond mainly to 4:11–5:6. There are good formal reasons for considering 5:12 as marking a turn to the final section of the composition. First is its use of the formula *pro panton* ("above all"). Whether or not it has specific contextual significance, such a phrase sometimes serves in epistolary convention to signal a final series of remarks (see notes). Second, the negative commandment (*mē*) has initiated other major portions of James' composition (2:1; 3:1; 4:11).

The more difficult question concerns the role of 5:12 itself. Does its content identify it as an isolated segment, so that its formal appearance as a beginning point is only formal, and 5:13 actually begins the final discussion in James? Most commentators tend to treat it this way, finding the theme of oath-taking only marginally connected either with what precedes or follows it (see, e.g., Dibelius, 248; Marty, 198; Vouga, 138; Adamson, 193; Cantinat, 241; Mussner, 211; Chaine, 125; Windisch, 32).

With a minority of commentators, however (see Laws, 218; Martin, 198), I see 5:12 as a genuine transition to the final section of the letter. This determination is based on my reading of what the final section of the letter is about. It is far from a disjointed series of exhortations. Rather, it is a unified discourse on the positive modes of speech in the community. The topic is speech: how can the tongue be used not for the destruction of humans, but for the building up of a community of solidarity?

In one sense, 5:12 is not an absolute beginning, for it is a negative command like those in 4:11 and 5:9, which also dealt with speech. In 4:11, James condemned slander and placed such behavior under God's judgment. In 5:9, he condemned grumbling speech against each other, placing it also under the threat of judgment. Now in 5:12, he forbids oaths, once more invoking God's judgment. There is certainly continuity between these commands. But 5:12 marks a beginning, nevertheless, for its primary significance is positive rather than negative. The opposite of slander and grumbling is silence. The opposite of taking oaths is plain speech.

The appropriate way to view this section of James as a whole, then, is as a discourse on positive modes of speech in the community. In 5:14, proper speech will be performative and expressed in action, but the reader who has been paying any attention to James at all will not be surprised at that (see 1:22–25; 2:14–26).

NOTES

12. *but above all*: Literally "before all": the preposition *pro-* plus the genitive expresses preference rather than spatial or temporal sequence (compare Plato, *Rep.* 366B; Josephus, *Ant.* 16:187). The construction with *pas* ("all") is found in some Hellenistic letters, usually in connection with the wish for health shortly before the final greeting (Marty, 199; Mussner, 211). The phrase occurs also at 1 Pet 4:8; *Did.* 10:4 (see also *pro pantos* in *Pol.Phil.* 5:3). The interpretive issue is whether the phrase has any significance beyond that of an "epistolary cliché" (see White, *Light*, 212). Is it a signal for the end of the letter—thus looking forward (so Francis, 125; Mitton, 191; Mussner, 211; Cantinat, 241;

Davids, 189; Vouga, 139; Laws, 220; Martin, 203)? Or is it being used to signal the importance of the prohibition against oaths—and thus looking backward (so Ropes, 300; Reicke, 56; Adamson, 194)? If the latter is the case, a further question concerns the strength of *de*: does James intend a contrast or a continuation, and if so, to what? The difficulties presented by such decisions encourage those seeking either to regard this verse as a gloss (Rendall, *Epistle of Saint James*, 68) or interpolation (Mayor, 165), or who see it as one more piece of evidence for James' essentially fragmented literary character (Dibelius, 248). If one recognizes, however, that James thus begins this final section of the letter with exhortations centering on the positive functions of speech (plain talk, prayer, confessing, correction), and that the prohibition of "grumbling against one another" in 5:9 also bore on improper speech, then this statement on oaths appears to continue the theme of speech started in 3:1–12 but now as applied directly to the community under harassment. The phrase *pro pantōn* indeed may give special significance to oath-taking (for reasons discussed below), but it *also* functions as a thematic transition to acts of speech within the community. Note also the sense of continuity provided by the fourth repetition in five verses of the vocative "brothers" (5:7, 9, 10, 12).

do not take oaths: As with other prohibitions in the present tense, this could also be translated as "stop taking oaths," but there is no reason to think this was a particularly severe problem faced by James. The combination of the verb *omnuein* ("swear") with *orkos* ("oath") is common (*Il.* 19:175; *T. Jud.* 22:3; Heb 6:16). The absolute prohibition is distinctive against the backdrop of Torah, where even Yahweh binds himself by oath (Exod 13:5; Num 14:16; Deut 1:8). Concern is shown for the manner or truth of any oath (see Lev 5:20–24; Num 30:3; Deut 23:22; Ps 23:4; Wis 14:29–30; Sir 23:11; Hos 4:15; Zech 8:17; Mal 3:5; Jer 5:2; see also Philo, *Decalogue* 84–95; *Special Laws* 2:2–38). The resemblance of the present prohibition to Lev 19:12 is noteworthy: *ouk omeisthe tō onomati mou ep'adikō, kai ou bebēlōsate to onoma tou theou hymōn* ("You shall not swear in my name wickedly, and you shall not profane the name of your God." This may be another instance where the context of Leviticus 19 helps James explicate the meaning of the royal law of love expressed by Lev 19:18 (Johnson, "Use of Leviticus," 397–98). Concern for oaths is found also in the Greek tradition (Epictetus, *Enchiridion* 33:5); the Pythagorean tradition forbade oaths entirely (see Diogenes Laertius, *Lives of Eminent Philosophers* VIII, 22; Jamblichus, *Life of Pythagoras* 9:28). And the same prohibition is associated with the Essenes: "Every statement of theirs is surer than an oath and with them swearing is avoided, for they think it worse than perjury. For they say that he who is not trustworthy except when he appeals to God is already under condemnation" (Josephus, *JW* 2:135; *Ant.* 15:370–72; but see also his account of their initiatory oaths in *JW* 2:139–43; and compare *CD* 9:9–10; 15:1–2, 8–10; 16:8–9; *1QS* 2:1–18; 5:8–11). Some rabbinic texts also testify to an extreme distaste for swearing (see *b.Bab.Bat.* 49a; *Numbers Rabbah* 9:35; *Exodus Rabbah* 5:4).

neither by heaven, nor by earth: For such oath formulae, see Philo, *Special Laws* 2:2 and *b.Sheb.* 35b. James' language most obviously resembles that in Matthew's Gospel. In Matt 23:16–22, Jesus attacks Scribes and Pharisees for their precise distinctions between kinds of oaths. In the Sermon on the Mount, Matthew has Jesus recall the tradition, "you shall not swear falsely but shall pay your oaths to the Lord," and then add this absolute prohibition: "But I tell you not to swear at all neither by the heaven (*mēte en ouranọ̄*), for that is God's throne, nor upon the earth (*mēte epi tẹ̄ gẹ̄*), for that is the footstool of his feet, nor (*mēte*) by Jerusalem, for it is the city of the great king, nor by the hair of your head, for you are not able to make a single hair black or white." The negative prohibition (*mē*), followed by the threefold *mēte, mēte, mēte* (in Matthew there is a fourth), makes for a strong formal parallelism between these passages.

nor any other sort of oath: This phrase extends the prohibition beyond the examples given and corresponds to *mē homosai holōs* ("do not take oaths at all") in the parallel passage of Matt 5:34.

rather, let your "yes" be "yes": Both James and Matthew 5:37 have this turn (in James, *ētō*; in Matt, *estō*); indeed, some MSS of James 5:12 supply "your speech" (*logos*) in agreement with Matt 5:37. The agreement between Matthew and James on the asyndetic *nai nai, ou ou* is especially striking. Characteristically, Matthew expands: "more than this is from the evil one." The sentiment here expressed is not unique to Matthew and James. A similar statement can be found in *Ruth Rabbah* VII, 6: "The yes of the righteous is yes, and their no is no." But the wording is so close as to suggest some sort of relationship. Does Matthew represent an earlier version of the saying (Mussner, 216), or does James (Dibelius, 251)? Determining priority is difficult (Davids, 190), and many commentators suggest that Matthew and James each depended on an earlier common source such as Q (Reicke, 56; Laws, 223; Marty, 202). This is reasonable, but the characteristic Matthean elements do appear to be secondary, particularly since they reflect his own thematic interests (Minear, "Yes or No," 7–8). An odd symptom of the complexity of tracing traditions is the fact that the logion appears also in Justin, *I Apol.* 16:5, and Clement of Alexandria, *Stromateis* 5,99,1; 7,67,5, associated with Matthew, yet in a form (using the article *to* before *nai* and *ou*) that is closer to James! The circulation of some such saying associated with Jesus is given further confirmation by Paul's Christological application in 2 Cor 1:15–20.

fall under judgment: See Josephus, *JW* 2:135, for a similar statement. Some MSS have a fascinating alternative reading: "fall into hypocrisy," reading *eis hypokrisin* rather than *hypo krisin*; this reading was in the text used by Oecumenius and Theophylact. There is a logic to this, since discussions of oath-taking emphasize the tendency of excessive oaths to lead to falsehood. Furthermore, the expression *hypo krisin* appears nowhere else in the LXX or NT. But precisely for these reasons, the alternative creates an "easier" reading and should be regarded as a correction. In fact, James has in several other places connected his negative commands with statements concerning judgment (see 2:4; 2:12–13; 4:11–12; 5:9). Bede makes reference here to the warning found in Matt 12:36.

13. *anyone among you suffering*: The *tis* in these clauses is indefinite rather than interrogative. Although they may be regarded as camouflaged conditionals (Mussner, 217), such rapid-fire questions and directives are common in the diatribe (compare, e.g., Philo, *On Joseph* 144; 1 Cor 7:18, 21; see Cantinat, 244–45; Marty, 204; Ropes, 303; Dibelius, 252). The verb *kakopathein* ("suffering"; see 2 Tim 2:9; 4:5) clearly picks up the *kakopathia* in 5:10. It means specifically to be enduring distress or hardship (see Xenophon, *Memorabilia* 1, 4, 11; 2, 1, 17; Philo, *On Dreams* 2:181).

let that person pray: As throughout this translation, "that person" attempts to provide a more inclusive (though awkward) substitution for "he" or "him," although sometimes these pronouns are unavoidable. Certainly, James has in mind both male and female members of the community. This is the first time that James has used *proseuchesthai*, introducing a section dominated by that verb (5:14, 16, 17, 18; see also *proseuchē* in 5:17). The verb denotes "prayer" in the broadest sense (Plato, *Symposium* 220D; Herodotus, *Persian War* 1:48; Dio, *Or* 52:1; Matt 14:23; Luke 1:10; 1 Cor 14:13–15). In the LXX, it tends to be reserved for prayer of petition (e.g., Gen 20:7, 17; Exod 10:17; Judg 13:8; 1 Sam 1:10; 2:1; Pss 5:3; 31:6; 108:4), as it does also in the NT (see Matt 5:44; 6:5–6; 24:20; Luke 18:1; 22:40; Rom 8:26; Phil 1:9; Col 1:3; 2 Thess 1:11) and in the present section (compare also James 1:5; 4:3). Although James does not specify the subject of prayer, it would make sense to suppose that it was either for relief from suffering or for the *hypomonē* to survive it (see 5:10).

is anyone feeling good: The translation of *euthymein* is not easy. It basically means to be in good spirits or cheerful (Euripides, *Cyclops* 530; Plutarch, *On Tranquillity of Soul* 2 [*Mor.* 465C]) but also means to give or take courage (see Acts 27:22, 25, 36). It does not occur in the LXX. The English translation "be cheerful" (RSV) is accurate but should not be understood simply as high spirits. It here stands in contrast to *kakopathein* and *asthenein* ("suffering and sickness"), so the translation "feeling good" seems more fitting.

let that person sing: It is tempting to translate "sing a psalm," and that may in fact be intended, but it is not said. The verb *psallein* meant originally to pluck the strings of a harp (Herodotus, *Persian War* 1:155; Lucian, *The Parasite* 17) and later—especially under the influence of the LXX—takes on the sense of singing in accompaniment of such harp-playing (see 1 Sam 16:16–23). In the LXX likewise, the verb is used largely with reference to such singing "to the Lord" (Judg 5:3; Pss 7:18; 9:3; 32:2; 104:2, etc.), so that *psalmos* ("that which is sung") becomes a technical designation for such songs (1 Sam 16:18; Job 21:12; see the titles of psalms). In the NT, there are three occurrences of the verb *psallein*: Rom 15:9 cites LXX Ps 17:50, "I will sing in your name"; 1 Cor 14:15 refers to singing "in the spirit and also with the mind"; and Eph 5:19 has: "address one another in psalms and hymns and spiritual songs, singing (*adontes*) and making melody (*psallontes*) in your hearts to the Lord." In the present case, it seems better to keep the precise content of the singing implicit, even though it is in all likelihood addressed "to the Lord." The RSV's "singing praise" is perhaps overly definite (see Adamson, 197). For singing in the Christian assembly (Reicke, 57), see 1 Cor 14:15; Rom 15:9; Eph 5:19–20; Col 3:16–17; Acts 16:25, and Pliny the Younger, *Letters* 10:96. Not surprisingly, James 5:13 became a favorite scriptural warrant: see, e.g., Origen, *Selecta in Psalmos* XLVII,7 (PG 12:1437); Cyril, *De Adoratione in Spiritu et Veritate* XII (PG 68:836); Athanasius, *In Interpretationem Psalmorum* 28 (PG 27:40).

14. *is anyone among you ill*: The verb *asthenein* means to be weak, as in some limb (Ps 108:29) or organ (Plato, *Lysis* 209E; Ps 87:9). The NT can use it in the sense of moral weakness (Rom 4:19; 1 Cor 8:7, 11–12), but the physical sense predominates (Matt 10:8; 25:36; Luke 9:2; John 4:46; 5:3; Acts 9:37; Phil 2:26) and is clearly intended here (see 5:15).

let that person call: The verb *proskalein* in the middle voice means to "summon" and has something of an official tone to it (see Plutarch, *Isis and Osiris* 9 [*Mor.* 354D]; compare Exod 3:18; 1 Sam 26:14; 2 Macc 4:28; Matt 10:1; 15:10; Luke 7:18; 16:5; Acts 2:39; 5:40; 6:2).

the elders: The only other designation for leaders that James has used is "teachers" (*didaskaloi*) in 3:1. The term "elder" (literally "older one," *presbyteros*) is attested for local leadership in papyri and inscriptions (LSMJ, 1462). In the LXX, it is used for local city council members (Josh 20:4; Ruth 4:2; Jdt 8:10; 10:6; also Luke 7:3). The designation "elders of the people" or "elders of Israel" is rooted in Moses' appointment of seventy to assist him in governing the people (Exod 19:7; 24:1) and is found in Lev 4:15; Num 11:16; 16:25; Deut 31:9; Josh 9:2; Judg 21:16; 1 Sam 4:3; 2 Sam 17:4. In the NT, the term is used for the members of the Jewish council (Matt 15:2; 26:3; Luke 22:52; Acts 4:5; 6:12; 23:14; 25:15; compare Josephus, *Ant.* 11:83; 12:406). But it also appears for leaders within the Christian movement (Acts 11:30; 14:23; 15:2, 23; 16:4; 1 Tim 5:1, 2, 17, 19; Titus 1:5; 1 Pet 5:1; 2 John 1; 3 John 1). The characterization "elders of the assembly" suggests something more than the older members of the community; it points to official leaders (Reicke, 57). Note the similarity to Acts 20:17, where Paul "called to him the elders of the church" in Ephesus. That elders of communities would visit the sick is also attested in rabbinic texts such as *b.Bab.Bat.* 116a; *b.Hag.* 3a; *b.Ned.* 41a.

of the assembly: In 2:2, James used *synagōgē* for the gathering/gathering place of the community. In wider Hellenistic usage, the *ekklēsia* referred to a gathered group of people (assembly) rather than to the place of meeting (see Herodotus, *Persian War* 3:142; Aristotle, *Politics* 1285A; Josephus, *Ant.* 12:164; *Life* 268). The same dynamic sense is found in the LXX (1 Kgs 19:20; 1 Macc 3:13; Sir

26:5) and in the NT for secular gatherings (Acts 19:32, 40). The term is also used in the LXX with specific reference to the congregation of Israel, especially when "convoked" for cultic activity, such as hearing the promulgation of the law (see Deut 4:10; 9:10; 18:16; 31:30). In the NT, *ekklēsia* is used for the assembly of believers when they physically come together (see 1 Cor 11:18; 14:4, 34), as well as for the "congregation" considered as the association of believers in a certain locality (1 Cor 4:17; Phil 4:15; Acts 15:22). It is in the broader sense that James uses the term here: the elders of the "association" are called together to form an "assembly" with the sick person.

after anointing him with oil: The aorist participle suggests that the anointing precedes the prayer. Olive oil (*elaion*) was used for a variety of anointings, including cosmetic (*Od*. 6:227; Ruth 3.3, 2 Sam 12.20; Ps 22:5), gymnastic (Thucydides, *Peloponnesian War* I,6,5; IV,68,5), and religious (Exod 40:15; Lev 2:1; 14:17; Num 3:3). There is some evidence for oil used medicinally in the Greco-Roman world (Menander, *Georgos* 60; Pliny the Elder, *Natural History* 23:39–40; Hippocrates, *Regimen* II, 65), but even more in Jewish literature (see Isa 1:6; Josephus, *Ant*. 17:172; *JW* 1:657; *T. Sol*. 18:34; Philo, *On Dreams* 2:58; *2 Enoch* 22:8–9 [though the function here is less certain]; *Life of Adam and Eve* 36:2; 40:1; *Test. Adam* 1:7); see also the Christian apocryphal writing, *The Gospel of Nicodemus* 19. In Luke's parable of the Samaritan, oil and wine are poured into the injured man's wounds (Luke 10:34). The most impressive parallel to James (as noted by Oecumenius and Bede) is found in Mark 6:13, where the emissaries sent out by Jesus to cast out demons are said to have "cast out many demons, and anointed many sick people with oil and healed them" (*ēleiphon elaiǭ pollous arrōstous kai etherapeuon*). Reicke judiciously notes that the practice here described is "rooted in traditional Jewish conceptions and has a point of contact with a suggestion by Jesus himself" (Reicke, 59).

in the name of the Lord: In 5:10, James said that the prophets had "spoken in the name of the Lord." In the discussion of that verse, it was noted that the expression communicated the source of the prophet's authority to speak. In the NT, a variety of activities is carried out "in the name of the Lord." Noteworthy among them is Paul's reference to "gathering together in the name of the Lord" (1 Cor 5:4), which seems to correspond to James' characterization of this community as having "a noble name invoked over them" (2:7). Even more impressive are those passages in Acts that speak of people being baptized "in the name of Jesus Christ" (Acts 2:38; 8:16; 10:48), of suffering "for the sake of the name of the Lord Jesus" (Acts 15:26; 21:13), of expelling demons by naming the name of Jesus (Acts 19:13), and, above all, of healing the sick "in the name of Jesus" (Acts 3:6; 4:10). James' language here obviously fits comfortably within that used in the earliest Christian movement, and "the Lord" whose name is invoked must surely be, as in 2:7, Jesus (Dibelius, 253).

let them pray over the person: Now the prayer of the group is directed to the individual member; for *proseuchesthai*, see the note on 5:13. Gathering together for such prayer is well attested in rabbinic literature (see Sir 7:35; *b.Bab.Bat.* 116a; *b.Ber.* 34b; *b.Sanh.* 101a; *Aboth de Rabbi Nathan* 41; *1QapGen* 20:21–22). The phrase *ep'auton* ("over him") is, however, unattested in the LXX or NT. Usually, prayer is said to be "in behalf" of someone (*hyper*; see, e.g., 2 Macc 12:44; Matt 5:44; Col 1:9; and James 5:16!) or "concerning someone" (*peri*; see Gen 20:7; 1 Sam 12:23; Jer 7:16; 44:3; Col 1:3; 4:3; 1 Thess 5:25; 2 Thess 1:11; 3:1; Heb 13:18). The phrase could mean either literally to pray "over" the prostrate sick person (see Chaine, 127) or to direct the prayer "towards" the sick one (Mussner, 219) in the sense of the "invocation of the Lord's name" (compare *to kalon onoma epiklēthen eph'hymas* in 2:7). There is certainly no reason to see this prayer as a form of exorcism, as Dibelius, 252, suggests. Indeed, the patristic discussions of the passage emphasize that such group prayer is the preferred alternative to magic (see Origen, *In Leviticam Homiliae* II,4 [PG 12:419]; Cyril, *De Adoratione in Spiritu et Veritate* VI [PG 68:472]; Procopius of Gaza, *Commentarium in Leviticam* XIX,19 [PG 87:763]).

15. *the prayer of faith*: The noun *euchē* can, in certain contexts, mean "oath/vow" (see, e.g., Xenophon, *Memorabilia* 2, 2, 10), and this is the dominant usage in the LXX (e.g., Gen 28:20; 31:13; Num 6:2; Deut 12:6; Ps 49:14; compare Acts 18:18; 21:23). Given James' prohibition of oaths in 5:12, such a meaning here is impossible, and *euchē* should be taken in its meaning of "prayer" (as in Xenophon, *Symposium* 8:15; Dio, *Or* 36:36), as is made clear immediately by the use of *euchesthai* in 5:16. The genitive *tes pisteos* is qualitative: the prayer spoken in faith or the prayer that is spoken out of faith. Compare "ask in faith" in 1:6, and contrast "ask wickedly" in 4:3.

will save the sick person: James uses the attributive participle of the verb *kamnein*, which when intransitive means "to be weary/fatigued (see Heb 12:3) or ill," either with respect to specific symptoms (Plato, *Gorgias* 478A; Lucian, *Toxaris* 60; 4 Macc 7:13) or simply in general; thus, "the sick" (*hoi kamnontes*), in Herodotus, *Persian War* 1:197; Plato, *Rep.* 407C). The verb *sōzein* has in this context its familiar ambiguity. At the most literal level, it means that the sick person will be healed. But in NT literature, especially when combined with "faith," it tends to mean "saved" in a religious sense. Indeed James' language here ("faith saves") is unmistakably part of early Christian argot, especially in connection with stories of physical healing. The phrase "your faith has saved you" (*hē pistis sou sesōken se*) is found in both Mark (5:34; 10:52) and Matt 9:22 in connection with Jesus' healings. In Luke, the expression is used even more frequently (Luke 7:50; 8:48; 17:19; 18:42), and in Acts, Luke explicitly connects "faith" to the power worked by "the name of the Lord" in healing (Acts 3:16; 4:9–10; 14:9), as well as to the joining of the Christian community (Acts 15:9, 11; 16:31). This is now the third time that James uses the language of "saving": in 1:21 he spoke of "the implanted word that is able to save your souls/lives"; in 2:14 he declared that faith without deeds could not "save"; now the two notions are joined: the prayer of the community is certainly a "deed of faith," and it is also "the name of the Lord" that has the power to save the life/soul of the sick person.

and the Lord will raise him up: The "him" is grammatical and should be read inclusively. James' language here again has a rich allusiveness. On one side, the use of *egeirein* ("to raise up") establishes a connection to the gospel accounts of Jesus' healings, a remarkable number of which involve this term: the paralytic (Matt 9:5–7; Mark 2:9; Luke 5:23–24; John 5:8); the man with the withered hand (Mark 3:3); the synagogue official's daughter (Mark 5:41; Luke 8:54); the widow of Nain's son (Luke 7:14); blind Bartimaeus (Mark 10:49); and Lazarus (John 11:29). On the other side, such language cannot but also recall the resurrection, whether of Jesus or the sick person. The connection is made explicitly in Luke's account of the healing of the lame man in Acts 3:1–10. Peter tells him, " 'In the name of Jesus Christ the Nazorean, walk,' and he took him by the right hand and raised him up" (3:7–8). Later, Peter declares that the resurrection of Jesus had effected the healing: "by faith in his name, has made this man strong, and the faith which is through Jesus has given the man this perfect health in the presence of you all" (3:16). And, before the Sanhedrin, Peter once more declares: "By the name of Jesus Christ the Nazorean, whom you crucified, whom God raised from the dead, by him this man is standing before you well . . . there is salvation in no one else, for there is no other name under heaven given among men by which we must be saved" (4:10–12). James' language shares this polyvalence, so that his reassurance can be read at two levels simultaneously: the Lord is able to "raise him up" from sickness, and thus "save him" by physical healing, *and* is able to "raise him up by resurrection" even if he should die and "save his life/soul" in the resurrection life (see James 1:18; 5:20).

if the person has committed sin: James uses a periphrastic construction: "if he has (become) a doer (*pepoiēkōs*) of sin." It was certainly part of the Deuteronomic tradition to understand God's blessings and curses in this-worldly terms and connected to human behavior (Deut 28:1–68; 30:1–19). In this view, sickness and distress are the direct result of sin (Deut 28:58–62). The prophet Ezekiel individualized the pattern but did not challenge its applicability (Ezek 18:1–29). Precisely such a link between sin and human distress is assumed by conventional Hebrew wisdom (Prov 3:28–35; 11:19; 13:13–23; 19:15–16; 23:19–21; Sir 1:12–13; 3:26–27; 11:14–20) and is placed in the mouths of Job's challengers (Job 8:1–22; 11:6; 22:1–30). Similar links between sin and sickness can be found in the rabbinic tradition (*m.Shab.* 2:6; *b.Shab.* 32a–33b; *b.Ned.* 41a; *b.Ber.* 5a). The equation is challenged in various ways by Qoheleth (3:16–22; 5:12–17; 6:1–9; 7:15; 9:11) and Job (9:13–21; 13:18–14:22; 21:4–26; 29:1–30:31). John's Gospel suggests a denial of the connection (John 9:1–3), but it is still found in 1 Cor 11:29–30, where Paul states: "For anyone who eats and drinks without discerning the body eats and drinks judgment upon himself; that is why many of you are weak and ill, and some have died." James, in contrast, does not directly attribute sickness to sin, for he uses a conditional: "and if this person has committed sin. . . ." Nevertheless, sin also is recognized here as a factor in illness, inasmuch as it involves a process of alienation that also requires "healing" as much as the body does.

he will be forgiven: Literally, "it will be released/forgiven with respect to him." The construction is impersonal (Mayor, 174). The construction, however, is problematic, as the textual variant suggests. It has the plural verb *aphethēsontai* ("they will be forgiven him"), clearly because *hamartias* in the previous clause is seen as an accusative plural rather than a genitive singular. The singular verb ("it will be forgiven him") appears to demand taking *hamartias* as the genitive singular: "if he has become a doer of sin." The plural form of *hamartia*, furthermore, appears in the very next verse! The singular *aphethēsetai*, therefore, should be taken as the "harder" and the preferred reading (compare Matt 9:2–6; 12:31; Mark 2:5–11; 3:28; Luke 5:20–24; 7:47–48; 12:10).

16. *therefore, confess sins to each other*: There are three significant textual variants in this part of the verse. Some MSS omit "therefore" (*oun*), possibly in order to make the already implicit connection to the previous statement more explicit. Other MSS add "from" to "sins." And others have *paraptōmata* ("transgressions") rather than "sins" (*hamartias*). This final alteration may be based on a reminiscence of Matt 6:14, where the forgiveness of transgressions by God is dependent on the human forgiveness of transgressions, with *paraptōmata* being used in both cases. The cognates *homologein* and *exomologein* have much the same range of meaning. *Homologein* is used predominantly in the LXX for "professing," with only one reference to "confessing your sins" (Sir 4:26). The same is true of the NT: the meaning "profess" is found in passages such as Acts 23:8; Rom 10:9–10; 1 John 2:23; 4:2, whereas "confessing sins" is found only in 1 John 1:9. In the LXX, the verb *exomologein* is used exclusively for the profession and praise of the Lord (see Gen 29:35; 2 Sam 22:50; 1 Chr 16:4; 2 Chr 5:13; Pss 6:6; 9:2; 70:22; Sir 39:6; Jer 40:11; Dan 3:25). In the NT, likewise, *exomologein* is used predominantly for "professing" (see Matt 11:25; Luke 10:21; Rom 14:11; 15:9; Phil 2:11). With the exception of the present passage, *exomologein* is used for the "confessing of sins" only in Mark 1:5; Matt 3:6; and Acts 19:18. The *practice* of acknowledging one's sins, however, is deeply rooted in Judaism, both for individuals (see, e.g., Lev 5:5; Num 5:7; Pss 38:8; *Pss. Sol.* 9:6–7; *1QS* 1:23–2:1) and for groups (Lev 16:21; 26:40; Deut 9:4–10; Baruch 1:15–2:10; Jdt 9:1–14; Tob 3:1–6; 3 Macc 2:2–20; 6:2–15). Evidence for the practice in Christianity appears also in the *Shepherd of Hermas*, which speaks of "confessing sins" (*Herm. Vis.* 1,1,3; *Herm. Sim.* 9,23,4) and "confessing sins to the Lord" (*Herm. Sim.* 3,1,5). The *Did.* 4:14 speaks of confessing transgressions in the assembly (*paraptōmata en ekklēsią*). See also 1 *Clem.* 51:3; 2 *Clem.* 18:3; *Barn.* 19:12. Perhaps the most distinctive aspect of the practice advocated by James is its *mutual* character: they are to confess to each other, not only "transgressions" of law, but "sins." Such mutual transparency is startling; some

MSS try to clarify by adding "each one's own sins" (*hamartias heautōn*). James is used to support such mutual confession and prayer in the community by Zachary, Patriarch of Jerusalem, *Epistula* (PG 86:3233); John Damascene, *Sacra Parallela* N II (PG 96:188), and John Cassian, *Conferences* XX,8.

pray for each other: As in 5:15, where some scribes replaced *euchē* with *proseuchē*, so here also some MSS "correct" the less familiar verb *euchesthai* to *proseuchesthai*. In fact, *euchesthai* is used widely in the sense of praying or entreating, especially "for/in behalf of" someone, both in the LXX (Exod 8:28; 9:28; Deut 9:20) and in the NT (Acts 26:29; 27:29; Rom 9:3; 2 Cor 13:7; 3 John 2).

you may be healed: The use of the plural verb indicates that James extends the need for healing from the individual sick person to the community as such: sickness and sin both create social alienation that requires remedy. In the NT, it is above all Luke-Acts that connects physical healing and social restoration (Johnson, "Social Dimensions of *Sōtēria*," 520–36). Jesus' ministry is portrayed in terms of healing (Luke 5:17; 6:18–19; 7:7; 8:47; 9:2, 11, 42; 13:32; 14:4; 17:15; 22:51; Acts 9:34; 10:38), and such physical healing is symbolic of social reconciliation (see esp. Acts 4:22, 30; 28:27). The instruction here in James most resembles that in Sirach 38:9: "My son, when you are sick, do not be negligent, but pray to the Lord, and he will heal you." The difference—and it is a significant one—is that Sirach is thinking in terms of the individual person, whereas James (as always) is thinking above all of the healing of the community.

a righteous person's prayer: Some MSS insert the connective *gar* ("for") to emphasize the assurance that prayer would bring healing. The characterization "righteous person" (*dikaios*) echoes the tradition of Torah for those who turned to Yahweh (see Pss 1:5–6; 2:12; 7:9; 32:1; 33:16; 36:39; 96:12; 145:8; Prov 4:18; 10:6, 16; 12:3; Wis 2:18; 3:1; Sir 35:6). It also picks up from "righteous one" (*dikaios*) in 5:6. Just as this readership can consider itself as "the poor," so can it also consider itself the community of "the righteous."

is able to have a strong effect: Although the general sense of this clause is clear, its precise translation is difficult. The neuter adjective *polu* ("much") functions as an adverb modifying *ischuein*, which basically means "to be strong": thus, "able to do much" (see Diodorus Siculus, *History* I, 60, 2; Josephus, *Apion* 1:77; *Ant.* 15:88; Phil 4:13; Matt 5:13). More difficult is the precise rendering of the participle *energoumenē*. Is it in the middle or passive voice (see Mayor, 177–79)? And is it to be read attributively as an adjective modifying prayer and thus yielding translations such as "the energetic prayer" (Dibelius, 256; Cantinat, 256; Laws, 234) and "active prayer" (Laws, 234)? Or should it be taken predicatively as modifying the verb "to be strong," yielding translations such as "when it is effective" (Mussner, 228), "very powerful in its operation" (Adamson, 199), "when it is exercised" (Ropes, 309), "when it is actualized" (Mayor, 178). In either case, the similarity with Gal 5:6, "faith working through (*energoumenē*) love" is noteworthy (Windisch, 33). Once more, James uses a term for prayer (*deēsis*) that emphasizes its petitionary quality (see 1 Kgs 8:28; 2 Chr 6:21; Pss 6:10; 21:25; 30:23; 87:3; Luke 1:13; Rom 10:1; 2 Cor 9:14; Phil 1:4), which the following example illustrates.

17. *a person like us in nature*: James uses *homoiopathēs* to modify *anthrōpos* ("person"). It means, literally, "to be of like feeling/passion" but has the sense of "like nature" (see Plato, *Rep.* 409B; *Timaeus* 45C; Wis 7:3; 4 Macc 12:13; Philo, *Confusion of Tongues* 7). Its function is clearly to assert the common humanity of Elijah and the readers, as in Acts 14:15: "we are also people of like nature to you" (*hēmeis homoiopatheis esmen hymin anthrōpoi*). James' language could be taken as a counter to the tendency to elevate the status of Elijah (see Mal 3:22–23; Sir 48:1–14; Mark 9:2–8; Matt 17:1–8; Luke 9:28–36), whose reputation for prayer was widespread (Sir 48:1–11; 2 Esd 7:109; *m.Taan.* 2:4; *b.Sanh.* 113a; *Esther Rabbah* VII, 13). But emphasizing the humanity of Elijah functions to affirm the possibilities available to them in their prayer.

yet he prayed fervently for it not to rain: The *kai* joining the clauses calls out for such translation (see BAGD 392g), for the statement responds to the implied concession in the previous clause: "*even though* Elijah was mortal, *nevertheless* he prayed." James uses the cognate construction *proseuchē proseuxato* (literally, "he prayed with a prayer") that is familiar from the Hebrew OT (Cantinat, 256; Moule, *Idiom Book* 177–78) and has the effect of intensifying the action of the verb: thus, "fervently" or "prayed and prayed" (Laws, 235). There are several textual variants for the phrase "for it not to rain," but the meaning is not significantly changed. James uses the articular infinitive construction that expresses purpose, literally, "so that it would not rain." The reference is to the prophecy of Elijah in the time of Ahab (1 Kgs 17:1): "As the Lord the God of Israel lives, before whom I stand, there shall be neither dew nor rain these years except by my word." Neither the MT nor the LXX make any mention of *prayer* in this statement, though the formula "as the Lord lives" might well be taken as an oath/prayer (*euchē*). For this tradition concerning the power of Elijah's prayer, see Rev 11:6: "these are the ones with the power to close up the heavens in order that it not rain during the time of their prophecy."

did not rain for three years and six months: The OT does not give the time sequence. Jewish traditions calculate the period of time diversely; see *Leviticus Rabbah* XIX, 1 and 5. The number given by James appears to be deduced from one statement and two implications. The statement is in 1 Kgs 18:1, that "the word of the Lord came to Elijah in the third year, saying, 'Go, show yourself to Ahab; and I will send rain upon the earth.'" Thus, the three years. Where do the six months come from? Possibly from the phrase, "after many days" in 18:1, which forms "after many days in the third year." Also, some time goes by before the word of the Lord is fulfilled and the rain actually comes (1 Kgs 18:45). In any case, the "three years and six months" tradition is found also in Luke 4:25: "There were many widows in Israel in the days of Elijah when the heaven was shut up three years and six months, when there was a great famine over the land." See also Sir 48:3: "By the word of the Lord he shut up the heavens," as well as 4 Ezra 7:39: "How then do we find that first Abraham prayed for the people . . . and Elijah for those who received the rain?"

18. *and he prayed again*: James once more makes explicit what was left implicit in the narrative of Elijah's encounter with the priests of Baal. Elijah prayed for the Lord to send down fire, and the Lord did (1 Kgs 18:37–38). But just before the rains came, Elijah went to the top of Mt. Carmel and "bowed himself down upon the earth and put his face between his knees" (1 Kgs 18:42). This gesture must be what James takes as his second prayer.

and the heaven gave rain: After Elijah's prayer on Mt. Carmel, there appeared a cloud from the sea (1 Kgs 18:44), and then "there was a great rain" (*kai egeneto huetos megas*). The phrase "the heaven gave" seems to be James' own addition and reflects his constant perception of God as "the giver of gifts" (see 1:5; 1:17; 4:6).

and the earth produced its fruit: This phrase also represents a haggadic expansion of the Elijah story as found in 1 Kings, which makes no mention of any consequences brought about by the renewed rain. The literary connection with James 5:7 seems patent: there also we have the farmer awaiting the precious fruit of the earth (*karpon tēs gēs*), which is given after a first and a second rain. The vivification of the earth expressed by fruit also establishes a parallel between sickness/dry land and health/fruit-bearing land (Davids, 197).

19. *if any among you wanders from the truth*: For the phrase *en hymin* ("among you"), see 1:5; 2:16; 3:13; 4:1; 5:13, 14. The situation is cast in a future conditional sentence, with the aorist subjunctive being used for both verbs in the protasis and the indefinite pronoun *tis* being used for both subjects: the condition could not be more generalized. James warned the readers in 1:16, "do not be deceived" (*mē planasthe*). Here, to "be deceived from the truth" is tautologous. James rather is playing on the sense of *planasthai* as "wandering astray," which can be either literal (Gen 37:15) or, as here, figurative. It is not surprising that some MSS supply either "the way" or "the way of truth" here, since that is what is clearly implied (compare, e.g., Deut 11:28; Prov 21:16; 28:10, and esp. Wis 5:6, *eplanēthēmen apo hodou alētheias*, "we wandered from the way of truth"). Although the best Greek text does not use "way" (*hodos*) here, it does appear in the next verse. "Truth" in this context does not mean theoretical correctness, but rather the proper "way" of behaving (see 2 Pet 2:15; *Did.* 6:1; *1 Clem.* 16:6). For the language about "the two ways" in Jewish and Christian moral exhortation, see the note on 1:8. James had earlier asserted that God gave birth by a "word of truth" (1:18) and had characterized envy and arrogance as "lying against the truth" (3:14).

and someone turns him back: In both these verses, the masculine pronouns are grammatical and can be read inclusively, particularly since they are introduced by the indefinite *tis*. The verb *epistrephein* is here active and transitive. And since the "wandering" should be understood in moral and religious terms, so should the "turning back" be taken as symbolic. James' language once more evokes that of the prophets, who called for a "turning back" to the Lord (see LXX Hos 3:5; 5:4; 6:1; Amos 4:16; Joel 2:12; Hag 2:17; Zech 1:3; Mal 2:6; 3:7; Isa 6:10; 9:12; 46:8; 55:7; Jer 3:12; 4:1; Ezek 18:30–32). In the NT, compare Matt 13:15; Luke 1:16–17; 22:32; Acts 3:19; 9:35; 11:21; 2 Cor 3:16; 1 Thess 1:9. The practice of fraternal correction is clearly similar to that described in Matt 18:15–18, which follows the parable of the lost sheep (18:12–14), with its implied ideal of "seeking the one that has wandered" (*poreutheis zētei to planōmenon*). Paul also advocates mutual correction in the community (Gal 6:1).

20. *let him know*: Or, "he should know"; some MSS have *ginōskete* ("you know/know you"), which appears to be a correction that seeks to eliminate the ambiguity later in the sentence (Metzger, 685). The third person imperative forms the apodosis to the condition posed by 5:19. This final reminder forms a bracket around the letter with 1:3, emphasizing once more the role that proper understanding plays in the exhortation as a whole (see note on 1:3).

a sinner from his erring way: This is the second time James has used the noun *hamartōlos*; the first was in the call to conversion in 4:8. But the composition has gazed steadily at the reality of sin as one of the options for human freedom, one that distorts and destroys authentic humanity (1:15; 2:9; 4:17; 5:15–16). The translation "erring way" reverses the adjective and noun in the Greek, which is literally "the error of his way" or "his way of error" (*planēs tou hodou autou*). It may be possible to detect here a faint allusion to LXX Lev 19:17b, which reads *elengmō elenxeis ton plēsion sou kai ou lēmpsē di'auton hamartian*: "You will earnestly reprove/correct your neighbor, and you will not bear sin on his account." The idea of "not bearing sin" corresponds rather well with "covering a multitude of sins" later in this verse, while *epistrephein* and *elenchein* are functionally equivalent (Johnson, "Leviticus 19," 398).

will save that person's soul from death: This translation is based on the critical Greek text of Nestle-Aland, 26th edition. Some MSS seem to reflect perplexity concerning the third person pronoun *autou*, since it could refer to the soul either of the converter or the converted person; they, therefore, place it after "death," making it an intensive: "death itself" (*thanatou autou*). The connection of sin and death is widespread (see Deut 30:19; Job 8:13; Pss 1:6; 2:12; Prov 2:18; 12:28; 14:12; Wis 2:24; Rom 5:12; 1 Cor 15:56; 2 *Bar.* 85:13; *T. Abr.* 10:2–15). The "rescue operation" by moral correction vividly recalls the imagery of 1:15, which describes the inexorable progress from desire to sin and from sin to death (*thanatos*). In Matt 18:15, the result of such correction is "gaining your brother" (*ekerdēsas ton adelphon sou*). Ezekiel also spoke of the prophetic rebuke in terms of life and death: "If you warn the righteous man not to sin and he does not sin, he surely shall live, because he took warning; and you will have saved your life" (Ezek 3:21). That mutual correction was a necessary part of genuine friendship and life together was also axiomatic for those living the philosophical life in the ancient world; see, e.g., Hierocles, *On Duties* 4.25.53; Dio, *Or.* 77/ 78:37–45; Plutarch, *How to Tell a Flatterer from a Friend* 30–37 (*Mor.* 70D–74E); Philodemus, *On Frankness* 37; PA 5:18; *1QS* 5:24–25.

   cover a multitude of sins: The exact meaning of this phrase is obscure. What does "cover" (*kalyptein*) mean here? The term occurs in the LXX for a variety of physical "coverings" (Gen 7:19; Exod 8:2), but only the reference to the cloud covering the tent of meeting (Num 9:15) or the mercy seat (Lev 16:13) seems to bear any possible cultic sense. In LXX Ps 84:3, Yahweh is praised for taking away the lawlessness of the people and "covering over all their sins (*ekalypsai pasas tas hamartias autōn*)." Similarly, Ps 31:1 begins "Blessed are they whose lawless deeds have been forgiven, and whose sins have been covered (*epekalyphthēsan*)" In these texts, "cover" seems to mean "remove from sight" in a sense synonymous with "forgive," for the psalm continues, "blessed is the person to whom the Lord does not count sin" (Ps 31:2). The combination *kalyptein plēthos hamartiōn* most resembles 1 Pet 4:8: "Above all, have sincere love in yourselves, because love covers a multitude of sins (*agapē kaluptei plēthos hamartiōn*)." The citation in 1 Pet 4:8, in turn, closely resembles the MT at Prov 10:12: "Hatred stirs up strife, but love covers all offenses." Strangely, however, it does not match the LXX translation of that passage, which has: "hatred stirs up strife, but friendship (*philia*) covers (*kalyptei*) all contention-lovers." In either case, the term "cover" here seems to have as much to do with "suppressing" as it does with "forgiving"; that is, it is preventative. The passage in 1 Peter seems dependent on Prov 10:12, though not directly from the LXX. Perhaps some oral version of the saying was in circulation; it finds its way also to *1 Clem.* 49:5 and *2 Clem.* 16:4. It is less certain that James has any dependence on Prov 10:12 (Davids, 200; Chaine, 137). If 1 Peter is set aside, it is difficult to find a reason to argue for such influence on the basis of the LXX (Ropes, 316). The final problem in this puzzling statement concerns its referent. Whose soul is saved and whose sins are covered? At least one commentator declares the text is too obscure to decide (Vouga, 146). Most, however, split the two referents: the soul saved belongs to the one corrected, the sins covered are those of the corrector (Dibelius, 258; Mussner, 233; Laws, 239; Ropes, 315–16; Adamson, 204). It is more likely, however, that both refer to the one corrected: his soul is saved, and his sins are covered (Mayor, 237–38; Martin, 220; Davids, 201). But the phrase "covers over a multitude of sins" is properly understood when it is taken, not as referring to sins of the past that are forgiven, but to sins of the future that the converted person is now no longer going to commit. "Covering over" here seems to work best when it means "suppress/prevent." The proper effect of correction in the community is that it "prevents the perpetuation of numerous sins in society" (Reicke, 63). Windisch, somewhat cryptically, calls this a "catholic concept" (35). The ending of James struck even some ancient scribes as abrupt, so they added *amen* ("amen") to the composition. But James is no more abrupt than the ending we find in Sirach 51:30 or Wisdom 19:22 (Cantinat, 263; see also Francis, "Form," 175).

COMMENT

The misuse of speech has been a constant theme running through this composition. In 1:19, James warned his readers to be "quick to hear, slow to speak, slow to anger." And in 1:26 he declared that anyone claiming to be religious who did not control speech had only a "foolish" form of religion. His explicit discussion of the power and perils of speech in 3:1–12 began with the sobering reminder that the profession of speaking (as a teacher) was a hazardous one and subject to greater judgment (3:1), for the tongue is the hardest of all things to control. James called it "the world of wickedness established among our members" (3:6) and showed great pessimism concerning the human capacity to subdue its evil tendencies (3:7).

Throughout his composition, furthermore, James shows just what kinds of speech reveal the "friendship with the world" that is enmity with God (4:4): heedless and self-deceiving speech (1:13–14), flattering and discriminatory speech (2:3), blaspheming speech (2:7), cursing speech (3:9), slandering speech (4:11), arrogant speech (4:13), recriminatory speech (5:9). All such modes of speech seek to assert the self at the expense of the truth and at the expense of others. It is speech in the service of envy and competition. It is speech that expresses the view of reality as a closed system and, by so expressing it, helps to perpetuate that view.

James also earlier attacks those forms of speech within the community of faith that reveal "double-mindedness," the attempt to live simultaneously by the measure of faith (the wisdom from above) and the measure of the world (the wisdom that is earth-bound, unspiritual, demonic). Such is the speech that claims a certain identity but does not express it in action (2:14), or worse, uses pious speech as a cover for inaction (2:15–16). Such is the speech that blesses God with one side of the mouth and curses a brother with the other side (3:9). Such is the speech that prays wickedly in order to satisfy envious cravings (4:3).

Now, at the conclusion of his composition, James returns explicitly to the ways speech can function positively within the community of faith. Like all Hellenistic moralists, James knows the power of speech (3:3–5). If it can "boast of great things" with respect to evil, perhaps also it can accomplish great things with respect to good. If speech can be an instrument of envy, competition, and violence, perhaps it can also be an instrument of peace, cooperation, and solidarity.

James' hope is based in the distinctive form of the gifts given humans by God. God brings humans (or this community) into being in the first place by a "word of truth" (1:18) with the express purpose of creating a community of "representative creatures." This word, furthermore, has been "implanted" in us and can become active as a force for good when "received with meekness"; it can, indeed, "save souls/lives" (1:21). James' language about this "word of truth," as we have seen, corresponds closely to his language about the "wisdom from above" that comes from God and is expressed in deeds of peace and righteousness (3:13–18), as well as to his language about "the spirit God made to dwell" in humans that is to seek peace through meekness and lowliness, rather than crave enviously and arrogantly (4:5–6).

From this perspective, James' prohibition of oaths is indeed appropriate in its place and does state something that is "above all" important about speech. The taking of oaths does not mean in the first place using profanity in speech, although there is a remote connection. What the contemporary world terms as "profane" speech is often (when it is not explicitly sexual and/or scatological) the corruption of more formal oaths and, therefore, not truly profane speech, but rather "profaned" speech, language that began as religious and solemn but that is now merely adornment. The effect of such language, however, is similar to James' implied complaint against oaths. Language that is laced with epithets loses both its denotative and connotative force; it must become ever more graphic even to be descriptive, ever more shocking even to achieve emotion.

The same problem attends the formal taking of oaths. An oath is a solemn utterance by which human speech invokes divine power as a warrant to its own truthfulness. Even ancient critics of oaths recognized how quickly such vows could become trivialized and a form of superstition (see notes). But any sort of oath-taking, even when practiced selectively, can represent a trivialization of speech. If speech is meant to be a primary symbol of the self, if it is from the heart's overflow that the tongue is meant to speak, then the invocation of a special realm (whether heaven or earth) or power (the name of the Lord) to buttress one's own speech becomes, paradoxically, an admission that one's own speech is untrustworthy without such warrant. The more towering the oath, the more impressive the power invoked to support my own statement, the more suspect my innate truthfulness appears. The moral effect of an oath can easily become the opposite of its intended purpose. Finally, the implied manipulation of the divine implied by such speech must appear particularly offensive to James (compare 1:26; 3:9; 4:3).

James' prohibition of oaths is, in reality, the encouragement of plain speech in the community of faith: "let your 'yes' be 'yes,' and your 'no', 'no.'" It is a call to simplicity and truthfulness. If a person's "yes" reveals the affirmation of the heart and the commitment of the hands, then it can be trusted. In the same fashion, if a person's "no" defines the boundaries of consensus and commitment, then it is equally to be trusted.

James places such speech in the first position because it is fundamental to every other sort of speech and action. Otherwise, the prayer in distress, the song of praise, the call for help, the confession of sins, the correction of the neighbor, can all become distorted, deceptive, and destructive, instruments of manipulation and competition. James forbids oaths because he desires a community of solidarity based in mutual trust; such trust is possible only where speech is simple and unadorned with false religiosity.

James turns next (5:13–16) to prayer within the community as an expression of truth. The person who is suffering should not say "I am being tempted by God" (1:13) or seek to retaliate against the source of distress (5:7) but, instead, let his "cries reach the ears of the Lord of armies" (5:4), for the Lord is the one who for the lowly "gives a greater gift" (4:6). The person who is feeling good should give expression to that truth by song, recognizing God as the generous giver (1:5) of every good and perfect gift (1:17), as the one who is, above all, compassionate and merciful (5:11) and the source of authentic human blessedness (1:12; 5:11).

The next part of James' discourse on speech within the community deals with the speech of the sick and the speech of the community in response to sickness. In the history of interpretation, this part of James has received disproportionate attention as a proof-text for the Sacrament of the Anointing of the Sick, formerly called "Extreme Unction." Roman Catholic interpreters were committed to finding the scriptural basis for that sacrament in this text. Protestant commentators were equally committed to the rejection of that claim. Extensive discussions of this topic are readily available (see, e.g., Mayor, 169–73; Chaine, 126–33; Bord, *L'extreme onction*). Like the attention given to the relationship between James and Paul in 2:14–26, the main effect of this preoccupation has been to distort the text and require it to address issues beyond its scope.

Most recent interpreters focus rather on the cultural context of the passage, seeking to locate the practices it encourages in Greco-Roman or especially Jewish usage (see notes). But no more than the earlier debates over the sacrament do such investigations draw us into a deeper consideration of the text's meaning within the composition as a whole.

The speech of the sick within the community, however, requires special attention, for the simple reason that sickness is a profound threat to the identity and stability of a community. Sickness is not the same thing as sin. Nor does James suggest that sickness derives from sin. But sickness is *analogous* to sin in its social effects. Therefore the healing of the sick person and the healing of the community must take into account the spiritual dimensions of this threat. The way in which James has intertwined the healing of illness and the forgiveness of sins testifies to his grasp of this reality.

Sickness presents a profound challenge to the community of faith: will it behave like friends of God or like friends of the world? According to the wisdom from below, the proper result of fierce competition is the survival of the fittest. The logic of envy is to claim strength at the expense of others. Envy, we have seen, leads to murder. Does someone fall sick? They are weak, leave them by the wayside. Their elimination leaves more resources for me; having to share my attention and resources with them distracts me and weakens me for my own struggle for supremacy and survival.

The logic of the world, therefore, is to isolate the sick from the healthy. The healthy organism recoils from the sick person to protect itself. Sickness then creates the opportunity for social alienation. This "natural reflex" of survival, however, also becomes the opportunity for sin, when it becomes the deliberate exclusion of the sick person from care and support, when the physical alienation imposed by sickness is embraced as a spiritual alienation from the sick.

It is not by accident, I think, that James here for the first time uses the term *ekklēsia*, for it is the identity of the community *as* community that sickness threatens. Will the community rally in support of the weak and show itself to be "merciful and rich in compassion," a community based in solidarity, or will it recoil in fear and leave the sick person to progressive alienation? We notice first that James empowers the sick themselves with respect to the community. When they are ill, *they* are to call the elders of the community. James' language has a formal quality: they are to *summon* the elders (5:14). James then enjoins the elders to pray over and anoint the sick person in the name of the Lord. In the elders, the *ekklēsia* is to respond to the weak member and overcome the alienation and inertia with which sickness threatens the life of the group.

The oil used for anointing is not a magic oil. It is the common olive oil that is widely used for medicinal purposes. There is no great gap between physical and spiritual healing. They must happen together. The oil gains its real power from the touch of human hands that apply it, that reach across pain and loneliness to reestablish communion. Likewise, prayer is not simply words said to God, but prayer "over" the sick person, a summons from the community that is willing to share its life and strength, its faith, with the one who is weak and whose sickness has probably also weakened his own faith and confidence. The community, through its elders, shares its faith by gathering together and supporting the sick person both physically and spiritually in the time of crisis.

In the actions of those gathered around the sick person, we recognize the practices of early Christians, rooted in the traditions of Israel and in the ministry of Jesus. As the notes indicate, there are remarkable parallels between James' language and the gospel traditions concerning Jesus' ministry of healing. Two of these in particular deserve attention. The first is the connection between healing and the forgiveness of sins: "if this person has committed sins, he will be forgiven" (5:15). What makes James intriguing in this respect is that he applies this not only to individuals but to the community as such: "Confess sins to each other and pray for each other that you may be healed" (5:16). Certainly, James has something more than the physical well-being of the members in mind. A community is healed as *ekklēsia* when, in trust and vulnerability, it is able to pray and confess sins together. Such speech establishes the community as based in "the word of truth" and restores it from whatever alienation has affected it from the sickness and sin.

Second, James shares the gospel tradition's immense confidence in the power of prayer to heal both individuals from their illness and communities from their alienation: "the prayer of faith will save the sick person and the Lord will raise him up" (5:15). This is a confidence in prayer and faith that most resembles Jesus' own: "Ask and it will be given to you; seek and you will find; knock, and it will be opened to you" (Matt 7:7). Is it by accident that this very saying of Jesus is echoed earlier in James: "Let him ask of God, who gives to all simply and without grudging, and it will be given to him. But let him ask in faith" (1:5–6)?

It is in connection with this confidence concerning the power of prayer that James points his readers to his fourth and final example from Scripture: the prophet Elijah (5:17–18). Elijah is used to illustrate the statement, "a righteous person's prayer is able to have a strong effect" (5:16b). In Elijah's case, this is demonstrated by the spectacular effects of drought and rainfall or, in biblical idiom, the "closing and the opening of heaven" (see notes). Such communication is perhaps not remarkable in the case of a prophet, who is, after all, the Lord's spokesperson. The prophet, above all, symbolizes a view of the world exactly opposite that of "the world," for whom reality is a closed system. The prophet's entire identity is predicated on the reality of God as the giver of gifts.

Two subtler aspects of James' characterization are worth remarking. Both have the effect of connecting Elijah more closely to the readers whom James is addressing and, thereby, of affirming that what happened for Elijah can happen also for them. The first is the description of Elijah as "a human like us in nature" (5:17). The Greek is literally "of like passion/feeling to us." What is important about this is not simply that it avoids making Elijah a semidivine figure, but that it empowers a community that is itself experiencing the same sort of stress and suffering that Elijah did in his battles with the priests of Baal in the days of wicked King Ahab. Elijah did not pray out of a posture of ostensible strength; he was beleaguered and isolated when he prayed. *That* is the lesson to readers who see themselves as oppressed by the powerful.

James' second touch is to imply that Elijah is a "righteous man" (*dikaios*) in 5:16b. The readers cannot but connect this to the charge against the rich in 5:6 that they had murdered the righteous person (*dikaios*). Elijah, in other words, was situated over against the powers of his world, as the oppressed poor are situated over against the rich. Yet Elijah's prayer was more powerful than them. *This* is the lesson to James' readers: the prayer that can raise the sick person and heal the community can also prove triumphant over the powers of evil in the world, for prayer is the openness of the human spirit to the powerful word of God that enables it to work. Indeed, the prayer of the community gathered in solidarity is already a victory over the world that defines itself by envy and competition. For prayer refuses that definition of reality. Prayer resists idolatry by insisting on the greater power of what is not seen than that which is seen. The prayer of the community gathered in solidarity triumphs over those forces that seek to divide and conquer, to isolate and eliminate, by insisting together on being "other" than that world, as being defined by what is totally "other" than that world, by seeking friendship with God rather than with that world (4:4).

James concludes the section and the composition with an encouragement to mutual correction within the community (5:19–20). This final example of plain speech in the community is perhaps most offensive to contemporary groups in which the strange ethos has taken root that regards every opinion as worthy of consideration and every behavior tolerable. It is not difficult to see how James, and indeed the entire ancient moral tradition, differed dramatically with respect to the obligation that communities and their members had to maintain the boundaries of their identity by mutual assistance. For many philosophers in James' period, such moral correction was of the very essence of the philosopher's vocation (see Epictetus, *Discourses* III, 22; Dio Chrysostom, *Oration* 77/78). Certainly, moral correction was at the heart of the prophet's call as well (see Ezek 3:1–11; 18:1–32).

Such correction has nothing to do with attitudes of moral superiority and smugness, or with slander and judging of others (4:11–12). Such attitudes are those of the world that operates by envy and competition, that seeks the elevation of one by the lowering of the other. No, James sees the plain speech of mutual correction as the correlative of confessing sins to each other and praying together. All humans are capable of self-deception and error (see 1:7, 14, 16, 22); each person needs the honest assistance of others in the path of righteousness. It is the understanding of mutual correction as an act of service that gives it a distinctive character and distinguishes it from mere criticism, carping, and busy-bodyness.

First, what is at stake is the community's own commitment to the "way of truth" as opposed to the "way of error." The ancient teachers understood how fragile an intentional community is and how devastating apostasy from its norms can be to the rest of the group. The "truth" here is that of the word, wisdom, and spirit, given to humans by God, for which and to which human freedom is responsible. Second, such correction has as its aim the "saving of the soul" of the erring comrade. This is the work of "the implanted word" that is received in meekness (1:21). Just as in the case of sickness, sin within the community has the effect of making the community recoil in self-defense: the sinner becomes increasingly isolated and increasingly alienated. To reach out with the word of truth is to "save" the other. Third, the effect of such correction is to "cover a multitude of sins." The notes discuss the options for understanding this difficult phrase. But it seems to me that the entire thrust of James' composition demands that we take this to mean that such correction will prevent a multitude of sins in the future, both the sins that the erring member might otherwise commit and the sin of the community that continues to fail in its speaking of truth to that erring brother.

Such is the noble task of correction within the community of faith. Such is the task that James has nobly performed for his readers. Such is the noble task to which this composition invites its readers, for the sake of "the noble name that has been invoked over you" (2:7). A community taking its lead from James can indeed be a "kind of firstfruits" of God's creatures (1:18).

BIBLIOGRAPHY

Althaus, P., "Bekenne einer dem andern seine Suendin: zur Geschichte von Jak 5,16 seit Augustin," *Festgabe für Theodor Zahn* (Leipzig: A Deichertsche Verlagsbuchhandlung, 1928) 165–94.

Baker, W. R., " 'Above All Else': Contexts of the Call for Verbal Integrity in James 5:12," *JSNT* 54 (1994) 57–71.

Bord, J. B., *L'extrème onction d'après l'épître de saint Jacques (V,14,15) examinée dans la tradition* (Bruges: Charles Beyaert, 1923).

Condon, K., "The Sacrament of Healing (Jas 5:14–15)," *Scr* 11 (1959) 33–42.

Dautzenberg, G., "Ist das Schwurverbot Mt 5,33–37; Jak 5,12 ein Beispiel für die Torakritik Jesu?" *BZ* n.s. 25 (1981) 47–66.

Eisenman, R., "Eschatological 'Rain' Imagery in the War Scroll from Qumran and in the Letter of James," *JNEST* 49 (1990) 173–84.

Francis, F. O., "The Form and Function of the Opening and Closing Paragraphs of James and 1 John," *ZNW* 70 (1970) 110–26.

Friesenhahn, H., "Zur Geschichte der Überlieferung und Exegese des Textes Bei Jak V,14f," *BZ* 24 (1938–39) 185–90.

Hoyos, P., "La Extrema Uncion en el Primer Siglo," *RevistB* (Brazil) 25 (1963) 34–42.

Johnson, L. T., "The Social Dimensions of *Sōtēria* in Luke-Acts and Paul," *SBLSP* 32 (1993) 520–36.

———, "The Use of Leviticus 19 in the Letter of James," *JBL* 101 (1982) 391–401.

Kilmartin, E. J., "The Interpretation of James 5:14–15 in the Armenian Catena on the Catholic Epistles: Scholium 82," *Orientalia Christiana Periodica* 53 (1987) 335–64.

Kutsch, E., " 'Eure Rede aber sei ja,ja, nein, nein'," *EvT* 20 (1960) 206–17.

Luff, S. G. A., "The Sacrament of the Sick—a First Century Text," *The Clergy Review* 52 (1967) 56–60.

Marconi, G., "La Debolezza in Forma di Attesta, Appunti Per Un'Esegesi di Gc 5,7–12," *RevistB* 37 (1989) 173–83.

Meinertz, M., "Die Krankensalbung Jak 5,14f.," *BZ* 20 (1932) 23–36.

Minear, P. S., "Yes or No: The Demand for Honesty in the Early Church," *NovT* 13 (1971) 1–13.

Reicke, B., "L'onction des malades d'après saint Jacques," *La Maison Dieu* 113 (1973) 50–56.

Rendall, G. H., *The Epistle of St. James and Judaic Christianity* (Cambridge: Cambridge University Press, 1927).

Sailer, J., "Jak 5,14 und die Krankensalbung," *TPQ* 113 (1965) 347–53.

White, J. L., *Light from Ancient Letters* (Philadelphia: Fortress Press, 1986).

Wilkinson, J., "Healing in the Epistle of James," *SJT* 24 (1971) 326–45.

INDEX OF SCRIPTURE REFERENCES

✦

Genesis

1:3   196
1:14–15   196
1:26–30   197
1:26–28   261, 262
1:26   262
1:28   261
2:15   303
3:10   238
3:22   284
3:24   280, 303
4:1   194
4:10   302
4:11   284
4:17   194
6:5   201, 271, 285
7:3   211
7:15   280
7:19   339
8:20   211
9:20   314
9:26   262
12:3   262
12:8   226
14:3   263
15:5   74
15:6   63, 74, 200, 243, 247–48
17:4–5   242
18:9   85
18:17   244
18:37   316
20:7   329, 332
21:1–2   85
21:1   212
21:23   200
22:1–18   242, 247–48
22:1   192, 193

22:2–9   63
22:2   195, 242
22:9   242
22:13   242
24:5   279
24:13   262
24:27   262
25:4   279
25:26   93
26:8   209
27:27   316
27:29   262
27:37   315
28:4   225
28:12   315
28:20   332
29:25   207
29:35   334
30:13   187
31:13   207, 332
31:41   207
37:15   337
37:28   193
37:35   285
38:26   242
42:21   212
45:27   280
48:16   226
49:15   314
50:3   285
50:24   212

Exodus

1:13   225
2:11   207
2:23–24   316
2:23   302, 316

348

3:6   93
3:7   302
3:15   93
3:16   212
3:18   330
3:20   284
4:21   271
4:31   212
5:8   302
6:5   316
8:2   339
8:28   335
9:24   259
9:28   335
10:17   329
12:39   312
13:5   327
13:22   262
15:13   200
15:27   262
17:12   315
18:10   262
18:21   283
19:7   330
19:10   285
19:21   284
19:22   284
19:24   294
20:5–6   188
20:7   50, 211
20:13–15   233
20:13   30
20:15   30
20:17   193
20:21   212
20:24   50
21:10   302
22:21–27   303
22:22   302
22:28   198
23:7–8   304
23:7   242
23:9–11   302
23:9   212
23:19   198
24:1   330
24:2   284
24:4   169
24:12   294
25:2–3   198
28:21   169

31:3   281
32:17   302
34:6   313, 321
35:31   281
36:21   169
40:15   331

Leviticus

2:1   331
2:12   198
4:4   284
4:12   211
4:15   330
5:3   212
5:5   334
5:20–24   327
5:23–24   304
6:4   302
7:19   211
11:24   212
11:32   211
14:15   284
14:17   331
14:26   284
14:32   284
15:13   211
16:9–15   212
16:13   296, 339
16:19–20   284
16:21   334
16:30   284
17:10   294
18:24   212
19:9–10   212
19:11   31
19:12   31, 231, 327
19:13–18   307
19:13   31, 231, 301–302, 308
19:14–18   40
19:14   31
19:15   7, 31, 52, 221, 223, 227, 228,
       231, 235, 304
19:16   31, 231, 293, 307
19:17   31, 231, 338
19:18   31, 40, 52, 61, 221, 230, 231,
       232, 235, 293, 316, 317, 327
19:33   212
19:35   302, 304
20:3   294
232:22   212

24:15 262
25:11 301
25:23 170
26:33 169
26:37 283
26:40 334
26:41 294

Numbers

3:3 331
5:3 212
5:7 334
6:2 332
8:7 211
8:21 285
9:15 339
11:2 302
11:10 285
11:16 330
12:3 201
12:8 292
14:12 294
14:16 327
14:18 313, 321
14:39 285
15:20–21 198
16:5 224
16:25 330
18:22 261
19:12 285
20:17 230
21:5 292
21:14 259
22:6 262
22:19 312
30:3 327
31:23 285
32:8 207
34:3 263

Deuteronomy

1:8 225, 327
1:13 270
1:15 270
1:17 228
1:45 285
2:7 284
2:12 225, 294
2:21 294
3:17 263

4:1 225
4:6 29, 179, 270
4:7 284
4:9 208
4:10 331
4:19 195
4:23 208
4:27 169
4:29 212
4:31 208
4:37 224
5:17–18 30, 233
5:21 193
6:3–4 224
6:4 188, 241
6:6 271
6:12 208
7:7 224
7:9 188
8:2 192, 285
8:14 208
8:20 294
9:1 224
9:2 283, 331
9:4–10 334
9:20 335
10:17–19 212, 304
11:4 294
11:14 315
11:26 262
11:28 195, 337
12:6 332
12:11 226
12:15 211
12:30–31 304
13:3 138
13:4 192
13:9 282
14:28–29 212
16:18–20 304
18:4 198
18:15–22 318
18:16 331
19:14 304
20:5–8 270
21:23 212, 262
23:22 327
24:10–16 302
24:12–13 304
24:14 302
24:17–18 212

24:17   304
24:19   301
25:1   242
25:7   279
25:13–16   304
26:12–15   212
27:6   178
28:25   169
28:64   169
29:19   282
30:4   169
30:19   338
30:20   188
31:9   330
31:30   331
32:17   241
32:19   282
32:26   169
32:39   294
33:14   197
33:19   200
33:29   187, 294
34:9   281

Joshua

2:1–21   245
2:11   245
2:13–14   245
2:16   245
4:5   169
6:17   303
6:25   245, 280
8:10   210
9:2   178, 330
9:22   207
14:7   168
15:2   263
15:8   260
18:16   260
20:4   330
24:10   294
24:14   200
24:30   50, 168

Judges

1:14   302
2:8   168
2:16   294
3:9   294, 302
4:3   302

5:3   329
6:7   302
6:14   294
6:23   239
7:3   270
10:18   313
13:8   329
15:11   262
15:19   245
18:6   239
19:5   315
19:6   294
19:8   315
19:20   239
20:31   193
21:16   330

Ruth

1:6   212
2:11   207
2:20   262
3:3   331
4:2   330
4:4   262

1 Samuel

1:3   303
1:10   329
2:1–10   185
2:1   329
2:6   294
2:7   286
2:21   212
2:27   167
4:3   294, 330
12:23   332
16:16–23   329
16:18   329
20:22   239
25:32   262
26:14   330
29:7   239

2 Samuel

6:21   262
7:8   168
7:25   168
7:29   168

12:20   331
12:30   188
15:27   239
17:4   330
18:28   262
22:50   334
24:22   260

1 Kings

1:48   262
3:5–15   179
8:15   262
8:28   336
17:1   336
18:1   336
18:32   318
18:42   337
18:44   337
18:45   336
19:20   330

2 Kings

2:24   318
5:9   239
5:11   318
9:20   197
19:31   282
20:17   300

1 Chronicles

16:4   334
17:4   168
21:19   318
22:18   283
28:2   239
29:10   262

2 Chronicles

2:11   262
3:18   318
5:13   334
6:21   336
20:7   244
36:16   318

Nehemiah

3:7   316
9:17   313, 321

9:20   302
9:25   303
11:30   260

Esther

1:1   286
4:17   211
8:15   230

Judith

5:19   169
8:10   330
8:33   212
8:35   239
9:3   211
10:6   330
12:16   211
12:18   260
13:16   211
16:17   300

Tobit

1:17   238
3:11   262
4:7   282
4:13   283
4:14   270
4:16   238, 282
5:7   312
7:17   282
10:7   295
10:13   195
13:13   169
14:9   234

1 Maccabees

1:26   316
1:40   185
2:52   242
3:13   330
4:30   168
4:46   239
7:42   278
8:4   313
8:16   282
10:18   169
10:24   185

10:25   169
11:30   169
11:32   169
12:6   169
12:20   169
13:36   165
14:10   169
14:29   283
15:2   169
15:16   169

2 Maccabees

1:1   169
1:2   168
1:27   169
2:18   188
2:26   318
3:13   230
4:25   230
4:28   330
6:14   313
6:28   317
8:12   313
8:15   226
8:35   201
9:12   283
11:16   169
11:22   169
11:34   169
12:44   332
15:10   231
15:21   313

Job

1:6–12   284
1:20–21   319
1:21–2:10   33
2:1–7   284
2:9–10   319
3:9   319
5:11   286
5:21   299
6:11   313, 319
7:3   319
7:16   313
8:13   338
8:15   319
9:4   313
9:14   319
9:31   333

13:18–14:22   333
13:28   299
14:2   186
14:14   313, 319
14:19   313, 319
15:3   237
15:30   187
15:31   313, 319
17:13   313, 319
19:3   292
19:20   299
20:26   319
21:4–26   333
21:12   329
22:21   313, 319
24:24   187
28:8   297
28:14   196
28:20–23   272
29:1–30:31   333
30:25   316
32:4   319
32:16   319
33:5   319
33:21   299
38:33   197
42:7–12   319, 320

Psalms

1:1   181, 187
1:2   29, 296
1:5–6   335
1:6   181, 338
2:12   187, 335, 338
3:5   302
3:8   294
4:2   200, 212
5:2–13   189
5:3   329
5:7   294
5:10   211
5:12   188
5:18   234
6:5   234
6:6   334
6:10   336
7:9   335
7:11   294
7:12   294, 321
7:18   329

9:2   334
9:3   329
9:5   200
9:6   294
9:19   222
9:21   294
9:30   222
9:35   207
9:39   185, 258, 286
11:2   271
11:3   211
11:6   299
11:7   273
12:4   222
13:3   261, 299
15:3   296
15:5   225
15:7   265
15:11   181
16:7   294
17:1–2   189
17:7   303
17:21   284
17:25   284
17:28   185, 286
17:42   302
17:50   330
18:8   209
18:10   273
20:10   300
21:3   302
21:22   294
21:25   336
22:5   331
23:4   284, 327
24:3   188, 312
24:5   188, 197
24:8   294
24:12   299
24:16   222
24:17   212
24:21   188
25:6   284
25:12   262
26:11   294
26:14   188, 312
27:1   302
27:9   294
30:6   197, 245
30:19   283
30:23   336

30:24   188
31:1   187, 339
31:2   339
31:6   329
32:1   335
32:2   329
32:12   224
32:13   222
32:20   188, 312
33:2   201, 262
33:13   270
33:14   33
33:16   335
33:19   185, 286
34:10   222
36:7   283
36:9   312
36:14   222
36:18   225
36:22   262
36:34   312
36:39   335
37:6   299
38:6   296
38:8   334
39:2   312
39:3   299
39:5   187
39:9   279, 296
39:11   197, 234
39:18   222
40:14   262
41:2   281
43:12   169
43:23   304
47:10   234
49:6   294
49:14   332
49:20   292, 293
50:12   285
50:6   242
50:8   272
50:12   211
55:9   188
59:13   211
61:2   283
61:6   283
61:11   282
61:13   61
64:14   302
67:6   294

67:19–20   262
68:2   294
68:17   222
68:21   219
68:37   188
70:22   334
71:13   294
71:18   262
72:13   285
72:27   278
73:20   222
74:8   294
76:19   260
77:19   292
77:70   168
78:5   282
81:3   185, 242, 286
83:5   187
83:7   294
83:12   282
84:3   339
85:5   274
85:15   313, 321
87:3   336
87:9   330
87:19   299
88:4   50, 168
88:21   168
88:52   280
88:53   262
89:17   284
91:10   280, 294
95:5   241
96:3   259
96:10   188
96:12   335
98:5   223
100:5   292, 293
100:7   283
101:18   185
102:8   321
102:15   186
103:15   315
104:2   329
104:26   168
104:42   50, 168
105:8   294
105:37   241
108:4   329
108:16   222
108:29   330

109:1   223, 225
110:4   321
111:1   187
111:8   315
117:1   50
118:1   29, 181
118:12   262
118:15   207
118:18   29
118:20   281
118:29   209
118:32   181
118:33   294
118:38   168
118:43   52, 198, 209
118:47   189
118:48   189
118:55   30
118:62   200
118:76   168
118:102   294
118:104   294
118:105   30, 209
118:109   30
118:113   189
118:121   200
118:131   281
118:142   30, 198
118:149   224
118:151   198
118:159   189
118:160   52
118:174   281
122:2   168
129:5   312
131:10   168
133:1   168
134:1   168
134:3   226
134:4   224
135:1   168
135:7   196
135:22   168
139:4   261
139:6   299
142:2   242
142:10   296
142:12   168, 294
143:10   168
143:15   187
144:8   321

145:4   294
145:8   335
146:2   169
146:6   201
148:3   196

Proverbs

1:7   33
1:8   224
1:15   181
1:16   201
1:18   301
2:6   33, 272
2:7   187
2:17   208
2:18   338
3:13   187
3:19–35   33
3:19   283
3:23   283
3:27–28   283
3:31   283
3:32   283
3:33   283
3:35   283
3:34   33, 38, 68, 73, 74, 86, 185, 269,
       280, 282, 283, 289
4:1   224
4:18   335
5:13   273
6:23   209
7:22   304
8:1–36   29, 33
8:13   283
8:22–31   179
8:30–36   272
9:8–12   270
9:10   179
10:6   335
10:12   33, 55, 73, 339
10:16   335
10:23   194
10:24   193
11:21   200, 275
12:3   335
12:13   256
12:27   211
12:28   338
13:3   256
13:10   270

13:23   295
14:12   338
14:21   225
15:1   33
15:28   280
16:26–27   259
16:27   300
16:32   313
17:6   188
18:8   293
18:21   262
19:4   179
19:11   313
19:17   33, 212
19:20   224, 270
20:9   188, 312
20:13   292, 293
20:26   260
21:3   33, 212
21:6   211
21:8   273
21:16   337
21:23   256
21:24   297
22:4   33
22:8   273, 275
22:21   52
22:22   225
25:1   274
25:8–9   180
25:15   313
25:20   299
26:22   293
26:28   273
27:1   33, 296
27:16   257
27:21   33, 177, 178
28:10   337
29:11   199
29:20   199
31:9   33, 212
31:20   33

Qoheleth

1:1–6   33
3:16–22   333
5:1   33, 199
5:12–17   333
6:1–9   333
7:9   33, 199

7:15   333
9:11   333

Sirach

1:1   33
1:8   270
1:14   33
1:22–24   199
1:22   242
1:26   33
1:28   181
2:1   33, 178
2:4   313
2:5   300
2:7–11   321
2:11   294, 313
2:12–16   29
2:15   189
3:17   270
4:1–6   238
4:1   222, 302
4:4   222
4:9   33, 212
4:26   334
4:29   199
5:1–8   29
5:4   313
5:15   280
5:9–13   262
5:11   33
5:13   33, 199, 262
5:15–6:17   244
6:9   280
6:19   279
6:23   224
6:34   270
6:37   315
7:3   275
7:6–7   221
7:34   285
9:17   270
10:7   283
11:18   296
11:27   209
12:11   208
13:3   222
14:1   256
14:4   303
14:10   282
14:14   302

14:16   211
14:19   299
14:23   209
15:11   192
16:22   200
18:11   313
18:13   234
19:6–12   33, 199
19:16   256
19:20   33
20:15   180
20:18   256
20:30   237
21:11   30
21:13   270
21:15   270, 303
22:16   315
22:20   180
22:27   256
23:1   262
23:4   262
23:7–8   33
23:10   284
23:11   327
24:1–34   33
24:1–23   35
24:1–2   185
24:23   29, 179
25:6   188
25:8   256
25:21   282
26:5   330–31
26:14   195
27:6   263
27:13   303
27:30–28:7   234
28:10   258
28:11   259
28:12–16   256
28:12   33, 262
28:22   259
29:1   234
29:6   302
29:8–9   33
29:8   212, 313
29:10   300
30:23   211
33:2   30
34:15   187
34:16   188
34:18   195

34:20–21 238
34:21–22 33, 212, 304–5
34:22 302, 309
35:2 33
35:6 335
35:8–10 221
35:12 294
35:13–15 212
35:19 313
36:14 198
37:1–6 244
37:2 279
38:9 335
38:34 198
39:6 334
41:14 237
41:25 180
42:13 299
44:17 178
44:19 242
44:20 242
44:22 242
44:23 169
45:5 30
46:14 212
47:8 188
48:1–14 336
48:1–11 336
48:3 337
48:18 258
51:23–30 35
51:30 340

Wisdom

1:1 200
1:6 33
1:11 292, 293
1:15 200
2:10 225
2:12 304
2:16 297
2:18 335
2:20 304
2:24 277, 282, 284, 338
3:1 335
3:4 33
3:5–6 178
3:12 207
4:2 212
4:12 193

5:6 181, 337
5:8 282, 297
5:18 275
6:1 224
6:17–19 194
6:23 271, 282
7:5 260
7:7 179
7:14 244
7:15–30 33
7:15–22 272
7:15 33, 270
7:18 197
7:25 296
7:26 208
7:27 244
8:7 200
8:20 212
9:2 198
9:6 178
9:13–18 272
9:13 296
10:5 212
10:16 283
11:3 283
12:10 202, 207
12:16 250
13:1 211
13:5 198
14:5 242
14:11 198
14:18 211
14:27 211
14:29–30 337
14:30 278
15:1 313
15:14 225
15:19 282
16:14 201
17:7 297
18:5 294
18:9 29
18:15 275
19:22 340

Isaiah

1:9 303
1:10 224
1:17 32
1:21–23 304

1:23   32
1:25   294
2:2   301
2:11   286
3:5   212
3:14–15   32, 212, 222
3:17   286
5:7–10   212
5:7   200, 303
5:8–9   32
5:9   303
5:15   286
6:10   338
7:13   224
9:12   338
10:1–2   222
10:10   299
10:33   286
11:2   29, 169, 281
11:14   185
13:6   299
13:11   286, 294
14:1   224
14:31   299
14:32   185
15:2–3   299
16:4   299
16:7   299
17:5   301
19:4   303
19:20   294, 302
22:14   285
22:21   188
23:1   299
23:6   299
23:14   299
24:4   285
24:11   299
25:11   286
28:1–5   188
29:14   29, 294
30:9   285
30:18   294
32:17   275
33:1   299
33:2   294
33:9   285
33:22   294
34:2   304
34:6   304
40:6–8   55

40:6–7   32
40:7   186, 191
40:8   191
40:13   50
40:27   93
40:31   312
41:8   244
42:19   168
43:5–6   32
43:6   295
43:10   224
44:20   195
44:28   296
46:8   338
47:11   299
48:1   224
48:20   50
49:3   168
49:4   280
49:23   312
50:9   299
50:10   270
51:2   242
51:8   299
52:5   226, 299
53:7   304
55:7   338
56:8   169
57:3   32, 87, 278
57:15   313
59:7   299
59:10   316
60:16   294
60:17   200
60:18   299
63:7   294
63:16   262
65:3   241
65:12   304
65:14   299
66:1   223
66:17   285

Jeremiah

2:27   304
2:34   304
3:6–10   278
3:9   32, 87
3:12   315, 338
4:1   338

4:13   285
4:20   285, 299
4:23   196
4:28   285
5:2   327
5:24   315
6:7   299
7:6   225
7:16   332
7:25   168
8:23   285
9:3   293
9:11   270, 272
9:18   285
9:23–24   185
10:20   285
10:23   187
12:3   303
12:12   285
13:17   285
13:27   32, 87, 278
14:2   285
14:8   313
14:14–15   318
15:3   304
15:7   169
15:15   313
15:20   294
16:9   286
19:6   304
20:6   318
20:7   286
21:10   315
22:3   225, 304
22:23   316
23:2   212
23:20   301
24:6   315
25:4   168
25:10   286, 294
26:8   294
26:10   303
26:27   294
27:11   234
27:24   283
27:38   234
32:34   304
34:14–15   318
40:11   334
41:17   169
44:3   332
44:17   318

Lamentations

1:1   285
1:4   285
1:5   286
1:7   286
1:11   316
1:21   316
3:14   286
5:15   286

Baruch

4:25   313
6:24   300

Ezechiel

3:1–11   345
3:21   338
5:1   318
6:2   315
7:27   285
8:7   262
12:23   316
13:17   315
14:8   315
14:14   319
16:7   238
16:38   32, 87, 278
16:49   303, 304
16:52   304
17:24   286
18:1–32   345
18:12   225
18:30–32   338
21:31   286
22:7   225
22:29   225
23:45   32, 87, 278
25:7   294
25:16   294
26:15   316
28:25   168
29:8   294
34:23   168
37:10   245
38:6   301
38:17   168
47:13   169

Daniel

1:4   270
2:28   301
2:40   261
3:25   334
3:35   168
6:21   294
6:23   294
9:6   318
10:14   301
12:12   188

Hosea

3:1   32, 87, 278
3:5   301, 338
4:15   327
5:4   338
5:5   286
6:1   228
6:6   296
6:13   315
7:10   286
7:13   292
7:14   299
9:1   278
9:6   299
10:2   285
10:12   275
12:5   285
12:7   284
12:8–9   212
14:1   283
14:9   286

Joel

1:2   224
1:5   285, 286
1:9–10   285
1:10   285
1:12   286
1:15   299
1:16   286
2:3   303
2:12   338
2:13   313
2:17   285
2:23   315
3:2   168

Amos

1:2   285
2:6–8   212
2:6–7   32
3:1   224
3:2   212
3:7   168
3:10   32, 299, 301
4:1   32, 222, 225
4:16   338
5:1   224
5:4–6   304
5:9   299
5:13   29
7:9   286
8:3   299
8:4–6   32
8:4   222, 225
8:8   285
9:4   315
9:11–12   118
9:12   226

Jonah

1:9   168
4:2   313

Micah

1:2   224
1:10   286
2:4   285, 299
2:12   93
3:1–4   212
3:4   302
3:7   292
4:1   301
6:1   224
6:9   294
6:10   301
6:15   301
7:7   312

Nahum

1:3   313
1:7   312

Habakkuk

1:3   299
1:4   225

1:16   304
2:3   312
2:7   297

Zephaniah

1:9   212
1:15   299
2:2   186
2:5   294
3:8   312
3:11   258
3:12   201, 286
3:17   294

Haggai

2:17   338

Zechariah

1:3   284, 338
1:6   168
3:3–4   201
6:14   312
7:8–10   212
7:10   225
8:7   327
9:16   294
10:1   315
10:3   212
10:12   234
11:2–3   285
11:2   299
11:4   304
12:7   294
13:2   303
13:3   318

Malachi

1:8   221
2:16   198, 338
3:5   212, 302, 327
3:7   338
3:13   292
3:15   283
3:22–23   336
3:24   168

Matthew

1:1   260
1:18   207
1:19   279
1:21   194
1:22   243
2:15   243
2:17   243
2:23   243
3:2   53, 316
3:6   334
3:8–9   249
3:9   210, 242
4:1–11   284
4:8   240
4:14   243
4:17   53, 316
5:3–11   187
5:3–5   201
5:3   52, 56, 225, 228
5:4   285
5:5   270
5:6   200
5:7   56
5:8   56, 285
5:9   56, 275
5:10–11   188
5:11   180, 271
5:12   32, 301, 318
5:13   335
5:16   60
5:21   233
5:22   260
5:27   233
5:29   260
5:30   260
5:34–35   31, 328
5:34   57, 328
5:35   223
5:37   328
5:43   52
5:44   329
5:48   178
6:2   275
6:5–6   329
6:5   275
6:7   210
6:10   297
6:16   275
6:24   279
6:14   334

6:19–20   299
6:26   303
6:28–31   299
7:1   31, 57, 293, 317
7:5   275
7:7   57, 344
7:8   181
7:11   180
7:14   188
7:16–20   274
7:16–17   263
7:16   56
7:21–23   56
7:21   249, 297
7.22   241
7:24–27   56
7:24   210
8:4   300
8:17   243
8:19   255
8:25   294
9:2–6   334
9:2   51
9:3   226
9:5–7   333
9:22   332
9:32–34   241
10:1   330
10:2   93
10:3   93
10:7   53, 316
10:8   241, 330
10:18   300
10:22   56, 188, 313
10:24–25   51
10:28   260, 294
10:40   202
11:6   187
11:18   241
11:19   60, 242
11:25   270, 334
11:29   201, 270
12:17   243
12:24–28   241
12:31   334
12:36   329
12:37   242
12:50   297
13:14   243
13:15   338
13:16   187

13:18   224
13:21   212
13:22   299
13:39   284
13:55   93, 96
14:23   329
15:2   284
15:7   275
15:10   330
15:19   224
16:3   223
16:5   208
16:17   187
16:25   51, 294
16:26   237
17:1–8   336
17:18   241
18:4   286
18:9   260
18:12–14   338
18:12–13   195
18:14   297
18:15–20   223
18:15–18   338
18:15   31, 338
18:19   273
18:23–34   301
18:26   313
18:29   313
19:7   241
19:16–17   188
19:18   233
19:19   52, 231
19:21   178
19:23–24   185, 298
19:28   169, 171
20:1–15   301
20:3   242
20:27   51
21:4   243
21:5   201, 270
21:21   56, 180, 223
21:22   180
21:31   297
21:33–34   301
21:33–41   314
22:37–39   235
22:37   189
22:39   31, 52, 231
23:8   255
23:12   56, 186, 286

23:13   256
23:15   260
23:16–22   328
23:33   260
23:34–37   318
23:34   270
24:3   52, 314
24:9   212
24:13   188, 313
24:14   300
24:20   329
24:23–33   31
24:27   52, 56, 314
24:32–33   317
24:33   53, 56
24:37   52, 314
24:39   52, 314
24:43   317
24:46   187
25:14   51
25:16   295
25:17   295
25:20   295
25:22   295
25:31   46, 250
25:36   238, 330
25:37   303
25:41   284
25:46   188
26:10   60
26:11   222
26:42   297
26:45   53
26:53   210
26:54   243
26:58   320
26:65   226
26:66   232
27:9   243
27:18   277
27:56   43

Mark

1:5   334
1:15   52, 53, 316
1:19   93
1:24   241
1:29   93
1:44   240, 300
2:5–11   334

2:7   66
2:9   333
2:11   55
3:3   333
3:4   51
3:17   93
3:18   93
3:28   334
3:35   96, 297
4:19   193, 299
4:38   55, 255
5:4   261
5:7   241
5:34   51, 239, 332
5:37   93
5:41   55, 333
6:3   93, 96
6:11   300
6:13   331
6:48   257
6:49   210, 280
7:2–5   284
7:14   224
7:21   224
8:14   208
8:23   181
8:35   51
8:36   237
9:2–8   336
9:2   93
9:27   55
9:35   56
9:45   188, 260
9:47   260
10:17   188
10:19   223, 302
10:25   185, 298
10:35   93
10:41   93
10:44   51
10:49   55, 333
10:52   51, 332
11:23   56, 180, 223
12:1–9   314
12:4   225
12:15   275
12:29   241
12:30   189
12:31   31, 52, 231
12:38–40   255
12:41   185

13:3   93
13:9   300
13:17   188, 313
13:20   224
13:28–29   317
13:33–36   187
13:34   60
14:33   93
14:49   243
15:10   277
15:28   243
15:40   93
16:1   93

Luke

1:10   329
1:14   260
1:16–17   338
1:24   194
1:33   320
1:51   283
1:53   298
1:68   212
1:73   242
1:78   212
3:8   242
3:19   231
4:2–13   284
4:13   177
4:21   243
4:25   336
4:33   241
4:43   52
5:3   330
5:14   300
5:17   335
5:20–24   334
5:22   224
5:23–24   333
5:26   97
6:8   224
6:9   51, 294
6:14   93
6:15   93
6:16   93
6:18–19   335
6:20–22   187
6:20   52, 56, 225, 228
6:21   286
6:22   188

6:23   32, 318, 319
6:24   185, 298
6:25   286
6:26   319
6:36   321
6:37   57
6:41   207
6:44   56
6:46   56
6:47–49   56
6:47   210
7:3   330
7:7   335
7:14   333
7:16   97, 212
7:18   330
7:23   187
7:25   299, 303
7:47–48   334
7:50   51, 239, 332
8:2   241
8:12   284
8:13   202
8:14   276, 299
8:15   178, 313
8:18   210
8:26–29   241
8:29   257
8:47   335
8:48–50   51
8:48   239, 332
8:54   333
8:55   245
9:2   330, 335
9:5   300
9:11   335
9:24   51
9:25   237
9:28–36   336
9:38   255
9:42   335
9:46–47   224
9:56   51
10:7   301
10:8–10   202
10:9   53, 316
10:11   53, 316
10:21   270, 334
10:22   197, 279
10:23   187
10:25   188

10:27   31, 52, 189, 231
10:30   177
10:34   331
11:9   180
11:10   181
11:27–28   187
11:28   210
11:41   211
11:49–51   318
11:50   32
12:4   294
12:10   226, 334
12:15   260
12:16–21   187, 298, 301
12:16   185
12:19   300
12:20   301
12:21   299, 300, 301
12:24   207
12:27–38   299
12:33   299
12:37–38   187
12:37   51
12:39   317
12:42–48   301
12:43   51, 187
12:51   210, 280
12:56   275
13:2   210
13:15   275
13:24–25   317
13:32   335
13:33   318
13:34   32
14:4   335
14:11   56, 186
14:12–14   298
14:12   185
14:14   187
15:14   278
16:1–8   301
16:5   330
16:19–31   222, 235, 298
16:19   299
16:26   315
16:30   242
17:3   31
17:10   51
17:15   335
17:18–37   187
17:19   51, 332

18:1   329
18:6   223, 224
18:7   313
18:14   186, 286
18:18   188
18:20   233
18:22   179
18:23–25   298
18:25   185
18:30   188
18:42   51, 332
18:43   97
19:10   294
19:11   210
19:12–27   301
19:18   301, 314
20:11   225
20:21   221
20:46   299
20:47   256
21:1–4   298
21:8   53, 316
21:9   273, 313
21:13   300
21:19   178, 188
22:29–30   169, 171
22:32   315, 338
22:40   329
22:42   197, 297
22:51   335
23:11   221
23:12   279
23:29   187
23:46   245
23:47   304
24:10   93
24:19   60
24:25   318
24:26   221
24:36   239
24:37   210, 280
24:38   224
24:40   240
24:44   243
24:49   188

John

1:13   198
1:29   194
3:2–14   54

3:3–5 198
3:3 52
3:12 272
3:15–16 188
3:19 60
3:20 221, 273
3:31 196
4:6 262
4:34 297
4:46 230, 330
4:49 230
5:8 333
5:29 188, 273
5:30 297
5:39 210
6:39–44 301
6:39–40 53
6:44 53
6:54 53
6:70 284
7:3–5 96
7:35 169
7:37 53
8:21 194
8:39 238, 242
8:44 289
8:46 231
8:49 225
8:56 242
9:1–3 333
10:1–9 317
10:25 60
10:36 226
11:24 53, 301
11:29 333
12:48 53
13:2 284
13:13–14 255
13:15 317
13:16 351
13:17 187
13:18 243
14:16 189
15:1 314
15:15 53
15:16 224
15:18 53
15:19 54
15:20 51
15:25 243
16:8–10 200

16:8 194
16:20–22 177
16:21 194, 212
16:23 180, 181
17:4 60
17:5 50, 221
17:12 243
19:24 243
20:11 209
20:19 239
20:29 187
20:31 188
21:25 181

Acts

1:3 52
1:4 52
1:13 93
1:14 97
1:16 243
1:22 224
2:17 53, 301
2:18 51, 168
2:19 296
2:21 226
2:33 52, 188
2:35 223
2:38 50, 331
2:39 52, 330
3:1–10 333
3:6 50, 331
3:7–8 333
3:14 304
3:15 188
3:16 178, 332, 333
3:19 338
4:9–10 332
4:10–12 333
4:10 50, 331
4:22 335
4:25 241
4:29 51, 168
4:30 335
5:3 271
5:4 273
5:9 317
5:17 271, 277
5:38 60
5:40 50
5:41 50, 225

6:2   330
6:7   112
7:2   242
7:5   52, 225
7:8   167, 169
7:9   277
7:10   212
7:11   212
7:17   52, 188
7:23   212
7:52   318
7:55   50
8:1   69
8:4   169
8:14   202
8:16   331
8:32–35   305
9:14–15   50
9:21   50
9:34   335
9:35   338
9:36   60
9:37   330
10:20   180, 223
10:30   221
10:34   52, 221
10:38   335
10:42   317
10:48   331
11:1   202
11:2   223
11:18   97
11:19   169, 212
11:21   338
11:30   51, 330
12:2   93, 97
12:3–17   97
12:6   317
12:9   210
12:17   97
12:20   230, 303
12:21   230, 299
13:1   51, 255
13:2   60
13:17   224
13:23   52, 188
13:32   52
13:45   271, 277
13:46–48   188
13:48   97
13:52   177

14:9   51, 332
14:15   211, 336
14:23   51, 330
15:1   97
15:2–23   51
15:2   330
15:5   97
15:9   223, 332
15:11   332
15:12–29   97
15:12–21   97
15:13–21   118
15:13   118, 224
15:14   118, 212
15:17   118
15:19   118
15:21   222
15:22   176, 331
15:23–29   97, 118, 170
15:23   118, 169, 330
15:25   118, 195
15:26   331
15:33   295
16:3   98
16:4   330
16:13   222
16:17   51, 167
16:19   226
16:25   330
16:31   332
16:36   239
17:5   277
17:11   202
17:18   241
18:18   98, 332
18:21   297
18:23   295, 315
19:13   331
19:18   334
19:32   331
19:40   331
20:3   295
20:16   98
20:17   51, 330
21:13   331
21:14   297
21:18   97
21:19   97
21:20–21   98
21:20   97
21:23   332

21:24   98
21:25   97
21:30   226
22:1   224
22:11   50, 221
23:8   334
23:21   188
23:26   169
24:25   200
26:2   176
26:5   211
26:6   52, 188
26:20   60
26:25   198
26:29   335
27:22   329
27:25   329
27:29   335
27:36   329
28:16   239
28:27   335

Romans

1:1   51, 168
1:4   50
1:5   50
1:7   195, 239
1:10   297
1:11   282, 315
1:16   202
1:17   200
1:21   211, 224
1:22   270
1:24   193, 201
1:25   197
1:29–31   60
1:29   201, 273
1:30   283, 293
1:31   274
2:1   60, 201, 241
2:2   255
2:3   60, 241
2:4   313
2:5   61, 301
2:6   61
2:7   178, 185, 313
2:8   271
2:9–10   200
2:11   52, 221
2:13   61, 206, 212, 242

2:17–29   249
2:23   185, 231
2:24   226
2:25–27   61
2:25   231
2:27   231
3:1   60
3:4   242
3:5   200, 280
3:8   255
3:13   261
3:16   285
3:20   30, 63, 242
3:22   200
3:24   62, 242
3:26   242
3:28   30, 242
3:30   242
4:1–25   63
4:1   63, 242
4:2   63, 242
4:3   231, 243, 280
4:4   301
4:5   200, 242
4:9   243
4:10   63
4:13–21   188
4:13   52
4:14   52
4:15   200
4:16   52, 63
4:19   207, 330
4:20–21   52
4:20   62, 180, 223
5:1   242
5:2–5   177
5:2–4   181, 183
5:2–3   185
5:3   60, 178, 313
5:9   242
5:10   280
5:11   185
5:12–13   194
5:12   194, 338
5:15   62
5:16   195, 255
5:17   201
5:21   188, 194
6:12   193
6:16   241, 278
6:22–23   188

7:5   194
7:7–8   193
7:8   30
7:12   61, 209
7:14   61, 209
7:16   61, 209
7:23   62
7:24   285
8:4   61
8:7   279
8:17   225
8:20   211
8:23   52, 198
8:25   178, 313
8:26   329
8:28–30   194
8:28   189
8:30   242
8:33   242
8:35   212
8:37   189
9:3   335
9:4   52, 188
9:8   52
9:9   52
9:11   273
9:14   212
9:17   231
9:20   60, 241
9:22   313
10:1   336
10:3   200, 283
10:4   320
10:9–10   334
10:9   50, 51
10:11   231
10:13   226
11:2   60, 231, 241, 278
11:4   280
11:11   232, 256
11:16   52, 171, 198
11:18   271
11:28   280
12:1   321
12:2   297
12:9   275
12:12   313
12:16   206
13:1–7   67
13:1   283
13:2   255

13:3   60
13:8   61, 243
13:9   30, 31, 231, 233
13:12   52, 53, 60, 201, 316
13:13   60, 271, 273
13:14   193, 202
14:1   224
14:3   61
14:4–5   178
14:4   61, 294
14:7   52
14:10   61
14:11   334
14:13   61
14:17   177
14:20   60, 211
14:22   239
14:23   62, 223
15:3   180
15:4   313
15:8   52, 188
15:9   330, 334
15:13   177
15:18   60
15:25–32   96, 97
15:32   297
16:1   238
16:5   52, 195, 198
16:8   195
16:9   195
16:12   195
16:19   270
16:25   315

1 Corinthians

1:1   297
1:2   50
1:3   239
1:4   282
1:10–31   229
1:10   50, 94
1:18   202, 294
1:19–20   270
1:20   272
1:21   51
1:25–27   270
1:27–28   224
1:29–31   185
1:30   200
2:6   178, 272

2:8   50, 221
2:9   188
2:14   53, 202, 272
3:3   271, 273
3:10   270, 282
3:13–15   60
3:13   60
3:16   60, 241, 278
3:18–19   270
3:18   60, 210, 280
3:19   212
3:20   211, 224, 270
3:21   185
4:4   242
4:7   180, 185
4:14–17   82
4:14–15   51
4:14   195
4:15   198
4:16   206
4:17   195, 331
4:20   52
4:21   202, 270
5:3–5   223
5:4   50, 333
5:6   60, 241, 278
5:8   201
6:1–8   223
6:1   273
6:2–3   60, 241
6:2   226, 278
6:4   226
6:5   196, 270
6:7–8   302
6:9–11   52
6:9–10   225
6:9   60, 195, 241
6:15   241
6:16   241
6:18   284
6:19   241
7:15   238
7:19   30, 61
7:23   206
7:34   245
7:37   212
8:2   210, 280
8:3   189
8:6   241
8:7   330
8:11–12   330

9:1   60
9:5   94, 97, 238
9:7   314
9:10   314
9:11   275
9:13   241, 278
9:24   241
9:25   188
10:12   280
10:14   284
10:20–21   241, 272
11:1   206
11:16   210
11:18   331
11:21   229
11:22   225, 229
11:27   232
11:29–30   333
11:31   180
11:34   255
12:3   50
12:11   197, 279
12:12   258
12:28–29   51, 255
12:31   240
13:3   60
13:4   313
13:7   313
13:12   208
13:13   51
14:4   331
14:6   237
14:13–15   329
14:15   330
14:24   231
14:33   273
14:34   283, 331
14:37   210, 280
15:3   194, 231
15:4   231
15:7   94, 101
15:10   241, 282
15:11   94
15:17   211
15:20–23   52
15:20   198
15:23   52, 198, 314
15:32   60
15:33   60, 195
15:35   60, 240
15:40   272

15:43   50, 221
15:44   272
15:46   272
15:50   225
15:56   194, 338
15:58   60, 241
16:1–4   94
16:3   282
16:10   60
16:15   52, 198
16:16   283
16:17   314

2 Corinthians

1:2   239
1:3   321
1:6   178, 313
1:10   257
1:12   272
1:15–20   328
1:15   177
1:20   52, 188
2:3   177
3:16   338
3:18   208
4:4   50
4:5   50, 51
4:6   221
5:1   272
5:2   282
5:10   273
5:12   185
5:21   200
6:1   202, 241
6:4   313
6:7   52, 198, 202
6:14   206
7:1   52, 284
7:4   177
7:6–7   314
7:10   200
7:11   273
8:2   179, 201
8:4   282
8:6   282
8:7   282
9:5   176
9:6   275
9:8   60
9:11–13   180

9:14   282, 336
10:1   270
10:10   314
10:13–15   185
10:15   201
10:17   185
11:4   202
11:9   212
11:15   60
11:18   185
11:25   295
12:14   300
12:19   195
12:20   60, 271, 273, 293
13:7   335

Galatians

1–2   94
1:3   239
1:4   194
1:6   95
1:10   51, 168
1:13   270
1:18   94
1:19   93
2:2   95
2:5   198
2:6   95, 221
2:7–9   95
2:9   95, 282
2:10   94, 95
2:11–14   95
2:12   95, 97, 109, 170
2:13   95
2:14   95, 198
2:16–17   242
2:16   30, 62, 63, 242
2:18   231
2:20   62
2:21   63
3:1–5   96
3:1   241
3:2   30, 63
3:5–6   242
3:5   30, 63
3:6   63, 243
3:8   242
3:10   30
3:11   212, 242
3:14–29   188

3:14   52
3:16   52
3:17   52, 63
3:18   52, 63, 225
3:19   52
3:21   52
3:22   52
3:24   242
3:28   196
3:29   52, 62, 225
4:3   96
4:7   225
4:9–11   30
4:9–10   62
4:12   206
4:14   202
4:19   51, 82, 198
4:20   231
4:23   52
4:26   170
4:28   52, 188
4:31   201
5:2–4   30
5:2   60
5:3   61, 62, 232
5:4   232
5:6   61, 135, 138, 243, 244, 335
5:12   30, 62
5:14   31, 52, 231
5:16–23   62
5:17   62
5:19–23   60
5:19–21   62
5:20–21   273
5:20   271
5:21   52, 225, 277
5:22–23   62
5:22   177, 313
5:23   202, 270
5:24   193
5:26   206
6:1   60, 270, 338
6:2   61
6:3   60, 210
6:4   60
6:7–8   275
6:7   60, 195
6:8   188
6:12   30
6:13   185
6:14   185
6:16   170

Ephesians

1:4   224
1:13   52, 188, 198
1:14   225
1:18   225
2:8   51, 282
2:9   185
2:14   189
4:2   202, 270, 313
4:6   241
4:11   51, 255
4:13   178
4:17   211
4:22   52, 201, 270
4:24   202
4:25   52, 201
4:26   199
4:27   284
4:31   199
4:32   206
5:1   206
5:2   189
5:5   52, 225
5:7   206
5:15   270
5:17   206
5:19–20   330
5:19   330
5:22   283
5:24   283
6:9   52, 221
6:11   284
6:23   239

Philippians

1:1   51, 168
1:2   239
1:4   177, 336
1:8   282
1:9   329
1:15   273
1:17   181, 271
1:26   314
2:3   176, 271
2:6   176, 330
2:7   168
2:9   201
2:10   50, 272
2:11   221, 334
2:12   195, 314

2:14   224
2:25   176
2:26   282
3:3   185
3:4   210
3:7   176
3:8   176
3:13   208
3:15   178
3:19   272
3:20   170
3:21   221
4:1   195
4:5   274
4:8   273
4:9   239
4:11   280
4:13   335
4:15   331

Colossians

1:2   239
1:3   329
1:5   52, 198
1:7   195
1:9   332
1:11   177, 178, 221, 313
1:28   178
2:1   258
2:4   207
2:16   30
2:18   211
2:21   30
3:5   193
3:8   52, 199, 201
3:10   202
3:11   196
3:12   202, 270, 313
3:16–17   330
3:17   50
3:18   283
3:25   52, 221
4:3   332
4:12   51, 178

1 Thessalonians

1:1   239
1:2–3   51
1:3   60, 178, 313
1:4   189

1:6   177, 202
1:9   338
2:1   241
2:9   314
2:11   51, 82
2:13   202
2:15   32, 318
2:19   52
3:2   315
3:6   282
3:13   52, 314, 315
4:15   52, 313, 314
5:2–3   187
5:2   317
5:12   60
5:13   60, 176
5:23   52, 239, 314
5:25   332

2 Thessalonians

1:2   239
1:4   313
1:5   52
1:6   212
1:11   60, 329, 332
1:12   50
2:1   52, 314
2:8   52
2:9   314
2:13   52, 198
2:16   189
2:17   60, 315
3:1   332
3:3   315
3:15   176

1 Timothy

1:2   51, 239
1:5   275, 285
1:8   209
1:16   313
1:18   51
2:5   241
2:8   224
3:3   274
3:6–7   284
3:15   198
4:1   241, 272
4:4   198
4:8   188

4:12 270
5:1 330
5:2 330
5:6 303
5:17 51, 330
5:18 231, 301
5:19–24 223
5:19 51, 330
5:22 212, 273
6:1 226
6:4 273
6:9 177, 193
6:11 284
6:14 212

2 Timothy

1:1 188
1:2 51, 239
1:3 208
1:4 208, 282
1:5 208, 275
1:6 208
2:1 51
2:5 188
2:6 314
2:8 208
2:9 329
2:10 313
2:12 313
2:15 52, 198
2:22 211
2:24 51
2:25 202, 270
3:1 52, 301
3:2 283, 297
3:4 279
3:6 193
3:10 313
4:3 193
4:5 329
4:8 188, 294, 317

Titus

1:1 51
1:2 188
1:4 239
1:5 51, 179, 330
1:15 211
2:5 273, 283
2:8 273

2:9 283
3:1 283
3:2 202, 270, 274
3:3 193, 201, 273, 276
3:7 225
3:9 211
3:13 179

Philemon

2 238
10 51, 198

Hebrews

1–2 72
1:2 53, 301
1:3–4 72
1:13 223
2:3 257
2:7–9 188
2:7 221
2:14 284
2:15 232
3:9 60
4:1 188
5:13 200
6:9 195
6:10 208
6:12 225
6:13 52, 188
6:15 313
6:16 327
6:17 197, 225
7:11 294
7:19 284
7:26 212
8:6 294
9:14 284
9:22 284
9:23 284
10:13 223
10:22 211
10:23 52
10:29 176
10:32 313
10:34 177
10:36 297
11:5–31 74
11:7 200, 225
11:8–16 170
11:8–10 53

11:9   225
11:11   52
11:17–19   53, 243
11:17   74
11:26   176
11:31   53, 245, 248
11:32–38   318
11:32–34   32
11:33   200
11:38   262
12:1   52, 178, 201
12:2   313
12:3   332
12:11   275
12:23   294
12:26   52
13:2   208
13:4   212
13:7   270
13:14   170
13:16   208
13:18   332
13:21   60

James

1:1–4:6   152
1:1–27   13, 14
1:1–2   8
1:1   8, 22, 29, 43, 48, 49, 50, 54, 85, 91,
     93, 118, 151, 167, 171, 255
1:2–27   37, 173–74, 175
1:2–25   236
1:2–18   174
1:2–12   140
1:2–8   176, 183, 203
1:2–4   9, 15, 79, 175, 183
1:2–3   190, 312
1:2   8, 9, 10, 27, 33, 51, 81, 118, 134,
     174, 175, 176, 182, 187, 190, 192,
     195, 204, 295
1:3–4   174, 200
1:3   5, 8, 20, 39, 51, 52, 60, 70, 182,
     188, 189, 190, 200, 206, 255, 295,
     321, 338
1:4–5   8
1:4   8, 60, 78, 83, 174, 182, 195, 243,
     247, 256
1:5–8   78, 175
1:5–7   15
1:5–6   86, 175, 344

1:5   33, 40, 43, 56, 76, 79, 83, 85, 86,
     127, 174, 175, 181, 182, 195, 204,
     248, 270, 272, 278, 282, 287, 321,
     329, 337, 342
1:6–11   83
1:6–8   42, 78, 192
1:6–7   210
1:6   8, 10, 39, 51, 56, 62, 79, 120, 141,
     145, 174, 182, 206, 207, 223, 257,
     295, 332
1:7–8   177
1:7   8, 50, 86, 182, 195, 295, 345
1:8   45, 68, 73, 76, 79, 87, 88, 175, 176,
     180, 187, 214, 261, 262, 264, 273,
     337
1:9–12   77, 184, 190, 203, 308
1:9–11   32, 40, 81, 83, 175, 189, 190,
     205, 228, 312
1:9–10   15, 190
1:9   51, 175, 189, 201, 222, 286, 297,
     298
1:10–12   4
1:10–11   10, 55, 296, 298
1:10   10, 79
1:11   7, 8, 82, 120, 208, 239, 258, 299
1:12–18   15
1:12–13   8, 9, 13, 174
1:12   5, 8, 15, 32, 35, 39, 44, 52, 56, 81,
     83, 86, 134, 138, 141, 175, 178, 189,
     190, 192, 203, 206, 210, 225, 228,
     233, 243, 283, 312, 319, 320, 322,
     324, 342
1:13–21   191–92
1:13–18   175, 200
1:13–15   189
1:13–14   44, 340
1:13   8, 10, 27, 42, 70, 71, 81, 85, 86,
     134, 138, 189, 192, 201, 203, 204,
     255, 261, 295, 321, 342
1:14–19   204
1:14–15   81, 174, 276
1:14   8, 42, 132, 175, 192, 210, 295, 345
1:15–18   4
1:15   10, 138, 143, 175, 197, 205, 231,
     298, 338
1:16–18   7
1:16   9, 51, 60, 83, 118, 175, 199, 210,
     295, 337, 345
1:17–20   140
1:17–18   82, 140, 199, 202, 204

1:17 5, 7, 8, 40, 43, 57, 62, 70, 71, 81,
    83, 85, 86, 87, 131, 136, 137, 138,
    139, 152, 175, 178, 179, 204, 205,
    209, 212, 248, 256, 272, 282, 287,
    321, 337, 342
1:18–21 206
1:18 7, 10, 52, 54, 83, 86, 141, 175,
    184, 191, 194, 199, 202, 205, 214,
    233, 238, 265, 271, 279, 287, 297,
    321, 333, 337, 341, 346
1:19–27 174
1:19–22 138
1:19–21 204, 205
1:19–20 15, 174, 175
1:19 5, 7, 9, 10, 23, 26, 28, 33, 35, 36,
    40, 41, 51, 71, 75, 81, 118, 138,
    195, 254, 265, 295, 321, 340
1:20 8, 33, 38, 39, 40, 42, 44, 81, 83,
    85, 86, 138, 175, 178, 187, 231, 321
1:21–22 174
1:21 8, 9, 51, 52, 55, 78, 79, 83, 86,
    191, 202, 222, 265, 270, 272, 287,
    294, 332, 341, 345
1:22–25 20, 28, 31, 41, 42, 53, 56, 61,
    81, 238, 239, 243, 244, 246, 318,
    326
1:22–24 15, 140, 152, 175, 205, 206,
    298
1:22–23 294
1:22 7, 8, 9, 83, 207, 210, 244, 245,
    295, 345
1:23 7, 8, 10, 27, 180, 187, 260
1:24 7, 8, 71, 83, 186, 207
1:25 7, 27, 30, 31, 42, 60, 61, 83, 178,
    206, 233, 235, 236, 256
1:26–27 8, 174, 175, 214, 218, 227,
    233, 236, 239, 247
1:26 33, 35, 36, 40, 42, 44, 60, 71, 81,
    83, 138, 175, 254, 256, 257, 264,
    271, 278, 280, 295, 303, 304, 315,
    323, 340, 341
1:27 5, 30, 32, 33, 36, 39, 41, 43, 53,
    71, 73, 77, 79, 82, 83, 84, 85, 86,
    118, 168, 175, 196, 201, 211, 214,
    224, 246, 259, 261, 273, 288, 321
2:1–5:20 37
2:1–5:11 18
2:1–26 217, 218, 236
2:1–13 219
2:1–11 13
2:1–9 40

2:1–8 xi
2:1–7 15, 83, 88, 175, 212, 218, 220,
    235
2:1–5 29, 88
2:1–4 91, 119, 185, 186, 233, 293
2:1 7, 9, 29, 31, 38, 39, 40, 48, 49, 50,
    51, 52, 63, 68, 82, 151, 214, 218,
    219, 220, 226, 228, 231, 235, 237,
    246, 253, 255, 292, 316, 326
2:2–7 306
2:2–4 8, 235, 236, 238
2:2–3 218, 219, 227, 246
2:2 187, 223, 300
2:3–6 255
2:3 5, 8, 9, 231, 295, 340
2:4 7, 9, 35, 206, 209, 218, 227, 228,
    239, 246, 270, 274, 309, 329
2:5–7 20, 32, 227, 246
2:5–6 77, 145, 190, 228, 298
2:5 9, 21, 27, 31, 39, 51, 52, 56, 62, 63,
    79, 81, 84, 85, 86, 118, 135, 185,
    188, 189, 190, 195, 213, 218, 219,
    220, 228, 230, 233, 235, 247, 288,
    321
2:6–7 82, 83, 229
2:6 9, 40, 77, 83, 88, 91, 273, 300,
    304, 309
2:7 9, 21, 35, 40, 44, 78, 79, 118, 230,
    270, 319, 331, 340, 346
2:8–13 218, 229, 230, 235
2:8–11 7, 86, 218, 246, 293
2:8–9 233, 235
2:8 7, 10, 27, 30, 31, 35, 38, 42, 44, 48,
    52, 61, 129, 209, 219, 220, 228, 232,
    236, 241, 256, 280, 301, 307, 317
2:9–11 61
2:9 7, 8, 31, 38, 52, 178, 194, 209, 219,
    231, 235, 236, 294, 298, 338
2:10–11 27, 35, 36, 39, 45, 70
2:10 8, 30, 61, 138, 139, 143, 206, 209,
    236, 256
2:11 8, 10, 30, 40, 139, 206, 209, 230,
    231, 236, 278, 321
2:12–13 8, 13, 203, 236, 307, 317, 329
2:12 7, 8, 9, 30, 86, 209, 236, 246, 265,
    309, 312
2:13–16 71
2:13 7, 8, 35, 44, 56, 82, 137, 141, 218,
    219, 222, 234, 271, 274, 297, 298,
    309, 321

2:14–26   13, 15, 74, 111, 114, 134, 143, 146, 175, 219, 229, 236, 237, 245, 298, 326
2:14–16   31, 33, 35, 36, 41, 42, 44, 45, 54, 56, 60, 81, 88, 119, 212, 219, 234, 236, 342
2:14   9, 10, 41, 51, 60, 136, 143, 145, 202, 218, 239, 246, 295, 332, 340
2:15–16   218, 219, 246, 247, 340
2:15   51, 82, 176, 179, 245, 249
2:16   8, 9, 10, 35, 246, 255, 270, 295, 337
2:17–18   35, 60
2:17   8, 28, 51, 231, 245, 258
2:18–26   62, 63, 238, 246
2:18–22   9
2:18–19   246
2:18   9, 48, 51, 60, 143, 237, 242, 246, 247, 248, 255, 270, 295
2:19–3:9   4
2:19–26   138
2:19–20   143
2:19   7, 51, 63, 84, 85, 86, 128, 129, 220, 231, 247, 273, 284
2:20–25   183, 209, 214, 246, 318
2:20–23   275
2:20   5, 8, 9, 10, 51, 60, 176, 218, 278, 280, 295
2:21–25   10, 20, 31, 53, 200, 218, 219
2:21–23   192, 248
2:21   35, 39, 60, 63, 74, 143, 145, 200, 244, 248
2:22   10, 31, 51, 60, 63, 178, 247, 256, 321
2:23   7, 10, 21, 27, 34, 35, 36, 42, 51, 63, 68, 71, 74, 85, 86, 128, 129, 141, 200, 220, 230, 244, 248, 279, 280
2:24   10, 31, 51, 60, 63, 74, 75, 141, 200, 206, 248
2:25   7, 8, 60, 200
2:26   8, 10, 51, 60, 70, 218, 239, 246, 253, 258, 280
3:1–12   13, 15, 28, 33, 35, 44, 81, 175, 253, 264, 268, 306, 327, 340
3:1–8   137
3:1–2   119, 254
3:1   8, 9, 51, 82, 91, 134, 137, 176, 203, 206, 254, 261, 263, 264, 265, 268, 292, 295, 312, 316, 317, 326, 330, 340

3:2   8, 134, 136, 178, 187, 232, 254, 264
3:3–4   28, 71, 42, 340
3:3   5, 7, 10, 264
3:4–5   254
3:4   9, 10, 38, 39, 264, 279, 301, 314
3:5–6   10, 254, 258, 264
3:5   8, 9, 40, 42, 239, 254, 264, 301
3:6   5, 7, 8, 10, 48, 77, 84, 121, 207, 209, 213, 224, 254, 264, 265, 268, 273, 280, 284, 288, 300, 340
3:7–10   265
3:7–8   254
3:7   8, 10, 42, 254, 262, 264, 340
3:8–9   7
3:8   5, 8, 27, 77, 79, 139, 181, 201, 254, 264, 268, 273, 274, 300
3:9–10   254
3:9   5, 35, 42, 44, 50, 73, 83, 85, 86, 88, 168, 197, 231, 254, 261, 264, 268, 295, 321, 340, 341
3:10–13   56
3:10   9, 10, 42, 51, 77, 79, 263
3:11–12   254, 268
3:11   9, 10, 120, 268, 271
3:12   7, 9, 10, 27, 51, 121, 127, 254, 263, 274
3:13–4:10   13, 15, 28, 31, 32, 73, 75, 88, 175, 254, 265, 267, 268, 275, 283, 287, 292, 304
3:13–4:6   33, 268, 269, 287, 308
3:13–18   33, 81, 179, 254, 268, 341
3:13–17   13, 36, 268
3:13–16   36, 44, 71, 265
3:13–14   269
3:13   7, 9, 40, 60, 73, 75, 79, 83, 202, 206, 240, 268, 269, 272, 274, 276, 289, 292, 295, 337
3:14–17   60, 268
3:14–16   277
3:14–15   82, 268, 269
3:14   9, 44, 185, 197, 234, 262, 268, 269, 295, 297, 303, 323, 337
3:15–17   28, 42, 287
3:15–16   8, 54, 269
3:15   7, 33, 42, 53, 77, 79, 83, 84, 127, 192, 280, 281
3:16–4:3   81
3:16   8, 35, 44, 71, 79, 83, 143, 181, 261, 268, 269, 271, 288
3:17–18   8, 35, 62, 83, 269, 281
3:17   8, 75, 76, 268, 281

3:18   7, 56, 83, 200, 268, 274, 275, 298
4:1–10   13, 254
4:1–6   38, 268
4:1–5   35
4:1–4   31, 204, 205
4:1–3   39, 44, 83, 211
4:1–2   44, 81, 83, 304
4:1   9, 10, 28, 38, 42, 44, 62, 73, 144, 258, 268, 269, 270, 280, 288, 308, 337
4:2   5, 7, 48, 74, 82, 141, 194, 202, 269, 288, 309
4:3   8, 35, 78, 86, 88, 175, 201, 269, 278, 288, 329, 332, 340, 341
4:4   8, 10, 20, 21, 32, 35, 38, 42, 44, 53, 54, 60, 69, 71, 74, 79, 82, 84, 85, 86, 87, 88, 128, 163, 176, 197, 205, 213, 224, 233, 244, 248, 265, 268, 269, 273, 280, 288, 289, 292, 295, 321, 340, 345
4:5–8   36
4:5–6   40, 269, 341
4:5   9, 33, 49, 71, 76, 79, 83, 86, 176, 230, 268, 269, 272, 277, 280, 281, 282, 287, 289, 295
4:6–10   29, 35, 36, 56
4:6   7, 8, 10, 33, 38, 44, 55, 62, 68, 73, 74, 75, 81, 82, 83, 84, 85, 86, 129, 141, 143, 230, 248, 268, 280, 286, 287, 288, 289, 297, 305, 312, 337, 341
4:7–11   7
4:7–10   7, 8, 46, 84, 268, 269, 287, 289
4:7–8   45, 71, 74, 269
4:7   8, 9, 45, 71, 76, 79, 84, 85, 268, 273, 279, 281, 287
4:8–9   269
4:8   8, 9, 38, 45, 46, 55, 56, 68, 73, 76, 79, 83, 85, 86, 87, 88, 135, 181, 264, 268, 271, 274, 275, 288, 289, 303, 316, 323, 338
4:9   268, 289, 298, 299
4:10   9, 44, 50, 55, 71, 73, 75, 82, 84, 86, 268, 269, 283, 287, 291
4:11–5:6   291, 292, 306, 311, 325
4:11–12   13, 30, 39, 44, 57, 70, 82, 232, 233, 236, 292, 306, 317, 329, 345
4:11   7, 9, 30, 31, 44, 51, 74, 75, 77, 79, 127, 206, 209, 231, 255, 291, 292, 294, 306, 311, 316, 326, 340
4:12   30, 35, 61, 73, 79, 83, 86, 202, 236, 238, 287, 307, 312, 321

4:13–5:6   13, 15, 91, 175, 292, 312, 322
4:13–16   9, 38, 44, 77, 79, 81, 85, 88, 187, 191, 292, 298, 306, 307
4:13–15   8
4:13   9, 10, 32, 120, 255, 292, 297, 298, 340
4:14–15   7
4:14   8, 9, 10, 33, 176, 306
4:15   7, 50, 86, 298
4:16   40, 44, 75, 82, 185, 308
4:17   79, 176, 194, 270, 279, 301, 308, 338
5:1–6   7, 9, 32, 41, 44, 77, 82, 83, 88, 187, 190, 204, 212, 292, 298, 305, 306, 308, 312
5:1   9, 10, 32, 285, 292, 294, 308, 312
5:2–3   7
5:2   10, 308
5:3   10, 53, 61, 261, 302, 308, 309, 312
5:4–6   323
5:4–5   321
5:4   7, 9, 10, 31, 50, 77, 79, 86, 121, 308, 309, 314, 341
5:5–6   292
5:5   7, 79, 203, 211, 233, 301, 308, 312, 315, 323
5:6   9, 49, 82, 83, 86, 233, 292, 305, 308, 309, 311, 312, 314, 320, 321, 335, 344
5:7–20   174
5:7–11   13, 15, 40, 175, 311, 321, 325
5:7–10   78
5:7–8   52, 312, 314
5:7   5, 8, 9, 10, 44, 50, 51, 52, 79, 121, 203, 279, 292, 301, 305, 311, 312, 318, 319, 322, 323, 327, 337, 342
5:8–10   7
5:8–9   56
5:8   8, 9, 50, 52, 53, 303, 322, 323
5:9–12   8
5:9   10, 31, 51, 52, 53, 57, 77, 79, 83, 128, 137, 233, 255, 293, 301, 311, 312, 314, 322, 323, 326, 327, 329, 340
5:10–11   10, 20, 41, 183, 209, 214
5:10   9, 39, 50, 51, 52, 79, 311, 312, 323, 327, 329, 331
5:11   5, 8, 9, 10, 31, 32, 33, 34, 49, 50, 52, 86, 178, 187, 292, 301, 311, 312, 314, 323, 324, 342
5:12–20   82, 146, 255, 311, 312, 325

5:12   9, 13, 31, 35, 51, 57, 138, 142,
   233, 292, 316, 317, 325, 326, 327,
   328
5:13–18   13, 15, 175
5:13–16   91, 342
5:13–14   9
5:13   119, 127, 318, 326, 330, 331, 337
5:14–16   83, 141, 143, 144, 146
5:14   50, 51, 82, 91, 119, 125, 141, 222,
   270, 319, 326, 329, 337, 343
5:15–16   338
5:15   7, 49, 50, 51, 55, 86, 194, 238,
   330, 335, 343, 344
5:16–18   209, 214
5:16   xii, 8, 9, 36, 44, 69, 119, 132, 194,
   279, 329, 332, 343, 344
5:17–18   7, 10, 20, 31, 32, 78, 183, 274,
   318, 344
5:17   7, 329, 344
5:18   10, 329
5:19–20   8, 13, 15, 28, 36, 71, 79, 81,
   82, 118, 345
5:19   9, 51, 119, 142, 270, 272, 338
5:20   7, 20, 31, 33, 35, 51, 55, 60, 68,
   73, 137, 176, 181, 194, 202, 238,
   285, 333

1 Peter

1:1   54, 169, 171
1:2   239
1:3–9   51
1:4   212
1:5   53, 301
1:6–7   54, 177, 182, 183
1:6   177
1:7   54, 177, 350
1:8   177
1:11   221
1:13   201
1:14   193
1:15   270
1:17   60, 170
1:18   270
1:20   53, 301
1:22   211, 273, 275
1:23–25   198
1:23   54
1:24   54–55, 186, 191
1:25   55
2:1–2   55

2:1   52, 201, 273, 277, 293
2:2   282
2:4   212
2:9–10   91
2:9   170
2:11   170, 195
2:12   270, 293
2:13–17   67
2:13   283
2:16   168
2:18   274, 283
2:20   212, 313
2:21–25   305
2:24   200
3:1   283
3:2   273
3:4   202
3:11   270
3:15   202, 270
3:16   293
3:17   297
3:20   313
4:7   53, 316, 320
4:8   55, 73, 326, 339
4:12   177
4:14   50, 180
4:16   50
5:1   51, 330
5:4   188
5:5   55, 68, 73, 283
5:6   55
5:8–9   284

2 Peter

1:1   51, 168
1:5–7   194
1:9   208
1:10   232
1:16   52, 314
2:3   255, 295
2:5   200
2:6   317
2:10   193
2:13   211, 276, 303
2:15   337
2:17   257
2:18   193
3:1   195
3:3   53, 301
3:4   52, 314

3:5   208
3:8   208
3:9   313
3:10   60
3:12   52, 314
3:14   212
3:15   313

1 John

1:7   284
1:9   284
2:7   195
2:15   54, 279
2:16–17   193
2:16   297
2:18   53, 301
2:23   334
2:25   52
2:28   52, 314
3:10   200
3:12   60
3:17–18   239, 250
3:17   54
3:18   54
4:2   334
4:7–10   189
4:18   178
5:2   189

2 John

1   51, 330
10   169
11   169
12   177

3 John

1   51, 330
2   335
7   50

10   60
15   239

Jude

1   51, 53, 93
3   101, 195
15   60
18   53, 193, 301
19   53, 272
21   188
23   53, 70, 259
25   212

Revelation

1:1   51, 240
1:4   239
2:2   60
2:10   52, 188
3:3   317
3:17   238, 285
3:18   238
3:20   53, 317
7:5–8   169
8:9   198
9:20   241
10:7   168
10:9–10   262
11:6   336
12:4   194
13:6   226
14:4   52, 198
16:9   226
16:18   257
18:11   285
18:15   285
18:19   285
19:5   168
21:12   169
22:3   51, 168
22:6   168
22:11   200

INDEX OF ANCIENT SOURCES

✦

I. GRECO-ROMAN

Aeschylus

Eumenides

307   294–95
1043   298

Persians

140   294

Prometheus Bound

119   280

Anacharsis

Letters

9:10–25   276

Apollonius of Tyana

Letters

81–82   256

Aristophanes

Knights

1011   294

Aristotle

Athenian Constitution

57:4   188

Dreams

459B–460A   208

Nicomachean Ethics

1095a   206
1099b   195
1101a   187
1108a   297
1125b   201
1127a   297
1129b   178
1137b   274
1142b   199
1156a   178
1157b   244
1166a   244
1168b   279

Poetics

1460a   207

Politics

1266b   303
1278b   318
1285a   330
1302b   271
1303a   271
1311b   185

Rhetoric

1383b   201
1386b   273
1380a   201, 232
1387b–1388a   271
1387b   287
1391a   317
1408a   207

Sleep and Waking

458a   274

On the Soul

415b   245

On the World

400b   257

Chariton of Aphrodisias

Chaereas and Callirhoe

6, 8, 3   286

Cicereo

De Amicitia

5:18   288
18:65   288
21:80   244
22:83   288

De Finibus

I, 13, 43–46   276
I, 43   28
III, 75   27

De Natura Deorum

I, 121–122   244
II, 34, 89   258
II, 60   261
II, 151   261

De Officiis

I, 22   261

Pro Roscio Amerino

XXVII, 75   194

De Senectute   28

Demetrius

On Style

I, 7   199
I, 9   199
V, 241   199
IV, 194   275

Demosthenes

De Corona

179   194

Dio Chrysostom

Orations

4:83–96   28
11:108   207
12:34   28, 258
17:2   208
17:3   320
21:8   278
35:2   207
35:3   207
35:11   207
36:36   332
36:50   257
40:38   196
47:21   231
49:9   276
52:1   329
71:2   198
77/18   20, 345
77/78:17–29   276
77/78:37–45   28, 339

Diodorus Siculus

History

I, 60, 2   335
III, 65, 1   313
IV, 3, 3   313

Diogenes Laertius

Lives of Philosophers

I, 40   270
I, 53   207
I, 70   199, 200
III, 79   200
III, 83   200
VII, 23   199
VII, 24   199
VII, 26   256
VII, 121   209
VIII, 22   327
VIII, 23   200
IX, 37   207
IX, 64   270

Dionysius of Halicarnassus

Roman Antiquities

VI, 23, 3   238

VI, 31, 1   273
VIII, 41, 5   238

Epictetus

Discourses

I, 1, 17   296
I, 6, 33   237
I, 6, 43   240
I, 9, 24   270
I, 11, 7   256
I, 12, 13   279
I, 12, 24–26   278
I, 12, 26   258
I, 14, 16   237
I, 22, 13   270
I, 22, 18   221
I, 30, 4   320
II, 1, 12   181
II, 1, 31   207
II, 6, 17   241
II, 9, 12   195
II, 9, 21   207
II, 11, 21   262
II, 14, 17–23   208
II, 14, 21   27
II, 15, 8   255
II, 16, 45   193
II, 17, 6   280
II, 18, 8   193
II, 18, 25   201
II, 19, 8   241
II, 19, 19   297
II, 20, 7   207
II, 20, 18   263
II, 25, 5   179
III, 5   18
III, 9, 21   193
III, 12, 13   274
III, 13, 9   275
III, 21, 12   296
III, 22   20, 345
III, 22, 2   296
III, 22, 9   207
III, 22, 61   271, 276
III, 22, 72   27
III, 23   18
III, 23, 57   20
III, 24, 9–10   278
III, 24, 40   295
III, 24, 43   297

III, 24, 51   237
III, 24, 65   283
IV, 1   18
IV, 1, 1   209
IV, 1, 3   27
IV, 1, 133   262
IV, 3, 9   27
IV, 4, 35   241
IV, 5   18
IV, 6, 14   299
IV, 6, 20   230
IV, 6, 23   195, 244
IV, 8, 27   297
IV, 12, 11   283

Enchiridion

33, 1–2   199
33, 5   327

Fragments

112   27
286   178

Euripides

Alcestis

199   316
209   313

Bacchae

689   298
894   241

Cyclops

530   329

Ion

243   272
309   167
402   198

Orestes

1046   243, 279

Suppliants

533   245

Heraclitus

Letter

2:7   283

On the Universe
Frag. 41   26

Hermetica
17   208

Herodotus
Persian War
1:24   276
1:45   304
1:48   329
1:50   185
1:92   198
1:96   177
1:155   329
1:197   332
2:19   197
2:28   207
2:37   278
2:39   262
2:121   299, 300
2:174   239
3:85   270
3:142   330
4:18   314
4:71   198
4:78   201
4:95   285
4:109   301
4:150   240
4:152   295
5:62   317
5:72   283
5:93   282
6:12   188
6:41   177
7:102   178
7:103   258, 295
8:26   188
9:94   202

Hesiod
Works and Days
480   301

Hierocles
On Duties
2, 9, 7   27, 192, 195
4, 25, 53   28, 339

Hippocrates
Regimen
II, 65   331

Homer
Iliad
1:177   275
2:135   299
3:332   294
6:42   260
19:175   327

Odyssey
1:30–35   192
3:441   294
4:767   298
6:207   262
6:227   331
17:267   317
19:234   221
21:259   273
22:408   298

Iamblichus
Life of Pythagoras
9:28   327
29:162   244
30:167   244

Julian
Orations
6:185A   193
7:212B   241
7:255A   207

Longinus
On the Sublime
32   200

Lucian of Samosata
Apology
9   193

The Cynic
15   276

The Dance

70 210

Demonax 20

2 208
51 199

Dialogues of the Dead

2:2 258
20 228

Dialogues of the Gods

10:1 194

Double Indictment

2 258

Hermotimus

5 258

Nigrinus 20, 24

6–7 208

The Parasite

17 329

Passing of Peregrinus

13 51

The Runaways

19 27

Timon

20 221

Toxaris

60 332

The Tyrannicide

4 210

Marcus Aurelius

Meditations

II, 17 296
VI, 30 212
VIII, 46 263

Maximus of Tyre

Discourses

36 20
36:2 28

Menander

Georgos

60 331

Musonius Rufus

Fragment 16 20

Philodemus

On Frankness

37 339

Philostratus

Life of Apollonius

I, 17 210
I, 33 177
III, 20 210
III, 42 210
VI, 11 199

Plato

Alcibiades

135D 296

Apology

26B 241

Euthydemus

284A 271
305E 186

Gorgias

448B 270
478A 332
497E 313
504E 237
513E 237
522E 279
525A 297

Laws

659A 262
679C 271
716D 27, 244
757A 244
759C 178, 273
767B 226
767C 197

777E 212
801B 299
823D 194
855E 282
862D 276
869B 232
869E–870A 277
896B 240
901A 303
943C 188
952E 295

Letters

7 (325B) 193
8 (352A–B) 176

Lysis

209E 330
214B 244

Meno

72A 201
77B 317

Minos

317C 230

Phaedo

61A 206
66C 28, 276
80D 296
83B 193
107B 225
253E 297

Phaedrus

232B 193
237D 202
246B–247C 257
247A 281
251A 241
252D 260
254A 274
254B–D 28
258B 285
274B 186
276B 314
278D 270
279B 27

Philebus

16C 195
65C 297

Protagoras

343B 198

Republic

347B 279
354A 187
366B 326
390B 239
395E 167
397E 181
407C 332
409B 336
429C 294
496C 211
500E 317
515E 193
519A 273
536C 206
546A 272
554D 181
560C 297
617D 261

Symposium

191D 202
210B 274
212A 194
213D 271
220D 329

Thaetetus

148B 232
151B 296
175A 222
177B 312
200E 240

Timaeus

29E 282
33B 208
45C 336
90D 207

Pliny the Elder

Natural History

23:39–40 331

Pliny the Younger

Letters

10:96 330

Plutarch

Adviee to Bride and Groom

14 (Mor 139F)   208
25 (Mor 141D)   208
28 (Mor 142A)   201

On Anger

3 (Mor 454F)   200
7 (Mor 461C)   200
9 (Mor 457D–458B)   293
9 (Mor 457D)   200
14 (Mor 462C)   200, 293
16 (Mor 464B–C)   200

On Borrowing

4 (Mor 829B)   194

On Brotherly Love   28

12 (Mor 484B–C)   244
14 (Mor 485D–E)   271
17 (Mor 487E–488C)   276

On Common Conceptions

46 (Mor 1084E)   272

Delays of Divine Vengeance

5 (Mor 551A)   200

Education of Children

13–20 (Mor 9F–14A)   208
14 (Mor 10B)   200, 208
14 (Mor 10F)   256

On Envy and Hatred   28

On Garrulousness   28

2 (Mor 502E)   199
3 (Mor 503C)   199
4 (Mor 503E–540C)   28
10 (Mor 507B)   259
17 (Mor 501E)   210
23 (Mor 515A)   256

Having Many Friends

8 (Mor 96F)   244

How to Profit by Enemies

1 (Mor 86C)   271
8 (Mor 90C)   200
9 (Mor 91B)   271

How to Study Poetry

8 (Mor 26B)   241
12 (Mor 33F)   257

How to Tell a Flatterer

15 (Mor 58C–D)   223
19 (Mor 60E)   201
22 (Mor 64A)   180
30–37 (Mor 70D–74E)   339

Isis and Osiris

9 (Mor 354D)   330

Letter to Apollonius

11 (Mor 107A–C)   296

Listening to Lectures

4 (Mor 39C)   256
8 (Mor 42A–B)   208
10 (Mor 43B)   297

On Love of Wealth

1 (Mor 523E)   297

On Moral Virtue

12 (Mor 452C)   258

Pericles

VI, 4   197

A Pleasant Life Impossible

8 (Mor 1091E)   177
22 (Mor 1102D–F)   195
22 (Mor 1102F)   27

Progress in Virtue

10 (Mor 81E)   210
14–15 (Mor 84B–85A)   208
14 (Mor 84B)   206

Sayings of Spartans

59 (Mor 213A)   169
Namurtes (Mor 230B)   177

Sign of Socrates

24 (Mor 593F)   313

Stoic Self-Contradictions

1 (Mor 1033B)   28, 206
27 (Mor 1046F)   27

Table Talk

1, 6 (Mor 623E)   295

Tranquillity of Soul   28

2 (Mor 465C)   329
8 (Mor 469B)   241
10 (Mor 470C)   271
11 (Mor 471A)   271
13 (Mor 472F–473B)   263
13 (Mor 472F)   27
13 (Mor 473B)   276

Uneducated Ruler

3 (Mor 780C)   209

Virtue and Vice

3–4 (Mor 101B–E)   29

Polybius

Histories

7, 4, 6   181

Pseudo-Isocrates

Demonicus   19

4   20
9   208
16–17   29
26   29
33   29
34   199

Seneca

On Anger

II, 10   263
II, 35, 1–6   276
III, 28, 1   241

On Benefits

II, 29, 4   261

On the Blessed Life

15:7   209

On Clemency

I, 1, 1   208
I, 1, 7   208
I, 6, 1   208
I, 6, 3   256

I, 7, 1   208
I, 15, 3   208

On Consolation

10:1–5   296

Moral Epistles   22

7:5   278
20:1   28, 263
23:2   27
40:14   199
75:7   210
87:25   27, 263
94:21   208
94:25   208

Natural Questions

I, 17, 2–3   208
I, 17, 4   208
VII, 31, 2   221

On Providence

2:1–6   178
2:2, 6   27

Shortness of Life

1:1–4   296
9:1–10:1   296

Strabo

Geography

16, 2, 42   299

Thucydides

Peloponnesian War

I, 6, 5   331
I, 99, 1   285
I, 128, 5   313
III, 45, 3   256
IV, 68, 5   331
V, 74, 2   285
VII, 77, 1   318

Xenophon

Anabasis

IV, 1, 21   312

Apology

14   295

Cyropaedia

I, 3, 18   230
I, 6, 20   225
II, 2, 112   297
III, 2, 19   242
IV, 3, 9   257
V, 4, 35   280
V, 5, 15   295
VIII, 2, 24   300

Memorabilia

1, 2, 23   276
1, 2, 24   276
1, 3, 11   278
1, 4, 11   329
2, 1, 3   188
2, 1, 4   193
2, 1, 17   329
2, 1, 26   201
2, 1, 33   244
2, 2, 10   332
2, 9, 1   273
4, 3, 10   261

Oecumenicus

14, 7   230

Symposium

4:47   262, 273
5:8   225
8:15   332

II. JEWISH

Aboth de Rabbi Nathan

1:7   249, 319
1:10   223
2:4   228
32   242
41   332

Apocalypse of Abraham

9:6   34
15:6   260

Apocalypse of Ezra

1:9   260

Aristeas, Letter of   24

3–5   38
17   198
31   206, 209
41   169
50–210   38
75   197
120–170   38
132   240
165   194
187–294   38
208   318
211   38
215   38
222   38
223   38
224   38
228   38
231   262
234   38
244   38
251   38
253   38
263   38
277–278   276
277   38

Ascension of Isaiah   318

1:3   260
4:14   260

2 Baruch

14:12   238
24:1   238
51:7   238
55:6   313
77:2   169
78:4   169
82:3   296
85:13   338

Deuteronomy Rabbah

II, 26–27   245
V, 6   223
VI, 8   293

Ecclesiastes Rabbah

V, 6, 1   245
V, 11, 1   245
VIII, 10, 1   245

1 Enoch

47:1   303
91:18   181
94:6–77   226
94:6–9   298
94:9   304
95:7   304
96:8   226, 304
97:1–10   298
97:5   303
97:8–10   226, 296, 304
98:1–16   226, 298
99:11–16   298
99:15   304
100:6   226
100:7–9   298
102:1–11   298

2 Enoch

22:8–9   331
30:15   181
42:10   181

Esther Rabbah

VII, 13   336

Exodus Rabbah

5:4   328
27:4   245
31:3   260
31:13   212

4 Ezra

7:12–18   181
7:39   337
7:61   296
7:77   238
8:32–36   238
9:7   238
13:23   238

Genesis Rabbah

XLIX, 4   249
LV, 4   249
LXI, 5   249

Josephus

Against Apion

1:77   335

1:237   285
2:10   222
2:119   317
2:175   222
2:177   273

Antiquities

1:19   294
1:20   222
1:221   169
1:222   211
2:10–18   277
2:294   262
3:80   313
3:91   240
4:167   303
4:211   222
5:5–30   245
5:205   257
6:18   295
6:179   297
6:299   278
7:271   304
7:332   179
8:129   231
8:208   258
8:266   201
9:55   313
9:210   180
12:81   208
11:83   330
12:164   330
12:271   211
12:406   330
13:66   262
14:111   297
15:15   195
15:88   335
15:370–372   327
16:43   222
16:187   326
16:376   273
17:154   237
17:172   331
18:328   312
18:357   258
20:199   98, 99
20:200   98, 99
20:201   99

Jewish War

1:240   195
1:565   58

1:591   226
1:657   331
2:135   327
2:139–143   327
6:64   256
6:103   317

Life

217   169
232   226
268   330
277   222
294–302   222
302   211
365   169

Jubilees

17:17–18   178
17:17   242
18:15–16   242
19:8–9   178
19:9   34
36:9–10   304

Leviticus Rabbah

16:4   259
19:1   336
19:5   336
34:3   260

3 Maccabees

2:6   177
3:12   169
3:17   313
5:11   198
6:7   282
6:11   211
7:1   169
7:20   222

4 Maccabees

1:1   39
1:4   200
1:7   39
1:10   39
1:16   39
1:17   39
1:18   200
1:20–29   276

1:22   39, 193
1:25–26   39, 194
1:26   297
1:32   272
2:5   39
2:6   200
2:16   39, 199
2:15   297
2:23   39
3:2   193
3:19   39
5:7   211
5:13   211
5:16–18   40
5:17   194
5:19–21   39
5:20   232
5:22–26   209
5:23   276
5:25   39, 294
5:34   271
5:37   39
6:35   39, 276
7:11   39
7:13   332
7:22   39, 178
8:6   274
8:19   284, 297
9:7–8   39
9:8   318
9:23   39
9:24   39
9:30   178
12:6   274
12:13   336
13:9   39
14:2   39, 230
14:20   39
15:17   179
15:24   39
15:28   39
15:31   39
16:20   39, 242
16:22   39
16:25   39
17:4   178
17:12   178
17:19   39
17:23   317–18

Mekilta on Exodus

Jith. Amal. 18:1   245

Midrash on Psalms

12:2   293

Mishnah

Peah 5:4   238
Peah 8:7   238
Peah 10:1   238
Demai 3:1   238
Shab. 2:6   333
Sanh. 7:4   99
Taan. 1:2   315
Taan. 2:4   336
Aboth 1:1   212
Aboth 1:2   35, 199, 212
Aboth 1:4   223
Aboth 1:5   35
Aboth 1:6   35
Aboth 1:9   35
Aboth 1:11   35
Aboth 1:12   35
Aboth 1:15   35, 199
Aboth 1:17   35
Aboth 1:18   35
Aboth 2:1   35
Aboth 2:4   293
Aboth 2:5   35
Aboth 2:6   35
Aboth 2:8   36
Aboth 2:9   35
Aboth 2:10   199
Aboth 2:11   35
Aboth 2:12   35
Aboth 2:13   35
Aboth 2:16   35
Aboth 2:21   35
Aboth 3:5   35, 209
Aboth 3:10   35
Aboth 3:14   35
Aboth 3:16   35
Aboth 3:18   35
Aboth 4:1   35, 199
Aboth 4:2   35
Aboth 4:4   35
Aboth 4:5   35
Aboth 4:7   35
Aboth 4:8   35, 294
Aboth 4:10   35
Aboth 4:11   35
Aboth 4:16   35
Aboth 4:21   35

Aboth 5:2   35, 242
Aboth 5:3   35, 178, 242, 243
Aboth 5:7   35
Aboth 5:9   35, 238
Aboth 5:12   199
Aboth 5:13   35, 212
Aboth 5:14   35
Aboth 5:18   35, 339
Aboth 5:19   35, 242
Aboth 5:23   35
Aboth 6:1   35
Aboth 6:2   209
Aboth 6:4   35
Aboth 6:5   35
Aboth 6:7   35
Yad. 1:1–4:8   284

Philo

On Abraham

19   244
60   193
70   258
167   249
235   42

Against Flaccus   41

26   257
45   222
47   222
48   222
143   238
176   258

Allegorical Laws

2:19   192
2:26   42
3:1   42
3:40   42
3:42–44   200
3:45–49   178
3:66   232
3:79   42
3:123–128   200
3:124   42
3:131   42
3:233   257
3:241   232

Cherubim

6   43
11   42

34   43, 91, 195
36   258
101   272
120   170

Confusion of Tongues

7   336
12   41, 199
17   43, 91
115   257, 258

Contemplative Life

2   193
25   208
29   208
74   193
75   208
85   208
88   208

On the Creation

14   42
16   197
23   42
24   42, 192
29   42
44   197
58   42, 180
77   197
86–88   257
88   261
128   222
138   197
171   240

Decalogue

21   41
28   42
32   42
54   261
55   211
60   257
65   240
84–95   327
93   262
153   276
173   258

On Dreams

1:25   42
1:123   303
2:21   42

2:42   42, 199
2:44   260
2:58   331
2:123   231
2:152   261
2:165   210
2:181   329

On Drunkenness

18   42
30   195, 197

Embassy to Gaius   41

56   209
166   261
229   222
312   222

Every Good Man is Free

7   42
45   209
159   193

Flight and Finding

38   41
136   256

On the Giants

51   180

On Husbandry

5   301
22–25   194
22   42
69   257
83   276

On Joseph

5–12   42, 277
5   276
10–11   276
20   222
144   329
149   221, 257
223   318

Life of Moses

1:6   207
1:19   207
2:8   207
2:9   294

2:48   207
2:216   222

Migration of Abraham

13   42
17   41
20   42
34   41
44–48   276
55   237
58   270
60   193
73   256
148   180

Noah's Work as Planter

50   178

Posterity of Cain

7   42
24   41, 42
30   42
86   237
88   256
101–102   230
116–119   276

Preliminary Studies

13   41, 42
14   42
67   207
172   193

Questions on Genesis

1:57   41

Rewards and Punishments

14   42
51   272
115–118   170
115   169

Sacrifices of Cain and Abel

32   42
131   294

On Sobriety

11   42
52   244

Special Laws

1:14   257
1:57   43, 212
1:311   241
1:315   211
2:2–38   327
2:2   42, 328
2:14   42, 199, 207
2:53   207
2:62   222
2:86   242
2:240   303
3:54   231
3:88   280
4:93–94   193
4:197   226

Unchangeableness of God

34–35   42
75   256

On the Virtues

66   226
162   297

Who is the Heir

5   42
177   262
217   299
256   317

Worse Attacks the Better

13   42, 199
21   42
27   42, 199
32   192
103   262
140   241

Psalms of Solomon

1:4–8   226
5:2   226
8:28   169
9:6–7   334
10:6   226
10:7   321
12:2   259
15:1   226
16:10   197
17:26–28   169

Qumran Writings

CD   36
CD 2:3   36
CD 3:2   36
CD 6:16   36, 212, 226
CD 9:9–10   327
CD 14:14   36, 212, 226
1QS 1:5   200
1QS 1:23–2:1   334
1QS 2:1–18   327
1QS 2:24   226
1QS 3–4   181
1QS 3:6–8   36
1QS 3:8–9   36
1QS 3:8   226
1QS 3:13–4:26   36
1QS 4:3   226, 272
1QS 4:9–26   281
1QS 4:9–11   36
1QS 4:18   36
1QS 4:24   36
1QS 5:1–3   36
1QS 5:3   226
1QS 5:8–11   327
1QS 5:16   178
1QS 5:24–25   36, 339
1QS 5:25   226
1QS 6:1   36
1QS 7:2   36, 199
1QS 7:9   36, 199
1QS 7:24–25   36
1QS 8:1   169
1QS 8:2   200
1QS 8:16   232
1QS 8:22–24   36
1QS 8:22   36
1QS 9:9–10   37
1QS 9:9   36
1QS 10:18   294
1QS 10:19   304
1QS 11:1   36, 226
1QS 11:9–15   200
1QH 1:36   226
1QH 2:32   226
1QH 2:34   226
1QH 3:25   226
1QH 4:30   200
1QH 5:13–14   258
1QH 5:13   226, 260
1QH 5:17–18   304
1QH 11:7–10   272

1QH 14:3   226
1QH 14:8   272
1QM 11:9   226
1QM 13:14   226
1QM 15:10   296
1QapGen 20:21–22   332
4QpHab 8:8–12   226
4QpHab 9:4–5   226
4QpHab 12:3–10   226
4QpPs37 2:8–9   226
4QpPs37 3:10–11   226

Ruth Rabbah

II, 1   245
VII, 6   328

Sentences of Pseudo-Phocylides   19, 31,
        52, 70

2–8   40
3–4   40
9–11   40
9   40
10   221
11   234
15   40
17   40
19   40, 302
20   40, 199
22–23   41, 212
26   41, 212
27   40, 260
28–29   41, 212
36   41
39   40
44–46   40
57   40, 199, 210
59–69   41
62   40
63   40, 199
69   41
70–75   40, 276, 282
75   40
88   40
89–96   41
98   41
110   40
116–121   40
116   296
123   40, 199
130   40

137   40
144   40
153–174   41
163   40
207–227   41
230   40

Sentences of Syriac Menander   37, 40, 70

13   37
31   37
33   37
35   37
145   37
176   37
179   37
180   37
240   37
250–251   37
301   37
304   37
310   199
311–313   37
314   199
355   37
422   37
424   37

Sibylline Oracles   34, 49

1:100–105   260
2:74   302
2:295   260
3:235   194
3:249   169
3:562   295
4:46   245
6:8   262
8:399–403   181

Sifra

Ked. Pireh 40, 4   223

Song of Songs Rabbah

I, 3, 3   245
I, 15, 2   245
IV, 1, 2   245
VI, 2, 3   245

Talmud

b. Ber. 5a   333
b. Ber. 5b   212

b. Ber. 6a   222
b. Ber. 8a   212
b. Ber. 34b   332
b. Ber. 64a   222
b. Shab. 15b   234
b. Shab. 32a–33b   333
b. Shab. 70b   232
b. Shab. 127a–b   293
b. Shab. 151b   333
b. Sheb. 31a   223
b. Sheb. 35b   328
b. Pes. 101a   222
b. Sukk. 49b   212
b. Hag. 3a   330
b. Meg. 14a–15a   245
y. Meg. 73d   222
b. Yeb. 47b   232
b. Ket. 5a   222
b. Ned. 41a   330, 333
b. Bab. Mez. 28b   222
b. Bab. Bath. 49a   328
b. Bab. Bath. 116a   330, 332
b. Sanh. 101a   332
b. Sanh. 113a   336
b. Hor. 8a   232

Tanchuma

29:4   319

Testament of Abraham

1:3   249
1:6   34
1:7   244
2:3   244, 334
2:6   244
4:1–11   249
7:1–7   196
10:2–15   338
13:4   313

Testament of Adam

1:7   331

Testament of Asher

1:2–5   45
1:3–5   181
1:3   45
1:4   45
1:9   45

2:1   45
2:5–10   45, 232
2:5   181
2:7   259
3:1   45
3:2   46
4:1   46
6:1   46
6:2   46
6:4   320
7:3   169

Testament of Benjamin

4:1   43, 44
5:2   45, 284
5:4   44
6:2   45
6:4   45, 281
6:5–6   44
6:5   262
6:7   46
7:1–2   277
7:1   45, 284
8:1   45
8:2   46, 211
9:1   46
10:8–10   44

Testament of Dan

1:6   45, 281, 297
1:7   45
1:8   45
2:1   313
2:2   44, 199
2:5   44
4:6–7   45
5:1–3   45, 281, 284
5:1   45
5:3   44
5:6   46, 283
5:7–13   46
6:1–2   45, 281

Testament of Gad

1:9   45
3:1   197
3:3   44, 283, 293
4:1   44
4:3   293
4:5–6   277

4:5   44
4:7   44
5:1–6   276
5:1   271
5:3   44
5:4   44
5:7   44
6:1   44
6:13   44
7:7   46

Testament of Issachar

3:1   46
3:3–4   293
3:3   179
3:4   44
3:5   46
3:8   44, 212
3:17   45, 284
4:1   46
4:5–6   44
4:6   279
6:1   45

Testament of Job   319–20, 324

1:5   34, 320
4:2–11   178
9:1–13:6   302
12:1–4   302
26:4–5   320
27:6–7   320
34:4   320
36:3   320

Testament of Joseph

1:2–7   276
1:3   44, 277
2:6–7   178
2:6   44
2:7   188, 313
3:9   46
4:6   44
4:7   44
6:7   44
7:1–8   194
7:1   316
7:4   44
9:2   303
10:2–3   44, 45, 281
10:6   44

11:1   44
17:8   297
19:1–12   46

Testament of Judah

13:2   44, 46, 283
13:3   45
14:2   46
14:3   45
15:5   46
16:1–3   45
17:1   44
18:2   46
18:3   283
20:1   45, 281
20:2   45
21:1–22:3   46
22:2   313
22:3   327
23:5   46
25:3   45

Testament of Levi

3:1–4:7   46
3:3   45
5:6   45
8:1–19   46
8:11   313
9:9   45, 46
13:1–2   44
13:9   44
14:1–4   46
14:5–7   46
14:7   44
17:11   44, 283
18:1–14   46
19:1   45

Testament of Naphthali

2:2   45
2:5   44
3:1   211
4:5   45
8:4   45, 281, 284
8:6   45

Testament of Reuben

2:1   45
3:5   44, 45, 281, 283

4:1   46
4:7   45
5:1   46
5:3   261
5:5   284
6:9   44

Testament of Simeon

2:7   44
3:1–5   276
3:2–3   277
3:3   44
3:5   45
4:4   46
4:5   46
4:8–9   276
4:8   44
6:1–7:3   46

Testament of Solomon

18:34   331

Testaments of the 12 Patriarchs   43, 49,
     69, 167, 194, 281

Testament of Zebulon

1:3   195
5:3   234
6:1   44
7:1–2   44, 212
7:2   274
8:1–3   234
8:1   44
8:5   44
9:7   321

III. CHRISTIAN

1st Apocalypse of James   68

25   102
42   102

2nd Apocalypse of James   68, 101

46   102
61–62   100, 101

Apocryphon of James   67

1–2   101
16   101

Apophthegmata Patrum   132

Apostolic Constitutions

II, 18   132
II, 55   132
II, 58   224
VII, 5   132
VIII, 14   132

Barnabas   79

4:14   66
5:2   66
9:6   240
18:1   69
19:3   69
19:4–5   69
19:4   68, 181
19:5–7   68
19:5   68, 181
19:7   69, 181, 262
19:12   334
20:1   69, 181
20:2   69

1 Clement   79, 103, 121, 128, 129, 135,
        136, 150

1   171
2:1   73
3–4   73
3:1   66
3:2   73
3:4   73
4:1   66
4:7   74
4:9–5:2   277
5:2   72
5:3   72
6:4   73
7:1   72
7:2–8:5   74
8:2   66
8:4   73, 212
9:2–12:8   74
9:2–4   72
9:2   72
10   245
10:1   68, 74
10:7   74
11   74
11:2   68, 181
12   74, 245
13:1   73, 201, 297

14:1   297
16:2   297
16:6   337
17:1   72
17:2   68, 74
17:3–4   319
17:6   296
19:3   72
21:5   297
23:2–3   68, 73
23:2   68, 181
23:3   66
24:1   72
25:1   72
28:3   66
29:1   74
30:2   73
30:3   74, 75, 293
30:5   75
31:1–2   75
31:2   74
33:3   315
33:5   73
35:5   293, 297
36:1   72
36:2   72
38:2   73
46:1   72
46:5   73
49:5   68, 73, 339
51:3   334
55:6   169
59:3   73
60:1   72
60:2   294
61:3   73
63:1   72

2 Clement   103

1:6   201
2:4   66
5:4   260
6:3–4   68, 128
6:8   319
11:2–5   68
11:2   66, 68, 181
11:5   181
13:1   226
13:2   226
16:4   68
17:4   339

18:3   334
19:2   68, 181

Didache   79

1–6   69
1–4   69
2:4   68, 69, 181, 262
2:5   69, 207
3:2   69, 199
4:3   68, 69, 221
4:4   68, 181
4:14   69, 334
5–6   69
5:1   69, 297
6:1   337
7–15   69
10:4   326

Didascalia Apostolorum

12   224

Letter to Diognetus   68

Gospel of the Hebrews   102

Ignatius of Antioch

Letters

Rom. 7:1   68
Eph. 3:2   274
Eph. 11:1   68
Eph. 15:1   68
Magn. 12:1   66
Magn. 15:2   274
Tral. 1:1   274
Tral. 3:1   222
Tral. 8:2   226
Pol. 4:2   222

Life of Adam and Eve

36:2   331
40:1   331

Martyrdom of Polycarp   68

Nicodemus, Gospel of

19   331

Protevangelium of James   120

1:1   169
1:3   169
9:2   103
25:1   67, 103

Pseudo-Clementine Literature   103–6,
   109, 112, 148

Ascents of James   104

Contestatio   104

Epistle of Clement to James   104

Epistle of Peter to James   103–4

Homilies   67, 103

II, 16   105
V, 5   241
XI, 35   105
XVII, 13–19   105

Recognitions   67, 103, 106

I, 33, 3   105
I, 55, 2   102
I, 69, 8   105
I, 70, 1   105
I, 71, 6   105

On Virginity   127

Sentences of Sextus   70–71, 79

6–8   70
7   70, 178
13–14   70
22   70
30   70, 183
52   71, 212
55   70
60   70
63   71
67–74   70
73   303
82–84   70
98   70
101   70
108–111   70
114   70
143–145   70
151–165   70
169–170   70
177   207

183   70
185–187   70
207–208   70
229–240   70
253   70, 199
257   70
264–274   70
277   70
294   70, 199
311   70
313   71
325   70
334   70
339   180
346   70
348–349   70
366   70
378   71
379   71, 212
428–429   70
429–430   199
432–433   70
449   70

Shepherd of Hermas   76–78, 128, 133, 135, 136

Mandates   76–78, 128, 133, 135, 136

1:3, 5   321
2:1   76
2:2–3   293
2:3   77
2:4   76
2:4, 6   76
2:7   76
3:1   76
4:1   76
4:1, 8–10   76
4:2, 2–4   76
4:4   76
4:4, 3   76
5:1, 1   78
5:1, 1–6   178
5:1, 2   78
5:1, 3   78
5:1, 6   78
5:2, 2   76
5:2, 3   78
6:2, 5   297
6:2, 7   76
7:6, 1   76

8:2   79
8:5   297
8:10   77, 79
9:1–5   76
9:1–4   78
9:1   181
9:4   76
9:6   181
9:7   76
9:7, 9   181
9:9   76
9:10   78
9:11   76, 77, 273
10:1, 4   77
10:2, 2   76
11:1   76
11:3   76
11:8   77
11:9, 13–14   222
11:11–12   77
11:12   211
11:13   76
11:14   77
11:21   77
12:2   76
12:4, 7   76, 284
12:5, 2   76, 284
12:6, 3   76
12:6, 5   76

Similitudes

1:1   171
1:3   76
1:8   77
2:2   77
2:5   77
3:1, 5   334
4:4, 5   77
4:4, 7   76
4:6   78
5:3, 6   76
5:6, 5   76
5:7, 1   76
5:7, 4   321
6:1   76
6:1, 1   79
6:2, 1   211
6:2, 2   77
6:4, 1   77
6:4, 4   211
6:5, 4   77

7:1   76
8:3–5   76
8:6, 4   78, 226
8:7, 6   78
8:7, 21   77
8:9, 4   76
8:11, 3   76
9:14, 6   78
9:15, 2   76, 78
9:18, 3   76
9:20   77
9:21, 2   76
9:23, 4   79, 334
9:24, 3   76
9:26, 2   77
9:27, 2   77
9:31, 4   76
10:4, 3   79

Visions

1, 1, 3   334
1, 3, 2   321
2, 2, 7   181
2, 2, 8   321
2, 3, 2   76
3, 1, 9   76
3, 2, 2   76
3, 3, 4   76
3, 4, 3   76
3, 8, 5   76
3, 8, 7   194
3, 9, 1   76
3, 9, 5   77
3, 9, 6   77
3, 10, 9   76, 181
4, 1, 4   76
4, 2, 3   321
4, 2, 5   76
4, 2, 6   76
5, 7   76
9, 10   79
11, 3   66

Teaching of Addai

F. 10a   101
F. 11a   101
F. 54a   101

Teachings of Silvanus   79

85   71
86   71
87   71, 194
88   71
89–90   71
89   71, 194
90   71
91   71
92–93   71
92   71, 194
95   71, 194
97–98   71
97   71
98   71
101   71, 195
102   71
104   71
105   71
108   71
110   71
111   72
115   71, 192

Thomas, Gospel of

12   101
54   225

IV. OTHER

Confucius

Analects

4:24   26
9:17   26

Psalms of Heracleides

192:8–9   100

Psalms of Serakoth

142:25–26   100

Sayings of Amen-Em-Opet

8   258
18   296

INDEX OF PRE-MODERN CHRISTIAN WRITERS (2ND TO 17TH CENTURIES)

✦

Alexander of Alexandria   130
Alulfus   139
Ambrose of Milan   135
Ambrosiaster   137
Andreas Bodenstein   141
Andrew of Jerusalem   132
Anselm of Laon   139
Antiochus Monachus   132
Antonius Melissa   133
Antony of Egypt   132
Athanasius   130, 132, 134, 234, 330
Augustine of Hippo   137, 138, 139, 141,
    196, 232, 320

Basil the Great   131, 133, 277
Bede the Venerable   xii, 139, 141, 179,
    185, 192, 196, 197, 199, 203, 209,
    232, 233, 241, 245, 258, 260, 276,
    279, 280, 282, 284, 293, 304,
    320–21, 329, 331
Robert Bellarmine   142
Bernard of Clairvaux   140

Caesarius of Cappadocia   234
Calvin, John   21, 142, 143, 144, 185,
    192, 221
Cassiodorus   129, 138, 304
Catena Graecorum Patrum   133, 203,
    232, 245, 321
Chromatius of Aquila   138
Clement of Alexandria   99, 100, 129, 328
Cornelius à Lapide   143
Cyprian of Carthage   135

Cyril of Alexandria   130, 131, 134, 135,
    196, 234, 256, 330, 332
Cyril of Jerusalem   131, 134

Damasus I of Rome   136, 137
Didymus of Alexandria   130, 134, 271
Dionysius of Alexandria   130, 133, 203
Dionysius Bar Salibi   132
Dionysius the Carthusian   139–40
Dorotheus of Palestine   131

Epiphanius of Salamis   105, 131
Erasmus of Rotterdam   140, 141, 142,
    144, 220, 277
Estius, G.   143
Eucherius of Lyons   138
Eusebius of Caesaria   99, 100, 101, 105,
    127, 129, 131, 168
Euthalius the Deacon   130, 133
Euthymius Zigibenus   134

Godfridus   140
Gregory the Great   138, 139
Gregory Nazienzus   131
Gregory of Nyssa   131
Gregory of Palamas   134

Haymo   140
Hegesippus   99, 100
Hesychius the Elder   133
Hesychius of Jerusalem   131, 134
Hilary of Poitiers   137
Hippolytus of Rome   105, 137

Innocent I   137, 139
Irenaeus of Lyons   105, 128
Isaiah of Egypt   132
Isho'dad of Merv   132
Isidore of Pelusium   134, 283
Isidore of Seville   139

Jerome   102, 116, 126, 137, 139, 141
Johannes Xiphilinus   235
John Cassian   138, 335
John Chrysostom   132, 133, 196, 204,
    205, 235, 245, 255, 313, 319
John Climacus   131, 132
John Damascene   131, 133, 134, 335
Julian of Halicarnassus   135, 243
Justin Martyr   47, 49, 105, 128, 222,
    226, 241, 328

Leontius of Byzantium   132
Liberius of Rome   137
Love, Christopher   144
Luther, Martin   125, 140, 141, 142, 144,
    148, 152, 163

Macarius of Egypt   132
Manton, Thomas   144
Marcellus of Rome   137
Mark the Egyptian   132
Martin of Legio   139
Maximus the Confessor   133
Meister Eckhardt   140
Melanchthon, Philip   142

Nicholas of Lyre   139
Niles the Abbot   132, 235, 282
Novatian   136

Oecumenius of Tricca   133, 168, 177,
    187, 198, 202, 203, 209, 232, 234,
    241, 245, 259, 260, 276, 280, 297,
    304, 305, 313, 328, 331

Pachomius   132
Palladius   132
Pamphilius of Caesaria   131

Paterius   138, 139
Peter of Alexandria   130
Polycarp of Smyrna   68, 171, 326
Procopius of Gaza   131, 256, 332
Pseudo-Andrew of Crete   168
Pseudo-Dionysius   140

Origen   93, 128, 129, 130, 131, 133,
    134, 135, 136, 256, 330, 332
Orsiesius   132

Radulphus Ardens   140
Rufinus   137

Scholia   133, 181, 196, 197, 202, 203,
    207, 209, 234, 260, 279
Serapion of Egypt   132
Severus of Antioch   133, 135
Sisoes of Egypt   132
Smaragdus   140
Sophronius of Jerusalem   131
Stephanus of Rome   136
Stobaeus, Johannes   28, 134, 240, 257,
    287
Strabo, Wilfred   139
Symeon Theophrastus   133

Taylor, Jeremy   144
Tertullian   33, 105, 135
Theodore of Mopsuestia   132
Theophylact of Bulgaria   133, 168, 187,
    198, 199, 202, 209, 232, 234, 241,
    245, 260, 305, 313, 315, 328
Thomas Aquinas   140
Thomas à Kempis   140
Thomas de Vio (Cajetan)   141, 169
Tyndale, William   142

Urban I of Rome   136

Wesley, John   144

Zachary of Jerusalem   131, 335
Zachary the Rhetorician   131, 135, 243
Zozimus   132
Zwingli, Ulrich   142

INDEX OF MODERN AUTHORS
(17TH TO 20TH CENTURIES)

✦

Achtemeier, P. 110, 114
Adamson, J. B. 118, 121, 159, 221, 230, 255, 259, 268, 271, 272, 275, 277, 280, 282, 292, 298, 299, 300, 302, 305, 309, 315, 316, 321, 326, 327, 330, 335
Agourides, S. C. 7, 116, 121
Aland, K. 4, 153, 154
Althaus, P. 346
de Ambroggi, P. 153, 154
Amphoux, C. B. 5, 6, 11, 12, 15, 198, 215
Anderson, H. 39, 46
Argyle, A. W. 117, 121

Baarda, T. 37, 46
Baasland, E. 8, 11, 12, 15, 20, 21, 24, 25, 33, 46, 116, 174, 215
Bacon, B. W. 80, 154, 250
Baird, W. 250
Baker, W. R. 346
Balch, D. L. 67, 80
Baltzer, K. 172
Barclay, W. 117
Barnett, A. E. 22
Barr, J. 117, 121
Barth, K. 156
Bartlett, D. L. 157
Bartmann, B. 64
Barton, G. 250
Bauer, W. 90, 106, 113
Baur, F. C. 90, 98, 106, 109, 110, 112, 115, 146, 148
Beck, D. L. 36, 46, 158
Behm, J. 154

Belser, J. E. 153
Ben de Rubies, J. F. 140
Bengel, J. A. 91, 106, 144, 145
Benoit, P. 157
Bergauer, P. 64, 160
Berger, K. 17, 18, 19, 20, 23, 25
Berger, P. L. 90
Bernays, J. 40, 46
Betz, H. D. 56, 57, 94, 106
Beyschlag, W. 149
Bianchi, U. 113, 115
Bieder, W. 159
Bischoff, A. 324
Black, M. 213, 215
Blenker, A. 12, 15
Boggan, C. W. 158, 309
Böhlig, A. 100, 106
Böhmer, J. 64
Bohnenblust, G. 289
Bonner, S. F. 17
Bord, J.-P. 342, 346
Bosch, J. S. 160
Bottini, G. V. 309
Boumann, H. 149
Boyle, M. O. 232, 250
Bratcher, R. G. 265
Braumann, G. 160, 201, 215
Braun, H. 153
Brinktrine, J. 251
Brooks, J. A. 160
Brosch, J. 119, 122
Brown, R. B. 159
Brown, R. E. 113, 115
Brown, S. K. 100
Brückner, W. 150

Bultmann, R.   111, 115, 119, 122
Burchard, C.   91, 106

Cabaniss, A.   12, 115, 159
Calmet, A.   146
Cameron, J.   145
von Campenhausen, H.   106, 119, 122,
    155
Cantinat, J.   44, 75, 199, 220, 221, 223,
    226, 230, 257, 272, 275, 276, 277,
    278, 280, 281, 289, 292, 294, 298,
    299, 300, 305, 313, 314, 315, 316,
    319, 321, 326, 329, 335, 336, 340
Capellus, J.   145
Capellus, L.   145
Cargal, T. B.   12, 13, 14, 83, 175, 215,
    289
Carr, A.   149, 265
Carrington, P.   67, 80
Carroll, K. L.   96, 106
Castelli, E. A.   112, 115
Cerfaux, L.   118, 122
Chaine, J.   4, 27, 153, 199, 218, 220,
    221, 223, 240, 257, 259, 274, 275,
    276, 277, 278, 279, 292, 297, 298,
    299, 300, 305, 314, 315, 316, 320,
    326, 332, 339, 342
Charles, R. H.   43, 47
Charue, A. M.   159, 265, 309
Cladder, H. J.   12, 15
Collins, J. J.   43, 47
Condon, K.   346
Cone, O.   154
Conzelmann, H.   119, 122
Cooper, R.   57
Coppieters, H.   289
Countryman, W.   229, 251
Cramer, J. A.   133
Cranfield, C. E. B.   159
Credner, K. A.   149
Crenshaw, J.   29, 47
Crossan, J. D.   96, 106
Cullmann, O.   50, 57, 103, 106

Dale, R. W.   152
Danby, H.   35, 47
Danielou, J.   113, 115
Darling, J.   144
Dautzenberg, G.   346
Davids, P. H.   11, 57, 117, 121, 160,
    193, 194, 208, 215, 221, 223, 230,
    231, 240, 243, 257, 270, 271, 272,
    273, 276, 277, 278, 280, 281, 292,
    298, 300, 304, 305, 314, 315, 319,
    320, 321, 327, 328, 335, 337, 339
Deems, C. F.   152
Deiros, P. A.   154
Deissmann, A.   22, 23, 25
Deppe, D. B.   55, 57
Descamps, A.   200, 215
De Wette, W. M. L.   148
Dibelius, M.   4, 5, 8, 9, 11, 13, 18, 19,
    23, 24, 25, 44, 50, 56, 67, 73, 75,
    76, 78, 85, 100, 111, 116, 121, 127,
    153, 155, 158, 159, 170, 171, 174,
    175, 178, 185, 186, 187, 189, 194,
    195, 196, 199, 206, 209, 221, 222,
    223, 224, 226, 230, 231, 239, 240,
    255, 257, 259, 260, 268, 271, 277,
    280, 281, 292, 293, 300, 302, 304,
    305, 314, 315, 316, 320, 326, 327,
    328, 329, 331, 332, 339
Dodd, C. H.   190, 215, 316, 324
Donelson, L. R.   118, 122
Donker, C. E.   251
Dugas, L.   289
Duplacy, J.   6, 12, 115
Dyrness, W.   251

Eckart, K.-G.   251
Edsman, L. M.   197, 198, 215
Edwards, R. A.   70, 80, 119, 122
Eglinger, R.   289
Eichholz, G.   64, 110
Eisenman, R.   157, 346
Eleder, F.   56, 57
Ellingworth, P.   72, 180
Elliott-Binns, L. E.   154, 156, 197, 215,
    265
Engelhardt, E.   289
Engelhardt, W.   106
Epp, E. J.   4, 6
Erdmann, D.   149
Ewald, H.   149

Fabris, R.   32, 47, 251
Feine, P.   149, 150, 154
Felder, C. H.   29, 158, 309
Feuillet, A.   304, 305, 309, 324
Filson, F. W.   265
Findlay, J. A.   290
Fine, H.   324

Fischel, H. A.   9, 26, 47
Fischer, H.   195, 215
Fitzmyer, J. A.   103, 107, 320, 324
Flusser, D.   157
Forbes, P. B. R.   12, 14, 15
Foster, O. D.   66, 80
Fowler, A.   16
Francis, F. O.   11, 16, 24, 25, 326,
   340, 346
Frankmölle, H.   12, 16, 21, 32, 33, 47,
   174, 215, 251, 309, 310
Freedman, D. N.   xi, xiii
Freyne, S.   117, 122
Friesenhahn, H.   346
Fry, E.   11, 16, 319, 324
Frye, N.   16

Gächter, P.   106, 107
Gamble, H. Y.   135
Gammie, J. G.   18, 25
Gard, D. H.   324
Gaugusch, L.   153
Gebser, A. R.   146
Gerhard, G. A.   172
Gertner, M.   157, 158
Geyser, A. S.   107, 159, 310
Goodenough, E. R.   41, 47
Gordon, R. P.   320, 324
Grafe, E.   153
Greeven, H.   215
Grimm, W.   290
Grosvener, M.   186, 252
Grotius, H.   144
Grünzweig, F.   154
Gryglewicz, F.   57, 58
Guthrie, D.   155

Haar, J.   160
Haas, C.   320, 324
Hadidian, D. Y.   121
Hagner, D. A.   72, 75, 80
Halston, B. R.   33, 47
Hands, A. R.   234, 251
Hanson, A. T.   157, 251
Harmon, H. P.   64, 160
von Harnack, A.   150
Harris, H.   109, 115
Hartin, P. J.   56, 57, 58, 120, 122
Hartmann, G.   12, 16, 159
Hauck, Fr.   153, 196
Haupt, E.   150, 151

Hays, R. B.   128, 191, 215
Hedrick, C. H.   101, 107
Hemer, C. J.   112, 115
Hengel, M.   64, 106, 107, 110, 111,
   112, 115, 117, 122
Herder, J. G.   145, 146
Hilgenfield, A.   160
Hill, C. C.   112, 115
Hirsch, E. D.   16, 89
Hock, R.   90
Hodges, Z. C.   251
Hofmann, J.   149
Hollmann, G.   154
Holtzmann, H. J.   150
Hope, C. H.   47
Hoppe, R.   33, 47, 160, 290
Horsley, R. A.   120, 122
van der Horst, P.   31, 40, 41, 47
Hort, F. J. A.   153, 185, 186, 187, 195,
   221, 224, 230, 239, 242, 245, 257,
   258, 259, 263, 268, 271, 272, 273,
   274, 275, 276, 277, 278, 279, 281,
   282
Hottinger, J. J.   146
Hoyos, P.   346
Hug, J. L.   149
Hultgren, A.   113
Huther, J. E.   149

Irmscher, J.   103, 104, 107

Jacobi, B.   146
Jacobs, I.   251
Jäger, G.   149
Jeremias, J.   64, 110, 115, 121, 122, 290
Johanson, B. C.   215
Johnson, L. T.   10, 19, 20, 21, 23, 25,
   28, 29, 31, 34, 46, 47, 48, 72, 89,
   96, 97, 107, 113, 115, 124, 157, 159,
   215, 226, 231, 251, 264, 266, 290,
   293, 310, 316, 318, 324, 327, 335,
   338, 346
Johnston, C.   64
Johnstone, R.   152
Jones, F. S.   104, 107
de Jonge, M.   43, 47
Judge, A. E.   23
Jülicher, A.   11, 150, 155

Karo, G.   251
Karrer, M.   160

Kawerau, G.   160
Keck, L.   105, 107, 158
Kee, H. C.   43, 48
Kelber, W.   96, 107
Kelly, F. X.   158, 310
Kennedy, E.   64
Kennedy, G.   9, 21
Kent, T.   16, 17
Kern, F. H.   18, 67, 80, 91, 107, 109, 115, 146, 147
Kierkegaard, S.   151, 152
Kilmartin, E. J.   346
Kilpatrick, G. D.   4, 233, 251
Kirk, J. A.   33, 48, 290
Kirn, O.   290
Kittel, G.   56, 58, 116, 122, 153, 160
Klijn, A. F. J.   5, 113, 115, 155
Kloppenburg, J. S.   119, 120, 122
Klopper, A.   64
Klostermann, E.   5, 6
Knowling, R. J.   153
Knox, R.   xi
Knox, W. L.   33, 48, 158
Köhler, A.   64
Köster, F.   53, 58, 172
Köster, H.   155
Kraft, R. A.   113, 115
Kübel, R.   64
Kubo, S.   161
Kühl, E.   64
Kuhn, T. S.   90
Kümmel, W. G.   94, 107, 109, 111, 115, 116, 124, 154, 161
Kürzdorfer, K.   158
Kutsch, E.   346
Kuttner, O.   64

Lackmann, M.   64
Lange, J. P.   152
Laws, S.   44, 75, 135, 157, 159, 221, 223, 230, 233, 240, 255, 256, 257, 258, 268, 275, 277, 278, 279, 280, 281, 282, 290, 292, 298, 300, 302, 304, 305, 314, 315, 317, 321, 326, 327, 328, 335, 336, 339
Layton, B.   113, 115
Leloir, L.   6
Liebermann, S.   117, 122
Lieu, J. M.   172
Lightfoot, J.   145
von Lips, H.   33, 48, 290

Little, D. H.   99, 100, 107
Lodge, J. C.   65
Lohse, E.   65, 154, 155
Loisy, A.   154
Longenecker, R. N.   53, 58, 251
Lorenzen, T.   65
Luck, U.   65
Luckmann, T.   90
Lüdemann, G.   105, 107, 112, 115
Luff, S. G. A.   346
Lyonnet, S.   94, 107

MacDonald, M. Y.   22, 90, 107
McGiffert, A. C.   150
Mack, B. L.   9, 21, 120, 123, 156
McKnight, S.   251
MacRae, G. W.   49, 102, 107, 113
Mader, J.   94, 107
Malherbe, A. J.   16, 19, 22, 23, 24, 25, 28, 29, 48, 170, 172
Malina, B. J.   29
Manns, F.   215
Marconi, G.   215, 251, 290, 346
Marcus, J.   157, 194, 216, 281, 290
Marrou, H.   17
Marshall, S.   216
Martin, D. B.   171, 172
Martin, R. P.   11, 99, 100, 117, 123, 171, 174, 185, 186, 194, 208, 221, 223, 230, 233, 257, 259, 271, 275, 276, 281, 298, 304, 305, 314, 316, 321, 326, 327
Marty, J.   75, 155, 194, 195, 197, 220, 221, 223, 225, 230, 232, 239, 242, 243, 255, 257, 259, 268, 271, 275, 278, 280, 281, 292, 293, 298, 300, 304, 305, 313, 314, 317, 319, 326, 328, 329
Marxsen, W.   155
Massebieau, L.   48, 50, 58, 151
Maston, T. B.   159
Matthaei, C. F.   133, 161
Maynard-Reid, P. U.   159, 310
Mayor, J. B.   4, 8, 9, 27, 66, 75, 110, 116, 117, 118, 121, 136, 149, 176, 186, 195, 199, 201, 206, 208, 209, 210, 221, 223, 224, 230, 239, 257, 258, 259, 260, 262, 275, 277, 278, 279, 280, 281, 293, 298, 299, 302, 304, 305, 313, 314, 315, 321, 327, 334, 335, 339, 342

Mayordomo-Marin, M.   310
Meeks, W. A.   23, 50, 51, 58, 90, 201, 216
Mehlhorn, P.   251
Meier, J. P.   98, 107, 117, 123
Meinertz, M.   161, 346
Menegoz, E.   65
Metzger, B. M.   4, 5, 6, 155, 223, 302, 338
Meyer, A.   12, 16, 158, 161, 167
Meyer, E.   154
Meyers, C. L.   117, 123
Meyers, E.   117, 123
Michaelis, J. D.   147, 221
Michaelis, W.   155
Michl, J.   290
Milikowski, C.   266
Milobenski, E.   290
Minear, P.   328, 347
Mitchell, A. C.   222, 251
Mitchell, M. M.   21, 112, 115
Mitton, C. L.   66, 80, 117, 293, 302, 326
Moffatt, J.   154
Morris, K. F.   157, 190, 216, 303, 310
Moule, C. F. D.   7, 155, 186, 192, 208, 336
Munck, J.   100, 107, 113, 115
Murray, J. A. H.   93
Mussies, G.   117, 123
Mussner, F.   4, 117, 154, 160, 195, 199, 221, 222, 230, 240, 245, 255, 257, 259, 268, 271, 276, 277, 280, 281, 292, 293, 296, 298, 300, 302, 305, 314, 317, 320, 326, 328, 329, 332, 335, 339

Nauck, W.   177, 216
Neander, A.   147
Neill, S.   109, 115
Neirynck, F.   119, 123
Nestle, E.   4
Netzer, E.   117, 123
Neyrey, J. H.   29, 90
Nicole, W.   65
Noack, B.   65, 159, 310
Noret, J.   161
Nötscher, F.   251
Nourry, N.   129

Obermüller, R.   160

O'Callaghan, J.   36, 48
Oesterley, W. E.   153
Olbricht, T. H.   21
Oosterzee, J. J.   152
Outtier, B.   5

Pagels, E.   49
Palmer, F. H.   216
Pardee, D.   170, 172
Paret, E.   290
Parry, St. J. R.   153
Peake, A. S.   154
Pearson, A.   145
Pearson, B.   161
Peel, M. L.   71, 72, 80
Perdue, G.   17, 19, 25
Perkins, P.   290
Peterson, E.   60, 252
Pfeiffer, E.   11, 16
Plummer, A.   153
Polhill, J.   92, 107
Polk, T.   152
Popkes, W.   91, 108, 156
Porter, S. E.   68, 80, 181, 216
Powell, C.   110, 116
Preisker, H.   153
Prentice, W. K.   108
Preus, J. S.   90
Preuschen, E.   324
Pricaeus   145
Prockter, L. J.   290

Quecke, H.   252

von Rad, G.   29, 48
Reicke, B.   11, 195, 199, 220, 221, 226, 232, 259, 276, 292, 300, 327, 328, 330, 331, 339, 347
Rendall, G. H.   117, 123, 153, 327, 347
Rendtorff, H.   160
Riegel, S. K.   113, 116
Riesenfeld, H.   216
Rivera, L. F.   157
Robbins, V. K.   17, 21, 128
Roberts, C. H.   36, 48
Roberts, D. J.   216
Robertson, A. T.   160
Robinson, J. A. T.   118, 123, 153
Robinson, T. M.   102
Rönsche, H.   252
Ropes, J. H.   4, 6, 9, 11, 17, 44, 75, 93,

116, 119, 133, 136, 155, 161, 181,
186, 194, 206, 220, 221, 223, 224,
226, 230, 232, 239, 240, 252, 254,
259, 260, 263, 271, 272, 273, 274,
276, 278, 279, 280, 281, 282, 292,
293, 295, 296, 297, 298, 299, 300,
302, 305, 313, 314, 315, 318, 319,
321, 327, 329, 335, 339
Rose, V. 50
Rosenmüller, J. G. 149
Rusche, H. 159, 216, 252

Sahlin, H. 168, 172
Sailer, J. 374
Salmon, G. 149
Sanday, W. 6
Sanders, E. P. 49, 58
Sanders, J. P. 159
Scatterfield, A. 145
Schammberger, H. 110
Schanz, P. 65
Schlatter, A. 153
Schmidt, W. G. 116, 149, 161
Schmidt-Clausing, F. 161
Schmitt, J. J. 278, 290
Schnabel, E. J. 29, 48
Schnayder, G. 266
Schneckenberger, M. 147
Schoedel, W. S. 102, 108
Schökel, L. A. 216, 290, 305, 310
Schoeps, H.-J. 110, 113, 116, 172
Scholes, R. 16
Schulthess, J. 146
Schwartz, E. 100, 107
Schwartz, G. 65
Schwegler, A. 148
Scott, E. F. 154
Seitz, O. J. F. 32, 48, 68, 76, 80, 157,
181, 216, 252
Sevenster, J. N. 117, 123
Shepherd, M. H. 57, 58
Shutt, R. J. H. 38, 48
Sigal, P. 157, 216
Siker, J. S. 53, 58, 131, 132, 161, 252
Simon, L. 160
Simon, M. 105, 108
Slingerland, D. 46, 48
Soards, M. L. 53, 58, 252
von Soden, H. 150
Songer, H. 18, 25
Souček, J. B. 65, 159

Souter, A. 135, 138
von Speyr, A. 160
Spicq, C. 290
Spitta, F. 48, 50, 58, 151, 231
Spittler, R. P. 320, 324
Staab, K. 133, 161
Stagg, F. 11, 16, 216
Stauffer, E. 106, 108, 157
Steck, E. 151
Stone, M. 117, 123
Storr, G. C. 145
Stowers, S. K. 9, 10, 17, 23, 25, 170,
172
Strecker, G. 104, 105, 108, 113, 116
Stringfellow, W. 160
Stuhlmacher, P. 65
Sundberg, A. C. 67, 80, 135

Talbert, C. H. 96, 108
Tasker, R. V. G. 154
Taylor, C. 76, 80
Thatcher, H. T. 120, 123
Theile, C. G. G. 146
Theissen, G. 23, 90, 229, 252
Thomas, J. 216
Thyen, H. 158, 159
Tielemann, Th. 65
Tobac, E. 65
Torrey, C. C. 172
Townsend, M. J. 276, 290
Travis, A. E. 65
Trocmé, E. 65, 96, 108, 255, 266
Tuckett, C. M. 68, 71, 80
Turner, N. 7, 8, 11

van Unnik, W. C. 290
Usteri, L. M. 65

Valla, L. 145
Van der Westhuizen, T. D. N. 252
Van Voorst, R. E. 104, 108
Via, D. O. 65
Vielhauer, Ph. 102, 103, 108
Vokes, F. E. 30, 48, 252
Vouga, F. 11, 168, 218, 221, 225, 226,
245, 255, 259, 271, 275, 278, 281,
292, 294, 298, 299, 300, 305, 315,
327, 339

Wachob, W. H. 21, 26, 225, 252
von Wahlde, U. C. 60
Walker, R. 65

Wall, R. 29, 48
Walter, N. 117, 123
Walther, W. 141, 161
Wandel, G. 266
Wanke, J. 266
Ward, R. B. 65, 158, 159, 223, 227, 249, 252, 310
Warner, M. 21
Watson, D. F. 21, 26, 252, 266
Weeden, T. 96, 108
Weiffenbach, W. H. 65
Weiss, B. 153
Weiss, J. 154
von Weizsäker, C. 150
Werner, K. 149
Wettstein, J. J. 145
White, J. L. 22, 26, 168, 172, 326, 347
Wiersma, S. 252
Wifstrand, A. 7, 11
Wikenhauser, A. 155
Wild, R. 70, 80
Wilkinson, J. 347
Williams, A. L. 108
Williams, F. E. 101, 108

Williams, R. R. 154
Wilson, B. R. 119, 123
Wilson, R. MacL. 102, 108
Windisch, H. 116, 220, 224, 230, 231, 252, 259, 276, 277, 280, 293, 294, 300, 305, 315, 320, 326, 335, 339
Wire, A. C. 112, 116
Wisse, F. 70, 80
Wolmarans, J. L. P. 266
Wolverton, W. I. 68, 80, 157, 216
Wordsworth, J. 6, 116, 123
Wright, N. T. 34
Wuellner, W. H. 12, 16, 21, 216

Young, F. W. 75, 80

Zahn, Th. 149, 150, 151
Zandee, J. 71, 72, 80
Zeller, E. 216
Zerwick, M. 186, 257
Zimmer, M. 65
Zmijewski, J. 159
Zodhiates, S. 160
Zyro, F. F. 290

412